UFOS AND POPULAR CULTURE

UFOS AND POPULAR CULTURE

An Encyclopedia of Contemporary Myth

JAMES R. LEWIS

ABC-CLIO

Santa Barbara, California
Denver, Colorado
Oxford, England

Library of Congress Cataloging-in-Publication Data
Lewis, James R.
    UFOs and popular culture : an encyclopedia of contemporary myth /
James R. Lewis.
        p.   cm.
Includes bibliographical references and index.
    ISBN 1-57607-265-7 (hard : alk. paper)
1. Unidentified flying objects.   2. Popular culture.   I. Title.
TL789 .L485   2000
001.942'03—dc21
                                                                                        00-010925
                                                                                        CIP

06   05   04   03   02   01   00   10 9 8 7 6 5 4 3 2 1

ABC-CLIO, Inc.
130 Cremona Drive, P.O. Box 1911
Santa Barbara, California 93116-1911

This book is printed on acid-free paper ∞.
Manufactured in the United States of America

CONTENTS

Foreword: UFOs—Folklore of
the Space Age, *Thomas E. Bullard,* ix
Introduction, xxvii
List of Contributors, xxxix

UFOs and Popular Culture:
An Encyclopedia of Contemporary Myth

FOREWORD: UFOS—FOLKLORE OF THE SPACE AGE

Thomas E. Bullard

Welcome to the most popular paranormal folklore of today.

Ever since pilot Kenneth Arnold sighted nine shiny objects that "skipped like saucers" over the ridges of Mt. Rainier on June 24, 1947, unidentified flying objects (UFOs) or flying saucers have held center stage in popular belief and imagination. Gallup Polls demonstrate that UFOs enjoy a lofty recognition level, with usually over 90 percent of the American public acknowledging acquaintance with the subject. In fact more people recognized the term "UFOs" than remembered the name of Gerald Ford in a poll taken just six months after he left the White House. UFOs have seeped so deeply into cultural awareness that they seem to be everywhere—in movies, TV shows, advertising, cartoons, and video games. Alien faces appear on greeting cards, toy tops of the 1950s were fashioned to look like flying saucers, a breakfast cereal bears the name "UFOs," salt and pepper shakers take the shape of alien heads, and where would the tabloids be without a weekly headline screaming "Extraterrestrials Infiltrate Congress" or something equally outlandish to shoppers as they stand in the grocery checkout lanes? Belief in UFOs was once an oddity, a badge of craziness in the routines of popular humor. But little by little this belief has become the norm, and nearly half the population now affirms that UFOs are real.

This popularity sustains an extensive publishing industry, with books on the subject numbering in the thousands. Whitley Strieber's *Communion,* an account of his UFO abduction experiences, spent several months on the best-seller list in 1987. A vast number of periodicals have come and gone over the years, many of them short-lived local newsletters, but a number of glossy magazines fill newsstand racks around the country today. UFOs have inspired many clubs and organizations, some of them large and widespread, such as the Mutual UFO Network (MUFON), which publishes a monthly magazine, the *MUFON UFO Journal,* and sponsors an annual symposium. The Center for UFO Studies (CUFOS), founded by astronomer J. Allen Hynek, continues Hynek's research by publishing the *International UFO Reporter* and a scholarly journal, *The Journal of UFO Studies.* The Fund for UFO Research gives grants for UFO study projects. The government has taken a long-term interest in the phenomenon, with the U.S. Air Force maintaining investigative units known as Projects Sign, Grudge, Twinkle, and Blue Book throughout the 1950s and 1960s and sponsoring a large-scale investigation at the University of Colorado from 1966 to 1968, the so-called Condon Committee. The city of Roswell, New Mexico, hosts an annual festival to celebrate the claims that a UFO crashed nearby in 1947, and thousands of people have visited the UFO museums in that city. On the Internet UFOs are said to be the second most popular subject, surpassed only by sex.

The saucers started to fly in North America but soon belonged to the world. The great European wave of 1954 established UFOs as a mainstay of popular belief on that continent, and some of the most sophisticated UFO research continues to come from there. One of the few government-sponsored investigation projects, and perhaps the only such effort to study the subject on its scientific merits without overwhelming political pressure or intellectual prejudice, originated in France during the late 1970s. Major waves in 1954 and 1957 popularized UFOs in South America, a continent that has remained a hotbed of abduction narratives and other bizarre stories, such as reports from northern Brazil between the 1970s and 1990s that UFOs injured or killed people who happened to be outdoors at night. No spot on earth can claim immunity from notable UFO visitations. Among many Australian encounters, an unforgettable example from 1978 includes the frantic messages of pilot Fred Valentich as he radioed flight control that a huge UFO hovered close above him, just before he disappeared without a trace. From New Guinea in 1959 a missionary, Father William Gill, and a company of some 40 parishioners watched a UFO hover nearby and saw its occupants wave in response to their own friendly gestures. A stream of stories issue out of Africa, and the Soviet Union hosted saucerian visitors from the 1940s onward, though only since greater freedom of the press began in the late 1980s have readers in the West learned of such activity in Russian skies. News of a massive UFO wave is breaking from the People's Republic of China at the start of the new millennium.

No one will deny the popularity and pervasiveness of UFOs, but how are they folklore? The reader may well stumble on that assertion. What is folklore about if not quaint beliefs of the past handed down by oral tradition, relics of bygone times surviving into the present but slowly dying out? Such an image comes to mind as soon as most people think of folklore, but the impression is a false one. Folklore can mean nothing more than "unofficial" culture, the beliefs and practices of people that stand apart from—and perhaps in opposition to—standard norms of the official culture. The medieval church had an official theology with accepted doctrines and rituals, but a folk religion existed side by side with this official version. The practitioners of folk religion considered themselves good Catholics, but the official religion did not serve all their needs, and they filled in the gaps with devotion to accessible holy figures such as the saints and the Virgin Mary, or relied on the magical potency of relics and charms to heal illnesses, foretell the future, and cast love spells.

These practices bordered on the heretical and led to divergent consequences—the church eventually embraced the cult of saints and devotion to the Virgin but lashed out against the white magic of amulets, charms, and remedies during the intolerant era of the Inquisition by condemning practitioners to be burned at the stake as witches.

In the modern secular age the consensus of scientific opinion sets the standards of truth for realities in the physical world. Most scientists dismiss UFOs as misinterpretations of conventional phenomena—meteors, aircraft, or the planet Venus mistaken for spaceships. If not honest mistakes, they believe, UFO reports must be deliberate deceptions or the products of deranged minds. The air force and other governmental agencies echo this verdict. A stamp of official disapproval slams shut the possibility that anyone really witnesses a phenomenon unknown to science or unrecognized by it. Against this conclusion stand the witnesses—several million of them, according to polls—who say they saw something too strange to explain in conventional terms and the believers who are convinced that the bulk of evidence simply outweighs the arguments of skeptics. The authorities of official culture state their case—where is the proverbial landing on the White House lawn, the alien artifact of unmistakable unearthly origin, the indisputable photographic evidence? They point out that human observers are leaky vessels, prone to miss much and add more, subject to see what they want to see rather than the sight before their eyes. Adherents of the unofficial view answer that they know what they saw, that it was no satellite or planet, and that the cumulative testimony of photography, radar, and witnesses reliable enough to send people to jail in a court of law add up to evidence aplenty that UFOs are genuine. These adherents fault scientists for refusing an open-minded investigation of UFOs and the government for knowing more than it tells, perhaps even conspiring to hide a secret that would turn the universe as we think we know it upside down. The battle lines have long since hardened. Just as proponents participate in a network of organizations supporting their beliefs, skeptics can join the Committee for the Scientific Investigation of Claims of the Paranormal (CSICOP), a group founded to combat "pseudoscientific" beliefs such as creationism, astrology, and UFOs.

Each side in this dispute holds its ground with stubborn determination, convinced that its view is the right one and its cause too important to compromise. After all, what could be more important than realizing that aliens are visiting the earth?— or, alternatively, than protecting scientific inquiry against a rising tide of irrational thinking? The strident tones of a crusade often characterize disputes over UFOs. What the folklorist cannot help but notice is the tension between two beliefs, one official and one unofficial and both passionately held amid perpetual skirmishing through half a century. Here is a relationship of oppositions that tags UFOs as the subject of folklore.

A "folk" does not mean a community of rustics hidden away in a mountain valley, cut off from the currents of the outside world. Any group of two or more people sharing an interest or a bit of knowledge constitutes a folk in the broadest sense of the word. UFO believers make up a distinctive folk because they share interests and beliefs and communicate them to one another. As evidence that folklore stays up-to-date rather than mired in the past, UFOs demonstrate modernization in both subject matter and the means of conveying it. Face-to-face contact still happens among the UFO folk, but they often turn to long-distance methods and stay in touch via written and telecommunications media such as newsletters, journals, the telephone, or the Internet. UFO believers may participate in a folk group only when the topic is UFOs; in fact, they may never communicate with one another concerning any other subject. But for part of their lives, these people bond together into a community of believers, far-flung but linked together by their special organs of communication, and through these channels the folk community shares its knowledge and thoughts, news and gossip. Through these contacts the group members keep up with the latest events, dispute interpretations, reinforce belief, and challenge dissidents—in fact, the community of UFO believers matches the activities of every other folk group. The skeptics comprise an equally self-contained folk since they bond together for the sake of combating supposedly dangerous and erroneous UFO beliefs.

The "lore" of folklore need not be age-old traditions handed down generation to generation. Jokes and urban legends thrive on the latest news and current fears as they circulate around the country or around the world at breakneck speed. All this lore needs is a folk to transmit it, and many people are willing to spread a good joke or some new and outrageous urban legend. Offices, schools, and families have their own folklore; so do truck drivers, teenagers, and astronauts. UFO lore likewise flourishes among its willing communicators. UFOs no longer belong just to ufologists; in the true democratic style of folklore this phenomenon has become the property of everyone. UFOs are at home in folk, popular, mass, and elite culture, with stories about them on the lips of astronomers and airline pilots, police officers and the neighbors outside for a summer barbecue. Personal experiences and rumors join movies, TV, books, magazine articles, the Roswell festival, and scholarly discussions as all levels of society intertwine in a give-and-take of claims and beliefs that knits together the fabric of UFO lore today.

Folklorists pay close attention to the forms of expression people use when they communicate. Some story types, or genres, attempt to entertain or amuse, others to convey belief or experience, still others to warn or educate. The typical UFO sighting report is a personal experience narrative, no different in its goal to provide a straightforward account of eyewitness observation than thousands of reports from people describing encounters with ghosts and fairies, or, for that matter, describing a wreck at the nearby intersection. Discussions of truth, accuracy, and interpretation may follow, but basic personal reports convey experience of all sorts and furnish the building blocks for the extensive folklore of paranormal encounters. More complex accounts such as abductions resemble legend narratives. Legends concern events that befall people out of the blue, so to speak, and warn that the world is full of dangers both unexpected and inescapable that strike the deserving and undeserving alike. Urban legends of crazy killers and kidney thieves convey this message of harm lurking always just around the corner in the everyday world. Abductions say the same thing but raise the stakes of human vulnerability when aliens intrude into the victim's home undeterred by locks or burglar alarms. The message rises to nightmarish pitch when people are unsafe in their own beds.

In a larger sense UFOs belong to the genre of myth. The term suffers from overuse and too many definitions, one narrow one being a sacred narrative about origins, another being a false or erroneous story. UFO reports do not necessarily fit either of these prescriptions. A more expansive sense of myth treats it as a system of knowledge that provides believers with their fundamental understanding of the world. Myth assumes certain key truths, and these deep central beliefs—for instance, in gods, modes of economic production, or alien visitors—serve as a conceptual refrain to which thinking always returns and from which answers to the most important questions arise. This description applies equally well to a scientific theory, but where scientific terms are well defined and delimit the application of the theory to some narrow subject such as biological evolution or the behavior of subatomic particles, mythical terms are flexible, operating as symbols with multiple meanings that expand rather than restrict applications. In a sense myth is a theory of everything—or, for believers, the true answer to everything. Myth is a full system made up of many parts. It is a pattern of meanings that relates the scattered, seemingly incomprehensible complexities of social, psychological, and physical experience and binds them together in a whole that satisfies both the intellect and the emotions, an understanding cast in human terms that is simply too good not to be true.

A religious mythology serves up a complete worldview, answering questions about how the world began and how it will end and how people should live in the meantime. The system settles all issues theoretical or practical. UFOs offer a less thoroughgoing system, but stories that began as mere accounts of odd sights in the sky have grown into a far-reaching explanatory scheme for the human condition past and present. There is a UFO-oriented way to understand just about everything. In this view ancient astronauts shaped the human past, bringing cultural skills and building monuments such as the Egyptian pyramids and Easter Island statues, instilling in ancient humans the idea of gods residing in the sky. Modern his-

tory has its UFO version as well. Ever since learning the truth of alien visitation in 1947, the government has conspired to conceal and manipulate that secret, its preservation the prime motive behind every government action. According to another claim, the saucer that crashed near Roswell introduced earthly engineers to technological marvels such as the microchip and laser, and an even wilder speculation alleges that the real purpose behind Ronald Reagan's "Star Wars" missile defense system was a need to fight off aliens, not Soviet rockets. UFOs determine the future as well, if ufologists are right about abductions. In one version the aliens carry out a vast program to create a race of hybrids, part human and part alien, as a way for the extraterrestrials to preserve their dying race. Little by little the hybrids infiltrate society, and one by one they replace humans, to raise the chilling prospect of a future dominated by beings whose primary mentality and loyalty will be alien rather than human.

One principal duty of the folklorist is monitoring the continuity of certain plots, themes, and images from the distant past into the present. Folkloric ideas and story patterns seem to be forever with us, popping up in one age after another in various guises and mutations but familiar all the same, somehow permanent features in the landscape of human thinking. A student of the subject never ceases to be surprised by encounters with old friends in unexpected places, such as a version of Cinderella among the Zuni Indians, or the near-universality of diminutive supernatural beings. Psychologist C. G. Jung explained such universals with a theory of archetypes of the unconscious, inherent patterns in the human mind that break into consciousness in symbolic form and lend similar shape to the myths and imagery of all peoples. Folklorists have not favored such a neatly packaged solution. Some of them prefer a theory of transmission, that stories and ideas have passed from one people to another throughout human history, with each recipient group selecting and adapting ideas to its own cultural needs. In this way cultural groups individualize their folklore, yet at the same time they all dip from a common pool. Other folklorists opt for multiple origins, arguing that groups originate many of their own ideas, but similar human needs and conditions of living inspire stories with similar conflicts and resolutions.

Old Themes Made New

Aside from any question of how similarities originate, a long list of similarities turns up in comparison of long-standing folkloric themes with the contents of UFO reports.

Strange sights in the sky. The most transparent continuity linking modern UFOs with previous ages lies in a timeless human fascination with unusual appearances in the sky. People in every era and place have paid attention to aerial oddities and read significance into them. In early times these phenomena had supernatural origins; later, with the growth of scientific thinking, such appearances became anomalies of nature; and technological visions dominate from the late nineteenth century down to the present. Supernatural interpretations prevailed from earliest times through the seventeenth century as witnesses saw a divine message or warning in any uncommon sight and regarded comets or eclipses as portents of war and forthcoming calamity. Such matters rated inclusion in historical records and count as the UFOs of the period.

In 1500 B.C. Egyptian Pharaoh Thutmose III prepared for battle against the Syrians when a ball of fire descended from the sky to strike and kill two enemy guards. Interpreting this "miracle of the star" as a favorable sign from the gods, Pharaoh attacked the dispirited Syrians and won a victory.

In 614 B.C. the prophet Ezekiel saw in a dream a great wheel within a wheel in the middle of the air, and conversed with angels. Other biblical phenomena of interest include the chariot of fire that carried Elijah into heaven, the pillar of cloud and cloud of fire that led the Children of Israel through the wilderness, and the star that the Wise Men followed to Bethlehem.

Julius Obsequens, a Roman writer of the fourth century A.D., compiled a *Book of Prodigies* that says for the year 100 B.C., "a circular object like a shield was seen to sweep across from west to east." The "flying saucer" shape was quite rare prior to 1947, but the *Royal Frankish Annals* from the time of Charlemagne report that while the Saxons besieged the Franks in 776 A.D., the armies saw "the likeness of two shields red with flame wheeling over the church." At this sight the pagan Saxons fled in panic.

Several accounts from Irish annals in the tenth century A.D. tell of ships in the air. In one case the parishioners leaving church after worship found an anchor stuck in the masonry of the building. The rope led to a ship floating in the air. After a while a sailor descended through the air as if swimming and tried to free the anchor. The people seized him and he protested that he was drowning until the bishop ordered his release. The man swam upward to the ship, which sailed away after the sailors cut the anchor rope.

For 979, the *Anglo-Saxon Chronicles* record "a bloody cloud, in the likeness of fire" that appeared about midnight on numerous occasions, then "about dawn, it glided away."

In China between the 1050s and 1060s a "pearl" appeared in various areas at night, floating above a lake and lighting the trees so that they cast shadows. One witness saw a door open in this "pearl" and a bright light shoot out through the opening (*Columbia Anthology of Traditional Chinese Literature*, p. 593).

In Dunstable, England, in 1188, "the heavens opened, and . . . a cross appeared . . . and it appeared as though Jesus Christ was fastened thereon" (*Annals* of Roger de Hovenden).

In May 1543 Conrad Lycosthenes recorded in his chronicle of prodigies that a great comet was seen one afternoon over a German village. It was bigger than a millstone and stretched out its tail to the north, "from whence a fire descending to the earth like a dragon, drunk clean up the brook that was next unto it." This object then flew into a field and consumed the grain, then mounted again into the sky.

On January 18, 1644, Governor John Winthrop wrote in his diary that three boatmen saw two lights rise out of the water and disappear over Boston after about fifteen minutes. A week later a light like the moon rose, and many witnesses saw it shoot out flames and sparkles.

With the advent of science and Enlightenment the predominance of supernatural explanations for aerial phenomena came to an end, though such beliefs persist into the modern era. A widespread rumor from the time of World War I attributed the safe retreat of British forces from Mons to luminous angels that descended and drove back the attacking Germans with showers of arrows. On October 13, 1917, in Fatima, Portugal, a series of apparitions of the Virgin Mary culminated with the sun spinning in the sky and seeming to fall from its place and then ascend again before a crowd of some 70,000 witnesses. A traditional folklore of mysterious lights continued among people not impressed by the scientific revolution. Folklorist Harry M. Hyatt collected a number of death-omen stories from Adams County, Illinois, in the 1920s, and one informant said that she once saw a big ball of fire in the sky and a small spark dropped from it. Two days later the informant's sister died and her baby a month later, signifying that the large and small lights served as tokens for the two deaths. Ghost lights appear in various parts of the country, the most famous of them being the Marfa Lights of Texas, the light at Hornet, Missouri, and the Maco Station and Brown Mountain Lights of North Carolina. The Maco Station light is said to be the lantern of a railway conductor killed in a train wreck, while the Marfa Lights have been entangled with UFO-related rumors such as an ability to stop vehicle engines or to incinerate pursuers if they draw too close.

The official interpretation of anything odd in the sky became naturalistic from the 1700s onward. In these terms astronomy or meteorology explained all appearances, and however unusual they were, these sights had to be nothing more than uncommon versions of conventional phenomena. Be that as it may, the scientific record had its leftovers, its excluded remainder that Charles Fort called a "procession of the damned." Fort became the chronicler of these misfits, searching through old newspapers, magazines, and scientific journals for those reports that strayed from the rigid categories of a scientific worldview, then waving his collection back in the face of officialdom to argue that the accepted understanding of the universe had holes in it after all.

On April 5, 1800, the *Transactions of the American Philosophical Society* for 1804 published an account of a luminous crimson object the size of a large house that sailed above Baton Rouge, Louisiana, in the evening. When this object passed over the heads of the witnesses at low altitude, they felt heat and heard a violent rushing sound after it disappeared, followed by an explosion.

On July 8, 1868, a writer to the *English Mechanic* (v. 7, p. 351) reported a "meteor" seen from Oxford in the twilight. Stationary at first, an object like an elongated white cloud appeared to set into motion and passed to the westward, deviating first to the south then back to the north during the four minutes before the object disappeared below the horizon. This appearance left a trail behind it and resembled the combination of flame and smoke that issues from a railroad engine.

On September 5, 1891, at 2 A.M., two ice deliverymen and a Methodist minister in Crawfordsville, Indiana, felt a sense of dread and looked up to see a shapeless monster some 20 feet long and 8 feet wide writhing and circling in the air about 100 feet overhead. It looked like a mass of white drapery and seemed propelled by several pairs of fins. No head or tail could be seen during the several hours this monster was visible, but it gave out a moaning sound and one witness reported a fiery eye (*Indianapolis Journal*, September 6 and 7, p. 1).

On January 27, 1912, for two and a half hours an amateur astronomer watched "an intensely black body about 250 miles long and 50 wide . . . and in shape like a crow poised" above the surface of the moon. "I cannot but think that a very interesting and curious phenomenon happened," he wrote to *Popular Astronomy* (vol. 20, pp. 398–399).

On August 5, 1926, explorer Nicholas Roerich wrote in *Altai Himalaya* (pp. 361–362) that while high in the mountains of Tibet, members of his party spotted a large eagle overhead. As everyone looked at the bird, they saw a silvery oval object farther up, moving at great speed. The object changed direction, and with their field glasses the witnesses saw the sun glint on the smooth surface.

No definite UFO accompanied this report from Venezuela, published in the December 18, 1886, issue of *Scientific American*, but the phenomenology resembles some of the most lurid modern accounts of radiation poisoning when humans come too close to a spaceship. A family of nine persons wakened to hear a loud humming sound and see a dazzling light shining into the house. No sooner had the inhabitants started to pray than violent vomiting commenced, accompanied by rapid swellings in the upper parts of their bodies. The swelling disappeared by the following day, but dark blotches appeared, and nine days later the skin peeled off to leave raw sores. Trees near the house also withered on the ninth day. The hair of the people fell out, but most profusely on the side facing the phenomenon, whatever it was.

A third conceptual revolution took hold around 1880 and soon converted most strange sights in the sky into machinery. Unusual meteors and other naturalistic mysteries continued to appear in the pages of newspapers and magazines, but the world awaited the news that some inventor, in an age of invention already rich with wonders, had at last created the most-anticipated wonder of the nineteenth century and solved the problem of aerial navigation. Quite a number of witnesses jumped the gun and began to see these flying marvels even before they left the ground. In the mid-1880s an expectant public in New York and New Jersey watched a nightly light in the west and believed that Thomas Edison had attached an arc lamp to a balloon, then raised it miles high, for no other reason than to impress the public with his wizardry. He received letters about his "Edison Star" for more than twenty years but dismissed it as the planet Venus.

A continuing thread of reports began in 1892 in Russian Poland, where border guards accused the Germans of spying on military installations from airships. The rumor of a dirigible airship with a powerful searchlight spread to various forts and cities deep within Poland. No nation on earth had an aerial device of such sophistication in 1892, but that minor limitation in no way interfered with spectacular reports:

A few nights ago the people of Warsaw were startled by an intensely bright light in the sky.

All eyes were turned upward, but nothing could be seen save a path of light that ended in a small focus. Suddenly the ray of light swept in another direction, and . . . the people could see, far up in the sky, a balloon. (*New York Tribune*, 31 March 1892, p. 1)

The airship scene shifted to the United States in 1896. On the evening of November 17, hundreds of Sacramento, California, citizens saw what seemed to be a bright arc light floating through the air, rising and falling as if it avoided church steeples and other tall objects. Some witnesses thought they saw the dark frame of machinery and a gas bag, and a few said they heard voices. Within a few days the airship, or at least its light, appeared over Oakland and San Francisco, and for the next two weeks reports spread throughout California and spilled over into Nevada. By mid-December most reports had come to a halt, but at the end of January 1897 the sightings resumed across middle and eastern Nebraska. After appearing in Omaha and Topeka, Kansas, late in March, the airship broke loose and toured the entire country for the next six weeks. Over the weekend of April 9–12 the ship put in appearances to large crowds in Chicago, St. Louis, Minneapolis, and Milwaukee. In Milwaukee the airship appeared about 9 o'clock.

It came from the northeast from out over the lake. There was no possibility of mistake this time. Thousands of people saw it, and in a few minutes they were following the machine as it floated over the city. It traveled toward the southwest until it reached a point directly over the City Hall, where it stopped for a quarter of an hour. Then the excitement in the downtown districts became intense. It was reported that attempts were being made to anchor the machine. (*Chicago Tribune*, April 12, 1897, p. 5)

Though such sightings were concentrated in the Midwest, nearly every state received a visit or two. All in all, at least 3,000 reports of airships appeared in newspapers between March and May 1897. Many people believed at first that some inventor had built a successful flying machine and was showing it off on his way to Washington for a patent. The story became harder to believe as reports spread in all directions and the ship appeared at the same time in places hundreds of miles apart. In some instances the reports were honest errors as people mistook bright planets or stars for the headlight of an airship, but hoaxing became widespread as well, with pranksters sending up kites with lanterns attached, or fire balloons, paper bags lofted by the hot air from a candle or other heat source, the burned-out carcasses of which sometimes turned up in vacant lots or corn fields.

Two famous hoaxes of the era were pure fabrications. One came from Aurora, Texas, on April 17, claiming that the airship crashed into a local windmill and exploded. The body of the pilot was found, and it was clear that "he was not an inhabitant of this world" but perhaps a native of Mars. Another originated with farmer Alexander Hamilton of Leroy, Kansas, who said that on April 19, a commotion in his cattle yard awakened him and he hurried outside with his family to see a cigar-shaped airship some 300 feet long descending slowly toward the ground. The ship shone a searchlight about, and inside a glassed-in undercarriage, he saw six strange beings. When the humans neared, the occupants turned the searchlight on the intruders and the airship began to rise. As it pulled away, it lifted a heifer by a rope around its neck, and the next day a neighbor brought in the butchered remains of a cow, found in a field with no footprints in the vicinity. A long list of the most respected citizens of Woodson County signed an affidavit that Hamilton had a well-deserved reputation for truth and veracity. Hamilton and the signers belonged to the same Saturday afternoon liars' club, it later turned out.

The events of 1896–1897 sketched the full outline of the modern UFO phenomenon fifty years before its official beginning. Numerous witnesses claimed that lighted mechanical objects of a design more advanced than anything on earth flew through the skies, with sightings coming in swarms or waves of hundreds or thousands of reports within a few weeks or months. Skepticism nestled side by side with credulity; rapid communication and the mass media relayed the stories far and wide. Landings and occupants figured into some reports, and a few tales implicated extraterrestrials as builders of the crafts. The great majority of the reports owed their existence to mistaken identity or hoaxes. Little has changed in the last hundred years.

The airships of 1897 combined balloons of the dirigible with wings and propellers of the airplane in an aerodynamically impossible design, but later phantom airships assumed a more practical configuration. Count Zeppelin flew his first dirigible in 1900, and the Wright brothers invented the first successful airplane in 1903. These experiments attracted little attention until 1908–1909, when early aviators gathered for public demonstrations and large crowds witnessed flying machines in action for the first time. The world went air-crazy, and people seemed to think of nothing else. A hit song of the day was "Come Fly with Me, Josephine, in My Flying Machine." Phantom aircraft returned to satisfy the public demand for flying machines and startled witnesses with an almost constant stream of isolated sightings, local waves, or large-scale waves from 1908 until 1918. Small waves in Washington state, Denmark, and New England in 1908 gave way to major waves in Britain, New Zealand, and New England (again) in 1909. Thousands of people in Boston saw the brilliant headlight of an airship supposedly flown by a Massachusetts inventor, though critics pointed out that the witnesses were in fact staring at Venus. As World War I approached, British witnesses saw German dirigibles shine searchlights across the countryside in 1913, and once the war broke out, phantom airplanes with bright lights soared over South Africa, Canada, and Norway. The Du Pont gunpowder works in Delaware became targets for spying aircraft in 1916, as did dock and industrial facilities in Minnesota and Wisconsin, while Massachusetts residents had aerial spies to worry about in 1917. In none of these cases was the alleged inventor or spy ever captured.

Another invasion of mystery aircraft occurred in the 1930s, with the most sustained activity in Sweden and Norway as large airplanes with one or more bright lights flew even through howling blizzards. These "ghost fliers" were thought to be smugglers or Soviet spies. The fliers appeared in late 1933 and the winter of 1934, then again in the fall, and thereafter visited for a month or two each year through 1937. During World War II, pilots in both the European and Pacific theaters saw singles or groups of luminous balls pace their aircraft while on night missions. Airmen kept a nervous eye on these objects, known as "foo fighters," as possible enemy secret weapons. No sooner did the war end than mysterious flying objects multiplied worldwide, but especially in Scandinavia once more, where silvery, metallic "ghost rockets" flew day and night during the summer of 1946. A few of these devices crashed into lakes, though efforts to recover the wreckage was never successful. The Swedish Air Force logged nearly 1,000 reports that year.

Silvery, metallic rockets relate to flying saucers as next of kin, and many ghost rocket reports read like descriptions of saucers seen on edge. The advent of flying saucers in 1947 brought out some 4,000 reports of strange objects in the sky, most of them literally saucer-shaped or something close to it, though cylinders, crescents, and various other shapes added variety to the descriptions, then as now. By the massive wave of 1952, most saucers presented themselves as luminous nocturnal disks, while some prominent reports from the 1957 wave included luminous torpedo or egg-shaped objects. The extended 1964–1968 wave featured close encounters with craft displaying more structure and complexity than most of their predecessors, while in the last twenty years triangular or flying-wing objects have grown commonplace. Even so, the general disk shape still tops the list of most common descriptions.

UFO history charts an unmistakable path of observations accommodating expectations. The past hundred years teach a lesson that the very definition of "advanced" operates as a moving target responsive to current ideals of cutting-edge design. The clunky airships of the 1890s improved into airplanes and rockets and secret weapons as observer expectations kept pace with rapid technological change, the mystery objects always one step ahead of reality until the idea of aliens sent flying saucers forward by a leap. Aliens promise to possess a technology beyond our reach, though perhaps not too far, and always within our imagining. Experiences gain credibility because the UFOs of an age assume the guises of the time and reflect its beliefs and expectations.

If interpretations and shapes vary over the years, the underlying preoccupations of the accounts stay the same. A tradition of interest in strange aerial sights extends throughout human history as a constant, even while specific forms and understandings adapt to the dominant con-

ceptions of the times. UFOs remained divine messages or natural anomalies when belief allowed no alternatives; later observations dutifully rewarded expectations of machines in flight. In most cases the scientific perspective unmasks the mystery of former sightings, revealing fiery appearances in the medieval night as auroras or strange meteors as just extreme examples of more conventional meteors. Even the flying monster of Crawfordsville was probably a flock of killdeer disturbed from their sleep by the new electric lights the town had installed. A touch of Venus and runaway imagination accounts for many an airship, or, for that matter, many a flying saucer, but human interest and the error it inspires persist down the ages to link all aerial oddities, explainable and unexplainable alike, into a long-lived folk tradition.

The Otherworld
"UFO" and "alien spaceship" are synonymous terms for most people. The current conception takes for granted that UFOs bring visitors from other planets to earth, and nothing seems more up-to-date than the idea that civilizations ahead of ours in technological progress have gotten the jump on us to come calling, even as we plan to call on them some day. Yet this most modern of ideas is also age-old in its way, with roots deep in folklore, religion, and mythology.

The mythological cosmos typically consists of three realms or levels: The gods reside in an upper realm or heaven, mortals live in the middle on earth, and the dead and evil entities occupy the underworld, or hell. This archaic cosmos tends toward compactness, with little distance between the three realms. They border one another so closely that in some traditions a great tree joins them all, growing on earth while its branches reach to the sky and its roots to the netherworld. Traffic between the realms is correspondingly simple, with gods and demons coming and going at will, while humans may reach heaven by climbing the world tree or a sacred mountain, or emerge into the netherworld after descending a cave or well. A basket lowered through a hole in the sky provides transport in some American Indian myths; a short sail by boat carries the Irish to the Land of the Blessed; and a rainbow bridge connects earth with Asgard, the home of the Norse gods. Distance never handicaps travel in mythology, just as the light years between stars pose no inconvenience for alien visitors.

Fairy lore contains an especially well-developed concept of an otherworldly realm, usually located underground but always adjacent to the human world with only the thinnest of barriers to separate the two. So close at hand is the residence of fairies that some folk superstitions warn against pouring hot water onto the ground, for fear of scalding the fairies below. On occasions of fairy festivals a mound or hill that marks the location of fairyland rises on pillars and a brilliant light shines from inside, a sight that closely resembles a landed UFO. Visitors to the underground fairyland describe a sky that is uniformly luminous but without a sun, like an earthly sky on a cloudy day, but also like the appearance some abductees report when a UFO flies them to an alien planet. Those UFO journeys share a surprising brevity, requiring less time than the morning commute or a drive to the local market. Time runs at a different pace in fairyland as well. A passerby who chances upon the fairies and joins in their dances or games for an hour or so may return home to find himself forgotten by all but the oldest residents, who recall him only as someone who disappeared twenty, fifty, or a hundred years ago. In these tales the bewildered stranger usually has only enough time to tell his story before he crumbles into dust. This widespread motif of the "supernatural lapse of time in fairyland" is the basis for Washington Irving's story of Rip Van Winkle. For students of UFO abductions, this physical time lapse appears to be a close relation to the mental time lapse of abductees such as Barney and Betty Hill, who could not account for two hours of a road trip until hypnosis released a mental block and they remembered that aliens captured and examined them during this interval.

A peculiarity of the fairy race is its lack of reproductive self-sufficiency. The fairies seem unable to reproduce themselves without human assistance, and fairy lore is full of stories about fairies kidnapping human babies, marrying mortals, or requiring a human midwife to deliver their babies. One of the most striking aspects of UFO abduction reports is evidence for a similar dependency among the aliens. They collect eggs and sperm from captives, impregnate a woman and then steal the fetus, grow the embryo in tanks of liquid, and later present the mother with a frail infant or child that is a hybrid combination of human and alien traits. The sexual preoccupations of aliens reflect similar interests of demons in the traditions of witchcraft. The incubus and succubus appeared to sleeping women and men (respectively) for sexual purposes, invading bedrooms in the night much as aliens do today, and demons sometimes flew witches away for the carnal revels of the Sabbat. Although modern abductions are no party, the new tradition resembles the old in a surprising number of details.

The transition to another realm also takes place in altered states of consciousness. A medieval account of the "Visions of Tundal" tells how a young man passed out at dinner and visited heaven and hell during his period of unconsciousness. An angel escorted him through hell, where he saw the torments of sinners and Satan himself, resembling a big cockroach squirming on his back in the midst of the fire. Heaven was beautiful and blissful, but no sun shone in the self-luminous sky. Formerly a diligent sinner, Tundal reformed after he wakened from his vision. This "tour of hell" tradition was widespread from the early Christian era to the Middle Ages and culminated in Dante's literary treatment, the *Divine Comedy*. Even today people who undergo a near-death experience describe an otherworldly visit as they sweep through a long tunnel to a heavenly place where they meet deceased friends and ancestors, with an occasional side trip to hellish scenes. Comparing these tours with UFO abductions turns up unmistakable parallels: Abductees lose conscious recall while an alien escort brings them inside the UFO, where they undergo a medical examination that is unpleasant, even akin to torture, at the hands of beings inhuman in appearance and inhumane in their treatment of captives. With a stretch of imagination the abductees who see the engine room of the ship are like Tundal when he glimpsed Satan. The sunless otherworld and life changes also characterize abduction accounts. These visionary tours belong to a larger tradition of initiation ordeals widespread in human cultures and probably of archaic origin. The initiation of the Siberian shaman and the vision quest of the Sioux begin with sickness or physical exhaustion. While the subject is delirious or unconscious the soul leaves his body and he meets spirits of the underworld to acquire knowledge and powers. In broad terms abduction accounts tell the same story.

Traditions of an otherworld near at hand coexisted with traditions of exotic distant places. When the followers of Alexander the Great invaded India, they brought back tales of the bizarre races of beings inhabiting this far-off land. Its population included the Dog-Headed Men; the Cyclops, or one-eyed men; the *Blemmyae,* men without heads having their faces located on their chests; and one-legged men who used their huge foot as an umbrella to shade themselves. This menagerie of monstrous beings reappeared in the travel literature of the Middle Ages, both in the fictitious journeys of Sir John Mandeville and in the genuine travels of Marco Polo. European explorers no sooner reached the New World than they rediscovered the monstrous races that had become traditional necessities in every faraway place. Some of these descriptions had likely factual sources—for example, the Dog-Headed Men were probably baboons—but the tradition created expectations that had to be met. The farther travelers wandered from the familiar territory of home, the more fantastic the inhabitants had to become—how else could you prove that you had gone anywhere at all?

Even as late as the beginning of the twentieth century, Sir Arthur Conan Doyle could write *The Lost World* and readers could believe that dinosaurs survived in some remote place. By 1933 the idea that King Kong ruled Skull Island had become a romantic fantasy. The earth had shrunk to human size as explorers reached every corner of the globe and rousted out the secrets from its surface. Monsters could still lurk beneath the sea, but the new home for the otherworldly had long since shifted from the earth to other planets. The idea of an inhabited universe is an old one. In the seventeenth century Bernard de Fontenelle speculated about the beings on other planets in his *Conversations Concerning the Plurality of Worlds,* while late in the following century the astronomer William

Herschel noted seasonal changes in the polar caps of Mars and concluded that the Martians enjoyed a climate similar to our own. So ingrained was the idea that God wasted nothing and therefore all heavenly bodies must be inhabited that Herschel took for granted vast populations living beneath the glowing atmosphere of the sun, and that Uranus, the planet he discovered, also provided a home for life.

Astronomers in the nineteenth century applied principles of physics to the other planets and found most of them either too hot or too cold for life as we know it, while the spectroscope revealed poisonous gases such as ammonia and methane in the atmospheres of the giant planets. Even as additional knowledge undermined the possibility of universal life, the likelihood increased that the planet Mars offered a hospitable home for living things. Its reddish surface had darker areas that observers interpreted as seas, also areas like snow at the poles and occasional clouds in the sky. The more astronomers learned about the planet, the more earthlike it seemed. Then in 1877, the Italian astronomer Giovanni Schiaparelli discovered thin linear features that stretched across the red areas from the seas. He called these lines *canali,* or channels, but the English translation of "canals" suggested an artificial origin to many readers. His drawings from 1877 and 1879 showed rather natural-looking features, but when the planet again swung into view during 1881–1882 the canals became much more remarkable—some of them appeared as double lines running in perfect parallel for hundreds or thousands of miles across the Martian surface, demonstrating that if they were real, the canals had to be artificial.

Many astronomers joined the dispute over the canals of Mars, arguing whether they were natural, artificial, or simply illusory. The answer seemed indisputable to Percival Lowell, a wealthy Bostonian who built an observatory in Arizona for the purpose of studying Mars. He saw a complex of canals more intricate than Schiaparelli's and arrived at a theory that Mars was inhabited by an advanced civilization fighting to survive on a dying planet. Lowell reasoned that Mars, being smaller than the earth and farther from the sun, would have cooled sooner; life would have evolved there sooner and intelligent forms appeared long before any comparable stage of development on earth. But Mars was now an old planet. Its seas had dried up, its atmosphere thinned. The dark areas visible from earth were tracts of vegetation, perhaps forests, while the reddish areas were deserts. No water remained but the polar caps, and this precious water had to be pumped with the seasonal melting of the snows to irrigate farmlands and through the canals to the ancient Martian cities left stranded in the deserts after the seas dried up. The canals themselves were not visible channels but tracts of cropland alongside a system of pipes. For now the Martians were surviving on their ingenuity, but their days were numbered. The drying process would continue to its inexorable end when all life became extinct on the planet.

The public was fascinated by Lowell's theory and the prospect of life on Mars, though most astronomers dismissed the canals as optical illusions—as in fact they turned out to be. Not everyone accepted the notion that technologically adept Martians would simply sit and wait to die out. Science fiction writer H. G. Wells scored a popular success with his 1897 novel, *The War of the Worlds,* which borrowed Lowell's theory but credited the Martians with a more ambitious program of self-preservation. In this novel the Martians built space cannons and fired cylinders to the earth. These cylinders opened to reveal Martians of an octopuslike appearance, having evolved into all head and hands. Despite earth's thick atmosphere and oppressive gravity, the invaders constructed tripodlike fighting machines that stalked across the landscape at express-train speed, incinerating cities with heat rays and exterminating large populations with poison gas. Not human armies but bacteria against which the aliens had no immunity defeated the Martians. This novel established the themes of much science fiction literature to follow, with the pulp magazines of the 1920s and 1930s often depicting bug-eyed monsters invading the earth. So plausible did the idea sound that some listeners panicked when they tuned in to the Orson Welles "War of the Worlds" radio broadcast of 1938.

When the flying saucers appeared, Mars leaped to mind as the likely source, its inhabitants suddenly concerned about the earth because the Martian astronomers had noticed the flashes of our nuclear explosions. At long last the primitives had advanced to the point where they posed a potential threat, and all-out surveillance became necessary. Writers of 1950s UFO literature worried that saucers frequented military installations, power plants, and other vital facilities, as if mapping the way for a surprise attack. Hollywood also favored the invasion idea with an outpouring of movies such as *Invaders from Mars, The War of the Worlds, Killers from Space, Invasion of the Body Snatchers, Earth versus the Flying Saucers,* and *I Married a Monster from Outer Space.* The dying planet theme often provided the motive for invasion, and while Mars was not always the source of the saucers, suspicion almost always fell on some nearby planet.

Our own advances in space exploration disintegrated any prospects for intelligent life in the solar system, but the universe remains a big place. Scientific opinion sanctions the belief that life springs up by natural processes wherever conditions are right, and so many planets probably exist that suitable conditions must be widespread and life must thrive in many star systems. UFOs reflect this reorientation of scientific belief and now originate from Zeta Reticuli, the Pleiades, or some other distant place where aliens keep their plausibility. The mileage has increased, the concepts have changed from supernatural to superscientific and from heaven or hell to faraway stars, but the old theme of visitation from other worlds repeats throughout human history without missing a beat.

Inhabitants of the Otherworld

Some of the most exciting stories about UFOs provide a glimpse of who—or what—travels inside. The contactees of the 1950s brought the reassuring news that the visitors were people just like us, only better-looking. George Adamski's man from Venus had long blond hair and looked for all the world like an angel without wings. These angelic beings continue to appear today, since abductees report that they sometimes meet tall, blond, blue-eyed humans, the "Nordics," who seem kind and wise in contrast to the cold, businesslike entities that carry out the examinations. UFO lore also has its monsters. After nightfall on September 12,

1952, near the end of a great wave of sightings, several children in Flatwoods, West Virginia, saw a luminous object land on a nearby hill. They called their mothers and a sizable troop including a woman, a young National Guardsman, several teenagers, children, and a dog started up the hill to investigate a possible plane crash. They found a glowing sphere the size of a house resting on the ground, then in another direction and closer by, they spotted two luminous eyes that seemed to belong to a raccoon. Turning the flashlight in that direction, the party saw a ten-foot-tall figure in some kind of space suit, with large round glowing eyes. The witnesses fled in panic and the Flatwoods Monster became one of the most popular newspaper stories of the year. This case remains one of the few genuine monster reports in UFO literature. For all the ugly creatures Hollywood invented to represent the inhabitants of other planets, for all the pervasiveness of these mass-culture images, one of the surprises of UFO lore is how seldom anything of the sort steps out of a flying saucer.

When UFOs land the usual occupants are "little men" or humanoids, beings of generally human form but short, often only three or four feet tall. Such beings often wore space suits or pilot's gear when they first appeared in considerable numbers during the 1954 wave in France and Italy. Similar creatures described as "hairy dwarfs" emerged from UFOs in South America that same year. America earned a distinguished place in the early history of humanoid activity on the evening of August 21, 1955, when a party of short, luminous beings with large ears and saucer-shaped eyes laid night-long siege to a farmhouse in Kelly, Kentucky. One family member went to the well for water about 7 P.M. and saw a saucer-shaped object descend into the nearby woods. Later a luminous figure approached along a dirt road, and the men of the house picked up firearms. When the creature looked in at a window, one of the men shot it through the screen. Yet bullets and shotgun blasts had no effect on the invaders, and for several hours they perched on the rooftop or in the trees and were seen by ten people before the unnerved family fled to town and contacted the sheriff about 11 P.M. The police and the press flocked to the

house and found ample evidence of a shootout but no sign of the strange creatures. Once the crowd departed and the family settled down to sleep, a luminous entity reappeared at the door and the siege resumed until near dawn, though at no time did the entities show any hostile intent.

Short humanoids man the ship in nearly every UFO report today. The military allegedly found them with the crashed saucer at Roswell, and they are the beings most likely to stop cars on lonely roads or invade bedrooms late at night to abduct humans. A standard description recurs in hundreds of abduction reports—the entities are short, three to five feet tall; their heads are large and bald, with pointed chins and grayish skin; the face consists of huge, elongated eyes, while the mouth, nose, and ears are small or vestigial. Sometimes the beings wear one-piece uniforms or jump suits; at other times their clothing seems skin-tight or even nonexistent, though witnesses seldom recognize any distinctive male or female traits.

This same variety of entities occupies the otherworld of folk tradition, with the populace of fairyland offering the richest examples. Only the Victorians regarded fairies as tiny beings. In genuine folklore one race of fairies, the Tuatha de Danann, was tall, beautiful, and godlike, while others, such as the brownies, were stunted, rough, and hairy. Some malevolent fairies looked thoroughly monstrous. Most fairy types were dwarfish in size, not small enough to sleep in the nectar cup of a flower but less than human size. Large heads characterized the dwarfs of German legend, and bright, notable eyes distinguished many Irish fairies. Ideas about the dead intertwined with beliefs about fairies so that they became cold, bloodless, and ghostly, with pallid skin never exposed to sunlight, and jealous of the living. A dependency went hand in hand with this jealousy, a willingness to kidnap humans and a need to replenish the race by stealing human children. Though best known in Celtic tradition, fairylike beings are nearly universal. A survey of American Indian mythology turns up a rich lore of small supernatural beings. Hawaiians know of the Menehune, the Japanese of kappas, while even the Pygmies of Africa tell legends of beings smaller than themselves. UFO occupants so closely parallel the inhabitants of fairyland that aliens, taken solely in the descriptive context of worldwide fairy legends, amount to nothing more than the latest update in a long-running tradition.

Apocalypse, Salvation, and the Millennium

When psychologists and sociologists discovered the contactee movement in the 1950s, they quickly decided that flying saucers served as vehicles not for aliens but for a new and distinctively modern religious movement. C. G. Jung was especially outspoken in recognizing flying saucers as elements in a developing salvation myth cast in technological terms. The experts were right about the religious intentions of contactees but dead wrong about the trend of UFO beliefs. Contactees flourished as a fashionable "New Age" religion in the 1950s, when platitudinous messages that nuclear testing was wrong and that the Space Brothers would help prevent nuclear war struck a responsive chord in people worried about the future but no longer comforted by conventional churches. The contactee movement survives today in groups such as the Unarius Society and the Raelians, while the mass suicide of Heaven's Gate members in 1997 spotlighted this contactee cult for a moment of notoriety. The fact remains that contactees reside on the fringes of UFO lore. Scientific ufologists rejected the principal claimants as hoaxers and con artists; most of the popular following listened for a little while and then moved on to other alternative religions. No church, theology, rituals, or ethics ever took root in this movement. UFOs have always been more about personal observations and experiences than any sort of formal religion; nevertheless, some persistent, seemingly spontaneous ideas entangle UFO lore with familiar religious themes concerning the last days and reconfiguration of the world.

A familiar cornerstone of Judeo-Christian and Islamic religious traditions is belief in an apocalyptic end of the world and restoration of humanity's original home in paradise. The thread of these beliefs probably stretches back to the ancient Persian prophet Zoroaster, who envisioned the forces of good and evil locked in ongoing conflict until the god of goodness triumphed in a great final battle. The earth would be destroyed and a new earth, cleansed of all evil, would become the home of the good, a place of perfection for sinless and immortal beings. Time and again the yearning for this purified and perfected state has inspired religious movements. Many Christians today expect Christ to return and rule the earth for a thousand years—the Millennium—after binding Satan and defeating the forces of the Antichrist. Between now and that blissful thousand years lies a time when evil multiplies and cataclysms begin the breakdown of the old, corrupt order. The recent excitement over the year 2000 owes much to this religious pattern, whether among the survivalists who prepare for a great catastrophe or the biblical literalists who read the turn of the calendar as the date of Christ's return. Secular visions of the future often copy the same religious model. Marxists believe that an age of turmoil and revolution will give way to an age when all people live together in harmony and communal ownership of goods. Technocrats foresee a time when science and technology will solve all human problems, creating abundance without toil or hardship, ending war and injustice, curing all diseases, and even abolishing death.

Though an integral part of Western religion, millennial hopes have inspired many peoples around the world. Such movements are especially common where external forces threaten and disrupt old, established ways of life. In 1890 the Ghost Dance movement spread among the Plains Indians. It promised to restore a vanishing culture by driving out the white man and bringing back the ancestors and the buffalo. Western contact confronted the people of New Guinea with the mystery of why only Europeans possessed the desirable material goods that outsiders brought. In their efforts to understand the strange favoritism of the gods, the natives created various millennial movements popularly known as cargo cults, wherein participants attempted various tactics, such as creating landing strips, to lure the airplanes of the gods to deliver the desirable cargo into native hands. Some millennial movements borrow ideas from Christian teachings, but peoples in eastern Brazil undertook arduous migrations to find the Land without Evil long before the first missionaries arrived.

These same themes resound with increasing insistence in UFO abduction reports. Although examinations and reproductive concerns seem to preoccupy the aliens first and foremost, a secondary purpose is to teach and instruct their captives, sometimes in a one-on-one conference, sometimes in an auditorium where an alien sage lectures a group of humans, sometimes through images shown on a screen or instilled in the brain. The message of the aliens rings an apocalyptic alarm: They warn of an impending catastrophe as humans continue their old habits of violence, materialism, and destructive exploitation of the earth. Sometimes the aliens underscore the danger by admitting that they speak from experience, having damaged or destroyed their own planet by similarly heedless practices. Abductees sometimes report radical changes in their attitudes and lifestyles; they become more humane and spiritually aware as a consequence of their encounters. Frightening as their methods seem, the aliens actually come as saviors striving to transform the consciousness of their captives toward ecological awareness and harmonious living with the earth. If this effort fails and cataclysms strike, the aliens have a backup plan. They sometimes assign individuals a task or mission to perform "when the time is right," inaccessible to memory until then but concerned with some helpful role in preventing or ameliorating the disasters to come. If all else fails the aliens themselves will intervene to rescue chosen individuals in the time of tribulation, according to some versions of the story.

We have every reason to expect a clean break with the past in modern UFOs. After all, they are mechanical and metallic—kick them and they go *clang*. They are spaceships manned by intellectually superior extraterrestrials here for exploration, scientific discovery, or similar no-nonsense purposes having nothing to do with fairy magic or insubstantial ghosts. At first glance nothing seems further removed from traditional folk beliefs. On closer inspection, the accounts of UFOs and their occupants sketch a phenomenon more magical than a straightforward nuts-and-bolts explanation allows. One minute a UFO reflects radar, registers on a photograph, or leaves apparent traces on the ground; the next minute that same craft may refuse to play by established rules of physics and perform in ways unfit for any material object. The reports often describe objects that travel at enormous velocity without atmospheric friction; turn at full speed and sharp angles; and stop instantaneously, then dart off again as fast as before without apparent acceleration. Some UFOs disappear in an instant rather than soar out of sight. No wonder scientists balk at the claim that UFOs are machines when they behave as if immaterial and without inertia. Abduction reports tell of a silence that surrounds the scene and captives that float into the UFO, while the aliens that visit bedrooms in the night may pass through a closed door in the time-honored fashion of ghosts.

So many claims seem surreal and dreamlike that critics cite these seeming impossibilities as proof that the whole experience results from the mind playing tricks, perhaps the result of a nightmare or hallucination. Proponents have countered with two responses. One begins with a quotation from science fiction author Arthur C. Clarke, that any technology sufficiently far advanced would seem like magic, and accepts that the strangeness we see is in fact advanced alien technology in action. The other results from the phenomenon becoming too bizarre even for ufologists. Some of them have despaired of explaining UFOs in purely physical terms and resorted to ideas such as alternate universes and objects that interchange the properties of matter and energy from minute to minute, or at the will of some mysterious godlike intelligence. In any case the folklorist recognizes a continuity where old-fashioned magical properties have become indistinguishable from super-scientific technology.

UFOs appear modern and different only on the surface. All in all, spaceships from the stars bring nothing new under the sun. They return age-old themes to the modern world—preoccupations with strange sights in the sky, concerns about last things, beliefs in other worlds and otherworldly visitors—expressed in space-age guise just as these same themes have found expression in the current idiom of every age. These issues sound out some of the deepest interests of human thinking—our place in the universe, whom we share it with, where we came from, and what will happen to us. UFO beliefs mix hopes of salvation and cosmic brotherhood with fears of invasion and violation from outside. They even repeat some of the time-worn specifics of previous beliefs such as super-natural kidnapping and the reproductive para-sitism of otherworldly beings to preserve a surprising continuity of the new stories with the old. In their revival of age-old themes, breadth of meaning, and depth of appeal UFOs seal their sta-tus as folklore and their stature as myth.

Folklore and Experience

What place do real UFOs—if any exist—hold within the perennial fabric of folk belief? Folk-lorists cannot say whether UFOs are genuine spaceships or only Venus and airplanes mistaken for something more, but they have gained respect for human experience as a necessary source and sustainer of tradition. The former understanding of folklorists sided with tradition as the basis for apparent experiences. By hearing ghost stories an individual learned to expect ghosts at midnight in a graveyard. That same individual passing a ceme-tery at night and seeing moonlight on a patch of fog might reshape the vague form to fit his expec-tations and fears, with the outcome a ghost com-plete with shroud and chains. The "witness" would then reinforce the belief of others by adding his testimony to tradition, though in fact the ghost amounted to mist and misperception force-fitted into an imaginative preconception, nothing more.

In recent years some investigators have turned this explanation upside down and argued that some traditions endure, even against the rational-istic opposition of official culture, because they have independent experience to back them up. Folklorist David Hufford investigated the "Old Hag" tradition of Newfoundland, a belief that a witch was responsible for experiences of people who wakened in the night unable to move while some evil presence entered the bedroom and choked the victim. The tradition with all its interpretations was well known and long established in New-foundland, but Hufford found that some of his stu-dents in Pennsylvania had suffered similar experi-ences, even though they knew nothing of the tradition. If the experience was widespread but the

tradition was not, the standard explanation that expectations create the experience quite simply fell apart. He established that "supernatural assault traditions" had worldwide distribution. The basic experiential features remained the same whatever the folk explanation might be, and included in part a physiological condition known as sleep paralysis. In this case the tradition seemed to begin with ex-perience and not the other way around.

A great deal of UFO lore depends on observa-tion. Tens of thousands of people have seen some-thing in the sky that they could not explain, and whether they reported the sighting or not, to them it became a UFO. In most of those cases the expec-tation led the way as it lent an aura of mystery and significance to an ordinary planet or meteor, a sight the witness would not imagine to be a space-ship without the preparation of tradition. In March 1967 a Soviet moon probe fell back into the atmosphere and burned up over several Midwest-ern states. The U.S. Air Force received about 70 re-ports of this reentry, and most observers gave an accurate description of half a dozen flaming, me-teor-like bodies high in the atmosphere. Some even recognized the nature of the objects. But there were a few individuals who saw something entirely different. One reported a UFO flying at treetop level with six lighted windows, fiery ex-haust, and riveted steel plates along the hull. Either this witness misinterpreted the reentry in terms of UFO expectations, or two of the most spectacular aerial sights of a lifetime occurred at once, and this witness missed one of them. A great many UFO reports have an experiential basis, but not necessarily an extraterrestrial one. They originate in the eyes of believers and take the shape of a spaceship, where another observer not under the influence of the UFO tradition looks at the same sight and sees nothing more than the evening star.

At the same time a remainder of reports contin-ues to puzzle the investigator, and the most deter-mined effort to find a conventional solution leaves behind evidence that refuses to fit. Even as fantastic a story as alien abduction defies the typical dynam-ics of folklore by varying very little from one narra-tor to another. Folk narratives typically exist as clus-ters of variants swarming around a core of ideas. Even tightly constructed forms such as jokes and urban legends multiply as different content fits into the same plot form, or similar content aligns itself with a different plot. Abduction reports are long, loosely constructed, and fantastic—ideal candidates for rampant variation, ready to satisfy the personal needs of anyone looking to escape the dullness of everyday life in fantasies of romance and adventure. In fact the accounts reflect few of these expectations. The episodes could exchange places and the story would make equally good sense, yet the episodes usually keep the same relative positions in one report after another. The same content recurs in story after story, down to some minor detail seldom if ever emphasized in any published or broadcast accounts, in some cases present in the reports for years before any investigators recognize or call attention to it. Despite all the aliens depicted in mass and popular culture, abductees limit their accounts to very few types and usually describe the rather bland and unimpressive small gray humanoids. All those opportunities for colorful fantasies languish unrealized as abductees usually depict themselves not as the heroes of their own adventure but as victims, taken and used and turned out with no sense of satisfaction, only feelings of resentment and confusion. Such an outcome is surprising for a fantasy, if fantasies these reports truly are. Proposals that abductees as a group are fantasy-prone or subject to suggestion while under hypnosis have proven doubtful when tested. Whatever they prove to be, abductions, like UFOs in general, appear more complicated than simple errors or creative imaginings.

Any final reckoning must balance the two sides that comprise the whole of the UFO mystery. On the one hand, Jung was right to call UFOs a modern myth. They answer big questions about life and the cosmos and tie them all together in a comprehensible whole with visitors from the sky at the center. They restore wonder and mystery, hope and dread to a world where modernization has stifled these emotions. UFOs challenge official knowledge with the grassroots experience of people who see things that the experts refuse to allow. In this rebellious resistance the folk assert the worth of their own knowledge and a democratic faith that officialdom holds less than full understanding of the world. Whatever else UFOs may be, they serve human uses. The vast lore accumulated around the UFO idea speaks less for the needs of reason than for the human needs of people who tell these stories.

On the other hand there are the UFOs themselves, whatever they may be, much entangled in the myth surrounding them. Folk, popular, mass, and elite cultures take their own approaches to the phenomenon, and the cumulative effect obscures the reality behind a multitude of expectations, wishes, and preconceptions. The UFOs of reality become lost behind the UFOs of belief, to be glimpsed only in distorted versions. Folklorists cannot settle the issue, but whether UFOs crumble into a collection of conventional occurrences or exist as an independent phenomenon, no one can hope to study UFOs without recognizing the role of human beliefs and concerns in UFO lore.

INTRODUCTION

I saw French astronomers erase a magnetic tape on which our satellite-tracking team had recorded eleven data points on an unknown flying object which was not an airplane, a balloon, or a known orbiting craft. "People would laugh at us if we reported this!" was the answer I was given at the time. Better forget the whole thing.

—Jacques Vallée, *Messengers of Deception*

This event, which prompted Jacques Vallee to begin investigating UFOs decades ago, embodies an all-too-common attitude toward this and similar phenomena: When we encounter the unknown, we rarely discuss it openly for fear of being laughed at or labeled a "kook." In some instances, we even attempt to erase all memory of the experience. Despite the high incidence of unusual activity in the world, it is clear that our perception is influenced by a social consensus that encourages us to ignore—even to ridicule—events that do not fit comfortably into the categories of our everyday reality.

However, at the same time that we as a society repress awareness of anomalous events, we are ultimately unable to exorcise our fascination with them, and they return to haunt us in our imaginings. Freed from social censure when the unknown cloaks itself in the guise of fiction, we revel in the unusual and the weird when they are explicitly acknowledged as products of human imagination—hence the runaway success of films like *Independence Day* and TV programs like *X-Files*. Literature, film, and other genres of imaginative expression create the illusion that we are taming anomalies by forcing them to fit into the Procrustean bed of familiar narrative structures.

However, the paranormal has an irritating propensity to keep breaking through the bonds within which we seek to confine it. With respect to

UFOs, it appears that just as soon as one unusual manifestation has been explained away as swamp gas, a weather balloon, or an unusual cloud formation, a new sighting comes along that seems to take us back to square one. Thus, despite the ongoing efforts of skeptics to dismiss them as anything other than misunderstood natural phenomena, UFOs stubbornly refuse to exit the stage of human experience. Like the sorcerer's apprentice who cannot stop his master's animated brooms from bringing more and more buckets of water, every attempt to deal a deathblow to UFOs seems, if anything, to have had precisely the opposite of the intended effect.

Why a New UFO Encyclopedia?
Whether UFOs are spacecraft piloted by aliens, products of the human imagination, or some other alternative, they are undoubtedly among the most fascinating phenomena of the modern world. As a writer who enjoys authoring encyclopedias on high-interest topics, I was intrigued by the prospect of developing a popular reference book on UFOs. However, when I originally proposed the idea, one of the first responses I received was, "Does the world really need another UFO encyclopedia?" This comment was an allusion to the many existing reference works on the subject. It seems that the very structure of this phenomenon—which humanity apprehends in the context of iso-

lated sightings, brief encounters, and the like—makes it particularly amenable to an A-to-Z treatment. As a consequence, more than a few UFO encyclopedias have been composed over the past 50 years.

The UFO field has not, however, remained static. Most earlier reference books were authored by empirically oriented ufologists who more or less assumed that flying saucers were physical craft piloted by extraterrestrials on a mission to collect data about our planet. Claims by so-called contactees to have received religious or quasi-religious messages from ufonauts were rejected as unworthy of serious consideration. Because of authors' "hardware" orientation, the marked tendency for many observers to impute occult and other imaginative meanings to the UFO phenomenon did not receive systematic attention in most reference books.

Mainstream ufology has, however, been forced to respond to new developments, particularly the emergence of alien abduction as an important topic. Abduction accounts have, in fact, come to dominate the field. A quick examination of UFO books published in the last 10 years reveals that books on abductions have come to outnumber books on all other subjects related to UFOs combined, and by a substantial margin. Some of the popular magazines devoted to UFOs have become almost exclusively concerned with abductions in recent years.

Because most existing UFO encyclopedias antedate the interest in the abduction phenomenon as well as downplay the religious meanings attached to flying saucers by an earlier generation of UFO contactees, I concluded that there really was room for a new, up-to-date treatment of the subject—one that would focus on so-called soft ufology, namely, UFO religions, folklore, mythology, and the like. I also felt that the many imaginative works to emerge out of an interest in UFOs and their hypothetical alien pilots—particularly as this interest has been reflected in films and other artifacts of popular culture—should be examined more extensively. Although ufological purists may object, most readers will be pleased with the result of this approach.

Many observers, skeptics, and ufologists alike appear to be obsessed with finding The Truth about UFOs, as if the phenomenon could be reduced to a single interpretation. Without necessarily dismissing this quest as irrelevant, the imaginative responses that emerge out of the human confrontation with the unknown are at least as fascinating as the simple question of whether or not UFOs are "real." Until the Space Brothers (a description coined by pioneer ufologist George Adamski) land on the White House lawn, UFOs will remain ambiguous phenomena. We can, however, gain a greater understanding of ourselves and of humanity by examining how our fellow terrestrials have imputed narrative and spiritual meanings to this ambiguity—an ambiguity that seems to reflect the resistance to interpretation of the human condition as a whole.

UFOs in the Human Imagination

The modern UFO era began on June 24, 1947, when Kenneth Arnold sighted nine objects in the sky near Mount Rainier, Washington. Arnold was a 32-year-old businessman and pilot who at the time was searching for a downed transport plane. He initially thought the objects were jets but was unable to discern any tails at the ends of what he at the time thought were airplane fuselages. Looking more closely, he noted that all but one of the objects looked like flat disks. The story of Arnold's sighting was reported in newspaper articles almost immediately. The term "flying saucers" was first coined by headline writers for this story.

It has been asserted that public interest in UFOs began with this event, but there is a long tradition of extraterrestrial-contact claims that predates Arnold's sightings by many decades. This tradition is contained in certain lineages of occultism that claim contact with spiritual masters from other planets. A useful example of this form of occultism is the "I AM" Religious Activity. The "I AM" activity is a popularized form of theosophy, reformulated to appeal to a broader audience than earlier theosophical organizations. The founder of the movement was Guy Ballard (1878–1939). He had long been interested in occultism and had studied theosophical teachings.

Ballard was engaged in mining exploration and promotion. In 1930, while he was working near Mt. Shasta—a giant volcanic cone in northern

California where strange occult events had been said to occur—he had his first substantive contact with a hidden world. While hiking in the woods around the mountain, Ballard reports that he encountered another hiker, who gave him a marvelous drink and introduced himself as the Ascended Master Saint Germain. The Compte de Saint Germain was one of the most famous occultists of modern times. Ballard was, he related, chosen as a messenger to restore to humankind the truths of reembodiment. Saint Germain imparted information about karma, the inner reality of the divine—which he referred to as the "Mighty I AM Presence"—occult world history, and the creative power of thought.

One New Year's Eve, the Master and Ballard joined a gathering inside a cavern in Royal Teton Mountain. The individuals at this assembly then became host to 12 Venusians who appeared in their midst in a blaze of light, not unlike a Star Trek beam-in. The Venusians played harp and violin music and showed the gathered terrestrials scenes of advanced technological achievements from their home world on a great mirror. These alleged events from the early 1930s were reported in Ballard's *Unveiled Mysteries,* which was published a dozen years before Kenneth Arnold's celebrated encounter.

The first noteworthy prophet to emerge in the wake of postwar flying saucer sightings was George Adamski. In the early 1940s he became intrigued with unidentified flying objects, long before they were much discussed by the public. He even claimed to have seen a UFO for the first time on October 9, 1946, the year before Arnold's sightings. Adamski further reported that on November 20, 1952, he experienced telepathic contact with a humanlike Venusian, and the following month he reported another contact in which a hieroglyphic message was given. These encounters were reported in *Flying Saucers Have Landed,* one of the most popular flying-saucer books ever written. Adamski gained a broad following and was soon in demand as a lecturer.

As we can see from Ballard's report of the Royal Teton gathering, religious and other revelations from Venusians were nothing new. Adamski was thus not an innovator in this regard. Rather,

Adamski's contribution was to connect the earlier notion of receiving information from extraterrestrials with the emergent interest in flying saucers. The Ballard example of Venusian spiritual masters also allows us to see that the human imagination had a predisposition to respond to flying saucers—viewed as alien spacecraft—in religious terms. Even much secular thinking about UFOs embodies quasi-religious themes, such as the cryptoreligious notion that the world is on the verge of destruction and that ufonauts are somehow going to rescue humanity—either by forcibly preventing a nuclear Armageddon or by taking select members of the human race to another planet to preserve the species. Psychologist Carl Jung was referring to the latter portrayal of ufonauts (flying-saucer pilots) when he called them "technological angels." The idea of positive, helpful extraterrestrials has been a common theme of much science fiction, from *Superman* (who, it will be remembered, was from another planet) to the friendly alien of Spielberg's *E.T. The Extra-Terrestrial.*

The influential Jung postulated a drive toward self-realization and self-integration that he referred to as the "individuation process." The goal of this process was represented by the Self archetype, an archetype characterized by wholeness and completeness. One of the concrete manifestations of this archetype can be a circle, and it was various forms of the circle that Jung referred to as "mandalas." According to Jung, mandala symbols emerge in dreams when the individual is seeking harmony and wholeness, which frequently occurs during periods of crisis and insecurity. Jung interpreted the phenomenon of flying saucers—which often appear in the form of circular disks—as mandala symbols, reflecting the human mind's desire for stability in a confused world.

Another line of thought regarding religious interpretations of the UFO phenomenon is that the Western tradition's marked tendency to imagine God as somehow residing in the sky gives us a predisposition to view unusual *flying* objects as well as beings from outer space in spiritual terms. In other words, the god of the Bible is, in a certain sense, an extraterrestrial being.

Not all spiritual beings are, however, beneficent. A more negative interpretation of UFOs is evident in recent claims of abduction by aliens. If in earlier UFO literature flying saucers were technological angels, in abductee literature ufonauts are technological demons. Abductees report being treated coldly and inhumanely by their alien captors— much as animals are treated when captured, tagged, and released by human zoologists. During their brief captivity, frightened abductees also often report having been tortured, usually in the form of a painful examination.

A careful reading of abduction narratives indicates that the patterns alleged to have been discovered by abduction investigators frequently have religious overtones or similarities with more traditional types of religious experience—similarities often ignored by UFO researchers. Hypnosis, which is generally used to explore the abduction experience, allows access to a subconscious level of an individual's psyche. This enables the hypnotic subject to recall repressed memories of actual events; it also makes it possible to derive memories of things that have never happened.

As Jung argued, the subconscious is a storehouse of religious ideas and symbols. Such symbols can become exteriorized through anxiety or stress. Thus, the cryptoreligious imagery brought to the surface by hypnosis—in this case torment by demonic beings, which is an initiatory motif— could be a confabulation of the subject's subconscious, perhaps worked into a UFO narrative in an effort to please the hypnotist. More literal demonologies have been proffered by conservative Christian observers of the UFO scene, many of whom view ufonauts as demons in disguise. A point often missed in analyses by mainstream ufologists is that the image of extraterrestrials as dangerous and evil—like the related image of aliens as superior spiritual entities—also antedates the Arnold sightings by a considerable margin.

To take a celebrated instance, on the night before Halloween in 1938, a radio announcer in New York broadcast the startling news that Martians had invaded the United States. Thousands of innocent people had already been slain by ray guns and by clouds of noxious gas released by the aliens. From their landing area in New Jersey, the announcer asserted, the Martians were rapidly advancing in all directions, setting the countryside

on fire and quickly overpowering any opposition to their onslaught. The broadcast set off a wave of hysteria across the Eastern Seaboard.

The announcer was Orson Welles, a brilliant actor who was reading an adapted-for-radio version of H. G. Wells's (no relation) 1898 novel, *The War of the Worlds.* Because a popular entertainer on a competing radio program had been replaced for the evening with a relatively unknown singer, many of the listeners who changed channels and tuned into Welles's broadcast missed the introduction in which the fictional nature of the play had been explained. The program was also presented in the style of, "We interrupt this program . . . ," which, in combination with the broadcaster's considerable talent, lent the drama a marked atmosphere of realism. An embarrassed Welles, fearful that his career had been ruined, made a contrite public apology for the broadcast.

Many analysts later concluded that the panic set in motion by the broadcast could be explained in terms of America's prewar jitters: The nation was on the edge of its seat as a consequence of events that would lead to world war. The fictional Martian invasion seemed to embody widespread but vague anxieties about a possible assault on American soil. These ambiguous fears were thus tapped and brought to the fore of the nation's consciousness by Welles's broadcast. However, this interpretation, while undoubtedly relevant, does not explain the seemingly *endless* public interest in extraterrestrial invasion that has been a staple of science-fiction literature almost from the very beginning of the genre and that continues to fascinate us even in the current post–Cold War era.

Inverted images of "friendly aliens" are reflected in the many portrayals of hostile aliens found in film and literature. The ugly, octopus-like extraterrestrials of H. G. Wells's imagination have their counterparts in innumerable invasion narratives, from straight horror movies like *The Blob* (which dropped to earth inside a meteorite) to such recent offerings as the box-office recordbreaker *Independence Day* and the short-lived TV series *Dark Skies.* Whereas friendly aliens appear to be projections of our fondest hopes, hostile aliens seem to embody our worst fears.

Skeptics and UFOs

While this discussion has stressed that the imaginative forms generated by the human mind's encounter with UFOs are both interesting and worthy of examination, this is not to completely dismiss the whole phenomenon as being merely the product of the human imagination. To the contrary, there appears to be an elusive reality behind as least some aspects of the UFO phenomenon—whatever it is—that resists ordinary modes of explanation. It is, therefore, of interest that ufology should be one of the primary targets of skeptical debunkers determined to exorcise humanity of its "superstitions."

The debate over UFOs has been bitter in the extreme. Ufologists have often been derided as profit-driven charlatans, their ideas lampooned as silly and irrational. For debunkers—those who set themselves up as the self-appointed guardians of human rationality—the response to the UFO phenomenon has been one of derision and contempt. However, the spectacle of debunking crusaders stridently assaulting ufology with the arrows of ridicule in the name of reason must surely give more objective observers cause for reflection.

What is truly unsettling about ufology, particularly the so-called extraterrestrial hypothesis (ETH—the notion that UFOs are spaceships piloted by technologically advanced aliens), is that, when stripped of overstatement and incautious speculation, it is really quite reasonable. Given the infinity of time, it is quite plausible to entertain the idea that intelligent species residing on other planets could have developed the technology to cross interstellar space and reach our world. What is so irrational about that? The answer is that there is *nothing* intrinsically unreasonable about the basic hypothesis.

Skeptical debunkers have, however, with a kind of intellectual sleight-of-hand, redefined "rational" and "irrational." Instead of referring to a line of reasoning that violates the canons of logic, skeptics have been able to get away with using "irrational" as if it meant "contrary to mainstream science." Hence theories like the ETH are irrational *by definition:* One can simply dismiss them without wasting the time it would take to give them serious consideration.

There are, of course, many problems with this attitude, not the least of which is that such an attitude is antiscientific. The very cornerstone of modern science is empiricism, which means that one approaches new phenomena with a view to investigating them. The methodology of most debunkers, however, is categorical rather than empirical: They approach paranormal experiences with the *assumption* that they cannot be real, and their "investigations" of such phenomena consist of little more than developing conventional explanations for strange and unusual events. This kind of tautological, a priori reasoning commits the fallacy of assuming the conclusion in the premise.

In this regard, we might recall the story of Galileo, who asked people to view the mountains on the Moon or to view the moons of Jupiter through his new telescope: Because these discoveries fundamentally violated the science of Galileo's day, people refused to examine the evidence for themselves. Rather than risk questioning established science, they dismissed the telescope as faulty or as some kind of trick. Galileo was eventually hauled before the Inquisition and required to recant his heretical views.

Lacking the equivalent of an Office of the Inquisition, contemporary champions of scientific orthodoxy have had to be more creative and resourceful than their medieval predecessors. In this regard, an incident reported by George Wingfield in Timothy Good's *Alien Update* with respect to crop circles is instructive.

Crop circles are any flattened area in a field of growing crops. The earliest examples of this phenomenon to come to public attention were circular (hence the name), but the shapes then became steadily more complex, so that a more adequate term might be "pictogram." The study of this phenomenon, now called "cereology," began in 1980, when the first circles to be observed appeared in a Wiltshire field, and the first article on them appeared in the *Wiltshire Times*, attracting the attention of a meteorologist, George T. Meaden, and a ufologist, Ian Mrzyglod. Between 1980 and 1987 a total of about 110 circles were reported. The numbers then soared: 112 or more in 1988; 305 in 1989; in 1990 about 1,000 were reported, from countries all around the world.

Meteorological explanations, involving "plasma vortexes"—something rather like an electrical whirlwind—have been offered to explain many cases of this phenomenon. Some speculations have involved the concept that these circles are places where UFOs have rested, others that the more complex diagrams are forms of alien graffiti. Yet others have claimed that the circles are natural phenomena—messages from Gaia, warning humans about an ecological crisis.

In 1991 a pair of English chums, Douglas Bower and David Chorley, hoaxed a crop circle. They were subsequently able to trick a prominent cereologist into declaring their artificially constructed wheat circle genuine. The hoax made international headlines, and skeptical debunkers had a field day.

In Winfield's words, "Their argument was that if an 'expert' can be taken in by a man-made formation, then every formation could be man-made and, *ergo,* the whole phenomenon is no more than a hoax." However, every year during the season when crops are mature enough that patterns can be created in them, several new circles are reported *every day.* Many others, of course, go unreported. Hence the "invisible army of unseen hoaxers, who are never caught, never acknowledged and never known to abandon their handiwork incomplete, could hardly have been responsible for *all* these formations."

Nevertheless, driven by an inscrutable passion to defend science and rationality via deceit and trickery, skeptics subsequently staged a number of other Doug and Dave–type hoaxes. For example, on the night of August 8, 1992, a crop circle was created near Froxfield, Wiltshire. No one, however, noticed it, and the farmer, who did not appear very interested in the phenomenon, gave signs that he was on the verge of harvesting the field. Desperate that their work might be for naught, the chief conspirator phoned Winfield on some other pretext and casually asked him for his evaluation of the Froxfield pattern. Aware that this particularly militant debunker always recorded such conversations, Winfield responded by asserting that he knew it was a fake, knew who did it, and that the farmer would shortly be bringing charges of criminal damage

against the hoaxers. Needless to say, the conversation ended rather abruptly.

As can be seen from this incident—and from many others that could be cited—skeptics who passionately denounce ufology in the name of science and reason appear to be caught up in a self-contradiction. In this regard, they represent a phenomenon on par, in a certain sense, with contactees who claim to convey messages from the Space Brothers. Once again, the human response to the UFO phenomenon is as interesting as the phenomenon itself.

A Brief History of the UFO Phenomenon

The first wave of UFO sightings in the United States occurred between late 1896 and the spring of 1897. At the time, people thought they were someone's aerial breakthrough. Only later were the "airships" speculatively linked with extraterrestrial visitors. During World War II UFOs were referred to as "foo fighters" and were feared to be secret weapons of the Axis powers. Immediately following the war, secret Soviet missile firings were blamed for the "ghost rockets" seen over northern Europe. Public interest in the UFO phenomenon did not, however, really take off until after Kenneth Arnold's sighting on June 24, 1947.

The first books with the expression "flying saucers" in their titles were published in 1950. Also, the first UFO organizations were formed in the early 1950s. Most were just saucer fan clubs, but some were more serious and undertook something like scientific investigations. These people referred to themselves as "ufologists." The early ufologists distanced themselves from contactees who claimed direct contact with benevolent Space Brothers.

By the mid-1950s the U.S. Air Force's Project Blue Book—set up to respond to civilian UFO sightings—had become little more than a debunking exercise. It conducted few, if any, field investigations. Most individuals involved in Blue Book were total skeptics. Some observers who discounted official pronouncements believed that the Air Force was covering up UFO secrets. By the end of the 1950s, the consensus of elite opinion was that the notion that UFOs represented anything more than hallucinations or misunderstood natural phenomena was ludicrous. Despite official dismissals, however, the sightings continued to occur. UFO waves erupted with alarming frequency between 1964 and 1973.

J. Allen Hynek, an astronomer, was for many years the Air Force's chief scientific adviser on UFOs. Hynek finally stepped forward to criticize Blue Book's shortcomings and argued for a fresh look at the phenomenon. James E. McDonald, an atmospheric physicist, got involved by going out and personally researching UFO sightings. Jacques Vallee, one of Hynek's students, became one of the two leading proponents (John A. Keel being the other) of a theory of occult ufology.

While all of this was going on, the Air Force handed over its UFO problem to the University of Colorado and physicist Edward U. Condon. Within months, the Condon Committee was engulfed in controversy amid charges that the committee's conclusion had been reached before the investigation began. The final report of the committee stated that there was no use further exploring UFOs, despite the fact that 30 percent of the project's own cases were left unexplained. Later that year Blue Book closed down, and public interest dropped. It would come to life again in the fall of 1973, in the midst of another wave of sightings.

The mid-1970s also saw the rise of a public debunking effort intended to address the public's growing interest. Certain individuals began claiming that aliens were inspired by visionary experiences. As investigations became ever more detailed, serious researchers found that, for all the hoaxes and unbelievable cases, there were also a significant number of plausible cases that resisted conventional explanation.

In the 1960s and particularly in the 1970s, close encounters dominated UFO reports as much as daylight disks and nighttime lights had in the 1950s. Now it became ever more difficult to distinguish a hoax from someone's genuine testimony because the content of both was extremely outlandish. Some individuals even claimed to have had sexual experiences with extraterrestrials.

In the late 1970s several American ufologists reinvestigated so-called crash-recovery cases. Eventually ufologists were prompted to examine the famous Roswell incident. This task stretched into the

1990s and involved the General Accounting Office of the U.S. government, which would report that all original documents were missing. The story of the Roswell crash is one of the most important narratives in the history of modern ufology, providing apparent evidence for the long-standing suspicion that certain government authorities know more about the phenomenon than the public has been led to believe. The Roswell case has also provided fuel for some of the wildest imaginable conspiracy theories, making JFK assassination-plot theories pale by comparison.

Roswell and Other Conspiracies

Americans have a tendency to resort to conspiracy theories as a way of explaining certain kinds of events and situations. Conspiracy theories are attractive because they explain complex social structures and the problems generated by them in an oversimplified way that puts faces on otherwise impersonal processes. We have, of course, seen a number of genuine conspiracies, from the Tonkin Gulf incident to Watergate. The spectacle of these exposés has fueled other conspiracy theories by making them appear more plausible.

Conspiracy theories are rampant in the larger UFO community. Beyond the intrinsic ambiguity of UFOs, conspiracy theories seem plausible in this arena because there appears to be a conspiracy of silence surrounding what the government—or, at least, what the military and the intelligence agencies—know about the phenomenon. Some of the evidence for an official conspiracy of silence regarding flying saucers comes from the Roswell story.

The narrative begins with the crash landing of what many claim to have been an alien spacecraft some 75 miles outside Roswell, New Mexico. In the early years of ufology, investigators generally depreciated rumors of flying-saucer crashes as little-men-in-pickle-jars stories. It was not until the publication of *The Roswell Incident* (1980) by William L. Moore and Stanton Friedman that the larger UFO community began to consider that such rumors might contain more than a grain of truth.

As the story goes, on the evening of July 2, 1947, the manager of a sheep ranch heard an unusual explosion during a violent electrical storm. Investigating, he found debris scattered over a wide area. The parts of the wreckage he examined had unusual properties, and some pieces were inscribed with unfamiliar hieroglyphics. He reported what he had found to the sheriff, who in turn contacted the local air base. After an initial investigation by the ranking intelligence officer, the public-information officer released the information that the U.S. Army Air Force had recovered the remains of a crashed flying saucer.

Shortly after this story had been released, however, the military retracted it. A news conference was quickly organized at which it was explained that there had been a mistake. The official interpretation, which all of the news media at the time accepted, was that the only thing that had crashed was a weather balloon. Meanwhile, according to the story, the army went out to the sheep farm in force, systematically collecting and removing as much debris as could be found. As part of this search, a second, larger crash site was discovered—a site at which, it was later claimed, the dead bodies of four ufonauts were found.

In addition to silencing their own people, the military was said to have exacted promises of silence from civilians, sometimes in heavy-handed ways. Thus, the event was shrouded in silence for over 30 years, until the publication of Friedman and Moore's book. Subsequent researchers turned up more evidence in the form of more people willing to break the silence.

The subject really exploded, however, with the publication of Majestic 12 (MJ-12). This is a document that appears to be a top-secret briefing on findings from the Roswell crash. The document was anonymously sent to a UFO researcher in 1984, who later released it to the public. MJ-12 set off a heated debate over its authenticity that has not died down to this day.

One interesting item of information to come out of the document was that arch UFO debunker Donald H. Menzel was working with the intelligence agencies and had inside information about the Roswell incident. Stanton Friedman followed up on this point and discovered that Menzel had secretly been associated with the Central Intelligence Agency and the National Security Agency

and had worked on a number of classified projects. The information about Menzel is particularly interesting. If in the unlikely event that MJ-12 is authentic and Menzel was in the know, then it would throw the three books he wrote debunking the UFO phenomenon into the category of misinformation—publications intentionally designed to throw serious researchers off the scent.

If the military had indeed acquired one or more extraterrestrial spacecraft, then the purpose of such disinformation would be that they (i.e., the military) would want to study alien technology as a way of getting the jump on the Soviets. This research would, however, have to be absolutely top secret. To derail both Soviet and domestic investigators, the government would have to take a stance of official disinterest in the UFO phenomenon. In addition, the intelligence agencies might hire respected scientists (Menzel was a Harvard astronomer) to author books that would help transform UFOs into a subject of derision—a subject no serious researcher would dare investigate. If the above conspiratorial scenario is correct, then this strategy has been remarkably successful.

As an ongoing part of the Roswell story, people interested in the UFO conspiracy have turned their attention to Area 51. Area 51 is located at a corner of the federal research reservation known as the Nevada Test Site. There, various projects connected with national security have been developed over past decades; these have included the U-2 and SR-71 spyplanes, the Stealth aircraft, and some of the technology for the Strategic Defense Initiative (SDI, the so-called Star Wars system of missile defense). Observers have reported seeing lights maneuvering over this area in the ways now considered typical of UFOs: at great speeds, with sudden changes of direction, silently hovering, and so on. There have also been daytime observations of craft that look like giant triangles.

The rumors about this area have developed far beyond what is usual even for UFO phenomena. There have been many claims that the technology that powers the giant triangles has been derived from investigations of crashed UFOs. Area 51 is also supposedly the final resting place of the flying saucer that crashed near Roswell. This bit of UFO lore was even incorporated into the film *Indepen-*

dence Day. One person claiming knowledge of Area 51 secrets, Robert Scott Lazar, was apparently subjected to a campaign of vilification and was effectively silenced when his critics were able to associate him with a Nevada brothel.

There have also been more radical rumors, such as that Area 51 scientists are working with living aliens as part of a secret agreement between certain agencies of the U.S. government and extraterrestrials. It has even been asserted that aliens have entered into a secret pact with the U.S. government, agreeing to provide the United States with advanced technology in exchange for unlimited access to U.S. citizens, whom aliens routinely abduct. The most bizarre of these rumors merge into implausible conspiracy theories rather like those of survivalists, neo-Nazis, and other extremists. By focusing public attention on these fringe elements of the UFO community, authorities can dismiss more plausible accusations as just more fabrications of the "crazies."

The Ancient-Astronaut Hypothesis

One important line of speculation that has split off from the mainstream UFO community is the ancient-astronaut school. The basic hypothesis of this subcommunity is that ufonauts visited our planet in the distant past. Many if not all of the powerful sky gods of traditional religions were really extraterrestrial visitors intervening in human history. Although this idea was around in the 1950s and 1960s, it was not until a series of books about the "chariots of the gods" authored by Erich von Däniken in the 1970s that this notion was popularized. Later writers such as Zecharia Sitchin have developed this view with greater sophistication, but none has been as influential as von Däniken.

This view, which seems to call into question the validity of religion, has been adopted by large segments of the New Age culture in a peculiar way that, for the most part, is not seen as contradicting metaphysical spirituality. Instead, believers see the Space Brothers as working in cooperation with spiritual forces to stimulate the spiritual evolution of this planet. There is also a tendency to view extraterrestrials as being more spiritually advanced than ordinary humans, and some New Age channelers claim to channel ufonauts.

One popular view is that the contemporary human race is the offspring of a union between aliens and native terrestrials. Some even believe that a distorted record of this event can be found in a few enigmatic verses in the Book of Genesis about the sons of God copulating with the daughters of men. This union produced an intermediate species that Genesis calls the Nephilim. Our space "fathers" have subsequently been watching over us, and will, according to some New Age notions, return to mingle with their distant offspring during the imminent New Age.

As part of ancient-astronaut thinking, it is also widely assumed that the technologically advanced civilizations of legendary antiquity such as Atlantis were inspired, founded, created, and/or administered by extraterrestrial visitors. However, not all ancient-astronaut thinkers paint such a rosy picture of our alien ancestors. Sitchin, the most influential writer in the ancient-astronaut school after von Däniken, for instance, asserts that humanity was created as a slave race by aliens exploiting the earth's resources.

As has already been pointed out, the ancient-astronaut school has, for the most part, been off by itself, separate from ufology. The reasons for this are complex. A major factor was that back in the 1970s, when von Däniken's ideas were first having a marked impact on the public consciousness, mainstream ufologists were still trying to make a case for ufology as a hard science. In contrast to mainstream ufologists' self-image as sober scientists, von Däniken appeared a flamboyant dilettante, willing to make bold assertions on the basis of thin evidence. Ufologists subsequently went out of their way to distance themselves from the ancient-astronaut school, and ancient-astronaut thinkers reciprocated in kind.

More recently, however, the face of mainstream ufology has been altered by the abduction phenomenon. More and more ufologists are accepting even some very strange abduction reports as valid close encounters, which makes ufology look less and less like a natural science. There have also been several recent books that have made the ancient-astronaut hypothesis look more respectable to the general public. *Forbidden Archeology* (1993), for example, is a serious work on the origins of the human race and material culture that calls establishment science into question. In addition to demonstrating the major role academic politics plays in shaping mainstream science, authors Michael A. Cremo and Richard L. Thompson also bring together extensive evidence indicating that ancient humanity had a high degree of technical sophistication. The ancient-astronaut school has been quick to embrace *Forbidden Archeology* as supporting its hypothesis of early contact between humanity and extraterrestrials

The importance of *Fingerprints of the Gods* (1995), in contrast, is less direct. In this work the author, Graham Hancock, argues for the existence of a technologically advanced civilization (e.g., Atlantis) in the time period preceding the earliest known urban societies. To support his point, he examines the many artifacts and architectural monuments that are difficult to account for within the limits of our currently accepted scheme of history. Hancock, however, uses the same evidence the ancient-astronaut school had compiled to demonstrate prehistoric contact with extraterrestrials and marshals it to support an alternative thesis. The author's dependence on ancient-astronaut evidence is even reflected in the title of his book, which is transparently a takeoff on *Chariots of the Gods?* Despite Hancock's rejection of the ancient-astronaut hypothesis, his highly popular book nevertheless showcases the very evidence that makes von Däniken and company's thesis plausible. And the long-range impact of *Fingerprints of the Gods* may well be to once again help bring the ancient-astronaut school back into the spotlight.

Occult/New Age Ufology

Ufology has had a long and ambivalent relationship with occult spirituality. Since the nineteenth century, the industrialized West has been home to a strand of alternative religiosity that has been variously referred to as the "occult," "metaphysical," or, more recently, as the "New Age movement." As was noted above with respect to Guy Ballard's "I AM" activity, there exists a predisposition within at least certain segments of this spiritual subculture to invest the UFO phenomenon with religious significance. Although scientifically oriented ufologists have generally despised occult ufology, it

has been the alternative spiritual subculture that has kept the topic of UFOs alive as a subject of popular interest, thus indirectly benefiting mainstream ufology. Because so many of the phenomena that the present volume will be examining have their roots in, or have been nurtured by, the New Age subculture, it will be useful to supply the reader with a little background.

The New Age is a synthesis of many different preexisting movements and strands of thought and can be viewed as a revivalist movement within a preexisting metaphysical-occult community. From another angle, the New Age can be viewed as a successor movement to the counterculture of the 1960s. One can pinpoint certain essential ideas that came to distinguish the New Age movement. None are particularly new ideas, their distinctiveness being in their having been brought together in a new gestalt.

First, there is the possibility of personal transformation. The New Age movement offers the possibility of a personal transformation in the immediate future. Although personal transformation is a common offering of some occult and New Thought groups, it is usually presented as the end result of a long-term process of alteration through extensive training in the occult life (in contrast to the immediate transformation offered by revivalist Christianity). Thus, the New Age, without radically changing traditional occultism, offered a new immediacy that had been lacking in metaphysical teachings.

The transformative process is most clearly seen in the healing process, and transformation often is first encountered as a healing of the individual, either of a chronic physical problem or of a significant psychological problem. Healing has become a metaphor of transformation within the New Age movement.

Second is the coming of broad cultural transformation. The New Age movement offers the hope that the world, which many people, especially those on the edges of the dominant culture, experience in negative terms, would in the next generation be swept aside and replaced with a golden era. As articulated by spokespeople like David Spangler, the hoped-for changes are placed in a sophisticated framework of gradual change relying upon human acceptance of the new resources and their creating a new culture. According to Spangler, a watershed in human history has been reached with the advent of modern technology and its possibilities for good and evil. At the same time, because of unique changes in the spiritual world, symbolized and heralded (but not caused) by the astrological change into the Aquarian Age, this generation has a unique bonus of spiritual power available to it. It is this additional spiritual energy operating on the world and its peoples that makes possible the personal and cultural transformation that will bring in a New Age.

It is, of course, the millennial hope of the coming of a golden age of peace and light that gave the New Age movement its name. This millennialism also provided a basis for a social consciousness that has been notably lacking in most occult metaphysics. Once articulated, the New Age vision could be and was grounded in various endeavors designed to assist the transition to the New Age. The New Age movement wedded itself to environmentalism, lay peace movements, animal rights, women's rights, and cooperative forms of social organization.

Most current New Age groups with a UFO emphasis are curiously untouched by this social consciousness. Instead, the millennial hopes of such groups seem focused on the coming of the Space Brothers, who will somehow magically destroy our social problems and establish a reign of truth and light on earth.

The third aspect is the transformation of occult arts and processes. Within the New Age movement one finds all of the familiar occult practices from astrology to tarot, from mediumship to psychic healing. Yet in the New Age movement the significance of these practices has been altered. Astrology and tarot are no longer fortune-telling devices but have become tools utilized for self-transformation.

The number of practitioners of astrology, tarot, mediumship, and psychic healing had been growing steadily throughout the twentieth century. Thus the New Age movement did not have to create its own professionals de novo; rather it had merely to transform and bring into visibility the large army of practitioners of the occult arts already in existence.

Possibly the most widely practiced New Age transformative tool is meditation (in its many varied forms) and related tools of inner development. In its utilization of meditation, the New Age movement borrowed insights from the findings of the human-potentials movement and transpersonal psychology, both of which, in isolating various practices for study, demonstrated that techniques of meditation and inner development could be detached from the religious teachings in which they were traditionally embedded.

Mediumship has become channeling, in which the primary role of the medium is to expound metaphysical truth rather than to prove the continuance of life after death. New Age mediums who channel Space Brothers—particularly those who found new religious groups—almost always present metaphysical teachings, but they also often make apocalyptic prophecies about the future and what humanity must do to prepare itself.

Fourth, New Agers see the self as divine. Within the New Age movement, one theological affirmation that has found popular support is the identification of the individual with the divine. Underlying this notion, which finds a wide variety of forms, is a monistic world in which the only reality is "God," usually thought of in predominantly impersonal terms as Mind or Energy. This is a tenet the New Age philosophy shares with such Asian philosophies as traditional Upanishadic Hinduism—not to mention the otherworldly philosophies of the ufonauts.

Through the 1980s the New Age became a popular movement that reinvigorated the older occult-metaphysical community and drew many new adherents to it while assisting the spread of occult practices (such as astrology and meditation) and ideas (such as reincarnation) into the general population far beyond the boundaries of the movement itself. The increasing public interest in UFOs is but one part of this expansion. Partially as a result of the long-range impact of the New Age, there has been a resurgence of UFO interest within the past several years—an interest reflected in the many recent alien-invasion movies and TV shows as well as in UFO-related segments of TV-tabloid shows devoted to the paranormal.

In the following pages, readers will find an overview of the folklore and popular culture aspects of the UFO phenomenon. Because the human imagination's response to the UFO phenomenon is at least as important as the question of what UFOs "really" are, extensive space has been devoted to examining how UFOs and aliens are represented in the medium of film. Readers will also find more than a few entries dealing with humanity's religious response to the alien "other." Finally, because close encounters and alien-abduction narratives are so central to contemporary UFO mythology, I have described the most well-known incidents in a separate set of entries.

It should be noted that many of the entries deal with extraordinary claims. To avoid stylistic awkwardness, most entries make selective use of qualifiers like "so-and-so *asserts* that . . ." or "so-and-so *claimed* that. . . ." In other words, the absence of these qualifiers should *not* be interpreted as implying that the author of the relevant entry necessarily accepts such statements as true. The UFO phenomenon is a fascinating topic that has resisted repeated attempts to dismiss it for the past 50 years. I would not be surprised if it continues its hold on the human imagination for the next 50 years and beyond. Enjoy!

CONTRIBUTORS

Pia Andersson is a graduate student in archaeology and religious studies at Stockholm University. She has written extensively on archaeology, archaeoastronomy, and "fringe" archaeology.

Jerome Clark is an independent writer and researcher. Among many other works, he is the author of the definitive *UFO Encyclopedia* and *Extraordinary Encounters: An Encyclopedia of Extraterrestrials and Otherworldly Beings* (ABC-CLIO, 2000).

Ryan J. Cook is a Ph.D. candidate in cultural anthropology at the University of Chicago, pursuing the cross-cultural study of the ways in which people employ UFOs to address issues in science and religion. He is currently doing research on ufology in Mexico.

Hilary Evans has been studying the paranormal for most of his life and has written several books exploring the social parameters of the field. He has been a council member of the Society for Psychical Research, London, and works in a historical picture archive.

Andreas Gruenschloss is associate professor *(Hochschuldozent)* in the Faculty of Protestant Theology at the University of Mainz. He holds advanced degrees from the University of Mainz, the University of Heidelberg, and the University of Chicago and is a specialist in the areas of interreligious hermeneutics, Buddhism, and new religious movements.

Christopher Helland is a Ph.D. student at the Centre for the Study of Religion at the University of Toronto. His research focuses upon the relationship between new religious movements and science, UFO religions being a primary example of amalgamation.

Kay Holzinger is a freelance writer. She has contributed to *The Encyclopedia of Cults, Sects and New Religions* and other reference works.

Aidan Kelly is an editor and independent scholar. He is the author of such works as *Crafting the Art of Magic* and *Religious Holidays and Calendars: An Encyclopedic Handbook.*

Pierre Lagrange is a former researcher at the Centre de Sociologie de l'Innovation of the Ecole des Mines of Paris, where he taught sociology of science (and of parasciences). He has published articles on the construction of paranormal phenomena and on science-parascience controversies. He is also the author of a book on the Roswell controversy.

James R. Lewis teaches religious studies at the University of Wisconsin, Stevens Point. His publications include *Cults in America* (ABC-CLIO) and *Witchcraft Today: An Encyclopedia of Wiccan and Neopagan Traditions* (ABC-CLIO).

Ryan T. O'Leary is a student of English and religious studies at the University of Wisconsin, Stevens Point.

Susan Palmer is an adjunct professor at Concordia University and a tenured professor at Dawson College, both in Montreal, Quebec. She has written or edited eight books and more than 60 articles on new religious movements.

Mikael Rothstein is assistant professor in the Department of History of Religions at the University of Copenhagen. He specializes in the study of new religions and is the author or editor of several books on the subject. He is editor-in-chief of *CHAOS,* a Danish-Norwegian journal on the history of religions.

Benson Saler is professor emeritus of anthropology at Brandeis University. His major ethnographic fieldwork has been among Maya-Quiché in Guatemala and Wayú (Guajiro) in northern Colombia and Venezuela. His publications include *Los Wayú (Guajiro); Conceptualizing Religion;* and a book coauthored with Charles A. Ziegler and Charles B. Moore, *UFO Crash at Roswell: The Genesis of a Modern Myth.*

John Saliba has taught at the University of Detroit Mercy since 1970. He has been studying new religious movements since the late 1960s and has published two bibliographies and several books on the subject. His latest book is *Christian Responses to the New Age Movement.*

Scott Scribner studied astronomy and cultural anthropology in Harvard University's Mount Hermon Liberal Studies Program and physics and sociology at Rensselaer Polytechnic Institute, where he was a student member of the Mars Survey Vehicle Development Group (Viking Lander). He is currently pursuing research on alien abduction narratives.

Bryan Sentes is a member of the English Department at Dawson College and a teacher of creative writing at Concordia University, both in Montreal, Canada.

Diana Tumminia teaches sociology at California State University, Sacramento. She publishes in the areas of social psychology, gender, race, and social class. She has written or coauthored numerous articles on the Unarius Academy of Science.

Greg Wheeler has a background in physics and holds advanced degrees in theology and clinical psychology from Fuller in Pasadena, CA. He maintains a private practice in Monrovia, California, and occasionally teaches. He is working on a book on what he calls first contact science.

John Whitmore is a graduate student in religious studies at the University of California, Santa Barbara. He has contributed to such collections as *The Gods Have Landed: New Religions from Other Worlds.*

Charles A. Ziegler holds advanced degrees in physics and cultural anthropology and is currently a member of the Anthropology Department of Brandeis University. His recent UFO-related publications include "UFOs and the U.S. Intelligence Community," in the journal *Intelligence and National Security,* and a coauthored book, *UFO Crash at Roswell: The Genesis of a Modern Myth.*

Michela Zonta is a graduate student in sociology at the University of California, Los Angeles. She has contributed to such reference works as *Angels A to Z* and the *Encyclopedia of Afterlife Beliefs and Phenomena.*

UFOS AND POPULAR CULTURE

ABDUCTEES

In recent times, the subject of UFO abductions has gained immense popularity, both with the public and with a small group of scholars and writers who have turned their attention to the UFO phenomenon. The number of people who claim to have been abducted by occupants of UFOs has been rising almost exponentially since the early 1970s, when the subject was first granted acceptance by the media and the ufological community. With the publication in 1987 of Whitley Strieber's *Communion,* interest in abductions and abductees exploded. Strieber's account, written with skill by an accomplished author, presented the bizarre details of UFO abduction in an accessible way, spurring the book to the top of the *New York Times* best-seller list. In the wake of this success, talk shows on radio and television fed the public interest in the abduction phenomenon with a steady diet of reports of individuals who believed that they, too, had been abducted.

Contemporaneous with the rise in popularity of Strieber's book was the work of UFO researchers who were dedicated to examining abductions. Individuals like Budd Hopkins, whose own book *Intruders* (1987) made it to the best-seller list, came to dominate the field of ufology. Hopkins and those who share his methodology believe that UFO abductions are a widespread phenomenon and are not always remembered by the victims. Hypnosis is the primary tool for retrieving these memories, which Hopkins and others argue reveal a specific pattern of action on the part of UFO occupants. In contrast to Strieber, who considers his own experiences to be mainly inexplicable, researchers who use hypnosis tend to have clearly defined theories about the nature and purpose of the abduction phenomenon. These theories have come to dominate the field of ufol-

ogy. A quick examination of UFO books recently published reveals that books on abductions have outnumbered books on all other subjects related to UFOs combined, and by a substantial margin. Popular magazines devoted to UFOs have become almost exclusively concerned with abductions in recent years.

The popularity of abductions has led to a proliferation of first-person accounts, both remembered consciously and retrieved through hypnosis, that are accessible to the researcher. These primary sources reveal a wealth of bizarre detail that is not wholly amenable to the neat theories of many ufologists. A careful examination of abduction narratives indicates that the patterns alleged to have been discovered by abduction investigators often have religious overtones or similarities with more traditional types of religious experience. In addition, the abduction experience is often given a religious meaning by the percipient, and these interpretations are habitually overlooked or ignored by the UFO investigator.

In coming to grips with the claims of abductees and researchers, the practice of hypnosis must first be considered. The use of hypnosis to investigate UFO abductions dates back to one of the earliest instances of the phenomenon—the story of the Betty and Barney Hill abduction in 1963. In the overwhelming majority of cases available for research, the memory of the abduction event was obtained or clarified through hypnosis. Typically, the abductee consciously recalls little or nothing about the experience. Certain telltale signs, such as unaccounted-for spans of time, uneasy feelings associated with UFOs, or the sense of a presence in the bedroom before falling asleep, serve to clue the vigilant researcher into the possibility that an abduction has occurred. Hypnosis is then generally used to explore the abduction experience.

Although the reliance on hypnosis is heavy among abduction researchers, most seem to be unaware of the difficulties inherent in the process. Hypnosis apparently allows access to a subconscious level of an individual's psyche, allowing him or her to recall repressed memories of actual events; but it also makes it possible to derive false memories of things that have never happened. Hypnotism greatly increases a subject's suggestibility, infusing him or her with a desire to please the questioner, making the subject very susceptible to leading questions. Although they sometimes recognize these limitations, researchers, with few exceptions, contend that hypnosis, when used competently, is an accurate tool for uncovering factual details of the abduction event. It is quite possible, however, that many, if not all, abduction memories are confabulations of the subconscious, guided by the preconceptions of the hypnotist. Noted UFO debunker Philip Klass favors this view and rather plausibly dismembers some better-known cases by applying this theory.

The nature of accounts obtained through hypnosis is important for understanding the religious characteristics of the abduction phenomenon. As psychologist Carl Jung argued, specifically in relation to UFOs, the subconscious is a storehouse of religious ideas and symbols. Such symbols can become exteriorized through anxiety or stress. Thus, the religious imagery and interpretation brought out by hypnosis could be confabulations of the subject's subconscious and perhaps worked into a UFO narrative in an effort to please the hypnotist. In his research, Jung noted that certain complexes of religious symbols appeared time and time again in widely separated subjects. The prevalence of similar patterns in part gave rise to his theory of a collective unconscious—a fund of ideas and imagery shared by all people. This theory may also help to explain the similar patterns, filled with religious overtones, that abduction researchers claim to find among their subjects.

The applicability of a Jungian form of analysis to UFO abductions is further strengthened by the markedly dreamlike character of the experience. Dreams are the most common arena in which religious symbolism is encountered. One of the signs noted by abduction researchers as indicative of an abduction event is the prevalence of dreams containing UFO- or alien-related imagery. In many of the cases in which the abduction is at least partially recalled prior to the use of hypnosis, it is recalled as a dream rather than as an objective event. For example, Kathie Davis, the main subject of Budd Hopkins's best-seller *Intruders,* consistently believes that her experiences were a series of dreams about UFO abductions. In his investigation, Hopkins hypnotically examines the alleged abduction events by directing her toward these dreams and asking her to recount their details. Hopkins explains that Davis remembers these events as dreams in order to shield her psyche from the unsettling implications of their reality. Unless one is strongly committed to a theory of extraterrestrial genetic engineers, as is Hopkins, it is difficult to dismiss Kathie Davis's contention that the events were in fact dreams.

The general characteristics of UFO abductions are:

1. The UFO is usually described as a domed disk with flashing or pulsating lights.
2. Unusual high-pitched sounds are often heard.
3. Witnesses sometimes see alien beings looking out of windows in their saucers. There is often the feeling that they are exerting some kind of hypnotic influence on the humans.
4. The aliens themselves are one of two types. The first type is the so-called gray race, or small, ugly beings. This type is described as having large heads and eyes with simple or nonexistent mouths, noses, and ears. They are between three and a half and five feet tall. The second, slightly less common type is tall (six feet or more) and thin, with pale skin and blond hair. Their eyes are described as Oriental or catlike and are often blue or pink. They are often said to be strangely beautiful. In some cases humans seem to be working together with the aliens in these UFOs.

5. The aliens often communicate with human witnesses telepathically but with each other by incomprehensible sounds.
6. They often make reference to having visited earth in the past and/or coming to earth because of atomic or nuclear activity.
7. The aliens usually assure the witnesses that they will not be harmed.
8. There is typically a loss of memory of parts of the experience and a resultant sensation of "missing time."
9. The method of entry of the witnesses into the UFO often involves a beam of light, but the precise mode of entry is not remembered.
10. Some witnesses report seeing the earth or other planets from outer space while aboard the UFO.
11. Sometimes the UFO is taken into a larger mothership.
12. Witnesses often experience great fear.
13. At some point during the experience witnesses say that they felt calm due to being reassured by their captors.
14. Witnesses often undergo an examination while lying on a table. Elaborate machines are used, and the body is often probed, poked, scraped, and injected with fluids. Ova and sperm samples may be taken. In many cases, symptoms of physical injury or disease are present following a UFO abduction.
15. Witnesses often see panels with many monitors.
16. After the examination the witnesses are often taken through the ship and see many incomprehensible things.
17. Witnesses often float through the air on beams of light, and they sometimes report floating through walls.
18. Some witnesses describe large assemblages of aliens in halls.
19. Sometimes the witnesses are shown strange, surreal landscapes.
20. There are often experiences that seem hallucinatory or visionary.
21. The witnesses often report extreme exhaustion after the experience.
22. The doors within the UFOs almost vanish seamlessly when they are closed.
23. In case after case, there are reports of sexual interactions between human abductees and UFO entities. These fall into two categories: experiments with human reproduction involving medical manipulations; and direct sexual relationships between abductees and their captors.

The notion of UFO abductions has become part of the belief systems of many New Age believers. As a religious system that generally denies the dark side of life, New Age belief in sinister aliens as quasi-demons is especially interesting. Alien abductions have also figured in the birth of at least one new religious movement: Claude Vorilhon (known as Rael to his followers), the founder of the Raelian movement, is said to be the offspring of a human mother and an alien being. Further, he founded the Raelian movement in 1973 as a result of an encounter with space aliens (referred to as Elohim by Raelians).

—*John Whitmore*

See Also: Alien-Abduction Narratives; Captivity Tales; Close Encounters; Fantasy-Prone Personality Hypothesis; Hopkins, Budd; Larson Abduction; Moody Abduction; Schirmer Abduction; Strieber, Whitley; Villas-Boas Encounter
Further Reading:
Baker, Robert A., and Joe Nickell. *Missing Pieces: How to Investigate Ghosts, UFOs, Psychics, and Other Mysteries.* Buffalo, NY: Prometheus Books, 1992.
Bryan, C. D. B. *Close Encounters of the Fourth Kind: Alien Abduction, UFOs, and the Conference at M.I.T.* New York: Alfred A. Knopf, 1995.
Bullard, Thomas E. *The Sympathetic Ear: Investigators as Variables in UFO Abduction Reports.* Mount Rainier, MD: Fund for UFO Research, 1995.
Evans, Hilary. *Visions, Apparitions, Alien Visitors.* Wellingborough, U.K.: Aquarian Press, 1984.
Hopkins, Budd. *Missing Time: A Documented Study of UFO Abductions.* New York: Richard Marek, 1981.
Klass, Philip J. *UFO Abductions: A Dangerous Game.* Buffalo, NY: Prometheus Books, 1988.
Mack, John E. *Abduction: Human Encounters with Aliens.* New York: Charles Scribner's Sons, 1994.
Ring, Kenneth. *The Omega Project: Near-Death Experiences, UFO Encounters, and Mind at Large.* New York: William Morrow, 1992.
Rogo, D. Scott, ed. *UFO Abductions: True Cases of Alien Kidnappings.* New York: Signet, 1980.

Strieber, Whitley. *Communion: A True Story.* New York: William Morrow, 1987.

ABRAHAM

According to the narrative in chapter 17 of Genesis, God appeared to Abraham, proclaimed that he would have a son, and that his descendants would be as numerous as the stars. After he finished speaking, the relevant passage asserts that "God ascended and left him." From the perspective of the ancient astronaut school, the image of God's ascension suggests an embodied being flying away in some sort of craft.

THE ABYSS

The Abyss is a high-suspense alien-encounter movie. A nuclear submarine is bumped by something and lodges on an undersea ledge. The U.S. Navy hires a deep-sea oil engineer and his estranged wife, who designed the submarine, to go down into the abyss and check the sub for survivors. Mysterious creatures float around the submarine who turn out to be nonterrestrial and who, in the end, save the day.

Most alien encounter movies fall into one of two subcategories: alien-invasion movies in which humanity must fight against hostile extraterrestrials; or technological angel–type movies in which friendly extraterrestrials try to help humanity in some way. A less common but not unusual third category includes films in which terrestrials help aliens.

The Abyss is in the second genre (aliens-as-angels). As is typical in many friendly-extraterrestrial movies, *The Abyss* includes a character who insists on viewing the aliens as hostile, thus bringing in the central theme of films from the first genre. There is also introduced an element of the third genre when the chief protagonist deactivates a nuclear warhead, saving the aliens from destruction.

Fox 1989; 140 min. Writer/Director: James Cameron; Cinematography: Mikael Salomon; Music: Alan Silvestri; Cast: Ed Harris, Mary Elizabeth Mastrantonio, Todd Graff, Michael Biehn, John Bedford Lloyd, J. C. Quinn, Leo Bermester, Kidd Brewer Jr., Kimberly Scott, Adam Nelson, George Robert Kirk, Chris Elliott, Jimmie Ray Weeks.

ADAMSKI, GEORGE

George Adamski (April 17, 1891–February 26, 1965) was the first of a new breed of flying-saucer witness to report UFO contacts, not to the military or to the police, but to the general public. In this way he also became the first person to gain celebrity by claiming to transmit spiritual wisdom from extraterrestrial visitors to humanity. He authored several books and articles detailing his travels with the Space Brothers, as he called the aliens he encountered. In these publications, Adamski reported their "revelation" of an occult philosophy identical to the one he had long propagated in other guises.

Adamski was born in Poland and moved to the United States with his family at the age of two. Little other information is available about his life from that point forward until he settled with his wife in Southern California and in 1936 founded the Royal Order of Tibet. He actually claimed to represent the Royal Order and to lecture on its behalf. Material originally composed and presented as the teachings of the Royal Order would later be modified slightly and propagated as the teachings of the Space Brothers. He was also briefly associated with the Order of Loving Service, a metaphysical group in Laguna Beach, California.

George Adamski with a picture of a "Space Brother" (American Religion Collection)

His day job was in a cafe near Mt. Palomar and its observatory. In the early 1940s he became interested in unidentified flying objects, long before they were much discussed by the public. On October 9, 1946, he reported seeing a UFO for the first time and in 1949 published *Pioneers of Space* to generate interest in the subject. On November 20, 1952, he reported telepathic contact with a humanlike Venusian and the following month reported another contact in which a hieroglyphic message was given to him. These encounters were reported in his second book (written with Leslie Desmond), *Flying Saucers Have Landed* (1953). This became one of the most popular flying-saucer books ever written. He gained a broad following and became a popular lecturer.

Adamski's many claims included one in which he and six others in 1946 had seen a large, hovering craft, and another during the following summer in which he saw a full 184 UFOs pass over him in groupings of 32 each. He also claimed that the government and scientists knew about spacecraft flying near earth and had in fact tracked one with radar as it was preparing to land on the far side of the Moon. Further, according to Adamski, science knew all planets to be inhabited by beings far more advanced but nonetheless human and had photographic proof that the "canals" on Mars were not natural phenomena but had been constructed by intelligent beings.

Some of his wilder (though by no means his wildest) claims concerned an event that supposedly took place on November 20, 1952, when, Adamski maintained, he had actually seen and spoken to a Venusian and had seen his spacecraft up close. During this meeting, he learned that many Venusians already lived, in disguise, upon the earth and that they came in peace—primarily out of a concern for humanity's warlike ways, especially nuclear testing, which, the alien told him, was "upsetting the harmony of the universe." Adamski's most extravagant claim, however, may have been that he traveled to Saturn aboard an alien craft, which he boarded on a U.S. Air Force base, in order to attend a conference with beings from other planets.

This is related to another of his claims: that he was supported by some of the world's highest offi-cials. Adamski said that he had had a secret meeting with the Pope at the Vatican in May 1963—a claim denied by the Vatican—and that he had had secret meetings with President John F. Kennedy and various White House personnel and UN leaders. Because all such meetings were clandestine, none of his statements about these events could ever be confirmed or discounted.

Adamski's following was gained from not only those interested in UFOs but also those interested in the knowledge, advice, and wisdom Adamski claimed to receive from the space people. In 1957 he organized the International Get Acquainted Club to bring his followers together. The pinnacle of his career was reached with a world tour in 1959, the publication of *Cosmic Philosophy* (1961), and the establishment of *Science Publications Newsletter* in 1962.

Adamski's career was plagued by charges of fraud that were supported by counterevidence to his claims. Even in the early 1950s, his assertions about the surface conditions on the various planets of the solar system contradicted then-known scientific data. According to investigator James W. Moseley, writing in *Saucer News,* witnesses of the first sighting Adamski reported were all close friends, and at least one recanted his story, admitting to having never seen such a craft and stating that he doubted any of the others had, either.

Perhaps the most blatantly contradictory story Adamski told was one in which he claimed that a flying saucer had actually given him a ride during an unscheduled train stop. The saucer, he said, landed as he was stretching his legs outside and picked him up, taking him to his destination and saving him a 20-minute wait. A check with the railway company on the part of Arthur C. Campbell, however, showed that neither had the train stopped during that trip in question, nor had the vestibule been opened at any point along the way. A final criticism that has been leveled against Adamski concerns his anti-Semitism and Nazi sympathies. Not coincidentally, all of the extraterrestrial humanoids he described were white, beautiful, and blond.

Finally, Adamski's work was also discredited in the eyes of many people when UFO researcher Moseley in 1957 stated that Adamski had faked his photographs, taken the "hieroglyphs" from an obscure scholarly work, and plagiarized old science fiction as space messages. Adamski's close associate C. A. Honey broke away in 1963 after confirming for himself apparent fraudulent activity.

Like many other contactee groups, the late Adamski's believers have no formal congregation or rituals beyond the informal International Get Acquainted Club he had created in 1957. Between 1958 and 1964, he published his metaphysical-extraterrestrial wisdom in courses and books. His teachings are today kept alive by various individuals and organizations who use the Internet, newsletters, and correspondence to maintain contact and disseminate information. Perhaps the most prominent of these is the Adamski Foundation; its website claims to be the "only authorized and original source for George Adamski information." Founded in 1965, it promotes a philosophy "pertinent to understanding that Human Life is the rule, not the exception, throughout the universe" and that humanity has the capacity for peace. Confidence in the validity of this philosophy comes from contact with benevolent beings from other planets in our solar system; a contact that has also produced, according to the foundation, "advancements in science, agriculture and human understanding" and that has the potential to usher the earth into a new age of peace.

—*Ryan T. O'Leary*

See Also: Contactees; Religions, UFO; Space Brothers
Further Reading:
Adamski, George. *Cosmic Philosophy.* Freeman, SD: Pine Hill Press, 1972.
———. *Flying Saucers Farewell.* New York: Abelard-Schuman, 1961.
———. *Inside the Space Ships.* New York: Abelard-Schuman, 1955.
———. *Pioneers of Space: A Trip to the Moon, Mars, and Venus.* Los Angeles: Leonard-Freefield, 1949.
Clark, Jerome. *The UFO Encyclopedia.* 2nd ed. Detroit: Omnigraphics, 1988.
Curran, Douglas. *In Advance of the Landing: Folk Concepts of Outer Space.* New York: Abbeville Press, 1985.
Flammonde, Paris. *The Age of Flying Saucers: Notes on a Projected History of Unidentified Flying Objects.* New York: Hawthorn Books, 1971.
Melton, J. Gordon. *The Encyclopedia of American Religions.* 3rd ed., 2 vols. Detroit: Gale Research, 1989.
Melton, J. Gordon, and George M. Eberhart, eds. *The Flying Saucer Contactee Movement, 1950–1990.* Santa Barbara, CA: Santa Barbara Centre for Humanistic Studies, 1990.
Stupple, David. "Mahatmas and Space Brothers: The Ideologies of Alleged Contact with Mahatmas and Space Brothers." *Journal of American Culture* 7 (1984): 131–139.
———. "The Man Who Talked with Venusians." *Fate* 32(1) (January 1979): 30–39.
Thompson, Keith. *Angels and Aliens: UFOs and the Mythic Imagination.* Reading, MA: Addison-Wesley, 1991.
Vallee, Jacques. *Messengers of Deception: UFO Contacts and Cults.* Berkeley: And/Or Press, 1979.

ADVERTISING

The end of the twentieth century witnessed a wave of fascination with UFO phenomenon that has no end in sight. As an indicator of the public's widespread familiarity with the phenomenon, UFOs and ufonauts have even begun appearing in TV ads. In one shoe ad, for example, a young man is abducted by aliens; while stretched out on the stereotypical alien "examination" table, he notices that his kidnappers show unusual interest in his Airwalk sneakers. In the final scene, he wakes up shoeless in the middle of a dark, lonely highway. Other TV ads involve a group of gray aliens interested in terrestrial automobile technology (Volkswagen's Jetta), and a Maytag commercial in which the supposed extraterrestrial origin of the new Maytag washer is indicative of cutting-edge technology.

All of these productions have a remarkably appealing edge of humor—involving a kind of "little green men" portrayal of aliens that makes for strikingly memorable ads. Beyond humor, the other theme of UFO-related ads is the notion that "our product is so good that even beings from other planets make the trip to earth to obtain it." The cutting-edge technology theme mentioned above is also common, though less so.

Yet other ads seem to use aliens and UFOs just to create a striking effect. One recent ad for hanging file folders, for instance, plays on the popular TV show *X-Files.* The picture in the ad shows part of a file cabinet, with files labeled "Alien Abduction" and the like. A little green hand with claws is seen reaching up out of one of the files. Likewise, a somewhat older AT&T ad shows a golf cart being lifted off of the ground by a beam of light from a UFO. The caption reads, "At a time like this, whose cellular phone would you rather own?" In both of these cases, there is no direct product-UFO connection—the alien image is simply intended to attract attention.

See Also: Humor and UFOs; Popular Culture
Further Reading:
Curran, Douglas. In Advance of the Landing: Folk Concepts of Outer Space. New York: Abbeville Press, 1985.
Nesheim, Eric, and Leif Nesheim. Saucer Attack! Pop Culture in the Golden Age of Flying Saucers. Los Angeles: Kitchen Sink Press, 1997.

AETHERIUS SOCIETY

The Aetherius Society is probably the best-known and -organized flying-saucer religion. It was founded by George King, who in May 1954 received a command from interplanetary sources to become "the Voice of Interplanetary Parliament." Since then, he continually received trance messages and/or telepathic communications from various beings, mainly from different planets in the solar system. His eminence Dr. George King, as the members of the society usually address him, has been lavished with innumerable titles, academic degrees, and honors. He has authored many books and, because of his teachings and works, is recognized as a charismatic leader by the society's members. Roy Wallis describes him in classical Weberian terms, namely, as a mystagogue who "offers a largely magical means of salvation." Members of the society, however, see salvation in terms of the laws of karma and understand Dr. King's role as that of a teacher who conveys messages and instructions from extraterrestrial beings, rather than that of a miracle worker or a dispenser of magical rites.

The Aetherius Society, which gets its name from the pseudonym of a being from Planet Venus who first contacted Dr. King, is a structured organization founded by King himself. It is run by a board of directors, which was chaired by King until his death in 1997. Some internal hierarchy exists, with several degrees of initiation and merit awards being available to members. Headquartered in Hollywood, California, the society has branches, groups, and/or representatives in North America (the United States and Canada), Europe (England), Africa (Nigeria and Ghana), and Australia. Its membership, though not very large, is thus varied. In the United States, members are more likely to be adult, middle-class, and white. One must add, however, that in some cities white members actually form a minority. Further, many of its ministers and priests are women and black. These factors, plus the society's presence on several continents, makes its overall membership cosmopolitan.

The society publishes Dr. King's books and taped lectures, a newsletter, The Cosmic Voice, which has been in print since 1956, and the quarterly Journal of Spiritual and Natural Healing, which a few years ago was replaced with The Aetherius Society Newsletter. This newsletter covers many topics, including information from the society's headquarters and various branches, activities of members, and columns on the Cosmic Teachings.

Among the many aims of the Aetherius Society are the spreading of the teachings (or transmissions) of the Cosmic Masters, the preparation for the coming of the next Master, the administration of spiritual healing, the creation of the right conditions necessary for contacts and ultimate meetings with beings from other planets, and the conduct of various missions and operations.

The beliefs of the Aetherius Society are rather complex. Reference to God is common in its prayers, though the planetary beings appear to occupy the central stage in the members' spiritual lives. Among its teachings are included those on the chakras, the aura, kundalini, karma, and reincarnation. Yoga and meditation are considered to be very important. George King is also said to be a master of yoga, a well-advanced stage that he achieved at an early age and later enhanced by practices given by a Master who resides on earth. Meditation, or Samadhi, is, according to the society, the experiential state of Adeptship, "when the soul is bathe in the Light of pure Spirit and one becomes a knower of truth." Mantras are also frequently repeated during services.

A common theme that runs through all the teachings of the Aetherius Society is spiritual service. The greatest yoga and the greatest religion is service to humankind. Many of the operations and missions upon which the society has embarked

Operation Prayer Power pilgrimage; the Aetherius Society on Holdstone Down, 16 September 1978 (Aetherius Society)

should be understood primarily as acts of service to the human race, which has at times placed itself on the edge of destruction.

Some of the teachings of the Aetherius Society has led one scholar, Robert Ellwood, to place the society within the theosophical tradition. The literature of the Aetherius Society in the late 1950s and early 1960s exhibits both great concern for the dangers of atomic warfare and fallout as well as excitement about UFO sightings. These features, plus accounts that the earth is under attack by evil cosmic forces and the interest in the coming of the next cosmic Master, has led Ellwood to conclude that "like the Adamski teachings, Aetherius can be thought of as apocalyptic theosophy." In both its literature and its regular prayer services, however, little if any prominence is given to an imminent apocalyptic scenario.

One of the Aetherius Society's central beliefs is the existence of a kind of pantheon of beings largely from other planets in the solar system. These beings live in a kind of paradise and are, scientifically and spiritually, millions of years ahead of the human race here on earth. In the society's literature there is mention of Four interplanetary Beings (Shri Krishna, the Lord Buddha, the Master Jesus, and Lao Tsu) who descended to earth as teachers. The Great White Brotherhood, made up of Masters from all races is, according to the Society, the spiritual hierarchy on earth and is made up of Adepts, Masters, and Ascended Masters. The function of these beings is mainly to preserve and develop spirituality upon earth.

Detailed descriptions of several Cosmic Intelligences, of their planetary habitats, and of the major types of spacecraft they use have been provided by George King. Motherships, scout patrol vessels, and special-purpose vessels are among those accounted for in the Aetherius Society's literature. The reason why these beings cannot land openly is because of the negative karmic effects created by human beings by their neglect of God's laws and the Teachings of the Masters.

There has been little attempt by the society's members to embark on an evangelization campaign; consequently, the Aetherius Society does not fit into the popular image of a new religion that indulges in heavy-handed recruiting tactics.

In practice much of the work is dedicated to conducting and/or maintaining several operations and/or missions, among which are: Operation Starlight, a mission carried out between 1958 and 1961 during which 19 select mountains were charged with spiritual energy that can be radiated to uplift our world by anyone who prays unselfishly on them; Operation Space Power, which involves the cooperation of the Aetherius Society with Interplanetary Beings to radiate spiritual power to earth during "Spiritual Pushes"; Operation Bluewater, which alleviated the effects of a warp in the earth's magnetic field, a warp produced by atomic experiments and the negative thoughts and actions of human beings that interfere with the natural flow of spiritual energies to earth; Operation Sunbeam, through which spiritual energy is restored to the earth as a token repayment for all the energy humanity has taken from it; Operation Prayer Power, which involves the storing of spiritual energy through prayer and mantra, an energy that can be released to relieve suffering anywhere on earth; and several past missions that saved the earth from evil extraterrestrial intelligences or entities (the Alien Mission and Operation Karmalight). These last two missions were almost entirely performed by Interplanetary Beings and are not being conducted or maintained by the society.

Probably one of the most interesting aspects of these missions is their technical aspect. Some of them required the designing and building of special equipment. Thus, for instance, Operation Prayer Power needs unique batteries and transmission systems that were designed by George King to, respectively, store spiritual energy safely and beam it effectively to trouble spots on earth.

The ritual of the Aetherius Society, which can be rather elaborate, is carried out on a weekly basis and on special commemorative occasions. The temple where the services are held (often a small room) is usually decorated with religious symbols that include a photograph of George King and a portrait of the Master Jesus. Every week the following services are held: a prayer meeting that includes a short meditation period, the recitation of the Twelve Blessings of Jesus, and petitions for the healing at a distance for anyone who has requested to be placed on the healing list; a service dedicated to Operation Prayer Power; a private healing service; and a regular Sunday service, during which taped instructions or lectures of Dr. King and messages from various planetary beings might be played. On a yearly basis the start and/or completion of several of the missions and operations are commemorated. Pilgrimages to the Holy Mountains, charged with spiritual power during Operation Starlight, are periodically made by devoted members of the society.

Several years after the death of its founder, the Aetherius Society still functions with little changes in its rituals and beliefs. The charisma of its deceased leader seems to be in the process of institutionalization, a development that, from a sociological point of view, is not surprising, for the society has a well-structured organization and a well-defined religious agenda. The society has, so far, continued to operate as a small religious movement or organization where belief in extraterrestrials who help humankind is central and spiritual healing is regularly practiced. Whether and when George King will be replaced by another Cosmic Master are not pressing issues in the minds of its members. The society's literature published since King's death has not dealt with the question of succession. The more common belief appears to be that George King will not be succeeded in the near future by another Master who will act as the Primary Mental Channel. In the unspecified future, however, a Cosmic Intelligence could come to earth and be the next Master.

—*John A. Saliba*

See Also: Ascended Masters; Contactees; Cults, UFO; Religions, UFO; Space Brothers

Further Reading:

Aetherius Society. *Temple Degree Study Courses.* Hollywood, CA: Aetherius Society, 1982.
The Aetherius Society Newsletter, 1992–1999.
Cosmic Voice, 1956–1999.
Ellwood, Robert. *Islands of the Dawn: The Story of Alternative Spirituality in New Zealand.* Honolulu: University of Hawaii Press, 1993, pp. 92–94.
King, George. *Life on the Planets.* Hollywood, CA: Aetherius Society, 1958.
———. *The Nine Freedoms.* Hollywood, CA: Aetherius Society, 1963.
———. *The Twelve Blessings.* Hollywood, CA: Aetherius Society 1962.
———. *You Are Responsible!.* Hollywood, CA: Aetherius Society, 1961.
King, George, with Richard Lawrence. *Contacts with the Gods from Space: Pathway to the New Millennium.* Hollywood, CA: Aetherius Society, 1996.
Saliba, John A. "The Earth Is a Dangerous Place—The World View of the Aetherius Society." *Marburg Journal of Religion* 4(2) (December 1999): 1–20.
The Story of the Aetherius Society. Hollywood, CA: Aetherius Society, n.d.
Wallis, Roy. "The Aetherius Society: A Case Study in the Formation of a Mystagogic Congregation." *Sociological Review* 22 (1974): 27–44.

AHO, WAYNE SULO

In 1957, Wayne Aho sighted a UFO and received a "cosmic initiation" in the desert of Southern California. This turned out to be the most important of the communications and contacts he had experienced since he was 12.

Aho began to publicly disseminate the messages he had received as well as a tape of "voices from Venus," which he recorded through the medium Enid Brady. One of his public lectures was held at the Pentagon. In 1958 Aho met Otis T. Carr, who was working on an interplanetary flying saucer and was selling shares for its realization. The enterprise ended with the arrest of both of them on charges of fraud. Aho, though, was proved to have been deceitfully lured into the partnership and was acquitted.

After a brief period in a mental hospital on Long Island, New York, he returned to his native Washington in 1961 and joined the community of ufologists in the Pacific Northwest. He also became involved in the New Age movement and, in 1965, created the New Age Foundation; 10 years later he founded the Cathedral of the Stars, Church of the New Age.

See Also: Contactees; Hoaxes

Further Reading:

Aho, Wayne S. *Mojave Desert Experience.* Eatonville, WA: New Age Foundation, 1972.
"Panorama: Major Wayne S. Aho." *Flying Saucer Review* 4(3) (May/June 1958): 30.
Sachs, Margaret. *The UFO Encyclopedia.* New York: G. P. Putnam's Sons, 1980.

AKAKOR

According to a document entitled *The Chronicle of Akakor,* Akakor was the capital city of the Brazilian people known as Ugha Mongulala. The *Chronicle* recounts that the Ugha Mongulala were visited by light-skinned gods who came from the sky in golden vehicles around 1300 B.C.E. The visitors came from a world called Schwerta, and they come once every 6,000 years to share their knowledge. Thirteen underground cities are said to have survived to this day—four of which are still inhabited by Indians. The Ugha Mongulala claim that the remaining cities contain technological equipment of the god-astronauts. In one of the underground cities it is claimed that there are three men and one female mummy with six fingers and six toes.

The *Chronicle of Akakor* was purportedly authored by Tutunca Nara and edited by Karl Brugger. It is sometimes cited as evidence for the ancient astronaut hypothesis. Translated from German and published in English in 1977 with a preface by Erich von Däniken, it was more likely an imaginative creation by Brugger. The *Chronicle* builds upon existing folklore about hidden underground cities in South America.

See Also: Ancient Astronauts; Inner Earth
Further Reading:
Brugger, Karl. *The Chronicle of Akakor.* New York: Delacorte Press, 1977.

AKASHIC RECORDS

The akashic records originally was a theosophical concept—now widely accepted throughout the New Age/metaphysical subculture—referring to the records of all world events and personal experiences. These events are transcribed in the form of complex images composed of pictures, sounds, and the like. These are indelibly impressed upon the "matter" of the astral plane (the akasha) and may be "read" only when the reader is in a special, altered state of consciousness. In such a frame of mind, one is able to tap the akashic records and receive direct information about past ages. Certain theosophical descriptions of Atlantis, for example, are supposedly received via this technique. Also, some psychics who do past-life readings claim to receive their information from the akashic records. Even information on one's extraterrestrial incarnations can be found in these records.

See Also: Atlantis; New Age; Occult
Further Reading:
Bletzer, June G. *The Donning International Encyclopedic Psychic Dictionary.* Norfolk, VA: Donning, 1986.
Shepard, Leslie A., ed. *Encyclopedia of Occultism and Parapsychology.* Detroit: Gale Research, 1991.

ALIEN

Alien was a 1979 movie from Fox studios. In it a human space crew on a galactic expedition finds the ruins of an old spacecraft built by aliens. One of the creatures comes to life. The rest of the film is a suspenseful battle between the crew and the most repulsive and vicious extraterrestrial ever filmed for control of their ship.

Although not an alien-invasion film, it appears to be derived from *It! The Terror from beyond Space,* a 1958 film with an alien-invasion theme. Also, *Alien* was such a popular piece that it subsequently influenced the entire genre, encouraging others to produce more films around the theme of hostile aliens.

Fox 1979; 116 min. Director: Ridley Scott; Writer: Dan O'Bannon; Cinematography: Derek Vanlint, Denys Ayling; Cast: Tom Skerritt, Sigourney Weaver, Veronica Cartwright, Yaphet Kotto, Harry Dean Stanton, Ian Holm, John Hurt.

ALIEN AUTOPSY FILM

On Friday, May 5, 1995, there was a premiere showing of a film alleged to have been made in 1947. It purported to show an autopsy performed on the body of an alien that was recovered from the flying-saucer crash at Roswell, New Mexico. The first showing of the film took place at 1 P.M. in a small auditorium in the Museum of London before an audience of 100. Everyone was physically searched for cameras before being allowed into the auditorium. There was no speaker or announcement to introduce the film. Before the film footage began, a few short statements appeared on the screen stating that the film had been acquired from the cameraman who originally shot the footage and that the copyright belonged to Merlin Communications, a company owned by Ray Santilli, a documentary film producer in London.

The black-and-white footage then started. The scene was apparently a small operating or autopsy room with plain, white walls and a table in the middle containing an unclad body lying face up. Two figures in white anticontamination suits with hoods and narrow, rectangular glass faceplates were standing in the room next to the table. Another person could be seen peering through a window into the room. He was not recognizable due to a surgical mask covering his face. The two doctors circled the operating table while the cameraman moved about in the room. He failed to get any really good shots of the body, and the film was not always in focus.

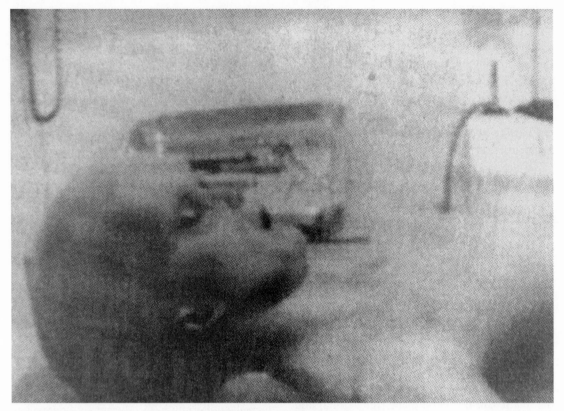

Video frame from the supposed "alien autopsy" film (Research Newsletter)

The alien shown in the film had a large head, and the open eyes were black orbs. The ears were low on the head. The nose was small and the mouth was small and open. The body was approximately four feet tall. It had a large, protruding stomach and stocky limbs. There was no hair on the body whatsoever. There were no external genitalia or secondary sexual organs. The feet had six toes, and the hands had six fingers. The forearms were longer than the upper arms. There was a large wound on one thigh, as well as a wound beneath the right armpit. The right hand was almost completely severed at the wrist.

The table on which the body rested was an operating table, rather than an autopsy table, which has channels to drain body fluids. A tray of instruments could be seen in the film laid out on a utility table. There was an old-style handsaw used for removing the cranial cap. Also included was a palpation hammer, which is used to check reflexes. A smaller table covered with a white cloth held a Bunsen burner underneath a flask, five test tubes in a test-tube stand, and a large beaker containing a dark fluid.

The area near the leg wound was inspected and the knee joint was manipulated with great care. One of the doctor's made a long, straight incision from the sternum to the pelvis. There was another incision from the lower part of the ear down the neck to the collar bone. The doctors removed the black lenses from the eyes in a matter of seconds. The skin on the skull was peeled back, and the cranium was opened. The chest and stomach were also opened. The doctors lifted organs clear of the body and dropped them into steel bowls. The entire film lasted about 20 minutes. According to the clock on the wall of the operating room, the two doctors completed the autopsy in about two hours.

In addition to the hospital autopsy, the film had footage of a preliminary autopsy in a tent, shots of debris from the crash, and pictures of the spacecraft wreckage as it was lifted onto a flatbed truck. The film footage of the tent autopsy was so dark and poorly reproduced that little could be seen except the two shapes of doctors, a shape on a table, and a lantern hanging from the tent pole. No one took the stage when the film was over to publicly answer questions.

After this initial viewing the film, or parts of it, were made available to various UFO researchers. UFO experts have viewed this film again and again, analyzing it in great detail. Ray Santilli claimed to have come across the film when he was in the United States searching for rare early footage of Elvis Presley. A U.S. Army cameraman allegedly had kept certain outtakes of the Roswell film. Santilli is said to have bought the film for about $100,000.

The hospital autopsy shown in the film is alleged to have occurred at Carswell Air Force Base near Fort Worth, Texas, the month following the flying-saucer crash. The doctors performing the autopsy in the film were identified as Detlev Bronk and Lloyd Berkner, both long since deceased. Although some have enthusiastically embraced the film as being authentic, others declare it to be a fraud. One of the immediate questions about the film is why did it not surface until nearly 50 years after it was made. The cameraman, who has never made a public appearance to authenticate the film, is alleged to have had it in a box in his home for all that time.

There are other questions about the autopsy procedure itself. The two doctors were performing an autopsy on a life-form unknown to them, yet they made no attempt to map the internal structure of the alien being; neither was a still photographer on hand to record each step precisely. The clock on the wall in the film showed that the autopsy took about two hours, despite the fact that it was conducted on a life-form they had never seen before and would probably never see again. Supporters of the film have suggested that perhaps the autopsy took 14 or 26 hours rather than two, but at no time in the film was the hour hand of the clock seen outside of those two hours.

When the security coding on the film was challenged as being more appropriate to Hollywood than the U.S. Army, the security codes disappeared from the film. That in itself suggests that the film was a hoax. Kodak officials offered to analyze a small segment of the film to determine when the

film was made—something that would aid in authenticating the film. However, Santilli did not make a film segment available to Kodak.

Another series of questions about the film's authenticity have to do with the setting of the film. Only two walls of the operating room appear in the film, leading one to believe that it was photographed in a two-walled set rather than an actual room. With the cameraman free to move around in an actual room, one would expect to see all four walls. A Bunsen burner can be seen in the film, although this apparatus is more appropriate to a chemistry laboratory than an operating or autopsy room. It has been suggested that the burner could have been used to burn the fat off surgical scalpels, but this action was not seen on the film. Moreover, if that was the function of the Bunsen burner, surely the flask would not have been in position over it. A palpation hammer, clearly seen on the instrument tray in the film, is used to test reflexes of the living and is not part of autopsy or surgical equipment.

The film was examined by a group of military photographers who found several significant discrepancies. First of all, a photographer would never be able to keep a portion of any top-secret military film because every frame of every reel must be accounted for. Second, the photographers said that in 1947 16mm color film was used for all important medical procedures as well as very special or important projects. It would not have been filmed in black and white. Furthermore, medical procedures were always filmed using two cameras in fixed positions, one looking down from the ceiling onto the operating table, the other elevated adjacent to the operating table. Third, a motion-picture cameraman would almost always be accompanied by a still photographer, and the two would work together as a team. The still photographer would invariably be visible at times in the motion picture. The experts in military photography also stated that the film was deliberately blurred so that no subject is visible in detail. The only conclusion to be drawn is that the alien autopsy film is a hoax.

In 1995, a one-hour video presentation entitled *Alien Autopsy: Fact or Fiction?* aired as part of the TV series *Sightings*. The video version carries the full autopsy film, purportedly unedited and uninterrupted, at the end of the presentation. This video can be rented at most video-rental outlets in the United States.

—*Kay Holzinger*

See Also: Hoaxes; The Roswell Incident
Further Reading:
Craft, Michael. *Alien Impact.* New York: St. Martin's, 1996.
Randle, Kevin D. *The Randle Report: UFOs in the 1990s.* New York: M. Evans, 1997.

ALIEN CONTAMINATION

This is a 1981 Italian film in which a cyclops creature from Mars spreads its eggs over the earth. The alien threat is discovered when a ship laden with the eggs (crated as coffee) docks in New York with every member of its crew dead. A team is assembled, which tracks the contamination back to South America.

While not at the top of anyone's viewing list, *Alien Contamination* is interesting as a piece that attempted to cash in on interest in the 1979 blockbuster *Alien* as a kind of pseudosequel built around the commonly used theme of the alien invasion of earth. While *Alien* was not a terrestrial invasion film, it, in turn, appears to have been at least partially based on the 1958 film *It! The Terror from beyond Space,* which featured an invasion plot.

Cannon 1981; 90 min. Writer/Director: Lewis (Luigi Cozzi) Coates; Cinematography: Guiseppe Pinori; Cast: Ian Culloch, Louise Monroe, Martin Mase, Siegfried Rauch, Lisa Hahn.

ALIEN FROM L.A.

In this 1987 comedy, a California girl travels to Africa when her explorer father disappears. She follows him down a hole that leads directly to the lost continent of Atlantis. The Atlanteans are immigrants from outer space, a notion taken from the 1978 film *Warlords of Atlantis.* The idea of aliens living inside the earth reflects the theme found in some UFO literature about flying-saucer bases being either under the earth or at the center of a hollow earth.

Cannon 1987; 88 min. Director: Albert Pyun; Writers: Albert Pyun, Debra Ricci, Regina Davis; Cinematography:

Tom Fraser; Cast: Kathy Ireland, Thom Mathews, Don Michael Paul, Linda Kerridge, William R. Moses, Richard Haines.

ALIEN NATION

In this 1988 film (which later became the basis for a TV series), hundreds of thousands of aliens in a flying saucer land in California, refugees from an outer-space slave state. They face the challenges of any immigrant minority. Some find avenues to get ahead in American society; others live in a kind of alien ghetto. One becomes an LAPD detective, teamed up with a bigoted human being out to revenge the death of his former partner (who had been shot by alien criminals). Part of the appeal of the film lies in the gradual development of an alien-human friendship between the two detectives.

Alien Nation is interesting for the manner in which it breaks out of traditional film portrayals of extraterrestrials, who are usually pictured one-dimensionally, as terrestrial friends or foes. Although ufologists who hold the extraterrestrial hypothesis have often speculated about the possible impact of the formal establishment of relationships with an alien race, few have speculated about what extended contact with extraterrestrials would mean.

Fox 1988; 90 min. Director: Graham Baker; Writer: Rockne S. O'Bannon; Music: Curt Sobel; Cast: James Caan, Mandy Patinkin, Terence Stamp, Kevyn Major Howard, Peter Jason, Jeff Kober, Leslie Bevins.

ALIEN-ABDUCTION NARRATIVES

In Seal Beach, California, a young boy propels his skateboard down Main Street while sporting a T-shirt picturing a terrified person being examined by large-eyed gray aliens under the caption "Alien Med-Lab." Nearby shops sell alien pins and curios, including votive candles "for protection against alien abduction." A six-year-old boy watches a TV program about UFOs and shortly afterward becomes terrified that they will attack earth. At a clinic for abused children, a little girl reports nightmares about "outer space men."

Major corporations such as General Motors, AT&T, Pepsi-Cola, and Mars Candies run expensive

TV commercials showing aliens coming to earth to steal our consumer products (thereby implying their products' desirability). These events—along with extensive Internet coverage—indicate the degree to which alien-abduction narratives (AANs) have seized the public imagination.

Although reports of visitations and abductions of humans by strange creatures have apparently occurred throughout recorded history, modern researchers agree that these reports have dramatically increased since 1947 in the case of UFO "sightings" and since 1966 for abduction narratives. The year 1966 also saw the publication of John Fuller's *The Interrupted Journey,* the abduction story of Betty and Barney Hill that is still considered paradigmatic for the modern form of the alien-abduction narrative. One of the most popular and influential explanations of AANs is that UFO stories constitute the basis of a new mythology that is developing in our highly technological age.

An AAN can refer to a single experience or to a group of experiences. They usually involve a claim that someone took the narrators out of their beds (or cars) and subjected them to medical examinations and other unusual experiences. In a typical AAN scenario, one or more individuals either come forward voluntarily, or they contact and are then interviewed by a specialist in this type of phenomenon. In each case, a narrative is presented consisting of a report of being kidnapped and experimented upon by "alien" creatures. Frequently, these accounts include expressions of trauma and terror as the "victims" are subjected to painful or humiliating procedures.

Several individuals have emerged to play leading roles as advisers to these narrators, who in many cases are alleged to display symptoms characteristic of post-traumatic stress disorder. These advisers include artist Budd Hopkins, historian Dr. David Jacobs, author Whitley Strieber, Harvard University psychiatrist John Mack, and clinical social worker John Carpenter, to name a few.

During the modern period of narratives about alien beings, several labels have been advanced to identify a person presenting some type of AAN. All of them introduce serious epistemological and methodological difficulties. In order to be precise about the subject matter under consideration, the term "narrator" is proposed to overcome some of these problems.

Since the early 1950s, some have been called "contactees." These include George Adamski, George King, and, more recently, Billy Meier. The characteristics of their narratives include:

- The narrator is an ostensibly ordinary individual who may have been on some spiritual quest.
- Benevolent or at least friendly beings present themselves by means of a sighting, apparition, or just voices. These beings conduct the narrator on a tour of some kind, during which he or she is lectured on humanity's future, morality, and other topics.
- These visitations or tours are repeated over a period of time and may increase in duration, complexity, and the importance of subjects revealed.

It is worth noting that this pattern fits even some traditional historical figures such as Joseph Smith, the founder of Mormonism.

In summary, the contactee narrative has gradually narrowed in meaning to denote persons claiming to have received religious or prophetic messages (involving religious awe, perhaps, but not terrifying experiences) from alien beings. In many of these cases, the use of this term today suggests that either mental illness or fraud was implied or suspected, but not necessarily.

Another contactee category is the "walk-in" or "host body" narrative. While sometimes engendering fear in others, these rarely involve a self-report of fear, in part because the original personality has been replaced. Examples include Marshall Applewhite, founder of the Heaven's Gate group, and Frederick Meier.

Contactee and walk-in narratives are not AANs, since they lack the elements of coercion and fear. It is not just contact, but abduction and its accompanying fear, that implies victimization, unwilling selection, and terror. Contactee narratives, and the activities that accompany them, have more in common with channeling.

Since the Betty and Barney Hill case in the 1960s, as documented in Fuller's 1966 book, the term "abductee" has increased in usage. It is still in general use today by those who hold to the extraterrestrial hypothesis (ETH) in the ufology field, whether skeptic, believer, or neutral. It is a term that carries with it the ideas of fear and unwillingness. However, not every abductee becomes a narrator. Some refuse to talk at all.

In his controversial work *Abductions: Human Encounters with Aliens* (1994), psychiatrist John Mack has adopted the term "experiencers." Although this appears to be an attempt at neutrality toward AANs, it unfortunately makes the unscientific assumption that an experience has occurred, when we have no independent evidence that this is the case.

In a 1996 article, Leonard S. Newman asserts that the origins of UFO abduction reports, since there is no consensus data on alien visitation that is even remotely convincing to conventional science, must be considered entirely terrestrial. If nothing else, this is just the null hypothesis of scientific study. The fact that Newman can confidently assert that UFOs are not of extraterrestrial origin succinctly illustrates the weakness of 50 years of UFO "research." Newman believes that a set of personal and cultural phenomena and processes parsimoniously explains the psychological symptoms reported by abductees. He agrees with Mack about the mental health of the vast majority of experiencers and does not deny the subjective power of their reports. However, Newman takes a different social-psychological approach and discusses the experiencer stories as narratives with a purpose.

As used here, the term "narrative" was defined in a 1994 paper by Newman and his mentor, Roy Baumeister, at Case Western Reserve University in Cleveland, Ohio. Narratives can be understood as a natural, everyday process of making sense out of one's experiences; that telling stories is a fundamentally social activity. Baumeister asserts that when we construct narratives about our lives, we operate out of four specific needs for meaning:

- We seek to find purpose to the events that befall us;
- We seek value and moral justification;
- We seek evidence of efficacy by showing a level of control over the environment; and
- We seek self-worth and affirmation

Narrative speech is the preferred mode for most people, and narratives can be subject to powerful social effects. Only a minority of people normally report their experiences abstractly, in what is called "paradigmatic speech." According to Newman, UFO abduction reports—whether obtained under relaxation or hypnotic regression—are narratives subject to many motivations and influences. Newman addresses the issue thus: If UFO abduction reports are not about UFO abductions, why would people recall something that did not happen to them in consensual reality, and, in particular, why would they recall something as traumatic as an alien abduction?

Many theories have been advanced to account for the occurrence of these narratives. These include:

- Extraterrestrial hypothesis. This is the most commonly understood explanation, the one that most closely fits the modern scientific worldview (or at least its popular equivalent). This hypothesis proposes that visitors from other physical places in the universe come to earth in flying vehicles and abduct humans for scientific purposes of their own.
- Psychosocial hypothesis. This category includes all attempts to understand AANs in terms of social science. For example, it considers the severe limitations of the hypnotic regression method and the existence of a cogent alternative psychological explanation, as discussed by Leonard Newman at the national convention of the American Psychological Association in Los Angeles in 1994. As Newman shows, regression hypnosis and abduction reports are far from convincing evidence of alien contact when seen from the perspective of conventional research psychology. Some of the therapeutic issues raised by AANs are similar to those encountered in investigations of near-death experiences, reincarnation, and so-called past-life regression, even satanic ritual abuse and multiple personality disorder. This area has been identified by sociologists as similar to the "wild psychotherapies."

- Religious-spiritual hypothesis. This category includes the view that AANs are part of a new modern mythology. It is based on the similarities between AANs and traditional religious narratives.

Below we offer some examples of the latter category.

First, AANs share with revealed religions a similar narrative status as viewed by science and ordinary common sense. When someone talks about visions or other highly personal experiences that have led them to a religious conversion (called "witnessing"), their testimony constitutes personal knowledge based on a perceived event that was real to them. AANs differ from such traditional witnessing in that they assume a modern technological worldview capable of acknowledging UFOs; but they are similar in disregarding the normal verification requirements of scientific or social consensus. In effect, the AAN may sometimes take the form of a verifiable event but, upon closer examination, will not yield weight to a testable hypothesis (e.g., that a so-called first contact has occurred). Instead, like any religious assertion, it inspires personal awe and transformation but remains aloof from scientific cosmology.

Abduction experiences cannot be corroborated (even the New Testament gospels are similar stories in this sense), so we don't know what really happened and still might not know even if we had been there. This is also the case with so-called past-life regression and other types of hypnotically obtained recollections, which are highly vulnerable to aggressive scientific critique. Even so, we have found debunking (the tool of the dominant scientific worldview) to be completely ineffective in dispelling the personally transforming effect of such experiences. Instead, as with religious belief, abrasive approaches tend to strengthen resolve. Consequently, belief systems growing out of AANs typically produce very powerful defensive protections—sometimes fundamentalist and even cultic—to ward off criticism.

Both AANs and religious stories can involve a dramatic reframing of a person's Weltanschauung. Consider the following two Bible passages (emphasis mine), and ask yourself: Could an AAN turn into a biblical account? Are the two forms of narrative interchangeable?

> On one such expedition I was going to Damascus, armed with full powers and a commission from the chief priests, and at midday as I was on my way, your Majesty [King Agrippa], I saw a LIGHT BRIGHTER THAN THE SUN COME DOWN FROM HEAVEN. It shone brilliantly around me and my fellow travelers. We all fell to the ground, and I heard a voice saying to me in Hebrew, "Saul, Saul, why are you persecuting me? It is hard for you [to resist]." Acts 26:12–14 (Jerusalem Bible)

> I know a man in Christ who, fourteen years ago, WAS CAUGHT UP—whether still in the body or out of the body, I do not know; God knows—right INTO THE THIRD HEAVEN [which is the highest]. I do know, however, that this same person—WHETHER STILL IN THE BODY OR OUT OF THE BODY [such distinctions were known even then], I do not know; God knows—was caught up into paradise and heard things which must not and cannot be put into human language. . . . In view of the extraordinary nature of these revelations, to stop me from getting too proud I WAS GIVEN A THORN IN THE FLESH [an implant?], an angel of Satan [literally: messenger from the adversary] to beat me and stop me from getting too proud. 2 Cor. 12:2–4, 7 (Jerusalem Bible)

Second, AANs appear across time and cultures. In cultures that practice shamanism, there are stories of "little people." Hinduism contains many tales of "space" beings. Buddhism has its cautions about encounters with "skandha demons." American Indians talk of the "little men." The Celtic cultures of Europe have their leprechauns. These similarities led Thomas Bullard to make his groundbreaking study of AAN folklore. But to his own surprise, Bullard found that AANs are not as culturally diverse as most folklore. We think there is merit in supposing this is due more to the context of a modern, media-driven society than to the content of the folklore.

What remains obscure is the psychosocial impact of folkloric traditions on individuals in the mass-media age and the possible mechanisms for triggering intrapsychic experience organized around mass media–driven folkloric icons. In the domain of mass psychology, far too much is assumed, and pitifully little is understood thus far, even in theory. Instead, media-savvy communicators draw on the known effects of careful manipulation of symbols to sell products and pedal influence. It may be easy to influence people but harder to offer insight when seeking to explain the power and cultural value of AANs in today's society.

Third, AANs have been the topic of millenarian anxieties. The 1995 collection *The Gods Have Landed* characterizes the UFO myth as millenarian, that is, concerned with the "end of time" both in its historical movements and its social dynamics. Christianity made linear time important, especially when measured on the clock toward the Endtime. Before the Christian era, the source of transcendent meaning tended to be "outside of time" (or perhaps in "missing time"). Narrators now as then become a new elect standing against the secular worldview. They await "revealed" aliens to vindicate them. Although this can be interpreted by the larger society as a trend toward irrationalism, we should take heed that this dismissive observation was very much the way the ancient Romans viewed the early Christians.

Fourth, AANs may be acquiring mythic status. In the 1950s, at the height of the early UFO flaps, Carl Jung wrote *Flying Saucers: A Modern Myth of Things Seen in the Sky.* Unfortunately, although Jung took the phenomenon seriously, his use of the term "myth" was characteristically misunderstood by our utilitarian culture. To the Western mind, a myth is a kind of lie. We do not see myths as the source of human experience—that which makes one the member of a group.

In modern times, initiation into adult society comes less from traditions ritually imbued by family and culture and more through random encounters with the mass culture of films, music, and television. Witness the nearly apocalyptic rhetoric of media events such as the death of Princess Di or the final *Seinfeld* episode. Perhaps societies driven by such hypostases of personality, like the United States, evolve a multimyth marketplace that eventually replaces the monopolistic functioning of traditional religious myth with an ongoing array of popular avant-garde religions. In such a context, the AAN has fertile ground to readily take form and multiply. Furthermore, if AANs are more like an antimyth—in opposition to established science

and religion—it raises a new possibility that resistance is growing to the desacralizing effect of science. I am reminded of Arthur Schopenhauer's famous edict: All truth passes through three stages. First, it is ridiculed. Second, it is violently opposed. Third, it is accepted as being self-evident.

And finally, AANs have raised issues of good and evil and thereby divide even AAN believers into denominations. In addition to some fundamentalist Christian attitudes toward AANs, an intense debate has arisen in the ufological community among those who give full credence to the claims of first contact and who yet differ about the intentions of the alleged sources of the phenomena. As a result, one faction fears alien invasion or human conspiracy or both (perhaps represented by Vallee, Jacobs, and Hopkins), another camp appears to welcome alien salvation (like Sprinkle and Boylan), and still a third stays on the fence (maybe Fowler and Strieber). Is this the beginning of first contact religion denominationalism?

It appears that there is an unlimited number of possible explanations for the AAN phenomenon. Most of them are untestable, not scientifically useful, or employ tests that are internal to the explanation itself and not extendable to other systems. The Rorschach-like nature of the AAN derives from the many ways of approaching it with a specific set of concepts: physical, metaphysical, religious. This is a blind alley. Even allowing for the possibility of hoax and deception will not cause the phenomenon to go away. The field still calls for an approach that studies the narratives strictly in terms of known human experience, not in terms of speculative theories.

Aliens are not attempting to solve our spiritual problems. Investing even a hypothetical alien lifeform with intense interest in human religious behavior can only be properly characterized as an anthropomorphic conceit. The reality is that we are engaged in our own spiritual struggles, on both the individual and social levels, and our intuitive faculties produce images reflecting that struggle. Then our cognitive processes impose sequences of order and meaning upon these images, resulting in narratives. Narrators and the "researchers" who shepherd them are fundamentalists, each after their own fashion: Christian, metaphysical, or materialist. And each in their own fashion is attempting to understand the implications of their respective stories.

The Christian tradition says that "God is not a god of the dead but of the living." Namely, our spiritual realm is not the realm of outer space or other dimensions but of the earth itself. We are led to other matters in our attempt to avoid the fears we feel as the result of our unwillingness to face ourselves and the consequences of our actions. The struggles embodied in AANs may come about because of a general failure to face reality. The eternal quality of the alien "presence" reflects the relevance of that presence only as a signal from ourselves to ourselves. When we are back about our own business as human beings, individually and collectively, the aliens will disappear.

Well before the advent of the computer sciences, German philosopher Rudolf Steiner claimed to see the spiritual effects of what he described as the "hyper-materialization of the modern worldview." This prophecy has an interesting connection to alien abduction narratives, for in the same essay where Steiner predicted that a "spidery network of automata covering the earth" would gradually attain its own consciousness, he also said that this development would bring about the arrival of "beings from the heavens" in response to an increasingly virtual (illusory) human existence. Whether AANs are a new reality or part of the illusion remains to be determined.

—*Scott R. Scribner*

See Also: Abductees; Captivity Tales; Close Encounters; Fantasy-Prone Personality Hypothesis; Missing Time

Further Reading:

Bullard, Thomas E. *UFO Abductions: The Measure of a Mystery, Volume 1: Comparative Study of Abduction Reports.* Mount Ranier, MD: Fund for UFO Research, 1987.

Fiore, Edith. *Encounters: A Psychologist Reveals Case Studies of Abductions by Extraterrestrials.* New York: Doubleday, 1989.

Fuller, John Grant. *Interrupted Journey: Two Lost Hours "Aboard a Flying Saucer."* New York: Dial Press, 1966.

Hopkins, Budd. *Missing Time: A Documented Study of UFO Abductions.* New York: Random House, 1981.

Jacobs, David M. *Secret Life: Firsthand Accounts of UFO Abductions.* New York: Simon and Schuster, 1992.

Lewis, James R., ed. *The Gods Have Landed: New Religions From Other Worlds.* Albany: State University of New York Press, 1995.

Mack, John E. *Abduction: Human Encounters with Aliens.* New York: Scribners, 1994.

Newman, L., and Baumeister, R. "Toward an Explanation of the UFO Abduction Phenomenon: Hypnotic Elaboration, Extraterrestrial Sadomasochism, and Spurious Memories." *Psychological Inquiry* 7 (1996): 99–126.

Ring, Kenneth. *The Omega Project: Near-Death Experiences, UFO Encounters, and Mind at Large.* New York: William Morrow, 1992.

Steiner, Rudolph. Lecture No. 14, Dornach, May 13, 1921. In *Materialism and the Task of Anthroposophy.* Hudson, NY: Anthroposophic Press, 1921.

Thompson, Keith. *Angels and Aliens: UFOs and the Mythic Imagination.* Reading, MA: Addison-Wesley, 1991.

Thompson, Richard. *Alien Identities: Ancient Insights into Modern UFO Phenomena.* Alachua, FL: Govardian Hill Publishing, 1993.

Vallee, Jacques. *Passport to Magonia: From Folklore to Flying Saucers.* Chicago: Contemporary Books, 1993.

ALLINGHAM, CEDRIC

Flying Saucer from Mars by Cedric Allingham was published in October 1954 and attracted much attention. In this book, Allingham claimed that he had seen a spaceship land in Scotland in February 1954 and had talked to a humanoid Martian from the spaceship. The book included some very poor photographs of the spaceship and the alien, as well as the sworn statement of a man named James Duncan, who claimed to have witnessed the entire meeting.

Allingham and Duncan both proved to be very hard to track down. Duncan was never located at all, and Allingham made only one public appearance in Kent in the company of astronomer and author Patrick Moore, an outspoken skeptic on the subject of UFOs. The publisher of *Flying Saucer from Mars,* which had also published several of Patrick Moore's books, announced in 1956 that Cedric Allingham had died of tuberculosis.

In 1969, journalist Robert Chapman concluded that Cedric Allingham had never existed and that *Flying Saucer from Mars* was a hoax. In the 1980s British ufologists postulated that Cedric Allingham was in fact a pseudonym for Patrick Moore, who was by this time a well-known TV personality. Moore, more than anyone else, had kept the Allingham contact claim alive by repeated reference to it. Furthermore, Moore was known as a practical joker, frequently writing letters to contactee periodicals that he signed with absurd pseudonyms such as L. Puller and N. Ormuss.

It finally came to light that Patrick Moore had indeed written *Flying Saucer from Mars* and had had a friend, Peter Davies, rewrite it to disguise his writing style. The picture of the author in the book was actually Peter Davies in disguise, and it was Davies who had posed as Allingham at the lecture in Kent.

—*Jerome Clark*

See Also: Contactees; Hoaxes

Further Reading:

Allingham, Cedric [pseudonym of Patrick Moore]. *Flying Saucer from Mars*. London: Frederick Muller, 1954.

Evans, Christopher. *Cults of Unreason*. New York: Farrar, Straus, and Giroux, 1974.

Girvan, Waveney. *Flying Saucers and Common Sense*. New York: Citadel Press, 1956.

ANCIENT ASTRONAUTS

As flying saucers and extraterrestrials have found their way into most aspects of contemporary society, the discipline of archaeology has also received its share of attention. Although contemporary academic archaeologists would hardly give the theory of ancient astronauts serious consideration, some of them would confess to having their interest in archaeology awakened by the books of Erich von Däniken. Today, the truth—or rather the *truths*—about our prehistoric past and origin is by no means either unanimous or coherent, as academia—with its multitude of disciplines—as well as many different religions, fight for dominance in explaining the wheres, hows, whens and whys of our origin. Around the world we find enigmatic remains of a bygone past that inspire not only the imagination of archaeologists but also people from all walks of life. Those who believe in UFOs and aliens from space have their own explanations of our origin and their own versions of how our historical remains should be interpreted.

The theory or set of theories about our past that include extraterrestrials is usually referred to as the "ancient-astronaut hypothesis." Other labels include "astroarchaeology," "cult archaeology," "science-fiction archaeology," "preastronautic," "prehistoric E.T. hypothesis," "paleo-SETI research," "archaeo-SETI,"

"exoarchaeology," and "extraterrestrial archaeology." Although academics seldom seek to delineate these unconventional interpretations of our past—dismissing these ideas as pseudoscience and fringe, fantastic, alternative, popular, or pseudoarchaeology—some of the more specific terms might tend to add to the confusion. "Astroarchaeology," for example, is often confused with "archeoastronomy," which is a completely different area of research, and therefore is a confusing label. Similarly confusing are the expressions "exoarchaeology" or "extraterrestrial archaeology," which have recently been proposed to designate future archaeology on other planets. Considering that the ancient astronaut hypothesis deals with the search for extraterrestrial visits in our own prehistoric past, the designation "ancient-astronaut theory," or one of the *pre-* or *paleo-* prefixes combined with "astronautics," "E.T." or "SETI," might be preferable.

It is uncertain exactly when the archaeology-related idea of ancient astronauts was first born, but since the middle of the nineteenth century there has been much speculation about the intelligence and possible technical know-how of our ancestors. As early as 1856, W. F. A. Zimmermann described the Ark of the Covenant in the Old Testament as an electronic generator in his book *Naturkräfte und Naturgesetze*. Three years later, John Taylor was the first in a long line of enthusiasts who wrote about the mathematical and astronomical calculations in the Great Pyramid of Egypt. Although these early speculations instigated ideas about our prehistory that are frequently found among contemporary ancient astronaut believers, the first explicit theory of prehistoric visits from outer space seems to have been put forward in early-twentieth-century religious literature. In 1913, in their *Man—Whence, How, and Wither,* theosophists Annie Besant and Charles W. Leadbeater relate that beings from the planet Venus at one time landed on earth. Charles Fort in his 1919 book, *The Book of the Damned,* explains that human beings on earth are the property of space aliens and that our owners now and then came to visit us. Even if Fort himself did not believe everything he wrote, many of his successors did, and his ideas have been quoted and referred to as scientific facts.

Near sunrise over Basel on 7 August 1566, "many large black globes were seen in the air, moving before the sun with great speed." (American Religion Collection)

During the 1950s and 1960s, there was much written about the high-technology of our ancient past. Among others, the Swede Henry Kjellsson, in his books *Forntidens Teknik* (1957) and *Försvunnen Teknik* (1961), talks about electronic batteries in Baghdad, metal columns in Delhi, radioactive material inside the Ark of the Covenant, and representations of electric light bulbs on the walls of the Dendera Temple in Egypt. He suggests that prehistorical remains from around the world point to an ancient advanced technological knowledge and discusses astronomy, ancient catastrophes, great floods, giants, and the mysteries of the Great Pyramid and the Sphinx. He also interprets legends, myths, folktales, and religious texts, suggesting they convey accurate data about our past rather than imaginary stories. Again, the author does not speak of beings from outer space but rather of an ancient high culture from the sunken continent of Atlantis. Nevertheless, he mentions most of the phenomena referred to by contemporary adherents of the ancient-astronaut hypothesis. Whereas some authors choose to omit the theory of aliens, others explicitly include the topic. The first UFO literature to come out of the 1950s frequently spoke about extraterrestrial visits in the past, but more for the purpose of emphasizing the fact that those visitors from the past were still among us today; see, for example, Desmond Leslie and George Adamski in their *Flying Saucers Have Landed* (1957), and George Hunt Williamson in *Roads in the Sky* (1960).

The best known of the numerous authors who have written about ancient astronauts is undoubtedly the Swiss author Erich von Däniken. His first book, *Erinnerungen an die Zukunft* (Chariots of the Gods?), was published in 1968 and turned out to be the beginning of a prosperous career in the field. Despite repeated strong criticism and unflattering allegations, von Däniken is still active today, writing books, lecturing, and planning future projects. Besides having inspired a whole generation of Swiss and German ancient-astronaut authors, he also motivated the American Gene M. Philips to found the Ancient Astronaut Society on September 14, 1973. The society was established to sponsor and coordinate activities on the subject all over the world. The next milestone came in 1976, when Zecharia Sitchin presented his theory of humanity's origins and early history in his book, *The Twelfth Planet*. Using the Old Testament and clay tablets from Sumeria as sources, he maintained, in contrast to von Däniken and others, that the space aliens that came to earth and created us did not come from another galaxy but from a twelfth planet in our own solar system. He describes the legendary battle between the gods—Marduk and Tiamat—as the twelfth planet's collision with what then became the earth and the Moon. This idea has inspired many ancient astronaut authors of late, as the theory of alien visitation is often combined with the theory of a great cosmic catastrophe in one way or another.

Today one can find ancient-astronaut interpretations on antiquity presented both as absolute truths connected with religious movements—for example, we find them as a tenet in the belief systems of the New Age movement and the Raelian religion—and as serious speculation within the UFO subculture, where magazines like *UFO Reality, UFO Universe, UFO Magazine,* and *Alien Encounters* often include articles about ancient-astronaut interpretations of prehistoric sites, relics, and artifacts as well as of legends, myths, and folklore. There also remain authors who, while writing on every other topic popular in the ancient-astronaut belief system, omit the idea of extraterrestrials as our creators and/or forefathers. Among these are John Anthony West, author of *Serpent in the Sky* (1979), and Graham Hancock, author of the popular *Fingerprints of the Gods* (1995). Richard Thompson—less famous for his theory of ancient astronauts than for his other writings—achieved a measure of academic respect with his coauthored *Forbidden Archaeology* (1993). Alan Alford, along the same lines as Zecharia Sitchin, maintains in *Gods of the New Millennium* (1996) that our cosmic creators origi-

nated on a planet within our own solar system. Many people were inspired by the 1976 NASA pictures of the so-called face on Mars and the surrounding area of Cydonia. Richard Hoagland is the leading name associated with speculation on these features of the Martian landscape. Other famous names in the contemporary ancient astronaut field are Colin Wilson, Peter LeMeshrier, Adrian Bailey, Maurice Cotterell, Robert Temples, Graham Phillips, David Rohl, and many more.

Beyond the abundance of authors writing on the subject, there is also a more organized attempt at coordinating worldwide interest in the ancient-astronaut hypothesis. In the summer of 1997, the Ancient Astronaut Society celebrated its twenty-fourth anniversary in Orlando, Florida, with a five-day conference and 22 lecturers. This meeting inspired a reorganization and, one year later, on June 17, 1998, the AASRA (Archaeology, Astronautics, and SETI Research Association) was founded in Ithaca, New York, by Erich von Däniken, Ulrich Dopatka, and Giorgio Tsoukalos. The AASRA claims it is

determined to prove, using scientific research methods, but in "lay-man's terms," whether or not extraterrestrials have visited earth in the remote past, asking questions such as: "Could it be that extraterrestrials have visited earth a long, long time ago?" "Could the knowledge of apparently highly advanced technology in ancient civilizations be related to alien contact?" "Did extraterrestrial visitors interfere with or influence human and cultural evolution?" "What traces do we currently find on earth or in our planetary system possibly indicating such visits?" and "What are the implications and consequences of proving we are not alone—and never have been!?"

Furthermore, if the paleo-SETI hypothesis ever was to be proven and accepted by the larger scientific community, the AASRA wishes to continue to help us incorporate it into our daily lives. AASRA distributes the membership journal *Legendary Times* bimonthly, and claims to have about 10,000 members worldwide. (http://www.aas-ra.org)

An arena much in vogue for ideas about extraterrestrial ancient visitations, as with all UFO-related topics, is the Internet. Using a standard Internet search engine and the phrase "ancient astronauts," one can find hundreds if not thousands of websites that mention ancient astronauts. On the Internet one also finds more unconventional versions of the ancient-astronaut hypothesis, as, for example, the so-called Wingmakers and their archaeological Ancient Arrow Project. This is how they introduce themselves, their archaeological excavation, and its result:

> Nearly 27 years ago, mysterious artifacts were found that led to one of the most intriguing scientific and anthropological discoveries ever made. A secret, unacknowledged department of the NSA [National Security Agency]—responsible for extraterrestrial contact and technology assimilation—took the discovery into their laboratory for the purposes of their own agenda. This secret organization is known as the Advanced Contact Intelligence Organization (ACIO) and has enjoyed complete anonymity until now. The discovery—referred to by the ACIO as the Ancient Arrow project—consisted of 23 chambers and connecting tunnels hollowed out deep within a huge, natural rock structure in a remote canyon of northern New Mexico. Inside this massive and well-hidden structure were incredible artifacts of a culture that was of indeterminate origins. In each of the 23 chambers were found wall paintings, various alien technologies, and strange, encoded hieroglyphs. By most appearances, the discovery was like a natural history museum from an alien race. It became known among the researchers as ETC or Extraterrestrial Time Capsule. Because of carbon-dating analyses, it was initially assumed that this time capsule was left behind by extraterrestrials that had visited earth in the 8th century AD. However, it wasn't until 1997 that the encoded language found within the site and its artifacts became accessible to the ACIO. It was then that it was determined that the time capsule was actually designed and built by a future version of humankind who were adept at interactive time travel. They called themselves, WingMakers. (http://www.wingmakers.com)

The WingMakers, who focus solely on an unknown, presumably prehistoric site, are not representative of the typical worldview and popular beliefs found among ancient-astronaut followers.

Most supporters of the theory of extraterrestrial visits in our past refer to the most grandiose and famous ancient remains around the world as evidence of the ancient-astronaut hypothesis. Most frequently mentioned are such monuments as the Sphinx and the Great Pyramid of Egypt, the monoliths in Baalbek, the temple of Angkor Wat in Cambodia, the statues of Easter Island, Machu Picchu and the straight lines and geoglyphs in the Nazca Desert in Peru, the ancient city of Tiahuanaco in Bolivia, the spheres in the jungles of Costa Rica, Palenque and Chichen-Itza in Mexico, Stonehenge, Avebury and Silbury Hill in England, and the menhirs of Carnac in France. Many cave paintings are also interpreted as supporting the ancient-astronaut hypothesis—paintings claimed to be representations of flying vessels and beings with helmets and space suits. Such paintings include the pictures in the Altamira caves in Spain, caves in France such as La Pasiega, Niaux, Les Trois Frérès, and Ussat, as well as caves in the Sahara, Australia, Peru, Italy, Brazil, and elsewhere. There has been much speculation about the depictions in the Dendera Temple in Egypt concerning ancient astronomical knowledge, electric light bulbs, and high-tension isolators, as well as other temple statues and paintings around the world.

Besides these famous prehistoric sites, this literature talks about "xenotechnology" and "oopas" (out-of-place-artifacts)—anomalous artifacts thought to be purposely ignored by established archaeologists. Usually mentioned are the so-called prehistoric batteries of Baghdad, the crystal skulls found in Mayan ruins, the deformed skulls at the Museum of Inca in Peru, objects similar to today's airplanes, and the like. The map of Piri'Reis is a frequent reference, as are artifacts found in strata much older than known civilized life. Furthermore, legends, folklore, and religious texts are reinterpreted so as to support the ancient-astronaut hypothesis. Several passages in the Bible, the ancient Mesopotamian *Epic of Gilgamesh,* the Mayan *Popol Vuh,* Hindu myths about Garuda and Shiva, the Sanskrit epic *Mahabharata,* and the Ethiopian *Kebra Nagast* are used to as evidence of the existence of ancient extraterrestrial visitations. One common version of the story is that space aliens arrived on earth once upon a time in the misty, distant past. They found the planet ideal for creation and, through insemination and genetic manipulation, created a hybrid of *Homo erectus* and themselves that became us. According to some theories, these space creatures lived on earth for a long time and are often associated with the lost continents Atlantis and Mu/Lemuria. Humans came to call them gods—gods who came from heaven and who could work miracles—though in fact they were simply using an advanced technology that human beings could not understand.

The belief in ancient astronauts being a flourishing segment of contemporary pseudoscientific archaeology, and pseudoarchaeology being a popular approach to interpreting our past, this phenomenon, needless to say, deserves academic attention. Because most contemporary scholars are reluctant to touch the subject of pseudoscience—and if they do, it is only to ridicule or criticize—an understanding of its origin, causes, definitions, and perhaps cure is not to be expected. To acquire such an understanding, we must look more closely at the nature of our current, existential situation. If we review fundamental questions about origins and the past, we can understand that the contemporary world is a state of crisis. There are several scientific theories about our prehistory and many preset religious ideas about what must have been. Pseudoscience arises through compromising and making these two basic approaches meet halfway.

The semireligious, pseudoscientific archaeology of the belief in ancient astronauts has connections with contemporary new religious movements as well as with the academic discipline of archaeology. Aiming to find one great, unified, and coherent theory of all aspects of our prehistoric past aligns ancient-astronaut believers with religious agendas rather than with academic science. Likewise, we find the idea of a conspiracy by the establishment as a prominent aspect of new religious movements as well as of pseudoarchaeology. The pseudoscientific basis for claiming something to be proof of something else frequently follows rules closer to religious reasoning than to the scientific method. The fact that ancient-astronaut researchers have already decided what their research will demonstrate beforehand is only the first of many obstacles to genuine science. But like the academic discipline of archaeology, they share the same goal—explaining our prehistoric past and

origin—using the same raw material and interpreting basically the same ancient sites and artifacts. Academics and pseudoarchaeologists accuse each other of practically the same things: basing conclusions on unreliable methods of measuring, selective collecting of data, denial of empirical facts that do not agree with the prevailing system of interpretation, lack of logic in argumentation, and so on. Either way, the battle for followers has begun. The winner might be decided less by solid, provable facts and scientific method—since these are hard to come by in the field of archaeology—than by rhetoric, marketing, and the potential of such theories for satisfying emotional needs.

Von Däniken plans to open the Ancient Astronaut Theme Park at Interlaken, Switzerland, in a few years, with full-size replicas of the pyramids at Palenque and Giza, the astronomical clocks of Stonehenge and Chichen-Itza, and a nighttime flight simulation over the Nazca lines in Peru. Conventional archaeology might thus be up for a challenge. Perhaps some of the state museums with their halls of silent artifacts are in dire need of a technological facelift to compete for the public's favor. In the meantime, we might try not to be ill at ease in the face of multiple truths, and patiently ponder the big issues. If a group of aliens created us, who then created the ones who created us? And who created the ones who created the ones who created us?

—*Pia Andersson*

See Also: 2001: A Space Odyssey; Akakor; Atlantis; Cargo Cults; Daniel, Book of; Deuteronomy, Book of; Dogu Statues; Elijah and UFOs; Ezekiel, Book of; Genesis, Book of; Gods and UFOs; Isaiah, Book of; Jacob and UFOs; Kings, Books of; Manna; Nazca Lines; Nephilim; Nimrod; Palenque Image; Psalms, Book of; Pyramids; Sirius Mystery; Vimanas; von Däniken, Erich

Further Reading:

Andersson, Pia. "'Fringe Archaeology': Contextual Truths about Our Prehistoric Past—A Closer Study of Pseudoscientific Archaeology." Seminar paper in Archaeology, Institution of Archaeology, Stockholm University, Stockholm, 2000 [English transl. by Olof Ribb].

Besant, Annie, and Leadbeater, C. W. *Man—Whence, How, and Whither: A Record of Clairvoyant Investigations.* Madras: Theosophical Publishing House, 1913.

Goran, Morris. *The Modern Myth, Ancient Astronauts and UFOs.* South Brunswick, NJ: A. S. Barnes, 1978.

von Däniken, Erich. *Chariots of the Gods? Unsolved Mysteries of the Past.* Trans. Michael Heron. New York: G. P. Putnam's Sons, 1970.

Thompson, Richard L. *Alien Identities.* Alachua, FL: Govardhan Hill Publishing, 1995.

THE ANDROMEDA STRAIN

The Andromeda Strain was a 1971 movie directed by Robert Wise and based on the novel by Michael Crichton. It tells of a deadly virus (Andromeda) that was accidentally carried from space to earth by a returning space probe. The microbe wipes out all but two inhabitants of a small town. The two survivors, the virus itself, and a team of scientists are isolated in a special germ-control laboratory, trying to find out how to combat the microorganism. When the virus mutates into forms harmless to humanity, technology rather than the virus becomes the foe. The fail-safe system of the research center must be defused if the research team is to survive.

The Andromeda Strain, while not about UFOs per se, is a close relative to UFO-type films that play on the hostile-invaders-from-outer-space theme. Instead of a giant, monster-like man in a spaceship, in this film the dangerous extraterrestrial is a virus.

Universal/Robert Wise Productions 1971; 131 min. Director: Robert Wise; Writer: Nelson Gidding; Cinematography: Richard Kline; Cast: Arthur Hill, David Wayne, James Olson, Kate Reid, Paula Kelly, George Mitchell.

ANGELS

While traditional societies have viewed every aspect of the world as being sacred, for reasons that are too complicated to develop in this short space the Judeo-Christian-Islamic family of religions divested the natural world of religious meaning. This left only the sky as the locus of sacrality. The celestial abode of the deity is evident in many places in Judeo-Christian scripture, from the passage about how the "Lord looked *down* on the Egyptian army" (Exod. 14:24) to Jesus's reference to God as "Our Father who art in *Heaven*" (emphases added). Angels, of course, are self-evidently celestial beings by virtue of their wings.

Painting of the Archangel Michael (Ascended Master Teaching Fellowship)

Decades ago the great psychologist Carl Jung noted religious themes in UFO discourse and dubbed flying saucers "technological angels"— that is, angels for an age that can no longer believe in the supernatural but that can believe in fantastic technological achievements. UFOs/flying saucers have been invested with religious significance almost from the beginning of their becoming a public phenomenon in the 1950s. This religious dimension of flying saucers is often expressed unconsciously, through certain themes in UFO literature. Of these, the *celestial* origin of the so-called Space Brothers is only the most obvious theme. Often, stories of encounters with space beings feature messages (e.g., of warning) to earthlings from advanced extraterrestrial civilizations. In this message-bearing role, they perform the central defining function of angels. Particularly in the 1950s when the threat of nuclear war seemed imminent, it was sometimes thought that the Space Brothers might intervene in human history to save us from our own self-destructive tendencies. In this redemptive activity, they were again playing a role traditionally reserved for angels.

Since the 1950s an entirely different concern has arisen to supplant the redemptive theme in ufological literature, namely, the abduction theme. Beginning rather modestly, stories by individuals who claimed to have been abducted by aliens grew steadily until the publication of Whitney Strieber's *Communion* in 1987. This fantastic, novelized account of abduction by aliens caused interest in the phenomenon to explode. At the time of this writing, more books on the abduction phenomenon are being published than books on all other ufological topics combined. These narratives almost always feature emotionless aliens subjecting abductees to some kind of painful operation, often sexual in nature. In these stories, extraterrestrials play the role of demons—that is, as fallen angels. Thus, if the earlier Space Brothers were technological angels, the kidnapping type of more recent decades are technological demons. The sexual or quasi-sexual themes in particular link modern extraterrestrials with the iccubi and succubi of the medieval period.

Another persistent topic in ufological literature has been the theme that the human race is the end product of genetic experimentation by aliens millennia ago with an earlier race of humanoid monkeys. This ancient-astronaut view sometimes includes a sexual theme, namely, that the aliens sexually abused our ancestors, or even that the extraterrestrials mated with human females to produce a superior race. As evidence for this peculiar view, advocates sometimes cite the Genesis verses about the Nephilim:

The sons of God saw that the daughters of men were fair; and they took to wife such of them as they chose. (Gen. 6:2)

The Nephilim were on the earth in those days, and also afterward, when the sons of God came in to the daughters of men, and they bore children to them. These were the mighty men that were of old, men of renown. (Gen. 6:4)

These sons of God, according to this line of interpretation, are the aliens that—by means of genetic manipulation or sexual insemination—produced the Nephilim, a superior terrestrial race. Interestingly enough, one of the traditional means of dealing with these verses was to say that the sons of God were fallen angels. This theme was particularly developed in the apocryphal Book of Enoch, which recounts how a group of angels desired mortal females, left heaven to mate with them, and fell from grace to become demons as a result. The offspring of this union were the Nephilim. Thus, in the genetic-manipulation-of-humanity theme of the ancient-astronaut theory, the Space Brothers once again play a role traditionally assigned to angels.

See Also: Ancient Astronauts; Hybrids, Alien-Human; Jung, Carl Gustav; Nephilim

Further Reading:

Jung, Carl Gustav. *Flying Saucers: A Modern Myth of Things Seen in the Sky.* Princeton: Princeton University Press, 1978.

Lewis, James R., and Evelyn Dorothy Oliver. *Angels A to Z.* Detroit: Gale Research, 1995.

Thompson, Keith. *Angels and Aliens: UFOs and the Mythic Imagination.* Reading, MA: Addison-Wesley, 1991.

ANGELUCCI, ORFEO MATTHEW

Born in 1912, Orfeo Angelucci was an enthusiastic amateur scientist who in 1946 sent several balloons aloft as part of a science experiment. A curious circular flying object hovered and maneuvered gracefully around his balloons. When the flying saucer craze started the next year, Angelucci was intrigued.

On May 24, 1952, Angelucci was driving home from work at an aircraft plant in Burbank, California, when he spotted a red, glowing, oval object. He began to follow it and got within 30 feet of it when it shot out two smaller objects and then streaked away. The smaller objects, fluorescent green and about three feet in diameter, approached Angelucci, who then heard a male voice say in English, "Don't be afraid, Orfeo, we are friends." The voice said that they had been observing him since his 1946 sighting. It said that the aliens loved all human beings because of an ancient kinship between their planet and earth.

On July 23, 1952, Angelucci experienced a dulling of consciousness followed by the sensation of being in flight. He was in a spherical object when the window opened and he saw the earth from space. He underwent a mystical experience and then returned to earth. Angelucci went public and spread the gospel through lectures and interviews. As a result he was ridiculed and alienated from family and friends. He was among the speakers at an August 1953 flying-saucer convention in Los Angeles. In 1955 he published his book, *The Secret of the Saucers*.

Psychologist and philosopher Carl Jung considered that Angelucci's experiences were visions rather than concrete happenings or conscious inventions. Angelucci lapsed into obscurity after the 1950s and is believed to have died in Los Angeles sometime in the 1980s.

—*Jerome Clark*

See Also: Contactees; Religions, UFO
Further Reading:
Angelucci, Orfeo. *The Secret of the Saucers*. Amherst, WI: Amherst Press, 1955.
———. *Son of the Sun*. Los Angeles: DeVorss, 1959.
Evans, Hilary. *Gods, Spirits, and Cosmic Guardians: A Comparative Study of the Encounter Experience*. Wellingborough, U.K.: Aquarian Press, 1987.
Jung, Carl Gustav. *Flying Saucers: A Modern Myth of Things Seen in the Sky*. Princeton: Princeton University Press, 1978.

ANTIGRAVITY

One item of UFO folklore that has become firmly entrenched in the popular consciousness is that the propulsion systems of flying saucers operate via some sort of antigravity device. Although this notion was popularized by contactees like George Adamski, the basic idea was formulated as far back as the seventeenth century by "science fiction" writer Syrano de Bergerac (not to be confused with the literary de Bergerac). Antigravity technology explained why their craft were able to hover in midair, seemingly without effort. The ufonauts' control over the force of gravity also conveniently explained why UFOs were able to make sharp, 90-degree turns at high speeds without squashing their pilots.

See Also: Adamski, George; Contactees
Further Reading:
Ritchie, David. *UFO: The Definitive Guide to Unidentified Flying Objects and Related Phenomena*. New York: Facts on File, 1994.

Thompson, Keith. *Angels and Aliens: UFOs and the Mythic Imagination*. Reading, MA: Addison-Wesley, 1991.

APOCALYPSE

Many current UFO-related religions have an apocalyptic component and a role for the Space Brothers to play in the Endtime. The term "apocalypse" has come to mean complete destruction, as in the title of the popular film, *Apocalypse Now*. Thus, in ordinary current usage, the term can refer to nonsupernatural mass destruction, such as would occur in the wake of an exchange of nuclear weapons.

The ancient Greek word for "revelation," apocalypse originally referred to a literary genre in which mysterious revelations were given or explained by a supernatural figure such as an angel. Apocalyptic literature generally includes an ac-

Cover of Gordon Cove's Who Pilots the Flying Saucers? *This English book tells us that UFOs are celestial warnings of imminent catastrophe. (Mary Evans Picture Library)*

count of an eschatological (end-time) scenario that includes wars, plagues, and other indicators of destructive violence, which is why it acquired its destructive connotations.

The first work to be formally called an apocalypse is the Apocalypse of John, more familiarly known as the Book of Revelation. Although the name comes from a Christian composition, the genre is much older, with Jewish apocalyptic literature appearing by at least the third century B.C.E. The earliest apocalyptic work was probably Zoroastrian.

Early Jewish apocalypses can be roughly divided into two principal groups. The first subgenre is what might be called "historical" apocalypses. These compositions, the most familiar of which is the Book of Daniel (the only apocalypse to be incorporated into the canonical scriptures), were extended prophecies presented in the form of allegorical visions (the Book of Revelation is clearly in this tradition). The other subgenre is narratives of otherworldly journeys, focused especially an ascent through a series of heavens, culminating in a vision of the throne of god.

In the contemporary period, the approach of the year 2000 on the Western calendar led to a heightened interest in popular belief about the possible end of the world, and most portrayals of the Endtime pictured an apocalyptic scenario. On the one hand, while there has been a steady production of predictions that the world is coming to an end over the last several centuries, their number slowly increased as the world reached the end of the second Christian millennium. There may or may not be a waning of such eschatological expectancy after the year 2001.

Much apocalyptic thought is tied to the Christian New Testament idea of a millennium, the predicted period of 1,000 years during which Satan would be chained and not allowed to pursue his evil work on earth. The arrival of the millennium has been a major theme in American Christian thought, the principal debate being whether the millennium would be brought in by a sudden act of God in the near future (prepremillennialism), emerge gradually as society became more Christian (postmillennialism), or not be a literal historical period (amillennialism).

Apocalypticism appears in every era and every culture but has become a uniquely vital theme in American religious life, especially since the rise of the Millerite movement in the 1830s. The failure of William Miller's predictions in the 1840s led directly to the Bible Students movement, built around the predictions of Charles Taze Russell, in turn succeeded by the prophetic proclamation of the Jehovah's Witnesses. Within the emerging fundamentalist movement of the late nineteenth century, prophecy conferences provided hope for the eventual triumph of beleaguered evangelicals locked in a losing confrontation with modernists for control of American Protestant churches. As evangelicalism prospered in the twentieth century, it produced literally thousands of books advocating an expectancy of the near end of the world as we know it.

Given the emphasis on this theme in American culture, it is no coincidence that a wide variety of American UFO prophets have received messages predicting an apocalyptic future. A closely related twist on this motif is represented in the frequent warnings about nuclear destruction that the Space Brothers communicated to humankind through contactees. This theme is also reflected in various ways in many films about contact with—or invasion by—extraterrestrial visitors.

See Also: Contactees; Eschatology; Millennialism; Space Brothers

Further Reading:

Cohn, Norman. *Cosmos, Chaos, and the World to Come: The Ancient Roots of Apocalyptic Faith.* New Haven: Yale University Press, 1993.

Eliade, Mircea, ed. *Encyclopedia of Religion.* New York: Macmillan, 1987.

Turner, Alice K. *The History of Hell.* New York: Harcourt Brace, 1993.

APPARITIONS

The term "apparition" usually refers to immaterial appearances of people; apparitions are also known as ghosts, animals, objects, and spirits. Despite much skepticism, reports of apparitions have always had a particular importance in folk belief and in the history of religion. UFOs exhibit many of the characteristics of apparitions, giving rise to speculation that UFOs are spiritual rather than physical phenomena.

Apparitions, which are not seen by everyone, usually involve noises, unusual smells, extreme cold, and the displacement of objects. Visual images, tactile sensations, voices, and the apparent psychokinetic movement of objects may also be included. Apparitions move through solid matter, appear and disappear abruptly, can cast shadows and be reflected in mirrors, seem corporeal or luminous and transparent, and can be lifelike or have limited movements.

Traditionally, apparitions manifest for a particular reason—to communicate a crisis or death, provide warning, comfort the grieving, convey needed information—and appear in places where emotional events have occurred. It has been shown that there are few differences between the characteristics of apparitions of the living and those of the dead. Apparition experiences can be of various types. They can be crisis apparitions, which typically appear to individuals who are emotionally very close to the agent, or apparitions of the dead, which usually occur within a short time after death. Sometimes apparitions are collective, occurring simultaneously to multiple witnesses, or they can be reciprocal, when both agent and percipient, who are separated by distance, experience each other simultaneously.

Numerous theories have tried to explain all types of apparitions, from the assertion that they are mental hallucinations to the notion of telepathy. Other theories refer to astral or etheric bodies, an amalgam of personality patterns, recording or imprints of vibrations, projections of the human unconscious or will and concentration, spirits of the dead, and localized phenomena with their own physicality, directed by an intelligence or personality. Again, any and all of these speculative theories could be applied to the UFO phenomenon.

See Also: Occult; Paranormal and Occult Theories about UFOs

Further Reading:

Cavendish, Richard. *The Encyclopedia of the Unexplained: Magic, Occultism, and Parapsychology.* New York: McGraw-Hill, 1967.

Green, Celia, and Charles McCreery. *Apparitions.* London: Hamish Hamilton, 1975.

Gurney, Edmund, F. W. H. Myers, and Frank Podmore. *Phantasms of the Living.* London: Kegan Paul, Trench, Trubner, 1918.

Myers, Frederic W. H. *Human Personality and Its Survival of Bodily Death.* Vols. 1 and 2. New ed. New York: Longmans, Green, 1954 [orig. publ. 1903].

ARCHETYPE

Noted psychologist Carl Jung observed that while some UFOs seemed to have objective, external reality, the circular form of many flying saucers made them concrete symbols of what he called the "Self" archetype. Psychological archetypes unconsciously predispose us to organize our personal experiences in certain ways. We are, for instance, predisposed to perceive someone in our early environment as a father because of the Father archetype. If our biological father is absent during our early years, someone else (e.g., one's older brother) is assimilated into this archetype.

A common mistake is to imagine the archetypes as being specific images or symbols. Archetypes are, however, more like invisible magnetic fields that cause iron filings to arrange themselves according to certain patterns. To take an example relevant to our concerns in these pages, Jung postulated the existence of a Self archetype that constitutes the unconscious basis for our ego—our conscious self-image or self-concept. This Self can be represented in a variety of ways, often in the form of four of almost anything (according to Jung, four is the number of wholeness and hence a symbol of the Self), a pattern Jung referred to as a "quaternity." The Self can, however, also be represented by alternate symbols, such as a circle or mandala.

These concrete manifestations of elusive archetypes are known as archetypal images or, when they appear in dreams, as archetypal dream images. Dreams are not the only arena in which archetypes can emerge. Jung also asserted that much of world mythology and folklore represented manifestations of the collective unconscious (the archetypal level of the human mind). He based this assertion on his discovery that the dreams of his clients frequently contained images with which they were completely unfamiliar but that seemed to reflect symbols that could be found somewhere in the mythological systems of world culture. Because much popular UFO literature can (and has) been characterized as modern folklore, we would expect it to embody archetypal images—implying that the circular pattern of the classic flying saucer embodies the Self archetype in its mandala expression.

See Also: Collective Unconscious; Jung, Carl Gustav; Mandala
Further Reading:
Jung, Carl Gustav. *Flying Saucers: A Modern Myth of Things Seen in the Sky.* Princeton: Princeton University Press, 1978.
———. *Psychological Types.* London: Routledge, 1933.
———. *Symbols of Transformation.* New York: Harper Torchbooks, 1956.

AREA 51

Area 51 is the unofficial but widely used name of a piece of U.S. Air Force land about 120 miles north of Las Vegas, Nevada. The designation is believed to have come from an old military map of the Nevada Test Site. The same area is also known as Dreamland and the Skunk Works. "The Box" is a term used by military and commercial pilots to refer to the square dimensions of a region in the sky above Area 51 that pilots must go around, no matter what the circumstances. The U-2 spyplane, SR-71 Blackbird, and the F-117 Stealth fighter-bomber were all put through their final test flights at Area 51. It is the location of the world's longest runway—27,000 feet.

Until the early 1980s, it was possible to drive up to the Groom dry lake bed, look across, and view the Air Force base in the distance. In the mid-1980s, the Air Force took jurisdiction over the Groom Mountains to keep Soviet spies from looking down on the base. At that point the base became officially nonexistent. It disappeared from U.S. Geological Survey maps, and the government has refused to refer to the base in any way.

The rumors about this area have developed far beyond what is usual even for UFO phenomena. There have been many claims that the technology that powers some of the test craft has been derived from investigations of crashed UFOs, and Area 51 is alleged to be the location of the flying saucer that crashed near Roswell, New Mexico, on July 2, 1947. This bit of UFO folklore was incorporated into the film *Independence Day*.

One person claiming knowledge of Area 51 secrets is Robert Scott Lazar. Lazar says that there is an even more highly secured facility located about 15 miles south of Area 51 called S-4. It is situated at the base of the Papoose Mountains next to the Papoose dry lake bed. According to Lazar, the installation is built into the mountain, and the nine hangar doors are angled at about 60 degrees. The doors are covered with a sand-textured coating to blend in with the side of the mountain and the desert floor.

Lazar claims to have worked at S-4 in the 1980s on disk-shaped flying craft that were based on a technology received from extraterrestrial beings, either voluntarily or involuntarily. Lazar says he personally worked on one of several fully operational flying disks at the facility. Lazar's disk was 16 feet tall and 40 feet in diameter. The center level of the disk housed control consoles and seats, both of which were too small and too low to the floor to be functional for adult human beings. Lazar claims to have been shown official briefing documents stating that the beings from whom the flying-saucer secrets came were from the Zeta Reticuli system. The beings were described as three to four feet tall, with grayish skin, large heads, and almond-shaped, wrap-around eyes. Lazar claims that these beings had been visiting earth for a long time, evidently around 10,000 years.

According to Lazar, security at Area 51 was tight. He says they worked on the buddy system, in which two individuals were assigned to be buddies and were allowed to converse with no one else. Staff members were followed by security even into the bathroom. Lazar claims that security monitored his telephone, and when they learned that he was having marital problems, they decided he was a security risk and canceled his clearance. It was after this that Lazar went public with his story.

Work with alien spacecraft technology supposedly accounts for the extremely high level of security at Area 51. Black Hawk helicopters patrol the public lands surrounding the base. Electronic sensors along the approaching roads detect the presence of vehicles. The surrounding public lands are monitored by armed men in camouflage fatigues who are the employees of the private security firm Wackenhut Corporation. On Wackenhut's board of directors are former FBI Director Clarence Kelley, two former CIA deputy directors, Frank Carlucci and Bobby Ray Inman, former Defense Intelligence Agency Director General Joseph Carroll, and former Secret Service Director James J. Rowley.

Wackenhut Corporation has about 30,000 armed employees. There have been reports of Wackenhut guards harassing and detaining citizens on public roads near Area 51 and confiscating cameras at gunpoint. Area 51 itself is posted with notices stating "Deadly Force Authorized." In addition to surveillance cameras, Area 51 has motion detectors in the ground and detectors that can sense the ammonia in human skin. In 1995 the Air Force obtained an additional 4,000 acres around Area 51, primarily the high points and mountains from which the curious had been watching for UFOs.

Robert Lazar's background has been checked, and there is evidence to discredit his story. Officials of the Los Alamos National Laboratory and EG&G, the firm where Lazar claims to have been interviewed by the Office of Naval Intelligence for his S-4 job, say that they have never heard of him. Lazar was effectively silenced when his critics were able to associate him with a Nevada brothel.

Since 1989 hundreds of persons have flocked to Rachel, Nevada, a tiny community near Area 51, after hearing stories that the U.S. government was experimenting with flying saucers there. Norio Hayakawa, former regional director of a California-based group called Civilian Intelligence Network, has organized many trips to the area surrounding Groom Lake. The degree of security at the area has convinced Hayakawa that the government is test-flying several state-of-the-art aircraft that resemble flying saucers. He also believes that several diamond-shaped aircraft that use some sort of pulse-detonation propulsion system are being tested in the area.

Gary Schultz, director of Secret Saucer Base Expeditions, claims that on February 28, 1990, he saw a metallic, disk-shaped object suddenly appear over the Jumbled Hills south of Area 51 and fly toward the Groom dry lake bed. Schultz believes that U.S. pilots are regularly being given instruction in maneuvering disk-shaped craft in the area.

Aviation Week and Space Technology reports that there have been many sightings of triangular-shaped, quiet aircraft seen with flights of Lockheed F-117A Stealth Fighters. On April 20, 1992, the NBC Nightly News with Tom Brokaw broadcast videotape made near Area 51 of a test flight of a new U.S. aerial craft that seemed to defy the laws of physics.

Abductees claim to have been taken to places described as underground facilities. Some abductees have seen what appeared to be U.S. military people involved, leading to rumors that they were taken to Area 51. There have also been more radical rumors, such as that Area 51 scientists are working with living aliens as part of a secret agreement between certain agencies of the U.S. government and extraterrestrials. The most bizarre of these rumors merge into implausible conspiracy theories rather like those of survivalists, neo-Nazis, and other anti-Semitic groups.

—*Michela Zonta*

See Also: Abductees; Conspiracy Theories; Hangar 18; *Independence Day;* Majestic 12; The Roswell Incident
Further Reading:
Craft, Michael. *Alien Impact.* New York: St. Martin's, 1996.
Randle, Kevin D. *The Randle Report: UFOs in the 1990s.* New York: M. Evans, 1997.

ARNOLD, KENNETH

The contemporary controversy over flying saucers began on June 25, 1947, when Kenneth Arnold, a young businessman and private pilot from Boise, Idaho, entered the office of the *East Oregonian* to talk to a journalist. Arnold was introduced to Nolan Skiff, then editor of "The End of the Week" column, who called in news editor Bill Bequette. Arnold had a strange story to report. The day before, on Tuesday, June 24, 1947, Arnold told the *East Oregonian* reporters that he had observed, during a trip in his own plane between Chehalis and Yakima, a chain of nine peculiar-looking aircraft in the region around Mt. Rainier. His first idea was that they were jet aircraft but "what I had just observed kept going through my mind."

There were nine of them flying in formation in two lines and moving "like a saucer would do if you skipped it across the water." They were flat, their fronts were circular, and their backs were tri-

22

Signed copy of The Flying Saucer as I Saw It, *Kenneth Arnold's account of his experience with a UFO (Mary Evans Picture Library)*

angular in the rear—but one of them looked crescent-shaped. They were traveling at least twice the speed of sound, Arnold guessed. In the last days of June 1947, breaking the sound barrier was still a dream and the subject of much speculation and discussion among pilots. Arnold's first thought was that they were some kind of new secret jets or guided missiles. But there was also another possibility that came to his mind after a moment: Soviet aircraft, as 1947 was a threshold year in the developing Cold War.

At Yakima, he told his story to pilots who remarked that the craft were bound to have been guided missiles from Moses Lake, Washington. Arnold recalled that "I felt satisfied that that's probably what they were. However, I had never heard of a missile base at Moses Lake." When he landed at Pendleton, Arnold learned that his story had arrived ahead of him. The Yakima pilots had telephoned Pendleton to notify them of Arnold's arrival and had related his adventure. (Contrary to what has often been written in UFO books, there were no reporters among these people). After discussing this with them and reaching the conclusion that these missiles were something out of the ordinary, Arnold—"armed" with his maps and calculations so as to give "the best description I could"—repaired to the local FBI office. He found the office shut.

Not having any luck with the FBI, Arnold decided to look up the journalists from the *East Oregonian*. One consideration in particular seems to have pushed him. As he explained to them, he had met, probably at the Hotel Pendleton where he was staying, a man from Ukiah, Oregon, who had said that he had seen a similar formation of craft there. Before leaving Pendleton, then, he went to the offices of the *East Oregonian*. He told Nolan Skiff and Bill Bequette about his adventure. Arnold described them as moving "like a saucer if you skipped it across the water." Skiff, skeptical to begin with, was rapidly convinced of Arnold's honesty. So was Bequette. The latter sent off, as he always did with local news, an Associated Press dispatch. The text of this dispatch, which was to have so many repercussions, was as follows:

PENDLETON, Ore., June 25 (AP)—Nine bright saucer-like objects flying at "incredible" speed at 10,000 feet altitude were reported here today by Kenneth Arnold, Boise, Idaho, pilot who said he could not hazard a guess as to what they were.

Arnold, a United States Forest Service employee engaged in searching for a missing plane, said he sighted the mysterious objects yesterday at 3 p.m. They were flying between Mount Rainier and Mount Adams, in Washington State, he said, and appeared to weave in and out formation. Arnold said he clocked and estimated their speed at 1,200 miles an hour.

Inquiries at Yakima last night brought only blank stares, he said, but he added he talked today with an unidentified man from Utah, south of here, who said he had seen similar objects over the mountains near Ukiah yesterday.

"It seems impossible," Arnold said, "but there it is."

It was as a direct consequence of this dispatch (in which the description of the movement of the objects became the description of their shape—"saucer-like") that the story was to be taken up and widely commented on by the press. From this moment on, Kenneth Arnold found himself under siege from reporters who, without ever having heard his story in detail, would, he claimed, extract a few details from him that were rushed immediately into print. As soon as Arnold's story became known, sightings of flying disks proliferated. As we have seen, the first AP dispatch was dated June 25 (toward the end of the morning). Starting from June 26 and over the days following, there were hundreds, perhaps even thousands, of newspaper articles devoted to flying disks.

Most of the time saucers were explained away by scientists and military experts who asserted that "the observers just imagined they saw something, or there is some meteorological explanation for the phenomenon." Statements quoted in these stories are filled with expressions like "mass hypnosis" and "foolish things." Saucers were compared to the Loch Ness Monster.

Following the initial reports of sightings in July, an ongoing newspaper debate about the phenomenon emerged. Everywhere actors were voicing their opinion—and the media were orchestrating the meetings. Reporters sought out actors, reported their observations, and brought them together. It was the readers at the other end of the process who had to draw their own conclusions from the debate. We do not know much about what readers thought. The saucers certainly became a popular topic. A Gallup poll taken on August 19, 1947, revealed that while only one out of two Americans had heard of the Marshall Plan, nine out of 10 had heard about the saucers.

The saucer craze created such a turmoil that the U.S. Army Air Force began an investigation in the early days of July. At the request of the Air Materiel Command, Arnold produced a written report detailing his sighting that he sent to Wright Field in Dayton, Ohio. A few days later, Arnold received a visit from two members of the military, Lieutenant Frank M. Brown and Captain William Davidson, who came from Hamilton Field in California. Brown and Davidson's aim was to bring back an account from—as well as an opinion about—Arnold. To this end, the enquirers, upon returning to their base, composed a report on what they had gathered. This report consists primarily of the details of the sightings and their impressions of the personalities of the witnesses. In 1948 Arnold's report landed on J. A. Hynek's desk. Hynek was an astronomer the Air Force had asked to study the reports so as to avoid any possible confusion with astronomical phenomena. Hynek's conclusion was that Arnold had seen some kind of aircraft. But Arnold heard nothing back about the eventual whereabouts of his report. He had to try other strategies to find a solution to his sighting. To this end, he accepted an invitation from a Chicago editor named Ray Palmer to go to Tacoma, Washington, and investigated another sighting. Ray Palmer was the editor of a pulp magazine called *Amazing Stories.* The case Arnold investigated turned out to be a crude hoax, at least from the point of view of the FBI investigators. Arnold called in the two military investigators who had interviewed him earlier (they asked him to contact them if he heard anything interesting). Afterward, Brown and Davidson died in an airplane crash.

From then on, the saucer story followed different paths. In January 1948 the newly formed U.S. Air Force launched Project Sign to investigate the sightings. This project, located in the Technical Intelligence Division at Wright-Patterson Air Force Base, was classified as secret, and the public had access only to the press reports.

But other actors entered the scene. For example, in the spring of 1948, Ray Palmer, while still concerned with the editing of *Amazing Stories,* founded with the aid of Curtis Fuller (editor in chief of the magazine *Flying*) a review completely devoted to the occult: *Fate.* What interests us is that the first issue featured flying saucers. And the article that followed the editorial was a reproduction of the report that Kenneth Arnold had given the U.S. Army a little more than a year prior. In the 1950s, amateur investigators began to challenge official explanations and launched fanzines and groups. Arnold kept up a strong interest in the subject.

The Kenneth Arnold affair is a challenge for social history and sociology. Unfortunately, it has been only randomly studied by historians. Ted Bloecher's pioneering work on the UFO wave of 1947 was not read outside UFO circles. Most historiographical works on UFOs, even if they are more sophisticated, have been conducted by amateurs who are not connected with the academic world. This is unfortunate, because when we read the historiographic studies published thus far on the UFO wave of 1947 we can see that the consequences of Arnold's story go beyond the simple historiography of UFOs. There is a strong possibility that it may open new perspectives on the sociology of contemporary scientific culture, in the following ways.

First, flying saucers are not just popular culture. Historians like Michel de Certeau have long criticized the tendency to see a clear-cut division between high culture and popular culture when historians study the alleged popular literature of the past centuries. And instead of taking this division for granted, historians like Natalie Zemon Davis and Roger Chartier have shown that we should describe how similar cultural elements are used in different ways. Thus, the divide between popular and elite culture is a *result* of the actors' actions, not the *basis* of their actions. Flying saucers are not a priori different from other cultural objects such as, for example, scientific facts. They become different in the course of controversy. Why should we describe flying saucers in a different way than we describe the "popular" culture of the sixteenth century?

In this perspective, the Arnold case has the same kind of importance for the social history of parasciences that the Menocchio case studied by historian Carlo Ginzburg has for the social history of the popular cosmologies of the sixteenth Century. Arnold provides us with the possibility of studying what is too quickly dismissed as "popular belief" with the same tools we use to study scientific knowledge. Moreover, in the same way Carlo Ginzburg identified the existence of a legitimate form of knowledge that was constructed and transmitted by actors like Menocchio, in Arnold we can identify a particular way of constructing the saucerian reality. Instead of taking categories like popular culture for granted, we should ask ourselves to describe the difference between the way we see saucers and the way we see scientific facts. Describing how Arnold saw the saucers and discussed their reality, and describing the way scientists describe scientific facts, helps us to identify a mode of seeing that is common to different social and cultural worlds.

Second, as a result of this methodological discussion, flying saucers should no longer be considered as secondary by-products of the Cold War. While historians explain how the actions of historical figures like Harry Truman and George Kennan played an important role in the birth of the Cold War era, they simply discard flying saucers as a by-product of this climate, and witnesses like Kenneth Arnold are merely victims of the cultural influence of the Cold War. Whereas the first are actors who create a context, UFO witnesses are reduced to cultural sponges responding to their environment. This asymmetrical sociological scenario, which proposes that some actors are constructing reality while others are under its influence, is clearly limited. On the contrary, witnesses such as Arnold are, like other actors (for example, the military or diplomats like George Kennan), constructing the same menace by different means. Whereas Kennan and Truman constructed their image of the Soviet world thanks to a complex network of diplomatic and military relations, witnesses like Arnold construct it from sightings and readings. The way the first category

sees the Red Menace is not necessarily better or less "popular" than the way Arnold sees it. If, for example, we turn away from Truman and Kennan and examine Air Force military experts, we find both strategies in the same milieu: While military experts build networks of intelligence agents who collect documents and construct the Soviet Red Plan in their office, Air Force pilots search the skies of Alaska for a Soviet presence. There is no great divide between the way in which Arnold and the Washington experts see the world; there are only many minor differences between the direction they look and the tools they use.

—*Pierre Lagrange*

See Also: Sociology of Ufology; Unidentified Flying Objects

Further Reading:

Aldrich, Jan L. *Project 1947: A Preliminary Report on the 1947 UFO Sighting Wave.* Chicago and Mt. Rainier, WA: Seguin and UFO Research Coalition, 1997.

Arnold, Kenneth, and Ray Palmer. *The Coming of the Saucers: A Documentary Report on Sky Objects That Have Mystified the World.* Boise, ID, and Amherst, WI: The Authors, 1952.

Bequette, Bill. "Boise Flyer Maintains He Saw 'Em." *East Oregonian,* June 26, 1947, p. 1.

———. "Experts Reach Deep into Bag to Explain 'Flying Discs.'" *East Oregonian,* June 28, 1947, p. 1.

———. "He'll Get Proof Next Time, Flyer Declares." *East Oregonian,* June 27, 1947, p. 1.

Bloecher, Ted. *Report on the UFO Wave of 1947.* Washington, DC: The Author, 1967.

Clark, Jerome. *The UFO Encyclopedia: The Phenomenon from the Beginning.* 2nd ed. Detroit: Omnigraphics, 1998.

Davis, Natalie Zemon. *Les Cultures du peuple. Rituels, savoirs er résistances au 16e siècle.* Paris: Aubier, Collection Historique, 1979.

Dean, Jodi. *Aliens in America: Conspiracy Culture from Outerspace to Cyberspace.* Ithaca and London: Cornell University Press, 1998.

Eberhart, Georges M. *UFOs and the Extraterrestrial Contact Movement: A Bibliography—Unidentified Flying Objects.* Metuchen, NJ, and London: Scarecrow Press, 1986.

Evans, Hilary, and John Spencer, eds. *UFOs, 1947–1987: The 40-Year Search for an Explanation.* London: Fortean Tomes, 1987.

Flammonde, Paris. *The Age of Flying Saucers: Notes on a Projected History of Unidentified Flying Objects.* New York: Hawthorn Books, 1971.

Fuller, Curtis G., et al., eds. *Proceedings of the First International UFO Congress.* New York: Warner Books, 1980.

Ginzburg, Carlo. *The Cheese and the Worm* (*Le Fromage et les vers, l'univers d'un meunier du XVI-siècle*). Paris, Flammarion, 1980.

Gross, Loren E. *Charles Fort, the Fortean Society, and Unidentified Flying* Objects: Fremont, CA: The Author, 1976.

Hall, Michael D., and Wendy A. Connors. *Alfred Loedding and the Great Flying Saucer Wave of 1947.* Albuquerque, NM: Rose Press, 1998.

Lagrange, Pierre. "Enquêtes sur les soucoupes volantes. La construction d'un fait aux Etats-Unis (1947) et en France (1951–1954)." *Terrain, Carnets du Patrimoine Ethnologique* 14 (March 1990): 92–112.

———. "A Forgotten Sociologist Named Kenneth Arnold." *Fortean Studies* 7 (2000).

———. "It Seems Impossible, but There It Is." In *Phenomenon: From Flying Saucers to UFOs—Forty Years of Facts and Research.* Edited by John Spencer and Hilary Evans. London: Futura Publications, 1988, pp. 26–45.

———. "L'affaire Kenneth Arnold. Note sur l'art de construire et de déconstruire quelques soucoupes volantes." *Communications* 52 (November 1990): 283–309.

Tulien, Thomas, ed. *The Sign Proceedings of Historical Group UFO History Workshop.* Scotland, CT: Sign Historical Group, 1999.

Westrum, Ronald M. "UFO Reporting Dynamics." In *UFO Phenomena and the Behavioral Scientist.* Edited by Richard F. Haines. Metuchen, NJ, and London: Scarecrow Press, 1979, pp. 147–163.

———. "Witnesses of UFOs and Other Anomalies." In *UFO Phenomena and the Behavioral Scientist.* Edited by Richard F. Haines. Metuchen, NJ, and London: Scarecrow Press, 1979, pp. 89–112.

THE ARRIVAL (1990)

In this 1990 film, an alien parasite turns an old man into a young vampire thirsting for female blood, a fact that the old (now young) man tries to hide from his schoolteacher-lover. This film is not to be confused with the 1996 film by the same name.

1990; 107 min. Writer/Director: David Schmoeller; Music: Richard Band; Cast: John Saxon, Joseph Culp, Robert Sampson, Michael J. Pollard, David Schmoeller, Stuart Gordon.

THE ARRIVAL (1996)

The Arrival was a 1996 film staring Charlie Sheen. A scientist working for the SETI project (*Search for Extra-Terrestrial Intelligence*), Sheen inter-cepts a major communication. Rather than taking his discovery seriously, his superiors destroy all records of the discovery, close down the project, and fire him. Sheen, however, is obsessed with the incident. He travels to Mexico, compares disturb-ing notes with an atmospheric scientist he hap-pens to stumble across (and who is murdered soon afterward), and eventually discovers a hid-den, mostly underground alien base. The extrater-restrials are engaged in a process of gradually in-creasing the temperature of the earth in order to make it uninhabitable to humans and hospitable to their own species. By taking on human guise, they have taken over certain key positions (includ-ing overseeing the SETI project) that make this manipulation possible. Sheen has several close calls but is eventually able to elude the aliens and warn his fellow terrestrials.

The Arrival was built around a creative rework-ing of the old covert-invasion-of-the-earth plot. Overshadowed by the roughly contemporary *Inde-pendence Day, The Arrival* was a much more richly textured movie. The ideas of the covert infiltration of the government and of a hidden, underground base for aliens are standard fare among conspir-acy-oriented members of the UFO community.

ASCENDED MASTERS

The concept of the Ascended Masters, or the Great White Brotherhood, was codified within theoso-phy by Helena Petrovna Blavatsky in the 1880s; from there it has been derived by the various reli-gious groups that descend from the Theosophical Society. Many people in the New Age movement believe that such Masters guide the spiritual progress of humanity. Within occult-oriented UFO groups, the Masters are frequently viewed as ufo-nauts. This is a development of an earlier idea, which was that at least some of the Masters were from other planets in our solar system, such as Venus.

The hierarchy proposed by Blavatsky, as re-vealed to her by the messages that she channeled from the Masters Koot Hoomi and El Morya, is as follows. First, the Solar Logos is the ruler of the various world systems. His agent Sanat Kumara is the lord of our world and is assisted by the three

Buddhas. Beneath the three Buddhas are the Masters, with whom human beings in this world could hope to have some contact. They are organized into three departments: Will, headed by Manu Vaivasvata; Love/Wisdom, headed by Bodhisattva Maitreya; and Intelligence, headed by Maha Chohan. Under these departments are then the Masters who can make divine attributes or virtues potentially available to human beings.

Under Will we find the Masters (1) Morya and Jupiter. Under Love/Wisdom come Masters (2) Koot Hoomi and Djual Khool (whom Alice Bailey claimed to channel and whom she usually called "the Tibetan"). Under Intelligence comes (3) the Venetian Master. These three numbered Masters are the Masters of the Major Rays. Then under Intelligence also come the Lesser Masters (4) Serapis, (5) Hilarion, (6) Jesus, and (7) Prince Rakoczi. The numbered Masters are also called the Masters of the Seven Rays, each corresponding to a color of the spectrum. (Writings by members of the so-called I AM groups and the Church Universal and Triumphant have reported contact with other Masters not listed above.)

The hierarchy is one of offices to be occupied, not of the individuals who currently hold those offices; and the individuals should perhaps best be understood as something like *boddhisattvas,* enlightened human beings being of service after being freed from the rounds of reincarnations. They are not angels or demigods but examples of what humans can become. It is worth noting that the person known as Apollonius of Tyana is believed by theosophists to occupy the office of Master Jesus of the Sixth Ray, and the person once known as Jesus of Nazareth is believed to have ascended in this hierarchy to the office of Boddhisattva Maitreya, so that the Buddhist belief in the return of Maitreya has been united with Christian belief in the Second Coming of Christ.

George King, founder of the Aetherius Society, proposed that these Masters were actually extraterrestrials who were members of a "space command" managing the affairs of the solar system. This concept has been built upon by other channelers and groups, such as Michael and Aurora El-Legion, who channel the so-called Ashtar Command.

See Also: The "I AM" Religious Activity; Mark-Age; Space Brothers; Theosophy
Further Reading:
Lewis, James R., ed. *The Gods Have Landed: New Religions From Other Worlds.* Albany: State University of New York Press, 1995.
Ransom, Josephine. *A Short History of the Theosophical Society.* Adyar: Theosophical Publishing House, 1938.
Stupple, David. "Mahatmas and Space Brothers: The Ideologies of Alleged Contact with Mahatmas and Space Brothers." *Journal of American Culture* 7 (1984): 131–139.

ASCENSION

Mythical tales often narrate divine, heroic, and human journeys to heaven, where the gods reside. As journeys symbolic of certain inner experiences, ecstatic techniques enabling such an ascent have been practiced throughout the world by the likes of shamans, healers, and medicine men. Similar practices have been documented in the spirituality of ancient religions, such as the religion of classical Greece. It is not difficult to see how the ancient astronaut school of thought could interpret at least some accounts of ascent to the realm of the gods as being brought into contact with ufonauts.

See Also: Ancient Astronauts; Gods and UFOs
Further Reading:
Lewis, James R. *The Encyclopedia of Afterlife Beliefs and Phenomena.* Detroit: Gale Research, 1994.
McDannell, Colleen, and Bernhard Lang. *Heaven: A History.* 1988; New York: Vintage, 1990.

ASHTAR COMMAND

The Ashtar Command is a new religious UFO movement based upon channeled messages believed to come from extraterrestrial beings. Its goal is the continued spiritual development of humanity, cumulating in the ascension of the earth's population into a galactic sister/brotherhood of light. Once ascended, humanity will be in direct contact with extraterrestrial and other ascended beings, participating in the spiritual development of the universe according to a plan laid out by a higher creator force.

The movement is loosely based upon early messages claimed to be received by George Van Tassel (1910–1978) in the 1950s. Van Tassel established a large UFO center near Landers, California, in the late 1940s. In 1959 alone up to 11,000 people had traveled to his center to attend UFO conventions and hear channeled messages from extraterrestrials. Channelers of the Ashtar Command claim that on July 18, 1952, Ashtar entered the solar system as Commander in Chief of the Ashtar Galactic Command to contact key military and scientific personal and warn them of the dangers of detonating a hydrogen bomb. Van Tassel was reported to be one of the key contactees.

Within the movement, Ashtar is regarded as a member of the Adam Kadmon; he is "an Ascended, Immortal, and 'Christed' Master" (see below for sources of quoted material). "He thus comes originally from what could be called the Twelfth Kingdom or the Celestial Throne Worlds of the Supreme Lord God Most High." The belief system stresses the spiritual aspects of Ashtar, recognizing him not "as a 'space god' but as an extremely highly evolved Son of God, a God realized Being and Ascended Master." Ashtar is regarded as the supreme commander and "elder statesman," responsible for multitudes of extraterrestrial forces. Those forces included higher spiritual beings such as Lord Melchizedek and Lord Metatron as well as multitudes of fleets and ships operating closer to the physical plane. This recognition of him as a divine being is a spiritualization of the Ashtar message that situates the belief system within a mythic framework that has developed the traditional I AM teachings into an accommodation of the UFO phenomenon.

At this time there was no specific movement created concerning the alleged contact between the Ashtar Command and humanity. Two notable individuals claimed to have received messages from Ashtar including Richard Miller in the 1950s and Tuella (Thelma B. Terrill) in the 1970s. Tuella has been credited with creating a resurgence in the belief of the Ashtar Command with publications that include *Ashtar: A Tribute* and *Project: World Evacuation*. In the 1980s several people began reporting contact with Ashtar through their channeling, and small groups were formed to receive the teachings and disseminate the messages. By the early 1990s Ashtar groups began using the Internet to unify the teachings, expand their mem-

bership base, and organize meetings. The movement's teachings can loosely be considered a development of the I AM Society and Blavatsky traditions that recognizes ascended beings of light from other planetary star systems.

The difficulty with the formation of a group in the 1980s can be attributed to the wide variation in messages reported to be received by channelers. By the mid-1990s some divisions within the Ashtar Command movement were claiming that an imminent landing of extraterrestrial ships would be taking place upon the earth and that the world population would experience direct contact with these beings. Yvonne Cole, who has been channeling from the Ashtar Command since 1986, warned participants in the movement that this event would occur in the latter part of 1994. According to Cole, when the landing occurred the international media would be notified of the event and broadcast a special message from the Ashtar Command worldwide. Due to "sensitization," most of humanity would accept the landings of UFOs as part of humankind's continuing evolution. Participants within the movement would act as advisers, counselors, and peacekeepers between the aliens and humanity. The world would be radically transformed by this contact, and humanity would be initiated into a higher level of existence.

With the absence of any landing of extraterrestrial forces, the movement set guidelines for the messages that could be considered authoritative teachings. They employed a mythic narrative to account for failed prophecy, claiming that messages that promoted fear, alien/government takeovers, or earth's devastation were from fallen beings. According to the narrative, decades ago a group of cadet trainees defected from the Ashtar Command and established their own form of negative extraterrestrial government. The beings made alliances with "others of a similar rebellious nature" and began operating upon the "lower planes closest to earth." Negative channeling, failed prophecy, and inconsistent messages were blamed upon these beings. It was also claimed that no more channels would be opened from the Ashtar Command to people who were not functioning upon the "level of the Soul."

Twelve guidelines were set, containing an overview of what the movement stood for and the role the Ashtar Command would play in its interaction with humanity. In this message it was stated that although there were millions of beings surrounding the earth in a "guardianship" they would not intervene with the planet's affairs unless there was a global catastrophe. However, the Ashtar Command was responsible for "encouraging the shift from fossil fuel to free energy, and non-polluting energy sources and transportation." They were also responsible for maintaining the stability "of your planet's polar axis" and "enhancing earth's para-magnetic harmonic resonance by creating crop circles for increasing production of food crops."

Within these parameters, the teachings of the movement and channeled messages shifted drastically from interest in physical contact with extraterrestrials to the development of basic metaphysical teachings concerning ascension and ascended beings. The teachings of the Ashtar Command have been summarized by Soltec (a primary channeler for the movement) as follows: "There is no particular philosophy to follow other than a belief in beings that are unseen, a view that the Earth is destined to transition into a new dimension and a desire for Unconditional Love to manifest in the hearts of all. For it is through love that 'Ascension' will take place."

To maintain the extraterrestrial or UFO dimensions of the belief system, in 1994 the Ashtar Command developed the concept of the Pioneer Voyage. The movement now taught that individuals could experience mass ascension and contact with the higher ascended beings through specific meditation and affirmation exercises. They believed that the human consciousness, or the etheric body, could be elevated from the physical dimension onto the command ships that were encircling the planet. Lift-off was now interpreted as a spiritual technique called "physical vibrational transfer." The movement incorporated an eight-step meditation/ritual process to accomplish this task. Drawing heavily from I AM movement teachings, the process involves specific affirmations that include calling to the "Mighty I AM Presence," calling upon Saint Germain, and repeating the mantra; "I

AM a guardian of the Light, I AM Love in action here co-operating with the Ashtar Command. I AM dedicated to the Kingdom of God on earth, Interplanetary fellowship, and universal peace."

The Pioneer Voyage was to occur only in a meditative state and would later be revealed to the individual in some form of conscious recall. Operating upon this spiritual level avoids any form of disconfirmation. Most individuals in the group initially felt that "they hadn't actually been anywhere or done anything" during their specific meditation for traveling to the guardian ships. However, a core group of seven individuals meeting in Sydney, Australia, claimed to have experienced the first voyage and provided a detailed account of life aboard the guardian ships, including floor plans, uniforms, and the general environment of existence in this higher realm. These experiences were posted on several websites, and soon other members began recalling their experiences and posting similar encounters. Individuals who did not recall their experiences were encouraged by others in the movement, being told they had been seen aboard the ship; although they could not consciously remember the event, they were in fact there.

Descriptions of the ship and its inhabitants vary slightly but remain focused within the general parameters established by the first group claiming contact. The ships are reported to be large enough to contain the entire population of the planet, having sleeping quarters, learning centers, recreation areas, and a command flight deck. The description of extraterrestrial beings aboard the ships varies from human ascended beings to more secular extraterrestrial descriptions. However, even the "iridescent, pale green figures with thin, long slender arms, not enough digits, and a tall, slender body with typical alien head" are regarded as evolved spiritual beings working in conjunction with the more "human" Ascended Masters that membership also reported in the spaceships. People report leaving their bodies behind and traveling in a quasi-physical manner to scout ships that are then flown up (sometimes by themselves) to the large guardian ships. The guardian ships operate upon the fifth dimension; therefore earth time is not a factor. In this manner, many individuals within the movement claimed to have spent several days or weeks aboard these ships while meditating for only 15 to 30 minutes.

According to the movement, the purpose of Lift-off is twofold. The first aspect relates to the spiritual development of the individual and concerns "the infusion of higher energies [that] will be carried forward with you and will help initiate change within your life and an opening to new directions and areas of Service. The recall of your experiences will hopefully validate, inspire, and regenerate you in profound ways" (from a message channeled by Soltec and posted at http://www.ambiencepublishing.com.au/directives.html). The second dimension is related to the large-scale ascension of the population of earth. Although based upon a spiritual dimension, the Ashtar Command believes that the guardian ships are deploying large electromagnetic grids around the planet that will allow for the spiritual development of humanity. The contact that has occurred between members of the Ashtar Command and higher ascended beings is viewed as a precursor to a larger event and also an experiment allowing for "the Command to perfect their techniques before approaching humanity."

The teachings and practices of the Ashtar Command can best be viewed as a syncretism between I AM types of movements and the UFO experience. The group has attempted to incorporate the acceptance and recognition of extraterrestrial beings within a spiritual framework of teachings that recognizes the connection between ascended beings with humanity. Issues concerning the role of the Great White Brotherhood, Saint Germain, Jesus, and other Ascended Masters are incorporated within a belief system that regards UFO experiences and sightings as the natural progression of the spiritual development of humanity.

—*Christopher Helland*

All quoted material comes from personal communications with the membership of the movement and from the following websites: The teachings of the Ashtar Command and their "twelve part overview of the Command's current tasks as they pertain to your world" can be found at several websites. These include The Ashtar Command official homepage at http://www.ashtar.org, http://ashtar-lightwork.tripod.com, http://www.spiritweb.org, http://members.netscapeonline.

co.uk/ashvarsheran/Pegasus.html, and http://www.ambiencepublishing.com.au/acommand.html. For a description of contact experiences reported by participants of the Ashtar Command concerning personal encounters, see: http://www.ambiencepublishing.com.au/acencounters.html.

See Also: Ascended Masters; Channeling; Contactees; Cults, UFO; The "I AM" Religious Activity; Religions, UFO; Theosophy; Van Tassel, George W.

Further Reading:

Clark, Jerome. *The UFO Encyclopedia.* 2nd ed. Detroit: Omnigraphics, 1998

Melton, J. Gordon. *Encyclopedia of American Religions.* 5th ed. Detroit: Gale Research, 1996.

Tuella [pseudonym of Thelma B. Turrell], ed. *Ashtar: A Tribute.* 3rd ed. Salt Lake City: Guardian Action Publications, 1989.

Van Tassel, George W. *I Rode a Flying Saucer! The Mystery of the Flying Saucers Revealed.* Los Angeles: New Age Publishing, 1952.

THE ASTOUNDING SHE-MONSTER

In this 1958 film, an alien spacecraft crash-lands in a forest. The female alien is surrounded by a radioactive forcefield and able to kill by touch. She unwittingly frees an heiress and a geologist who are being held captive by a gangster. The geologist then disposes of the monster with a homemade acid bomb that eats through her protective metal suit.

The Astounding She-Monster is an uninspired cross between the hostile-alien-invader idea and other kinds of narratives that feature a femme fatale as the chief antagonist. The theme of a shipwrecked alien also resonates with ufological speculation about crashed flying saucers, though it is unclear whether the UFO community influenced Hollywood or vice versa.

Hollywood International Productions 1958; 60 min. Director: Ronnie Ashcroft; Writer: Frank Hall; Cast: Robert Clarke, Keene Duncan, Marilyn Harvey, Jeanne Tatum, Shirley Kilpatrick, Ewing Miles Brown.

ASTRAL PROJECTION (OUT-OF-BODY EXPERIENCE) AND UFOS

Astral projection, also known as etheric projection or out-of-the-body traveling, refers to the ability of the consciousness to travel outside the physical body while still alive. Out-of-body experience is the scientific expression for astral projection, which is the older occult terminology. Certain aspects of astral projection appear to relate to the UFO experience.

The astral body is said to be an exact replica of the physical body, only more subtle. It is the body that one is said to inhabit after death. It is further said that it is capable of detaching from the physical body at will or under special circumstances. It can also spontaneously leave the physical body during sleep, trance, or coma, under the influence of anesthetics or drugs, or as the result of accidents. The astral body, or the human double, is the vehicle of consciousness and the instrument of passions, desires, and feelings that are conveyed to the physical body through this invisible, intangible medium. When it separates from the denser, physical body, it takes with it the capacity for feeling.

The astral body is said to be composed of subtle elements, etheric in nature, that correspond to what the Yogis consider the vital centers of the physical body, more connected with the life force than with matter. During astral projection, individuals are said to experience bright lights and pass through walls. These same types of experiences are reported by UFO abductees. While abductees claim that their alien kidnappers have transported their physical bodies aboard extraterrestrial spacecraft, perhaps these accounts are rooted in the same source as the phenomenon of astral projection.

See Also: Abductees; Occult; Paranormal and Occult Theories about UFOs

Further Reading:

Muldoon, Sylvan J., and Hereward Carrington. *The Phenomena of Astral Projection.* London: Rider and Company, 1969.

———. *The Projection of the Astral Body.* New York: Samuel Weiser, 1970.

Shepard, Leslie A., ed. *Encyclopedia of Occultism and Parapsychology.* Detroit: Gale Research, 1991.

ASTROLOGY

Astrology, literally the study (or science, depending on how one translates the Greek word *logos*) of the stars (*astron*), has existed for millennia. Although astrology and UFOs are not necessarily connected, their proximity in the metaphysical subculture means that many believers in astrology also believe in the existence of UFOs. To the extent that these belief systems are spiritually oriented, contemporary astrology and ufology reflect a traditional tendency to locate the realm of the sacred in the celestial realms.

Despite the widespread presence of astrology in contemporary society, most people are familiar with only a tiny portion of this subject, namely, the 12 signs of the Zodiac as they relate to the person-

The Astronomy *by Charles-Nicolas Cochin the Younger (1715–1790) (Dover Pictorial Archive Series)*

ality of individuals and the use of astrology for divinatory purposes. The Zodiac (literally: "circle of animals") is the belt constituted by the 12 signs—Aries, Taurus, Gemini, Cancer, Leo, Virgo, Libra, Scorpio, Sagittarius, Capricorn, Aquarius, and Pisces.

The notion of the Zodiac is ancient, with roots in the early citied cultures of Mesopotamia. The first 12-sign Zodiacs were named after the gods of these cultures. The Greeks adopted astrology from the Babylonians, and the Romans, in turn, adopted astrology from the Greeks. These peoples renamed the signs of the Mesopotamian Zodiac in terms of their own mythologies, which is why the familiar Zodiac of the contemporary West bears names out of Mediterranean mythology.

From a broad historical perspective, zodiacal symbolism can be found everywhere, and zodiacal expressions are still in use in modern English (e.g., "bull-headed," an allusion to Taurus; "crabby," an allusion to Cancer; and so on). The popularity of Sun sign astrology (the kind found in the daily newspaper) has kept these ancient symbols alive in modern society, so that even such things as automobiles have been named after some of the signs (e.g., the Ford Taurus).

Astrological symbolism has also been associated with several UFO abduction experiences. In one case, a Southern California woman claimed that during her abduction her back had been marked with a symbol resembling the astrological glyph for Jupiter. In certain other cases, hypnotized abductees recall seeing the symbol for the planet Saturn.

When Samuel Eaton Thompson met a group of Venusians in 1950, they revealed to him that the reason for the earth's problems is that earthlings are all born under different astrological signs. On other planets, all the people are of the same astrological sign—that of the planet. It seemed that earthlings had lived lives on other planets before being exiled to the earth. Thompson learned that all people who fulfill their mission in life return to the planet of their sign when they die.

See Also: Occult; Thompson, Samuel Eaton
Further Reading:
Lewis, James R. *Astrology Encyclopedia.* Detroit: Gale Research, 1994.

DeVore, Nicholas. *Encyclopedia of Astrology.* New York: Philosophical Library 1949.

ATLANTIS

Within the contemporary metaphysical/New Age subculture, it is widely assumed that the technologically advanced civilizations of legendary antiquity such as Atlantis are thought to have been inspired, founded, created, and/or administered by extraterrestrial visitors. Alternately, some have speculated that at least some ufonauts are human beings who survived the sinking of Atlantis by escaping into space on flying saucers.

The Atlantis story is part ancient myth and part modern legend. Atlantis, as an island in the Atlantic, first appears as a parable in two of Plato's Dialogues. Plato asserted that the story of Atlantis had been brought to Athens from Egypt by the Greek poet Solon, so many have supposed there may have been some historical basis for Plato's tale. However, it could also be that Plato was simply using the legend of Atlantis as a narrative lead-in to the meat of his analysis—without being particularly concerned about the legend's historical truth—as he does with other myths elsewhere in his Dialogues. For the Greek philosopher, the story of Atlantis was primarily a morality tale: In many ways parallel to the biblical story of the Garden of Eden, Plato's narrative of Atlantis describes a kind of earthly paradise that was destroyed by the gods after its rulers became puffed up and greedy. Thus, as with many other versions of the flood myth that is told worldwide, the Atlantean deluge was explained as a form of divine punishment.

However, it should also be noted that the cataclysm that destroyed Atlantis was not just confined to the island nation; it devastated other areas of the world as well. In particular, in *Critias,* Plato indicates that the Athenian army that threw back the Atlantean invaders was destroyed in the same cataclysm: "But afterward there occurred violent earthquakes and floods, and in a single day and night of rain all your warlike men in a body sank into the earth, and the island of Atlantis in like manner disappeared, and was sunk beneath the sea." Thus, the Atlantean cataclysm was presumably also a universal cataclysm that had an impact on the entire world, or at least that with which Plato was familiar, namely, the Eastern Mediterranean.

Several contemporary scholars have proposed alternate sites for the legendary isle. Most compelling is the theory, originally advanced early in the twentieth century, that Plato's story of Atlantis actually describes the destruction of Cretan civilization by a volcanic explosion in 1470 B.C.E. An alternative argument, put forward by Eberhard Zangger in *The Flood from Heaven* (1992), is that the myth refers to the Achaean destruction of Troy in the fourteenth century B.C.E.

There has been some interest in Atlantis over the centuries, but the Christian civilization of traditional Europe tended to discourage such speculation. After the Americas were encountered by Europeans, several writers penned works arguing that the newly discovered continents were Plato's Atlantis. Subsequently, interest in the ancient tale of a sunken isle waned. In terms of belief in the existence of an antediluvian world, Atlantis is more of a modern than a traditional myth—a myth that did not achieve widespread currency until the late nineteenth century, more than two millennia after Plato's time.

Contemporary interest in the legend began with Ignatius Donnelly's *Atlantis: The Antediluvian World* (1882), in which he proposed that the human race and human civilization had begun on that island and had initially spread elsewhere by colonization, then by refugees when the island was destroyed by a natural cataclysm. Donnelly's ideas were adopted as an integral element of theosophy in Helena Petrovna Blavatsky's *The Secret Doctrine.* The most important author who spread interest in Atlantis was, however, Lewis Spence (1874–1955), a Scottish occult scholar who wrote five books on Atlantis between 1924 and 1943.

From these sources, the focus on Atlantis passed to Edgar Cayce, who used it as a parable, much as Plato had, in his readings. After Cayce's death, two compilations of such material were released by the Association for Research and Enlightenment, *Atlantis: Fact or Fiction,* and *Edgar Cayce on Atlantis.* These two paperbacks were the source for most beliefs about Atlantis within the New Age movement. Cayce predicted that evidence

for the historical existence of Atlantis would be found offshore from North America in the 1960s. To date, however, the most that has been discovered is a roadway-like series of stones on the ocean floor—stones that might be a natural phenomenon rather than an artifact of human design.

In the early 1980s, Frank Alper, in *Exploring Atlantis,* extensively discussed the material he claimed to have channeled on how the Atlanteans used crystals to power their civilization. Discussions such as Alper's further served to secure a place for the Atlantis legend in New Age thinking. For many contemporary metaphysical writers, Atlantis was a highly technological society that destroyed itself through misuse of its technology—perhaps even through misuse of its crystal technology.

In the late 1990s, however, these views underwent modification as the result of a new school of Atlantology, which champions the view that Antarctica was the site of the ancient nation. The assumption at work here, which is based on the geological theories of the late Charles Hapgood, is that the earth's crust has been displaced in such a way that Antarctica was shifted from a temperate climate zone to its current location at the South Pole.

This perspective has been popularized by the relatively recent *Fingerprints of the Gods* (1995), which argues for the existence of a technologically advanced civilization—Atlantis—in the period preceding the earliest known citied societies. To support his point, author Graham Hancock examines the many artifacts and architectural monuments that are difficult to account for within the limits of our currently accepted scheme of history. Like Donnelly before them, for Hancock and other Atlantologists the ancient civilizations of Egypt and Mesoamerica were either Atlantean colonies or areas where survivors fled after the sinking of Atlantis.

The advantage of this new site for Atlantis is that it avoids the problem of the nonpresence of ancient ruins in the beds of the Atlantic Ocean: Whatever remains of Atlantis is hidden beneath the southern polar ice cap. Given the inaccessibility of this new site for the antediluvian world, the legend of Atlantis is likely to continue to provide fuel for the human imagination well into the current millennium.

For roughly the same reasons, Antarctica is an ideal location for imaginatively placing a "secret" UFO base. One of the more well-known proponents of this notion was Albert Bender, who claimed to have visited a large extraterrestrial installation hidden beneath the ice of the southernmost continent. Antarctica was also supposedly the site of a portal through which UFOs passed, according to certain hollow-earth enthusiasts. If it has not already been asserted, it is only a matter of time before someone comes up with the idea that UFO bases existing at the South Pole represent the residue of Atlantean civilization.

See Also: Akakor; Fingerprints of the Gods; Inner Earth; Pyramids

Further Reading:

Alper, Frank. Exploring Atlantis. Farmingdale, NY: Coleman Publishing, 1982.

Cayce, Edgar. Edgar Cayce on Atlantis. New York: Paperback Library, 1968.

Donnelly, Ignatius. Atlantis: The Antediluvian World. New York: Harper and Brothers, 1882.

Hancock, Graham. Fingerprints of the Gods. New York: Crown, 1995.

Zangger, Eberhard. The Flood from Heaven. New York: William Morrow, 1992.

ATMOSPHERIC LIFE-FORMS

Sir Arthur Conan Doyle may have been the first writer to conceive of life-forms that existed only in the upper atmosphere. In 1931, Charles Fort proposed in his book Lo! that some of the unknown things seen high in the sky or close to the earth could be living things from somewhere else. This concept has occasionally been used in an attempt to explain at least some types of UFO phenomena, perhaps most notably by Kenneth Arnold, whose 1947 sighting of a UFO over Mt. Rainier, Washington, began the modern era of UFO research.

While climbing Mount Everest in 1933, Frank Smythe saw two dark objects floating in the sky. They looked like balloons but had short wings and pulsated in and out as though they were breathing. They hovered silently for a minute or two before being obscured by mist. John Philip Bessor of Pennsylvania wrote the U.S. Air Force in 1947 offering his theory about the nature of flying disks.

He claimed they were a form of space animal capable of materialization and dematerialization that may be carnivorous.

Countess Zoe Wassilko-Serecki wrote in the September 1955 issue of American Astrology magazine that creatures live in the upper atmosphere—large luminous bladders of colloidal silicones that assume different shapes depending on whether they are stationary or moving. They feed on energy and have appeared more frequently in the lower atmosphere since power production became widespread.

In 1958 Trevor James Constable wrote They Live in the Sky, in which he claimed that aerial entities live in the upper atmosphere and are occasionally visible as meteors or UFOs. Constable even made infrared photographs of the animals. In 1959 Kenneth Arnold, who first spotted flying saucers in 1947, concluded that UFOs are space animals: living organisms in the atmosphere that have the power to change their density and appearance. In 1962 John M. Cage theorized that UFOs are sentient life-forms that follow airplanes much as dolphins follow ships.

The concept has fallen recently into disfavor, simply for being nonparsimonious. However, the existence of such life-forms, whether indigenous to earth or arriving from elsewhere, is not impossible; and certain types of Fortean phenomena, especially immense falls of organic matter, might well be evidence in favor of such a possibility. The subject should probably not be considered to be closed; there continues to be speculation and even controversy over it.

—Jerome Clark

Further Reading:

Clark, Jerome. The UFO Encyclopedia, Volume 2. Detroit: Omnigraphics, 1992.

Shepard, Leslie A., ed. Encyclopedia of Occultism and Parapsychology. Detroit: Gale Research, 1991.

THE ATOMIC SUBMARINE

This 1959 film featured a submersible flying saucer piloted by a cyclops-like monster, who, of course, is intent on taking over the world. The action takes place under the Arctic ice cap, where some people in the UFO community have speculated an alien base may lie. The extraterrestrial is opposed by the crew members of an atomic submarine, who, of course, manage to save the world from the alien threat. This is a low-budget film built around the most common of all sci-fi plot devices: the invasion-of-earth-by-hostile-aliens theme. Despite the low budget and hackneyed theme, this film has received surprisingly good reviews.

> Gorham Productions/Allied Artists 1959; 80 min. Director: Spencer Gordon Bennet; Writer: Orville H. Hampton; Cinematography: Gilbert Warrenton; Cast: Arthur Franz, Dick Foran, Bob Steele, Brett Halsy, Joi Lansing, Paul Dubov, Tom Conway.

ATTACK OF THE 50 FOOT WOMAN (1958)

The 1958 film *Attack of the 50 Foot Woman* has become a cult classic. A woman released from an insane asylum is witness to a flying-saucer landing in the desert. She is zapped with a ray that makes her grow. She tears up the town looking for her faithless husband. When the huge woman finds her husband with another woman, she squeezes them both to death. The sheriff arrives to kill her with a riot gun.

While the flying saucer is an ad hoc device included for the sole purpose of providing the means by which the heroine is transformed into "bikini-clad colossus," there is some resonance with the archetypal theme of individuals who are transformed by their contact with UFOs.

> Woolner/Allied Artists 1958; 72 min. Director: Nathan (Hertz) Juran; Writer: Mark Hanna; Cinematography: Jacques Marquette; Cast: Allison Hayes, William Hudson, Roy Gordon, Yvette Vickers, George Douglas.

ATTACK OF THE 50 FOOT WOMAN (1993)

The 1958 cult movie *Attack of the 50 Foot Woman* was remade in 1993 for Home Box Office. Rather than getting crushed by his huge wife in the end, the 50 Foot Woman's husband this time is condemned to an eternity of wearing a Star Trek uniform in a male consciousness-raising encounter group.

> HBO 1993; 89 min. Director: Christopher Guest; Writer: Joseph Daugherty; Music: Nicholas Pike; Cast: Daryl Hannah, Daniel Baldwin, William Windom, Frances Fisher, Cristi Conaway, Paul Benedict, Lewis Arquette, Xander Berkeley, Hamilton Camp, Richard Edson, Victoria Haas, O'Neal Compton.

AUTOMATIC WRITING

Automatic writing is a form of mediumship in which writers (or sometimes typists) record information from sources other than their own conscious mind. Automatic writing was very popular during spiritualism's heyday in the nineteenth century, a popularity that has continued into the present in such altered forms as New Age channeling. The popular author Ruth Montgomery, for example, claims to produce many of her books with the aid of automatic writing.

In the nineteenth and twentieth centuries, and even today, most practitioners assert that automatic writing represents communications from disembodied entities, usually the souls of deceased human beings. In the contemporary metaphysical subculture, many people have claimed to have received such messages from embodied beings, including extraterrestrials. For example, the leader of the group that was featured in the classic study *When Prophecy Fails* received her messages from the Space Brothers via automatic writing.

As currently used, the expression "automatic writing" is often used to refer both to automatic writing and inspirational writing. The actual recording of characters in true automatic writing is not under the control of the writer, so that the handwriting is often quite different from her or his ordinary handwriting. In inspirational writing, by way of contrast, words and ideas flow into the writer's mind, so that she or he acts as a recorder (as if one was a court reporter, recording whatever was said in a courtroom). In inspirational writing, the handwriting and sometimes even the writing style is the said to be the writer's own; only the content of the writing is from the Other Side. In true automatic writing, the writer usually does not know what she or he is writing. A tingling is sometimes felt in the hands or arms. Most often, automatic writing takes place at a greater speed than one's normal writing.

> *See Also:* Channeling; Occult; *When Prophecy Fails*
> *Further Reading:*
> Grattan-Guinness, Ivor. *Psychical Research: A Guide to Its History, Principles, and Practices.* Wellingborough, U.K.: Aquarian Press, 1982.
> James, William. "Notes on Automatic Writing." In *The Works of William James: Essays in Psychical Research.* Edited by Frederick Burkhardt (gen. ed.) and Fredson

Bowers (text ed.). Cambridge: Harvard University Press, 1986 [orig. publ. 1889].

Muhl, Anita. *Automatic Writing.* New York: Helix Press, 1963.

Stevenson, Ian. "Some Comments on Automatic Writing." *Journal of the American Society for Psychical Research* 72(4) (October 1978): 315–332.

AZTEC CRASH

The so-called Aztec Crash was a hoax modeled on a popular film and a report about a saucer crash. Frank Scully, a columnist for *Weekly Variety,* became the victim of this hoax, which was dreamed up by Silas Newton and Leo GeBauer. Newton was a veteran con artist who got the inspiration for this hoax from the publicity for a 1949 science-fiction film entitled *The Flying Saucer.* The producer of this film, Mikel Conrad, promoted the view that the spaceship seen in the movie was an actual alien craft held by the government. In publicizing the film, Conrad got an "FBI agent" who swore that the story was true. This prompted the U.S. Air Force to launch an investigation into the matter. Conrad admitted to the investigating officer who contacted him that he had concocted the tale to promote the movie. Newton followed this controversy in the Los Angeles newspapers.

Newton also learned of a report of two prospectors in Death Valley who allegedly saw a UFO spin out of control and crash into a sand dune. Two humanoid occupants emerged from the craft and fled, with the prospectors in pursuit. The miners eventually gave up the chase and returned to the scene of the crash only to find the saucer gone.

In August 1949 Newton and his accomplice were demonstrating an oil-detecting device in the Southwest, including Aztec, New Mexico. Shortly thereafter Newton, representing himself as a Texas oilman, told the Death Valley prospector story to Frank Scully, but he changed its location and said that the two men were scientists who had forced the UFO down with sophisticated instruments. Newton told Scully that he had heard the story directly from the scientists involved. Newton presented GeBauer to Scully, saying that he was "Dr. Gee," a government scientist specializing in magnetics who had participated in the recovery operation.

The story that appeared in *Weekly Variety* under Scully's byline on October 12, 1949, was that on March 25, 1948, a flying saucer crashed on a rocky plateau east of Aztec, New Mexico. The bodies of 16 small, humanlike beings dressed in the style of 1890 were found inside by Air Force investigators, who determined that they were from Venus. Soon afterward a crash occurred in Arizona, and 16 bodies were taken from that wreckage. A third spaceship went down near Phoenix, leaving two dead occupants. In 1950 Scully elaborated on the story in his book *Behind the Flying Saucers.*

The September 1952 issue of *True* magazine exposed the hoax in a story by J. P. Cahn. Cahn revealed that Scully's sources were both in fact con artists who used the flying-saucer story as a ruse to attract the attention of potential investors in a bogus oil-detection scheme allegedly linked to extraterrestrial technology. Scully responded to Cahn's charges by attacking Cahn's character and avoiding the substantive issues of the case. He also claimed that Dr. Gee was a composite of eight men who had given him pieces of the story.

In 1953 Newton and GeBauer went on trial in Denver for conspiracy to commit a confidence crime. They were given suspended sentences and ordered to make restitution to investors. Newton's confidence career didn't end there, however. In February 1955 he was tried for selling $15,000 in worthless securities in a Utah uranium claim. In March 1958 he was again in court in Denver on a $100,000 uranium swindle. As late as 1970 he was under indictment in Los Angeles on two counts of grand theft. When he died in Los Angeles in 1972, there were at least 140 claims filed against Newton's estate by individuals who claimed that he had "borrowed" money from them to exploit oil or mining claims. His estate totaled $16,000; claims filed against it exceeded $1.35 million. Many of the claims alleged that Newton salted the claims or pumped oil into the ground at night to pump it back up the next day for the benefit of investors.

In 1987 *UFO Crash at Aztec* by William S. Steinman and Wendelle C. Stevens was published. It was based on speculation, rumor, and unnamed informants. In it, Newton and GeBauer were painted as honorable men whose good names were destroyed by the government and the press for daring to divulge information on UFOs.

See Also: Hoaxes; The Roswell Incident
Further Reading:
Good, Timothy. *Above Top Secret: The Worldwide UFO Cover-up.* New York: William Morrow, 1988.

Moseley, James W. "UFOs Out West." In *UFOs, 1947–1997: From Arnold to the Abductees: Fifty Years of Flying Saucers.* Edited by Hilary Evans and Dennis. London: John Brown Publishing, 1997, pp. 53–59.
Scully, Frank. *Behind the Flying Saucers.* New York: Henry Holt, 1950.
Steinman, William S., and Wendelle C. Stevens. *UFO Crash at Aztec: A Well Kept Secret.* Tucson, AZ: UFO Photo Archives, 1986.

BAD CHANNELS

Bad Channels, a low-budget comedy, was aptly named. A rock station disc jockey finds his studio invaded by a space creature with a large head that shrinks attractive female listeners to put into specimen jars for transport back to his planet. Precisely what the captives will be used for is never spelled out. Although the movie's details bear no relationship with the world of ufology, the film's overarching motif—alien abduction—was the dominant theme of UFO literature in the early 1990s, when *Bad Channels* was produced.

Full Moon Entertainment 1992; 88 min. Director: Ted Nicolaou; Writer: Jackson Barr; Cinematography: Adolfo Bartoll; Cast: Paul Hipp, Martha Quinn, Aaron Lustig, Ian Patrick Williams, Charlie Spading, Tim Thomerson.

THE BAMBOO SAUCER

In this 1968 film a flying disk buzzes the United States and lands in communist China. The aliens piloting it perish from earth germs. A team of Americans searching for the flying saucer in Red China comes across a Russian team with the same mission. As both groups fear being discovered by the Chinese, they form an uneasy alliance. The climax has three of the humans escaping in the flying saucer and heading into outer space.

This film is more about the Cold War than it is a sci-fi movie. It is, nevertheless, interesting to speculate where the idea of a crashed saucer originated, given the rumors about Roswell that had been circulating since the late 1940s.

NTA/Harris Associates 1968; 103 min. Director: Frank Telford; Producer: Jerry Fairbanks; Cinematography: Hal Mohr; Cast: Dan Duryea, John Ericson, Lois Nettelton, Nan Leslie.

BARBARELLA

Barbarella was a 1967 film starring Jane Fonda. It was based on a risqué French comic-strip heroine. Although not about flying saucers or alien invaders, it is a useful example of how the outerspace sci-fi genre is an inkblot for our human projections, including sexual fantasies.

Marianne Productions 1967; 98 min. Director: Roger Vadim; Writer: Terry Southern; Cinematography: Claude Renois; Music: Charles Fox; Cast: Jane Fonda, John Phillip Law, David Hemmings, Marcel Marceau, Anita Pallenberg, Milo O'Shea.

BARKER, GRAY ROSCOE

Gray Barker was the founder of a popular UFO magazine, *The Saucerian,* and the author of *They Knew Too Much About Flying Saucers.* He was born on May 2, 1925, in Riffle, West Virginia. In 1947 he graduated from Glenville State College in West Virginia. He taught public school for a year and then began selling theatrical equipment and working as a theater booker.

In 1952 Barker wrote his first magazine article, an account of the so-called Flatwoods Monster, a UFO encounter that occurred in West Virginia. It was published in *Fate* magazine. That year he joined the International Flying Saucer Bureau (IFSB), headed by Albert K. Bender of Bridgeport, Connecticut, and became one of its most active members. Barker wrote frequently for *Space Review,* the publication of the IFSB.

In late 1953 Albert Bender closed down the IFSB, allegedly due to a threat he received from three men dressed in black (this was the origin of the so-called men-in-black, or MIB, phenomenon). Gray Barker's book about the Bender incident, *They Knew Too Much About Flying Saucers,*

Film still of Jane Fonda in Barbarella, *1967 (The Del Valle Archive)*

was published in 1956. When the IFSB dissolved, Barker started his own magazine, *The Saucerian*. It became one of the most popular UFO magazines, with a circulation of 1,500. Barker considered himself an entertainer and folklorist rather than a factual reporter and was a gifted writer with a gentle, understated sense of humor.

One of Barker's best friends was James W. Moseley, publisher of a rival magazine, *Saucer News*. Moseley and Barker pretended to be feuding and sniped at each other in the pages of their magazines. Together, Barker and Moseley were responsible for one of the most notorious hoaxes of the 1950s. They obtained a piece of State Department stationery and wrote a letter to contactee George Adamski, signing it "R. E. Straith." The letter stated that the State Department had on file a great deal of evidence confirming Adamski's claims and encouraged his work. After receiving this letter, Adamski sent a registered letter addressed to Straith at the State Department. When the return receipt indicated that

the letter had been accepted, it was assumed that Straith was real. The Straith letter was announced in an article in the March/April 1958 issue of *Flying Saucer Review*. Adamski partisans around the world celebrated this validation of his work. The Straith letter created Barker and Moseley's desired effect of throwing long-term confusion into the UFO field.

In 1959 Barker entered the book-publishing field. His first offering was Howard Menger's *From Outer Space to You*. In 1962 he published Albert K. Bender's *Flying Saucers and the Three Men*. This was a wild story that told of Bender being abducted by monstrous aliens and taken to the South Pole. Barker also published several paperback compilations, such as *The Strange Case of Dr. M. K. Jessup* and *Gray Barker's Book of Saucers*.

The last issue of Barker's magazine, which had changed its name to *Saucerian Bulletin* in 1956, appeared in 1962. Barker sold the magazine to James Moseley, who incorporated it into *Saucer News*. In 1970 Barker wrote and published *The Sil-*

ver Bridge, a fictionalized account of UFO-related events. Barker published a tabloid, *Gray Barker's Newsletter,* in the 1970s. In 1981 he compiled and published *A UFO Guide to "Fate" Magazine.* Gray Barker died on December 6, 1984. Following Barker's death, Moseley confessed to writing the Straith letter with Barker.

See Also: Bender, Albert K.; Flatwoods Monster; Men in Black
Further Reading:
Barker, Gray. *MIB: The Secret Terror among Us.* Clarksburg, WV: Saucerian Books, 1983.
———. *The Silver Bridge.* Clarksburg, WV: Saucerian Books, 1970.
———. *They Knew Too Much about Flying Saucers.* New York: University Books, 1956.
Dove, Lonzo. *The "Straith" State Department Fraud.* Broadway, VA: The Author, 1959.
Menger, Howard. *From Outer Space to You.* Clarksburg, WV: Saucerian Books, 1959.

BATTERIES NOT INCLUDED

In this 1987 film a real-estate developer plots to destroy a tenement in New York while its few remaining residents struggle to save the building. The residents are aided by tiny but mechanically inclined flying saucers. In this film, the UFOs are not piloted by aliens but appear to be mechanical life-forms themselves. They even reproduce!

Amblin/Universal 1987; 107 min. Director: Matthew Robbins; Writers: Matthew Robbins, Brad Bird, Brent Maddock, S. S. Wilson; Cinematography: John McPherson; Music: James Horner; Cast: Hume Cronyn, Jessica Tandy, Frank McRae, Michael Carmine, Elizabeth Pena, Dennis Boutsikaris.

BATTLE IN OUTER SPACE

In this 1959 Japanese film, earth is under attack from an alien planet, evidenced by the facts that Venice's lagoon is emptied and all of the water is dumped on the city. New York is burned, and the Golden Gate Bridge is destroyed by a space torpedo. Two spaceships are sent out to do battle with the enemy on the Moon and in space.

Toho 1959; 90 min. Director: Inoshiro Honda; Writer: Shinichi Sekizawa; Cinematography: Hajime Koizumi; Cast: Ryo Ikebe, Kyoko Anzai, Minoru Takada, Koreya Senda, Leonard Stanford, Harold Conway, George Whitman, Elise Richter, Hisaya Ito, Yoshio Tsuchiya.

BATTLE OF THE WORLDS

This is a 1961 Italian film in which a professor ridicules the claims of his colleagues that a meteorite is about to collide with earth. It turns out that he is right: The meteorite stops and launches flying saucers against earth. The professor finds that the meteor has been sent by an alien planet, the inhabitants of which have died. The meteorite is manned by computers that are mechanically carrying out what they have been programmed to do. The professor is fascinated by the wealth of information the central computer must contain. He gains access to it but is blown up with the contraption as military leaders on earth fire upon it.

Ultra Film/Sicilia Cinematografica; 95 min. Director: Anthony (Antonio Margheriti) Dawson; Cast: Claude Rains, Maya Brent, Bill Carter, Marina Orsini, Jacqueline Derval.

BENDER, ALBERT K.

In April 1952 Albert K. Bender, a 31-year-old factory worker from Bridgeport, Connecticut, formed the International Flying Saucer Bureau (IFSB) to gather information about flying saucers and acquaint people who were interested in flying saucers. The organization quickly grew to an international membership of 1,500. In October 1952 Bender published the first issue of *Space Review,* the IFSB magazine. In February 1953 Gray Barker was appointed as the IFSB's chief investigator.

In September 1953 Bender related a theory about UFO origin to someone. Shortly thereafter three men dressed in black, who Bender claimed were members of the U.S. government, allegedly called on Bender and told him the actual origin of UFOs and warned that he would be imprisoned if he repeated it to anyone. The men informed Bender that the U.S. government had known what UFOs were since 1951 and would reveal the frightening secret within four years. Bender was so upset by this incident that he was sick for three days afterward.

The October 1953 issue of *Space Review* was the last. It carried this notice: "The mystery of the flying saucer is no longer a mystery. The source is already known, but any information about this is being withheld by orders from a higher source. We would like to print the full story in *Space Review*, but because of the nature of the information we are very sorry that we have been advised in the negative. We advise those engaged in saucer work to please be very cautious."

Over the next year and a half, UFO enthusiasts in Canada, New Zealand, and Australia left the field under suspicious circumstances; the implications were that they were silenced by mysterious, dark-suited strangers. Gray Barker did more than anyone else to keep the Bender mystery alive by featuring it in his popular magazine *The Saucerian*. In 1956 Barker published a book about the mystery, *They Knew Too Much About Flying Saucers*.

Gray Barker persuaded Bender to write his own book about the mystery and offered to publish it. *Flying Saucers and the Three Men* appeared in 1962, and many readers found it to be unbelievable. In it Bender said that the three men were actually aliens in disguise and that their mission was to extract an element needed on their home planet from seawater. These aliens took Bender to their base in the Antarctic and told him that God does not exist and that human beings do not survive death. The aliens completed their mission and left earth in 1960, thereby freeing Bender to tell all.

Those who knew Bender understood that something had genuinely frightened him and caused him to shut down his organization in 1953. Gray Barker speculated that Bender could have come across some military secret, causing agents from an intelligence agency to visit him and make him keep quiet about it. Possibly Bender wrote the fictitious account of the visit of the three aliens to end the harassment from enthusiasts who were trying to get him to reveal his secrets.

See Also: Barker, Gray Roscoe; Men in Black
Further Reading:
Barker, Gray, ed. *Bender Mystery Confirmed.* Clarksburg, WV: Saucerian Books, 1962.
Bender, Albert K. *Flying Saucers and the Three Men.* Clarksburg, WV: Saucerian Books, 1962.
Rojcewicz, Peter M. "The 'Men in Black' Experience and Tradition: Analogues with the Traditional Devil Hypothesis." *Journal of American Folklore* 100 (April-June 1987): 148–160.
Schwarz, Berthold Eric. "The Man-in-Black Syndrome." *Flying Saucer Review* 23(4) (1977): 9–15 (pt. 1); 23(5) (1978): 22–25 (pt. 2).

BERMUDA TRIANGLE (DEVIL'S TRIANGLE)

The Bermuda Triangle is an area in the Atlantic Ocean within which unusual events occur—particularly the disappearance of ships and airplanes without a trace. In geographical terms, the watery expanse is triangulated by Bermuda, Florida, and Puerto Rico (i.e., if one were to draws line between these three locations on a map, one would trace the boundaries of the Bermuda Triangle).

Folklore about the area usually begins with Columbus. As the explorer's ships sailed through the area, the crew was said to have seen strange lights in the sky—probably meteors—and the compass supposedly went haywire. Most auspiciously, on October 11, 1492, lights were seen in the direction in which land was discovered the next day.

A second historical mystery that has been retroactively incorporated into the Bermuda Triangle myth is the discovery of the *Mary Celeste* in 1892. The ship was discovered off the coast of Portugal with no crew members aboard, some 400 miles off its original route from New York to Genoa. It had probably been abandoned on the high seas during a storm that the captain had incorrectly judged as being too strong to weather.

The legend of the Devil's Triangle was launched in modern times with the disappearance of Flight 19—five U.S. Navy Avenger bombers—on December 5, 1945. A rescue plane was also lost. Lieutenant Charles Taylor, an experienced pilot leading a group of rookies on a routine training mission, had compass problems. Familiar with the area, he likely felt he could continue the mission by dead reckoning. He eventually concluded that the group had wandered into the Gulf of Mexico by mistake, so he ordered them to turn east. Eventually the group ran out of gasoline and plummeted into the ocean. Any survivors drowned in a storm that had formed during the mission. No wreckage was found until many years later.

One popular explanation for these disappearances is that some sort of still-active machinery from Atlantis lies at the bottom of the ocean that periodically obliterates passing craft, or, alternately, that periodically opens a "doorway" to another realm—a time warp of sorts from which one never returns. Another popular explanation is that a secret undersea UFO base is located in the area and that there is something about the comings and goings of UFOs that is responsible for the destruction of ships and planes. Even an official U.S. Navy report noted that the Avengers had disappeared "as if they had flown to Mars."

Subsequent to Flight 19, some 200 other incidents were attributed to the mysterious "energies" present in the area. The Bermuda Triangle received its name from an article by W. Gaddis that was published in *Argosy* magazine in 1964. Ten years later, a sensationalistic book by Charles Berlitz, *The Bermuda Triangle,* became a bestseller, and the area became enshrined in paranormal folklore.

See Also: Atlantis; Time Travel
Further Reading:
Berlitz, Charles. *The Bermuda Triangle.* Garden City, NY: Doubleday, 1974.
Kusche, Lawrence David. *The Bermuda Triangle Mystery—Solved.* New York: Harper and Row, 1975.

BETHURUM, TRUMAN

Truman Bethurum was a prominent contactee of the 1950s. Born in Gavalin, California, on August 21, 1898, he worked as a laborer until the early 1950s. In the early-morning hours of July 28, 1952, Bethurum was napping between shifts as a heavy-equipment operator in the Nevada desert. He was allegedly awakened by eight small men who took him to a nearby flying saucer, where he met the captain, a beautiful woman who appeared to be in her forties. They were from the planet Clarion, which is in our solar system but is never seen because it is always on the other side of the moon. The Clarionites were a peaceful people who were visiting the earth out of concern that human beings might destroy earth and its inhabitants in a nuclear war.

Bethurum began a new career as a flying-saucer celebrity when his first published account of his alleged encounter with space people appeared in *Saucers* magazine in 1953. Thereafter he received an income from writing and lecturing. In August 1953 at a convention sponsored by Flying Saucers International, Bethurum told his story in public for the first time. His book, *Aboard a Flying Saucer,* was published in 1954.

Bethurum had numerous supporters in contactee circles, but few mainstream ufologists believed his claims were authentic. Most UFO researchers dismissed him as a charlatan. Bethurum refused to surrender a letter allegedly written by the captain of the flying saucer and typed on Clarion paper for analysis to authenticate it. He also refused to take a polygraph test concerning his claims.

In November 1955 Bethurum claimed the captain of the saucer visited him in astral form and instructed him to solicit contributions to buy a large section of land and establish a commune. The commune was established in Prescott, Arizona. Bethurum died on May 21, 1969, in Landers, California.

—*Jerome Clark*

See Also: Contactees; Religions, UFO; Space Brothers
Further Reading:
Bethurum, Truman. *Aboard a Flying Saucer.* Los Angeles: DeVorss, 1954.
Flammonde, Paris. *The Age of Flying Saucers: Notes on a Projected History of Unidentified Flying Objects.* New York: Hawthorn Books, 1971.
Jacobs, David M. *The UFO Controversy in America.* Bloomington: Indiana University Press, 1975.

BIGFOOT (SASQUATCH; THE ABOMINABLE SNOWMAN)

Despite its links to ancient Native American stories about Sasquatch in the Pacific Northwest region of the United States and Canada, the documented history of such beings seems to have begun only this century. In 1901 a newspaper in British Columbia carried a story about the sighting of a "monkey man" by a Vancouver Island lumberman. Various similar stories followed: a "Yellow Top" apelike creature in Ontario, a killing of a seven-foot hairy creature in Newfoundland, and so on. In 1958 the term now in common usage, "Bigfoot," appeared in conjunction with a sighting (widely considered a hoax) of giant tracks in northern California.

Hairy bipeds are generally taller than humans although they are humanoid, have a thick dark or yellowish fur, and glowing eyes that appear red, green, or yellowish. It is perhaps this last characteristic that has fueled discussion about the link between Bigfoot and UFOs. Hundreds of such combined sightings have been reported in the Pacific Northwest well into the 1990s. One of the most notable accounts comes from Uniontown, where on October 25, 1973, a young man and two boys saw a UFO land and, upon hearing screaming sounds, focused their attention on two apelike creatures with glowing eyes. As is often the case, one of the witnesses claims to have shot one of the creatures multiple times, certainly injuring it. But upon further investigation the creatures were not to be found, and the UFO quickly vanished. The witnesses and an officer who had responded to their call did walk the area and reported a sulfur-like smell and the nagging feeling that they were being watched or followed by an invisible entity.

In another account, two hikers in the Anza Borrego Desert in Southern California reported waking in the middle of the night to the sound of an explosion. Their investigation over the top of a nearby ridge revealed the adjacent valley to be full of entities with glowing red eyes marching along as a red, circular flying saucer hovered above. Perhaps the strangest of experiential claims comes from a trio that had purchased a ranch in a remote area of Colorado. Repeatedly, alone or in groups, they would see a tall, furry creature on the ranch, sometimes shooting at it. They found footprints, strands of hair, mutilated cattle, and in one instance a black box on the ground beneath a bright light in nearby trees. Two creatures, this time blond and wearing tight-fitting "flight suits," suddenly appeared in the light and warned one of the ranchers away from the box, then apologized for the inconvenience they had caused. The would-be ranchers moved back to Denver shortly afterward.

It may be that reports of Bigfoot are greatly exaggerated. Nevertheless, the preponderance of reports and the accompanying dearth of physical evidence has led Dr. Scott Rugo to speculate that UFOs and Bigfoot, among others, are merely "psychic projections."

See Also: Chupacabras; Mythology and Folklore
Further Reading:
Clark, Jerome, and Loren Coleman. *Creatures of the Outer Edge.* New York: Warner Books, 1978.
Hunter, Don, with René Dahinden. *Sasquatch.* Toronto, Ontario, Canada: McClelland and Stewart, 1973.
Keel, John A. *Strange Creatures from Time and Space.* Greenwich, CT: Fawcett Gold Medal, 1970.
Rogo, D. Scott. *The Haunted Universe: A Psychic Look at Miracles, UFOs, and Mysteries of Nature.* New York: Signet, 1977.
Sanderson, Ivan T. *Abominable Snowmen: Legend Come to Life.* Philadelphia: Chilton Books, 1961.
Slate, B. Ann, and Alan Berry. *Bigfoot.* New York: Bantam Books, 1976.

THE BLOB

The first and, in almost everyone's opinion, the better *Blob* film was made in 1958. A meteor brings a blob of space protoplasm to earth. The Blob consumes some of the inhabitants of a small American town and becomes elephant-sized. When two teenagers report that the Blob has eaten the town's doctor and nurse, no one believes them. One teenage boy rallies a group of his friends who have also seen the Blob, and they try to warn the police but are laughed off. Finally the teenagers discover that the Blob does not like cold. They stun it with electricity and squeeze it into a transport plane, from whence it is dropped into the Antarctic. This film gave Steve McQueen his first starring role. *The Blob* was remade in 1988. In this version the Blob was not an alien organism but a product of the military. There was also a 1971 comedy film sequel—*Beware! The Blob*—in which the Blob stalks a Midwestern town in search of victims.

Although not about UFOs per se, *The Blob* is built around the same general theme as movies like *The Arrival* and *Independence Day*, namely, hostile aliens invade the earth and threaten the very existence of humankind. Even a casual overview of films involving extraterrestrials will make it clear that aliens are almost always portrayed as being either super-good or super-evil—there is almost no such thing as morally ambiguous extraterrestrials in Hollywood. *The Blob* clearly falls into the evil-alien genre.

Original—Tonylyn Productions/Paramount 1958; 83 min. Director: Irvin S. Yeaworth Jr.; Writer: Theodore Simonson, Kate Phillips; Cinematography: Thomas E. Spalding; Cast: Steve McQueen, Aneta Corsaut, Olin Howlin, Earl Rowe.

Sequel: Jack H. Harris Enterprises 1971; 88 min. Director: Larry Hagman; Cinematography: Al Hamm; Producer/Writer: Anthony Harris; Cast: Robert Walker,

Publicity illustration for Paramount's 1958 film The Blob, *starring Steve McQueen (The Del Valle Archive)*

Gwynne Gilford, Godfrey Cambridge, Carol Lynley, Shelley Berman, Burgess Meredith, Gerrit Graham.

Remake: Tri Star; 92 min. Director: Chuck Russell; Writer: Frank Darabont, Chuck Russel; Cinematography: Mark Irwin; Cast: Kevin Dillon, Candy Clark, Joe Seneca, Shawnee Smith, Donovan Leitch, Jeffrey DeMunn, Del Close.

See Also: Contactees; Cults; UFO; Religions, UFO; Space Brothers

Further Reading:

Lewis, James R. *The Encyclopedia of Cults, Sects, and New Religions.* Amherst, NY: Prometheus Books, 1998.

Melton, Gordon. *Encyclopedia of American Religions.* 5th ed. Detroit: Gale Research, 1996.

BLUE ROSE MINISTRY

The Blue Rose Ministry is the organizational vehicle for Robert E. Short, who channels ufonauts. He was brought to public attention during the 1967 annual contactee gathering at Giant Rock, California, formerly hosted by George Van Tassel. Just before Short's channeling session began, a red-orange UFO was sighted by the crowd and was visible for about two minutes. Korton, the channeled entity speaking through Short, asserted that he was from Jupiter and that the craft they had seen was a scout ship from the mothership. The Blue Rose Ministry produces books and tapes of Short's channelings. Its goal is to bring people into closer attunement with enlightened being in the cosmos.

THE BRAIN FROM PLANET AROUS

In this 1958 film a large flying evil superbrain arrives on earth from another planet and overpowers a nuclear scientist, entering his body. The scientist's girlfriend becomes alarmed by his strange new behavior. A good alien brain arrives on earth in pursuit of the first and takes temporary possession of the scientist's dog. It then tells the girlfriend how to kill the evil brain by landing a blow on the side of its head. She does this, and the scientist returns to normal.

Although not exactly recommended viewing, *The Brain from Planet Arous* is interesting as an early example of the rare film that brings both good and bad aliens into the plot. This tendency to dichotomize our projections is reflected in a certain subpopulation of the UFO community that believes that different sets of ufonauts—some good (friendly) and some evil (hostile)—pilot different sets of flying saucers. Rarely does the human imagination portray extraterrestrials as morally ambiguous.

Marquette Productions 1958; 80 min. Director: Nathan H. Juran; Producer/Cinematography: Jacques Marquette; Screenwriter: Ray Buffum; Cast: John Agar, Joyce Meadows, Robert Fuller, Thomas B. Henry, Ken Terrell.

THE BROTHER FROM ANOTHER PLANET

In this 1984 film a mute alien materializes in New York in black human form, discovers alienation, ends a drug racket, and, after disposing of a pair of extraterrestrial bounty hunters (who appear as white Anglos) who are after him, decides to stay. The only things about the alien that set him apart other than his muteness are his three-toed feet and the E.T.-like ability to repair electronic devices just by touching them.

The Brother from Another Planet is less a sci-fi flick than it is a morality tale about human oppression and inequality. It is, however, interesting in that it brings both good and bad aliens into the plot—a departure from the marked tendency of Hollywood to portray extraterrestrials as either completely friendly or completely hostile. It is also one of the first films to cast a black person as an alien, in contrast to almost all earlier movies, in which humanoid extraterrestrials were Anglos.

A-Train Films 1984; 109 min. Writer/Director: John Sayles; Cinematography: Ernest R. Dickerson; Music: Mason Daring; Cast: Joe Morton, Dee Dee Bridgewater, Ren Woods, Steve James, Maggie Renzi, David Strathairn, Tom Wright, Herbert Newsome, Leonard Jackson.

BROTHERHOOD OF THE SEVEN RAYS

The Brotherhood of the Seven Rays was established in 1956 by George Hunt Williamson. In that year Williamson and some associates traveled to Peru to establish the Abbey of the Seven Rays. The monastery opened in the 1960 and continued into the 1970s. Students who came to live at the center in Peru had to accept the cosmic Christ as one who came to earth and who is due to return in the near

future. Meditation, fasting, and contemplation were practiced. The group had a communal meal daily. Novices of both genders underwent baptism by immersion before becoming friars and were anointed with oil before becoming monks. No narcotics or stimulants (including chocolate) were used, and no meat was eaten. Marriage was allowed. The Brotherhood had two orders: The Order of the Red Hand was dedicated to preserving arcane knowledge at a scriptorium at the monastery in Peru; the Ancient Amethystine Order's purpose was to cure humanity of its ills and the earth of its drunken state. The U.S. headquarters of the Brotherhood was in Corpus Christi, Texas. The Brotherhood had ceased to function by 1980.

George Hunt Williamson had been an archaeologist and student of theosophy. He witnessed George Adamski making his first contact with a being from Venus in the California desert in 1952. In 1953 Williamson published his own story, *The Saucers Speak,* in which he claimed contact with Martians by means of automatic writing. Williamson also claimed to have been in touch with the ascended masters, who were once human and who now teach humans about spiritual realities.

See Also: Contactees; Cults, UFO; Religions, UFO; Space Brothers
Further Reading:
Melton, Gordon. *Encyclopedia of American Religions.* 5th ed. Detroit: Gale Research, 1996.
Williamson, George Hunt. *The Brotherhood of the Seven Rays.* Clarksburg, WV: Saucerian Books, 1961.

BRYANT, ERNEST

Ernest Bryant of Scoriton, England, wrote a letter in 1965 to the Exeter Astronomical Society, saying that he had seen a light-blue light that hummed and clattered; when he investigated, he found metallic scraps in the area where the UFO had been. Later, as the investigation progressed, he said it was the second contact he had experienced. The first involved three extraterrestrial beings that landed in a field near his house. They were Venusians who told of the unimaginably happy life on their planet and warned that the evil planet Epsilon wanted to use humans for reproductive purposes. They gave Bryant a tour of their ship, then waved goodbye, promising to return.

Bryant made sketches of the beings, one of which looked remarkably like a young George Adamski, the controversial occult contactee of the 1950s who claimed to have been befriended by a Venusian named Orthon who took him on space adventures throughout the solar system. Bryant also claimed to see a purple gown with an embroidered rose in the alien craft, which had been given to Adamski at a conference on Saturn. Some members of the Adamski Society believed he had acquired a new, youthful body, whereas others decided that it was a trick of "mischievous space people."

Back on earth, the metallic scraps were found to be ordinary pieces of aircraft equipment, and the small tube found by Bryant with the inscription reading "Brother to Brother" in classical Greek was a gardening gadget. Soon the word "hoax" began to spread about the incident, but no one would be able to question Bryant because he died of a brain tumor. His wife, however, told investigators that he had planned to write a sci-fi novel sounding very much like his UFO stories.

See Also: Contactees; Hoaxes; Space Brothers
Further Reading:
Buckle, Eileen. *The Scoriton Mystery.* London: Neville Spearman, 1967.

"UFO abduction" in the 1930 cartoon strip Buck Rogers in the 25th Century *(American Religion Collection)*

Keel, John A. *UFOs: Operation Trojan Horse.* New York: G. P. Putnam's Sons, 1970.
Story, Ronald D., ed. *The Encyclopedia of UFOs.* Garden City, NY: Doubleday, 1980, pp. 324–326.

BUCK ROGERS IN THE 25TH CENTURY

In this 1979 film, based on a 1930 comic strip, an evil princess plans to conquer earth but is foiled by Buck Rogers, who uses a mixture of old-fashioned heroics and modern technology. Although not directly relevant to UFOs, the Buck Rogers sto-

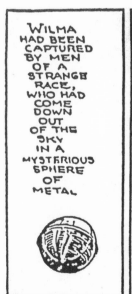

Table examination and "mindscan" during a UFO abduction in the 1930 cartoon strip Buck Rogers in the 25th Century *(American Religion Collection)*

ryline helped to shape our image of outer space and has influenced, to a greater or lesser extent, most subsequent sci-fi films and TV shows involving space travel.

Universal 1979; 90 min. Director: Daniel Haller; Writer: Glen Larson, Leslie Stevens; Cinematography: Frank Beasoechea; Cast: Gil Gerard, Pamela Hensley, Erin Gray, Henry Silva, Tim O'Connor, Joseph Wiseman.

CAPE CANAVERAL MONSTERS

In this 1960 film an alien life force arrives in Florida to interfere with the U.S. space program at Cape Canaveral by taking over the bodies of humans and turning them into zombies. It is an *Invasion of the Body Snatchers* type of film that some commentators have tried to explain in terms of the American fear of Soviet infiltration. The basic notion that hostile, human-looking aliens are taking over the earth is widespread among the more paranoid segments of the UFO community.

CCM 1960; 69 min. Director/Writer: Phil Tucker; Cinematography: Merle Connell; Cast: Scott Peters, Linda Connell, Jason Johnson, Katherine Victor, Frank Smith.

CAPTIVITY TALES AND ABDUCTIONS

Although the United States is not the only country that has been troubled by hostages, the other nations of the world appear to be less enthralled by the spectacle of the bondage of its citizens. Furthermore, unlike in most other countries, the manner in which our government deals with American captives has marked political repercussions: The hostage crisis that emerged in the wake of the Iranian revolution hurt Jimmy Carter's presidency, and Ronald Reagan's ill-advised arms-for-hostages deal led to Iran-contra, the worst scandal of his career. This nation's interest in captivity can also be seen in our ongoing obsession with American POWs who may or may not still be in Southeast Asia, our invasion of Grenada for the ostensive purpose of "rescuing" American medical students, and the central role that the captivity-rescue motif plays in many of the stories found in our entertainment media.

This country's broader obsession with the theme of bondage (e.g., a seemingly endless fascination with hostages and hostage stories) has led certain scholars to attempt to locate the historical origins of this fixation. The approach generally taken has been to postulate a chain of influences reaching back to the narratives composed in colonial New England by former captives of Native Americans. In other words, in an effort to explain why the North American imagination is more enthralled with captivity than are other societies, the dominant tendency has been to refer to the unique situation of a 250-year conflict between Euro-Americans and aboriginal Americans—a conflict in which, particularly during periods of full-scale war, Native Americans often captured large numbers of settlers. This explanation immediately strikes one as intuitively correct, especially if one is familiar with the primary material on which the argument is based.

But was the imagination of the Puritans (from whom the first set of Indian-captivity tales emerged) simply overwhelmed by the sheer number of captures (as some writers have argued), or were the Puritans ideologically predisposed to give significance to situations of bondage? On this issue, several different scholars have called attention to Puritan preoccupation with captivity themes, a preoccupation antedating Puritans' migration to America. For the Puritans (and, to a lesser extent, for all Christians of that period), imprisonment was a comprehensive metaphor through which the whole of human existence could be viewed.

Saturated with such imagery, Puritans naturally would be interested in the experience of colonists who had been captured by Native Americans. The Puritans imposed a theological gloss on these narratives. At one level, the overall pattern of Indian-captivity tales (capture, bondage, and ransom) could be viewed as parallel to the three stages of conversion (contrition, despair, and salvation)—parallels that were not lost on the Puritans. The aptness of this structural parallel also dovetailed nicely with the Puritans' tendency to identify their enemies with God's enemies (Native Americans, in other words, were viewed as minions of Satan), hence Indian captivity was a singularly appropriate symbol for bondage to sin.

The published captivity tales were extremely popular. The Puritans believed that secular fiction was a waste of time, but they could, with a clear conscience, read stories composed by former captives of American Indians. These captivity tales were the closest thing to an action-adventure story available to the early colonists. However, tales of captivity at the hands of American Indians, both historical and fictional, continued to be produced long after the Puritan worldview had lost its hegemony.

This American fascination with captivity, which, it has been noted, continues up to the present day in the form of our fascination with hostages, made it almost inevitable that tales of alien abduction should originate in the United States. Once mainstream ufologists finally gave in and began to consider this phenomenon a part of serious ufology, alien abduction quickly came to occupy center stage. To the historically informed observer, it is not surprising that abduction books have become the best-selling of all UFO publications in the history of modern ufology.

See Also: Abductees; Alien-Abduction Narratives; Close Encounters

Further Reading:

Axtell, James. *The European and the Indian: Essays in the Ethnohistory of Colonial North America.* Oxford: Oxford University Press, 1981.

Slotkin, Richard. *Regeneration through Violence: The Mythology of the American Frontier, 1600–1860.* Middletown, CT: Wesleyan University Press, 1973.

VanDerBeets, Richard. *The Indian Captivity Narrative.* Lanham, MD: University Press of America, 1984.

CARGO CULTS

Millenarian movements await an imminent, collective, and ultimate liberation, usually—but not exclusively—*within* this world. This liberation implies the founding of a perfect age or pure country or kingdom and the construction of a totally "new

person" *(Homo novus).* Likewise, the so-called cargo cults of Melanesia and New Guinea relate to a dawning state of material, organizational, and spiritual well-being, and the expected abundance of supernaturally acquired supplies is often turned into the central characteristic of the approaching millennium.

For the Melanesian cargo cults in colonial and postcolonial times, the formerly unknown consumer goods and commodities of Western civilization ("cargo"; in pidgin, *kago*) became objects of religious concern, partly by offering a substitute or compensation for current insufficiencies. The formative cargo cults were centered around the fascinating "alien cargo" discharged from ships and airplanes: cotton-cloth, rice, canned food, razor blades, knifes, guns, axes, and many other supplies. Their basic intention focused on the acquisition of such exotic goods. Because the process of industrial production remained hidden to the indigenous people, and because the colonial personnel obviously did not have to "work" for their appropriation, the cargo had to be of unknown supernatural origin. Therefore, a plausible interpretation was the new belief that these goods were originally gifts from the ancestors or culture heroes of primordial times—now mysteriously stolen by the agents of colonial power. Innumerable prophets declared imminent arrivals of other ships: The true indigenous consignees would then get their share, and specific rituals (partly an imitation of colonial ritual practice, partly derived from traditional religions or Christian missions) would help to speed the eschatological process, which would finally lead to a new and just order in the world.

In various forms of modern UFO faith, a similar cargoistic strand is inherent. However, here it is the supposed superior technology of the space aliens (passing between parallel worlds, velocity beyond the speed of light, teleportation, or "beaming," etc.) as well as the higher or paranormal spiritual faculties (enlightenment, higher consciousness, time travel, astral projection, telepathy, etc.) that—together with other gifts and supplies (especially unknown cosmic energies)—exercise an exotic charm. As in the case of cargo cults, an imminent and utterly transformed new cosmic order is linked with the arrival of a radically different range of material and spiritual goods. And in both cases, the cargo is believed to issue from a supernatural source: the realm of higher spiritual beings.

Starting with George Adamski, Orfeo Angelucci, George Van Tassel, Daniel Fry, and other early contactees, the alien visitors are always presented as—according to the human perspective—supernormal beings with supernormal powers and technologies, which they are ready to disclose and share for the gradual benefit of earthly humankind. A "ground crew" of chosen individuals and prophets is selected to spread the Space Brothers' gospel. In many cases the alien visitors are associated with legendary culture heroes and gods of antiquity: They become identified with the Ascended Masters of theosophy and are viewed as founders of ancient civilizations on the sunken continents of Atlantis and Mu (or Lemuria). Several instances in ancient religious texts and myths or archaeological artifacts are thus reinterpreted as "Memories of the Future" (cf. Erich von Däniken).

In ufological expectations, the hope for an eschatological transfer of the space aliens' supernatural technology to earth is often combined with the idea of a restitution of the original paradise. A superabundant Heaven on Earth is in sight, and a primordial, paradisiacal harmony is going to be established on this planet. There will be spiritual growth and perfection (enlightenment, cosmic consciousness) and—at the same time—technological progress and perfection (advanced technological supplies and scientific programs to overcome earth's ecological problems). Contemporary human science and technology will be either elevated or partly destroyed, as in the case of nuclear weapons and powers. A golden age is expected, and the imagery of the perfect garden is wed with the dream of a scientific miracle. As Norman Poulsen, the founder and leader of the Californian Sunburst Community, once stated on behalf of the coming Millennium: "The by-product of living a life of harmony with the Spirit is to have physical abundance." In UFO faith, there exists a remarkably consistent imagery connected with this cargoistic future. For example, in the *Appeal to Earth Dwellers* (1992: 56ff.) ("Aufruf an die Erdbe-

wohner," by W. and Th. Gauch-Keller), a Swiss-German ufological mission-brochure related to Ashtar and the Ashtar Command, the so-called New Time—after the Great Evacuation into the millions of spaceships hovering around earth—is portrayed in the following way:

> With the help of our Star Brothers and Sisters [*Sternengeschwister*] and with the newly mastered techniques of materialization, dematerialization, prognosis, etc. we will create . . . everything needed for our life. Telepathy will be everyday language, and time as we know it on earth today will no longer be valid. . . . We will not only be able to use these supernormal techniques but we will also learn how to engage in intergalactic space travel. We will master the use of free cosmic energies and we will manifest things, food, etc. by free will. Everything will be possible, when we live and act according to the cosmic/divine laws.
>
> After the Transformation, we will live in a half-ethereal and/or ethereal body—like our Space Brothers and Sisters. Our body atoms will oscillate in such a high frequency that we will become invisible to normal physical eyes. . . .
>
> A long era of peace, love and harmony will dawn (thousand year reign), since in this new resonating frequency wars and destructive thoughts can no longer exercise control over human minds. Any oppression of people will vanish, because these lower vibrations will cease to exist.

The benevolent Space Brothers and Space Sisters function as angelic mediators and culture heroes: They are essentially angels in space suits, and with their highly advanced faculties, training programs, and supernormal science it takes only a very short time to lead humans up to the realms of highest enlightenment (cf. ascension and the transformation of the person into a new cosmic being and a member of the Galactic Federation). When this ufological millennium breaks through, its new cargo will not manifest itself in an abundance of material wealth of the Western kind but as a completely superior technology with special materials hitherto unknown to humankind and with a release of unknown energies of the universe. Spiritual progress and technological advance are amalgamated into one, creation will be brought to its end, and a truly Galactic Society will be established.

However, ufological eschatologies also differ with respect to the degree in which cargoistic hopes are integrated into the apocalyptic framework. In Christian millenarian eschatology (cf. Revelation of John) there are two basic models: According to premillennialism or postmillennialism, the eschatological hope can either be concentrated on deliverance or salvation from this world (e.g., rapture of the chosen 144,000 before the millennium) or on salvation within this world (final establishment of the heavenly reign on earth after the millennial interim period and the ultimate defeat of Satan).

Analogous patterns can also be found in ufology:

1. On the one hand, there is a dominant "Big Beam" scenario: Earthly souls will finally be evacuated and taken up into flying saucers or giant motherships. The millennial hope is focused primarily on salvation *from* this earth. A prominent example of this option was the Heaven's Gate group, which declared its final departure as "the last chance to evacuate earth before it is recycled" and thus displayed a strong this-worldly pessimism. In their opinion, only a complete removal to the "Level Above Human"—a beaming-up of souls after they "discarnated" from their bodily "containers"—could promise salvation, and this left no place for any kind of world-changing cargoism.

2. On the other hand, one can find a strongly optimistic hope concerning Planet Earth—with a paradisiacal Heaven on Earth at its center. This scenario, in which the transfer of Space Alien Cargo becomes a central feature in the millennial process, is shared by most esoteric and contactee versions of UFO faith. Often these variants of UFO millenarism also imply a general rapture, but the Big Beam is in most cases reduced to a contained period of time: a few years—if not days, or even hours. Earth dwellers are temporarily beamed up to a safe place in the space ships, but they will be brought back when Mother Earth is finally cleansed, rejuvenated, and trans-

formed to her original integrity. Since the Paradise is to be restored on earth, and a joyful, almost hedonistic life in cargoistic abundance is in sight, the Great Tribulation as well as the Big Beam will be only a short intermezzo.

Without doubt, an important attraction of the contactee version of UFO faith is rooted in its capacity to synthesize various elements of esoteric, spiritualistic, and theosophical or Christian traditions and to reconcile them with aspects of contemporary science, space technology, and cosmology—the result being a strong re-enchantment of heaven (cf. caring and loving angelic aliens). When millenarianism and cargoism are linked within the ufological vision of a spiritual and technological miracle, "the images of modern technology and scientific achievement will be retained, so that the prophesied new Order can even be articulated as the very apex of Modernity rather than [exclusively] that of a Great spiritual Return, and at times it can bear a strong ring of Science Fiction [or some 'science mythology'] about it" (G. Trompf). In certain Western contexts of relative powerlessness, sociocultural discomfort, and obscurity, these promises of a new (compensatory) appropriation of power, knowledge, and control can be very attractive. Furthermore, such a cargoistic utopia does not seem alien to a culture of narcissism, and it is fully compatible with the optimistic fantasies of technological evolution and increasing scientific control that are still dominant in modern industrial societies.

—*Andreas Gruenschloss*

See Also: Contactees; Cults, UFO; Eschatology; Millennialism; Religions, UFO; Space Brothers

Further Reading:

Gauch-Keller, W., and Th. Gauch-Keller. *Aufruf an die Erdbewohner* [Appeal to Earth Dwellers]. *Erklärungen zur Umwandlung des Planeten Erde und seiner Menschheit in der Endzeit.* Ostermundingen/CH, 1992.

Gruenschloss, Andreas. "'When We Enter into My Father's Spacecraft'—Cargoistic Hopes and Millenarian Cosmologies in New Religious UFO Movements." *Marburg Journal of Religion* 3(2) (1998); URL: www.uni-marburg.de/fb03/religionswissenschaft/journal/mjr/ufogruen.html

Lewis, James. ed. *The Gods Have Landed: New Religions from Other Worlds.* Albany: State University of New York Press, 1995.

Tromf, Garry, ed. *Cargo Cults and Millenarian Movements.* Berlin and New York: Mouton de Gruyter, 1990 (esp. "Introduction" and the essay "The Cargo and the Millennium on Both Sides of the Pacific").

CARR, OTIS T.

Otis T. Carr was born in Elkins, West Virginia, on December 7, 1904. In 1955 Carr founded OTC Enterprises in Baltimore. Two years later he announced that he had invented a space vehicle powered by an electric accumulator. He claimed to have learned his secrets from inventor Nikola Tesla, whom Carr had met while working as night clerk at the New York hotel where Tesla resided.

Carr hired Norman Evans Colton as his promotion man. Carr and Colton became regulars on Long John Nebel's radio show in New York City. These shows were humorous, with Nebel highlighting Carr's unintelligibility. On one show, Carr stated that he could not begin to enumerate the discoveries made as a result of Nikola Tesla's work. Asked to tell the audience just one of these, Carr responded, "That's funny. I cannot remember even one." Carr and Colton sent out regular information bulletins to investors. Hundreds of thousands of dollars came Carr's way from people who wanted to invest in free-energy systems.

In 1958 contactee Wayne Sulo Aho became involved with OTC Enterprises. Carr and Aho went on a nationwide lecture tour of the United States, explaining why rockets would never reach other planets; why Washington officials would not reveal the facts about UFOs; why Tesla's works had been hidden for 50 years; and how the OTC free-energy devices actually worked. Many investors were attracted from the contactee and occult circuit as a result of these appearances.

In 1958 Carr moved his operation to Oklahoma City. Carr and Colton advertised that a six-foot prototype saucer-shaped spacecraft would be flown to the Moon and back in 1959. On Sunday, April 19, 1959, a crowd converged on Frontier City amusement park in Oklahoma City, where the vehicle was to take its maiden flight. However, Carr

was in the hospital with a mysterious throat ailment, and the spacecraft developed a "mercury leak" that caused the flight to be canceled. Shortly thereafter, a fire destroyed the saucer.

Carr and several of his associates, including Wayne Aho, were charged with violating state regulations on stock sales. Carr was convicted of illegally selling stock and fined $5,000. Unable to pay, he was confined to jail to work off his obligation at a dollar a day. Eventually charges against Aho were dropped. Colton, who had fled Oklahoma prior to the charges being filed, formed the Millennium Agency to sell orders to construct free-energy machines that would be able to draw electricity from the atmosphere without the use of any fuel.

See Also: Contactees; Hoaxes
Further Reading:
Curran, Douglas. *In Advance of the Landing: Folk Concepts of Outer Space.* New York: Abbeville Press, 1985.
Flammonde, Paris. *The Age of Flying Saucers: Notes on a Projected History of Unidentified Flying Objects.* New York: Hawthorn Books, 1971.
Nebel, Long John. *The Way Out World.* Englewood Cliffs, NJ: Prentice-Hall, 1961.

THE CAT FROM OUTERSPACE

In this 1978 Disney film an extraterrestrial cat is stranded on earth when his spaceship breaks down. One man attempts to raise the $120,000 in gold needed to repair the spaceship while another tries to steal the cat's collar, which is the source of his super-powers. This is a Disneyesque movie in which a cute, friendly alien is involved in a drama with good and bad earthlings.

Disney 1978; 103 min. Director: Norman Tokar; Writer: Ted Key; Cinematography: Charles F. Wheeler; Cast: Ken Berry, Sandy Duncan, Harry (Henry) Morgan, Roddy McDowal, McLean Stevenson.

CATTLE MUTILATIONS

Cattle and other animal mutilations and their alleged link to UFOs have been one of the more surreal aspects of ufology for over 30 years. The first reported animal mutilation occurred in the San Luis Valley, Colorado, on September 9, 1967, when rancher Harry King found his sister's horse decapitated near his home. The head and part of the

Drawing of a UFO abducting a cow (Katherine Hollaud)

neck were stripped clean of flesh, with only a white, clean skeleton left. The horse's body, however, was untouched. Because of the sharpness of the incision, the medical examiner thought that it had been cauterized by a laser beam, even though no laser technology existed in 1967 that could have made the cut. In addition, many of the horse's internal organs were missing, such as the heart, lungs, and thyroid. Most confusing of all, no blood was found on the skin or the ground. The mystery was amplified by the reported sighting of a UFO just before the mutilation occurred. King's mother claimed that a "large object" had passed over the ranch on the night of the mutilation.

Since 1967 animal mutilations, mostly of cattle, have been reported by the thousands, and they continue to this day. In late 1973 farmers in Kansas and Minnesota began reporting deaths of cattle under apparently mysterious circumstances. Certain factors were found common to all mutilations: There seemed to be no visible cause of death; soft body parts had, it was claimed, been removed with surgical precision; the cattle were systematically drained of blood, often through small holes punched in their jugular vein; internal organs— especially sex organs—seemed to have been cut

away; evidence of residual radiation or tranquilizing chemicals (it was claimed) were discovered; some animals were found with broken legs and backs pushed into the ground, as if they had been dropped from above; there were no footprints near the carcasses; and, finally, UFO sightings were common in the areas where the mutilations occurred. Various earthly interpretations have been put forward to explain the phenomena. A veterinary lab at Colorado State University insisted the deaths were the work of animal predators.

In December 1973 a group of sheriffs met and decided, from essentially no evidence, that the deaths were probably the work of "cultists." Other law-enforcement officials were more skeptical, and the Kansas State University Veterinary Hospital proved that the animals had died of blackleg, a bacterial disease. Nevertheless, many rural people had come to believe that "Satanists" had sacrificed the cattle, and this rumor persisted.

By the late 1970s these rumors had spread to other states and into Canada. Newspapers were claiming thousands of deaths. The four major schools of thought on the causes of the deaths blamed them on cultists, secret government experiments, UFOs, and hysteria. Circumstantial evidence began to turn up that seemed to link cultists with these supposed deaths.

Around this time, federal prisoner Kenneth Bankston claimed that the work was done by a secret order of devil worshipers called the Sons of Satan. He said that the cult used PCP and then amyl nitrate to sedate the cattle. Hypodermic needles were utilized to draw out the animal's blood. The cult, according to Bankston, used the sex organs for fertility rights. He asserted that footprints were concealed by wrapping the cow's feet in cardboard. Subsequently, blowtorches melted the snow, obliterating the tracks. This explanation was also debunked, as the people implicated by Bankston were discovered to have been in jail at the time of the mutilations. Furthermore, because of the large number of mutilation reports—1,500 cattle in 22 states between 1975 and 1977—it was physically impossible for cultists to have accomplished the feat.

In 1975 Donald Flickinger, an agent for the U.S. Bureau of Alcohol, Tobacco, and Firearms, was assigned to investigate reports of a nationwide Satanist network engaged in animal and human sacrifice. He could find no supporting evidence. Investigations of speculations about government experiments led to a similar dead end.

Further attempts at more earthly explanations have not yielded much in the way of results. Journalist Linda Howe produced a documentary and a book linking cattle mutilations to UFOs. According to Howe's research, mutilations have been reported dating back to the 1700s, implying that this is not a new phenomenon.

Howe's evidence for extraterrestrial involvement seemed to keep mounting. A rancher in Waco, Texas, claimed that he saw two four-foot-high creatures while searching for his missing cow. The creatures were described as having egg-shaped heads, no hair or nose, with eyes angled upward. He asserted they carried the cow between them. Other "evidence" came from a woman named Judy Doraty, who, under hypnosis, reported memories of an abduction. While driving with family members, she saw a craft beaming down a light. After pulling over and exiting the car, she saw a calf being drawn toward the light. Then she was pulled into the craft. The occupants then asserted she wasn't supposed to be there. They told her that they were trying to fix a pol-

Illustration from "Dragons of Space," by Aladra Septama, in Amazing Stories Quarterly *(Mary Evans Picture Library)*

lution problem caused by humans, in which nuclear testing or wastes caused a chemical composition change. This pollution had gone from the water to plants and animals, and people would die if nothing was done. So the aliens were studying the reproduction system of the animals to determine the extent of the contamination. After they were done examining the cow, they dropped it to the ground. Then the aliens abducted her daughter and examined her, taking tissue scrapings from her mouth before putting her and her mother back in the car. No one else in the car remembered the encounter. Ufologists have speculated that the aliens, since humans eat cows, were studying them to figure out how man-made radiation is affecting humans.

Theories about extraterrestrials who mutilated cattle thus merged with abduction beliefs. By the early 1990s there had arisen a subculture believing firmly in a complex mythology that asserted evil aliens were in cahoots with the U.S. government and were being permitted to abduct cattle and humans in exchange for advanced technological information.

There have been further investigations, by a former FBI agent, Kenneth Rommel, and by two journalists, Daniel Kagan and Ian Summers. Using different methods, they arrived at converging conclusions: that there is no significant evidence that there have ever been any cattle deaths from anything but natural causes; and that the rumors about such deaths have been created and perpetuated by incompetent investigators, uncritical reporters, and people who were personally benefiting from exploiting the "mutology" subculture. However, the myth of cattle mutilations appears to be as durable as any other myth that meets what is apparently a type of religious need in an American subculture.

—*Jerome Clark*

See Also: Abductees; Chupacabras; Mythology and Folklore; Satanism and UFOs

Further Reading:

Howe, Linda Moulton. *An Alien Harvest: Further Evidence Linking Animal Mutilations and Human Abductions to Alien Life Forms.* Littleton, CO: Linda Moulton Howe Productions, 1989.

Kagan, Daniel, and Ian Summers. *Mute Evidence.* New York: Bantam Books, 1984.

Owen, Nancy H. *Preliminary Analysis of the Impact of Livestock Mutilations on Rural Arkansas Communities.* Fayetteville: University of Arkansas Department of Anthropology, January 1980.

Rommel, Kenneth M. *Operation Animal Mutilation.* Report of the District Attorney, First Judicial District, State of New Mexico. Santa Fe: District Attorney, June 1980.

CHANNELING

"Channeling" is the modern term for what spiritualists traditionally termed "mediumship"—an event or process in which an individual "channel" is able to transmit information from a nonordinary source, most often from a nonembodied spirit. Channeling was popularized in UFO circles as the psychic communications from "Space Brothers" and was only later applied to New Age mediums. While some channelers retain full consciousness during their transmissions, most of the prominent New Age channelers are what spiritualists refer to as "trance mediums"—mediums who lose consciousness while a disembodied spirit takes over the channeler's body and communicates through it. These spirits frequently claim to be spiritually advanced souls whose communications consist of metaphysical teachings. The teaching function of this communication contrasts with traditional nineteenth-century mediums, who were more concerned with transmitting messages from departed relatives and with demonstrating the reality of life after death.

As vehicles for communications from the other world, channels are merely the most recent manifestations of a phenomenon that can be traced back at least as far as archaic shamanism. Ancient shamans mediated the relationship between their communities and the Other World, often transmitting messages from the deceased. Modern channelers also sometimes view themselves as being in the tradition of ancient prophets, transmitting messages from more elevated sources. Unlike the prophets, however, New Age channelers rarely claim to be delivering messages directly from God; neither do they usually rail against the sins of society, as did the Hebrew prophets. Most often their communications come from intermediary beings—ranging from deceased religious figures to the inhabitants of flying saucers—and consist of some form of New Age philosophy, which they explain to their listeners.

See Also: Automatic Writing; Contactees; New Age; Space Brothers

Further Reading:

Klimo, Jon. *Channeling.* Los Angeles: Jeremy P. Tarcher, 1987.

Roberts, Jane. *The Seth Material.* Englewood Cliffs, NJ: Prentice Hall, 1970.

Sixteenth-century woodcut by Hans Sebald Beham depicting Mercury, patron muse of artisans, riding a celestial chariot (Dover Pictorial Archive Series)

Ryerson, Kevin, and Stephanie Harolde. *Spirit Communication: The Soul's Path.* New York: Bantam Books, 1989.

CHARIOTS OF THE GODS?

Chariots of the Gods? is the title of Erich von Däniken's now classic book that in the late 1960s and early 1970s brought the ancient-astronaut hypothesis into public awareness. This hypothesis holds that in the more or less distant past technologically advanced extraterrestrials intervened in terrestrial history, giving birth to human civilization. Other writers had postulated the idea before von Däniken, but none as persuasively as the famous Swiss author. *Chariots of the Gods?* is an uneven work—some of von Däniken's speculations are plausible, others implausible—but there are enough real mysteries in the human past to lead even the most cautious reader to consider the possibility that perhaps aliens really did visit earth in the historical past. *In Search of Ancient Astronauts,* a TV special based on *Chariots of the Gods?* aired in January 1973. Before the end of the year, the Ancient Astronaut Society had been founded.

See Also: Ancient Astronauts; Gods and UFOs; von Däniken, Erich

Further Reading:

Goran, Morris. *The Modern Myth, Ancient Astronauts and UFOs.* South Brunswick, NJ: A. S. Barnes, 1978.
von Däniken, Erich. *Chariots of the Gods? Unsolved Mysteries of the Past.* Trans. Michael Heron. New York: G. P. Putnam's Sons, 1970.

CHEN TAO

The Taiwanese religious movement known as Chen Tao was briefly in the news when its leader announced that God would appear on television on March 25, 1998, and then in person on March 31, 1998. In Chinese, *chen* (or *zhen*) means "right" or "true," and *tao* (*dao*) means "way."

The history of Chen Tao goes back roughly four decades to a spiritual self-improvement association based in urban southern Taiwan, called the Association for Research on Soul Light. The group sought to locate, quantify, and cultivate spiritual light energy using technological devices and traditional Chinese practices like *qigong;* its mixture of Buddhism-Taoism and high-technology attracted a good number of students, academics, and white-collar professionals (several thousand by one account).

Among them was sociology professor Hon-ming Chen, who joined the association in the early 1990s. In it he found an explanation for his reportedly lifelong visions of spheres of golden light. Through these golden spheres God the Heavenly Father wished to communicate several things to him: first, that he had a special role to play as spiritual teacher and critic of degraded popular religion; and second, that he was to deliver messages about the end of the world and the return of Christ.

Chen succeeded to prophetic leadership of the group in 1995, refashioning Chen Tao's steady-state cosmology by coupling the Buddhist conception of reincarnation according to merit with a cyclical model of history, bringing in a biblical apocalypse as an exclamation point. According to Chen, the Endtime is brought about by the collective negative karma of all living beings. God, as a loving father, creates and re-creates the cosmos and sends Christ and Buddha, first to teach us, and then, at the end of each cycle, to save those who have followed the Right Way and attempted to rebalance their karmic books. But God also grants His children complete free will, allowing souls to take on bodies, to be seduced by the lusts of corporeality, and thus to create negative karma for themselves, to injure other living beings, and ultimately to propel the material cosmos to repeated destructions. Evidence provided by the damage to our natural environment and the degradation of our civilization is cited by Chen to bolster his claim that ours are the last days and that Christ will soon arrive in God's spacecrafts.

He proclaimed that the Kingdom of God descended first on the group's headquarters in Taiwan in 1995, and then on the North American continent. One site in particular (Garland, Texas) was singled out by Chen as the location of the repeated creations and salvations of humanity. Chen moved to this Dallas suburb in the spring of 1997, followed by up to 160 Chen Tao members that fall. In Garland, Chen made public his prophecies concerning the two televised theophanies, statements

Chen Tao leaders announcing God's imminent return in a UFO, Garland, Texas (Ryan J. Cook)

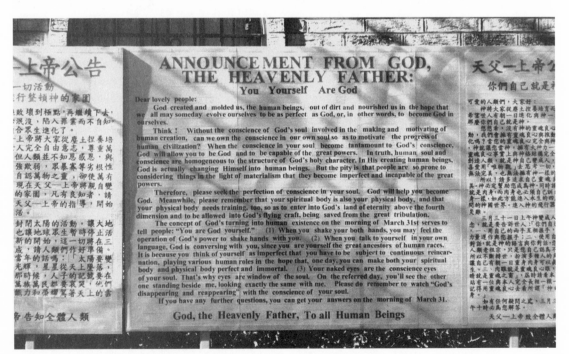

A close-up of the text displayed behind the Chen Tao leaders (Ryan J. Cook)

that for several weeks in the spring of 1998 earned his group headlines around the world. The news media (mostly on their own accord, but also at Chen's earnest invitation) came in droves, hyping Chen Tao as the next Heaven's Gate.

When events failed to take place exactly as predicted on March 25, Chen held a press conference at his Garland home at which he stated that the news media and audience worldwide could consider the prophecy nonsense. However, he and his followers hung on until God's scheduled appearance on March 31. When the Heavenly Father once again did not appear as promised, press interest dissolved almost entirely, and many followers returned to Taiwan. A small remnant of the group moved to Upstate New York in April 1998 to await the prophesied saucer salvation, then set for late 1999.

—*Ryan J. Cook*

See Also: Contactees; Cults, UFO; Millennialism; Religions, UFO

Further Reading:

Chen, Hon-ming. *Practical Evidence and Study of the World of God and Buddha.* Privately published, 1996.

Cook, Ryan J. "Reporters in Godland, TX: The Role of the Mass Media in a New Religious Movement's Adaptation to Suburban America." Paper presented at Center for Studies on New Religions annual conference, Bryn Athyn College of the New Church, Bryn Athyn, PA, 1999.

Wicker, Christine. "Leader Tells Listeners That They Are God." *Dallas Morning News,* April 1, 1998.

CHILDERS, LEE

Lee Childers was a baker in Detroit, Michigan, and a fan of science-fiction comic books. He appeared before a local flying-saucer club in 1958 and declared he could travel in space simply by closing his eyes and entering another state of consciousness. He demonstrated his technique to the audience and traveled to the Moon, Venus, and Mars during the next 10 minutes.

Douglas Hancock, a member of the U.S. Army Band, heard and believed Childers's stories. In October 1958, when Hancock was in New York, he introduced himself to a local flying-saucer club and persuaded them to bring Childers from Detroit to lecture. When Childers went to New York in December 1958 to talk to the Bureau of UFO Re-

search and Analysis, he was calling himself "Prince Neosom" and said he was from the planet Tythan, which was eight and a half light years from earth.

Prince Neosom appeared on the Long John Nebel radio show in New York, claiming he had replaced a stillborn earth child at birth. A doctor witnessed the exchange, but he had his memory wiped out by the aliens. Nebel saw Prince Neosom as a ludicrous charlatan and ordered him to leave the studio. Childers continued to tell his tales in New York to whomever would listen and then returned to Detroit.

A New York ufologist decided to expose Childers's charade by sending Douglas Hancock a telegram stating that Prince Neosom had been promoted to King. He signed the telegram "Mission for Space Unification." Douglas Hancock telephoned the message to Childers, who said he had already been given the news and was surprised the Mission for Space Unification had taken so long to tell Hancock about it.

On January 9, 1959, Douglas Hancock was committed to the psychiatric ward of St. Albans Hospital in Long Island and eventually given a Section 8 discharge from the army. Lee Childers left his wife and five children in Detroit and married one of the women he had traveled with in New York. His new wife became known as Princess Negonna. The two soon faded into obscurity.

See Also: Contactees; Hoaxes

Further Reading:

Mapes, D. O. *Prince Neosom, Planet: Tyton* [sic]. Buffalo, NY: The Author, January 22, 1959.

Nelson, Buck. *My Trip to Mars, the Moon, and Venus.* Mountain View, AR: The Author, 1956.

CHRISTIANITY

To some Christians, and to many ufologists who would not consider themselves religious Christians, UFOs are present in the Bible. John Saliba summarizes such beliefs in the following way:

Many incidents recorded during the Exodus of the Israelites from Egypt provide excellent cases of multiple witness sightings. The parting of the Red Sea is said to have been caused by unidentified flying objects and the cloud that guided them across the wilderness (Exod. 13:21) is compared to contemporary cigar-shaped UFOs. In the same way

Ezekiel's ascension (2 Kings 2) in a 'chariot of fire' is one of the biblical narratives most often quoted to document the existence of flying saucers in biblical times. In the New Testament, the appearance of the angels to the shepards at the birth of Jesus (Matt. 17:1–8), the scene described at the baptism of Jesus (e.g., Matt. 3:13–17), and his ascension in a cloud (Acts 2:9) are all similarly explained as UFO experiences.

This interpretation requires that biblical texts be read as trustworthy, historical narratives. From a scholarly point of view, however, incidents such as Ezekiel's ascension must be interpreted as myths, not as historical events. Using ufology as a hermeneutical principle for biblical interpretation, therefore, is no academic venture but an expression of religious creativity. Furthermore, although a few theologians have embarked down the ufological highway, this is not a popular approach among most Christians. Theological discussions regarding the possible existence of extraterrestrial beings is old and well known, but theological analyses of UFOs and flying saucers are unusual. One thus has to say that even though some links exist, traditional Christians (of whatever church or denomination) on the one hand, and ufologically interested groups on the other, are usually not in dialogue with one another.

Nevertheless, some Christian denominations, primarily within fundamentalist groups but also in the charismatic movement, have actually adopted a theological position on UFOs. These groups consider UFOs to be dangerous and negative. In several cases, UFOs are considered to be agents of Satan or outright satanic beings. They are here, it is said, to distort peoples' minds so that they may be confused when Christ returns. This notion places UFOs in the same eschatological scene where it is usually found but, in this case, in the role of a negative, destructive force. UFOs do not carry saviors. They are here to enslave us on behalf of Satan. They are not rejected as superstition or irrational absurdity. On the contrary, UFOs are interpreted according to Christian mythology, which portrays Satan as doing whatever he can to destroy God's plan of salvation. Along with his demons he will do whatever he can, in whatever disguise needed, to delude people.

This interpretation of UFOs is held within the limits of traditional Christian demonology and serves the same purpose as the positive evaluation of UFOs in other religions or religious groups; the belief system (in this case Christian) is confirmed. In this way UFO sightings and UFO reports may well urge members of these Christian groups to strengthen their hold on their own faith. Considering that UFOs are usually praised by people belonging to occult subpopulations that conservative Christian groups regard as satanic anyway, this pattern is not very surprising.

—*Mikael Rothstein*

See Also: Demonological Explanations of UFOs

Further Reading:
Peters, Ted. "Exo-theology: Speculations on Extraterrestrial Life." In *The Gods Have Landed: New Religions from Other Worlds.* Edited by James R. Lewis. Albany: State University of New York Press, 1995.
Saliba, John A. "Religious Dimensions of the UFO Phenomenon." In *The Gods Have Landed: New Religions From Other Worlds.* Edited by James R. Lewis. Albany: State University of New York Press, 1995.
Weldon, John, and Zola Lewitt, *UFOs: What on Earth Is Happening?* California: Harvest House, 1974.

CHUPACABRAS ("GOAT SUCKER")

The Goat Sucker phenomenon is one that encompasses a weird series of reports of mysterious animal deaths and sightings of strange beasts believed responsible for these deaths. The phenomenon began in Puerto Rico, but as Goat Sucker incidents died down there, new reports starting coming in from Mexico, Texas, and Florida.

The Puerto Ricans who found the first animal victims labeled the killer a *chupacabras,* or "goat sucker," and felt the deaths were connected to ancient native legends. Because Puerto Rico was the scene of a wave of UFO sightings before and during the time of the attacks, the two phenomena became associated, and at least some people were convinced that UFOs were the source of the Goat Suckers.

Puerto Rico has an extensive history of UFO sightings. Laguna Cartagena was the scene of many UFO sightings in 1990 and 1991. There were many sightings of triangular-shaped UFOs in

1994. On May 19, 1995, a witness saw a brilliantly lighted UFO fly over a Puerto Rican town. In Barranquites, many witnesses saw a huge, glowing disk with a row of windows hovering over a radio transmitter on November 18, 1995. Some of these witnesses saw several small, unidentified creatures during the sighting.

The first of the mysterious animal deaths was reported on March 11, 1995, when eight sheep were found with puncture marks in their chests. All were drained of blood. Fifteen days later, the first Chupacabras sighting occurred. A local man noticed a creature perched in a tree. He described the creature as having a rounded, hairless head, large slanted black eyes, thin, clawed hands, and a tail. The creature hissed at the man before leaping from the tree and running into heavy vegetation. The man reported feeling sleepy and faint afterward. On April 2, 1995, a large group of people saw a three-foot-tall grayish creature. One of the children was reported to have passed out after seeing the creature.

Descriptions of the Chupacabras have been gathered from many people. Although there are some similarities among all the reports, there are enough variations that it can be certain that the same creature was not seen in all cases. The creature is described as being three or four feet tall, with a pear-shaped body, described as similar to that of a kangaroo or a bipedal dinosaur. It has thin forearms ending in three-fingered hands with long claws. The hind legs are described as large and strong; the feet also have long claws. Some reports state that the creature has no tail. If a tail is mentioned, no description is given. The head is large and oval with large, slanted eyes. The eyes have been described variously as black, red, or glowing in the dark. The mouth is small, with long fangs protruding upward and downward. Some reports say that the creature has small, pointed ears, but others make no mention of ears. The creature is covered with hair, either entirely black or gray with black spots. Some have claimed that it can change color to blend in with the environment. There is a row of spines or quills from the head down to the middle of the back.

By August 1995 about 150 animals ranging from pet birds and chickens to cows and horses

had been found drained of blood. They had large, circular puncture marks on their haunches, necks, or the tops of their heads and an unknown viscous substance on their bodies. On November 1, 1995, a report was made to the police in Puerto Rico that a goat had been found with an eye missing and with a strange wound on the neck. There was no evidence of blood in the body, and it did not appear to have been attacked by dogs. In a separate incident that same day, the owner of a junkyard found all of his sheep and geese dead.

On November 2, 1995, a Puerto Rican woman told a reporter that her dog had been killed during the night. The woman's neighbor's two cats had also been found, drained of blood. On November 6, 1995, two Puerto Rican fishermen saw a horrible, devil-like creature with large ears, large, luminous eyes, large claws, and wings. The men fled along the shore and were pursued by the creature flying above the trees. Reaching a house, one of the men grabbed a machete. The creature landed on a hut, then jumped to the ground and ran into the woods, leaving deep footprints. On November 7 Victor Ortiz reported that the Chupacabras had killed a cat, injured two sheep, and eaten a lamb. This time there were no footprints, although there were signs of a fierce fight. During November and December 1995 the slaughter of animals was being reported almost daily by various media reporters. Puerto Rican authorities did nothing about the attacks, which continued to be reported through 1996.

In March 1996 40 animals in a rural area northwest of Miami, Florida, were killed. A woman in the area reported that she had seen a dog-like creature standing up, holding two short arms in the air. On May 10, 1996, there were more reports from Florida that the creature had been sighted or that pets had been attacked. A Goat Sucker attack was reported in southern Texas in May 1996 after a pet goat was killed with three puncture wounds in the neck. Although some thought these were the telltale signs of the beast and evidence that it had migrated into Texas, a local veterinarian thought that the goat had been bitten by a dog and that the bites had become infected.

In the spring of 1996 Chupacabras attacks began to be reported in Mexico. A farmworker in

Jalisco, Mexico, was treated in a local clinic after having been attacked and bitten by a creature three feet tall with a huge snout and dark, velvety skin. This was the first report of an attack on a human. Chupacabras reports became widespread throughout Mexico. On May 2, 1996, a Chupacabras sighting was reported in Juarez. It was described as looking like a kangaroo with a row of spikes from the top of its head to the small of its back. It had three-clawed hands and feet. Some witnesses claimed it had a tube that projected from the mouth that was the sucking device. On May 3, 1996, a giant batlike creature was reported to be terrorizing a village in northern Mexico. The blood-drained bodies of goats were being found daily. Farmers and livestock owners in the area were forming armed squads to patrol the area at night. Others were warned to stay inside at night to avoid being attacked.

Dead cows and sheep were found in Sinaloa, Mexico, in May 1996. A flying creature about one and a half feet tall was reported to have been seen in the area. Police in the area were reportedly confronted by a creature they described as having a humanlike face with red eyes. They opened fire on it, but it jumped a fence and disappeared. Several people in the Sinaloa area are reported to have survived Chupacabras attacks. They were engulfed by a shadowy figure and then lost consciousness. They were left with marks on their bodies that resembled large bullet holes. On May 12, 28 rams were found dead in Mexico, all with puncture marks on their bodies. A spokesman for the Mexican Department of Agriculture attributed the attacks to dogs or coyotes.

There are several theories concerning what the Goat Sucker is and where it came from. One theory is that the Goat Sucker is a product of highly sophisticated genetic manipulation by human agencies. Scientists have produced new hybrids of plants and animals via genetic engineering. An article in *UFO Universe* stated that American scientists had been experimenting in Puerto Rico for years, experiments that included thalidomide and contraceptive drugs that caused many birth defects. The genetic-engineering theory does explain why Goat Suckers did not appear until 1995, but there is no physical evidence to support the theory.

Another theory is that the Goat Sucker is a mutation of aliens. The close association of some of the Goat Sucker sightings and UFO reports is something that suggests this. A third theory is that Goat Suckers are primates that have escaped from a research center on Puerto Rico. There have been documented cases of rhesus monkeys escaping research facilities, but these monkeys are small and do not fit the descriptions of the Goat Suckers. Moreover, they are not carnivorous.

A newspaper suggested that the Goat Suckers were vampire bats that had arrived via cargo ships from South America. However, the descriptions of the Goat Suckers, again, do not suggest a bat. A common explanation by veterinarians and government officials for the animal deaths is wild dog attacks. Dogs, however, rip their prey apart to eat them, rather than sucking their blood. A final theory is that the Goat Sucker is a heretofore unknown natural creature whose habitat has been disturbed and has therefore come out into an area where it can be seen and reported by humans for the first time.

There is an additional possibility that the Goat Sucker is nothing more than urban legend; that many animals have died is the only factual evidence surrounding the Goat Sucker phenomenon. These animals could have died of many different causes, including disease, dog attack, and human attack.

—*Kay Holzinger*

See Also: Bigfoot; Cattle Mutilations; Mythology and
    Folklore
Further Reading:
Corrales, Scott. *Chupacabras and Other Mysteries.*
    Murfreesboro, TN: Greenleaf Publications, 1997.
———. *The Chupacabras Diaries: An Unofficial Chronicle
    of Puerto Rico's Paranormal Predator.* Derrick City, PA:
    Samizdat Press, 1996.
Lara Palmeros, Rafael A. "Chupacabras: Puerto Rico's
    Paranormal Predator." *INFO Journal* 76 (Autumn
    1996): 12–16, 18.

CLOSE ENCOUNTERS

In 1972 astronomer and ufologist J. Allen Hynek proposed a three-tiered classification system for UFO sightings, which has since become standard nomenclature. Objects or brilliant lights that ap-

Painting, by Michael Buhler, of Linda Napolitano (a.k.a. Cortile) being abducted from her New York apartment by aliens (Mary Evans Picture Library)

pear less than 500 feet away from witnesses, and which usually do not physically affect their environment, he called Close Encounters of the First Kind (CE1). The best examples involve multiple witnesses who sight objects genuinely hard to explain away in conventional terms.

Close Encounters of the Second Kind (CE2) were defined by Hynek as sightings in which a physical effect on either animate or inanimate matter is manifested. In theory, a CE2 should produce the most hard evidence that can be tested in the laboratory. This is not, however, always the case; because of the fringe nature of UFO research, investigators seldom possess proper scientific training or adequate funds. The most common CE2 effect is vehicle interference—cars stop, power goes off, and so on. Other effects include paralysis of the witness and traces of a ship's landing, such as singed grass or damaged trees. Occasionally, a CE2 encounter may produce physical illness or even death in the experiencer.

A Close Encounter of the Third Kind (CE3) is an encounter with the occupant of a UFO. In the early days of UFO research, some serious investigators ignored or minimized CE3s, fearing little-green-men–type ridicule from the mainstream press. But even as early as the 1950s, some ufologists maintained the importance of these encounters, usually preferring to concentrate on brief, frightening meetings, where the aliens, if they spoke at all, spoke unintelligibly. Today, of course, CE3s are at the center of UFO research. Not just encounters, but abductions, experiments, and even cross-species breeding are becoming more and more commonly reported experiences. Ufologists disagree whether these are actual events— literal, physical interactions with extraterrestrials—other kinds of paranormal experiences, or purely subjective experiences, arising from social and psychological factors.

Rather than referring to all face-to-face encounters as CE3s, some writers have introduced further differentiation within Hynek's last category so that abductions are designated Close Encounters of the Fourth Kind (CE4), to distinguish more or less friendly meetings from encounters in which aliens are said to intervene forcefully in the lives of human subjects. People have reported being captured, taken on board UFOs, and subjected to humiliating physical examinations. Alien-abduction narratives date back to the 1940s. They differ from the contactee cases, in which a person claims to have entered into a voluntary, friendly relationship with alien beings. Abductees usually describe their experiences in negative or fearful terms, at least at the outset. Some writers even take the close-encounter designation one step farther—Close Encounters of the Fifth Kind (CE5)—to refer to sexual encounters with aliens. Alternately, some researchers want to use the CE5 designation to refer to two-way communications between researchers and ufonauts.

UFO researchers Ted Bloecher and David Webb identify seven different categories of CE3s, including nonvisual contact with aliens (telepathy and the like) as well as CE3s that do not involve spacecraft at all. These latter are sometimes called "ground-level abductions" and might include encounters with Big Foot, mothmen, or the men in black—what John Keel has called "ultra-terrestrial" beings.

Four out of five CE3s involve humanoid aliens—usually little gray men, but some are reptilian or robotic. The nonhumanoid encounters, some would say, create the greatest plausibility problems. The French American ufologist Jacques Vallee was the first to observe that if one or two details were changed many CE3s would be indistinguishable from stories of fairies, little people, and demons from previous centuries.

—*Jerome Clark*

See Also: Abductees; Demonological Explanations of UFOs; Mythology and Folklore
Further Reading:
Bryan, C. D. B. *Close Encounters of the Fourth Kind: Alien Abduction, UFOs, and the Conference at M.I.T.* New York: Alfred A. Knopf, 1995.
Emenegger, Robert. *UFOs Past, Present, and Future.* New York: Ballantine Books, 1974.
Hall, Richard H., ed. *The UFO Evidence.* Washington, DC: National Investigations Committee on Aerial Phenomena, 1964.
Heard, Gerald. *The Riddle of the Flying Saucers: Is Another World Watching?* London: Carroll and Nicholson, 1950.
Rogo, D. Scott, ed. *UFO Abductions: True Cases of Alien Kidnappings.* New York: Signet, 1980.
Schwarz, Berthold E. *UFO-Dynamics: Psychiatric and Psychic Dimensions of the UFO Syndrome.* 2 vols. Moore Haven, FL: Rainbow Books, 1983.

CLOSE ENCOUNTERS OF THE THIRD KIND

This $22 million 1977 film made astronomer J. Allen Hynek's term a household word. The commercial and critical success of this movie put writer-director Steven Spielberg on the way to becoming the most popular film director of all time. The film follows three related stories: a man who witnessed a UFO and becomes obsessed with the encounter, a woman whose son was abducted by UFOs, and a scientist investigating worldwide reports of strange phenomena. At the end of the movie, they all converge at Devil's Tower in Wyoming to witness a huge spaceship land and

A UFO hovers over scientists, politicians, and bureaucrats near Devil's Tower National Monument in Wyoming in the 1977 film Close Encounters of the Third Kind *(The Del Valle Archive)*

small humanoids emerge. Except for the ending, the film is true to reported sightings. Some UFO skeptics thought the film's popularity would lead to a rise in UFO sightings, though that prediction failed to materialize.

Like certain other films such as *Fire in the Sky*—and, more recently, the TV program *X-Files*—*Close Encounters* drew its inspiration from existing UFO lore. At the same time, the success of the final production promoted broader interest in the phenomenon, helping to make UFOs less of a marginal and more of a mainstream phenomenon.

Columbia/EMI 1977; 135 min. Writer/Director: Steven Spielberg; Cinematography: Vilmos Zsigmond; Cast: Richard Dreyfuss, Teri Garr, Melinda Dillon, Francois Truffaut, Bob Balaban, Cary Guffey, J. Patrick McNamara.

COCOON

In director Ron Howard's 1985 film, four aliens in human guise have a mission to revive and rescue a group of aliens lying underwater in boulder-like cocoons off the Florida coast. They do so, storing the cocoons temporarily in the swimming pool of their rental house. Unbeknownst to them, three members of a nearby retirement home sneak onto the property regularly to swim. Swimming in the pool with the cocoons rejuvenates the three geezers to the extent that they take up such unlikely activities as break dancing. In the finale, some 30-odd members of the retirement home leave earth with the aliens.

A sequel—*Cocoon: The Return*—that came out three years later was not directed by Ron Howard. The old-timers who left earth with aliens at the end of that film return for a visit at the beginning of this one. The plot involves raising the remaining cocoons from the bottom of the ocean. No reviewer regards the sequel as being in the same league as the original.

The original movie was more focused on bringing attention to the state in which our culture leaves our elderly. Nevertheless, in terms of themes resonant with contemporaneous UFO lore, the film alludes to ancient-astronaut thinking when the chief alien tells the story of why the hibernating extraterrestrials became cocooned in the first place (a terrestrial station of aliens overtaken by

radical earth changes). The rejuvenation of the old people also seems to be a theme that reflects the numerous stories of human beings being healed by contact with aliens.

Original—Fox/Zanuck Brown Productions 1985; 117 min. Director: Ron Howard; Writer: Tom Benedek; Cinematography: Don Peterman; Music: James Horner; Cast: Wilford Brimley, Brian Dennehy, Steven Guttenberg, Don Ameche, Tahnee Welch, Jack Gilford, Hume Cronyn, Jessica Tandy, Gwen Verdon, Maureen Stapleton, Tyrone Power Jr., Barret Oliver, Linda Harrison, Herta Ware, Clint Howard.

Sequel: Fox 1988; 116 min. Director: Daniel Petrie, Writer: Stephen McPherson; Cinematography: Tak Fujimoto; Music: James Horner; Cast: Don Ameche, Wilford Brimely, Steve Guttenberg, Maureen Stapleton, Hume Cronyn, Jesseca Tandy, Gwen Verdon, Jack Gilford, Tahnee Welch, Courteney Cox, Brian Dennehy, Barret Oliver.

COLLECTIVE UNCONSCIOUS

Noted psychologist Carl Jung postulated a drive toward self-realization and self-integration that he referred to as the "individuation" process. The goal of this process was represented in images characterized by wholeness and completeness, such as circles. Jung referred to circles as "mandalas," a term originally reserved for circular meditation diagrams. According to Jung, mandala symbols emerge from the collective unconscious in dreams when the individual is seeking harmony and wholeness, which often occurs during periods of crisis and insecurity. Jung interpreted the phenomenon of flying saucers—which often appear in the form of circular disks—as mandala symbols, reflecting the human mind's desire for stability in a confused world.

The collective unconscious, an expression coined by Jung, refers to the storehouse of myths and symbols to which all human beings have access. Much of traditional Jungian analysis focuses on the interpretation of dreams. Jung found that the dreams of his clients frequently contained images with which they were completely unfamiliar but that seemed to reflect symbols that could be found somewhere in the mythological systems of world culture. The notion of the collective unconscious was used to explain this phenomenon.

Jung's unique contribution to modern psychology begins with the observation that the basic

Artist's impression of objects sighted in the sky near Nuremburg, 14 April 1561 (American Religion Collection)

structure of many symbols and myths is nearly universal, even between cultures that had no historical influence on one another. Most traditional societies, for example, tell hero myths, utilize circles to represent wholeness, the sky to symbolize transcendence, and so on. Jung theorized that this universality resulted from unconscious patterns (genetic or quasi-genetic predispositions to utilize certain symbolic and mythic structures) that we inherited from our distant ancestors. The reservoir of these patterns constitutes a collective unconscious, distinct from the individual, personal unconscious that is the focus of Freudian psychoanalysis.

Jung referred to unconscious, predisposing patterns for particular myths and symbols as "archetypes." Hence, one can talk about the mandala (i.e., the circle) archetype, the hero archetype (the latter made famous by the late Jungian thinker and myth expert Joseph Campbell), and so forth. Jung asserted that his notions of the collective unconscious and the archetypes were on par with the theory of instincts. In other words, one examines certain kinds of behaviors and theorizes that they are the results of certain biological drives, although it is, of course, impossible to directly observe such drives and instincts.

Jung's ideas have sometimes been invoked to explain certain experiences or certain cultural-historical facts that seem to indicate the existence of a spiritual dimension, such as conscious life after death. Thus, the fact that people report similar experiences during near-death experiences, for instance, can be explained in terms of universal symbols from the collective unconscious. Similarly, the fact that different cultures at different periods of time all report similar phenomena—from abduction by fairies and aliens to the appearance of circular objects in the sky—indicate that such phenomena reflect archetypal patterns in the human mind rather than constituting evidence that such entities really exist in the external world.

See Also: Archetype; Collective Unconscious; Mandala
Further Reading:
Hall, Calvin S., and Vernon A. Nordby. *A Primer on Jungian Psychology.* New York: New American Library, 1973.

Jung, Carl Gustav. *The Archetypes and the Collective Unconscious.* 2nd ed. Bollingen Series 20. Princeton: Princeton University Press, 1968.

Samuels, Andrew, Bani Shorter, and Fred Plaut. *A Critical Dictionary of Jungian Analysis.* London: Routledge and Kegan Paul, 1986.

COMMUNION

This is a 1989 film adaptation of the "nonfiction" book of the same name in which science fiction and fantasy writer Whitley Strieber comes to believe that during trauma-induced amnesiac fugues he was in contact with beings possibly from another world. In a final encounter, the hero discodances with the aliens.

Strieber's book *Communion* was a best-seller. The movie was less well received. Next to Budd Hopkins, Strieber has done more than any other single person to popularize the idea of alien abduction. *Communion* supposedly records his own abduction experience. Despite the claim that the narrative is nonfiction, it is difficult not to view *Communion* as a dramatization of the phenomenon, particularly considering Strieber's background as a science-fiction writer.

Phesantry Films 1989; 103 min. Director: Philippe Mora; Writer: Whitley Strieber; Music: Eric Clapton; Cast: Christopher Walken, Lindsay Crouse, Frances Sternhagan, Joel Carlson, Andreas Katsulas, Basil Hoffman, Terri Hanauer.

COMMUNION FOUNDATION

Whitley Strieber, author of *Communion: A True Story* and *Transformation: The Breakthrough,* founded the Communion Foundation in 1989 in response to his readers' fascination with abduction phenomena. Himself an "abductee," Strieber says the purpose of the foundation is to provide help and support for abductees and to generate funding for further research in abduction phenomena. One service the Communion Foundation provides is magnetic-resonance imaging for those who believe they have alien implants in their bodies. With a parallel interest in the contactee experi-

Christopher Walken starred as Whitley Strieber in the 1989 film adaptation of Strieber's book Communion. *(The Del Valle Archive)*

ence, the foundation takes a positive approach to alien abduction. This attitude is in direct contradiction to the general view held by ufologists and most abductees. Strieber blames the negative attitude of investigators, who, he says, are hostile to the benevolent "visitors" and try to scare abductees into thinking their experience was traumatic. He warns readers and members to avoid ufologists.

See Also: Abductees; Strieber, Whitley
Further Reading:
Strieber, Whitley. *Communion: A True Story.* New York: Beach Tree, 1987.
———. *Transformation: The Breakthrough.* New York: William Morrow, 1988.

CONDON COMMITTEE

By the late 1950s the U.S. Air Force was ready to shed itself of its UFO burden. Most Americans felt that the Air Force's Project Blue Book had lost credibility because its explanations of UFO sightings reflected a desire to "solve" reports at any cost. Some people felt that UFOs were a scientific problem and not a military problem and, therefore, an issue with which the Air Force should not be dealing. But the Air Force did not want a public backlash if it dropped Blue Book precipitously. The Air Force thus needed to find someone else to take to project off its hands. But no organization was interested in accepting the Air Force's offer of the UFOs.

On September 28, 1965, E. B. LeBailly, the Air Force director of information, essentially endorsed J. Allen Hynek's idea for Blue Book to assemble a panel of civilian scientists to take a fresh look at the problem. On February 3, 1966, six scientists met to discuss what the project should do about the UFO phenomenon. The scientists did not believe that the reports were actually caused by something as extraordinary as extraterrestrial spacecraft, and they thought something could be learned if selected sightings were investigated "in more detail and depth than has been possible to date." They urged the Air Force to work with a few selected universities to provide scientific teams to conduct UFO research.

The Air Force, however, had problems finding schools willing to dedicate time and manpower to

a subject as controversial as UFOs. Finally, the University of Colorado agreed to take on the project, under the direction of physicist Edward U. Condon. On October 6, 1966, the contracts with the Air Force were signed and the University of Colorado UFO Project, later called the Condon Committee, began. On November 11 Hynek and Jacques Vallee gave an extended briefing to Condon and his staff. They then adopted a rating system that would allow investigators to eliminate explainable sightings and examine only the extremely unusual. The general public saw the committee as a hard-working group searching for the truth. Unfortunately, there was a different agenda at the highest levels. Project coordinator Robert Low and Condon were extreme skeptics, and one of the members of the committee quit because he did not want to be involved in a "sham investigation."

After Condon's meager enthusiasm had been established publicly, members of the project who were still working diligently discovered that in the end, no matter what they had to report, Condon could put forward his personal opinions as if they were the project's conclusions—this despite the fact that Condon had not been involved in even one field investigation. Through all of this turmoil, the committee still plodded on with investigations.

After a confidential memo from Condon to Low surfaced that decried the uselessness of the project, Condon fired several of the best people from the committee. Condon also attempted to intimidate into silence or to discredit other individuals who had expressed criticism of his high-handed approach. For example, when Robert M. Wood, an aerospace engineer, wrote Condon a letter politely criticizing the project's weaknesses, Condon contacted McDonnell Douglas, Wood's employer, and attempted to persuade the chief executive officer to fire him. Condon's personal attitude was perhaps best expressed in a speech given before the April 1969 meeting of the American Philosophical Society in which he asserted that "publishers who publish or teachers who teach any of the pseudo-sciences [e.g., ufology] as established truth should, on being found guilty, be publicly horse-whipped, and forever banned from further activity in these usually honorable professions."

When the final report was released—announcing that all UFOs could be explained by ordinary means—it was assailed by critics who claimed that the results had, in effect, been rigged. Controversial aspects of Condon and Low's behavior during the life of the project, including the notorious memo, were presented as evidence that the investigation was seriously flawed. The report itself had many anomalies also, the most notable of which was that about 30 percent of all cases were left unexplained—yet Condon stated in the introduction to the report that there were no instances indicating anything but the most conventional explanations for UFOs. Throughout, the report states that the field investigators' own beliefs in the possibility that UFOs—in the sense of "mechanical devices of unknown origin"—could be the explanation for certain activities. Because the Condon report was so controversial, many people tried to start their own committees, hoping to be funded by the government. Unfortunately, the Condon Committee would be the last significantly funded UFO study. The controversy surrounding Condon's work also fed the conspiratorial view that the government was not interested investigating, but only in debunking, the UFO phenomenon.

See Also: Conspiracy Theories

Further Reading:

Brittin, Wesley E., Edward U. Condon, and Thurston E. Manning. *A Proposal to Air Force Office of Scientific Research for Support of Scientific Study of Unidentified Flying Objects.* Boulder: The Authors, November 1, 1966.

Craig, Roy. *UFOs: An Insider's View of the Official Quest for Evidence.* Denton: University of North Texas Press, 1995.

Hynek, J. Allen. *The UFO Experience: A Scientific Inquiry.* Chicago: Henry Regnery, 1972.

Jacobs, David M. *The UFO Controversy in America.* Bloomington: Indiana University Press, 1975.

Saunders, David R., and R. Roger Harkins. *UFOs? Yes! Where the Condon Committee Went Wrong.* New York: World Publishing, 1968.

CONEHEADS

This 1993 movie was a spin-off of *Saturday Night Live* sketches. The bald, pointy-headed aliens from Remulak explained their oddities to earthlings by asserting that they were French. In the movie, the aliens, Beldar and Prymaat, crash-land and must try to blend in with the terrestrials until they are rescued many years later—enough time elapses for them to have a baby who grows to teenhood on earth—by fellow Remulakians. Beldar is subsequently recruited to lead a campaign against terrestrials, but after so many years away from Remulak he and his family have adopted the earth as their home world. As a consequence, Beldar tricks the invasion force into calling off the attack and resettles among humankind with his family.

Reviewers tended to pan this movie. It is, however, an excellent big-screen adaptation of the original *Saturday Night Live* skits, and it certainly makes no pretense at being more than an entertaining comedy. In terms of the human-alien contact nexus, the general theme of the movie is the conversion of hostile aliens into friendlies via their adaptation to terrestrial culture—not unlike an interstellar *Shogun.* It might also be noted that there are other Hollywood productions in which extraterrestrials save the earth from fellow aliens (e.g., *Teenagers from Outer Space*), though, unlike *Coneheads,* the usual motivation for turning against their own kind is the development of an alien-human romance (a subtheme in *Coneheads,* in which the daughter is infatuated with an earthling). Beyond the ideas of alien infiltration and invasion, the film's principal theme of adaptation to and adoption of terrestrial culture has no real equivalent in UFO literature.

Paramount 1993; 86 min. Director: Steven Barron; Writers: Dan Aykroyd, Tom Davis, Bonnie Turner, Terry Turner; Cast: Dan Aykroyd, Jane Curtin, Laraine Newman, Jason Alexander, Michelle Burke, Chris Farley, Michael Richards, Lisa Jane Persky, Sinbad, Shishir Kurup, Michael McKean, Phil Hartman, David Spade, Dave Thomas, Jan Hooks, Chris Rock, Adam Sandler, Julia Sweeney, Danielle Aykroyd.

CONQUEST OF EARTH

This is the third of the *Battlestar Galactica* film series. The commander of Battlestar Galactica tries to make contact with a scientist and so prepare earth for an imminent Cylon attack while at the same time keeping earth's location a secret from the Cylons by destroying their probe before it can communicate with its base. This is an unexceptional film in the timeworn hostile-aliens-plan-to-invade-the-earth genre. This film is listed here only because this is one of the recurring themes found in certain forms of UFO literature.

Glenn A Larson/Universal 1980; 99 min. Directors: Sydney Hayers, Sigmund Neufeld Jr., Barry Crane; Writer: Glen A. Larson; Cinematography: Frank P. Beascoechea, Mario DiLeo, Ben Colman; Cast: Kent McCord, Barry Van Dyke, Robyn Douglass, Larne Greene, Patrick Stuart, Robbie Rist, Robert Reed, John Colicos.

CONSPIRACY THEORIES

As has been demonstrated in several studies, Americans have a historically conditioned propensity to gravitate toward conspiracy theories as a preferred explanatory mode. This tendency goes back at least as far as the American Revolution. Conspiracy theories are attractive because they can explain complex social structures and the problems generated by them in an oversimplified way that puts faces on otherwise impersonal processes. We have, of course, seen several genuine conspiracies, from the Tonkin Gulf incident to Watergate. The spectacle of these exposés has fueled other conspiracy theories by making them appear more plausible.

Conspiracy theories are rampant in the larger UFO community. Beyond the intrinsic ambiguity of UFOs, conspiracy theories seem more plausible in this arena because there actually does appear to be a conspiracy of silence surrounding what the government—or, at least, what the military and the intelligence agencies—know about the phenomenon. Widespread publicity about the Roswell incident has served to fuel such speculations. These rather plausible hypotheses contrast markedly with the wild conspiracy theories one finds at the fringes of the UFO subculture. The most extreme of these theories asserts that aliens have entered into a secret pact with the U.S. government, agreeing to provide the United States with advanced technology in exchange for unlimited access to U.S. citizens, whom aliens routinely abduct. An alternate school of UFO conspiracy thinking views such radical scenarios as the end product of a disinformation campaign conducted against the UFO community by U.S. intelligence agencies.

Cover of W. Mattern's UFO's Letzte Geheimwaffe des Dritten Reiches? *This Nazi sympathizer proposed that UFOs were manifestations of the Third Reich's secret weapons. (Mary Evans Picture Library)*

The history and development of UFO conspiracy theories are a tangled web. To citizens who paid more than casual attention to the UFO phenomenon, it was clear by the latter 1950s that the government was more interested in explaining away reported anomalous events than in conducting investigations of them. It was this debunking approach that provided fertile ground for conspiracy thinking. Beyond this generalization, it is difficult to select an initial event that led to later theories.

In the late 1970s a New Mexico businessman with a physics background, Paul Bennewitz, came to feel that he had picked up extraterrestrial electromagnetic signals used to manipulate abductees. He also filmed what he believed to be UFOs near Kirtland Air Force Base. Bennewitz contacted base officials, who, after several meetings, informed him that they had decided against considering the matter further.

In 1980 William L. Moore, coauthor of *The Roswell Incident,* was contacted by an individual who claimed to represent a group of 10 "insiders" opposed to continued government secrecy about UFOs. This individual, code-named "Falcon," informed Moore that a living extraterrestrial humanoid (referred to as an "extraterrestrial biological entity," or EBE) had been recovered from a flying saucer that had crashed two years after the well-known Roswell crash. The Air Force was eventually able to communicate with "EBE-1." This led, in turn, to projects conducted under the auspices of the National Security Agency, which electronically communicated with aliens. In April 1964 a UFO landed at Holloman Air Force Base. Moore was further informed that no less that nine alien races were exploring our planet. According to Falcon, the familiar "grays" had come from Zeta Reticuli 25,000 years ago to help shape human evolution.

Falcon noted that the government was closely following Bennewitz's activities and, further, had made him the target of a disinformation campaign. Moore would later be brought into this campaign. Building on his existing suspicions, Bennewitz was informed, among other things, that the government and evil extraterrestrials had entered into agreement to take over the planet. Furthermore, the aliens were mutilating and slaying people as well as cattle, utilizing the organs for the purpose of revitalizing and lengthening their lives—they were even said to be eating human flesh. Human and extraterrestrial scientists were working together in underground laboratories, creating androids and engaging in inhumane experiments on people and animals. Aliens were also abducting human beings in massive numbers for the purpose of installing mind-control devices. Bennewitz believed these wild allegations, tried to warn others, and was eventually hospitalized.

The Falcon also informed Moore and others that he was aware of at least two UFO crashes beyond the Roswell incident in which bodies had been found. As part of an agreement established between the EBEs and the government, aliens can mutilate cattle and are permitted to land at a particular base. In exchange, the United States re-

ceives advanced technological information. Falcon also asserted that the entertainment media were being used to prepare the public for the idea of contact with friendly aliens.

In 1983 Linda Moulton Howe, the Denver-based producer of the documentary "Strange Harvest" and the most prominent person investigating the UFO angle on cattle mutilations, was put in contact with Sergeant Richard Doty (a.k.a. "Falcon") in connection with a UFO special she was developing for HBO. Flying to Albuquerque on April 9, she eventually met with Doty, who, after taking her to a building at Kirkland Air Force Base, stated that "my superiors have asked me to show you this," then handed her a few sheets of paper containing instructions that she could read them in his presence but not take them or make copies. The document, entitled "A Briefing Paper for the President of the United States on the Subject of Unidentified Flying Vehicles," did not specify the date it was prepared, the agency that prepared it, or the president for whom it was presumably written.

The briefing paper discussed various UFO crashes—the familiar Roswell crash and others in Kingman, Arizona, and Aztec, New Mexico. The occupants were invariably the classic short "grays" familiar from abduction literature. They were described as beings from another solar system that had been coming to the earth for thousands of years. The human race was the outcome of their genetic experiments. Elsewhere, other aliens, referred to as "Talls," were mentioned.

The paper also mentioned some highly classified projects that dealt with recovered crash materials and ongoing communications efforts, including Snowbird (reverse engineering of a spacecraft aliens had given to the military), Aquarius (coordinating research and contact efforts), Sigma (the effort to communicate with extraterrestrials), and Garnet (aimed at assessing the alien impact on human evolution). The aliens were also said to have been responsible for human religious beliefs, with one paragraph noting, "Two thousand years ago extraterrestrials created a being" that was sent to earth to teach peace and love.

Among other revelations congruent with existing UFO conspiracy theories, the briefing paper

*The U.S. government's ongoing secretiveness about UFO-related information has contributed to the development of UFO conspiracy theories. (*Research Newsletter*)*

asserted that Project Blue Book (set up by the Air Force to investigate UFO reports) had been initiated for the sole purpose of diverting public attention away from what was really happening. Doty also informed Howe that "MJ-12" (Majestic 12) referred to a board composed of intelligence officials, scientists, and military officials who ultimately decided policy regarding the extraterrestrial project. In the end, Doty promised to supply Howe with films of the crashes, of extraterrestrial corpses, and of the first official meeting between military officers and the aliens for her to use in her documentary. Doty also indicated that Howe might be allowed to interview an alien.

Howe was naturally excited and informed HBO about the unexpected development. Almost immediately, however, delays began cropping up. HBO, for instance, asked Howe to supply it with a legally binding letter of intent from the government to release the film footage. When Howe contacted Doty, he responded, "I'll work on it." HBO also informed Howe that it would not authorize the funds without the evidence in hand. Blocked in both directions, Howe waited. Gradually, her ongoing contact with the military decreased (Doty

called her to say that he had been taken off the project) until her contract with HBO expired in October. She continued to be contacted with more news of delays, though by then she had for all intents and purposes dropped the matter.

In 1989 Moore "revealed" that Howe had been the target of an elaborate intelligence campaign designed to discredit her and to spread disinformation to the larger UFO community. The military was said to have feared that Howe would include Bennewitz's information about his having intercepted low-frequency electromagnetic emissions from around the Kirkland complex in her film. As a consequence, a sting operation was supposedly set in motion to drive a wedge between Howe and HBO.

It was in the midst of Moore's ongoing contact with Doty and others that Moore's associate, Jaime Shandera, received a roll of 35mm film containing the Majestic 12 document. The document was sent anonymously. Dated November 18, 1952, MJ-12 appears to be a top-secret briefing on findings from the Roswell crash for President Dwight Eisenhower. Shandera and Moore released it to the public three years later. MJ-12 set off a heated debate over its authenticity that has not completely died down to this day. To some, the MJ-12 document looked like another disinformation scheme.

In 1988 Moore provided two of his sources, including "Falcon," for "UFO Cover-up . . . Live," a two-hour program that aired in October 1988. Subsequently judged a laughable embarrassment, the two informants, their faces shaded, asserted that the EBEs liked traditional Tibetan music and strawberry ice cream.

Meanwhile, the least reputable conspiracy theories—those supposedly derived from government disinformation—had begun to take hold within the UFO community. John Lear, a pilot with a CIA background, began claiming that certain unnamed sources were supplying him with information that made the Doty-related data tame by comparison.

In addition to the usual information about flying-saucer crashes and reverse engineering being conducted at Area 51, Lear claimed that a secret government agency beyond the knowledge and control of even the U.S. president had entered into an agreement with EBEs to receive alien technology in exchange for limited permission to kidnap citizens, with the provision that the extraterrestrials supply the agency with a list of abductees. In 1973, however, the agency supposedly discovered that thousands of individuals were being kidnapped who were not on the list. Tensions arising from this discovery led to a confrontation in the late 1970s in which several scientists and Delta Force soldiers were said to have been slain.

Since then the military has frantically been searching for a way to counter the aliens, while the aliens progressively place mind-control transplants in their human abductees. Lear also recounted the familiar tales about aliens utilizing organs from human beings and cattle for experimentation and for the purpose of revitalizing and lengthening their lives. It is clear that one of Lear's most important sources was Bennewitz.

Lear went further than Bennewitz by linking earlier UFO conspiracy thinking to political conspiracy theories associated with the extreme right. In Lear's conspiratorial vision, an evil secret government was trying to utilize EBEs and

their technology to control the world. Lear was also receiving information from physicist Robert Lazar. In a story by George Knapp that aired November 11 and 13, 1989, on the ABC-TV affiliate in Las Vegas, Lazar claimed to have worked on alien-related technology at Area 51. Lazar's story seemed to support at least some of Lear's basic story.

The next step in this rapidly expanding UFO conspiracy theory was supplied by Milton William Cooper, who in late 1988 began sharing information he had supposedly picked up as a U.S. Navy petty officer on a computer network devoted to anomalous phenomena. Cooper claimed to have seen two documents that basically set forth the same litany about Roswell, Area 51, secret government agreements, and so forth that were already familiar to the UFO community. Cooper, however, went several steps beyond the existing conspiracy theory on May 23, 1989, when he produced his 25-page "The Secret Government: The Origin, Identity and Purpose of MJ-12," which he presented as a lecture a few weeks later.

According to Cooper, President Harry Truman, afraid of an alien invasion, established ongoing contacts with the other nations of the world but hid what was going on from ordinary citizens. To facilitate international cooperation, the Bilderbergers, a secret society centered in Switzerland, was established. It quickly became the world's so-called secret government. Meanwhile, there were innumerable UFO crashes of more than one extraterrestrial race, with whom the secret government entered into agreements.

A race of large-nosed grays from a planet orbiting Betelgeuse sporting trilateral insignia on their uniforms entered into a formal treaty with President Eisenhower. Tying in UFO conspiracy theories with certain right-wing conspiracy notions, the emblem of the Trilateral Commission is taken directly from the alien flag. One part of the treaty was the by now standard provision that aliens could abduct human beings as they saw fit. The government would conceal the alien presence. In exchange, the aliens would provide advanced technological knowledge. Also, humans and extraterrestrials would jointly operate secret underground bases in the U.S. Southwest.

In congruence with the scenarios of previous UFO conspiracy theories, officials soon learned that the extraterrestrials were abducting far more people than had been agreed and were not returning all of them. They also mutilated and even killed animals and humans. Furthermore, they were in cahoots with the communists and seeking to control American society via religions, witchcraft, and occultism. In response, Eisenhower established the "Jason Society," composed of 35 people, to respond to the alien threat. Cooper claimed that in 1969 a conflict erupted in one of the hidden laboratories, resulting in the hostage-taking of scientists and the deaths of several soldiers who attempted to free them. The alliance was reestablished two years later.

The United States and the Soviets jointly reached a decision that they would begin to control the population by wiping out "undesirables." Diseases like AIDS were introduced. To raise funds, the CIA became involved in selling drugs. This venture was so successful that today the CIA controls all of the drug markets in the world. A hidden Soviet-American-alien base is located on the other side of the Moon. Plugging in to the most popular U.S. conspiracy topic of all time, Cooper claimed that President John F. Kennedy was assassinated because he demanded that MJ-12 stop selling drugs and because he was going to tell the public about the extraterrestrials. Kennedy was supposedly assassinated by a Secret Service agent.

At present, an invisible empire run by the intelligence agencies peddles drugs and promotes street crime as a way of encouraging antigun legislation. Furthermore, via CIA mind control, mentally imbalanced people are directed to massacre children and others in order to push public opinion in the direction of supporting extreme gun-control legislation. Using its control over the mass media, the secret government is influencing the general public so that it will eventually accept martial law. At that point, citizens will be rounded up and sent as slave labor to the colonies on Mars and the Moon.

By the fall of 1989 Cooper was on the lecture circuit, relating his wild tales to crowds eager to have their wits scared out of them. Lear and others did likewise. More mainstream ufologists, who normally expected some craziness on the fringes of the UFO community, became alarmed when Cooper and Lear began attracting media attention. Such outlandish conspiracy stories went well beyond the "high weirdness" of even the abduction literature and tended to discredit "serious" ufology.

As ufologists sought to distance themselves from the conspiratologists, the community was rocked by the revelation that Moore had been intimately involved in promulgating disinformation. On July 1, 1989, Moore gave a lecture at the Mutual UFO Network (MUFON) meeting in Las Vegas in which he confessed, among other things, to providing false information to Bennewitz that fed the paranoia of this already distressed individual. Moore had become involved in hopes of being allowed access to the "real" data about what the government knew about UFOs.

Moore further shocked the audience by noting a series of ufologists "who were the subject of intelligence community interest between 1980 and 1984." Dennis Stacy, editor of *MUFON UFO Journal,* would later write, "A couple of people even stumbled out of the lecture hall, gripped by a combination of shock, anguish and tears." In the following months Moore's behavior was blasted as outrageous by many of his former colleagues.

Although some members of the UFO community were ready to declare Moore's lecture a watershed, marking the end of the most extreme conspiracy theories, it is clear that such notions will not simply evaporate. Conspiracy theories are almost by definition immune to falsification. In the case at hand, it is far too easy for conspiratorialists simply to dismiss Moore's public confession as yet another, more subtle form of government dissimulation and to continue walking down the road with their worldview intact.

—*Jerome Clark*

See Also: Area 51; Cattle Mutilations; Condon Committee; Hanger 18; Majestic 12; The Roswell Incident
Further Reading:
Avery, Michael. *UFOs: Opposing Viewpoints.* San Diego: Greenhaven Press, 1989.
Barker, Gray. *They Knew Too Much about Flying Saucers.* New York: University Books, 1956.
Bartholomew, Robert E. *Ufolore: A Social Psychological Study of a Modern Myth in the Making.* Stone Mountain, GA: Arcturus Book Service, 1989.

Billig, Otto. *Flying Saucers—Magic in the Sky: A Psychohistory.* Cambridge: Schenkman, 1982.

Clark, Jerome. *The UFO Encyclopedia.* 3 vols. Detroit: Omnigraphics, 1990, 1992, 1996.

Cohen, Daniel. *Myths of the Space Age.* New York: Dodd, Mead, 1977.

Hall, Richard. *Uninvited Guests.* Santa Fe, NM: Aurora Press, 1988.

Hamilton, William. *Cosmic Top Secret.* New Brunswick: Inner Light Publications, 1991.

Jung, Carl Gustav. *Flying Saucers: A Modern Myth of Things Seen in the Sky.* Princeton: Princeton University Press, 1978.

Randle, Kevin D. *The Randle Report: UFOs in the 1990s.* New York: M. Evans, 1997.

Randles, Jenny, and Peter Hough. *The Complete Book of UFOs: An Investigation into Alien Contacts and Encounters.* New York: Sterling, 1996.

Schwarz, Berthold Eric. *UFO Dynamics: Psychiatric and Psychic Dimensions of the UFO Syndrome.* 2 vols. Moore Haven, FL: Rainbooks, 1983.

CONTACT

This 1997 film, based on a novel by scientist Carl Sagan, is, as the title suggests, about first contact between humanity and extraterrestrials. Sagan, an archdebunker of UFOs and anything suggestive of the paranormal, was, perhaps paradoxically, enthusiastic about the SETI project. In the movie adaptation of his book, Jodi Foster plays a SETI scientist who—in the face of underfunding and the specter of professional ostracism—succeeds in receiving the first message from another planet.

What comes through is a reflected broadcast of one of the earliest TV broadcasts from earth—the 1936 Olympic Games held in Hitler's Germany—along with instructions for building a giant piece of alien technology that seems to open a doorway to a distant world. After a failed start and other misadventures involving religion Foster makes an unusual, dreamlike voyage to another world. Upon her return, she is unable to "prove" that she has successfully traveled to the stars and back and ends up defending her experience in language that sounds remarkably similar to religious language.

1997; 150 min. Director: Robert Zemeckis; Writers: James V. Hart and and Michael Goldenberg; Cast: Jodi Foster, Matthew McConaughey, James Woods, John Hurt, Tom Skerritt, William Fichtner, Angela Bassett, Rob Lowe.

CONTACTEES

Some UFO narratives are more elusive than others. The stories told by the so-called contactees belong to one of the more unambiguous trails of ufology. This does not mean that the UFO prophets who came to bear this designation provide an easily overlooked field. On the contrary, what it means simply is that the basic notions and the average ideology of these characters are quite similar and that their claims are rather robust and therefore easier to handle than more ambiguous ufological notions.

Modern tales of human encounters with benevolent, superhuman beings from other worlds belong to the oldest traditions. Judaism, Christianity, and Islam, for instance, all tell of human interaction with angels. Also, in theosophy, which encompasses Hindu, Buddhist, as well as older European occult and metaphysical traditions, direct contact with spiritually advanced Masters is essential. Persons who have claimed close encounters with space people in the years following World War II operated within these traditions. These individuals emerged during the early 1950s and soon became central figures in the evolving UFO movement. Some of the more prominent were Truman Bethurum (1898–1969), Daniel Fry (b. 1908), George Van Tassel (1910–1978), Howard Menger (b. 1922), and Orfeo Angelucci (b. 1912), not to forget the mentor of them all—George Adamski. But many more were probably active, and some have never come to the attention of scholars or the public. Today only a few traditional contactees operate with the same enthusiasm as ever, some with a deliberate religious claim, others with a more secular position. One such contactee of some fame (or notoriety) is Eduard Maier of Switzerland. Contemporary religiously inclined contactees were George King of the Aetherius Society, who died in 1997, and Ruth Norman of Unarius, who died in 1993.

The basic components of the contactee narrative are the following: Contactees usually describe how a strange telepathic message or a peculiar intuition made them visit an isolated location and how flying saucers would then land nearby. The ufonauts that emerge are described as human beings, but not of an ordinary kind. Rather, they are

Rael (Claude Vorilhon), founder of the Raelian Movement, claims contact with extraterrestrials. Here he stands in front of the scale model of the Embassy of the Elohim. (Raelian Movement)

extraordinarily beautiful in physical appearance as well as in mentality. They are usually Caucasian, blond, tall, often wearing shoulder-length hair. They are dressed in jumpsuits, although other kinds of clothing are sometimes described. The occupants may come from Venus, Mars, Jupiter, Saturn, or the Moon, but more distant stars may also be mentioned as their home. Basically, it is believed that human beings such as those that inhabit the earth live in many different places in the universe, but their spiritual and technological level of development is very different. People on earth are seen as rather primitive, whereas those paying visits are of a superior standing. They preach a gospel of love, peace, and responsibility and urge humans on earth to focus on spiritual development. They are often representatives of interplanetary associations, and it is the obligation of the contactee to motivate or prepare the people of earth to join these universal congregations. First, however, the inhabitants of earth need to evolve, to reach for higher spiritual levels of living and understanding.

Contactees owe much to theosophy. The Space Brothers of contactee narratives, for instance, have the same features and preach the same ideology as the Mahatmas of theosophical lore. The role of the contactee also resembles the role of the theosophical leaders; in traditional theosophy only a chosen few would receive messages from the Adepts, and it would be these individuals' obligation to pass on to others what they had learned. Further, theosophical leaders would serve as preachers themselves and guard the Mahatmas' message on a daily basis, just as the contactees would undertake the responsibility for spreading the Space Brothers' message. Concepts such as Cosmic Wisdom, which are characteristic of theosophy, are also very common in contactee literature. The traditional ways of theosophical beliefs have, through ufology, been translated into a modernized version.

It is almost impossible to distinguish contactees from other kinds of prophets, visionaries, and seers. However, the very term "contactee" signifies that the individual's function is as a mediator between what is human, and what is superior to humanity is what really counts. With this focus, "charisma" does not relate to the individual but rather to the office held by him or her. The contactee is not primarily a preacher but a prophet who works on behalf of superhuman entities, or at least considers his actions inspired by them. Indeed, contactees may be viewed as equivalents of the Judeo-Christian tradition's prophets and understood within the larger context of the so-called prophet pattern. Contactees may also be understood in terms of other religious types. There are, for instance, elements that resemble shamanism in many of the contactees' claims. The shaman travels to the land of the spirits, where he or she obtains power or knowledge, brings it back, and uses it to improve, heal, or develop conditions in the land of the living. Similarly, many of the contactees travel to distant worlds, either in terms of a "journey in the spirit" or aboard a flying saucer, where they behold all kinds of marvels, returning wiser and full of inspiration. Contactees may also be perceived as modern equivalents to spiritualist mediums. Contrary to what is occasionally supposed, contactees cannot be regarded as mystics.

The contactee movement was born on November 20, 1952, when George Adamski had his first encounter with a man from another world: Along with six companions, Adamski drove to the California desert hoping to see a flying saucer and perhaps even communicate with its passengers. Adamski had seen strange crafts in the sky before; among other things, he claimed that in August 1947 he had seen 184 saucers flying in formation high above him. Soon the small group in the California desert saw a large, cigar-shaped craft rising from behind a mountain, followed by another craft that suddenly appeared in the sky. At this point Adamski left the group and set off alone by foot. Shortly, Adamski saw someone waving to him at a considerable distance. He walked closer and realized that he was in the presence of a man from space—"a human being from another world." The man, who laid the foundation for the appearance of the typical Space Brothers described above, was about five feet, six inches tall, weighed about 135 pounds, and appeared to be in his late twenties.

This incident was published in Adamski's bestseller of 1953, *Flying Saucers Have Landed,* and was referred to, along with later contacts, in two subsequent volumes. People soon gathered around

him, believing his story to be true. On behalf of the
Space Brothers, as he referred to the visitors, he
taught that people on earth should turn away from
their warlike ways; in particular, all experiments
with nuclear testing should be abandoned. This
was new—as were nuclear weapons themselves—
but the rest of Adamski's teaching was easily recognizable. In fact, most of what he said, including
his metaphysical teachings and recollections of
meetings with people on other planets, had been
with him for a long time prior to his arrival on the
flying-saucer scene. In the words of scholar of new
religions, J. Gordon Melton, "George Adamski,
teacher of cosmic philosophy . . . developed an interest in the occult and first emerged into public
light, when he founded the Royal Order of Tibet
through which he taught a course in the mastery
of life."

Further, Melton notes, ufologist and editor Ray
Palmer (1910–1977) claimed that Adamski's account of meeting a Venusian had been submitted
to him by Adamski in 1944 as a science-fiction
story—some eight years prior to the alleged encounter in the desert. Strange hieroglyphs that
Adamski claimed to have seen aboard a spacecraft
later turned out to be copied from an obscure anthropological work, his alleged photographs of
spaceships were exposed as frauds, and, finally, in
1963 it was revealed how Adamski had re-edited
his Royal Order of Tibet material to make it appear
as if his lessons had come from the Space Brothers. This seems to confirm that theosophy formed
the starting point as well as the core element in
Adamski's UFO-related teachings and that science
fiction also had an impact. The Royal Order of
Tibet was, not surprisingly, in the theosophical
tradition.

Despite the fact that Adamski's claims were less
than accurate, he gained a following that has lasted
to this day, initially through his organization, the International Get Acquainted Program, which
Adamski set up in 1958, and later in the George
Adamski Foundation (GAF) International/Adamski
Foundation formed in 1965. Groups of devoted followers deny all allegations of fraud, and the notion
of benevolent Venusians, Saturnians, and Martians
is still alive. Concluding an article on Adamski,
UFO-movement historian Jerome Clark writes: "In

the end, however, the amount of disconfirming evidence must be judged so overwhelming as to require a leap of faith to see Adamski as a truthful,
even if misguided, teller of interplanetary tales."

Adamski set the stage for a long line of contactees. A simple listing shows that the classical
contactee stories by his successors were published
between 1953 and 1959. In this connection it is interesting to note that the first published account in
1953 recalls an alleged incident from the year before, whereas the stories published by other contactees *after* Adamski's first book had appeared
(apart from King) would recall incidents *prior* to
Adamski's alleged experience. In short: Almost
every contactee tried to see himself as the "first" or
as the "original." Similarly, most new religions will
argue that they are based on primordial revelations, that they represent an original message or
an original knowledge.

Urging earth people to abandon their path of
nuclear war and conflicts, the Space Brothers of the
1950s said what everybody on earth dreamed of
but was unable to do anything about. In this sense,
the Space Brothers may be interpreted as figments
of the Cold War imagination, entering the scene
just as the inhabitants of earth were planning their
self-destruction. Several contactees related how
their space friends had told of previous disasters
brought about due to humans' poor knowledge and
understanding, thereby providing a mythological
basis for their ideal of cosmic peace and spiritual
development. George King, for instance, published
such a tale of destruction, the Maldek myth, in
1963, shortly after the 1962 climax of the confrontation between the United States and Soviet
Union (the Cuban missile crisis). The dualism described in the myth (the confrontation between the
White and the Black magicians) may well reflect
that conflict—indeed, the great terror of those
days—was fear of the atomic bomb. Further, during 1954–1955, when King began his mission, the
Cold War was building up, and the world had recently witnessed a terrible war. The historical conditions for evoking peace-loving Cosmic Masters
could hardly have been better. Adamski's different
narratives are of the same kind.

The wise Space Brothers would always emphasize the need for peace and loving compassion to-

ward other people. In one of his descriptions, Adamski tells of how a Master, during a confidential talk on board a huge mothership in orbit around earth, explained to him why the Space Brothers were so worried about the wars and "explosions" on earth. One reason is simple concern for the people of earth, but the whole cosmic balance may be disrupted should radiation and other lethal emissions escape earth's gravity. If this should happen, most of the earth's population would instantly vanish, the soil would loose its fertility, and the waters would become polluted. But the planet itself would also be in great danger. There are reasons to believe, said the Master, that earth, under such circumstances, would be in danger of loosing "its balance in our Milky Way." War, and especially nuclear explosions, were envisioned as the threat above all other threats. Not only did the contactees come up with a solution to the flying saucer enigma; they also added an ideological dimension to the alleged phenomenon that would address many peoples' emotional needs. Adamski dedicated his book, *Inside the Space Ships,* to "A better World," and George King would explain that his work was all in the service of mankind in order to prevent devastating catastrophes.

The stories told by the contactees have often been ridiculed. Today, some 50 years after the emergence of these characters, it is easy to dispute many of their claims on a rational basis: The contactees' descriptions of cities on the Moon, agriculture on Venus, bureaucracy on Mars, and sports and typical ways of relaxation among Saturnians appeal to few people today. Similarly, most people find it hard to accept that contactee Truman Bethurum carried a camera during several of his meetings with the space woman, Aura Rahnes from planet Clarion, but that he either forgot to use it, was short of film, or avoided taking pictures because he was asked not to do so by the space people. Similarly, most people find it strange to learn that Adamski's camera was unable to take sharp pictures because of "magnetism," although the technically advanced Venusians, Martians, and Saturnians he met with did their best to help him improve his camera. At the time of their emergence, though, such claims were not as naive as they seem today. Several of the contactees gathered

enthusiastic followings, and new dimensions were added to the UFO milieu.

The contactees claimed to be messengers for people from other planets, but it is worthwhile to see them as producers of messages themselves who simply chose the myth of the flying saucer as a way of expressing their personal hopes and desires or whatever motif they may have had. In any case, the UFO was chosen as the central feature because this particular symbol had become popular at that time. In fact, it is possible that the spaceship myth, which was popularized by the early contactees, was formed as some kind of unconscious response to the great confusion that surrounded the "flying saucers" of the day. In 1947 people had a hard time understanding what flying saucers were, but, thanks to the contactees, this question was solved: Flying saucers were spaceships, and their purpose for coming to earth was evident, as the occupants themselves had explained their motives. Since the days of the classic contactees, the UFO myth has disseminated into modern popular religion in many other ways. It is possible, however, to see the current "channeling" movement as the direct modern successor to the original contactees.

Modern channelers have much in common with spiritualists of past centuries. Contrary to spiritualism, however, channeling is not focused on contacting the spirits of deceased people. Rather, modern channelers serve as media between people on earth and highly developed beings of other realms. Sometimes such beings are highly evolved souls, guardian angels, or discarnate beings from mythological worlds such as Lemuria or Atlantis, but frequently the beings that manifest themselves through their earthly mediums are from distant planets or stars. As in the case of traditional contactees, groups of devotees gather around such individuals. The emphasis is always on the entity that reveals itself through the medium, but in fact the mediums themselves also very often end up as subjects of devotion. The channeling movement is clearly inspired by a broader New Age ideology, but at the same time it is easy to detect a development that owes much to traditional contactees. The important difference, of course, is that the channelers have escaped the problem of proving the nuts-and-bolts claims of the contactees of the 1950s. They never meet their space companions in physical form but restrict the communication to a mediumistic trance that places the ideological or religious claim within the same realm as most religious systems. In this sense, the contactees have turned the contactee experience inward and put an emphasis on introspective experience rather than encounters via the ordinary senses.

—*Mikael Rothstein*

See Also: Adamski, George; New Age; Space Brothers; Theosophy

Further Reading:

Adamski, George. *Inside the Space Ships.* New York: Abelard-Schuman, 1955.

Adamski, George, and Desmond Leslie. *Flying Saucers Have Landed.* New York: British Book Centre, 1953; London: Werner Laurie, 1953.

Angelucci, Orfeo. *The Secret of the Saucers.* Amherst, WI: Amherst Press, 1955.

Bethurum, Truman. *Aboard a Flying Saucer.* Los Angeles: DeVorss, 1954.

Clark, Jerome. *The UFO Encyclopedia.* 2nd ed. Detroit: Omnigraphics, 1988.

Evans, Hilary. *Gods, Spirits, and Cosmic Guardians: A Comparative Study of the Encounter Experience.* Wellingborough, U.K.: Aquarian Press, 1987.

———. *Visions, Apparitions, Alien Visitors.* Wellingborough, U.K.: Aquarian Press, 1984.

Gibbons, Gavin. *They Rode in Space Ships.* London: Neville Spearman, 1957.

King, George. *Life on the Planets.* Hollywood, CA: Aetherius Society, 1958

Melton, J. Gordon, and George M. Eberhart, eds. *The Flying Saucer Contactee Movement, 1950–1990.* Santa Barbara, CA: Santa Barbara Centre for Humanistic Studies, 1990.

Vallee, Jacques. *Messengers of Deception: UFO Contacts and Cults.* Berkeley: And/Or Press, 1979.

COSMIC CIRCLE OF FELLOWSHIP

The Cosmic Circle of Fellowship was formed in Chicago in 1954 by William A. Ferguson. Ferguson was a mail carrier who learned the techniques of absolute relaxation and became adept at relaxing his body, mind, and conscious spirit. In 1937 Ferguson wrote *Relax First* and then began to teach relaxation techniques to others.

On July 9, 1938, while lying in a state of absolute relaxation, Ferguson's body was charged with energy and carried away to the seventh dimension. He stayed there two hours, and his soul became illuminated. When he returned to normal waking consciousness, he found that his physical body was no longer where he had left it, and he could not be seen or heard by his wife and his friend. He placed his noncorporal being back where his body and been and soon regained physical three-dimensional form.

One week later Ferguson was carried away to the center of all creation and experienced the sixth dimension. He saw creation in action: Rays of pure intelligent energy of all forms and colors were flowing throughout a cube of pure universal substance. In the 1940s Ferguson began to gather a group primarily related to cosmic-healing techniques, especially the "clarified water device" taught to Ferguson by Khauga (his tour guide). This device, thought to impart healing properties to water, got Ferguson in trouble with the American Medical Association. In 1947 Ferguson was convicted of fraud in relation to the clarified water device and served a year in prison.

Also in 1947, the being named Khauga (also identified as the Spirit of Truth, the angel who gave the Book of Revelation to St. John, and a perfected being from the Holy Triune) took Ferguson on a trip to Mars. Upon Ferguson's return, family and friends could not see or hear him until he went into the next room, lay on a cot, and was rematerialized. He delivered a message that the Martians were sending an expedition to earth. Within a few months many UFOs were reported, and several people claimed to have made personal contacts with their inhabitants.

In 1954 Ferguson was taken aboard a Venusian spacecraft, where he learned that spacecraft normally function in four dimensions and are therefore invisible to us, but they can also function in three dimensions. When they disappear suddenly, they have merely changed back into the fourth dimension. Ferguson joined with Edward A. Surine and Edna I. Valverde and in 1954 formed the Cosmic Circle of Fellowship. The group incorporated in the state of Illinois in 1955. In 1958 Ferguson started traveling around the country, founding Circles in other cities, including Washington, Philadelphia, New York, and San Francisco.

The doctrine of the Cosmic Circle of Fellowship holds that the Father of Creation is pure intelligent energy and that the Mother of Creation is pure universal substance. Creation occurs as the rays of life of the Father impregnate the substance of the Mother. Khauga is revered as the Comforter and the leader of the Universal Brotherhood of the Sons of the Father, members of which are drawn from the various solar systems. The Universal Brotherhood is preparing earth for the Second Coming of Jesus. Members believe that as the New Age comes in, materialism and evil will be overthrown and man will be lifted into fourth-dimensional consciousness. Ferguson's relaxation techniques remain the major way to consciousness-expansion. Since Ferguson's death in 1967 the Chicago group has continued to publish his writings

See Also: Astral Projection and UFOs; Contactees; Religions, UFO; Space Brothers
Further Reading:
The Comforter Speaks. Potomac, MD: Cosmic Study Center, 1977.
Ferguson, William. A Message From Outer Space. Oak Park, IL: Golden Age Press, 1955.

THE COSMIC MAN

This 1959 film explores the idea of a benevolent alien trying to set earth to rights. The Cosmic Man arrives on earth to spread his message of peace and love and to warn humanity against destroying itself. He is greeted with suspicion and hostility because he is different. Essentially, this is a low-budget version of *The Day the Earth Stood Still*.

The theme of benevolent aliens that approach earth with a message of concern about our self-destructive tendencies—particularly about our potential for setting off a nuclear holocaust—was central to much of the flying-saucer contactee literature of the 1950s and 1960s. Although the importance of Cold War concerns for interpreting certain films of this period have often been overemphasized, it is clearly relevant when applied to movies and contactee accounts built around the theme of warnings about atomic war from space.

Futura 1959; 72 min. Director: Herbert Greene; Writer: Arthur C. Pierce; Cinematography: John F. Warren; Cast: Bruce (Herman Brix) Bennett, John Carradine, Angela Greene, Paul Langton, Scotty Morrow.

COSMIC STAR TEMPLE

The Cosmic Star Temple was founded in 1960 in Santa Barbara, California, by Violet Gilbert; it has since relocated to Grants Pass, Oregon. Gilbert had been a student of theosophy and a member of the "I AM" Religious Activity. She was made aware of the Space Brothers in 1937. Following a request for healing in 1938, she prepared for eight months for a trip to Venus, which she took in January 1939. She received a complete physical healing during the three-and-a-half-week trip. She was also given instructions in healing and in reading the Akashic records. The Akashic records are the records of all that has happened and are inscribed on the universal ethers. Gilbert also made a trip to Mars in 1955.

In 1960 she went public and founded the Cosmic Star Temple. A major aspect of the temple's work is healing. Gilbert also reads the Akashic records of individuals, which give information about their previous incarnations. The teachings of the Cosmic Star Temple include material from New Thought metaphysics, spiritualism, and theosophy. Gilbert teaches that the Space Brothers are beneficent. Their purpose is to keep us from destroying ourselves and to share their advanced knowledge.

See Also: Akashic Records; Contactees; The "I AM" Religious Activity; Religions, UFO; Space Brothers; Theosophy
Further Reading:
Gilbert, Violet. My Trip to Venus. Grants Pass, OR: Cosmic Star Temple, 1968.
Melton, Gordon. Encyclopedia of American Religions. 5th ed. Detroit: Gale Research, 1996.

COSMOLOGY

Cosmology—the quest for a comprehensive model of the origin, structure, and destiny of the known universe—might simply be called the "ultimate theory of everything." In practice, however, cosmological research aims at a theory of everything physical. To some theoretical astrophysicists these statements are equivalent, but others might wonder if the discovery of a successful Grand Unified Theory would provide any kind of ultimate answers for anyone else.

For most of human history there has been no significant distinction between scientific and philosophical approaches to the cosmological question. However, the Copernican revolution split the river of cosmology into at least two branches. Giordano Bruno derived a philosophical cosmology from the bare bones of awareness that the earth was a planet revolving around a star in a larger universe of similar stellar bodies. Galileo observationally refuted numerous, long-held, a priori cosmological beliefs while redrawing the accepted (i.e., geocentric) theories of the universe. In the process astronomers, determined to be free of church and philosophical hegemony over discovery, gradually banished metaphysical constructs from the arena of mathematical and physical cosmology.

Philosophical cosmology today remains a separate and sometimes not even "parallel" universe of thought, sometimes interacting with scientific cosmology but more often trailing as a weak afterthought. Usually, cosmologists will issue a disclaimer, stating such questions as What happened before the Big Bang? or Where is the universe expanding into? or Who or what caused the Big Bang? as unanswerable paradoxes because they are asking the "wrong" questions.

Ironically, in the larger, traditional sense of cosmology as the ultimate theory of everything, it may be the average nonscientist asking the wrong questions who ends up asking the biggest questions of all. Not surprisingly, such individuals are also submitting to the world highly controversial evidence that, if accepted, would contradict most everything science tells us about the universe. Such are the implications if even *one* of the reports of UFOs, crop circles, or alien abductions proves to be a First Contact event.

In practice, contemporary cosmological theories tend to have a very narrow focus. Basic astrophysical models contend in the literature for ascendancy, and the current "leader" is often determined by interpretations of physical findings, ever changing and based on the degree of congruence between theoretical predictions and evolving observational data and mathematical tools.

A typical example of the primary interests of scientific cosmology at the beginning of the twenty-first century is the determination of the true value of the Hubble Constant (a function of the amount of matter in the universe). This research objective generates numerous projects searching for "dark," or normally undetected, matter in the universe. Immense effort is invested to assess the number and size of black holes and other by-products of stellar evolution. Also of interest is the existence and relative occurrence of various elementary particles such as WIMPs (weakly interacting massive particles) and mass relevant forces, factors, or constants in quantum-mechanical processes (such as the half-life of a proton), which might yield a different total-mass result. These and many other approaches (finding distant, red-shifted objects to determine "flatness," etc.) seek to conclude whether the universe is "closed" (i.e., likely to contract back upon itself) or "open" (i.e., likely to expand infinitely).

Rapid developments in astrophysics are generating new entries for a successful cosmological model, and some theorists express great confidence that one of these models will produce a "perfect fit" for observational data and solve a wide array of mathematical conundrums across the physical-science spectrum.

The question of how an observer with such ultimate concerns could exist at all is usually less scientifically compelling (although certainly of at least theoretical interest to many) than the physical data the scientist seeks about the cosmos. Often described as the "Anthropic Principle," this cosmological question considers whether the fundamental constants of our universe interact with the conditions necessary to evolve sentient life, as well as whether the existence of the questing astrophysicist is just one possible outcome of infinite-universe configurations. Although the fundamental importance of these conceptions to establishing an expected frequency of sentient life-forms in *this* universe is acknowledged, methods for testing such hypotheses are still developing as part of the newly emerging discipline of astrobiology.

The discipline of astrobiology encompasses a vast number of questions about the exact nature of "life" and its genesis as part of the evolution of planetary systems. From this base, the development of sentient life in the universe and the frequency of advanced civilizations beyond that remain highly speculative questions. Whether and how such civilizations might eventually interact across the vast space-time oceans separating solar systems is often held as unanswerable without any evidence that another life-form even exists somewhere other than earth. Consequently, a bold, direct step toward answering this question has recently taken form as the SETI project (Search for Extra-Terrestrial Intelligence).

SETI's modern birthday is marked by the culmination of Project Ozma on April 8, 1960, and the development of the now-famous Drake Equation, which was a first attempt at deriving an estimate of the number of advanced civilizations in our galaxy (i.e., those with a roughly similar stage of technical development to our own). Morrison and Cocconi also conjectured that extraterrestrial civilizations might leave an electromagnetic footprint (intended or unintended), which could be detected as radio signals on earth given adequate technical skills (and sufficient professional tolerance among fellow astronomers). Ironically, as the equipment improved, the staffing and computing time necessary to process the signals became harder to fund. This led to the most successful public-participation science experiment to date, the Seti@home distributed computing project.

The cosmological quest no doubt started with early mythological explanations for the dazzling celestial objects so prominent in ancient dark skies. If we consider the universe from a perspective of our own mortal existence, we might suppose that one primary focus of the cosmological agenda is to establish a theory for the existence of sentient life—in particular, our own. This might transform the classic cosmological question—Why is there something rather than nothing?—into something more like Why are we here asking this question at all? Thus, the rebirth of scientific cosmology has actually contributed to the rebirth of metaphysics. This form of cosmological thinking is of little interest to scientific cosmologists, who tend to see it as an anachronism of protocosmology, based on casual and subjective observations of unsophisticated cultures from the past.

The awareness of order in the night sky, and the development of cities and agricultural regions de-

pendent on seasonal changes, have been credited with stimulating the development of systematic observational methods and more advanced mathematics. The building of astronomical structures (the current focus of archeoastronomy) to mark recurring celestial events instituted a transition into meaningful models of the so-called heavenly sphere. Many of these structures remain as symbolic placemarkers reminding us that ancient civilizations were deeply concerned with the sky as the sole representative of the unobservable universe. Even if these cultures seemed only to seek astrological predictions and omens in recurring celestial events, clearly the relationship with the universe was intensely personal.

From a philosophical perspective, early cosmological thought (what might be considered a kind of autistic phase—when all our human mental dynamics were splashed on the sky as the behavior of powerful gods) was an attempt to answer the more immediate question of purpose—Why do humans exist? The next phase of metaphysical cosmology disciplines this immaturity while depersonalizing celestial phenomena. The deities leave the sky, and the questions center more on when certain unusual objects next rise or set. The question of existence is divorced from the sky and is addressed more by various theological belief systems.

Today, the possibility that other sentient beings coexist on other planets in our galaxy inevitably leads to numerous questions about every observed cosmological phenomenon. Are we unique? Or are we an example of more widespread cosmological principles?

Interestingly, many scientists have had some difficulty transferring the concept of uniform physical laws in physics to the domain of biology. Although this may be a legacy of theologically based anthropocentrism, it has frequently been argued that biological systems, being massively more complicated than physical structures such as planets and subject to the random-selection forces of evolution, could statistically rarely come into existence, even in a universe of seemingly infinite proportions. Factors limiting favorable conditions for the development of sentient life are formidable and, unmitigated, can yield a far lower favorability factor for such evolution. Pessimistic Drake Equation parameters winnow the number of sentient beings to a small fraction of all biological creation, and of those sentient beings, only a small proportion would reach the level of potential interstellar communicants. In this view, we are a lonely outpost of consciousness in the cosmos.

Given the current assessment of scientific cosmology—that the probability of contact with an extraterrestrial intelligence is an extremely low probability event, unlikely to occur during the lifetime of a planetary civilization—it is not surprising to find scientists uninterested in reports of alien spacecraft and visitors. This would likely be so even without the contribution of any conspiracy theory proposing active efforts to discredit such reports.

Consequently, the gap is immense between the strongest and best-validated, observationally based contemporary cosmological theories on the one hand, and the universe implied by contentions that earth has been more or less under continual visitation by one or a variety of extraterrestrial beings on the other. Those claiming direct experience of something extraterrestrial have, until recently, found themselves acutely confined by the power of their own witness and the contradictory pronouncements of normal science. Those doing normal science do not feel there is a gap anymore than there is a gulf between science and various religious beliefs about the universe. From this point of view, there simply is no relationship between them.

Clearly, this explanatory gap is not easily reconciled. As a result, contemporary reviews of cosmological theories would make little or no mention of UFOs, crop circles, ancient alien artifacts, or other indirect evidence of extraterrestrial visitation or contact. Such evidence, if confirmed, would require a radical revision in cosmological models, not the least of which would be to vastly upsize the estimate of intelligent beings organized into advanced technical civilizations capable of visiting a variety of planets at vast interstellar distances.

Of course, we would expect that contact with any representatives of an advanced extraterrestrial civilization would be fruitful and might lessen the load of future incremental theory-building by giving up some new data from the work of the more advanced science. So far, most of the cosmological information forwarded by those claiming contact with such beings has not alleviated any of the arduous scientific work of earth's principle cosmological investigators. This has no doubt reinforced the sullen view of the scientific community that ufology is a waste of time.

It is not surprising, then, that the primary role of contemporary scientific analysis has been one of "saving the phenomena" by providing a variety of explanations for narratives, forensic artifacts, and anomalous detection data (radar, infrared, electromagnetic-field signatures, etc.) provided by UFO researchers. The position of governmental agencies with the capacity for advanced analysis and understanding of such evidence has been to strongly promote conventional scientific explanations for all UFO-type data.

A more pernicious view—that of a worldwide government-level cover-up of confirmed extraterrestrial contact and promotion of a business-as-usual attitude—could certainly be dismissed as merely reflecting the natural consequence of this wide and passionately felt gulf in perspectives. Yet the vast number of individuals claiming experiences with contact phenomena believe either that the explanations of conventional science are wrong, or that the scientists involved are but the hand-maidens of such conspiracies. Thus is created a kind of mirror conclusion, which views the agenda of scientific cosmology as benighted at best and as a clever ruse at its most conspiratorial.

The UFO question therefore has become one of the most interesting areas of investigation for social scientists who see the societal manifestations in our time of "cosmological uncertainty" as perhaps a stage of development to be expected as the universe beyond earth is increasingly explored. This phase of human intellectual development might be considered the age of First-Contact Science (FCS), a proposed discipline connecting the astronomical and space-science advances of this period in history with changes in human awareness and belief systems about the prevalence of extraterrestrial life, its possible purposes, and the likelihood that earth may be of interest to advanced civilizations.

Despite the best efforts of sanctioned, establishment cosmology to debunk popular alien-visitation mythology and to provide scientific explanations for UFO sightings, contact narratives, and crop-circle communications, these events continue to be reported.

The FCS approach would suggest that our civilization, with the capacity for probing the basic facts of the universe and to conduct local space travel, has become unavoidably aware of the larger context beyond the visible plane of earth's surface. Although most aspects of human culture strive to keep that awareness below the "blue sky of denial," the recurrent themes of space travel and distant planets have already done their work. Every step farther out into the universe tends to increase the awareness and "readiness" of human consciousness for First Contact, which in turn makes it a growing preoccupation of our time.

With every new discovery of another extrasolar planetary system, variations of life existing under extreme conditions using novel survival strategies, and intriguing new cosmological concepts that offer plausible mechanisms for interstellar communication and travel, the currency that life on earth may not be particularly unique rises in value. With this understanding, it is also easier to assume that a society just a few thousand years more advanced than earth might develop the capacity to visit distant planets. Furthermore, our own defense industry's efforts to advance stealth technology lend credence to the idea that such very advanced technologies (compared to our own) would likely be capable of eluding verifiable detection by our current methods.

The broad scope suggested by FCS would include everything that is currently considered ufological: UFOs buzzing cities, blasting out cryptic symbols in corn and wheat fields, abducting various people at random, mutilating cattle, and so on. FCS goes beyond the domain of so-called traditional ufologists to include every scientific investigation that seeks answers about nonhuman sentience: Ongoing astronomy projects such as the search for sun-and-earth type systems, SETI, and even local space exploration itself are the subjects of study as part of this growing planetary awakening to the possibility that we're not alone in the universe.

FCS must be a scientific discipline, because without the controls of a scientific community the experiences of "encounter" become the private knowledge domain of an interpreter who then speaks to the outside world. This results in the constant revival of a peculiar brand of ufology that makes no claims to consensus understanding, only to the explication of hidden mysteries. This is, in fact, the oldest of cosmological traditions— not a doorway to the universe, but a descent into the labyrinthine, murky caves of First-Contact Religion (FCR).

Although both FCS and FCR could be dismissed by some as ephemeral pursuits born of ignorance, there are lessons in the productive tension between these views. It is the paradoxical fact that the more we learn about the cosmos, the more the experience of a living cosmology eludes us. Perhaps because modern cosmology lacks a metaphysical dimension, the attraction of various belief systems—some riding the backs of frankly antiquated cosmological models—is increasing rapidly.

The German language shows this contrast more clearly in its distinction between Weltbild (the "world picture" of science) and Weltanschauung ("world outlook" or "world orientation" of our lives). Although we currently lack proof of extraterrestrial life (or, for that matter, certain knowledge of God), our growing astronomical knowledge stimulates our intuition. This faculty—fertilized by cultural and religious traditions about nonterrestrial beings—produces the widespread belief that "they are out there." For good or ill, this dialectic is shaping our modern Weltanschauung and subsequently generating forms of FCR.

Richard Grossinger's lyrical analysis of the tradition he calls "occult astronomy" centers on a loss of direct meaning inspired by the stars and its replacement by a physical-spiritual split—a division of meaning into scientific and religious spheres. Into the breach fall our modern "unclassified" phenomena—the alien-encounter and -abduction narratives—which are part witness testimony, part personal experience, and part mystery story. As

Jacques Vallee has said, "The UFO mystery mirrors our fantasies and expresses our secret longings for a wisdom that might come down from the stars."

Whether such knowledge comes down from the stars, or we find it there ourselves, First-Contact Science implies that as a planetary culture we are destined to make the search.

—Greg Wheeler

Further Reading:

Baugher, J. On Civilized Stars: The Search for Intelligent Life in Outer Space. Englewood Cliffs, NJ: Prentiss-Hall, 1985.

Barrow, J., and Tipler, F. The Anthropic Cosmological Principle. New York: Oxford University Press, 1986.

Davies, P. The Accidental Universe. Cambridge: Cambridge University Press, 1982.

Hawking, S. A Brief History of Time: From the Big Bang to Black Holes. New York: Bantam, 1988.

Kaku, M. "A Theory Of Everything?" In Mysteries of Life and the Universe. Edited by W. Shore. Harvest Books, 1994.

Mack, John E. Abduction: Human Encounters with Aliens. New York: Charles Scribner's Sons, 1994.

Neugebauer, O. Astronomy and History: Selected Essays. New York: Springer-Verlag, 1983.

The Night Sky: The Science and Anthropology of the Stars and Planets. San Francisco: Sierra Club Books, 1981.

Wheeler, G., and S. Scribner. "Remembering Shadows in Plato's Cave." Continuum 5(2): 8.

———. "Take Me or Leave Me Alone: Frames, Filters, and Paradigms for the Age of First Contact." Continuum 4(1) (1996): 10–14.

CREEPING TERROR

The monster in this 1964 movie is constructed of foam with men inside making it crawl. It emerges from a crashed spaceship in the Colorado desert and begins eating people—a real yawner. Its only significance is that it represents a projection of humanity's worst kind of image onto an imaginary extraterrestrial, namely, a monster who eats people. The closest thing to this kind of being in UFO literature is found in the recent discussion of the Chupacabras ("Goat Sucker"), an alien monster whose menu is primarily animals but who also spices up its diet with an occasional human victim.

Teledyn/Metropolitan International Pictures 1964; 75 min. Director: John Sherwood; Writer: Arthur Ross; Cinematography: Maury Gertsman; Cast: Vic Savage, Shannon O'Neill.

CRITTERS

In this 1986 Gremlins-imitation film, a group of Krites escape from an intergalactic prison and head for earth. In Kansas, a normal family finds its farm under siege as the hungry, dangerous fur balls with teeth close in. The mother, father, and daughter are injured, and it is up to the son to fend off the monsters, which he does with home-made fireworks. A pair of shape-shifting alien bounty hunters also come to round up the Krites. There was a series of sequels. The third Critters movie took place in a big city. A family on a picnic returns to its city tenement with Krite eggs, which hatch and allow the furry little monsters to wreck a laundry room.

The many sequences in which the Krites are being shot with shotguns in the movie are reminiscent of the Kelly-Hopkinsville Close Encounter, which took place at Kelly, Kentucky, on the evening of August 21, 1955. In that encounter the beings identified as aliens were repeatedly knocked down (but never, apparently, slain) with blasts from shotguns.

New Line/Smart Egg/Sho Films 1986; 86 min. Director: Steven Herek; Writers: Don Opper, Stephen Herek, Dominic Muir; Cinematography: Tim Suhrstedt; Music: David Newman; Cast: Dee Wallace Stone, M. Emmet Walsh, Billy Green Bush, Scott Grimes, Nadine Van Der Velde, Terrence Mann, Billy Zane, Don Opper.

CROP CIRCLES

The phrase "crop circle" applies to a variety of patterns in various crops of grain, including wheat, rye, and barley, without tracks leading to or from the patterns. The first crop circles were so called because they appeared as flattened circles in grainfields. The study of this phenomenon has been dubbed "cereology."

The first known example appeared in Queensland, Australia, in 1965. The first English example was discovered in 1972; one was discovered in Switzerland in 1975. By 1997 crop circles were reported from 24 countries all over the world in a number approaching 5,000. In England, where the first circle appeared very close to highway A34 near Hampshire, the connection with UFOs was made instantaneously. The original idea was that

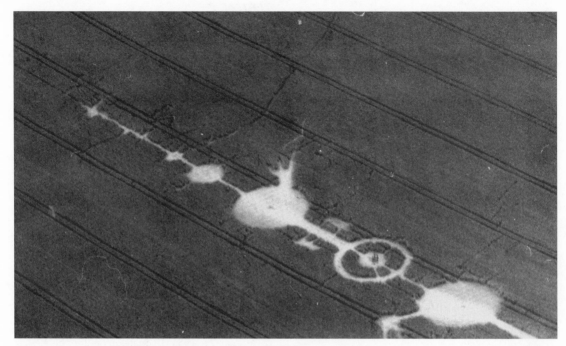

Over the years, crop circles gradually evolved into complex pictograms. This pictogram was discovered in July 1990 at Alton Barnes, Wiltshire, England. (American Religion Collection)

the strange circles in the fields were landing marks left by alien spacecraft. Later on, as the crop circles developed into more complex formations, it was believed that the patterns were designed by aliens aboard spacecrafts by means of some kind of beams that were directed toward the fields from high altitude.

The interpretation of the phenomenon has changed along with the alterations of the phenomenon itself. Originally, crop formations were circles, but today they appear in virtually any shape, from the simple to the highly complex. Among the most advanced crop formations, one encounters patterns or designs otherwise familiar from computer-generated models of complex geometric patterns, or fractals. Hence the original term "crop circle" has been abandoned in favor of more prestigious designations such as "pictograms" or "geoglyphs," meaning "signs on the ground."

There has also been a change in interpretation in other ways. Rather than seeing the crop formations simply as evidence of the alien presence, many ufologists believe that they carry a message to humanity. For this reason the emphasis has moved from "proof" to "contact": The challenge is

to solve the riddle and understand what is contained in the extraterrestrial messages. The UFO (understood as a physical vehicle) is less important; the intellectual, emotional, or even spiritual balancing with the extraterrestrials become of paramount importance.

Some ufologists hold that the messages are hard to understand because the aliens know that humans will need to unravel their message gradually in order to grasp it—not to say appreciate it. An overly straightforward communication would be disastrous, but by placing the crop formations in the fields the visiting aliens gradually educate us to understand and accept their presence. This idea is so important that it has inspired an important development in ufology: the Close Encounter of the Fifth Kind, which means a mutual communication, a deliberate contact. In 1992 Dr. Stephen M. Greer, the leader of a small team of ufologists aiming at a direct contact with the circle makers high above, and following a close-encounter experience, stated that: "The interim result which we are taking back home from this project is that definitively structured spaceships are observed in connection with these circles, that a well-motivated and prepared group can interact with them and that the circle-makers are nonterrestrial visitors who produce these circles by using an advanced technology" (cited in *The Cosmic Connection*).

Some people in the New Age community, however, do not link the crop formations to UFOs at all. Some believe that they are signs from Mother Earth, who is believed to be a goddess, that she has suffered beyond her limits, and that pollution and the exploitation of natural resources must cease.

When the phenomenon reached a peak in England in 1990, farmers demanded compensation from the state, claiming that it was the responsibility of authorities to protect them against alien vandalism. Some of the crop formations were rather large and caused the farmers considerable loss of income. Other farmers were more creative. They fenced off their field and sold tickets to people who wanted to see the strange phenomenon, or perhaps meditate inside the formations, as many New Agers felt like doing. Finally, of course, some people deliberately produced formations in their fields to attract interest. Some Christian ministers think that the crop circles pose a special challenge. They take them to be expressions of the devil's presence and therefore counteract them with prayer, holy water, and sometimes even exorcism.

In 1991 two elderly men came forward and confessed that they were the circlemakers and that they had been making them for years. They were fully aware that a network of circlemakers had come into being, but they wanted the world to know that they had been the first (in England at least). The two men had used rather simple tools for their trick (ropes and pieces of wood), but later circlemakers used high-tech surveying equipment. Crop-formation enthusiasts responded that whereas fake circles naturally could be attributed to human action, "real" formations necessarily had to be the work of higher intelligences. Indeed, people responded to the confession of the two old pranksters that it would be impossible for even a large group of people to produce the large number of reported crop formations and that no human capacity was skillful enough to produce the fantastic patterns that later

appeared in the fields. At the same time, other observers hypothesized that rare meteorological phenomena—certain stationary, descending atmospheric vortexes—might cause phenomena similar to those presented as UFO-related crop circles, and to some observers the original circles are satisfactorily explained in this way.

The way UFOs are connected with crop circles is a good example of how one unexplained phenomenon may be explained through another unexplained phenomenon—and vice versa. The crop formations nourished the UFO myth, and the UFO myth adds reason and meaning to the otherwise incomprehensible signs in the grainfields. It is also important to note that the central scene for the development of crop circle–UFO ideologies is an area in southern England where legends and rumors relating to all sorts of beliefs in the paranormal have firm roots. Further, the media have served as a willing carrier of stories of unbelievable events.

Finally, it should be added that crop circles were described in a publication predating the current UFO myth by centuries—in 1678. The story goes that a farmer invoked the devil to mow his crops but found that the Evil One had created circles in his field. It is very likely that the old story of the devil making the circles and the contemporary story of UFOs doing so are in fact the same narrative, shaped according to the prevailing worldview. Indeed, many people prior to industrialism's breakthrough testified that they had seen the devil in physical form, just as people of modern times tell of experiences with strange spacecraft. The crop-circle story is probably a detail in this larger continuum.

—*Mikael Rothstein*

See Also: Hoaxes
Further Reading:
Delgado, Pat, and Colin Andrews. *Circular Evidence.* London: Bloomsbury, 1989.
Hesemann, Michael. *The Cosmic Connection: Worldwide Crop Formations and ET Contacts.* London: Gateway Books, 1996.
Meaden, George Terence. *The Circles Effect and Its Mysteries.* Bradford-on-Avon, U.K.: Artetech, 1989.
Noyes, Ralph, ed. *The Crop Circle Enigma.* Bath, U.K.: Gateway Books, 1990.
Randles, Jenny, and Paul Fuller. *Crop Circles: A Mystery Solved.* London: Robert Hale, 1990.

CULTS, UFO

New religious forms that incorporate flying saucers and/or the Space Brothers into their doctrine are often placed into the generic category of UFO cults. The meaning of the word "cult," however, is ambiguous. One should also note that, as commonly used, the term is highly pejorative.

The word "cult" is etymologically related to such terms as "culture" and "cultivate" and has several related meanings. In the first place, it can refer to a system of worship and devotion found within the fold of a larger religious body, as in the cult of the Virgin Mary. Second, it can refer to particular movies (e.g., *The Rocky Horror Picture Show*), public personalities, and other phenomena that attract cult followings. Prior to the religious-cult controversy of the 1970s, "cult" was also a value-neutral sociological term referring to small, informal religious groups, particularly transitory groups in the metaphysical-occult subculture that gathered around charismatic religious leaders.

By the mid-1970s "cult" had become a pejorative term, applied to any unpopular religious group. All cults, according to this stereotype, are formed by charismatic, egotistical leaders for the sole purpose of benefiting the founder. Because of its pejorative connotations, mainstream scholars working in the field tend to avoid the term, preferring the label "new religion" or "new religious movement."

See Also: Cargo Cults; Contactees; Religions, UFO
Further Reading:
Lewis, James R. *Cults in America*. Santa Barbara, CA: ABC-CLIO, 1998.
———. *The Encyclopedia of Cults, Sects, and New Religions*. Amherst, NY: Prometheus Books, 1998.

DALEKS—INVASION EARTH 2150 A.D.

The hero of this 1966 British film is Dr. Who, an absent-minded old inventor. A London bobby mistakes Dr. Who's time machine for a police box and is transported with Dr. Who and his two granddaughters to the desolate earth of the future. There they find out that the Daleks, mutated aliens sitting inside mobile transporters, have conquered earth and are planning to rip out its core with a huge bomb and use the planet as a spaceship. The time travelers join the underground resistance movement and manage to divert the bomb by creating a magnetic forcefield that destroys the Daleks, who are sucked into the earth's core.

This is a not particularly imaginative variation on the timeworn plot of noble earthlings versus evil alien invaders—tolerable for Dr. Who fans but otherwise unremarkable. Like space travel, time travel is a useful plot device for sending heroes and heroines into exotic settings. The UFO community did not traditionally give much attention to time travel. This changed when certain segments of this community became interested in the lore surrounding the Philadelphia experiment, a time-travel experiment that was supposedly carried out by the U.S. Navy on a ship in Philadelphia harbor.

AARU (United Kingdom) 1966; 81 min. Director: Gordon Fleming; Writer: Milton Subotsky; Cinematography: John Wilcox; Cast: Peter Cushing, Bernard Cribbins, Ray Brooks, Andrew Keir, Jill Curzon, Roberta Tovey.

DAMON ENCOUNTER

A few miles outside Damon, Texas, on the night of September 3, 1965, two deputy sheriffs driving home saw two lights in the sky. The lights approached them, and they saw a triangular-shaped UFO 150 feet away and 100 feet high. They drove into Damon, then drove back to see if the object was still there. Once again, they saw the lights approach them, and this time they took off in fear. One of the deputies had suffered an injury that night when his son's pet alligator bit his index finger. After the encounter, the injury was inexplicably healed. The next day one of the deputies was approached by two menacing strangers who told him not to repeat the story. This encounter with the proverbial men in black occurred before any newspaper accounts appeared.

See Also: Healing; Men in Black
Further Reading:
Clark, Jerome. *The UFO Encyclopedia.* 2nd ed. Detroit: Omnigraphics, 1998.
Clayton, William. "It Looked Like a Football Field!" In *Flying Saucers.* Edited by David C. Whitney. New York: Cowles Communications, 1967, pp. 18–19.

DANIEL, BOOK OF

Daniel 2:31–33 describes a statue made of gold, silver, bronze, iron, and tile, seen by King Belshazzar in a dream that Daniel is interpreting. The statue is destroyed by a stone that turns into a mountain. Attempts to interpret this as a UFO sighting seem to ignore the fact that it is described as a dream within what is considered by historians to be a work of political fiction.

Daniel 7 describes a dream in which Daniel sees four beasts emerge from the sea. Verse 7:7 says, "I saw the fourth beast, different from the others, terrifying, horrible, of extraordinary strength; it had great iron teeth with which it devoured and crushed." Verses 7:9–10 continue: "Thrones were set up, and the Ancient One took his throne. . . . [It] was flames of fire, with wheels of burning fire. A surging stream of fire flowed out from where he sat." Could this be a disguised report of a UFO sighting? That seems possible, but this is presented as a dream within a work of fiction, set in Babylon during the Captivity (ca. 586–536 B.C.) but actually written in Maccabean times as a commentary on political developments. Verse 7:13, which introduces the "Son of Man," is often interpreted as a prediction of the coming of the Messiah.

See Also: Ancient Astronauts

Further Reading:

Downing, Barry H. *The Bible and Flying Saucers.* Philadelphia: J. B. Lippincott, 1968.

Goran, Morris. *The Modern Myth, Ancient Astronauts and UFOs.* South Brunswick, NJ: A. S. Barnes, 1978.

THE DAY MARS INVADED EARTH

In this 1962 film Martians are quietly killing off humans and replacing them with alien minds and resurrected humanoid bodies in order to prevent the exploration and colonization of Mars by earth. In stark contrast to the standard Hollywood scenario, the Martians end up triumphant in this one. The timeworn interpretation of films involving extraterrestrial infiltration is that they reflect Cold War fear of infiltration by communists. The problem with such interpretations is that they fail to explain why in the post–Cold War period such plots continue to inform imaginative creations, from the film *The Arrival* to the TV series *Dark Skies.* The same basic theme is popular in some of the more paranoid segments of the UFO community.

API 1962; 70 min. Director: Maury Dexter; Writer: Harry Spalding; Cinematography: John Nickolaus; Cast: Kent Taylor, Marie Windsor, William Mims, Betty Beall, Lowell Brown, Greg Shank.

THE DAY THE EARTH STOOD STILL

In this classic 1951 film an alien named Klaatu and his robot Gort arrive in Washington, D.C., in a flying saucer to warn earth to stop its atom-bomb testing or be blown apart. The alien is gunned down by soldiers. Gort kills the soldiers and reactivates the alien, who places Gort and several other robots in society as police robots. He then leaves in his saucer, warning earthlings that they must either live in peace or be destroyed by the robots. There is a subplot in which Klaatu attempts to discover what humans are really like by taking a room in a boarding house where he befriends a woman and her son. The woman is the one who saves earth by saying, "Gort! *Klaatu barada nikto,*" after the alien's death, thereby stopping the robot from destroying earth.

Friendly extraterrestrials approaching earthlings with a message of concern about our potential for nuclear holocaust was a central theme in much of the flying-saucer contactee literature of the 1950s and 1960s. There has been an overemphasis on the importance of Cold War concerns for interpreting certain films of this period on the part of certain commentators. It is, however, clearly relevant when applied to movies and contactee accounts built around the theme of warnings about atomic war from outer space. *The Day the Earth Stood Still* is also the single most significant box-office film to embody the "technological angels" theme articulated by Carl Jung. Jung may even have had this film in mind when he wrote about flying saucers as quasi-divine beings—technological saviors for an age that could no longer believe in traditional supernatural beings.

Fox 1951; 92 min. Director: Robert Wise; Writer: Edmund H. North; Cinematography: Leo Tover; Music: Bernard Hermann; Cast: Michael Rennie, Patricia Neal, Hugh Marlow, Sam Jaffe, Frances Bavier, Lock Martin, Billy Gray.

DELVAL UFO, INC.

Delval UFO, Inc., was founded in 1972 by Anthony and Lynn Volpe. It is a New Age UFO contactee group whose members seek to commune with space beings on all levels of existence. In doing this they hope to help in preparing humanity for the imminent New Age. There is one group that meets monthly in Ivyland, Pennsylvania. The group maintains contact with approximately 400 people across the United States, plus members in Canada, Australia, and Japan through its periodical, *The Awakening.*

See Also: Contactees; Religions, UFO; Space Brothers

Further Reading:

Melton, Gordon. *Encyclopedia of American Religions.* 5th ed. Detroit: Gale Research, 1996.

Volpe, Anthony, and Lynn Volpe. *Principles and Purposes of Delval UFO, Inc.* Ivyland, PA: The Authors, n.d.

DEMONOLOGICAL EXPLANATIONS OF UFOS

When the modern UFO era began in the late 1940s, the predominant interpretation of the phenomenon—beyond hypotheses that simply tried to explain UFOs away, such as mass hallucination and swamp gas—was the extraterrestrial hypothesis: UFOs are real, physical craft piloted by intelligent life-forms from other planets. By the time interest in UFOs had become something of a fad in the 1950s, some Christian fundamentalists were offering a more supernatural hypothesis, namely, that UFOs were the products of demonological activity. This peculiar line of interpretation was taken up in the latter 1960s by a handful of more mainstream ufologists associated with the *Flying Saucer Review;* these were ufologists who adhered to a form of occult spirituality in which evil beings could emerge from other dimensions or from parallel universes with the purpose of opposing the spiritual evolution of humankind.

The notion of some form of conscious demonic force has been a part of the human imagination since prehistoric times. The belief that malicious entities lie behind natural disasters and other unpleasant aspects of human life is still prevalent in many traditional societies. Although natural explanations have gradually supplanted metaphysical explanations, demons still survive in the mythology of Carl Jung's collective unconscious and in other schools of the study of the mind that interpret evil forces as projections of human fear and/or as hallucinations.

Toward the latter part of Jung's lifetime, this great psychological theorist became interested in the flying-saucer phenomenon, particularly the archetypal themes reflected in certain kinds of UFO literature. Even much secular thinking about UFOs embodies quasi-religious themes, such as the notion that the world is on the verge of destruction and ufonauts are somehow going to rescue humanity—either by forcibly preventing a nuclear Armageddon or by taking select members of the human race to another planet to preserve the species. Jung was referring to the latter portrayal of flying saucers when he coined the expression "technological angels." In more recent years the earlier contactee literature—which was dominated by friendly aliens trying to save humanity from self-destruction—has been supplanted by abductee accounts.

If in the earlier literature flying saucers were technological angels, in abductee literature ufonauts are portrayed as technological demons. Abductees, most of whom appear to have been genuinely traumatized by their experience, report being treated coldly and inhumanely by their alien captors—much like animals are treated when captured, tagged, and released by human zoologists. During their brief captivity, frightened abductees also often report having been tortured, usually in the form of a painful examination.

A careful reading of abduction narratives indicates that the patterns alleged to have been discovered by abduction investigators often have religious overtones or similarities with more traditional types of religious experience—similarities often ignored by UFO researchers. Hypnosis, which is generally used to explore the abduction experience, allows access to a subconscious level of an individual's psyche. This enables the hypnotic subject to recall repressed memories of actual events but also makes it possible to derive "memories" of things that have never happened. As Jung argued, specifically in relation to UFOs, the subconscious is a storehouse of religious ideas and symbols. Such symbols can become exteriorized through anxiety or stress. Thus, the cryptoreligious imagery brought out by hypnosis—in this case torment by demonic beings, which is an initiatory motif—could be a confabulation of the subject's subconscious, perhaps worked into a UFO narrative in an effort to please the hypnotist.

More literal demonologies are proffered by conservative Christian observers of the UFO scene. The Greek word "daimon" was introduced in the Roman and Hellenistic world to indicate evil forces and thus entered early Christian writings with the negative connotation of impure spirits. The Judeo-Christian tradition elaborated the concept of the devil as the fallen angel who tempted Adam and Eve and was forever banished from Paradise. Early Christian literature also drew upon the belief system of their neighbors in the depiction of demons. The belief in evil powers as the source of

Illustration from "Amazing Stories Quarterly" of a human couple being abducted by demonic aliens (Mary Evans Picture Library)

sicknesses and problems for humans is found in all of the earliest Christian literature, and Christian theology acknowledges evil as a necessary alternative for the fulfillment of free will.

Among some contemporary fundamentalist Christians, one finds a tendency to regard everything that departs from a rather narrow interpretation of doctrinal correctness as being part of a satanic plot to lure humanity down the road to perdition. The UFO phenomenon is portrayed as being an integral part of this plot. In the words of David Ritchie, author of *UFO: The Definitive Guide to Unidentified Flying Objects and Related Phenomena:*

> Certain elements of belief appear so frequently in UFO contact reports that one must suspect that they form part of a belief system or systems that the UFO phenomenon is engineered (if one may use that word) to encourage. Those elements include collectivism; the unification of human society into some kind of global regime; veneration, bordering on worship, of nature and of natural objects; faith in occult principles and practices, such as mediumism or "channeling"; discouragement of traditional Judeo-Christian religious beliefs, such as the doctrine of the divinity, crucifixion and resurrection of Christ; and a syncretic set of religious beliefs with identifiable parallel in Buddhism, Hinduism and shamanism.

Ritchie's analysis exemplifies the conservative Christian position on UFOs, which is that ufonauts are not extraterrestrials at all but rather demons in disguise whose real purpose is to extend Satan's empire at the expense of traditional Christianity. Clearly this view is persuasive only if one adheres to similar theological assumptions. Hence, this form of literal demonology is not likely to dominate mainstream ufological interpretations of the UFO phenomenon in the foreseeable future.

See Also: Abductees; Angels; Mythology and Folklore
Further Reading:
Jung, Carl Gustav. *The Archetypes and the Collective Unconscious.* 2nd ed. Bollingen Series 20. Princeton: Princeton University Press, 1968.
Lewis, James R. *The Encyclopedia of Afterlife Beliefs and Phenomena.* Detroit: Gale Research, 1994.
Ritchie, David. *UFO: The Definitive Guide to Unidentified Flying Objects and Related Phenomena.* New York: Facts on File, 1994.

DERENBERGER, WOODWARD W.

Woodrow W. Derenberger was a contactee whose story attracted widespread attention in the late 1960s. On November 5, 1966, Derenberger, a 50-year-old sewing-machine salesman, was driving home to Parkersburg, West Virginia, when he was forced to stop by a large, wide object that blocked the path of his panel truck. The object, which was presumably a spaceship, was charcoal in color and shaped like two glass coverings of a kerosene lamp joined together at the bottoms. A tanned, dark-haired man in an overcoat stepped out of the ship, walked over to the side window of Derenberger's truck, and had a brief conversation with him. This man, who called himself "Cold," finished with the message "we will see you again," returned to the craft, and left. Shaken, Derenberger raced home, related the encounter to his family, and then called the local police as well as the media.

The next day Derenberger held a news conference that was widely reported because of a UPI dispatch. The salesman had no history of being either dishonest or mentally unbalanced, and he initially struck many observers as sincere. This apparent sincerity, in combination with a rash of contemporaneous UFO sightings up and down the Ohio River Valley, seemed to corroborate Derenberger's strange narrative and initially gave his tale a certain air of plausibility. UFO investigators subsequently arrived in Parkersburg, including a four-man team from the National Investigations Committee on Aerial Phenomena (NICAP). By then, Derenberger had become a local celebrity and was beginning to expand on his story with information provided during new visits with Mr. Cold and a fellow alien, Carl Ardo. As the salesman's tale grew to include trips to Cold's home world—trips that were later detailed in a book he coauthored with Harold W. Hubbard, *Visitors from Lanulos*—most serious observers, including the NICAP team, concluded that Derenberger's increasingly elaborate narrative was more the product of fantasy than the residue of a genuine encounter.

The case might have dropped into obscurity were it not for a handful of people whose testimony kept Derenberger's tale alive. Chief among these was the independent UFO writer John A.

Keel, who persistently supported Derenberger and who continued to portray the salesman's claims as plausible in his writings. Derenberger also received support from a Parkersburg psychiatrist associated with NICAP who claimed he, too, had been contacted by "Indrid Cold." Another source of support was Gray Barker, a publisher of occult and contactee-related literature who had been ejected from NICAP. Perhaps as a way of getting even, Barker vigorously defended Derenberger against NICAP's critical conclusions. Finally, during a radio talk show, a young man named Tom Monteleone called in and informed Derenberger that he, too, had been to Lanulos. Though Monteleone would later claim that his phone call was a prank intended to ridicule the salesman's story, his initial claims of sincerity provided Derenberger with an independent source of support. Monteleone later became a science-fiction writer and authored a play based on his experiences as a contactee. As for Derenberger, the light of publicity gradually faded, and a decade later he was still residing in Parkersburg, earning a living as a used-car salesman.

See Also: Contactees; Hoaxes; Space Brothers
Further Reading:
Barker, Gray. The Silver Bridge. Clarksburg, WV: Saucerian Books, 1970.
Bord, Janet, and Colin Bord. Life Beyond Earth? Man's Contacts with Space People. London: GraftonBooks, 1991.
Derenberger, Woodrow W., and Harold W. Hubbard. Visitors from Lanulos. New York: Vantage Press, 1971.

DESTROY ALL PLANETS

In this 1968 Japanese film aliens, whose spaceships turn into giant flying squids, are attacking earth. Gamera, a flying, fire-breathing space turtle, saves the day, assisted by two little boys in a miniature submarine. Battling monsters is practically a trademark of Japanese sci-fi films—it is as if all subsequent Japanese producers have been trying to cash in on the classic appeal of Godzilla. In this movie, the battling-the-monsters theme is overlaid upon an invasion-of-the-earth-by-hostile-aliens theme. Unless the ufological community in Japan is substantially different from American ufology, this film is less relevant to the concerns of contemporary UFO speculation than other alien-invasion movies.

Daiei 1968; 75 min. Director: Noriaki Yuasa; Writer: Fumi Takahashi; Cinematography: Akira Kitazaki; Cast: Peter Williams, Kojiro Hongo, Toru Takatsuka, Carl Crane, Michiko Yaegaki.

DEUTERONOMY, BOOK OF

Some passages in the Book of Deuteronomy have been suggested as indirect evidence for ancient UFOs. Verse 3:11 mentions a giant iron bed owned by a king, preserved in an Ammonite town. Verse 9:2 mentions the Anakim as "tall people." Neither seems to be strong evidence for either UFOs or ancient astronauts, though it is sometimes cited as such.

See Also: Ancient Astronauts
Further Reading:
Downing, Barry H. The Bible and Flying Saucers. Philadelphia: J. B. Lippincott, 1968.
Goran, Morris. The Modern Myth, Ancient Astronauts and UFOs. South Brunswick, NJ: A. S. Barnes, 1978.

DEVIL GIRL FROM MARS

The setting for this 1954 British film is a remote Scottish inn in which an escaped killer takes shelter. A Martian arrives in her spaceship dressed in a vinyl jumpsuit and miniskirt. She explains that Mars has been taken over by women. Aided by her robot, she circles the inn with an invisible electronic shield and demands healthy earthmen to take back to Mars for breeding purposes. The killer heads for London in her spacecraft but manages to blow it up, killing himself and the Martian.

Commentators have described Devil Girl from Mars as a spoof on The Day the Earth Stood Still, though the relationship would not be transparent to the casual moviegoer. From the standpoint of the film's relationship to UFO concerns, it is interesting to note that the theme of kidnapping earthlings to replenish an exhausted gene pool is a staple of contemporary speculation about alien abductions of human beings.

Danziger Productions 1954; 76 min. Director: David McDonald; Writers: John C. Mather, James Eastwood; Hugh McDermott, Hazel Court, Patricia Laffan, Peter Reynolds, Adrienne Corri, Joseph Tomity, Sophie Stewart, John Laurie, Anthony Richmond.

Movie poster for the 1954 film Devil Girl from Mars *(The Del Valle Archive)*

DOGU STATUES

Statues crafted by the Jomon people of Japan have an oddly mechanical appearance. In his books *Astronauts of Ancient Japan* and *The Six Thousand Year Old Space Suit,* author Vaughn M. Greene argues that these statues are actually space suits worn by extraterrestrials who visited earth thousands of years ago. In his work, Greene also examines Shinto folklore and mythology that appear to support this line of analysis.

See Also: Ancient Astronauts
Further Reading:
Goran, Morris. *The Modern Myth, Ancient Astronauts and UFOs.* South Brunswick, NJ: A. S. Barnes, 1978.

DOIN' TIME ON PLANET EARTH

The misfit younger brother of a clean-cut hunk due to marry into a socially prominent family is informed by his computer that the reason he feels so out of place with his family is that he is an extraterrestrial. Two UFO enthusiasts claim to be fellow aliens and explain that all the world's misfits and losers are the descendants of ancient astronauts. They convince him that he is the leader destined to take them away from earth, but in the end he decides that earth needs weirdos like him.

Cannon 1988; 83 min. Director: Charles Matthau; Writer: Darren Star; Cinematography: Timothy Suhrstedt; Cast: Adam West, Candice Azzara, Hugh O'Brian, Matt Adler, Timothy Patrick Murphy, Roddy McDowall, Maureen Stapleton, Nicholas Strouse, Andrea Thompson, Hugh Gillin, Gloria Henry.

DOLLMAN

A 13-inch-tall alien appears in the South Bronx, where he is caught up in a struggle between a crack-dealing gang and a neighborhood-watch group. This is an unimaginative twist on the time-worn theme of the helpful alien that saves the day for earthlings. The "cutesy" shortness of the hero clashes with his characterization as a tough guy. There is no particular resonance with UFO literature except as it reflects the tendency to portray aliens as short people.

Full Moon Entertainment 1991; 86 min. Director: Albert Pyun; Writer: Chris Roghair; Cinematography: George Mooradian; Cast: Tim Thomerson, Jackie Earle Haley, Kamela Lopez, Humberto Ortiz, Nicholas Guest, Judd Omen.

DON'T PLAY WITH MARTIANS

In this 1967 French film Martians land on a small island off the coast of France in the presence of two incompetent reporters and a social worker with extrasensory perception. The Martians eventually leave, taking with them a newly born set of sextuplets who, it turns out, are the offspring of one of the Martians. An unexceptional film, it is interesting for ufological purposes only in that the notion of human-alien hybrids would later become an important theme in both abduction literature and ancient-astronaut literature.

Fildebroc/Les Productions Artistes Associes 1967; 100 min. Director: Henri Lanoë; Writers: Johanna Harwood, Philippe de Broca (based on a book by Michel Labry); Cinematography: René Mathelin, Haydée Politoff, Pierre Dac, Frédéric de Pasquale.

DR. ALIEN

In this 1988 film an alien poses as a science teacher on earth to study human sexuality so that she can repopulate her world. She injects a college student with a green liquid, causing him to grow a tentacle from his forehead. He becomes irresistible to women, which gets him in trouble with his girlfriend. This is a B-grade comedy that tries to make up for its many weaknesses with top-heavy actresses. In terms of resonances with UFO literature, it is worth noting that an important subtheme of abduction literature is the marked interest extraterrestrial abductors seem to take in human sexuality.

Phantom 1988; 87 min. Director: David DeCoteau; Writer: Kenneth J. Hall; Cinematography: Nicholas von Sternberg; Cast: Billy Jacoby, Olivia Barash, Stuart Fratkin, Troy Konahue, Arlene Golonka, Judy Landers.

DR. X

A physician in southern France, Dr. X (so called because of his wish to remain anonymous), reports that his experiences with UFOs began on November 2, 1968. He was awakened in the middle of the night by his son's cries about something shiny in his room. X attributed the lights that were indeed flashing through the shutters to an imminent storm. It was not until he was downstairs filling a bottle that he realized there was no accompanying thunder for the light. From a terrace outside his living room he saw two luminous cylindrical objects in the rainy sky. They were silvery white on top and deep red on the lower half. Each had an antenna on top and on the bottom next to a white column of light extending to the hill below. He said they seemed to "sucking in the atmospheric electricity" that entered through the antennae. Soon afterward

they merged and moved into a position directly over him, then disappeared in a bang, leaving a luminous thread that did the same. It was 4:05 A.M.

Back in bed, X drew sketches of his encounter and awakened his wife to tell her the story. She noticed suddenly that an axe injury to his leg sustained three days earlier had completely healed. (Injuries from a land-mine explosion 10 years earlier soon began to heal as well.) Curiously, Dr. X experienced amnesia regarding his encounter when he awoke the next day at 2 P.M., only to recover his memory in a fall he had foretold while sleep-talking: "Contact will be reestablished by falling down the stairs on November 2."

What is extraordinary about Dr. X's story is the apparent physical evidence produced. On many occasions since 1968, a reddish isosceles triangle has abruptly appeared around his navel and that of his son a few hours later. These stigmata have been medically documented and continue to this day. Dr. X's stories have also come to include poltergeists, levitation, and an encounter with a man traveling with a three-foot, mummy-skinned creature. The man has apologized for the trouble X has endured and provided him with teleportation and time-travel experiences.

See Also: Healing; Time Travel

Further Reading:

Michel, Aimé. "The Strange Case of Dr. 'X'." In UFO Percipients: Flying Saucer Review Special Issue No. 3. Edited by Charles Bowen. London: Flying Saucer Review, 1969, pp. 3–16.

———. "The Strange Case of Dr. 'X'—Part 2." Flying Saucer Review 17(6) (November-December 1971): 3–9.

Schnabel, Jim. Dark White: Aliens, Abductions, and the UFO Obsession. London: Hamish Hamilton, 1994.

Vallee, Jacques. Confrontations: A Scientist's Search for Alien Contact. New York: Ballantine Books, 1990.

EAGLE RIVER PANCAKE TALE

Joe Simonton, a 54-year-old plumber from Eagle River, Wisconsin, looked out his kitchen window on the morning of April 18, 1961, to find a bright-chrome, disk-shaped vehicle (like two saucers back-to-back) with no windows parked in his driveway. Curious and unafraid, he went out to meet the short man in the saucer's doorway, who was holding an empty jug and silently gesturing for some water. After handing the filled jug to the man, Simonton noticed two other men in the saucer near control panels and dressed in black suits. One was cooking pancakes. Simonton's efforts to strike up a conversation resulted in the cook handing over four hot pancakes. Shortly afterward, the saucer abruptly flew away.

What ensued when Simonton told his story has been called a local wonder, a national joke, and a food fight. His reputation as honest and genuine gained him considerable local support. On the national level the U.S. Air Force, the National Investigations Committee on Aerial Phenomena (NICAP), the Aerial Phenomena Research Organization, and Project Blue Book all became involved. Various samples of the pancakes, minus one cardboard-tasting bite, were sent away for analysis; one report from the Food and Drug Administration returned the verdict that "the article is an ordinary pancake of terrestrial origin." NICAP for its part was reluctant to investigate due to the "contact" nature of the claim and its sensitive and difficult task of presenting believable accounts of encounters. Critical reviews of NICAP's head, U.S. Marine Corps Major Donald E. Keyhoe, were rampant in UFO-related publications. But the modesty of Simonton's claim ultimately won him the status of having had a close encounter of the third kind. Skeptics still maintained that he had merely experienced a hallucination followed by delusion.

The question is . . . does this generally produce pancakes?

See Also: Contactees; Hoaxes
Further Reading:
Foght, Paul. "Inside the Flying Saucers . . . Pancakes." *Fate* 14(8) (August 1961): 32–36.
Lewis, James R. *Doomsday Prophecies.* Amherst, NY: Prometheus Books, 1999.
Lorenzen, Coral, and Jim Lorenzen. *Encounters with UFO Occupants.* New York: Berkley Medallion, 1976.
Vallee, Jacques. *Passport to Magonia: From Folklore to Flying Saucers.* Chicago: Henry Regnery, 1969.

THE EARTH DIES SCREAMING

In this 1964 British film a test pilot returns from a flight to discover that England has been devastated. He joins up with other survivors and travels to London, where they are attacked by robots who kill people and resurrect the corpses as mindless zombies. Eventually the test pilot discovers the power source of the robots and destroys the transmitter station that is controlled by aliens from a distant planet.

The director of this film, an uninspired film that does not live up to its sensational title, was also the director of two other alien-invasion movies. Other than the tired, overworked theme of extraterrestrial invasion, the only other connection with the UFO phenomenon is that some contactees and abductees have reported encounters with beings that seemed to be robots under the command of ufonauts (e.g., the Pascagoula abduction).

Lippert/Planet 1964; 62 min. Director: Terence Fisher; Writer: Henry Cross; Cinematography: Henry Cross; Cast: Willard Parker, Virginia Field, Dennis Price, Thorley Walters, Vanda Godsell, David Spencer, Anna Falk.

EARTH GIRLS ARE EASY

In this 1989 film a Hollywood manicurist is having trouble with her unresponsive, fickle fiancé when a spaceship crash-lands in her swimming pool and disgorges three colorful, hairy, fun-loving aliens that move in for the weekend. They make a trip to the beauty shop, where they are shaved into reasonable approximations of humanity, and everyone goes on the town. Even reviewers who liked this movie called the script "stupid." The film has a few themes that overlap with themes found in the UFO community, such as a idea of a flying-saucer crash and the notion of human-alien intimacy.

Panavision 1989; 100 min. Director: Julien Temple; Writer: Julie Brown, Charlie Coffey, Terrance McNally; Cinematography: Oliver Stapleton; Music: Nile Rodgers; Cast: Geena Davis, Jeff Goldblum, Jim Carrey, Damon Wayans, Julie Brown, Michael McKean.

EARTH VERSUS THE FLYING SAUCERS

Earth versus the Flying Saucers was a black-and-white, grade-B science-fiction film based very loosely on Donald E. Keyhoe's best-selling book, *Flying Saucers from Outer Space.* When Henry Holt, the publisher of *Flying Saucers from Outer Space,* sold the movie rights to Clover Productions, the author was assured that the film would be a documentary. Keyhoe never saw the film's title until the picture was finished. He did not serve as technical director and never spoke with the producer or the director, Fred F. Sears. Keyhoe made an unsuccessful attempt to have his name removed from the film's opening credits when he learned that the plot consisted of hostile aliens trying to take over the world only to be foiled by a heroic scientist who invents an antimagnetic weapon that can shoot down the spaceships.

Earth versus the Flying Saucers embodies the alien-invasion plot that commentators have connected with Cold War fears. It should be remembered that the notion that flying saucers were some sort of communist spying device was one of the first hypotheses put forward to explain the

Hugh Marlowe and Joan Taylor in the 1956 film Earth versus the Flying Saucers *(The Del Valle Archive)*

craft sighted by Kenneth Arnold in 1947. *Earth versus the Flying Saucers* is also interesting as one of the first films to recast the classic *The War of the Worlds* alien-invasion theme in terms of the emergent flying-saucer phenomenon, transforming ufonauts from beings of ambiguous intent into hostile enemies.

Columbia 1956; 81 min. Director: Fred F. Sears; Writers: George Worthington Yates, Raymond T. Marcus; Cinematography: Fred Jackman; Cast: Hugh Marlowe, Joan Taylor, Donald Curtis, Morris Ankrum.

EGGS, FLYING

One recurring motif in many mythological systems—one that at first glance seems astonishing—concerns flying eggs or egg-shaped structures in the sky or atmosphere. It is often said that these artificial structures may be of "supernatural" origin. A comparison with modern UFO sightings seems possible. The creation myth of the pre-Greek Pelasgians concerned the all-mother Eurynome, who was later identified with Thetis, on whom Ophion, acting in the shape of a dragon, had engendered an egg that drifted in boundless Chaos before all the material world hatched from it. Eurynome, according to Robert Graves, meant "Wide Wanderer."

Orphic myths related that at the beginning the goddess of the black-winged night bore a silver egg, which drifted in the primeval Ocean until Eros (also called Phanes, the "Revealer") was born from it. Helen of Troy was also born from an egg, since Zeus in the form of a swan had seduced her mother, Leda. In Egyptian myth, Ptah, the lord of the earth, and Geb, father of Isis and Osiris, were born from golden eggs.

Tibetan Buddhist writings speak of a golden "world egg." Other Tibetan legends tell of a flying egg that has neither arms nor legs nor feathers but does have a voice. Hindu scriptures tell that Brahma awoke from a deep sleep in a flying egg that shone like the sun. The Melaniden are said to be descendants of gods who arrived in metallic eggs on the "white island" in the early Gobi Sea.

Thai mythology calls the first people "P'an Ku," who came out of an egg that a divine bird had laid on a mountaintop. Similar "eggs of origin" can be found in the legends of Polynesia, Tahiti, the Solomons, and Easter Island, as well as those of the Incas, whose mother-goddess was said to have landed in a golden egg.

—*Aidan A. Kelly*

See Also: Mythology and Folklore
Further Reading:
Chevalier, Jean, and Alain Gheerbrant. *The Penguin Dictionary of Symbols.* London: Penguin, 1996.
Cirlot, J. E. *A Dictionary of Symbols.* New York: Dorset Press, 1991.

ELECTROMAGNETIC HYPOTHESIS

A line of thought parallel to the extraterrestrial hypothesis (the theory that some UFOs are spaceships from other planets) is the electromagnetic hypothesis (EMH—the theory that UFOs and close-encounter experiences are caused by electromagnetic phenomena and their interaction with the human nervous system). The EMH, as developed since the 1970s by its more noted proponents—Michael Persinger, Paul Devereux, Albert Budden, and their coresearchers and colleagues—draws on diverse disciplines (e.g., Budden lists medicine and clinical ecology, electromagnetics, bioelectromagnetics, neurology, psychology, physical geology, meteorology, atmospheric physics, and electrical engineering, among others) in order to explain not only UFO phenomena but apparitions in general, including hauntings, poltergeist activity, and even visions of the blessed Virgin Mary. In general, the EMH proposes that fields of electromagnetic radiation (EMR) generated by natural or artificial sources can cause light phenomena and a wide range of physiological and psychological effects, which, when combined with the background beliefs of the witness, create encounter experiences of the kind mentioned above.

As developed primarily by Persinger and Devereux, the EMH relates fault lines and tectonic activity with UFO reports and close encounters. Their studies purport to discover a close correlation among not only fault lines, seismic activity, and UFO reports but also among these geological features and light phenomena, such as earthquake lights, mountain-peak discharge, and ball lightning. Though many geologists and physicists question the nature and even existence of such phenomena, EMH proponents refer to measurements of a range of EMR generated by tectonic stresses and to eyewitness descriptions (even photographic evidence) of unclassified aerial phenomena (UAPs). The appearance, behavior, and visible effects of UAPs are those generally attributed to UFOs. UAPs appear as opaque, metallic, or variously colored glowing spheres, ovoids, squiggles, or even inverted Christmas trees. Being almost without mass, they accelerate and stop instantaneously, hover, or fly in straight or irregular lines, achieving speeds clocked, in one instance, at 600 miles per hour. Being a kind of electrical plasma phenomena, they appear on radar and emit a broad band of EMR, giving rise to electromagnetic effects associated with flying saucers, namely, burns, scorching, melting, and electrical interference, as well as those more subliminal effects on the nervous system that result in the imagery and narrative of a close-encounter experience. Being a mysterious (if natural) phenomena, UAPs and their haunts (as it were) have been associated with many ancient or traditional holy sites, such as stone circles in England and Wales, monasteries and temples in Greece and China, and holy mountains, like Mt. Shasta in California. Tectonic stresses and the earth tremors that result from them have likewise been long associated with marked behavior in animals, giving rise to research into the possible causal grounds for this connection between geological activity and the nervous systems of higher organisms, including human beings.

Michael Persinger and others have experimented extensively with the effects of EMR on the brain. Persinger, for example, has developed a chamber wherein a subject is seated and fitted with a specially designed helmet that induces small changes in the electromagnetic fields of targeted regions of the brain, thereby modifying the electrochemical reactions of the neurons, resulting in modifications of consciousness. Depending on the strength of the field, the region of the brain stimulated, the subject's background, and even the imagery decorating the chamber, subjects report a wide range of perceptual effects, including intense emotions of fear or anger, flashing lights, feelings of being observed by an unseen presence, sensations of sudden intense cold or of being touched or moved, and so on. More extreme reactions include auditory or visual hallucinations, such as hearing authoritative God-like voices or the appearance of skinny, wax-like humanoids. As these effects are those associated with ghost sightings, poltergeist hauntings, and UFO abduction experiences, researchers propose that the energies released by geological activity or perhaps by the light phenomena supposedly caused by this activity lead to experiences interpreted by the experiencer as an encounter with a ghost, UFO and its pilots, or with some other form of apparition whose character and behavior is culturally determined by the experiencer's background.

Proceeding from the research of Persinger and others, Albert Budden has expanded and refined the EMH to include artificial sources of EMR and the electromagnetic pollution they are seen as causing. The historically recent increase of EMR in the environment has resulted in an "electromagnetic smog" from sources such as wireless communications technologies and radar, power lines, high-tension cables, transformers, substations, and junction boxes. Anxiety over electromagnetic pollution is hardly a fringe phenomenon, as the health effects of EMR have been the subject of studies and concern both within single nations (e.g., a Swedish study of 50,000 subjects to determine a link between proximity to high-tension power pylons and forms of cancer) and internationally (e.g., studies conducted by the World Health Organization). By natural and artificial sources of EMR, singly or together, along with other factors, Budden attempts to explain in detail how "hallucinatory/visionary perceptions are caused ultimately by the actions of [electromagnetic] fields in the environment on the human system, although physiological factors that are involved point to synergistic mechanisms." In Budden's view, artificial and natural electromagnetic fields interact to produce those UAPs his coworkers identify as the source of UFO reports and close-encounter experiences.

—Bryan Sentes

Further Reading:
Budden, Albert. Electric UFOs. London: Blandford, 1998.

———. *UFOs: Psychic Close Encounters.* London: Blandford, 1995.

Devereux P., A. Roberts, and D. Clarke. *Earth Lights Revelation.* London: Blandford, 1989.

Evans, Hilary. *Gods, Spirits, and Cosmic Guardians: A Comparative Study of the Encounter Experience.* Wellingborough, U.K.: Aquarian Press, 1987.

———. *Visions, Apparitions, Alien Visitors.* Wellingborough, UK: Aquarian Press, 1984.

Persinger, M. A., and G. F. Lafreneire. *Space Time Transients and Unusual Events.* Chicago: Nelson Hall, 1977.

Vallée, Jacques. *Dimensions.* New York: Ballantine, 1989.

———. *Passport to Magonia: From Folklore to Flying Saucers.* Chicago: Henry Regnery, 1969.

ELEMENTALS

The term "element" has come to be associated with the atomic elements. Prior to the modern era, and dating back to at least the time of the ancient Greeks, this term referred to the four classical elements: earth, air, water, and fire. It seems that by these elements the ancients meant to refer to states of matter as understood in modern times: solid, gas, liquid, and (for lack of a better term) energy.

The Western occult tradition, especially as it was mediated through the Theosophical Society to the contemporary metaphysical/New Age subculture, postulated that these "states" were the result of the activity of small, invisible spirits, or elementals. While some branches of the occult tradition view elementals as transitory and soulless, others see them as representing a conscious life that evolves from elementals through fairies to angels.

One strand of speculation added two additional classes of elemental beings: those who dwell underground; and lucifugum ("fly-the-light"). Such "flying lights" suggest a parallel to contemporary UFOs. Another point of comparison is the obvious parallel between the "little men" of fairy lore and the little beings associated with flying saucers. These parallels support the contention that modern UFO lore is little more than traditional folklore in contemporary garb.

See Also: Angels; Demonological Explanations of UFOs; Mythology and Folklore; Occult; Theosophy
Further Reading:
Lewis, James R. *Witchcraft Today: An Encyclopedia of Wiccan and Neopagan Traditions.* Santa Barbara, CA: ABC-CLIO, 1999.

Shepard, Leslie A., ed. *Encyclopedia of Occultism and Parapsychology.* Detroit: Gale Research, 1991.

ELIJAH AND UFOS

Various passages regarding the prophet Elijah have been suggested as possibly being evidence for ancient UFO or extraterrestrial activity. 1 Kings 18:12 has been suggested to be referring to transportation by a UFO, as have all passages about people parting waters or walking dryshod across some water. Verse 18:38 has been interpreted as chemical fire or some weapon fired from a UFO; and so have 2 Kings 1:12 and Lev. 9:24. The famous passage in 2 Kings 2:11, "a flaming chariot and flaming horses came between them, and Elijah went up to heaven in a whirlwind," has of course been interpreted as an abduction by a UFO. The tendency here is obviously to try to interpret

Elijah being taken up in a chariot—a poetic rendering of a UFO experience? (American Religion Collection)

all biblical miracle stories in terms of extraterrestrial technology.

See Also: Ancient Astronauts
Further Reading:
Downing, Barry H. The Bible and Flying Saucers. Philadelphia: J. B. Lippincott, 1968.
Goran, Morris. The Modern Myth, Ancient Astronauts and UFOs. South Brunswick, NJ: A. S. Barnes, 1978.

ESCAPE TO WITCH MOUNTAIN

Escape to Witch Mountain is a Disney film about two children who are actually aliens with superhuman powers but who have no memory of who they are. A villainous ogre kidnaps them, intending to profit from their powers of telepathy. They are befriended by a man played by Eddie Albert, who helps them escape in his camper. In the conclusion, the camper takes to the skies to make its escape.

Escape to Witch Mountain is built around a standard sci-fi theme, namely, aliens and good humans team up to help each other and to defeat bad humans. (Another variation on this plot structure is when humans and good aliens team up to defeat bad aliens.) Although this movie and its sequel, *Return from Witch Mountain,* are unexceptional, it is interesting to note that one of the standard traits of ufonauts in both contactee and abductee literature is the exceptional telepathic powers of the extraterrestrials.

Disney 1974; 97 min. Director: John Hough; Writer: Robert Malcolm Young; Cinematography: Frank Phillips; Cast: Eddie Albert, Ray Milland, Donald Pleasance, Kim Richards, Ike Eisenmann, Denver Pyle.

ESCHATOLOGY

As the world approached the end of second millennium, a diverse range of religious thinkers were prompted to speculate that humanity—indeed, the entire earth—was nearing the Endtime, when life and the world as we know it is completely destroyed and/or transformed. Often those who anticipate such a radical intervention transformation also hold an apocalyptic view, meaning that this world will end in terrible destruction. The Book of Revelation, which contains an outline of Endtime events, pictures the end as a time of violence and destruction. In New Age religions that have an UFO component, ufonauts (the presumed pilots of UFOs) are often seen as carrying out this redemptive activity, rescuing humanity (or select groups of humanity) from the final destruction.

Eschatology (from *eschaton-logos,* "study of the last things") is the technical theological term for the study of the end of time. Religious eschatology always involves the idea of redemption or salvation and is a part of the doctrine of most world religions. It can be subdivided into individual eschatology (concerned with the fate of individual souls, or the judgment of the dead and their ultimate destination) and cosmic eschatology (which can be either restorative of the old pure primordial order or utopian—establishing a perfect system that never before existed).

Western notions of the eschaton date back to Zoroastrianism, in which individual and cosmic eschatologies merge. The souls of the dead are provisionally assigned a state of bliss or suffering. Their final status is determined at the end of the world. Once the forces of light will have completely overturned darkness, the resurrection of the dead will occur. This optimistic vision of the end of the world is an original contribution to the religious thought of the Western world.

Early Jewish eschatology as documented in the prophecies of the Old Testament aimed at the restoration of the old golden age. Persian and Hellenistic ideas influenced Judaism during the first diasporas, leading to the development of several different messianic and/or apocalyptic ideas. These sometimes contradicted each other, and only in later centuries were they harmonized into a coherent system. The Messiah who is expected to come is a descendant of the House of David and/or a divine being referred to as the "Son of Man." He represents the redeemer of a peaceful world, whereas the apocalypse envisions the annihilation of the present age.

Judaism influenced the eschatology of early Christianity, providing the notion of the Messiah as the redeemer of a new age. The Messiah will replace the present age with the "kingdom of God" upon the day of judgment and the resurrection of the righteous. Throughout the centuries, various Christian movements have developed their own millenarian doctrines that anticipated the end of the world and the coming of a new golden age. It was the redeemer role in which ufonauts were cast by UFO contactees that prompted psychologist Carl Jung to refer to flying saucers as "technological angels."

See Also: Angels; Apocalypse; Cargo Cults; Jung, Carl Gustav; Millennialism; Religions, UFO
Further Reading:
Eliade, Mircea, ed. Encyclopedia of Religion. New York: Macmillan, 1987.
Lewis, James R. The Encyclopedia of Afterlife Beliefs and Phenomena. Detroit: Gale Research, 1994.
Van Der Leeuw, G. Religion in Essence and Manifestaton, Volume 1. Gloucester, MA: Peter Smith, 1967 [trans. of first German ed., 1933].

E.T. THE EXTRA-TERRESTRIAL

One of the most successful movies of all time, E.T. broke the mold for alien-contact films. A flying saucer arrives on earth not to conquer it but to obtain plant specimens. An alien botanist is stranded on earth when his spaceship is forced to take off without him because it is being stalked by government men. A boy finds the strange-looking but obviously frightened being in his tool shed and lures him into his room with candy. The boy and his brother and sister make a plaything of the alien and try to conceal him from the authorities and other grown-ups. They also assist the alien in contacting his planet. Meanwhile, the government men are searching for the alien they know was left behind. When the government men get to him, E.T., whose health has been deteriorating, apparently dies. He revives, however, when put into a decompression chamber with the boy who found him. The two escape just in time to meet the alien ship that has come to take E.T. home.

Many details of this movie come from UFO folklore: Aliens are short, lizardlike creatures with big eyes and strange powers. The portrayal of the corrupt government people who, in their pursuit of knowledge about extraterrestrials, run roughshod over human feelings and the rights of American citizens also reflects the image found in conspiracy-oriented UFO literature.

Universal 1982; 115 min. Director: Steven Spielberg; Writer: Melissa Mathison; Cinematography: Allen Daviau; Music: John Williams; Voice: Debra Winger; Cast: Henry Thomas, Dee Wallace Stone, Drew Barrymore, Robert MacNaughton, Peter Coyote, C. Thomas Howell, Sean Frye, K. C. Martel.

EVOLUTION OF THE SOUL

One commonplace idea found in the contemporary New Age–occult subculture is that the Space Brothers are here to help the planet or to help humanity "evolve." This statement reflects the belief in what we might call "spiritual" evolution, or the evolution of the soul. This statement also reflects the widely held assumption that ufonauts share the spiritual worldview of members of the New Age subculture.

Traditional religions have tended to emphasize the sharp transition from a nonenlightened or nonsaved state to enlightenment or salvation. In contrast, modern metaphysical spirituality emphasizes gradual growth, expansion of consciousness, and learning across time, including growth across many different lifetimes. Thus, in contrast with traditional Hinduism and Buddhism—which view reincarnation negatively, as a cycle of suffering out of which one should strive to liberate oneself—in the contemporary metaphysical subculture reincarnation is viewed positively, as a series of opportunities for expanded spiritual growth. This gradual spiritual expansion constitutes a kind of evolution of the soul, and the metaphor of spiritual evolution is often expressed in the literature of this subculture.

See Also: Karma; New Age; Reincarnation; Space Brothers; Theosophy
Further Reading:
Eliade, Mircea, ed. Encyclopedia of Religion. New York: Macmillan, 1987.
Lewis, James R. The Encyclopedia of Afterlife Beliefs and Phenomena. Detroit: Gale Research, 1994.
Shepard, Leslie A., ed. Encyclopedia of Occultism and Parapsychology. Detroit: Gale Research, 1984.

EXODUS, BOOK OF

To any reader with an ancient-astronaut orientation, the biblical account of the Hebrew exodus from Egypt contains passages that might be interpreted as reflecting the intervention of the "Space

Brothers" in human history. The parting of the Red Sea, for example, seems so extraordinary that it has been attributed to extraterrestrials. More relevant are the descriptions of God leading the Hebrews with a pillar of smoke by day and a pillar of fire by night—both suggesting the image of rocket engines. Yahweh is also decidedly a sky god, as many passages make clear. For instance, the Hebrews are fed by manna that drops from above, and in the Red Sea account it says that in the morning watch God "looked down" on the Egyptians—a passage that clearly places Yahweh in the sky. The most suggestive passage, however, is probably the description of God's "landing" on Mt. Sinai (Exod. 19:16–20):

> On the morning of the third day there were thunders and lightnings, and a thick cloud upon the mountain. All of the people in camp heard a sound like a loud trumpet blast, and trembled. The Moses brought the people out of camp to meet God, and they took their stand at the foot of the mountain. Mount Sinai was wrapped in smoke, because the Lord was descending upon it in fire. The smoke of it went up like the smoke of a furnace, and the whole mountain quaked. As the sound grew louder and louder, Moses spoke, and God answered him in thunder. And the Lord Landed upon Mount Sinai.

Although this passage as well as the others mentioned could be interpreted in multiple ways, it is particularly easy to imagine the event described here as the landing of some great rocketship.

See Also: Ancient Astronauts
Further Reading:
Downing, Barry H. *The Bible and Flying Saucers.* Philadelphia: J. B. Lippincott, 1968.
Goran, Morris. *The Modern Myth, Ancient Astronauts and UFOs.* South Brunswick, NJ: A. S. Barnes, 1978.

EXTRATERRESTRIAL BIOLOGICAL ENTITIES

Extraterrestrial biological entities (EBEs) is supposedly the U.S. government's official designation for ufonauts. The term has been used in contexts, most famously in the so-called Majestic 12 document, which recounts, among other incidents, the recovery of a crashed saucer and the bodies of dead EBEs near Roswell, New Mexico.

See Also: Majestic 12; The Roswell Incident
Further Reading:
Clark, Jerome. *The UFO Encyclopedia.* 2nd ed. Detroit: Omnigraphics, 1999.

EXTRATERRESTRIAL EARTH MISSION

The history of this group dates to 1986, when the extraterrestrial spirit named Avinash walked into the body of John, a channel and a metaphysical teacher in Seattle, Washington. A walk-in consists, as explained by Ruth Montgomery, in the translocation of a spirit from an abandoned body to a new body. Avinash moved to Hawaii with a female walk-in, Alezsha, and there they met Ashtridia, herself a walk-in. The teaching of Avinash was focused on the importance of removing the limitations to obtaining a new reality. Through contacts they established with a spaceship, the three walk-ins realized they possessed extradimensional abilities.

Upon moving to Sedona, Arizona, they encountered nine other walk-ins with whom they collaborated for a while. After the group disbanded, the three that remained—Avinash, Arthea, and Alana—experienced a series of walk-ins through which they repeatedly changed their personalities. The spirits that "walked in" are alleged to be extraterrestrial ones. In the latter part of 1987, the three original entities, now named Aktivar, Akria, and Akrista, organized a series of public meetings and created the Extraterrestrial Earth Mission. They produced video- and audiotapes that described the role of mankind in the creation of the universe and addressed human weaknesses.

A few months later a new series of walk-ins took place and the group, now guided by Savizar and Silarra, turned into a New Age organization. They dedicated their activity to discovering the many unaware masters of the earth and helping them create a new earth. Teaching the superconscious technique was one of the aspects of their mission; through it individuals can manifest their desires. Subsequent walk-ins in 1990 and 1993 marked new phases in the mission's activity. The new entities Drakar and Zrendar moved to Hawaii and started the Christ Star Project, according to which they are trying to create a new model of civilization in Maui. Supporters of the Extraterrestrial Earth Mission exist in the United States and Canada. Meetings are organized during which various extraterrestrial entities speak to the audience through Drakar and Zrendar.

See Also: Contactees; Extraterrestrial Walk-Ins; Religions, UFO
Further Reading:
Lewis, James R. *The Encyclopedia of Cults, Sects, and New Religions.* Amherst, NY: Prometheus Books, 1998.
Melton, J. Gordon. *Encyclopedia of American Religions.* 5th ed. Detroit: Gale Research, 1996

EXTRATERRESTRIAL HYPOTHESIS

The extraterrestrial hypothesis (ETH) is the theory that the core of the UFO phenomenon is constituted by spacecraft piloted or otherwise under the control of extraterrestrial aliens. This theory became popular in the 1950s and has since been the most familiar nonnaturalistic explanation put forward for UFOs. However, as the years have gone by without universally convincing evidence for the ETH, and because so many UFO encounters do not strike observers as physical experiences in the normal sense, several observers have adopted alternative explanations. For example, some ufologists have postulated that UFOs come from another dimension rather than from another planet. Yet others have adopted occult or quasi-spiritual interpretations.

Further Reading:
Boylan, Richard. *Close Extraterrestrial Encounters: Positive Experiences with Mysterious Visitors.* Tigard, OR: Wild Flower Press, 1994.
Clark, Jerome, and Loren Coleman. *The Unidentified: Notes Toward Solving the UFO Mystery.* New York: Warner Books, 1975.

EXTRATERRESTRIAL INCARNATIONS

Most variations in the theory of reincarnation include the notion that one may incarnate in a variety of different forms, human or animal. In classical Hinduism, an ordinary human being might even incarnate as a demigod, such as Yama. As ideas about the inhabitants of UFOs and extraterrestrials were adopted by—and integrated into the ideology of—the West's metaphysical subculture, it was natural that speculation about possible incarnations on other planets would eventually be integrated into that subculture's general worldview. In more recent communications with the Other Side, New Age channelers have even claimed to have received information from, among other sources, extraterrestrials. Thus, while generally overshadowed by the more exotic notion of extraterrestrial walk-ins, it is not uncommon to speak with people who claim to have had such lifetimes.

See Also: New Age; Reincarnation
Further Reading:
Guiley, Rosemary Ellen. *The Encyclopedia of Ghosts and Spirits.* New York: Facts on File, 1992.
Lewis, James R. *The Encyclopedia of Afterlife Beliefs and Phenomena.* Detroit: Gale Research, 1994.

EXTRATERRESTRIAL WALK-INS

A walk-in is an entity that occupies a body that has been vacated by its original soul. An extraterrestrial walk-in is a walk-in who is supposedly from another planet. The walk-in situation is somewhat similar to possession, although in possession the original soul is merely overshadowed—rather than completely supplanted—by the possessing entity. The contemporary notion of walk-ins was popularized by Ruth Montgomery, who developed the walk-in notion in her 1979 book, *Strangers among Us.* According to Montgomery, walk-ins are usually highly evolved souls here to help humanity. In order to avoid the delay of incarnating as a baby, and thus having to spend two decades maturing to adulthood, they contact living people who, because of the frustrating circumstances of life or for some other reason, no longer desire to remain in the body. The discarnate entity finds such people, persuades them to hand over their body, and then begins life as a walk-in.

The walk-in concept seems to be related to certain traditional South Asian tales about aging yoga masters taking over the bodies of young people who die prematurely. Another possible source for the contemporary walk-in notion is the well-known (in theosophical circles) teaching that Jesus and Christ were separate souls. According to this teaching, Jesus prepared his physical body to receive Christ and, at a certain point in his career, vacated his body so as to allow Christ to take it

Cover for issue 6 of UFO Review, *"Aliens Walk among Us," 1979 (Mary Evans Picture Library)*

over and preach to the world. An underlying notion here is that Christ was such a highly evolved soul that it would have been difficult if not impossible for him to have incarnated as a baby. Even if he could have done so, it would have been a waste of precious time for such a highly developed soul to have to go through childhood.

Ruth Montgomery, more than any other single person, is responsible for popularizing the contemporary notion of walk-ins. She describes the phenomenon rather dramatically:

> There are Walk-ins on this planet. Tens of thousands of them. Enlightened beings, who, after successfully completing numerous incarnations, have attained sufficient awareness of the meaning of life that they can forego the time-consuming process of birth and childhood, returning directly the adult bodies. A Walk-in is a high-minded entity who is permitted to take over the body of another human being who wishes to depart. . . . The motivation of a Walk-in is humanitarian. He

returns to physical being in order to help others help themselves, planting seed-concepts that will grow and flourish for the benefit of mankind.

In 1983 Montgomery published another book, *Threshold to Tomorrow,* containing case histories of 17 walk-ins. According to Montgomery, history is full of walk-ins, including such famous historical figures as Moses, Jesus, Muhammad, Christopher Columbus, Abraham Lincoln, Mary Baker Eddy, Gandhi, George Washington, Benjamin Franklin, Thomas Jefferson, Alexander Hamilton, and James Madison. In fact, it seems that almost everyone manifesting exceptional creativity and leadership would be identified by Montgomery as a walk-in. In her words, "Some of the world's greatest spiritual and political leaders, scientists, and philosophers in ages past are said to have been Walk-ins."

In a later book, *Aliens among Us* (1985), Montgomery developed the notion of extraterrestrial walk-ins—the idea that souls from other planets have come to earth to take over the bodies of human beings. This notion dovetailed with popular interest in UFOs, which had already been incorporated into New Age spirituality. Following Montgomery, the New Age movement came to view extraterrestrial walk-ins as part of the larger community of advanced souls that has come to earth to help humanity through a period of crisis. This basic notion fit nicely into the teachings of Heaven's Gate, explaining away the founders' personal histories as the histories of the souls who formerly occupied the bodies of Marshall Applewhite and Bonnie Lu Nettles.

It should be noted that the walk-in idea—a notion implying a radical disjunction between soul and body—would have provided Applewhite with an essential ideological component in his conceptualization of the final-ascension scenario. Heaven's Gate members would let go of their physical containers and ascend spiritually (rather than physically, as he originally theorized) to the waiting saucers. Once aboard, they would consciously "walk-into" a new physical body and join the crew of the Next Level spacecraft. This scenario is related in one of the group's Internet statements: "Their final separation is the willful separation from their human body, when they have changed enough to identify as the spirit/mind/soul—ready to put on a biological body belonging to the Kingdom of Heaven." This entering into their "glorified," or heavenly, body takes place aboard the Next Level spacecraft above the earth's surface. Presumably, these new physical bodies would be supplied to Heaven's Gate members out of some sort of "cloning bank" maintained aboard the spaceships.

See Also: Extraterrestrial Earth Mission; Extraterrestrial Incarnations; Extraterrestrial Walk-Ins; Heaven's Gate; New Age; Star People
Further Reading:
Lewis, James R. *The Encyclopedia of Afterlife Beliefs and Phenomena.* Detroit: Gale Research, 1994.
Montgomery, Ruth. *Aliens among Us.* New York: Putnam's, 1985.
———. *Strangers among Us: Enlightened Beings from a World to Come.* New York: Coward, McCann, and Geoghegan, 1979.
———. *Threshold to Tomorrow.* New York: G. P. Putnam's Sons, 1983.

EXTRATERRESTRIALISM

Extraterrestrialism is a theory developed by rabbinical scholar Yonah Fortner that the earth has been populated by various races of aliens for tens of thousands of years. Fortner maintains that these aliens have guided human culture in its development. Fortner began reading Chaldean literature when he was eight years old. He eventually became fluent in several ancient languages. His theory of extraterrestrialism arose from his study of ancient manuscripts. He outlined his theory in a series of articles for *Saucer News.*

According to Fortner, the Chaldeans met alien prophets known as the Elohim. The Elohim and the Chaldeans intermarried. At the same time, another race of aliens, the Titans, was living in Central Asia and Nigeria. The Titans later left earth but maintained communication with the Chaldeans. Another race of aliens, the Serpent people, is believed by Fortner to have been on earth since before life formed on the planet. They were a malevolent people who were forced underground when the Titans arrived.

One extraterrestrial named Y'hova arrived on earth in 1340 B.C. Y'Hova told a human malcon-

tent named Abraham that he (Y'hova) was the true God and that Abraham and his family must leave the city and offer up sacrifices to Y'hova. Y'Hova became the God of the Christians and Jews. Fortner states that this God of Israel is a very ancient and perhaps nearly immortal being who does not come from our visible universe but from another dimension.

See Also: Ancient Astronauts
Further Reading:
Clark, Jerome. *The UFO Encyclopedia.* 2nd ed. Detroit: Omnigraphics, 1999.
Goran, Morris. *The Modern Myth, Ancient Astronauts and UFOs.* South Brunswick, NJ: A. S. Barnes, 1978.

THE EYE CREATURES

In this low-budget 1965 film a teenager saves America from invasion by multieyed aliens. *The Eye Creatures* is an uninspired cross between the hostile-alien-invader idea and a monster movie. As noted, the idea of a hostile extraterrestrial invader is standard fare among many members of the UFO community.

Azalea 1965; 80 min. Director: Larry Buchanan; Cast: John Ashley, Cynthia Hull, Warren Hammack, Chet David, Bill Peck.

EZEKIEL, BOOK OF

It is well known that many passages in Ezekiel have been suggested to be references to UFOs or extraterrestrial activity. These include the following:

A stormwind came from the north, a huge cloud with flashing fire, enveloped in brightness, from the midst of which gleamed something metallic. Within it were four living creatures that looked thus: their form was human, but each had four faces [of a man, lion, ox, and eagle] and four wings . . . the soles of their feet sparkled and gleamed like polished bronze. [Verses 1:4–10]

In among the living creatures were something like living coals of fire, torchlike, moving among the creatures. The fire gleamed and sent out flashes of lightning. As I looked at the creatures I saw wheels on the ground beside each one. They sparkled like chrysolite. All four looked the same, built one inside the other, and they could move in any direction

Model of Ezekiel's spaceship (Ancient Astronaut Society)

without veering. All four had rims, which were full of eyes all around. When the creatures moved, the wheels moved with them; when they were raised from the ground, the wheels rose also. . . . Over their heads something like a firmament was visible, looking like crystal. . . . I heard the sound of their wings, like the roaring of mighty waters. [Verses 1:13–24]

Chapter 10 repeats this entire description almost exactly. Certainly the temptation to perceive these passages as a description of some sort of alien airship is obvious. Historical scholars offer more prosaic interpretations of Ezekiel's symbolism—not that the symbolism is entirely understood.

And this from verses 3:12–14: "The spirit lifted me up; I heard behind me a loud rumbling as the glory of the Lord rose from its place. It was the sound made by the wings of the living creatures striking each other and by the wheels beside them." Again, this does sound like an attempt to describe a machine. Verses 8:1, 11:24, and 40:1–2 are also about being lifted up and have also been interpreted as referring to transportation by a UFO. However, they are more probably referring to a shamanic vision-journey, one that is psychological, not physical.

See Also: Ancient Astronauts
Further Reading:
Downing, Barry H. *The Bible and Flying Saucers.* Philadelphia: J. B. Lippincott, 1968.
Goran, Morris. *The Modern Myth, Ancient Astronauts and UFOs.* South Brunswick, NJ: A. S. Barnes, 1978.

FAIRIES

Fairies are a kind of nature-spirit that, under different names and guises, are found in every part of the world. Often pictured as small humanoid beings with wings, they present the appearance of being miniangels. Because many popular images of extraterrestrials picture them as being small and because fairies have the power to fly, there is a strand of ufological speculation that connects fairies with UFOs. Fairies are also supposed to have abducted humans, and the phenomenon of crop circles was traditionally termed "fairy rings."

Unlike angels, fairies have always had a mixed relationship with humanity. As nature-spirits concerned with natural processes, they do not normally seek out human contact, but when they take a liking to someone they will help her or him in various ways. But they have also been pictured as mischievous beings that enjoy playing pranks on people. This mixed relationship between humanity and fairies also suggests certain parallels between humanity and ufonauts.

Fairies—*fayes* in Old English—is thought to be derived from *fatae*, the ancient-Greek fates who were pictured as three-winged women. *Fay-erie* was originally the "erie" state of enchantment that could be induced by the fays and only later became interchangeable with the beings themselves. The fays were originally but one class of spirit-being, and it was perhaps the general association of "little people" with enchantment that enabled the term "fairy" to become the generic term for fays, brownies, elves, pixies, and the like.

An older theory is that fairy lore represents a distant memory of an earlier and more primitive race (e.g., the aboriginal Picts of the British Isles) that continued to interact with the dominant invaders (e.g., the Celts) for many centuries before disappearing altogether. Fairy folklore, in other words, is the imaginative residence of "real" contact between two races. This theory could plausibly be extended to cover contact between humanity and an extraterrestrial race—that is, fairy folklore is the residue of contact with aliens.

To demonstrate the intensive interaction between humans and fairies, one has only to look at some of the themes explored in Katherine Briggs's comprehensive fairy encyclopedia: Fairy Borrowing, Fairy Thefts, Dependence of Fairies Upon Mortals, Fairy Brides, Fairy Loans, and so on. A close examination of this folklore—particularly the tales about fairies abducting humans—makes plausible the notion that fairy lore is a residual memory of interactions with extraterrestrials.

There are several alternative fairy-beings that bring out other characteristics of this type of spirit. Pixies (pigsies, piskies), for example, are said to be small, winged fairies, with large heads and pointed ears and noses—traits attributed to certain aliens. Pixies are said to enjoy playing pranks on people, being especially fond of misleading travelers. The latter habit has given rise to the expression "pixie-led," a state in which one goes around in circles and cannot seem to find one's way back to the beaten path.

Gremlins are technological fairies, associated particularly, but not exclusively, with airplanes. Traditional fairies, who are usually thought of as connected with nature, are said to dislike technology, but gremlins seem to have adapted to the modern age. Some sources claim that gremlins are spirits of the air, others that they live underground around airfields. Although descriptions vary, they are usually pictured as being about a foot tall, green in color, with webbed feet (which they use to cling to airplane wings). They sometimes go about naked, while others are clothed like aviators, with suction cups on the bottoms of their boots; again, the traits of gremlins resonate with the characteristics of some reports of extraterrestrials.

See Also: Angels; Demonological Explanations of UFOs; Elementals; Mythology and Folklore
Further Reading:
Briggs, Katharine. *An Encyclopedia of Fairies.* New York: Pantheon, 1976.
Lewis, James R. *Witchcraft Today: An Encyclopedia of Wiccan and Neopagan Traditions.* Santa Barbara, CA: ABC-CLIO, 1999.
Shepard, Leslie A., ed. *Encyclopedia of Occultism and Parapsychology.* Detroit: Gale Research, 1991.

FANTASY-PRONE PERSONALITY HYPOTHESIS

In 1988 two articles in the *International UFO Reporter,* written by Australian ufologist Keith Basterfield and American sociology graduate student Robert Bartholomew, offered an original and controversial hypothesis of abduction phenomena. The articles described abductees as fantasy-prone personalities (FPPs)—people so susceptible to imaginary images that they lose the ability to distinguish fantasy from reality. Otherwise healthy and normal, by psychological standards these personalities experience "transient memory losses, road hypnosis, amnesias, lucid dreams, out-of-body experiences and imaginary companions—within the context of their supernatural worldview." The authors estimate that about 4 percent of the world's population is fantasy-prone.

According to a later article, Basterfield and Bartholomew argued that contact with and abduction by aliens is purely in the minds of those who have experienced such phenomena. They went so far as to say that the scars and wounds are products of a fantasy-prone mind. In multiple-abductee cases, the authors claim that all contactees/abductees would be found to be fantasy-prone if subjected to psychological testing.

The reaction in the ufological world was mostly skeptical, though many were impressed by the hypothesis. One of the criticisms was based on the probability of having multiple FPPs together in a single abduction case. If only one of the purported abductees was not an FPP, that person would deny any abduction. It is entirely unlikely, according to the critic, that three, four, or five FPPs would be together at a given time, which makes the FPP hy-

pothesis irrelevant to multiple-person abduction cases. Another criticism found fault with the notion that mind power alone can produce the deep wounds that abductees have revealed.

Basterfield and Bartholomew suggested that their hypothesis could be proved if thorough psychological tests were administered, looking at hypnotic susceptibility, vividness of mental imagery, creativity, and the like. In 1989 at the University of Connecticut, the FPP hypothesis was tested formally, and the researchers found no correlation between UFO experiences and fantasy-proneness.

See Also: Abductees; Contactees
Further Reading:
Evans, Hilary. *Visions, Apparitions, Alien Visitors.* Wellingborough, U.K.: Aquarian Press, 1984.
Rodeghier, Mark, Jeff Goodpaster, and Sandra Blatterbauer. "Psychosocial Characteristics of Abductees: Results from the CUFOS Abduction Project." *Journal of UFO Studies* 3 (new series, 1991).
Stillings, Dennis, ed. *Cyberbiological Studies of the Imaginal Component in the UFO Contact Experience.* St. Paul: Archaeus Project, 1989.
Wilson, Sheryl C., and T. X. Barber. "The Fantasy-Prone Personality: Implications for Understanding Imagery, Hypnosis and Parapsychological Phenomena." In *Imagery: Current Theory, Research, and Application.* Edited by Anees A. Sheikh. New York: John Wiley, 1983, pp. 340–387.

FATIMA APPARITION

The Fatima apparition was a series of religious miracles that occurred in Fatima, Portugal, in 1916 and 1917 that roughly fifty years later was reinterpreted by some to be UFO phenomena. The incidents began in the spring of 1916 when three local children saw a white light approach them and transform into the figure of a transparent, luminous young man who said, "Fear not. I am the Angel of Peace. Pray with me." There followed a series of miraculous visitations from the angel and the Virgin Mary.

On August 13, 1917, a crowd of about 18,000 came to the site to see the saints contact the children. Although authorities detained the children, the crowd heard thunder and saw lightning in the clear blue sky. A cloud hovered above the oak tree where the apparitions usually appeared. On September 13, 1917, the children were in attendance

The Fatima vision of Our Lady has often been interpreted as a UFO sighting. (American Religion Collection)

when a luminous globe sailed across the sky and a white cloud enveloped the oak tree and the children. A rain of white roses fell out of the heavens but dissolved just before landing. The crown could hear one of the children talking with the Virgin Mary.

On October 13, 1917, the crowd had swelled to 70,000 despite a driving rain. Suddenly the rain stopped and a patch of sky appeared in the clouds. In the middle of it was something resembling the sun. It was steel-colored and looked as bright as the sun, but the people were able to look straight at it. It began to spin rapidly, casting out beams of different-colored light for about five minutes. The object then turned red and appeared to be hurtling down toward the crowd. Then it zigzagged higher in the sky and began shining as the sun normally does. The remaining clouds broke up naturally.

The Fatima apparition first appeared in the context of UFO literature in a 1962 French book, *Les Extraterrestres* by Paul Thomas. Thomas compared the Fatima events to contemporary UFO sightings and came to the conclusion that they

were identical. Other ufologists reading Thomas's book speculated that either aliens impersonated Roman Catholic deities or the local people had interpreted the appearance of UFOs bearing aliens in the context of their Roman Catholic worldview. Later skeptics speculated that both religious visions and UFO encounters are hallucinatory events dictated by the viewer's own culture.

See Also: Apparitions; Mythology and Folklore
Further Reading:
Delaney, John J., ed. *A Woman Clothed with the Sun: Eight Great Appearances of Our Lady in Modern Times.* Garden City, NY: Hanover House, 1960.
Evans, Hilary. *Visions, Apparitions, Alien Visitors.* Wellingborough, U.K.: Aquarian Press, 1984.
McClure, Kevin. *The Evidence for Visions of the Virgin Mary.* Wellingborough, U.K.: Aquarian Press, 1983.

FILM AND TELEVISION

As with literature and popular culture more generally, on films and television the impact of UFOs has been large or small, depending upon how one defines the UFO category. As a phenomenon that can be dated to Kenneth Arnold's sighting on July 24, 1947, UFOs have exercised comparatively little direct influence. There is, however, an older tradition of interest in space travel and in possible encounters with alien beings that predates UFOs by several centuries. This larger interest has had a much broader impact on the human imagination.

The theme of alien invasion, for example, which provides the basic plot for countless science-fiction films, is at least as old as H. G. Wells's 1898 novel *The War of the Worlds.* Thus, while the UFO phenomenon of the 1940s and 1950s may have stimulated writers to compose quantitatively more alien-invasion stories, the basic plot of such tales has a much older origin.

The larger theme within which the UFO phenomenon best fits is the encounter with extraterrestrials. The great bulk of relevant films are less interested in probing the mystery of what it might mean to actually encounter extraterrestrials than in exploring human nature using the foil of aliens. Thus, while many twentieth-century aliens may not be represented in anthropomorphic ways, they still tend to have all of the thoughts and feelings of human beings. As in sci-fi literature, there are only a handful of basic plot outlines that an alien-encounter film can follow:

1. Alien invasion tales in which humanity must fight against hostile extraterrestrials, either against an overt invasion (*The War of the Worlds; Independence Day*), or against a covert infiltration of society and the government by aliens that look like human beings (*Invaders from Mars; Invasion of the Body Snatchers; They Live; The Arrival*).
2. "Technological angel"–type tales in which friendly extraterrestrials try to help humanity in some way (*The Day the Earth Stood Still; The Hidden*).
3. A less common but not unusual third category is constituted by stories in which terrestrials help aliens (*Enemy Mine; E.T.*).
4. Tales in which aliens are simply stand-ins for human beings, giving an exotic backdrop for a rather ordinary narrative (*Star Wars*).
5. Stories that attempt to come to grips with a truly alien Other (*Alien; Contact*).

These are not, of course, mutually exclusive categories, and many of the better films mix two or more of these together as subplots, making for a more complex overall narrative. We might also note that filmmakers, unlike certain sci-fi novelists, tend to shy away from stories that attempt to come to grips with a truly alien Other.

Although one can point to several exceptional films and programs, there does not seem to have been anything like a regular or a systematic utilization of UFO lore in sci-fi TV shows or box-office movies until very recently. The top-selling *Independence Day*, for example, distinguishes itself from earlier similar films in utilizing everything from abduction lore to such staples of UFO conspiracy theorizing as Area 51 and Roswell. The whole genre, in fact, seems to have been impacted by the runaway success of *X-Files*, a show that relies heavily on the paranormal claims that are actually popular in contemporary culture—particularly claims about UFOs and extraterrestrials.

Prior to *Independence Day*, the one major box-office hit to draw heavily from the contemporary UFO phenomenon was *Close Encounters of the Third Kind* (1977). This $22 million production placed astronomer J. Allen Hynek's encounter terminology into common parlance. Its commercial and critical success put writer-director Steven Spielberg on the way to becoming the most popular film director of all time. Except for the very ending, the film is true to reported sightings.

One of the products of the cultural imagination that groundbreaking psychologist Carl Jung may have had in mind when he referred to UFOs as "technological angels" was the 1951 classic *The Day the Earth Stood Still*. In this film, an alien named Klaatu and his robot Gort arrive in Washington, D.C., in a flying saucer to warn earth to stop its atom-bomb testing or be blown apart. Later, several less memorable films were made in imitation of *The Day the Earth Stood Still*. Stories of friendly extraterrestrials that approach earthlings with a message of concern about our potential for a nuclear holocaust were central to much of the flying saucer–contactee literature of the 1950s and 1960s.

In television, one of the few shows to draw elements directly from popular interest in the flying-saucer phenomenon was *My Favorite Martian* (an alien with antennae who could receive communications telepathically and who, furthermore, had intervened in terrestrial history in the past), though the novelty of the situation was not fully exploited. The other program that occasionally featured items of genuine UFO lore was *The Outer Limits*, a sort of *X-Files* of the 1960s.

One of the few films to use the expression "flying saucer" in its title was the 1956 B-grade movie *Earth versus the Flying Saucers*, which was based very loosely on Donald E. Keyhoe's best-selling book *Flying Saucers from Outer Space*. Beyond this handful of films and TV programs, it becomes progressively more difficult to tie relevant sci-fi movies directly to the UFO community. There were any number of very forgettable alien-invasion films that were more in the tradition of *The War of the Worlds* than productions appropriating aspects of the contemporaneous interest in flying saucers. Of these, one of the best was *Invasion of the Body Snatchers*.

The 1950s also witnessed the emergence of horror movies incorporating the theme of a monster or monsters from outer space, such as *The Blob*. This has remained a handy device to explain the origins of an unusually horrifying creature up to the present. Taking little or nothing from UFO folklore, this plot device gives filmmakers a convenient explanation for everything from the superpowers of a Superman or a Starman, to the unearthly attributes of the Andromeda Strain or the queer traits of the characters encountered in *The Rocky Horror Picture Show*, to the enlargement of the female protagonist in *Attack of the 50 Foot Woman* or the primal power of Natasha Hentridge's character in *Species*.

What all of this indicates in terms of the lines of influence between the UFO phenomenon, the electronic entertainment media, and the culture more generally is that UFOs have had relatively little direct impact on films and TV until recently. Prior to the 1990s mainline productions and programs embodying concepts and lore unique to the ufological community numbered one or two dozen, at most. Still, one could argue that widespread interest in the UFO phenomenon—particularly in the 1950s—was partially responsible for the many alien-encounter/alien-invasion films to be produced in the decades following Kenneth Arnold's famous sighting. While the argument certainly has merit, it is impossible to assess the extent of this influence. For instance, to refer again to the H. G. Wells paradigm: Where does the influence of the much older *The War of the Worlds*-type interest end and the impact of the newer ufological interest begin?

The reverse influence is similarly complicated. The great majority of our fellow citizens—even those skeptical about UFOs—are quite confident that intelligent extraterrestrial life exists somewhere in the cosmos. The widespread acceptance of this unproven hypothesis is at least partially the result of generations of people who have been exposed to the notion in countless science-fiction books, films, and TV programs. It is also clear that films about contact with aliens have fed popular interest in UFOs, but, once again, the extent of this influence is probably impossible to measure.

In terms of the general public's awareness of UFOs and ufology, however, we seemed to have crossed an important threshold in the 1990s. *Fire in the Sky* was the first box-office film built around the theme of an alien abduction that followed the account of an alleged real abductee. Not too many years later, the TV series *X-Files* began—a series that features an FBI agent whose interest in the paranormal was initiated by the abduction of his sister at a young age. The 1990s also witnessed the emergence of many TV-tabloid programs, such as *Sightings* (a name alluding to UFO sightings), that regularly discuss paranormal activities, including UFOs.

Older ufology was represented by attempts to document sightings and by the many people (i.e., contactees) who claimed to have received messages from friendly extraterrestrials that were here to warn us against destroying ourselves. The new ufology focuses on the abduction phenomenon and paranoid conspiracy theories about secret government tests of alien technology, even of official collusion with less-than-friendly aliens. The writers and producers of *X-Files* have clearly picked up on themes from more recent ufology and helped to popularize them. The notion of alien abduction—to pick one prominent idea from the new ufology—has become so widely familiar that it can be featured in advertisements and greeting cards.

The broad cultural awareness of alien-abduction themes and UFO-related conspiracy theories is clearly the direct result of the presentation of this information in the entertainment media. Without *Sightings, X-Files, Fire in the Sky, Independence Day*, and the like, items of data reflecting the new ufology would have remained confined to the ufological community. There is thus more discussion about UFOs at present than during any previous period, including even the 1950s. And whatever the other influences at work promoting this awareness may be—perhaps the new millennium, humanity's continuing exploration of the solar system, and other factors—it is clear that relevant films and TV programs have had the most significant impact in this regard.

See Also: Literature and the Alien Image; Popular Culture
Further Reading:
Guffey, George R. "Aliens in the Supermarket: Science Fiction and Fantasy for 'Inquiring Minds.'" In *Aliens: The Anthropology of Science Fiction*. Edited by George

E. Slusser and Eric S. Rabkin. Carbondale: Southern Illinois University Press, 1987.

Nesheim, Eric, and Leif Nesheim. *Saucer Attack! Pop Culture in the Golden Age of Flying Saucers.* Los Angeles: Kitchen Sink Press, 1997.

Rovin, Jeff. *Classic Science Fiction Films.* New York: Citadel Press, 1993.

FINGERPRINTS OF THE GODS

Fingerprints of the Gods (1995) is a relatively recent popular book that argues for the existence of a technologically advanced civilization (e.g., Atlantis) in the period preceding the earliest known citied societies. To support his point, author Graham Hancock examines the many artifacts and architectural monuments that are difficult to account for within the limits of our currently accepted scheme of history. *Fingerprints of the Gods* was poorly received by ancient-astronaut researchers, who felt that the author had taken the evidence they had compiled for prehistoric contact with extraterrestrials and marshaled it to support an alternative thesis. The author's dependence on ancient-astronaut evidence is even reflected in the title of his book, which is transparently a takeoff on *Chariots of the Gods?*. Hancock does not, however, acknowledge the work accomplished by his predecessors. In the few places where he bothers to mention the ancient-astronaut school, it is to dismiss Erich von Däniken and company out of hand.

See Also: Ancient Astronauts; Atlantis; von Däniken, Erich
Further Reading:
Hancock, Graham. *Fingerprints of the Gods.* New York: Crown, 1995.
von Däniken, Erich. *Chariots of the Gods? Unsolved Mysteries of the Past.* Trans. Michael Heron. New York: G. P. Putnam's Sons, 1970.

FIRE IN THE SKY

This 1993 film is based on the Walton abduction. A group of workingmen are driving back from a hard day's logging when a spaceship looms overhead. One man gets out of the pickup to investigate. A grapple descends from the spacecraft to abduct him. The others leave him behind in their haste to escape. When the man is reported missing, the sheriff wants to charge his coworkers with murder, which convinces them to relate the story of the sighting. Weeks later, the man reappears, dazed and battered, and tells his story of being probed and examined by aliens inside the saucer.

Before *Fire in the Sky*, the Walton abduction was already one of the best-known abduction incidents. The film served to give it even more prominence. Like *Close Encounters of the Third Kind,* it is one of the few box-office films to have been derived directly from UFO lore. Unlike many stories that portray alien abductions as morally ambivalent experiences, *Fire in the Sky* emphasizes the horror of the experience. As a corollary to this portrayal, aliens come across as immoral, evil beings. *Fire in the Sky* is probably more responsible for making the public aware of the alien abduction phenomenon—particularly as a negative, frightening experience—than any other single mainstream production before *X-Files*.

Paramount 1993; 98 min. Director: Robert Lieberman; Writer: Tracy Torme; Music: Mark Isham; Cast: D. B. Sweeney, Robert Patrick, Craig Sheffer, Peter Berg, James Garner, Henry Thomas, Kathleen Wilhoite, Bradley Gregg, Noble Willingham.

FIRST MAN INTO SPACE

A man returns from space covered in a strange type of dust he collected while flying through a meteor field. Eventually this organism kills the spaceman yet continues to inhabit his body. The organism must have human blood to survive and becomes a sort of alien vampire that even breaks into a blood bank. The astronaut's brother maneuvers the organism into a decompression chamber and kills it. *First Man into Space,* although not about UFOs per se, is a close relative to UFO-type films that play on the hostile-invaders-from-outer-space theme. Instead of a giant, monsterlike man in a spaceship, in this film the dangerous extraterrestrial is a microscopic organism.

Anglo-Amalgamated 1959; 78 min. Director: Robert Day; Writers: John C. Cooper, Lance Hargreaves; Cinematography: Geoffrey Faithful; Cast: Marshall Thompson, Marla Landi, Bill Edwards, Robert Ayres, Bill Nagy, Carl Jaffe.

FLASH GORDON

Flash Gordon was a classic 13-part 1936 serial based upon Alex Raymond's comic strip originally created in 1934. It starred Buster Crabbe, the former Olympic swimmer. This film influenced all subsequent space movies, including images of aliens. In 1980 Universal released a $40 million film remake of the same name, which flopped. While the Flash Gordon story was not about UFOs, the courageous explorer left a mark in our collective imagination. The long-range influence of Flash Gordon (as well as Buck Rogers, another serial star) parallels that of *Star Trek*.

Starling Productions/Famous Films 1980; 111 min. Director: Mike Hodges; Writer: Lorenzo Semple Jr.; Music: Howard Blake; Cast: Sam Jones, Melody Anderson, Chaim Topol, Max von Sydow, Ornella Muti, Thimothy Dalton, Brian Blessed.

FLATWOODS MONSTER

The so-called Flatwoods Monster was the name the press applied to one of the most famous alien encounters of all time. It occurred near Flatwoods, West Virginia, on the evening of September 12, 1952. Three boys saw a slow-moving, bright-red, round object come around a hill and stop above another hill. It then dropped suddenly behind the hill. An orange light could be seen to flare up. The boys thought they had seen a meteorite or a flying-saucer crash and went off to find it. They were joined by five other people and a dog along the way.

As they neared the site, the dog ran ahead out of sight. It began barking furiously and then turned tail and ran back past the group of people. The party noticed that the ground was shrouded in a foul-smelling mist that caused their eyes to water. Those at the head of the group saw a ball of fire the size of a house resting on the ground. Those in the rear did not see the ball of fire because their attention was distracted by what at first appeared to be just two small lights on the branch of an oak tree to their left. A member of the party turned a flashlight on the lights. They saw an entity about six feet tall. It had no arms or other appendages but had a distinct "head" shaped like an ace of spades. The head had a large circular window through which they could see darkness; two pale-blue lights like eyes shone out fixedly. The entity began to move around in cir-

Drawing of the Flatwoods Monster (CUFOS)

cling movements. It appeared to be gliding rather than walking.

The witnesses saw this entity for a few seconds. One of them fainted; the others dragged him off as they fled the scene. Later, when members of the party accompanied by representatives of the local press revisited the scene, they found nothing but noted a gaslike odor on the ground, which irritated the nose and throat. Returning to the scene when it became light, a witness saw skid marks about 10 feet apart between the tree where the entity had been sighted and place where the ball of fire had sat. In that area a large area of grass lay flat. In the skid marks only the tall grass was pushed down; no impression was made in the ground. The witnesses to the monster were obviously terrified, and they were not accused of consciously fabricating the story. No evidence or confession of hoax has ever come to light.

See Also: Barker, Gray Roscoe

Further Reading:

Barker, Gray. *They Knew Too Much about Flying Saucers.* New York: University Books, 1956.

Keyhoe, Donald E. *Flying Saucers from Outer Space.* New York: Henry Holt, 1953.

Teets, Bob. *West Virginia UFOs: Close Encounters in the Mountain State.* Terra Alta, WV: Headline Books, 1995.

FLIGHT TO MARS

In this 1951 color movie, interplanetary explorers crash-land on Mars, where there exists an advanced underground society very similar to that of humans. Martian leaders help fix the rocket while secretly scheming to copy its atomic-powered design for an invasion fleet. Its overlap with UFO thinking is confined to the theme of hostile aliens plotting to invade earth.

Monogram 1951; 72 min. Director: Lesley Selander; Writer: Arthur Strawn; Cinematography: Harry Neumann; Cast: Cameron Mitchell, Marguerite Chapman, Arthur Franz, Virginia Huston, John Litel, Richard Gaines.

FLYING, MAGICAL

One of the principal attributes of UFOs is that they fly (hence the names, e.g., unidentified *flying* objects; *flying* saucers). Many religious traditions, particularly within Western religion, associate the power of flight with spiritual beings—from gods to angels to demons. It was partially this attribute that led psychologist Carl Jung to characterize UFOs as "technological angels." Picking up on Jung's line of interpretation, one major school of thought has come to view modern UFO lore as traditional folklore in modern guise. The rise of the abduction as the dominant mode of encountering ufonauts suggests an alternate model for UFOs as technological *demons.*

The flight of demons and witches, typically with the aid of a broomstick, fork, or shovel, was a popular belief during the Middle Ages and the Renaissance, when it was claimed that the devil, his demons, and witches could fly and transport others through the air. Witches were also said to ride demons who were transformed into such animals as goats, cows, horses, and wolves, and the devil could carry people through the air with no visible means of transport. The speed of flying broomsticks and forks was said to be very high.

See Also: Ancient Astronauts; Angels; Gods and UFOs; Jung, Carl Gustav

Further Reading:

Gordon, Stuart. *The Encyclopedia of Myths and Legends.* London: Headline, 1993.

Lewis, James R. *Witchcraft Today: An Encyclopedia of Wiccan and Neopagan Traditions.* Santa Barbara, CA: ABC-CLIO, 1999.

FLYING DISC MAN FROM MARS

A 12-episode serial, *Flying Disc Man from Mars* was released in 1951. It is the story of Professor Mota who arrives on earth to prepare for its invasion by Mars. He first has to rebuild his disk-shaped spacecraft with the enforced aid of an earth scientist. From his flying saucer, Mota intends to bomb earth into submission. A scientist saves the day by diverting an atomic bomb so that it falls on Mota's hideout inside a volcano.

The saucer in this serial is a squat, cigar-shaped structure, which first appeared in the 1942 serial *Spy Smasher.* The studio reused the earlier footage of the saucer wherever it could and filmed no new flying scenes at all for *Flying Disc Man from Mars.*

Republic 1951; 167 min. Director: Fred C. Brannon; Writer: Ronald Davidson; Cinematography: Walter Strenge; Cast: Walter Reed, Lois Collier, Gregory Gay, James Crave, Harry Lauter, Richard Irving.

THE FLYING SAUCER (1950)

This 1950 movie was the first to feature flying saucers. Mikel Conrad directed, produced, and starred in the film. The plot revolves around U.S. and Russian scientists who clash over their search for a huge flying saucer that is hidden under a glacier. Commentators have tended to use this film as a concrete demonstration of how Cold War fears of invasion and fears of invasion from outer space were linked in the popular imagination.

Witches concoct an ointment to be used for flying to the Sabbath in this fourteenth-century illustration. (Dover Pictorial Archive Series)

Colonial 1950; 120 min. Director: Mikel Conrad; Cast: Mikel Conrad, Pat Garrison, Hanz von Teuffen.

THE FLYING SAUCER (1964)

The Flying Saucer is also the name of a 1964 Italian film in which several characters see Martians land on earth. They are subsequently locked up in a lunatic asylum when they press their claims. Although a comedy, the film speaks to a very real fear, namely, that any serious claim of seeing a UFO will be judged as being either a hoax or as an indication of mental imbalance.

Dino De Laurentiis 1964; 93 min. Director: Tinto Brass; Writer: Rudolfo Soego; Cinematography: Bruno Barcarol; Cast: Alberto Sordi, Monica Vitte, Silvano Mangano, Eleonora Rossi Drago, Guido Celano, Alberto Fogliani.

FLYING SERPENTS

There have been reports of enormous aerial serpents from the Middle Ages into the twentieth century. Flying serpents have been reported in England, Nebraska, Chile, Texas, South Carolina, Indiana, Norway, Denmark, and Brazil. The serpents were seen circling the sun, hovering over a steamboat, coiling up, and making striking movements. Flying serpents have been variously reported as having feathered wings and several pairs of fins. Flying serpents have been reported in such periodicals as *Flying Saucer Review, Amazing Stories, Saucer News,* and *Doubt.*

Further Reading:
Mackal, Roy P. *Searching for Hidden Animals.* Garden City, NY: Doubleday, 1980.
Wilkins, Harold T. *Flying Saucers on the Attack.* New York: Citadel Press, 1954.

FOO FIGHTERS

Foo fighters were unexplained phenomena sighted by aircraft pilots and other military personnel during World War II in both the European and Far Eastern theaters of operation. The phenomena were balls of light that would fly near or with the aircraft and maneuver rapidly. The term comes from a cartoon character named Smokey Stover, who repeated the maxim, "Where there's foo, there's fire." Foo fighters were variously believed to be new German or Japanese weapons, flares, balloons, flak, or St. Elmo's fire (an electrical discharge resembling a flame that is sometimes seen at prominent points on a ship's mast at sea). Had the term "flying saucers" been popularized at the time, that label probably would have been used instead. Indeed, within two weeks of the Kenneth Arnold sighting of June 24, 1947, the expression "flying saucer" had come to define all UFO phenomena, including foo fighters. Following are some examples of foo-fighter sightings:

On February 26, 1942, a Dutch sailor on the Timor Sea near New Guinea was scanning the sky for enemy aircraft. He saw a large illuminated disk 4,000–5,000 feet overhead. He observed the object for the next three hours. It remained at a constant altitude, circling above. Then it suddenly flew off at about 3,000 miles per hour and disappeared from view.

On March 25, 1942, a tailgunner on a Royal Air Force bomber over Holland saw a luminous orange disk or sphere following his plane. The gunner fired at the object when it came within 150 yards. He apparently hit the object with no affect. Shortly thereafter the object flew away at a speed of about 1,000 miles per hour.

In December 1944 a pilot reported that a foo fighter chased his plane 20 miles down the Rhine Valley. He was flying at 260 miles per hour and making evasive turns to starboard and port, but two balls of fire kept right up with his plane.

See Also: Arnold, Kenneth; Ghost Rockets
Further Reading:
Arnold, Kenneth, and Ray Palmer. *The Coming of the Saucers: A Documentary Report on Sky Objects that Have Mystified the World.* Boise, ID, and Amherst, WI: The Authors, 1952.
Gross, Loren E. *Charles Fort, the Fortean Society, and Unidentified Flying Objects.* Fremont, CA: The Author, 1976.
Lore, Gordon I. R. Jr., and Harold H. Deneault Jr. *Mysteries of the Skies: UFOs in Perspective.* Englewood Cliffs, NJ: Prentice-Hall, 1968.

FORBIDDEN ARCHEOLOGY

Forbidden Archeology (later condensed and reissued as *The Hidden History of the Human Race*) is, despite its considerable scholarship, a popular work on the origins of the human race and material culture that calls the establishment view into question. In addition to demonstrating the major role academic politics plays in shaping accepted science, authors Michael A. Cremo and Richard L. Thompson also bring together extensive evidence indicating that ancient humanity had a high degree of technical sophistication. The ancient-astronaut school has been quick to embrace *Forbidden Archeology* as supporting its hypothesis of early contact between humanity and extraterrestrials, and the authors have reciprocated by speaking at gatherings of the Ancient Astronaut Society and having their work published in *Ancient Skies,* its official periodical.

See Also: Ancient Astronauts; *Fingerprints of the Gods*
Further Reading:
Cremo, Michael A., and Richard L. Thompson. *Forbidden Archeology.* Los Angeles: Bhaktivedanta Book Publishing 1996 [orig. pub. 1993; condensed and reissued as *The Hidden History of the Human Race*].
Thompson, Richard L. *Alien Identities.* Alachua, FL: Govardhan Hill Publishing, 1995.

FORBIDDEN PLANET

Forbidden Planet was a 1956 MGM film starring Walter Pidgeon, Leslie Nielson, and Anne Francis.

It also featured Robby the Robot, who became a popular hero. In a plot based on Shakespeare's *The Tempest,* a team of astronauts takes a saucer-like spaceship to the planet Altair Four to find out what became of a lost expeditionary force. Although not about UFOs per se, this was an important film for influencing all subsequent views of space and spacecraft.

MGM 1956; 98 min. Director: Fred M. Wilcox; Writer: Cyril Hume; Music: Bebe Barron, Louis Barron; Cinematography: George Folsey; Cast: Walter Pidgeon, Anne Francis, Leslie Nielsen, Warren Stevens, Jack Kelly, Richard Anderson, Earl Holliman, George Wallace.

FORT, CHARLES HOY

Charles Hoy Fort was the first person to collect and publish reports of anomalous aerial phenomena as well as unexplained physical phenomena. He was also a satirist who ridiculed scientists' labored attempts to explain anomalies conventionally. Born in 1874 in Albany, New York, Fort worked as an editor and writer. His first memorable book, *The Book of the Damned,* was published in 1919. It contained data regarding phenomena that were unexplained by science.

American novelist and playwright Booth Tarkington wrote the introduction to Fort's *New Lands*

Commander John J. Adams (Leslie Nielsen) and his crew get their first look at the planet Altair-4 in the 1956 film Forbidden Planet. *(The Del Valle Archive)*

(1923) and coined the adjective "Fortean," meaning anomalistic. Fort's third book on anomalies, and the last to deal with UFOs, was called *Lo!* (1931). This book was the first ever to mention reports now known as close encounters of the third kind, involving a UFO seen at a distance less than 500 feet and involving observation of or interaction with occupants of the UFO.

On January 26, 1931, Fort's close friend, Tiffany Thayer, announced the formation of the Fortean Society, which survived until Thayer's death in 1959. The first issue of *The Fortean Society Magazine,* which would later be renamed *Doubt,* appeared in September 1937. Charles Fort died on May 3, 1932.

While Charles Fort laid the groundwork for ufology, since his death Forteans and ufologists have gone their separate ways. Ufologists limit their interests to UFOs only, whereas Forteans are interested in all anomalies, including such things as the Bermuda Triangle and Bigfoot encounters. Although the Fortean Society and *Doubt* are now defunct, there are currently at least three Fortean magazines: *INFO Journal* (published by the International Fortean Society), *Fortean Times,* and *Strange.* All three include UFO reports in their issues.

See Also: Fortean Society
Further Reading:
Fort, Charles. *The Book of the Damned.* Revised by Mr. X. London: John Brown Publishing, 1995.
———. *The Books of Charles Fort.* New York: Henry Holt, 1941.
Knight, Damon. *Charles Fort: Prophet of the Unexplained.* Garden City, NY: Doubleday, 1970.

FORTEAN SOCIETY

The Fortean Society was established on January 26, 1931, in New York City by Tiffany Thayer, a close friend of anomalist Charles Hoy Fort. Thayer read Charles Fort's second book, *New Lands,* at the age of 21 and wrote an enthusiastic letter to the author. Fort and Thayer began corresponding regularly. The two met seven years later when Fort returned to New York from London, and they became close friends.

Charles Fort himself played only a minor role in the society Thayer named after him, refusing

even to become a member. Fort died a year and a half after the society was established, bequeathing his notes to Thayer. The Fortean Society conducted irregular and informal meetings headed by Thayer.

In September 1937 it began publication of *The Fortean Society Magazine,* which changed its name to *Doubt* in 1944. The periodical cataloged such Fortean data as strange animals, UFOs, archaeological mysteries, and falls of various objects from the sky. Thayer also used the magazine as a vehicle to express his views on vivisection, politics, fluoridation of drinking water, vaccination, and anything else that struck his fancy.

In 1941 the Fortean Society published a 1,125-page volume, *The Books of Charles Fort.* The book went through several printings over the years and introduced Charles Fort to new generations of readers. Tiffany Thayer died of a heart attack on August 23, 1959, and the Fortean Society died with him.

See Also: Fort, Charles Hoy
Further Reading:
Gardner, Martin. *Fads and Fallacies in the Name of Science.* New York: Dover Publications, 1957.
Gross, Loren E. *Charles Fort, the Fortean Society, and Unidentified Flying Objects.* Fremont, CA: The Author, 1976.
Knight, Damon. *Charles Fort: Prophet of the Unexplained.* Garden City, NY: Doubleday, 1970.

FRANKENSTEIN MEETS THE SPACE MONSTER

In this 1965 film an android space pilot is attacked by an alien princess with a laser gun and her dwarf attendant when they land on earth in search of humans to replenish their dying planet. The attack short-circuits the android, which goes temporarily haywire, and the aliens begin their kidnapping mission. The princess has a ferocious pet space monster that terrorizes her earthling captives before the android gets rewired and frees them. It also destroys the aliens and their spaceship. This interesting film demonstrates how the theme of alien abduction entered the cultural imagination long before abductions became the dominant phenomena associated with UFOs.

Vernon-Seneca Films 1965; 80 min. Director: Robert Gaffney; Writer: George Garret; Cinematography: Saul

Midwell; Cast: James Karen, Nancy Marshall, Marilyn Hanold, David Kerman, Robert Reilly, Lou Cutell.

FRY, DANIEL WILLIAM

During the 1950s heyday of the flamboyant contactees of Southern California, Daniel Fry was a well-known and controversial celebrity on the circuit. Born in Verdon, Minnesota, in 1908, Fry was orphaned at the age of nine and went to Pasadena, California, to live with his grandmother.

In 1950 Fry was employed by Aerojet at the White Sands Proving Ground in New Mexico. On July 4 of that year, Fry missed the last bus to Las Cruces, where other White Sands employees had gone to celebrate the holiday. He was alone when a flying saucer appeared and hovered just above the ground. A voice started talking to Fry and invited him to board. The vehicle turned out to be a remote-controlled cargo carrier. The being speaking to Fry, who identified himself as Alan, was in the mothership located 900 miles above the earth. Fry accepted the invitation and was flown to New York and back in 30 minutes. Fry learned that Alan and his people were former residents of earth who had fled an ancient conflict.

In April 1954 Fry told his tale to a contactee gathering and was approached by a representative of New Age Publishing about writing a book. The book, *White Sands Incident,* was written and published within two months. On June 1, 1954, Fry held a press conference and impressed at least some reporters with his solidness and sobriety, as well as his willingness to submit to a lie-detector test. A few days later Fry took the test and failed. Fry disputed the interpretation of the polygraph operator in an article in *Saucers* magazine.

Soon Daniel Fry was a star attraction at the First Annual Flying Saucer Convention in Los An-geles. He was billed as the "scientist who rode a flying saucer from White Sands." Fry claims to have been contacted again in 1954 by Alan while at his secluded cabin near Merlin, Oregon. In 1955 Fry founded Understanding, Inc., which published the magazine *Understanding.* It reported on space messages and occult teachings. The organization and the magazine still exist.

An interesting chapter in Fry's life involved the National Investigation Committee on Aerial Phenomena (NICAP). NICAP secretary Rose Hackett Campbell harbored procontactee sympathies and granted Fry the honor of being a "charter member" of NICAP. Fry habitually identified himself as such. In 1957 NICAP challenged prominent contactees, including Fry, to undergo polygraph examinations. Fry and most others declined. Eventually NICAP sent out a form letter that disavowed any association between it and Fry and rejected Fry's claims as improbable. It also revoked Fry's regular membership (which he had obtained by paying dues) for misusing NICAP's name in ways that implied its endorsement of his views.

Daniel Fry claims to have met Alan personally in 1961. He turned out to look like a normal white male in casual clothes. Daniel Fry currently lives in Arizona and still makes occasional public appearances.

—*Jerome Clark*

See Also: Contactees
Further Reading:
Flammonde, Paris. *The Age of Flying Saucers: Notes on a Projected History of Unidentified Flying Objects.* New York: Hawthorn Books, 1971.
Fry, Daniel W. *Alan's Message: To Men of Earth.* Los Angeles: New Age Publishing, 1954a.
———. *The White Sands Incident.* Los Angeles: New Age Publishing, 1954b.
Gibbons, Gavin. *They Rode in Space Ships.* London: Neville Spearman, 1957.

LE GENDARME ET LES EXTRATERRESTRES

In this 1978 French comedy film, a police sergeant is confronted by the occupants of a flying saucer that has landed in St. Tropez. The aliens look exactly like human beings, but when someone knocks on them they sound hollow, like empty gasoline cans. They drink motor oil. The lone theme overlapping UFOs is the idea that ufonauts can appear as ordinary human beings.

SNC 1978; 91 min. Director: Jean Girault; Writer: Jacques Vilfrid; Cinematography: Marcel Grignon, Didier Tarot; Cast: Louis de Funes, Michel Galabru, Maurice Risch, Jean-Pierre Rambal, Maria Mauban, Guy Grosso, Michel Modo, Jacques François.

GENESIS, BOOK OF

Verse 6:4: "Then the Nephilim appeared on earth, after the sons of heaven had intercourse with the daughters of man, who bore them sons. They were the heroes of old, the men of renown." This passage in interpreted as referring to interbreeding between humans and extraterrestrial visitors. A more conventional explanation is that it is a vestige of the stories about the loves of gods and humans (e.g., Leda and the Swan, and all of Zeus's other exploits) remaining in the Bible out of the common Greek and Hebrew heritage from the civilizations of the second millennium B.C. Verse 15:17 refers to a smoking brazier and flaming torch that pass between the halves of Abram's sacrifice. This is far-fetched as a UFO report, sensible as ritual symbolism. Verses 19:24–27, the destruction of Sodom and Gomorrah, has been interpreted as being an atomic explosion from a bomb dropped by a UFO, though the radioactivity in that area would have to be higher than it is now for that to have been true.

See Also: Ancient Astronauts

Further Reading:
Downing, Barry H. *The Bible and Flying Saucers.* Philadelphia: J. B. Lippincott, 1968.
Goran, Morris. *The Modern Myth, Ancient Astronauts and UFOs.* South Brunswick, NJ: A. S. Barnes, 1978.

GHOST LIGHTS

Ghost lights are luminous phenomena that are classed separately, for several reasons, from ball lightning and UFOs. They are often supposed to be supernatural, and the lore about them therefore laps over into occult and superstitious beliefs. They are associated with the dead, fairies, black dogs, and religious visions. Attempts to photograph them have failed, suggesting that they are a psychological rather than physical phenomena.

Many of the descriptions of such lights from before 1947 suggest that, they would have been described as UFOs had the sightings been made later. Much research, including some by J. Allen Hynek, has gone into investigating them and their connection, if any, with UFOs. They have been explained variously as swamp gas (like the will-o'-the-wisp), ball lightning, and luminous clouds. Ufologist Jerome Clark is of the opinion that they are probably a grab bag of many different phenomena.

See Also: Green Fireballs
Further Reading:
Clark, Jerome. *The UFO Encyclopedia.* 2nd ed. Detroit: Omnigraphics, 1999.
Ritchie, David. *UFO: The Definitive Guide to Unidentified Flying Objects and Related Phenomena.* New York: Facts on File, 1994.

GHOST ROCKETS

Ghost rockets describe the numerous cigar-shaped objects sighted in Northern Europe in

1946. There were nearly 1,000 such sightings in Norway and Sweden that year. The majority of these observations were of light phenomena, luminous or fiery balls or cigar-shaped objects, often trailing smoke.

There were aerial sightings and radar trackings of the objects as well as crashes witnessed. There were no reports of occupants of these objects. At the time, many believed that ghost rockets were Soviet experiments with captured German V-2 rockets, although records since have shown that Russia had a primitive rockets technology at the time and was not the source of these ghostly missiles. Meteors explained a few of the reports, but not those of specifically structured craft.

In the 1980s Swedish ufologists investigated the ghost-rocket wave of 1946. They concluded that it was not a postwar hallucinatory phenomenon but that people saw real physical objects. They also postulated that the crashed objects disintegrated themselves and might have been made of a kind of magnesium alloy that would disintegrate easily.

See Also: Foo Fighters

Further Reading:

Birdsall, Mark Ian. *A Research Paper Pertaining to the Phenomenon Known as Ghost Rocket and Foo Fighter.* Leeds, U.K.: Quest Publications, 1988.

Gillmor, Daniel S., ed. *Scientific Study of Unidentified Flying Objects.* New York: Bantam Books, 1969.

Gross, Loren E. *UFOs: A History—1946: The Ghost Rockets.* 3rd ed. Fremont, CA: The Author, 1988.

GHOSTS

Although ghosts and UFOs are not necessarily connected, their common classification as paranormal phenomena means that many believers in ghosts also believe in the real existence of UFOs. The notion of ghosts is found throughout history and in all cultures. Ethymologically, "ghost" is linked to the German word *geist,* or spirit, indicating a broader connotation of the original word. In fact, ghosts have been viewed in different ways— as a soul, as breath, as good, and/or as evil. Most typically, ghosts are believed to be the souls of the dead who return to the living world for a variety of reasons, such as revenging their own unjust death, reclaiming their goods, accomplishing some un-

finished task, revealing some sort of truth, protecting their families, and so on.

Ghosts have been viewed differently in different civilizations. In the West, the appearance of ghosts was considered frightening, a source of evil or a demonic force. In Eastern Europe, there was a good deal of popular lore about the ghosts of the dead who come back to attack the living in the form of vampires. In Indian culture, both Hinduism and Buddhism acknowledge the existence of some sort of ghosts. Ghosts, like evil spirits, haunt cemeteries and live in trees.

Although it is typically believed that ghosts appear at night, there are many traditions of daylight and twilight appearances. There have been various theories to explain the phenomenon of ghosts as tricks of light and shade or as one's imagination. Psychological theories tend to explain the belief in the appearance of ghosts as dreams, projections of one's subconscious, or hallucinations.

Ghosts, which are not seen by everyone, usually involve noises, unusual smells, extreme cold, and the displacement of objects. Also visual images, tactile sensations, voices, and the apparent psychokinetic movement of objects may be included. Ghosts move through solid matter, appear and disappear abruptly, can cast shadows and be reflected in mirrors, seem corporeal or luminous and transparent, and can be lifelike or have limited movements. UFOs exhibit many of these same characteristics, giving rise to speculation that UFOs are spiritual rather than physical phenomena.

A new approach to ghosts developed in the nineteenth century with the birth of spiritualism. Mediums—intermediaries who communicated with the spirits—viewed ghosts as souls of the dead. In more recent times channeling, a new form of mediumship, has become popular in New Age circles. Among such New Age mediums, it is interesting that this unusual way of conversing with the dead has been extended to other classes of beings, including extraterrestrials. Thus, not only do UFOs exhibit ghostly traits, but human beings attempt to communicate with ufonauts via the same method they communicate with spirits of the dead.

See Also: Apparitions; Channeling; Demonological Explanations of UFOs

Further Reading:

Cavendish, Richard, ed. *Encyclopedia of the Unexplained: Magic, Occultism, and Parapsychology.* London: Arkana Penguin Books, 1989.

Lewis, James R. *The Encyclopedia of Afterlife Beliefs and Phenomena.* Detroit: Gale Research, 1994.

Ritchie, David. *UFO: The Definitive Guide to Unidentified Flying Objects and Related Phenomena.* New York: Facts on File, 1994.

THE GIANT CLAW

In this 1957 movie a giant bird arrives from outer space to hatch an egg. It also wreaks havoc by doing such things as grabbing a train and flying off with it dangling from its beak. The bird is radioactive and has an antimatter shield that prevents conventional weapons from harming it and ensures it does not show up on radar. A device is developed to pierce the antimatter shield and the monster is killed, sinking into the ocean with one claw upraised. The movie is unintentionally hilarious due to its atrocious special effects and the goofy design of the bird, which has huge feet, turkey feathers on its wings, a long neck, and glassy eyes.

The notion that alien animals, in addition to intelligent extraterrestrial ufonauts, also exist and can survive on earth and be a threat to humankind is an old idea to Hollywood but a new notion within the UFO community, confined almost entirely to reports associated with the activity of the Chupacabras ("Goat Sucker"). This may be an example of how a theme of the human imagination has filtered down to be a concrete, empirical claim.

Clover 1957; 76 min. Director: Fred F. Sears; Cast: Jeff Morrow, Mara Corday, Morris Ankum, Louis D. Merrill, Edgar Barrier, Robert Shayne, Morgan Jones, Clark Howat.

A giant bird from "some godforsaken antimatter universe" goes on a rampage in major cities around the world in the 1957 film The Giant Claw. *(The Del Valle Archive)*

GIANT ROCK SPACECRAFT CONVENTION

The Giant Rock Spacecraft Convention was an annual event held from 1953 to 1977 at Giant Rock in the desert of Southern California. It was hosted by contactee George Van Tassel and was the most important contactee gathering on the circuit. In addition to Van Tassel, other participants included George Adamski, Wayne Aho, Orfeo Angelucci, Truman Bethurum, Daniel Fry, and George Hunt Williamson. These contactees, their followers, and curiosity-seekers would meet at the convention, sell and buy literature and metaphysical materials, listen to the latest claims, and try to outdo each other in spouting their own views and theories. The gatherings were colorful, entertaining, and harmless. In the 1950s the conventions attracted 10,000 persons. Audiences waned in the 1960s. The convention was not continued after the death of Van Tassel on February 9, 1978.

See Also: Contactees; Van Tassel, George W.
Further Reading:
Barker, Gray. *Gray Barker at Giant Rock.* Clarksburg, WV: Saucerian Publications, 1976.
Curran, Douglas. *In Advance of the Landing: Folk Concepts of Outer Space.* New York: Abbeville Press, 1985.
Reeve, Bryant, and Helen Reeve. *Flying Saucer Pilgrimage.* Amherst, WI: Amherst Press, 1957.
Van Tassel, George W. *I Rode a Flying Saucer! The Mystery of the Flying Saucers Revealed.* Los Angeles: New Age Publishing, 1952.

GLITTERBALL

Two boys find an alien and help it contact its home planet in this 1977 film. In the climax the mothership returns to rescue it. This is clearly a precursor if not *the* precursor to Steven Spielberg's classic *E.T.,* this is one of the few films in which earthlings rescue aliens rather than vice versa. Beyond the basic idea of an extraterrestrial arriving on earth from a spaceship, there is little or no direct link between this film and UFO thinking.

Mark Forstater Productions/Children's Film Foundation 1977; 56 min. Director: Vincent McEveety; Writers: Arthur Alsberg, Don Nelson; Cinematography: Leonard J. South; Cast: Dean Jones, Don Knotts, Julie Sommars, Jacques Marin, Roy Kinnear, Bernard Fox.

GODS AND UFOS

Subscribers to Erich von Däniken's ancient-astronaut theory often try, as he did, to interpret every celestial event in ancient literature as being a manifestation of UFOs, extraterrestrials, or something akin to them. As a blanket explanation for all ancient mystical and mythic writings, this approach is clearly inadequate. However, for *some* passages about ancient gods, goddesses, heroes, and the like, the interpretation that these represent a UFO sighting or a memory of one is not utterly impossible. A more cautious, selective application of the ancient-astronaut hypothesis to celestial events mentioned in religious texts will have to take place before the theory stands any chance of serious consideration by mainstream scholars.

See Also: Ancient Astronauts; von Däniken, Erich
Further Reading:
Goran, Morris. *The Modern Myth, Ancient Astronauts and UFOs.* South Brunswick, NJ: A. S. Barnes, 1978.
von Däniken, Erich. *Chariots of the Gods? Unsolved Mysteries of the Past.* Trans. Michael Heron. New York: G. P. Putnam's Sons, 1970.

GRAYS

Different contactees have reported ufonauts with a variety of appearances, from handsome humanoids to ugly beasts. One of the most popular types reported is the so-called grays. As the name suggests, this category of alien is gray in color. Hairless and about four feet tall, their heads appear disproportionately large for their bodies, which are thin with long, with spindly arms and legs. The eyes are large, black, and insect-like. They have little or no nose and small, lipless mouths. Grays have often been reported by abductees and are by far the most popular alien type, particularly in the industrialized West.

See Also: Abductees; Close Encounters
Further Reading:
Clark, Jerome. *The UFO Encyclopedia.* 2nd ed. Detroit: Omnigraphics, 1999.
Ritchie, David. *UFO: The Definitive Guide to Unidentified Flying Objects and Related Phenomena.* New York: Facts on File, 1994.

GREEN FIREBALLS

Aerial phenomena described as "green fireballs" were sighted between 1948 and 1951 in the U.S.

Southwest, just as the UFO craze was beginning to grow. The military investigated these because of their proximity to government research installations but came to no publicly announced conclusions. The failure to mount a careful investigation means that these phenomena, whatever they were, cannot be explained as either being or not being UFOs.

See Also: Ghost Lights

Further Reading:

Maccabee, Bruce, and Edward Walters. *UFOs Are Real . . . Here's the Proof.* New York: Avon Books, 1997.

Walters, Ed, and Frances Walters. *The Gulf Breeze Sightings: The Most Astounding Multiple Sightings of UFOs in U.S. History.* New York: William Morrow, 1990.

GREEN, GABRIEL

Gabriel Green was born November 11, 1924, in Whittier, California. He received his higher education at Los Angeles City College and Woodbury Business College. He founded the Amalgamated Flying Saucer Clubs of America in 1957 and has served as its president since 1959. He lectures widely at UFO conferences on such topics as channeling, psychic phenomena, spirituality, past-life regressions, the New Age, the Higher Self, universal economics, and the Second Coming. His book *Let's Face Facts About Flying Saucers* was published by Popular Library in 1967.

See Also: New Age

Further Reading:

Biographical Sketch of Gabriel Green. Northridge, CA: Amalgamated Flying Saucer Clubs of America, 1974.

Green, Gabriel, and Warren Smith. *Let's Face the Facts about Flying Saucers.* New York: Popular Library, 1967.

Jacobs, David M. *The UFO Controversy in America.* Bloomington: Indiana University Press, 1975.

A painting by Michael Buhler of a typical abduction scene with the gray aliens described by many (Mary Evans Picture Library)

GROUND CREW/PLANETARY ACTIVATION ORGANIZATION

The Ground Crew is an online UFO religious movement that is attempting to prepare humanity for large-scale first contact between earth and the Galactic Federation, a universal organization of extraterrestrial beings. According to the movement's teachings, this contact is imminent, and members of the group will play key roles as intermediaries between these extraterrestrial forces and the earth's population.

The teachings of the Ground Crew began being posted online in 1996 under the direction of Sheldon Nidle. Nidle claims to have had extraterrestrial and UFO experiences shortly after his birth on November 11, 1946. These experiences include various telepathic communications, teaching sessions aboard extraterrestrial spacecraft, and knowledge from "direct core implants." According to Nidle's biography, at the age of 14 he demanded that communication between himself and the Sirians be stopped due to the conflict he was experiencing between extraterrestrial and terrestrial knowledge. He attended Ohio University and the University of Southern California, receiving an M.A. in Southeast Asian government, as well as an M.A. in American politics and international public administration. He began, but did not complete, a Ph.D. program, instead researching alternative electrical energy sources. He claims that in the mid-1980s he was again contacted by extraterrestrial forces and now speaks for those forces as a representative and lecturer for the Galactic Federation.

The teachings of the Ground Crew began as an urgent call to humanity to prepare for an immediate planetary transformation. Earth was to experience the effects of photon belts, which would surround the planet and assist in its transformation back to a pristine state. During this transformation, major cities and human structures would be destroyed, and the population of the planet that was not evacuated to underground chambers or removed aboard spacecraft would perish in the upheaval. According to the early teachings of the Ground Crew, without extraterrestrial intervention from the Galactic Federation most of humanity would be destroyed.

In the early sessions Sheldon Nidle channeled excited messages from the Galactic Federation on at least a weekly basis, claiming that even as he spoke special extraterrestrial forces were drilling huge underground chambers for the population. Massive motherships were preparing for millions of passengers, and the membership of the Galactic Federation was rejoicing at the prospects of initiating another species into a universal deep-space brotherhood. The specific day for the scheduled First Contact was December 17, 1996.

Participants of the Ground Crew were assured of their significance and told of their urgent roles. Certain members would be special "councilors" who would aid individuals having difficulty accepting the mass landings and rapid transformation of the planet. Others would be elevated to bureaucratic positions, being a sort of earthly ambassador responsible for relations between extraterrestrial species and humans. Training for these positions would begin while the membership slept, through sophisticated and advanced technology brought by the Galactic Federation specifically for this purpose. After First Contact, the remaining training would be implanted within the individuals, so they had no need to experience any anxiety regarding their lack of formal preparation concerning their anticipated role. Each member within the organization was praised for their willingness to accept this predicted responsibility and encouraged to spread the word and recruit as many people as possible, since many needed positions had not yet been filled.

Despite members' being assured that all was fully ready to begin the mass landing on the chosen date, December 17 came and went without the manifestation of the anticipated contact. Messages from the Galactic Federation continued to guarantee the participants that they would be appearing relatively soon, stating it would like to land on the planet before the start of the Gregorian New Year. To prepare for the final phase of the operation, the federation instructed all the elements of the fleet to be put on final standby status and for the defense forces to put their full suppression operation into immediate effect.

Although the New Year began and the ships did not arrive, messages from the Galactic Federation continued to forecast a scenario anchored within a time frame based upon a relatively quick resolution. The spring of 1997 was now seen as the appropriate period for First Contact and planetary evacuation; however, this event was also delayed due to a solar storm and the instability of the planet. Over these several months the messages presented by Nidle to participants in the organization remained exciting and entertaining, giving glimpses into the future life they would lead as members of a universal brotherhood equipped with the technology to travel throughout the cosmos. Descriptions were presented of other members of the Galactic Federation, including Arcturians and Mintakans, amphibiod species, horse-like sentient beings, and other humanoid space travelers. Renditions of spaceships, planetary environments, Galactic Federation uniforms, and even the uninhibited sexual nature of our Space Brothers and Space Sisters were presented to the membership, keeping spirits high and anticipation palpable.

Despite the failed prophecy concerning the mass landing scenario on a specific day, a new date was set to coincide with the arrival of the Hale-Bopp comet on May 5, 1997. The comet was in fact, "a large spaceship that contains a crew of over 200,000 sentient beings" (SN, Feb. 22, 1997). Along with the crew, the ship contained a "cloaking and holographic systems that imitate what a comet should look like" and 10,000 ambassadors who would play a special role in the formal initiation of the earth population into the Galactic Federation. The mass landing would coincide with the arrival of the ambassadors and the detailed scenario outlined by Nidle would be completed. Millions of ships would participate in the mass landing event, despite the "traffic jam" that was now occurring in the upper atmosphere of the planet.

Although members of the Ground Crew were told that a special delegation was being sent to meet with the 10,000 ambassadors who would be landing near Ayers Rock, Australia, it became a nonevent after the mass suicide of the membership of the Heaven's Gate group. In an effort to distance themselves from the belief system of Heaven's Gate, Valerie Donner, a core member of the Ground Crew, dismissed the act and stated

that the Heaven's Gate leader had "narcissistic tendencies" and that their channeled information was accurate, whereas the HG group practiced "ridiculous acts of self-destruction." Instead of the mass landings of millions of spacecraft along with the ambassadors we are told that, "a shuttle from the ambassador's star ship, carrying key personal [sic] landed . . .just south of Ayers Rock in Australia . . .[which was] met by a special shuttle from the Galactic Federation Fleet." A "special ceremony" was conducted and "vital papers" were exchanged (SN, May 3, 1997). This message was posted by Sheldon Nidle two days before the scheduled event was to take place and after May 10, 1997 there is no further mention made concerning the Hale-Bopp comet or its 10,000 ambassadors.

Despite the repeated failure of any recognizable landing of extraterrestrial spaceships, Nidle and the Ground Crew remained focused upon an imminent landing scenario: "Our command team is completely dedicated to a policy of no more delays and no more unforeseen developments" (SN, May 13, 1997). The prophetic failure was justified using several reasons, including a development of an earlier Ground Crew revelation. Early in the channeled messages of Nidle, reference is made to the negative attitude and shortsighted outlook of the planetary leaders of earth. Nidle claims that earth governments are aware of the extraterrestrial forces looming in the upper atmosphere of the planet, yet they choose to ignore the implications of this event and deny the existence of these forces to the planetary population. On December 18, 1996, Nidle claims that the bureaucratic rulers of earth are in fact "illegal surface governments" that "continue to interfere with the divine plan." By September 1997 it is revealed that the governments are in fact corrupted by "their previous secret relationship to reptoids, dinoids, [and] other similar forms of then dark sentient beings." Yet followers are assured that governments pose no real threat to their well-being, although a gnostic-type myth is presented concerning galactic wars, hidden subterranean civilizations, Atlantis, and Lemuria. By June 1997 blame for the failed landings is clearly laid upon these otherworldly forces, which conspired with "planetary elites." Maintaining channeling of epic proportions, the membership is told of secret experimental weapons and interstellar dogfights between the Galactic Federation and a desperate ruling class bent on maintaining its sovereignty over planet earth. Although the Galactic Federation "underestimated" the power and connections of the earth elites, participants are assured that, "our mission cannot be stopped, or even slightly deterred by their nefarious actions" (SN, June 17, 1997).

Thus messages from Nidle begin to recognize that a specific date for a mass landing was perhaps too specific and not reflective of the "right divine time." "Please do not overly concentrate on any specific mass landing date" (SN, June 7, 1997), participants are told, "a major part of this non-specific way is to not be attached to specific dates. We will come in the right divine time" (SN, June 14, 1997).

"In the past several months, many of you have addressed a great deal of vitriol over the galactic concept of 'soon' and the promise of our coming. We would now like to dispel this form of criticism of our actions . . . You are a most short-sighted and impatient set of humans . . . All that is needed now is your continued full cooperation and enduring support of our most sacred task" (SN, Aug. 9, 1997).

Soon a very important shift begins in the focus of the Ground Crew's message. Although the original channeling began with an urgent recognition that without the direct intervention of spaceship and extraterrestrial forces most of humanity would be destroyed, the onus was now placed upon the membership to assist in the transformation of the planet without the intervention of these forces. Messages began to contain a greater spiritual dimension, including references to the Great White Brotherhood, Ascended Masters, the I AM Self, archangels, and Elohim. It was revealed that the prophesized earthly catastrophes and potential for cataclysmic disaster had been altered by the "immense turning to the light of the planetary population" (SN, Sept. 30, 1997). Emphasis shifts concerning the role of the participants from being one solely focused upon aiding the Galactic Federation after a mass landing scenario to more stringently include "the interim period" before the landings are to occur. Membership is now consistently told that salvation is a "two way street" and

that "we ask that you do not think that we are some sort of a rescuing army."

In December 1997 Nidle began restructuring the Ground Crew. One of the core members, Valerie Donner, was removed from the organization; however, when she left, she took with her the rights to the Ground Crew name and website. Donner had been an ardent supporter of the Nidle message and also a channeler of messages from spiritual beings. Although the reason for this falling-out is not clear—both parties presented alternate accounts of the event—the separation did not occur over the failed arrival of the Galactic Federation. Valerie Donner maintains a Ground Crew website and posts channeled messages, "straight from the heart" along with the weekly insight of the "Great One." Donner continues to "watch the skies" for UFOs, but her message remains focused upon personal spiritual transformation. Although she believes we are living in the end times and "we will have extraterrestrial brothers and sisters visit us here," her focus can be considered more "new age" in content, often referring to Angels, fairies, talking with plants, and telepathic communication.

Donner claims that several hundred people visit her web site daily to receive her channeled messages of spiritual healing, personal transformation, ascension, and "peace, joy, and harmony." Her web site is well maintained and offers standard New Age items for sale, including essential oils, books of channeled messages, and personal consultations for $85 an hour over the phone. Her belief in UFO activity permeates throughout her messages, which contain statements such as, "it flew by faster than any UFO I have ever seen." She certainly continues to believe in the Galactic Federation as described by Nidle, "What are the Galactic Federation, Spiritual Hierarchy and God thinking about all of this drama," yet she remains attached to her "messages from the heart" and prefers poetry over spaceship descriptions, "Get your act together—and do it soon. God wants you to have it all with a silver spoon. Can you believe it? 1997 was a bust! I'll bet 1998 begins with some big spiritual thrust." (VD, Dec. 29, 1997)

With the loss of the Ground Crew name and website, Nidle founded a new movement, the Planetary Activation Organization. A website was quickly established, membership was informed of the changes, and the organization was restructured to make the messages channeled by Nidle the only source for information concerning the Galactic Federation. A detailed bureaucratic organization was set in place that included special representatives within a hierarchical structure, with Nidle occupying the apex. Small organizations—Planetary Activation Groups—were established under Subgroup Coordinators, Regional Coordinators, and the Main Coordinator. Along with Planetary Activation Groups and Planetary Activation Workers, membership could also participate to maintain communication between the groups.

With a restructured organization in place, Nidle began to focus upon the need to create a "Web of Light," the purpose of which was to unite similar-minded groups within a network concerned with the environment, government conspiracies, and UFO's. The role of the membership now begins to focus upon building and maintaining this new network, along with their spiritual transformation. Messages channeled by Nidle continue to maintain a belief in the existence of UFO forces and the Galactic Federation, yet new insights are given into the spiritual evolution of humanity and the role the Planetary Activation will play in bringing about these "spiritual" earthly transformations.

Messages began to focus on topics such as the creation of reality, the "matrix," illusion, and the true self of the individual. The individual is recognized as a god-like being created specifically for a divine purpose that is now coming to fruition. The negative earth rulers are identified as an ancient "world wide order of secret cabal" who have been creating the reality matrix of humanity for millennium. The Galactic Federation now plays the role of the enlightened being responsible for slowly removing the influence of these negative entities from the population. Nidle reported that "Star Gates" were being placed in the upper atmosphere to aid in the transformation and special "Galactic Exploration and Medical Teams" were assisting people when they slept. Although switching the majority of the channeled messages to spiritual transformation, Nidle continues to incorporate the UFO dimension in an appeal to those members fixated to this component of the myth. The Galac-

tic Federation remains, "dedicated to massive first contact as soon as possible" with the repositioned and reordered ships available, "at a moments notice, we are fully prepared to appear on your shores" (SN, Feb. 23, 1999).

Humankind's exalted and fully developed spiritual role now makes earth a vitally important planet for the universe. Nidle reveals with excitement and pride that earth is in fact a special "showcase" planet that will act as a switch in the spiritual transformation of the Milky Way Galaxy (SN, Jan. 25, 2000). "Mother earth contains a crystal that drives the energies that are sustaining the galaxy . . .[earth is] one of the most auspicious places in the universe" (SN, May 5, 2000). Nidle's teachings have now become so anthropocentric that the "Time Keepers" of heaven who exist throughout the galaxy have even modified a special day count more "appropriate to *your* need" (emphasis added).

Messages continue to be presented with excitement and at a fever pitch. Despite the failed prophecies, the movement continues to develop and expand its member base, claiming to have hundreds of Planetary Activation Groups in over 29 countries.

The greatest difficulty concerning the study of this movement is also one of the most interesting—its virtual composition. It is impossible to gauge the increases and decreases in membership without observable and empirical data. Membership may have declined drastically with the continued failed prophecies of 1996 and 1997, yet the movement generated sufficient income to maintain its website and a core group of devoted religious virtuosi. Along with the lack of empirical data, archived transcripts of the movement may be altered or simply disappear. The movement's most notorious period of failed prophecy is no longer posted online, and new members within the movement may never be exposed to this component of Nidle's channeling.

—*Christopher Helland*

See Also: Channeling; Contactees; Cults, UFO; New Age; Religions, UFO
Further Reading:
Daniels, Ted. *A Doomsday Reader: Prophets, Predictors, and Hucksters of Salvation.* New York: New York University Press, 1999, chap. 12.
Donner, Valerie. URL: http://www.thegroundcrew.com.
Planetary Activation Organization, URL: http://www.paoweb.com.

HANGAR 18

Hangar 18 is a notorious storage building at Wright-Patterson Air Force Base in Ohio, where, rumor has it, the military has been storing the bodies of aliens recovered from crashed UFOs, particularly from Roswell. There is no public knowledge of this, or any admission by the military that any such thing is going on; this is usually explained away as being the result of a conspiracy the hide the truth from the public. Ufologists have put together a reasonably plausible trail of testimony to back up the idea that at least something was going on. Skeptics claim it is all a fantasy.

See Also: Area 51; Conspiracy Theories; The Roswell
    Incident
Further Reading:
Randle, Kevin D. *The Randle Report: UFOs in the 1990s.*
    New York: M. Evans, 1997.
Ritchie, David. *UFO: The Definitive Guide to Unidentified*
    Flying Objects and Related Phenomena. New York:
    Facts on File, 1994.

HANGAR 18

This is a 1980 film in which two astronauts are targeted by the White House as scapegoats for the loss of a space shuttle that actually collided with a UFO. They try to blow the cover-up of the alien craft's crash-landing in Texas. A NASA investigator sides with the astronauts after discovering and decoding alien plans to invade the United States.

This film resonates with several important ideas in ufological thinking. Beyond the theme of hostile aliens invading the earth, the whole idea of U.S. authorities trying to hide the fact of a flying-saucer crash reflects a major subject of popular thinking about UFOs. Even the name of the film—*Hangar 18*—is taken directly from UFO conspiracy lore.

Sunn Classic 1980; 97 min. Director: James L. Conway;
Writer: David O'Malley; Cast: Darren McGavin, Robert

Vaughn, Gary Collins, James Hampton, Philip Abbott, Pamela Bellwood, Tom Hallick, Cliff Osmond, Joseph Campanella.

HANSEN, MYRA

Myra Hansen, under hypnosis, reported that in the spring of 1980 in rural New Mexico, west of Las Cruces, she, along with her six-year-old son, saw five UFOs descending into a cow pasture. Two white-suited creatures emerged from the UFO and mutilated a cow with an 18-inch knife. Then she and her son were abducted and taken to separate ships, where she was given a physical examination, including a vaginal probe. They were then taken to an underground base filled with vats full of floating human body parts. Finally, they were taken aboard the craft and flown back to the landing site.

See Also: Abductees; Alien-Abduction Narratives; Close
    Encounters; Inner Earth

HARMONIC CONVERGENCE

Harmonic convergence refers to the period August 16–17, 1987, during which many New Agers believed that a strong cosmic force climaxed, resulting in a collective shift in human mental orientation. This shift was supposedly characterized by a move from tribal to planetary consciousness, from separation to unity, from fear to love, and from conflict to cooperation. During the harmonic convergence, many participants, including Jose Arguelles, the person who laid the theoretical foundation for the gathering, saw UFOs, as if the Space Brothers were somehow aware of and participating in the event.

The basic idea is contained in Arguelles's *The Transformative Vision* (1975), in which he claims that modern humankind has depreciated the relationship to the earth as an organism and has instead favored a materialistic culture. According to Arguelles, civilization is soon to be replaced by a planetary culture through a process called "climax of matter," a concept developed from his study of Mayan prophecies and the Mayas' calendar system. It is claimed that this process began with a period of nine 52-year cycles that had its origins in the arrival of Hernando Cortés in Central America and culminated in 1987. Arguelles argues that the spread of civilization follows a harmonic wave pattern, which was supposed to peak on August 16–17, 1987. The energy released into the planet's life during this event was viewed as a prelude to the real intergalactic harmonic convergence in 2012.

According to Arguelles, the harmonic convergence would result in the demilitarization of the planet, as well as in a cessation of environmental pollution, whereas sociocultural changes would be denoted by an increase in the actualization of human potential and the emergence of parapsychological abilities.

See Also: New Age; Space Brothers
Further Reading:
Arguelles, Jose. *The Transformative Vision.* New York: Muse Publications, 1992 [orig. ed. 1975].
Melton, J. Gordon, et al. *New Age Almanac.* Detroit: Gale Research, 1991.

HEALING

Although individuals who get too close to alleged UFOs have become sick with burns, radiation illness, and certain other symptoms, abductees also sometimes report that their alien kidnappers also heal them, should they have been sick or disabled at the time of the abduction. This characteristic of the abduction experience has its parallel in fairy lore.

See Also: Close Encounters; Fairies

HEAVEN'S GATE

On March 26, 1997, the bodies of 39 men and women were found in a posh mansion outside San Diego, all victims of a mass suicide. Messages left by the group indicate that they believed they were stepping out of their "physical containers" in order to ascend to a UFO that was arriving in the wake of comet Hale-Bopp. They also asserted that the comet, or parts of it, would subsequently crash into the earth and cause widespread destruction. In a taped message, the leader further noted that our calendars were off—that the year 1997 was really the year 2000, as if everyone was in agreement that the world would end precisely two millennia after the time of Jesus. The deaths of Heaven's Gate members embody a sinister aspect of apocalyptic religiosity, one that propels millenarians to engage in radical acts of preemptive violence as a way of invoking the final end.

Heaven's Gate—formerly known as Human Individual Metamorphosis—originally made headlines in September 1975, when, following a public lecture in Waldport, Oregon, more than 30 people vanished overnight. This disappearance became the occasion for a media event. For the next several months, reporters generated story after story about glassy-eyed cult groupies abandoning the everyday lives to follow the strange couple who alternately referred to themselves as "Bo and Peep," "the Two," "Do and Ti," and other bizarre monikers.

Bo and Peep founded one of the most unusual flying-saucer religions ever to emerge out of the occult-metaphysical subculture. Bo (Marshall Herff Applewhite) and Peep (Bonnie Lu Nettles) met in 1972. In 1973 they had an experience that convinced them that they were the two witnesses mentioned in Revelation 11 who would be martyred and then resurrected three and a half days later—an event they later referred to as "the Demonstration." Preaching an unusual synthesis of occult spirituality and UFO soteriology, they began recruiting in New Age circles in the spring of 1975. Followers were required to abandon friends and family, detach themselves completely from human emotions as well as material possessions, and focus exclusively on perfecting themselves in preparation for a physical transition (i.e., beaming up) to the next kingdom (in the form of a flying saucer)—a metamorphosis that would be facilitated by ufonauts.

Bo and Peep were surprisingly effective at recruiting people to their strange gospel, though their activities did not attract much attention until the Waldport meeting. Six weeks later the group was infiltrated by University of Montana sociologist Robert Balch and research assistant David Taylor. Balch and Taylor presented themselves as interested seekers and became pseudofollowers in order to clandestinely conduct field research. As they would later report in subsequent papers, the great majority of people who became involved with Bo and Peep reflected marginal individuals living on the fringes of society or those who had been deeply involved with occult spirituality for some time.

Doctrinally, Heaven's Gate represented a syncretism of Christian and occult ideas. Almost from the beginning of the UFO craze in the late 1940s–early 1950s, certain segments of the occult-metaphysical subculture adopted flying saucers, transforming them and their presumed extraterrestrial pilots into spiritual beings that had come to earth to help us along the path. Because earlier theosophical writings had portrayed certain spiritual masters as originating from Venus and other planets, this transformation was not difficult. The connection to this tradition is easy enough to discover: Before meeting Applewhite, Nettles had belonged to the Theosophical Society and had attended New Age channeling sessions at which extraterrestrial beings may have been channeled.

For his part, Applewhite—the son of a Presbyterian minister who had aspired to a ministerial career—seems to have supplied some distinctly Christian elements. Of particular importance was the notion of physical resurrection: In the early phase of their movement, Applewhite and Nettles taught that the goal of the process they were teaching was to prepare followers to be physically taken aboard the spacecraft, where they would enter a cocoon-like state, eventually being reborn in a transformed physical body. The notion of resurrection is central to Chapter 11 of the Book of Revelation, the biblical passage Applewhite and Nettles came to view as describing their particular ministry: "At the end of the three days and a half the breath of life from God came into them; and they stood up on their feet to the terror of all who saw it. Then a loud voice was heard speaking to them from heaven, which said, 'Come up here!' And they went up to heaven in a cloud, in full view of their enemies. At that same moment there was a violent earthquake" (Rev. 11:11–13).

In the early phase of their movement, Applewhite and Nettles prophesied that they would soon be assassinated. Using the above passage as a script for future events, they further predicted that they would be resurrected three and a half days later and taken up into a flying saucer. The Two asserted that this Demonstration would prove the truth of their teachings. As for their followers, they taught that Heaven was the literal, physical heavens, and those few people chosen to depart with the Two would, after their physical transformation, become crew members aboard UFOs.

Applewhite and Nettles taught that aliens had planted the seeds of current humanity millions of years ago and have come to reap the harvest of their work in the form of spiritually evolved individuals who will join the ranks of flying-saucer crews. Only a select few members of humanity will be chosen to advance to this transhuman state. The rest will be left to wallow in the spiritually poisoned atmosphere of a corrupt world.

Applewhite would later teach that after the elect had been picked up by the Space Brothers the planet would be engulfed in cataclysmic destruction. In 1993, using the pseudonym Total Overcomers Anonymous, the group ran an advertisement in *USA Today;* their portrayal of the postrapture world was far more apocalyptic than Applewhite and Nettles had taught in the 1970s: "The earth's present 'civilization' is about to be recycled—'spaded under.' Its inhabitants are refusing to evolve. The 'weeds' have taken over the garden and disturbed its usefulness beyond repair."

For followers of the Two, the focus of day-to-day existence meant a disciplined regime referred to as the "overcoming process" or, simply, the "process." The goal of this process was to overcome human weaknesses—a goal not dissimilar to the goal of certain spiritual practices followed by more mainstream monastic communities. For Applewhite, however, it appears that stamping out one's sexuality was the core issue. Furthermore, it is clear that his focus on sexual issues was tied to the problems he had experienced in the past as a direct result of his own sexuality.

Despite the outward success of Applewhite's early academic and musical career, he had been deeply troubled. Married and the father of two children, he secretly carried on a double life as a homosexual. Guilty and confused, he is said to have longed for a platonic relationship within which he could develop his full potential without being troubled by his sexual urges. He eventually divorced his wife and, in 1970, was terminated by St. Thomas University. Devastated, Applewhite became bitter and depressed.

He met Nettles in 1972 at a hospital where he was seeking help for his sexual and psychological problems. Nettles and Applewhite quickly became inseparable. For a short while they together operated a metaphysical center. After the center folded, they continued holding classes in a house they called Knowplace. In 1973 they began traveling in search of a higher purpose. They eventually camped out in an isolated spot near the Oregon coast and, after six weeks, came to the realization that they were the two witnesses prophesied in Revelation 11.

In the spring of 1975 they recruited their first followers, beginning with a metaphysical teacher named Clarence Klug and 23 of his students. As the first step in the transformational process taught by the Two, their followers abandoned everything that tied them to their everyday life, including jobs, families, and most possessions except for cars and camping supplies (necessary for leading a quasi-nomadic lifestyle). Mirroring their own process, they placed males and females together in nonsexual partnerships in which each was instructed to assist their partner in the overcoming process. They also attempted to tune in to the next level, again reflecting the process that Applewhite and Nettles had experienced during their six-week retreat.

The group developed quietly until media interest increased in the wake of the Waldport meeting. This new attention awakened fears that Bo and Peep might be assassinated before they could fulfill their mission. They subsequently canceled a planned meeting in Chicago and split the group into several autonomous "families" consisting of a dozen or more individuals. These families were then sent on their way, traveling, camping out, begging for food, and occasionally recruiting new members. Many of the faithful fell away during this period. Around the end of 1975

or the beginning of 1976, the Two reemerged, gathered together the remnants of their following, and eventually began a new round of recruiting activities.

In the face of strong ridicule, however, Nettles abruptly announced that "the doors to the next level are closed," and their missionary activity ceased. The harvest had ended with less than 100 individuals engaged in the process. Another change was the subsequent announcement that the Demonstration had been canceled because followers had not been making rapid enough progress in the overcoming process: Rather than focusing on the time when they would be taken up by the saucers, they must concentrate on their own development. To this end, the Two developed more practices and disciplines to help their followers overcome their human weaknesses. For example, in one exercise known as "tomb time," followers would go for days without saying anything except "yes," "no," or "I don't know" (other communications took place via written notes). Followers also began to wear uniform clothing.

The seminomadic period ended within a few years when two followers inherited a total of approximately $300,000. They then rented houses, initially in Denver and later in the Dallas–Fort Worth area. Each house, which they called a "craft," had the windows covered to prevent the neighbors from watching their activities. Followers adhered to a strict routine. With members immersed in the intensity of their structured lifestyle, the teachings of the Two became more and more real.

The group's strict segregation from society was suddenly altered in 1983 when many followers visited their families on Mother's Day. However, these members dropped out of contact as soon as they left. It was during these visits that they communicated to their families that they were learning computer technology. Another change took place in 1985, when Nettles died of cancer. The group surfaced again in 1994 when, thinking the liftoff would begin in a year or two, it held another series of public meetings. It was as part of this new cycle of missionary activity that the *USA Today* ad appeared.

Details about how the group came to attach apocalyptic significance to Hale-Bopp are tantalizingly scanty. For whatever reason, someone outside the group had come to the conclusion that a giant UFO was coming to earth, "hidden" in the wake of the comet. This individual then placed his opinion on the Internet. When Heaven's Gate retrieved this information, Applewhite took it as an indication that the long-awaited pickup of his group by aliens was finally about to take place. The decision that the time had come to make their final exit could not have been made more than a few weeks before the mass suicide.

The idea that the group might depart via suicide had emerged in Applewhite's thinking only within the last few years. The earlier idea—an idea that had set Heaven's Gate apart from everyone else—was that groups of individuals selected to move to the next level would bodily ascend to the saucers in a kind of "technological rapture." Applewhite may have begun to rethink his theology after his beloved partner died because, in order to be reunited with Nettles, her spirit would have to acquire a new body aboard the spacecraft. Although the death of Nettles may or may not have been the decisive influence, he later adopted the view that Heaven's Gate would ascend together spiritually rather than physically.

In the end, however, Applewhite seems to have hedged his bets. Using the scenario described in chapter 11 of Revelation as a kind of script, it was clear that the group considered the possibility that they might be physically resurrected three and a half days after they died. This would explain why the letter sent to a former member informing him that they had taken their own lives was timed to arrive three and a half days after the first set of suicides (people killed themselves in three waves of 15, 15, and nine). It also explains why the group was uniformly dressed in new clothes, with packed suitcases at their feet.

See Also: Apocalypse; Cults, UFO; Extraterrestrial Walk-Ins; New Age; Occult; Religions, UFO
Further Reading:
Introvigne, Massimo. *Heaven's Gate: Il paradiso non può attendere.* Turin, Italy: Editrice Elle Di Ci, 1997.
Lewis, James R., ed. *The Gods Have Landed: New Religions From Other Worlds.* Albany: State University of New York Press, 1995.
Vallee, Jacques. *Messengers of Deception: UFO Contacts and Cults.* Berkeley: And/Or Press, 1979.

HERMANN, WILLIAM J.

It began as a rash of sightings in late 1977 and early 1978. William J. Hermann saw a disk-shaped object on five occasions near his home in Charleston, South Carolina, before he was finally brought aboard the ship by humanoid beings on March 18 for examination and a tour. Only five feet tall, with large, bald heads, oversized eyes, and pale skin, they wore red suits and spoke English to him, claiming they were from Zeta Reticuli. Their most ominous message was a warning for humans to shape up or be destroyed. Despite channeling alien writings and publishing some of his own, Hermann's accounts are generally considered dubious.

See Also: Channeling; Contactees; Hoaxes
Further Reading:
Bullard, Thomas E. *UFO Abductions: The Measure of a Mystery, Volume 1: Comparative Study of Abduction Reports;* and *Volume 2: Catalogue of Cases.* Mount Rainier, MD: Fund for UFO Research, 1987.
Stevens, Wendelle C., and William James Hermann. *UFO . . . Contact from Reticulum: A Report of the Investigation.* Tucson, AZ: Wendelle C. Stevens, 1981.

THE HIDDEN

This is the tale of a seasoned cop and a benign alien posing as an FBI agent who team up to track down and destroy a hyperviolent alien life-form. The original appeared in 1988. A sequel, *The Hidden II,* came out in 1994.

The basic structure—earthling and good alien versus bad alien—is a standard Hollywood plot. Most alien-encounter movies fall into one of two subcategories: alien-invasion movies in which humanity must fight against hostile extraterrestrials; or "technological angel"–type movies in which friendly extraterrestrials try to help humanity in some way. *The Hidden* is a not uncommon blend of the two.

New Line/Heron 1988; 98 min. Director: Jack Sholder; Writer: Bob Hunt; Music: Michael Convertino; Cinematography: Jacques Haitkin; Cast: Kyle MacLachlan, Michael Nouri, Clu Gulager, Ed O'Ross, Claudia Christian, Clarence Felder, Richard Brooks, William Boyett.

HIGDON, E. CARL

E. Carl Higdon, Jr.'s close encounter with "men" who took him to their home planet began with a simple hunting outing. On Friday, October 25, 1974, the resident of Rawlins, Wyoming, had an elk in his sights when he realized his bullet had fallen to the ground just 50 feet from him as if it had hit some invisible object. When he investigated, he saw a very tall humanoid figure with no chin, ears, or brows under a tree wearing a black coverall. The figure offered Higdon some pills and a ride back to his home planet 163,000 light-years away. Higdon accepted. They traveled via a cubicle that was small but held three humanoids and five elks. There, Higdon and the figure (named Ausso One) floated over to a mushroom-like tower before Higdon heard the verdict that he wasn't "any good for what [they] need[ed]." Back on earth, Higdon suffered severe amnesia and physical pain in the two days following his encounter.

See Also: Abductees; Close Encounters
Further Reading:
Gansberg, Judith M., and Alan L. Gansberg. *Direct Encounters: The Personal Histories of UFO Abductees.* New York: Walker, 1980.
Lorenzen, Coral, and Jim Lorenzen. *Abducted! Confrontations with Beings from Outer Space.* New York: Berkley Medallion, 1977.

HILL, BETTY AND BARNEY

Betty and Barney Hill's close encounter began with a late-night drive at the end of a vacation. On September 19–20, 1961, they were returning to their home in Portsmouth, New Hampshire, from Quebec, when in the White Mountains they began to see a bright light in the sky. Thinking it was an airplane, Barney was startled to discover through binoculars that the craft was wingless and appeared to have a particular interest in their car. Gun in pocket, Barney got out of the car and saw for the first time 11 figures in the flattened, circular disk hovering less than 100 feet above the ground. He remembers being terrified of capture and running back to the car. As they drove away, they heard several beeping sounds from the trunk.

The story the Hills tell was two to three years in the making and involved many hours of hypnosis therapy. As they looked back on it, they remembered feeling drowsy and not knowing what had happened to them as they completed their five-hour drive home. The problem was that it had

taken them seven hours. Such "missing time" would become a common characteristic of abductee experiences, though they were on the leading edge and had never even heard of such an experience before. In the days following their trip, Barney experienced severe anxiety, and Betty had intensely vivid nightmares.

In one, she and her husband were accompanied by several men up a ramp and into a metallic, disk-shaped structure. One of them explained in English that they should not be afraid. They would be tested and released shortly. The figures wore uniforms and had gray skin, dark eyes and hair, and were about five feet tall. The examination was hurried, consisting of a skin scrape, a sample of her fingernail, a nervous-system check, and a pregnancy test. When the figure was able to wave away Betty's pain, she instantly lost all fear and began to converse with him. She was at first allowed to take evidence of their visit with her and, following her own failure to understand a sky map that the being showed her, attempted to convince the being to meet with astronomically knowledgeable humans at a later date. Abruptly she was rebuked, and her evidence (a book) was taken back. They said they would make it so she and her husband would not remember the incident and returned them to their car.

As medical and psychological problems continued to nag at the Hills, they sought psychiatric help. After speaking with several physicians, they underwent hypnosis in January 1964 with Dr. Benjamin Simon, despite their fears that it would be a traumatic experience. Betty told essentially the same story from her dreams three years earlier in her session. Betty also produced a drawing of the three-dimensional map she had been shown. Surprisingly, because he has always maintained his skepticism about UFOs, Barney also relayed an abduction experience. There were minor differences between the stories relating to the number of men, the details of the initial encounter on the ground, and some of the events inside the spacecraft. Dr. Simon was suspicious of UFO stories in general and specifically of the possibility that Barney was merely deriving his story from Betty's dreams. This would become a commonly held theory in explaining away the validity of their claim.

By and large the Hills kept their thoughts and fears about the encounter to themselves for four years after it occurred. They had reported a sighting of a strange flying object to Pease Air Force Base the day after, and they did write to Donald E. Keyhoe, a retired Marine Corps major with connections to the National Investigation Committee on Aerial Phenomena (NICAP). But the general public was largely unaware of their story until a journalist for the *Boston Traveler,* using tapes of public statements they had made to small audiences, wrote an article detailing their claims of having been abducted. The story immediately became an international affair. Shocked, the Hills first considered legal action, then, after some time, seemed to embrace their new fame. They cooperated on books and movies about their story.

After Barney's death in February 1969, Betty continued her public appearances and began to report many new sightings. For better or worse, much of what happened after this point provided rich material for those intent on debunking the Hills' claim. Betty's credibility came under criticism as she seemingly mistook stars, streetlights, and airplanes for UFOs during many of her escorted excursions to a "landing area" near Portsmouth. She was not without allies, however. In her defense, stories of an unidentified object appearing on Air Force radar the night of their encounter began to surface. Also, the star map that Betty had produced was taken up by an amateur astronomer, Marjorie E. Fish, and shown to correspond to a section of space including the stars Zeta 1 and 2 Reticuli. Endorsed by Walter Webb (an interested investigator of the case) and Stanton T. Friedman (a scientifically trained ufologist), the story drew the attention of none other that Carl Sagan, eminent astronomer from Cornell University, who argued that the pattern match was merely a product of chance.

Official reports by Project Blue Book and NICAP attributed the sighting to a temperature inversion making Jupiter appear brighter than usual and to a concoction stemming from subconscious fears. Webb, who had worked for NICAP, provided more positive evaluations of the event. In 1965 he pointed out the smoothness with which the details of the story fit together under hypnosis and to two pieces of physical evidence: a circular shape on the skin around Barney's groin area that subsequently developed unusual warts, and a pink substance that appeared on Betty's dress. He went on to say that the Hills' psychological stress and confusion following the encounter was consistent with posttraumatic stress disorder, commonly manifested in abductees. Attempts to debunk continue to this day. If nothing else, it is a testament to the fascination of abduction stories and the breakthrough brought about by two folks out for a drive in 1961.

See Also: Abductees; Close Encounters

Further Reading:

Dickinson, Terence. *Zeta Reticuli Update.* Fredericton, New Brunswick, Canada: UFO Research Institute, 1980.

Fuller, John Grant. *Interrupted Journey: Two Lost Hours "Aboard a Flying Saucer."* New York: Dial Press, 1966.

Gansberg, Judith M., and Alan L. Gansberg. *Direct Encounters: The Personal Histories of UFO Abductees.* New York: Walker, 1980.

Jacobs, David M. *Secret Life: Firsthand Accounts of UFO Abductions.* New York: Simon and Schuster, 1992.

HIMMELSKIBET

Himmelskibet is a Danish film made in 1917 in which a professor takes his son to Mars, where they find the inhabitants to be peace-loving, white-robed vegetarians. A Martian woman returns with them to earth, where they make a plea for peace. This is a straightforward "technological angels" portrayal of extraterrestrials in which the aliens try to save humanity from themselves. This type of film would reach its apex in *The Day the Earth Stood Still.*

Nordisk 1917; 97 min. Director: Holger Madsen; Writers: Ole Olsen, Sophus Michaelis; Cinematography: Louis Larsen, Frederik Fugisang; Cast: Nicolai Neiiendam, Gunnar Tolnaes, Zanny Petersen, Alf Bluetecher, Frederik Jacobsen, Svend Kornbeck, Birger von Cotta Schonberg, Harald Mortesen, Lilly Jacobson, Nils Asther.

HOAXES

Over the years hoaxes have played a minor role in UFO reporting. There were so few of them that Project Blue Book, the original U.S. Air Force project investigating UFOs, didn't even have a category for hoaxes; they simply fell into the "other" category. There have, however, be several hoaxes that have given rise to significant paranormal folklore, such as the information received by a UFO writer about the Philadelphia experiment. Some of the best-known hoaxes are described below.

On March 29, 1880, the *Santa Fe Weekly New Mexican* reported that a large, fish-shaped balloon passed over Galisteo Junction, New Mexico. Judging by the sounds, the occupants of the balloon were having a party. Several items fell to the ground from the balloon. One was a flower with a piece of paper with strange characters. Another was a cup. A day later a Chinese man showed up in town and found that the paper attached to the flower was a message from his fiancée, a passenger on an airship that had flown from China on a maiden voyage to America. There was no such voyage between China and America in 1880, and the technology of such flights was unknown at that time.

On June 6, 1884, cowboys in Nebraska reported seeing a blazing object crash to earth, burning grass and fusing sand on which it fell. One of the witnesses was blinded by the bright light. The *Lincoln* (Nebraska) *Daily State Journal* suggested that the object was a spaceship from another planet. Several days later the paper said that the remains of the spaceship had dissolved like a spoonful of salt. No evidence of the occurrence could be found.

On November 27, 1896, the *Stockton* (California) *Evening Mail* reported that two men were confronted by naked, seven-foot-tall beings that tried to carry them into a nearby airship. The attempt reportedly failed because the aliens were weightless and therefore unable to carry the men.

On April 19, 1897, the *Dallas Morning News* reported that an airship crashed into a windmill in Dallas, killing its Martian pilot, who was to be buried in the local cemetery. Later investigation into the story concluded that the paper had run the story in an effort to boost the town's flagging economy.

On April 23, 1897, the *Yates Center* (Kansas) *Farmers Advocate* reported that three men had seen the occupants of an airship rustle a calf, the remains of which were found the next day in a neighbor's pasture. All the men involved later confessed that the story was a fabrication.

Fred L. Crisman wrote to science-fiction editor Ray Palmer, stating that on June 21, 1947, he and Harold Dahl had seen doughnut-shaped UFOs disgorge metallic materials. Palmer sent Kenneth Arnold to investigate. Arnold believed the story and had two military intelligence officers come up to listen to the story. Dahl confessed to the officers that the story was a hoax. On the way back to their base, the officers' plane crashed, killing both men.

In 1949 two con artists, Silas Newton and Leo A. GeBauer, developed a scheme that would help them peddle a bogus oil-detection device. Representing themselves as a Texas oilman and a government scientist, they contacted *Variety* columnist Frank Scully and told him their fabricated story: On three occasions the U.S. government had recovered crashed spaceships that contained bodies of Venusians. Scully hurriedly wrote and published *Behind the Flying Saucers*, which became a best-seller, as Newton and GeBauer had planned. Newton and GeBauer were portrayed in the book as having credentials to have access to the deepest official secrets. This gave them enormous credibility with their potential investors. When Donald E. Keyhoe investigated Newton and GeBauer's story, he found it was a hoax.

According to a letter written to the editor of the *Steep Rock* (Ontario) *Echo,* on July 2, 1950, an anonymous man and his wife, picnicking on the shore of Steep Rock Lake, Ontario, saw a UFO on the water. Hatch covers were open on the top, and there were 10 queer figures on it, each three and a half to four feet tall. As they moved back and forth they did not turn around but just changed the direction of their feet. Several Canadian newspapers ran the story. It appeared in *Fate* in 1952 and was thereafter cited regularly in UFO literature. When the story was investigated in the 1970s by the Aerial Phenomena Research Organization, it was found to be entirely fictitious and written to entertain readers of the magazine.

In July 1953 a barber in Atlanta, Georgia, in order to get his name in the newspapers and win a $10 bet, bought a monkey, killed it, shaved it, and cut off its tail. He put this carcass in the roadway and flagged down a passing motorist, saying that he had just hit the occupant of a flying saucer. He did make the papers. When the actual identity of the body was determined, the barber was fined for littering a public highway with the body of an animal.

October 1954 saw the publication of a book called *Flying Saucers from Mars,* which related the meeting of the author, Cedric Allingham (a pseudonym, it turned out), with a spaceman whose saucer allegedly landed in Scotland in February 1954. Contactee George Adamski's followers hailed the book as confirmation of Adamski's claims of flying saucers. No one had any luck in contacting Cedric Allingham, however. It turned out that the actual author of *Flying Saucers from Mars* was Patrick Moore, whose purpose in writing the book was to spoof Adamski and show how gullible his supporters were.

In 1955 and 1956 UFO writer Morris K. Jessup received a series of letters from someone named Carlos Allende, who wrote that levitation was a known process mastered by human technology. Allende stated that an experiment at a Philadelphia dock had rendered a destroyer invisible and caused it to reappear at a U.S. Navy dock in Virginia. As a result of this experiment, half of the crew of the ship had gone insane. Jessup did not take this seriously. A year later, however, he got an invitation to come to the Office of Naval Research (ONR) in Washington. It seems the ONR had received a copy of Jessup's book *Case for the UFO,* which had annotations, seemingly from three different people, regarding making a navy ship invisible. Jessup read the annotations and told the navy they looked very similar to the letters he had received from Carlos Allende. One day in 1969 one Carl Allen showed up at the Tucson headquarters of the Aerial Phenomena Research Organization and said that the annotations in the book were his. His purpose was to encourage ONR research and discourage Jessup's investigations.

On the night of December 29, 1956, four followers of contactee Howard Menger supposedly met a spacewoman at Menger's paint shop in Washington, New Jersey. The building was unlighted. However, the door accidentally opened, and light fell on the "spacewoman's" face, revealing that she was Connie Weber, a cohort of Menger who later married him.

On November 5, 1957, Reinhold Schmidt claimed that he had been taken aboard a blimp-shaped flying object near the Platte River in Nebraska by two men who spoke German. After a very brief stay in a mental hospital, Schmidt became a lecturer on the contactee circuit. In October 1961 Schmidt was convicted of grand theft for bilking a widow out of thousands of dollars for a mining venture involving crystals from a spaceship.

In December 1957 Gray Barker and James W. Moseley wrote a letter on State Department stationery and signed it "R. E. Straith." The letter was addressed to George Adamski and said that the State Department knew that his meetings with the Space Brothers were true and they supported his efforts. Adamski informed his followers that Straith existed, despite denials by the State Department. Moseley confessed to the hoax after Barker's death in December 1984.

In 1958 and 1959 Otis T. Carr collected hundreds of thousands of dollars from investors for the production of a flying saucer. When the saucer failed to materialize, Carr was convicted of illegally selling stock and sent to prison.

In February 1962 14-year-old Alex Birch of Mosborough, England, produced photos that he had taken over his backyard. It showed five out-of-focus domed disks hovering in the air. The photograph and accompanying story were published in the *Sheffield Post* on June 20, 1962. Alex and his father showed the picture to the Air Ministry in London. The ministry claimed the images were due to a temperature inversion. Alex's father fiercely defended his son's honesty until October 6, 1972, when Alex confessed in a televised interview that he had created the photo by superimposing images painted on glass over the background scenery.

In the mid-1960s in Spain, unknown persons began posing as extraterrestrials from the planet Ummo. The produced hundreds of technically sophisticated documents, photographs, and artifacts and sold them to European UFO enthusiasts. A small but devoted Ummite cult still thrives in Europe.

In 1967 14-year-old Ronnie Hill of North Carolina sent a color photograph of a space suit–clad, large-headed little man holding an unknown device and standing in front of a spherical UFO to

John Keel, a writer on UFOs. Keel wrote to the boy, who said that the UFO had landed in his family's backyard on July 21, 1967. All parents, teachers, 4-H leaders, and Boy Scout leaders whom Keel asked attested to the boy's honesty. The photograph was examined by several professional photographers in New York City and apparently stood up. However, it turned out that the figure was a small model; the "UFO" was an egg.

In 1967 a prank was cooked up by students at the Royal Aircraft Technical College in Farnborough, England. They molded six five-foot-wide disks out of fiberglass and placed them along a straight line 220 miles long at 1 degree of latitude. U.S. Air Force intelligence officers took photographs, and chemists analyzed a liquid that seeped out from the disk before the hoax was uncovered.

In September 1969 the supermarket tabloid *National Bulletin* reported that the Apollo 11 astronauts had seen UFOs after their landing on the Moon on July 16, 1969. It printed an alleged transcript of radio communications between the astronauts and mission control as evidence of this sighting. Investigation revealed that *National Bulletin* could produce neither documentation nor the reporter whose byline appeared on the article.

In 1970 British UFO debunkers perpetrated a hoax in Warminster, where UFOs allegedly appeared with high frequency. They shined a light beam from a purple high-intensity spotlight. Another member operated a bogus magnetic-field sensor, which buzzed, seeming to indicate the presence of a strong magnetic field. A third debunker posing as a UFO enthusiast took photographs of the object. The hoaxers fooled *Flying Saucer Review* and French astrophysicist Pierre Guerin. The debunkers then criticized the investigators who had failed to interview the witnesses or examine the basic data critically.

In 1971 a biochemist showed ufologist Paul Cerny a photo he had taken five years earlier at Diamond Peak in Willamette Pass, Oregon. The photo showed a disk-shaped object, yellow on top, with two stripes, dark and light, underneath. The man insisted it was a UFO. It was sent to the labs at NICAP, whose analysts concluded that something like a bird feeder or a landmark had been photographed.

In January 1978 *Official UFO* magazine featured an article recounting the destruction of Chester, Illinois, by UFOs on the night of August 2, 1977. This was easily enough debunked by reporters from the mainstream press who interviewed residents of Chester after their reported demise. Publisher Myron Fass insisted that the incident had actually occurred but that the aliens had rebuilt the town and erased the citizens' memories of the events.

In 1978 Aaron David Kaback contacted ufologist Leonard H. Stringfield to recount his experience with a recovered flying saucer in November 1965. He claims he was on duty at Fort Riley, Kansas, when he was ordered to hike out with some other enlisted men to guard a large oval object about 40 feet in diameter with a fin and an exhaust port and a row of squares all around its rim. An investigator from Citizens against UFO Secrecy found that Kaback had received a hardship discharge from the service in July 1965. After this was found out, Kaback claimed that the incident had occurred on December 10, 1964. The commanding officer of Fort Riley, who Kaback claims handed him a clip of ammunition and ordered him to guard the craft, was contacted and had no idea about any incident involving a UFO.

In 1979 a literary hoax appeared in the form of *An Account of a Meeting with Denizens of Another World 1871* by David Langford. It purported to be the experiences of a man named William Robert Loosley. Loosley, it turned out, was a real man, but his experiences as related in the book were the invention of Langford. The hoax fooled few, if any, readers.

In September 1979 in Lake City, Minnesota, a farmer named Curtis Olson found a circle of flattened corn 50 feet in diameter. The stalks were flattened in a pattern radiating from the center. In the center of the circle some stalks were missing, and others were charred. Olson thought a UFO was responsible. Eight years later Olson's uncle, David Olson, confessed that he had flattened the corn using a posthole tamper and his burlap-covered feet as a practical joke. His nephew rejected his confession, sticking to the UFO explanation.

In September 1991 "Doug and Dave" (Douglas Bower and David Chorley) hoaxed a crop circle. They were subsequently able to trick Pat Delgado, a prominent cereologist (one who studies crop circles) into declaring their artificially constructed wheat circle genuine. The hoax made international headlines. Crop-circle enthusiasts subsequently charged the English government with conducting a disinformation campaign.

One of the more interesting items of UFO lore is the story that a flying saucer crashed near Roswell, New Mexico, on July 2, 1947. Remains from the crash, including bodies of dead ufonauts, were allegedly picked up by the military, and all witnesses were told to remain silent about what they knew. The Roswell story has subsequently been the topic of several books and has provided fuel for much recent speculation. In August 1996 Fox Network aired a program that focused on film footage supposedly taken during the autopsy of one of the ufonauts from Roswell. The subject of the film appeared to be a short humanoid with large (in proportion to his body) head and eyes, six digits on each hand and foot, and a burned leg. During the operation a relatively indistinct substance—rather than definite organs—were taken from the body cavity. The FOX program, hosted by Jonathan Frakes of *Star Trek: The Next Generation* fame, presented a series of commentators who appeared to support the contention that the film was, indeed, genuine footage of an alien autopsy. After much debate, and as a result of certain later revelations, the general consensus of ufologists is that the film is almost certainly a hoax.

—*Jerome Clark*

See Also: Alien Autopsy Film; Crop Circles; Philadelphia Experiment
Further Reading:
Evans, Hilary. *Gods, Spirits, and Cosmic Guardians: A Comparative Study of the Encounter Experience.* Wellingborough, U.K.: Aquarian Press, 1987.
Flammonde, Paris. *The Age of Flying Saucers: Notes on a Projected History of Unidentified Flying Objects.* New York: Hawthorn Books, 1971.
Korff, Kal K. *Spaceships of the Pleiades: The Billy Meier Story.* Amherst, NY: Prometheus Books, 1995.
Nickell, Joe, with John F. Fischer. *Secrets of the Supernatural: Investigating the World's Occult Mysteries.* Buffalo, NY: Prometheus Books, 1988.
Plank, Robert. *The Emotional Significance of Imaginary Beings: A Study of the Interaction Between Psychopathology, Literature, and Reality in the Modern World.* Springfield, IL: Charles C. Thomas, 1968.
Stein, Gordon. *Encyclopedia of Hoaxes.* Detroit: Gale Research, 1993.

HOPKINS, BUDD

Budd Hopkins (b. 1931) is the author of several widely read books on UFOs. Having graduated from Oberlin College in 1953, he lives in New York City and also has a successful career as a painter and sculptor. Some of his works are in the permanent collections of major museums, and he has won many prestigious awards. In 1964 Hopkins and two companions observed a UFO. He has been following his curiosity about them ever since. His investigations led him to become one of the first to discover the "missing time" phenomenon, experienced by people who under hypnosis recall being abducted by aliens. His first book was called *Missing Time.* His second, *Intruders,* recounts incidents of sexual experimentation by aliens on unwilling human subjects and suggests that the aliens may be trying to create a hybrid race. The books are, of course, quite controversial. In 1990 Hopkins created the Intruders Foundation in New York City.

See Also: Abductees; Close Encounters
Further Reading:
Bryan, C. D. B. *Close Encounters of the Fourth Kind: Alien Abduction, UFOs, and the Conference at M.I.T.* New York: Alfred A. Knopf, 1995.
Hopkins, Budd. *Intruders: The Incredible Visitations at Copley Woods.* New York: Random House, 1987.
———. *Missing Time: A Documented Study of UFO Abductions.* New York: Richard Marek, 1981.

HOWARD THE DUCK

Howard the Duck, based on a comic-book character, is an alien from a parallel world who is accidentally beamed to Cleveland. For the first half of this 1986 film, Howard tries to fit into human society. The second half has him fighting space demons. The central theme of the movie—the struggles of an alien attempting to adjust to earth life—has no direct correspondence to ufological speculation. In the second half of the movie, however, Howard takes on the role of a technological angel who saves humanity from an invasion by evil aliens.

Lucasfilm/Universal 1986; 111 min. Director: Willard Huyck; Writer: Willard Huyck, Gloria Katz; Music: John

Barry, Sylvester Levay; Visual Effects: Chip Zien; Cast: Lea Thompson, Jeffrey Jones, Tim Robbins.

THE HUMAN DUPLICATORS

In this 1965 film a giant alien invader takes over a laboratory in which a scientist has created a race of androids. Its plan is to produce a series of look-alikes of leaders so that a blanket alien takeover can be arranged. FBI agents fight back, destroying the alien and its robots with a laser beam. The basic plot of invasion via clandestine infiltration of the government is a staple of certain UFO conspiracy literature. Some interpreters view such themes as reflective of Cold War paranoia.

Woolern Brothers/Independenti Regionali 1965; 82 min. Director: Hugo Grimaldi; Writer: Arthur C. Pierce; Cinematography: Monroe Askins; Cast: George Nader, Barbara Nichols, George Macready, Dolores Faith, Huge Beaumont, Richard Kiel, Richard Arlen.

HUMOR AND UFOS

And this is why the flying saucers are not landing. 'Cause we're so damn *stupid!* They know us. They know that if they hang out with us, sooner or later we're gonna take 'em out, get 'em drunk, beat the shit out of 'em, and take their damn saucer."

—*Gallagher*

Beginning with the UFO craze of the 1950s flying saucers and extraterrestrials have been the subjects of a seemingly endless series of jokes and cartoons. Like sex, death, and certain other topics that simultaneously arouse aversion and curiosity, the UFO phenomenon is one of those uncommon subjects that we make less anxiety-producing by making it the target of humor. What makes UFOs such a rich source of both comedy and speculation is that there is some trickster-like quality about the phenomenon that, in Michael Grosso's words, "seems contrived to run the human mind through an ontological blender." ("Mind in the UFO Blender," in Paul Pursglove, ed., *Zen in the Art of Close Encounters.*) As he says at greater length later in the same essay,

The whole thing seems driven by some metaphysical imp of the perverse. There is just enough physicality and externality to the

phenomenon to seduce us into believing stories about nuts-and-bolts technologies, flying saucers, Zeta Reticulins, anti-gravity machines, holodecks and hyperspace; on the other hand, there's just enough that is psychic, paranormal and archetypal about the phenomena to support spinning tales of psychoid, etheric, imaginal, spiritual and psychokinetic worlds.

It is the ultimate irreducibility of the phenomenon that makes even dedicated, hardware-oriented ufologists welcome a good laugh at the expense of the UFO field.

One phase of the phenomenon that appears to be an attempt at communication from the ufonauts is the so-called crop circles—fields of grain that have been bent down in patterns that can be discerned from the air. Many ufologists initially welcomed the appearance of these agriglyphs, as they came to be called, but to date no one has convincingly interpreted their meaning. Who knows? Perhaps the crop circles are just so much alien graffiti that the Space Brothers create in a spirit of play. Or maybe the makers of the agriglyphs are practical jokers who enjoy giving human beings more unfathomable mysteries about which to speculate. The writer of *ET 101*, who claims to have channeled the book from "Mission Control," responding to a query regarding crop circles from Jean Mundy ("Hey UFOLKS, Allee, Allee, All in Free-ee!" in *Zen in the Art of Close Encounters*) wrote:

In response to your question concerning the meaning of the crop circles, the Intergalactic Council refuses to comment because these symbols are a direct communication to the genetic structures of this planet and were intended to bypass the linear mind. Therefore, explaining to the linear mind what they mean is counterproductive.

Mission Control, on the other hand, was glad to offer an explanation. They said, loosely translated, they mean, "Wake up and smell the coffee. Kiss the old world goodbye, and let them eat Mandelbrot."

Even though there is something about the phenomenon itself that almost seems to invite a tongue-in-cheek response, much UFO-related humor revolves around using hypothetical aliens as foils for laughing at human foibles. This is clearly the approach in most film and TV comedies built around humorous extraterrestrials. Some of the best UFO comedy was featured at Leo Sprinkle's annual Rocky Mountain Conference on UFO Investigation at the University of Wyoming. The following, "From an *Ersatz Dodo Comedy Team* Performance," are excerpted from Pursglove's compilation cited above:

Trans-Personals
Single White Male seeks Multiple Blue Female for late night close encounters of any kind. I like star-gazing, semi-automatic writing, missing time. Let's start a new race that will populate the stars. No weirdos.

Dear E.T. Landers,
As an alien who abducts humans with regularity, I find it increasingly difficult to quit. I've tried everything; hypnosis, drugs and the "patch." However abduction has been good to me over the years. I met my wife when I abducted her eight years ago and we've been happy ever since. But her family has put pressure on me recently to quit. At first they took me for a sort of savior and their daughter as one of the chosen few. However, as they realized over the years that I can't solve my own problems, much less the earth's, they have become increasingly rude and bossy. And now my wife has become suspicious that my abductions are just an excuse to meet "chicks." What should I do?
Signed: A Little Blue Green Man

Dear Blue,
Your wife is right, abductions are a great way to meet "chicks." I myself have met some wonderful aliens on any number of hot abductions. Although I certainly don't consider myself a "chick," I have no problem with . . . "squeeze mamma." As for trying to quit, I've heard this can be difficult. Although I've never quit doing anything in my life, I do use the patch.

Much UFO-related humor relies upon the above approach, namely, placing extraterrestrials in terrestrial situations—but with some twist taken from UFO folklore. A series of recent greeting cards called "The Grays" put out by Hallmark, for example, has standard gray extraterrestrials greeting the recipient with some word of birthday (or other holiday) cheer, incorporating some reference to abduction or other UFO lore. One such

card pictures three grays on the cover with little frowns on their faces, saying, "We hate to abduct guys your age." Inside the card, the sequel message reads, "It takes forever to find a hair sample on your head"—an allusion to the tissue, hair, and other samples typically taken during an alien abduction. Another card pictures three happier extraterrestrials seated at the controls of a spacecraft. One gray turns in his seat, faces the reader, and says, "Make your birthday one of those nutty, irresponsible days when you do anything you want just for the fun of it." The inside of this card reads, "You know, like when we made those guys build Stonehenge"—an indirect reference to the ancient-astronaut hypothesis.

The same basic strategy—inserting aliens into a familiar human situation, usually through the use of some common item of UFO folklore—is utilized by such prominent cartoonists as Gary Larson and Gahan Wilson. In one *Farside* cartoon, for example, the foreground is occupied by a chicken that is being drawn through the broken roof of a chicken coop and into a flying saucer via some kind of antigravity beam. In the background, an old woman is standing in the doorway of her house, shouting, "Paw! Paw! Get the shotgun! The aliens are stealing the chickens again!" Many Larson cartoons rely on the same juxtaposition of ordinary with extraordinary elements to set up a comic situation.

Similarly, in a *New Yorker* cartoon by Gahan Wilson, a frazzled individual sits in an examination room in his undershorts with four stereotypical grays. Speaking with a thermometer in his mouth, the man says, "I had a touch of the flu last February, and that funny ache in my thumb still flares up when it's damp, but, thanks to the diet and exercise program you recommended, I feel better all around since the last abduction." In another *New Yorker* cartoon, the stereotypical gray-suited businessman is coming home at the end of the day. Responding to what the reader presumes was his wife's "How did it go today, Honey?" he says, "Actually, it was a day not without interest. As I approached my office, I was mysteriously drawn into an alien spacecraft which transported me at the speed of light to the far reaches of the universe. There I was the subject of bizarre sexual experiments which continued until I was returned to earth just in time to catch the 5:27 back home."

The same basic approach, with an added touch of what we might call "role inversion," is frequently deployed in a masterful way by Larson. In one memorable cartoon, a particularly ugly extraterrestrial is stepping off a spaceship as frightened human beings run away in every direction. The alien, obviously delighted with his accomplishment, exclaims, "One step for a Zork! A giant leap for Zork-kind!" Similarly, in another *Farside* cartoon, a man who has clearly been stranded on a isolated island that is barren except for a few palm trees notes the approach of a spacecraft and gasps, "Thank God, I'm saved." The craft then lands, brings the trees on board (who turn out to be stranded aliens), and takes off without him.

See Also: Popular Culture
Further Reading:

Curran, Douglas. *In Advance of the Landing: Folk Concepts of Outer Space.* New York: Abbeville Press, 1985.
Guffey, George R. "Aliens in the Supermarket: Science Fiction and Fantasy for 'Inquiring Minds.'" In *Aliens: The Anthropology of Science Fiction.* Edited by George E. Slusser and Eric S. Rabkin. Carbondale: Southern Illinois University Press, 1987.
Pursglove, Paul David. *Zen in the Art of Close Encounters: Crazy Wisdom and UFOs.* Berkeley: New Being Project, 1995.

HYBRIDS, ALIEN-HUMAN

The notion of extraterrestrials attempting to create alien-human hybrids is a major theme in both the ancient-astronaut school of thought and in contemporary abduction literature. The difference between these two orientations is that ancient-astronaut thinkers posit that the human race is the offspring of a union between aliens and native terrestrials (presumably an ape-like ancestor, perhaps even Neanderthals)—a hybridization that was successfully carried out millennia ago. In contrast, abduction literature portrays ufonauts as *currently* conducting genetic experiments with the human beings they kidnap. Prominent abduction researcher Budd Hopkins, for instance, speculates that "at the center of this ongoing genetic experiment is a systematic attempt to create a hybrid species, a mix of human and alien characteristics."

NBC's 1995 "Visitors of the Night," *starring Markie Post, portrayed alien abduction as part of a scheme to produce human-alien hybrids, a common theme in abduction literature. (NBC)*

The convergence as well as the divergence between these two perspectives are interesting. In the ancient-astronaut school, the purpose of such hybridization was to speed up the evolution of the human race by imparting alien intelligence to terrestrial ape men. The ultimate purpose of such experimentation in abduction literature is unclear, unless it is simply to satisfy the curiosity of extraterrestrial scientists. It is, of course, possible to reconcile these two schools of thought by postulating that our alien ancestors were of a different race than the current aliens that abduct human beings. Perhaps our celestial ancestors were well-intended and the current crop of extraterrestrials visiting the earth are more sinister.

If the whole notion of visiting extraterrestrials is just a human fantasy, then there must be something extremely attractive about the idea of human-alien hybridization for this theme to crop up in two distinct arenas of ufological speculation. Perhaps this concept draws energy from some archetype of forging a bond between human (terrestrial) and celestial (alien) elements, as with the classical heroes who were half-mortal and half-divine. The theme of such hybridization even finds expression in certain imaginative works, such as the movie *Species*.

See Also: Abductees; Close Encounters; Hopkins, Budd; Sex

Further Reading:

Bryan, C. D. B. *Close Encounters of the Fourth Kind: Alien Abduction, UFOs, and the Conference at M.I.T.* New York: Alfred A. Knopf, 1995.

Hopkins, Budd. *Intruders: The Incredible Visitations at Copley Woods.* New York: Random House, 1987.

———. *Missing Time: A Documented Study of UFO Abductions.* New York: Richard Marek, 1981.

THE "I AM" RELIGIOUS ACTIVITY

Although it has been asserted that public interest in UFOs began with Kenneth Arnold's sighting of flying disks near Mt. Rainer, there is a long tradition of extraterrestrial-contact claims that predates Arnold's sightings by many decades. This tradition is contained in certain lineages of occultism that claim contact with spiritual "masters" from other planets. A useful example of this form of occultism is the "I AM" Religious Activity.

"I AM" is a popularized form of theosophy, reformulated to appeal to a broader audience than earlier theosophical organizations. The founder of the movement was Guy Ballard (1878–1939) who was born in Kansas. He had long been interested in occultism, and had studied theosophical teachings. He married Edna Wheeler (1886–1971) in 1916, and three years later their son Donald was born.

Ballard was engaged in mining exploration and promotion. In 1930, while he was working near Mt. Shasta—a giant volcanic cone in northern California where strange occult events had been said to occur—he had his first substantive contact with a hidden world. While hiking in the woods around the mountain, Ballard reports that he encountered another hiker, who gave him a marvelous drink and introduced himself as the Ascended Master Saint Germain. The Compte de Saint Germain was one of the most famous occultists of modern times. Ballard was, he related, chosen as a messenger to restore to humankind the truths of reembodiment. Saint Germain imparted information about karma, the inner reality of the divine—which he referred to as the "Mighty I AM Presence"—occult world history, and the creative power of thought.

One New Year's Eve, the Master and Ballard joined a gathering inside a cavern in Royal Teton Mountain. The individuals at this assembly then became host to 12 Venusians who appeared in their midst in a blaze of light, not unlike a *Star Trek* beam-in. These Venusian "Lords of the Flame" played harp and violin music and showed the gathered terrestrials scenes of advanced technological achievements from their home world on a great mirror. These events from the early 1930s were reported in Ballard's *Unveiled Mysteries,* which was published a dozen years before Kenneth Arnold's celebrated encounter. This incident and other reported encounters makes the I AM movement the first popular religious group to make extraterrestrial contacts a central tenet. Furthermore, Ballard essentially created the image of the golden-haired, angelic Venusian that Adamski would bring into the saucer age.

Ballard returned to Chicago in 1931 to propagate Saint Germain's message. Saint Germain's teachings had certain distinctive characteristics that contributed to the remarkable spread of the I AM Activity. Among its tenets are the American setting and nationalistic overtones. According to I AM, the Masters are found in the romantic American West—Mt. Shasta, the Grand Tetons, and Yellowstone.

It is believed that humanity began in America and that this is the seventh and last cycle of history, under the Lord of the Seventh Ray—Saint Germain. The history of this epoch will also end in America, which will be the vessel of light to bring the world into new and paradisiacal times.

I AM makes rich use of vivid colors, which characterize the rays of the Masters and the spiritual characteristics of people. In addition, I AM bookshops and centers are bright with color diagrams and lights. Ballard's writing is packed with color words. Ballard, who was fascinated by mines and gold, loved to depict the Masters' retreats as underground.

Color is very important because of the vibratory action of each color. Everything is constituted by energy and electrons, which manifest in different qualities through various colors. Also, sound-talking can be considered energy, which can be largely destructive and, as a matter of fact, has done much to get humanity into its current troubles. I AM followers believe that constructive activity can be brought forth by surrounding oneself with harmonious colors.

These revelations were spread during the lectures of the three Ballards, who traveled in the 1930s as "Accredited Messengers" of the Masters. Further messages from the Ascended Masters, especially from Saint Germain and the Master Jesus, were sometimes produced in public or private. The main teaching is that the "Mighty I AM Presence" is God in action, which is immediately available. It is also said that one's "individualized Presence" is a pure reservoir of energy, from which power can be drawn at will.

Saint Germain and Jesus are considered the mediators between the "I AM Presence" and humans. The Ascended Masters, at one time, were all human beings who became able to transcend the physical world through purification of their lives. The goal of human life is represented by ascension.

The deeds and desires of a person are reflected by each individual's karma-made aura, which is generally both dark and light. When it is dark, it reaches a point where the person can no longer be of much service or make much progress. Thus, the person dies physically to begin another life. Through purification of thought and feeling, the causal (higher spiritual) body becomes fully luminous and draws the individual into the Ascension, acting like a magnet. Through the Ascension, the person joins the Ascended Masters, with whom he shares their unconditioned state of Joy and Freedom.

In 1938 the I AM Activity was given a dispensation, according to which persons who had devoted themselves so much to the movement that they had not given all they might to personal purification could, upon normal death, ascend from the after-earth state without reembodiment. It is believed that manifestation of constructive activities can be brought forth through one's acknowledg-

ment and use of the power of qualification and visualization through music and contemplation. This can be done also through Decrees, which are Affirmations, or prayers, used only for constructive purposes. It is said that all that is destructive comes from human beings and that records of past karmic debts can be consumed by the use of the "Violet Consuming Flame," which is like the grace of the New Testament. Through the use of this "Sacred Fire," humans can be liberated from the toils of what has gone before.

The I AM activity worked publicly from 1937 to 1940 to establish a group of devoted followers numbering over 1 million. With the death of Guy Ballard on December 29, 1939, the movement began to decline. Edna Ballard claimed that her husband had become an Ascended Master. However, the fact that Guy Ballard had experienced a physical death rather than bodily Ascension threatened the movement's credibility. The following year a sensational trial of the leaders of the movement took place, after some members of Ballard's personal staff accused the Ballards of obtaining money under fraudulent pretenses. The indictment was overturned in 1944 by the U.S. Supreme Court with a landmark decision on religious liberty. The case was finally dismissed after Justice William O. Douglas, in stating the majority opinion, asserted, "Men may believe what they cannot prove. They may not be put to the proof of their religious doctrines or beliefs."

—*Michela Zonta*

See Also: Contactees; Occult; Theosophy
Further Reading:
King, Godfre Ray [Guy W. Ballard]. *Unveiled Mysteries*. Chicago: Saint Germain Press, 1934.
Lewis, James R., ed. *The Gods Have Landed: New Religions From Other Worlds*. Albany: State University of New York Press, 1995.
Melton, J. Gordon. *An Encyclopedic Handbook of Cults in America*. New York: Garland, 1992.

IMPLANTS, ALIEN

Alien implants are relatively small bits of matter that have been found embedded in the bodies of some UFO abductees. In many cases, abductees claim to actually remember having the material implanted in them—most often in the head—

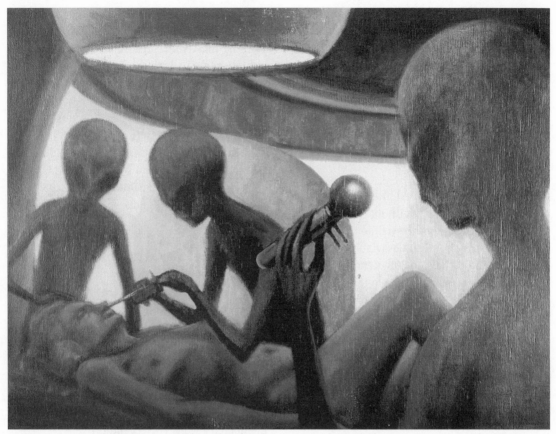

A painting by Michael Buhler of aliens inserting an implant in the victim's nose, an experience commonly recalled by abductees (Mary Evans Picture Library)

during an abduction by beings assumed to be aliens. It has been hypothesized that the implants are actually devices that allow extraterrestrials to track their human subjects, not unlike the manner in which zoologists tag wild animals.

A relatively recent topic in the UFO subculture, it has been further speculated that these devices not only broadcast information about the subjects' bodies to extraterrestrials but also allow aliens to influence or even to control abductees. None of the embedded material recovered from abductees' bodies has thus far been decisively demonstrated to be extraterrestrial in origin.

Dr. Roger K. Leir, a Ventura, California, podiatrist, and Derrel Sims of the Huston UFO Network cofounded the Foundation for Alien-Human Research for the purpose of studying implants. Among their reported findings is that—contrary to what one would normally anticipate—nerve cells *were*, but inflammatory cells were *not*, found in the soft tissue surrounding embedded objects. Removed implants were also highly magnetic.

See Also: Abductees; Close Encounters; Hoaxes
Further Reading:
Craft, Michael. *Alien Impact.* New York: St. Martin's, 1996.
Randle, Kevin D. *The Randle Report: UFOs in the 1990s.* New York: M. Evans, 1997.

INCIDENT AT RAVEN'S GATE

In this 1988 Australian film unusual things happen in the Outback. Cassette players are emitting the wrong music. Dead birds are falling out of the sky. Huge circular burns are appearing in isolated pastures. Lights are seen in the sky. The ambiguous finale suggests that intangible alien visitors are to blame. *Incident at Raven's Gate* has some of the atmosphere of a high-tension horror movie, and it resonates with the paranoid conspiracy thinking of certain segments of the UFO subculture.

FGH International 1988; 93 min. Director: Rolf De Heer; Writers: Rolf De Heer and Marc Rosenberg; Cinematography: Richard Michalak; Cast: Steven Vidler, Celine Griffin, Ritchie Singer, Vincent Gil, Saturday Rosenberg, Terry Camilleri, Max Cullen.

INDEPENDENCE DAY (ID4)

Released in July 1996, this film broke box-office records. *ID4* was a straight-out shoot-'em-up alien-invasion flick. Though well done as action-adventure films go, the runaway success of *ID4* was due at least partially to 20th Century Fox's intensive marketing efforts. At the time of this writing, *ID4* was the second largest income-earner in film history.

For the UFO buff, *ID4* draws on everything from the Roswell incident to Area 51, both staples of UFO conspiracy thinking. Mention is also made of the alien-abduction phenomenon. What is interesting to the ufologically informed observer is that even as recently as five or six years prior to the creation of *ID4* the writers would probably not have brought the Roswell–Area 51 theme into the script. However, the growing interest in UFOs and UFO-related conspiracies—stimulated, in part, by the runaway success of *X-Files*—has made these notions more reputable (on par, in a certain sense, with Kennedy assassination conspiracies). In other words, the presence of such references in a box-office film like *ID4* indicates that ufology and UFO-related speculation has become somewhat more mainstream—or, at least, that the general public is more aware of UFOs and ufology than in the past.

20th Century Fox 1996: 145 min. Director: Roland Emerick; Writer: Dean Devlin; Music: David Arnold; Cinematography: Karl Kindenlaub; Visual Effects: Volker Engel, Douglas Smith; Cast: Bill Pullman, Will Smith, Randy Quaid, Jeff Goldblum.

INITIATION

Some observers have noted that UFO abductions share certain characteristics with initiation rituals in traditional societies. Initiation in the most general sense refers to a rite in which the initiate undergoes a transformation in religious or social status. The most widespread initiatory ritual is the puberty rite, in which the individual becomes an adult member of the community. The second widely practiced rite classified as an initiatory ritual is initiation into specialized groups, particularly initiation into secret societies.

A third and final class of rites and experiences classified as an initiation is the transformation of an individual into a shaman or medicine man. Shamans are the religious specialists of certain traditional societies; they act as healers and diviners. There are several different traditional ways in which one becomes a shaman. Often it is simply inherited, and the shaman is initiated in public. At other times the person to become a shaman is chosen by spiritual forces. Sometimes the chosen individual does not particularly wish to take up a shamanic vocation. This "supernatural" election frequently involves a serious illness, in which the person comes close to death. The death theme is emphasized in certain traditions in which the individual has a vision of himself as being slain, dismembered, reconstructed, and revived.

In any one of these initiations, individuals may be ritually tortured as part of their rite of passage. Torture is a way of symbolically slaying the old self so that the new self may be born. It is in the torment aspect of this experience that initiation seems to come closest to the abduction experience.

See Also: Abductees; Close Encounters; Shamanism
Further Reading:
Eliade, Mircea, ed. *Encyclopedia of Religion.* New York: Macmillan, 1987.
Lewis, James R. *The Encyclopedia of Afterlife Beliefs and Phenomena.* Detroit: Gale Research, 1994.
Van Der Leeuw, G. *Religion in Essence and Manifestation, Volume 1.* Gloucester, MA: Peter Smith, 1967 [transl. of first German ed., 1933].

INNER EARTH

Over the years various claimants have had a uniting theme of UFOs coming from highly advanced people who live inside the earth. Almost all treatments of the inner-earth legend (a.k.a. the hollow earth) mention Admiral Richard E. Byrd's flight

Some observers have compared abduction with initiation. The theme of initiatory torture is particularly relevant. (American Religion Collection)

over the North Pole on February 19, 1947. Hollow-earth enthusiasts believe that he flew into an opening at the top of the world that led into the interior of our planet. These accounts sometimes go farther than this to claim that Admiral Byrd met with advanced beings that asked him to deliver a message to the surface world. However, upon Byrd's return to Washington he was ordered to remain silent about his experience by his superiors.

This basic scenario is reflected in the apocryphal *A Flight to the Land beyond the North Pole; The Missing Diary of Admiral Richard E. Byrd.* After landing inside the earth and being brought before a spiritual Master, the Master informs Byrd that, "I shall tell you why you have been summoned here. Our interest rightly begins just after your race exploded the first atomic bombs over Hiroshima and Nagasaki, Japan. It was at that alarming time we sent our flying machines, the "Flugelrads," to your surface world to investigate what your race had done." "Flugelrads" are obviously meant to refer to UFOs—advanced aerial vehicles mistakenly identified as extraterrestrial spacecrafts. This impression is further reinforced by the Master's remark that "in 1945 and afterward, we tried to contact your race, but our efforts were met with hostility. Our Flugelrads were fired upon, yes, even pursued with malice and animosity by your fighter planes." Like many of the flying saucer contactees of the 1950s, Byrd is then given a message of warning and hope for the inhabitants of the surface world.

Similarly, in 1943, Richard S. Shaver of Barto, Pennsylvania, related through *Amazing Stories* magazine his interactions with a race of giants that lived in a vast series of underground caverns. According to Shaver, this race had superior science and technology and possessed spaceships that were sometimes seen in our atmosphere. Other inner-earth contactees included Maurice Doreal, a reader of *Amazing Stories* who claimed to have had many visits with the Master who lived inside Mt. Shasta and the survivors of the lost continent of Atlantis. Doreal said that they possessed an extraordinary technology including spaceships.

Residents of San Carlos, Costa Rica, reported flashing lights and strange noises coming from an inactive volcano. There were several sightings of UFOs seeming to enter the mountain. Costa Rican officials allegedly attempted to investigate, but their efforts were repeatedly frustrated by flash floods or thunderstorms that seemed to come out of nowhere. Finally, searchers persisted in getting to the top of the mountain and saw that the bottom of the crater was a gigantic airlock. They watched a huge flying saucer emerge from the open crater. They learned that the source of these flying saucers was not extraterrestrial but from the interior of the earth.

The year 1960 saw the publication of *Our Paradise inside the Earth* by Iowa evangelist Theodore Fitch. This book placed the Garden of Eden inside the earth and claimed it was populated by small men who fly saucers. *The Hollow Earth: The Greatest Geographical Discovery in History* by Raymond Bernard (pseudonym of Walter Siegmeister) was published in 1964. It reported on the conspiracy to keep the truth about the hollow earth, flying saucers, and holes in the earth's poles that provided access to the interior of the earth secret from the human race. Various Nazi groups since World War II have maintained that Adolf Hitler escaped and established a base for flying saucers inside the South Pole.

See Also: Atlantis; Contactees; Shaver Mystery

Further Reading:
Beckley, Timothy Green, ed. *The Smoky God and Other Inner Earth Mysteries.* New Brunswick, NJ: Global Communications, 1993.
Bernard, Raymond [pseudonym of Walter Siegmeister]. *The Hollow Earth: The Greatest Geographical Discovery in History.* New York: Fieldcrest Publishing, 1964.
Commander X. *Underground Alien Bases.* New Brunswick, NJ: Abelard Productions, 1990.
A Flight to the Land Beyond the North Pole: The Missing Diary of Admiral Richard E. Byrd. New Brunswick, NJ: Inner Light Publications, n.d.
Friedrich, Christof [pseudonym of Ernst Zundel]. *Secret Nazi Polar Expeditions.* Toronto, Ontario, Canada: Samisdat, 1978.
Gardner, Martin. *Fads and Fallacies in the Name of Science.* New York: Dover Publications, 1957.
Kafton-Minkel, Walter. *Subterranean Worlds: 100,000 Years of Dragons, Dwarfs, the Dead, Lost Races, and UFOs from Inside the Earth.* Port Townsend, WA: Loompanics Unlimited, 1989.

INTERNATIONAL UFO MUSEUM AND RESEARCH CENTER

A story that hit the media in July 1947 was that the military had recovered a crashed flying saucer near Roswell, New Mexico. Remains from the crash, including bodies of dead ufonauts, were allegedly picked up by the military, and all witnesses were told to remain silent about what they knew. The government claimed that the reported saucer was merely a downed weather balloon. The Roswell story languished for years, but starting about 1990 UFO researchers painstakingly interviewed witnesses and pieced together whatever evidence remained (which does not including saucer parts). The incident subsequently became the topic of several books and has provided fuel for much speculation.

One of the institutions to emerge out of this incident is the International UFO Museum and Research Center in Roswell, New Mexico. The museum opened in the fall of 1992, and on July 1, 1996, it recorded its 100,000th visitor. One of the more interesting incidents associated with the museum occurred in 1996, when the September issue of *Penthouse* magazine featured pictures that it claimed were photos of a genuine alien from a saucer crash. As it turned out, however, the pictures were photos of an alien prop in the International UFO Museum.

See Also: Hoaxes; The Roswell Incident
Further Reading:
Craft, Michael. *Alien Impact.* New York: St. Martin's, 1996.
Randle, Kevin D. *The Randle Report: UFOs in the 1990s.* New York: M. Evans, 1997.

INTERPLANETARY CONNECTIONS

This organization publishes books and issues transcripts and tapes of the channeling sessions held by Darryl Anka. Originally a designer and also the brother of singer Paul Anka, Darryl Anka saw a spaceship on two occasions in the early 1970s. He was interested in channeling and had his first experience as a medium in 1983, when he channeled Bashar and Anima; he understood then that the spaceship he had seen was Bashar's.

Bashar and Anima are members of a society that communicates by telepathy; Bashar means "leader" in Arabic, and Anima is a Latin term taken from Jungian psychology that refers to the representation of the feminine in the male psyche. Bashar originally came from a planet that is in a different dimension and, as such, is impossible to see by humans. He speaks on behalf of his society, and his purpose is to help humanity in a period that he considers transitional. He particularly focuses on the concept of guilt and on its limiting effects on mankind.

See Also: Channeling; Contactees; New Age
Further Reading:
Anka, Darryl. *Bashar: Blue Print for Change—A Message from Our Future.* Simi Valley, CA: New Solutions Publishing, 1990.
Melton, J. Gordon. *Encyclopedia of American Religions.* 5th ed. Detroit: Gale Research, 1996.

INTRUDERS

Intruders is a movie about three people who meet as a result of psychiatric therapy for unexplained lapses of time. The plot unfolds as they each share their experiences with the skeptical psychiatrist,

Alien images from the 1992 CBS special Intruders *(CBS)*

who finally brings them together as a result of their similar graphic discriptions of alien encounters with white-faced, bug-eyed creatures. This entire movie flows more or less directly out of recent reports of alien abduction.

1992: 162 min. Director: Dan Curtis; Cast: Richard Crenna, Mare Winningham, Susan Blakely, Ben Vereen, Steve Berkoff, Daphne Ashbrook.

INVADERS FROM MARS

In the original 1953 version of *Invaders from Mars,* a little boy sees a flying saucer bury itself behind his house. His father goes out to investigate and returns a changed man. When his mother changes, too, the boy finds radios in their necks. The kid seeks the help of a psychologist and an astronomer. They find that the flying saucer is operated by green creatures and captained by a Martian who controls the earthlings. The ending has the boy waking up having dreamed it all and then hearing a flying saucer land.

The 1986 remake has nothing to add to the original film except a lot of spectacular special effects, which fail to improve it. Jimmy Hunt, child star of the 1953 version, gives a cameo in this one as a cop.

The basic idea of aliens invading the earth by taking over human beings would be developed in its classic form in the later film *Invasion of the Body Snatchers.* This is another form of the infiltration plot that commentators have connected with fear of communist takeover. The notion of aliens posing as human beings is a staple theme in the UFO subculture.

Cannon 1986; 102 min. Director: Tobe Hooper; Writers: Dan O;Bannon, Don Jakoby; Music: Christopher Young; Cinematography: Daniel Pearle; Cast: Hunter Carson, Karen Black, Louise Fletcher, Laraine Newman, Thimothy Bottoms, Bud Cort, James Karen.

INVASION

Two humanoid aliens and their human prisoner crash-land outside an English hospital. A doctor admits the prisoner for treatment, but aliens arrive and demand that the prisoner be handed over to them immediately. When the doctor turns down this request, the aliens surround the hospital with

an impenetrable forcefield. This is a very human drama that has very little direct connection between this film and the UFO subculture, except that it reflects the human tendency to anthropomorphize everything, including extraterrestrials.

Merton Park 1966; 82 min. Director: Alan Bridges; Cast: Edward Judd, Yoko Tani, Valerie Gearon, Lydon Brook, Tsai Chin, Barrie Ingham.

INVASION OF THE ANIMAL PEOPLE

In this 1960 film a spaceship lands and releases a giant stone-age monster, which goes on a rampage. After much carnage, the aliens recapture it and return to their distant planet.

The notion that alien animals, in addition to intelligent extraterrestrial ufonauts, also exist and can survive on earth and be a threat to humankind is an old idea to Hollywood but a new notion within the UFO community, confined almost entirely to reports associated with the activity of the so-called Chupacabras ("Goat Sucker"). This may be an example of how a theme of the human imagination has filtered down to be a concrete, empirical claim.

Gustaf Unger Films/A. B. Fortuna 1960; 73 min. Director: Virgil W. Vogel, Jerry Warren; Cast: Robert Burton, Barbara Wilson, John Carradine.

INVASION OF THE BODY SNATCHERS

The classic film *Invasion of the Body Snatchers* was made in 1956. It was adapted from Jack Finney's novel, *The Body Snatchers.* In it, a doctor played by Kevin McCarthy returns to his hometown from a medical convention and finds everything disturbingly different. He discovers that an invasion of parasite aliens (pods) has replaced humans with soulless counterfeits.

The 1978 remake featured Donald Sutherland, Leonard Nimoy (as a psychiatrist who says, "People are changing. They're becoming less human.") and Jeff Goldblum. The director of the 1956 film, Don Siegel, has a cameo in this one as a cabbie (and pod). The location is changed from small town to big city (San Francisco), where urban alienation makes it virtually impossible to distinguish between pods and people. Kevin McCarthy

Film still from the 1956 version of Invasion of the Body Snatchers, *starring Kevin McCarthy and Dana Wynter (The Del Valle Archive)*

makes a cameo appearance as the doctor of the earlier film, still trying to inform the world of the danger of the pods.

This is another form of the infiltration plot that commentators have connected with Cold War fears. The notion of aliens posing as human beings is a staple theme in the UFO subculture. Although not the first film to feature people being taken over by alien invaders, it was the first really good film to make use of this theme.

Invasion of the Body Snatchers also represents a trend to substitute extraterrestrial factors for supernatural factors in movies, particularly in horror movies. In other words, in an earlier era the rough equivalent to a tale like *Invasion of the Body Snatchers* would be a horror story about demonic spiritual entities attempting to take over by possessing ordinary human beings. In our highly secularized world, it is more plausible to entertain the idea that aliens are at work behind the scenes. This strategy has become commonplace in horror

movies from *The Blob* (which fell to earth in a meteor) to *The Rocky Horror Picture Show* (the haunted house is actually an extraterrestrial spaceship).

Walter Wanger Productions 1956; 80 min. Director: Donald Siegel; Writers: Sam Peckinpah, Daniel Mainwaring; Cinematography: Ellsworth Fredericks; Cast: Kevin McCarthy, Dana Wynter, Carolyn Jones, King Donovan, Donald Siegel, Larry Gates, Jean Willes, Whit Bissell.

Remake: Solofilm Company 1978; 115 min. Director: Philip Kaufman; Producer: Robert H. Solo; Screenwriter: W. D. Richter; Cinematography: Michael Chapman; Cast: Donald Sutherland, Brooke Adams, Leonard Nimoy, Veronica Cartwright, Jeff Goldblum, Art Hindle.

INVASION OF THE LOVE DRONES

In this sexploitation film of 1975, the spaceship of the alien Dr. Femme runs on sexual energy. She therefore has to create a race of love drones with which to cause a worldwide orgy to fuel the invasion of earth. Such films are useful for demonstrating the point that space and unknown aliens have served as almost a blank screen onto which we project our hopes and fears. In this case, extraterrestrials serve to embody our sexual projections.

A Sensory Man Production 1975; 72 min.
Director/Cinematography: Jerome Hamlin; Writers: Jerome Hamlin, Conrad Baunz, Michael Gury; Cast: Eric Edwards, Viveca Ash, Bree Anthony, Tony Blue, Sarah Nicholson, Jamie Gills.

INVASION OF THE SAUCERMEN

In this 1957 comedy, little green aliens are harassing teenagers at the local Lover's Lane. When two teenagers accidentally run over one alien, the others seek revenge by framing the teens for the murder of the town drunk, who was actually injected with alcohol, which the little green men excrete from needles in their fingertips. The teenagers must convince the authorities that the creatures exist before the aliens can multiply and take over the world. The climax has the teenagers turning their headlights on the aliens and evaporating them.

A film built around the theme of alien invasion—a theme shared by Hollywood and the UFO community—it is interesting that at least one close encounter—the Munroe Falls hit-and-run—is built around the experience of running over an alien.

Malibu 1957; 69 min. Director: Edward L. Cahn; Music: Ronald Stein; Cast: Steven Terrell, Gloria Castillo, Frank Gorshin, Lyn Osborn, Ed Nelson, Angelo Rossitto.

INVASION OF THE STAR CREATURES

This is a 1962 film in which two American soldiers on army maneuvers encounter two Amazon women who, under the control of aliens, plan to conquer earth. The aliens, called Star Creatures, invade the army base, but the Amazons fall in love with the soldiers and cancel their hostile plans. The Star Creatures are sent back into space. The basic plot is taken from countless other alien-invasion films, a theme projected onto ufonauts, perhaps out of fears of a communist invasion.

American International 1962; 81 min. Director: Bruno DeSoto; Writer: Jonathan Haze; Cinematography: Basil

Bradbury; Cast: Bob Ball, Frankie Ray, Gloria Victor, Dolores Reed, Mark Ferris.

ISAIAH, BOOK OF

In verse 4:5, the traditional manifestation of the Lord to Israel, as a cloud by day and a pillar of fire at night, has been suggested to be a reference to a UFO. The same interpretation is applied to this description wherever it appears in the Pentateuch. Scholars consider it to be merely a story-telling device. Verses 6:1–4 are the passage in Isaiah that has supplied the Jewish and Christian liturgies with the *Trishagion:* "Holy, holy, holy is the Lord of Hosts. Heaven and earth are filled with his glory." True, the Seraphims described here sound like Ezekiel's living creatures, but both appear to be based on traditional visual imagery.

There are many passages in Isaiah, such as 66:15, that refer to the Lord riding in the clouds or whirlwinds, wrathfully punishing enemies and evildoers. This same imagery appears in Greek mythology. It was a writing convention, and it is difficult to see such passages as UFO reports.

See Also: Ancient Astronauts
Further Reading:
Downing, Barry H. *The Bible and Flying Saucers.* Philadelphia: J. B. Lippincott, 1968.
Goran, Morris. *The Modern Myth, Ancient Astronauts and UFOs.* South Brunswick, NJ: A. S. Barnes, 1978.

IT CAME FROM OUTER SPACE

In this 1953 film aliens crash-land on earth in a ship that looks like a meteorite. It was originally filmed in 3-D, and the fiery meteor seemed to burst from the screen and zoom directly toward the viewers. An astronomer witnesses the event, but when he tries to tell people about the aliens, no one will believe him. The aliens' spaceship has broken down, and they need human beings as mechanics. Their modus operandi is to replace local people with alien doubles who behave in a similar manner to the originals except for a zombie-like stare when not in the company of human beings. Eventually, the locals attempt to destroy the aliens, but the astronomer has found out that they mean no harm to the world and protects them in the final confrontation. When the spaceship is repaired, the aliens take off for outer space, having returned the missing citizens and reclaimed their doubles. This theme resonates with themes in the UFO subculture, such as flying-saucer crashes and the infiltration of human society by alien-controlled human beings.

Universal 1953; 81 min. Director: Jack Arnold; Writer: Harry Essex; Music: Herman Stine, Henry Mancini;

Cinematography: Clifford Stine; Cast: Richard Carlson, Barbara Rush, Charles Drake, Russell Johnson, Morey Amsterdam, Joseph Sawyer.

IT CONQUERED THE WORLD

In this 1956 film an idealist makes radio contact with a dying race of intelligent creatures on Venus.

Film still of Lee Van Cleef battling a monster from Venus in the 1956 film It Conquered the World *(The Del Valle Archive)*

Believing he'd be saving humankind from itself, he guides the cucumber-shaped, fanged Venusian to earth, only to discover that it intends to transform humanity into zombie slaves. The largely immobile alien hides out in a cave, giving birth to bat-mites, which fly and implant stingers in the backs of human necks, bringing them under telepathic control. A scientist foils the invasion. Coming out in the same year as *Invasion of the Body Snatchers*, it seems to embody the same fear of invasion-by-infiltration that commentators have associated with Cold War fears.

Sunset Productions 1956; 68min. Director: Roger Corman; Writers: Charles B. Griffith, Lou Rusoff; Cinematography: Federick E. West; Cast: Peter Graves, Beverly Garland, Lee Van Cleef, Sally Fraser, Russ Bender Jonathan Haze, Dick Miller, Karen Kadler, Paul Blaisdell.

JACOB AND UFOS

Jacob was the third patriarch of Israel, after Abraham and Isaac. He had two remarkable experiences with angels that in retrospect have been interpreted as UFO encounters. In the first, Jacob dreams about a stairway to heaven, which has been interpreted as a UFO sighting. At the end of a long day of traveling, Jacob laid his head on a stone and slept:

> And he dreamed that there was a ladder set up on the earth, and the top of it reached to heaven. And behold, the angels of God were ascending and descending on it! . . . Then Jacob awoke from his sleep and said, "Surely the Lord is in this place and I did not know it." And he was afraid, and said, "how awesome is this place! This is none other than the house of God, and this is the gate of heaven." (Gen. 28:12–17)

Scholarly commentary on this verse asserts that the image of the ladder is more accurately rendered as a stairway or ramp. The image seems to allude to a ziggurat (a temple build in a stepwise fashion). The gods contacted humanity at the top of the ziggurats, and the temple priests ascended and descended the tower in service to the divinities. Jacob's dream applies this image to God and to God's ongoing interactions with the earth. This dream emphasizes, among other things, that Yahweh is a sky god who resides in the celestial regions.

Jacob is also known for a wrestling match between himself and an angel. This has been interpreted as an encounter with an extraterrestrial. In his wrestling match with the angel, Jacob seems to get the upper hand until his opponent knocks his leg out of joint. Nevertheless, Jacob continues to cling to his opponent until he receives a blessing:

> And Jacob was left alone; and a man wrestled with him until the breaking of the day. When the man

saw that he did not prevail against Jacob, he touched the hollow of his thigh; and Jacob's thigh was put out of joint as he wrestled with him. Then he said, "Let me go for the day is breaking." But Jacob said, "I will not let you go, unless you bless me." And he said to him, "What is your name?" And he said, "Jacob." Then he said, "Your name shall no more be called Jacob, but Israel, for you have striven with God and with men, and have prevailed." (Gen. 32:24–28)

This unusual story of hand-to-hand combat with the dark angel—variously identified as a man, an angel, a demon, God Himself, or, from an ancient-astronaut perspective, an extraterrestrial—has naturally tended to puzzle commentators. If the attacker is indeed an angel as the dominant line of interpretation suggests, one wonders why a man so blessed by God would be attacked by God's messenger. One explanation is that in some (nonextant) original version, the "angel" was a spirit or demigod. According to this line of interpretation, later priestly editors, in an effort to remove a seeming affront to strict monotheism, obscured the true identity of Jacob's assailant.

See Also: Ancient Astronauts; Angels

Further Reading:

Downing, Barry H. *The Bible and Flying Saucers.* Philadelphia: J. B. Lippincott, 1968.

Goran, Morris. *The Modern Myth, Ancient Astronauts and UFOs.* South Brunswick, NJ: A. S. Barnes, 1978.

JESSUP, MORRIS KETCHUM

Morris K. Jessup, born in 1900, dropped out of a doctoral program in astronomy and ended up running an export business and writing about ancient and modern mysteries. From 1955 to 1957 he published three highly speculative books on UFOs, connecting the "little people" of folklore with extraterrestrials. He claimed to be the recipient of communications from one "Allende," who was privy to government secrets about UFOS. It turned out that Carl Allen, born in 1925, was the mysterious person who provided annotations to Jessup's books. Despite this debunking, myths and legends about Jessup live on. An untreated chronic depressive, Jessup committed suicide in 1959. Some have claimed contact with his ghost as a spirit guide.

See Also: Mythology and Folklore; Philadelphia Experiment

Further Reading:

Barker, Gray, ed. *The Strange Case of Dr. M. K. Jessup.* Clarksburg, WV: Saucerian Books, 1963.

Flammonde, Paris. *The Age of Flying Saucers: Notes on a Projected History of Unidentified Flying Objects.* New York: Hawthorn Books, 1971.

Genzlinger, Anna Lykins. *The Jessup Dimension.* Clarksburg, WV: Saucerian Press, 1981.

JUNG, CARL GUSTAV

Eminent psychologist and philosopher Carl Gustav Jung (1875–1961) was interested in the subject of UFOs since 1946 and read every book he could get on the subject. He was an honorary member of the Aerial Phenomena Research Organization (APRO) and belonged to the National Investigations Committee on Aerial Phenomena.

Born at Kesswil, Switzerland, Carl Jung is considered the originator of analytical psychology. He studied medicine at the University of Basel, Switzerland, and received his M.D. in 1902 at the University of Zurich. Between 1907 and 1913 Jung became a disciple of Sigmund Freud, but their collaboration did not last.

In July 1954 *Die Weltwoche,* a weekly magazine published in Zurich, published two letters by Dr. Jung regarding flying saucers. The letters were equivocal in the extreme. These letters were translated into the French and appeared in the Swiss UFO magazine *Courrier Interplanetaire.* The French version was translated into English, abridged, and published in England's *Flying Saucer Review.* By the time the piece appeared there, Jung's qualifying remarks had been removed.

More than three years later, *Flying Saucer Review's* version was reprinted in the APRO bulletin. An Associated Press (AP) writer in Alamogordo, New Mexico (where APRO had its office),

Cover of Carl Jung's 1958 book Flying Saucers: A Modern Myth of Things Seen in the Skies *(Mary Evans Picture Library)*

read the APRO bulletin and issued a release that Carl Jung stated UFOs are real and show signs of intelligent guidance by humanoid pilots. This release made no mention of the fact that the statement made by Jung had occurred four years previously and gone through two translations and additional alteration. The story appeared in newspapers all over the world, including the *New York Times.*

Seeing the AP story, Jung wrote APRO and asked for a copy of the *Flying Saucer Review* article it had reprinted. After reading this article, Jung told AP that people who think they have seen flying saucers wanted to see them because they are in need of fantasy. AP released this in a follow-up story. Not to be outdone, United Press International interviewed Jung about UFOs and was given the statement, "I have formulated my position on the question of the reality of UFOs in the phrase: 'Something is being seen, but it is not known what.'" Jung's major concern was not with physical UFOs but with the way observers conceive of them. However, he also states that UFOs cannot be accounted for with a purely psychological explanation because they show up on radar screens and photographic plates.

Jung postulated the existence of a collective unconscious and discussed mythology and religion in terms of the "primordial images," or "archetypes," in the collective unconscious that every human being inherits. He believed that religion represented a fundamental element of the psychotherapeutic process as well as of life. Jung's focus was, however, always on the psychological aspect of religion.

In 1959 Jung's book *Flying Saucers: A Modern Myth of Things Seen in the Sky* was published in English. Jung was interested in how the human response to UFOs was unconsciously cast in religious terms—for example, being saved or rescued by friendly ufonauts placed UFOs in a soteriological ("saving") role usually reserved for gods or angels. It was this kind of response that led Jung to refer to UFOs as "technological angels."

See Also: Angels; Archetype; Collective Unconscious; Mandala

Further Reading:

Cavendish, Richard, ed. *Encyclopedia of the Unexplained. Magic, Occultism, and Parapsychology.* London: Arkana Penguin Books, 1989.

Jung, Carl Gustav. *Flying Saucers: A Modern Myth of Things Seen in the Sky.* Princeton: Princeton University Press, 1978.

———. *Memories, Dreams, Reflections.* New York: Vintage Books, 1965.

———. *Symbols of Transformation.* New York: Harper Torchbooks, 1956.

KARMA

Many New Age religions—including UFO-oriented spiritual groups—assume the basic validity of reincarnation and the accompanying notion of karma. The many different religious systems in or originating in South Asia (India) all assume the basic validity of the law of karma. In its simplest form, this law operates impersonally like a natural law, ensuring that every good or bad deed eventually returns to the individual in the form of reward or punishment commensurate with the original deed. (The term derives from the Sanskrit root word *kr,* which means to "act," "do," or "make.")

Karma refers both to the personality patterns that result from past actions and to the forces at large in the cosmos that bring reward or retribution to the individual. It is karma that compels human beings to take rebirth (to reincarnate) in successive lifetimes. In other words, if one dies before reaping the effects of one's actions (as most people do), the karmic process demands that one come back in a future life. Coming back into another lifetime also allows karmic forces to reward or punish one through the circumstance in which one is born. Hence, for example, an individual who was generous in one lifetime might be reborn as a wealthy person in her or his next incarnation.

For the most part, the mainstream of South Asian thinking does not view the cycle of death and rebirth as attractive. Hence the ultimate goal of most Indian religions is to escape the cycle of death and rebirth. While many contemporary Westerners would view the prospects of reincarnation positively, the traditional South Asian view is that returning to live another life is distinctly undesirable: Because life in the physical body always involves suffering, we should strive to escape the wheel of rebirth.

See Also: Extraterrestrial Incarnations; New Age; Reincarnation
Further Reading:
Feuerstein, Georg. *Encyclopedic Dictionary of Yoga.* New York: Paragon House, 1990.
Zimmer, Heinrich. *Philosophies of India.* New York: Bollingen, 1951.

KEEL, JOHN ALVA

John Alva Keel is a controversial figure. Born in 1930, he became a professional writer at age 16 and has made a living at that trade ever since. His many books are filled with wild speculations, considered by many to be quite in the tradition of James Churchward but also invested with a curious aesthetic quality. In some ways, he offers another version of the "paraphysical" explanation for UFOs favored by Jacques Vallee and Carl Jung. He continues to write on UFOs and many other topics.

See Also: Jung, Carl Gustav
Further Reading:
Keel, John A. *Disneyland of the Gods.* New York: Amok Press, 1988.
———. *The Mothman Prophecies.* New York: Saturday Review Press/E. P. Dutton, 1975.
———. *UFOs: Operation Trojan Horse.* New York: G. P. Putnam's Sons, 1970.
Michell, John. *Eccentric Lives and Peculiar Notions.* San Diego: Harcourt Brace Jovanovich, 1984.

KELLY-HOPKINSVILLE INCIDENT

At a farmhouse in Kelly, Kentucky, on the evening of August 21, 1955, Billy Ray Taylor came inside and excitedly reported to the other 10 occupants of the house that he had seen a flying saucer. He said it was at an altitude of about 40 feet when it dropped to the ground at the end of the fields. The others did not go outside to investigate, thinking he had merely seen a shooting star.

An hour later the dog started barking, and two of the men went out to investigate. The dog ran under the house, and the men saw a figure approaching from the field. The creature was three and a half feet tall with a large head, and its arms reached almost to the ground. It had glowing yellow eyes and talons at the ends of its fingers. One man grabbed a rifle and the other a shotgun. When the creature was within 20 feet of them, both fired. The creature reportedly did a flip and scurried off to the side of the house, where it disappeared in the darkness. A while later the same or a similar creature appeared at a side window, and one of the occupants of the house fired at it through the screen with the shotgun. The creature flipped over and could no longer be seen.

The men decided to go out to investigate. As the first one went out through the door, a clawlike hand reached down and touched his hair. This man was yanked back inside by his wife, and another man went out and fired the shotgun at the creature, which flipped back over the roof. Another creature was seen in a maple tree. The men shot it, knocking it off the limb, and it floated to the ground. Another creature appeared from around the corner of the house, and the men shot it from extremely close range. The shotgun pellets made a sound as if they had hit a metal bucket. The creature flipped over and ran away.

After more attempts to drive the creatures away failed, the occupants of the house got into two cars and drove to the police station in nearby Hopkinsville. By this time it was after 11 P.M., and the witnesses were near hysteria. Local police, state police, a deputy sheriff, newspaper personnel, and military police responded to the site, but no evidence was found other than damage to property caused by the firearms. Everyone except the occupants left at 2 A.M. The creatures were again periodically seen at the windows for about two more hours. There was no evidence that the witnesses had been drinking. They were genuinely scared, with elevated pulse rates. The seven adult witnesses signed statements as well as composite drawings of the creatures. No evidence of a hoax has ever surfaced.

Further Reading:
Davis, Isabel, and Ted Bloecher. *Close Encounter at Kelly and Others of 1955.* Evanston: Center for UFO Studies, 1978.
Hynek, J. Allen. *The UFO Experience: A Scientific Inquiry.* Chicago: Henry Regnery, 1972.
Matyi, J. Robert. *My God, They're Real!* Port Washington, NY: Ashley, 1979.

KENTUCKY ABDUCTION

On the night of January 6, 1976, in the small town of Liberty, Kentucky, three friends were driving home just after 11:15 P.M. when a brightly colored object took control of their car. Even though the car's engine was not running, the car was moving at 85 miles per hour. Then a bright light flashed into the car, and the three women went blank. Tears flowed from their eyes, their skin tingled, and they had severe headaches. They could not recognize any of the surrounding landscape, then, in what seemed like no more than a moment, the landscape became familiar again. When they returned home, they noticed that the kitchen clock read 1:25 A.M., but their watches said 6 A.M. They could not remember what happened in the time they seemed to have lost. Under hypnosis they claimed that they were split apart from each other and examined by aliens with a scalding liquid that was poured over them. That evening there were numerous reports by local residents of a brightly colored object in the sky.

See Also: Abductees; Close Encounters; Time Travel
Further Reading:
Lorenzen, Coral, and Jim Lorenzen. *Abducted! Confrontations with Beings from Outer Space.* New York: Berkley Medallion, 1977.
Stringfield, Leonard H. *Situation Red, the UFO Siege!* Garden City, NY: Doubleday, 1977a.
Turner, Karla. *Taken: Inside the Alien-Human Abduction Agenda.* Roland, AR: Kelt Works, 1994.

KILLER KLOWNS FROM OUTER SPACE

In this 1988 film the aliens are grotesque clowns who arrive in a circus-tent-shaped flying saucer and wrap their victims' corpses in cotton candy. Easily, this is one of weirder extraterrestrials-as-technological-demons films.

Transworld/Sarlui-Diamant 1988; 88 min. Director: Stephen Chiodo; Writers: Stephen Chiodo, Charles

Chiodo; Cinematography: Grant Cramer; Cast: Suzanne Snyder, John Allen Nelson, Royal Dano, John Vernon, Michael Siegel, Peter Licassi.

KILLERS FROM SPACE

This is a 1954 black-and-white film in which a scientist surviving a plane crash is captured and brainwashed by big-eyed aliens and forced to assist them in their evil plan for world domination. The scientist's wife and assistant both notice that he has turned to espionage. He is given an injection of truth serum to establish the truth, but when he tells it no one believes him. The brainwashing wears off, the scientist returns to the cave where he was brainwashed, and he shuts off the dynamo that is their power source, killing them.

Many commentators have noted Cold War fears reflected in both concern about UFOs and in certain sci-fi movies of the 1950s. While this line of interpretation has been overworked, it is more appropriate for some films than others. The capture and brainwashing of the scientist in *Killers from Space,* for example, seems to reflect the American experience during the Korean War.

Planet Filmways, Inc. 1954; 80 min. Director: W. Lee Wilder; Cinematography: William Clothier; Cast: Peter Graves, Barbara Bestar, James Seay, Frank Gerstle, Steve Pendleton, John Merrick.

KINGS, BOOKS OF

In addition to the passages on Elijah, other passages in 1 Kings and 2 Kings have been interpreted as referring to UFOs or extraterrestrials. 1 Kings verses 19:9–14 explain that God is not "in" physical phenomena but instead is heard as a "tiny, whispering voice." To interpret this as a UFO phenomenon goes exactly against the sense of the passage; but seeing it as referring to communication from an extraterrestrial is somewhat more logical. However, neither believers nor scholars will agree that God can be explained as an extraterrestrial.

See Also: Ancient Astronauts
Further Reading:
Downing, Barry H. *The Bible and Flying Saucers.* Philadelphia: J. B. Lippincott, 1968.
Goran, Morris. *The Modern Myth, Ancient Astronauts and UFOs.* South Brunswick, NJ: A. S. Barnes, 1978.

KISS ME QUICK!

In this 1964 sexploitation film, an alien comes to earth in search of females because those on his planet are barren. He visits Dr. Breedlove, an expert at creating artificial women, and takes one of his creations back with him. Although not meant to be anything more than titillation, it is interesting how this film anticipates one of the themes of more recent UFO lore about alien abductions, namely, the notion that somehow the DNA of extraterrestrials has somehow become exhausted and that the alien abductors renew themselves with human DNA.

Fantasy Productions 1964; 80 min. Director/Writer: Russ Meyer; Cinematography: Lester Kovac; Cast: Jackie DeWitt, Fred Coe, Althea Currier, Claudia Banks.

KLARER, ELIZABETH

Elizabeth Klarer saw her first UFO in October 1917 with her sister at their farm in South Africa in the Drakensberg Mountains. Twenty years later, while flying with her pilot husband, she saw another UFO. On the morning of December 27, 1954, a flying saucer returned to the farm and came so close that she could see a handsome occupant looking at her with a hypnotic stare. On April 6, 1956, she was drawn by a strange compulsion to go back to the farm. The next morning the saucer was waiting for her along with the good-looking occupant. The man's name was Akon, and he told her that he came from the planet Meton in the Alpha Centauri system. Klarer had a romantic and sexual relationship with Akon. She lived for four months on Meton, during which she gave birth to her and Akon's son, Ayling, whom she had to leave on the planet because of the different "vibratory rates" between the earth and Meton.

See Also: Contactees; Sex
Further Reading:
Bord, Janet, and Colin Bord. *Life Beyond Earth? Man's Contacts with Space People.* London: GraftonBooks, 1991.
Evans, Hilary. *Gods, Spirits, and Cosmic Guardians: A Comparative Study of the Encounter Experience.* Wellingborough, U.K.: Aquarian Press, 1987.
Klarer, Elizabeth. *Beyond the Light Barrier.* Cape Town, South Africa: Howard Timmins, 1980.

KRONOS

In this 1957 film Kronos is a 100-foot-high energy-accumulating alien robot who comes to earth to drain it of all power sources. He arrives on a California beach and marches inland, sucking up energy as he goes. The military try to H-bomb Kronos, but the robot merely absorbs the energy, causing him to become even larger. A scientist finds a way of short-circuiting Kronos, which causes the robot to absorb its own energy and disappear. Although the contemporary UFO community has not claimed that extraterrestrials are here to drain us of energy, there is a recurring theme in some UFO literature that aliens are here because they must want something, either from human beings or from our planet.

Regal 1957; 78 min. Director: Kurt Neumann; Writer: Lawrence Louis Goldman; Cinematography: Karl Struss; Cast: Jeff Morrow, Barbara Lawrence, John Emery, George O'Hanlon, Morris Ankrum.

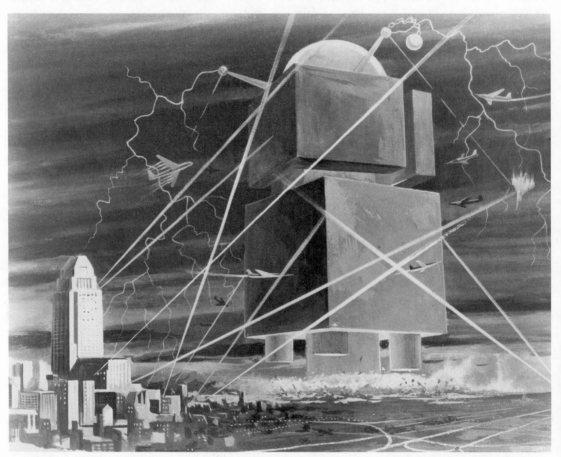

A machine created by an alien race designed to siphon energy from earth battles with the earthlings in the 1957 film Kronos. (The Del Valle Archive)

LARSON ABDUCTION

On August 26, 1975, three friends left Fargo, North Dakota, on their way to Bismarck. Terry O'Leary, Jackie Larson, and Sandy Larson suddenly saw a brilliant flash light up the sky and heard sounds of what they thought to be thunder, only louder. They then observed eight to 10 orange glowing objects flying from south to west, the highest being significantly larger than the others. The three then felt something strange when they looked at the objects, almost as if they were frozen for a second. The strangest aspect of the situation was that Jackie, who was sitting in the front seat, was now in the center of the backseat. Later, when Jackie was hypnotized, she claimed that robotlike figures abducted her and it felt like they pulled her brain from her body. They told her that they would be back for her again. When they came back they did a more complex abduction, taking her to a different planet—one that she described as "a barren desert with a building in the middle." When the second abduction was done the abductors told her (through telepathy) never to tell anyone because they would not believe her.

See Also: Abductees; Close Encounters
Further Reading:
Jacobs, David M. *Secret Life: Firsthand Accounts of UFO Abductions.* New York: Simon and Schuster, 1992.
Lorenzen, Coral, and Jim Lorenzen. *Abducted! Confrontations with Beings from Outer Space.* New York: Berkley Medallion, 1977.
Turner, Karla. *Taken: Inside the Alien-Human Abduction Agenda.* Roland, AR: Kelt Works, 1994.

LASERBLAST

In this 1978 film a loner finds a laser gun and a mysterious pendant left behind by a fleeing, lizard-like alien. When he wears the pendant, he is taken over by the alien and revenges himself on everyone who has mistreated him. He is finally killed by aliens that have been searching for the original owner of the laser gun. This is an interesting variant on the classic theme of tapping an evil power that eventually kills the wielder of the power. *Laserblast,* in other words, is an aliens-as-technological-demons movie.

> Irwin Yablands, Co. 1978; 87 min. Director: Michael Rae; Writer: Franne Schacht, Frank Ray Perilli; Music: Richard Band, Joel Goldsmith; Cast: Kim Milford, Cheryl "Rainbeaux" Smith, Keenan Wynn, Roddy McDowall.

LAST DAY MESSENGERS

The Last Day Messengers, under the leadership of Dave W. Bent, is centered in Fort Lauderdale, Florida. He channels the Great White Brotherhood (a.k.a. the Ascended Masters), and for the most part his teachings reflect the general worldview of the New Age–metaphysical subculture. The name of the group comes from the teaching that we are in the final period before Christ returns and physically cleanses the planet. In preparation for His return, individual human beings must cleanse their consciousnesses.

See Also: Channeling; Contactees; New Age
Further Reading:
Lewis, James R. *The Encyclopedia of Cults, Sects, and New Religions.* Amherst, NY: Prometheus Books, 1998.
Melton, J. Gordon. *Encyclopedia of American Religions.* 5th ed. Detroit: Gale Research, 1996.

LEE, GLORIA

Gloria Lee was a martyr of the early contactee movement. She was born in Los Angeles on March 22, 1925, and worked as a child actress. When she grew up she became an airline stewardess. In 1952 she married aircraft engineer William Byrd. After her marriage she worked as a ground hostess at Los Angeles International Airport.

While at the airport in September 1953 Gloria Lee received a message by automatic writing from an entity that identified itself as J. W., a resident of Jupiter. She continued to receive messages by automatic writing and then telepathically. Once, when she was hanging out wash in her backyard in Westchester, California, she received a telepathic message to look above. She saw a large flying saucer heading north toward Santa Monica. At J. W.'s recommendation, Gloria joined a psychic development group. Her experiences there convinced Gloria of J. W.'s existence.

In 1959 Gloria Lee established the Cosmon Research Foundation, which published and distributed J. W.'s teachings, including her first book, *Why We Are Here!*, which was widely read in contactee circles. The following year Gloria Lee visited the Mark-Age Meta Center, a newly organized contactee group in Florida. There she found out that J. W. had been incarnated in the person of Jim Speed, whom Gloria met at the center. Gloria Lee published her second book, *The Changing Conditions of Your World* in 1962.

She had received plans for a spaceship telepathically from J. W. with instructions to present the plan to government scientists. In September 1962 she traveled to Washington, D.C., to carry out this mission. Lee said that J. W. and other extraterrestrials were disturbed about the fighting and nuclear weapons on earth. The space people were going to invade the earth and establish a peace program. When officials in Washington refused to look at her blueprints, Lee checked into the Hotel Claridge and began a fruit-juice fast for peace while waiting for the officials to arrive. No one ever showed up. On November 28 Lee's husband, fearing for her health, summoned an ambulance. She died in the hospital on December 2. She was survived by her husband and two children, ages five and seven. Cosmon Research, with 2,000 members, disbanded upon her death.

On December 12, 1962, Yolanda (Pauline Sharpe) of the Mark-Age Meta Center was contacted by Gloria Lee. The conversation was published as *Gloria Lee Lives!* On January 21, 1963, Verity, a medium with the Heralds of the New Age in New Zealand, also claimed contact with Gloria Lee. She produced a book of Lee's dictations called *The Going and the Glory.*

See Also: Automatic Writing; Contactees; Religions, UFO

Further Reading:
Lee, Gloria. *The Changing Conditions of Your World, by J. W. of Jupiter, Instrumented by Gloria Lee.* Los Angeles: DeVorss, 1962.
———. *Why We Are Here: By J. W., a Being from Jupiter through the Instrumentation of Gloria Lee.* Los Angeles: DeVorss, 1959.
Mark-Age MetaCenter. *Cosmic Lessons: Gloria Lee Channels for Mark-Age.* Miami, FL: Mark-Age MetaCenter [1969–1972].
———. *Gloria Lee Lives! My Experiences since Leaving Earth.* Miami, FL: Mark-Age MetaCenter, 1963.
Melton, J. Gordon. *The Encyclopedia of American Religions.* 3rd ed. 2 vols. Wilmington, NC: McGrath Publishing, 1978.

LIFEFORCE

This is a 1985 British film based on Colin Wilson's novel *The Space Vampires.* A space girl is discovered by a space team investigating Halley's comet. On being brought to earth she comes back to life and sets about vampirizing the inhabitants of London for their life force. This is another variation on the ufological notion that aliens somehow need human life force in order to survive.

London Cannon Films 1985; Director: David A. Prior; Cast: Jack Vogel, Renee Cline, Jeffrey Smith, William Hathaway-Clark, Perry Roberts.

LITERATURE AND THE ALIEN IMAGE

As with popular culture more generally, the impact of UFOs on the literary imagination can be said to be large or small, depending upon how one delimits the UFO category. As a specific, contemporary phenomenon that can be dated to Kenneth Arnold's sighting of flying disks on July 24, 1947, UFOs have exercised little direct influence on the literary imagination. There is, however, a much older layer of interest in space travel and in possible encounters with extraterrestrial beings that antedates the modern UFO craze by several centuries. This larger interest has had a much broader impact.

The theme of alien invasion, for example, which provides the basic plot for countless science-fiction

Cover of a 1954 Norwegian book, De Flygende Tallerkener *(Mary Evans Picture Library)*

novels and popular films, is at least as old as H. G. Wells's 1898 novel, *The War of the Worlds.* Thus, although the UFO phenomenon of the 1940s and 1950s may have stimulated writers to compose more alien-invasion stories, the basic plot of such tales has a much older origin. Even in the science-fiction literature roughly since 1950, one notes a marked tendency to avoid bringing anything like contemporaneous UFOs into the narrative. This is because, as many observers have noted, the conscious goal of better sci-fi authors was to compose "plausible fictions"—an aim that could easily work at cross purposes with the "flying-saucers-are-real!" emphasis of most ufological literature. The same observation holds true, though to a lesser extent, for films and TV narratives.

Literature dealing with space flight and extraterrestrials is automatically categorized as science-fiction literature. As a genre, sci-fi is marginalized because it is generally regarded, rightly or wrongly, as a less serious body of literature—a product of popular culture rather than of high culture. Thus, any piece that attempts to come to grips with UFOs will, by definition, never be a candidate for the Noble Prize in literature—at least not before the Space Brothers land on the White House lawn.

The larger sci-fi theme within which the UFO phenomenon best fits is the encounter with the alien extraterrestrial. This basic notion goes at least as far back as *Other Worlds,* the seventeenth-century novels by Savinien Cyrano de Bergerac, who encountered humanoid aliens on the *Moon* (1656) and the *Sun* (1662). Aliens were, in fact, almost always human or humanoid until the late nineteenth century. The image of extraterrestrials as ruthless competitors with humanity did not emerge until after Charles Darwin's nineteenth-century notions about the struggle for survival between species had been popularized. The first major work of literature to embody this negative image was Wells's *The War of the Worlds.*

By far most authors are less interested in probing the mystery of what it might mean to actually encounter extraterrestrials than in exploring human nature via the foil of aliens. Thus, while many twentieth-century aliens may not be represented in anthropomorphic ways, they do tend to have all of the thoughts and feelings of human beings. It is only comparatively recently that authors have explored what it means to encounter the irreducible otherness of an alien being that shares no common background with humanity.

With few exceptions, there are only a handful of basic plot outlines that the alien-encounter story can follow:

1. alien-invasion tales in which humanity must fight against hostile extraterrestrials, either against an overt invasion, as with *The War of the Worlds,* or against a convert, infiltration of society and the government by aliens that look like human beings
2. "technological angel"–type tales in which friendly extraterrestrials try to help humanity in some way
3. stories in which terrestrials help aliens (a less common but not unusual third category)
4. tales in which aliens are simply stand-ins for human beings, giving an exotic backdrop for a rather ordinary narrative
5. stories that attempt to come to grips with a truly alien Other

These are not, of course, mutually exclusive categories, and many of the better sci-fi tales mix two or more of these together as subplots, making for a more complex overall narrative.

See Also: Film and Television; Popular Culture

Further Reading:

Cohen, Daniel. *Myths of the Space Age.* New York: Dodd, Mead, 1977.

Curran, Douglas. *In Advance of the Landing: Folk Concepts of Outer Space.* New York: Abbeville Press, 1985.

Slusser, George E., and Eric S. Rabkin, eds. *Aliens: The Anthropology of Science Fiction.* Carbondale: Southern Illinois University Press, 1987.

MAC AND ME

MAC and Me is a 1988 film inspired by *E.T.: The Extra-Terrestrial*. MAC is an acronym for *mysterious alien creature*. He is a cute alien with big eyes and a squeaky whistle that is stranded on earth and takes refuge with a boy and his family, who protect him from the authorities. In the finale, it is the human who dies and is resurrected by the alien. Resurrection incidents are barely disguised religious themes, indicating that both E.T. and MAC are manifestations of the ufonaut-as-technological-angel motif. The film was largely financed by McDonald's, which gets very prominent product placement.

Orion 1988; 94 min. Director: Stewart Raffill; Writer: Stewart Rafill; Music: Alan Silvestri; Cast: Christine Ebersole, Jonathan Ward, Katrina Caspary, Lauren Stanley, Jade Calegory.

MAGONIA

The archbishop of Lyon in 840 A.D. complained about the foolishness of the local people, who believed that "there is a certain region called Magonia whence come ships in the clouds." Jakob Grimm, knowing the term from other contexts, commented that it seemed to be formed from "magus" and so to mean the "magic land." In any event, the term was revived by Jacques Vallee in his *Passport to Magonia* in order to have a neutral term that meant "wherever it is that UFOs come from." Vallee argued that the saucer myth is merely the modern form of a type of folklore that has persisted for centuries and need not involve extraterrestrials at all. Much debate has ensued over whether the Magonia reference is meant to be a physical or merely a psychological reality.

See Also: Mythology and Folklore

Further Reading:
Ritchie, David. *UFO: The Definitive Guide to Unidentified Flying Objects and Related Phenomena.* New York: Facts on File, 1994.
Vallee, Jacques. *Passport to Magonia: From Folklore to Flying Saucers.* Chicago: Henry Regnery, 1969.

MAJESTIC 12

In December 1984 Jaime Shandera, a member of a research team looking into the reality of flying saucers, received a package wrapped in plain brown paper at his Burbank, California, home. Delivered by the U.S. Postal Service, this package had no return address, but it was postmarked Albuquerque, New Mexico. In the package was an exposed but undeveloped roll of 35mm film. Shandero developed the film and found that the photographs were of official-looking documents purporting to be briefing papers for President-elect Dwight D. Eisenhower on the subject of Operation Majestic 12.

One of the documents was a brief, top-secret memorandum dated September 24, 1947, from President Harry Truman to Secretary of Defense James V. Forrestal, instructing him to set up a super-secret project that would go by the code name Operation Majestic Twelve. The other documents were descriptions of UFO sightings and the crash of a UFO and recovery of the bodies of four aliens near Roswell, New Mexico, in 1947.

The documents would be a great find if authentic—but were they? After years of exhaustive study, no one is yet prepared to state flatly that they are photographs of genuine government documents. Some detractors have declared that they are frauds.

According to the documents, Majestic 12 (MJ-12, the Maji, and Majic) comprised 12 of the nation's most prominent scientific and political figures. These men had the final say on anything to do with extraterrestrial investigations. They held high military rank by protocol and could come and go as they pleased on any U.S. military base in the world. They were experts in the fields of astrophysics, astronomy, mathematics, medicine, linguistics, military strategy, engineering, diplomacy, and international protocol. Shandera's documents named the members as:

1. Admiral Roscoe H. Hillenkoetter, the first director of the CIA upon its formation in September 1947. After his retirement from government, Hillenkoetter joined the private National Investigations Committee on Aerial Phenomena (NICAP). As a member of NICAP, Hillenkoetter publicly stated that UFOs are real and that through ridicule people are led to believe that UFOs are nonsense.

2. Dr. Vannevar Bush, organizer of the National Defense Research Council and the Office of Scientific Research and Development, which led to the production of the first atomic bomb.

3. James V. Forrestal, who became secretary of defense in July 1947 (at the time of the Roswell incident) but resigned in March 1949, one month before his death at Bethesda Naval Hospital—reportedly a suicide. According to the MJ-12 documents, more than a year passed before Forrestal's MJ-12 position was filled by General Walter Bedell Smith, former U.S. ambassador to Moscow and President Eisenhower's chief of staff.

4. General Nathan F. Twining, commander of the Air Material Command at Wright-Patterson Air Force Base. It was Twining's recommendation that resulted in the creation of the UFO study group named Project Sign.

5. General Hoyt S. Vandenberg, Air Force chief of staff. Vandenberg ordered the destruction of the Project Sign report that UFOs were real. Many UFO researchers believe this was done to maintain security for MJ-12.

6. Dr. Detlev Bronk, an internationally known physiologist and biophysicist who chaired the National Research Council and was a member of the medical advisory board of the Atomic Energy Commission. The alien autopsy film of Ray Santilli allegedly showed Dr. Bronk as one of the two surgeons performing an autopsy on an alien victim of the Roswell crash.

7. Dr. Jerome Hunsaker, chairman of the Departments of Mechanical and Aeronautical Engineering at the Massachusetts Institute of Technology; he also chaired the National Advisory Committee for Aeronautics.

8. Sidney W. Souers, executive secretary to the National Security Council and a retired rear admiral who had been Director of Central Intelligence.

9. Gordon Gray, secretary of the army and a special assistant on national security affairs to President Truman.

10. Dr. Donald Menzel, a Harvard professor of astrophysics and UFO debunker.

11. General Robert M. Montague, base commander at the Sandia Atomic Energy Commission facility in Albuquerque, New Mexico.

12. Dr. Lloyd V. Berkner, executive secretary of the Joint Research and Development Board. He headed a study that resulted in the creation of the Weapons Systems Evaluation Group. Berkner was a member of the 1952 CIA-sponsored panel headed by Dr. H. P. Robertson that concluded that UFOs did not constitute any direct threat to national security. He was also allegedly the other surgeon in the alien autopsy film. These men were all dead at the time the MJ-12 papers surfaced and thus were unable to answer any questions about their role, if any, in such a group.

It was Donald Menzel's inclusion on the list that led most ufologists to doubt its authenticity. On the fourth page of the document photographs received by Shandera, there is a reference to Dr. Menzel stating that he believed the origin of the spacecraft seen was outside of this solar system. This statement was totally contradicted by Menzel's public position, which was that extraterrestrial spacecraft did not exist and that all supposed UFO sightings could be explained by mundane means. Menzel's first UFO-debunking book was published in 1953. It was followed by two others, both proclaiming that every UFO sighting could be explained mundanely.

However, perhaps Menzel's alleged position as stated in the MJ-12 documents was not as contradictory as it first seemed. There was another side to Dr. Donald Menzel that would not be suspected by readers of his books. Menzel had a long, continuous association with the National Security Agency and its predecessor U.S. Navy group. He had a "Top Secret, Ultra" security clearance, had done work for the CIA, and was a world-class expert on cryptanalysis. Well into the presidency of John F. Kennedy, Menzel continued to advise the White House on matters of national security and NASA.

Ufologist Stanton Friedman was the investigator who discovered that Menzel had secretly been associated with the CIA and the National Security Agency and that he had worked on several classified projects. Partly as a consequence of this investigation, Friedman is one of the staunchest supporters of the authenticity of MJ-12. Many other people feel that MJ-12 is disinformation—an item of data with enough truth in it to convince people of its reality but that otherwise leads investigators astray so that more important information is not discovered.

Jaime Shandera and William L. Moore, a Roswell investigator, discovered another document in the National Archives in 1985 that also refers to MJ-12. It was a top-secret memorandum dated July 14, 1954, from Robert Cutler, special assistant to the president, to General Nathan Twining, informing him of a change in date of an MJ-12 briefing. The authenticity of this document was called into question because it was found between two folders in a Records Group to which it was totally unrelated. Some claim that it was planted there for Shandera—perhaps by the same person who had sent him the film.

The MJ-12 documents tell of a civilian pilot flying over the Cascade Mountains in the state of Washington on June 24, 1947, who observed nine flying disk–shaped aircraft traveling in formation at a high rate of speed. This was not the first such sighting, but it was the first to gain widespread attention in the public media. Hundreds of reports of sightings of similar objects followed. The military attempted to ascertain the nature and purpose of these objects in the interests of national defense. Little was learned about the objects until a report was received that one had crashed in a remote region near Roswell, New Mexico. On July 7, 1947, a secret operation was begun to assure recovery of the wreckage of this object for scientific study. During the course of this operation, four small, humanlike beings were found dead and badly decomposed near the crash site. The bodies and the wreckage were removed for study. The cover story was given to the press that the object that had crashed was a weather balloon.

According to the MJ-12 documents, General Twining and Dr. Rush analyzed the wreckage and concluded that the disk was most likely a short-range reconnaissance craft, as it was small and lacked provisions. Project members were divided as to the source of the craft. Some suggested Mars, whereas Dr. Menzel allegedly held that they came from another solar system. The craft lacked conventional methods of propulsion and guidance, such as wings, propellers, and jets. There was also a lack of wiring, vacuum, and other electronic components. The propulsion unit was apparently completely destroyed in the crash.

The documents went on to say that Dr. Bronk analyzed the bodies and concluded that the biological and evolutionary processes responsible for their development were quite different from those postulated in *Homo sapiens*. Dr. Bronk termed them "extraterrestrial biological entities," or EBEs.

Several additional government documents that mention MJ-12 have become public, including a pay record for Bob Lazar (see entry for Area 51), a man who claimed to work with UFOs. All such documents have been branded fakes by debunkers. None, however, has been absolutely proven to be fake, and the numbers of such documents seem to be increasing.

—*Kay Holzinger*

See Also: Conspiracy Theories; Extraterrestrial Biological Entities; The Roswell Incident
Further Reading:
Clark, Jerome. *The UFO Encyclopedia.* 2nd ed. Detroit: Omnigraphics, 1998.
Craft, Michael. *Alien Impact.* New York: St. Martin's, 1996.
Randle, Kevin D. *The Randle Report: UFOs in the 1990s.* New York: M. Evans, 1997.

MAN FROM PLANET X

In this 1951 film an alien arrives on earth in search of assistance for his freezing planet. The Man from Planet X, however, finds the humans heartless and cold. They refuse to help, thus condemning all life on Planet X to extinction, and even bombard the alien and his ship with bazookas.

Man from Planet X came out in the early years of the UFO era, before ufonauts became associated with such sinister activity as abducting human beings and performing strange experiments on them. In sharp contrast to earthlings, the Man from Planet X is a kind and good being—a "technological angel" confronted with the evil of fallen humanity.

Mid-Century Films 1951; 70 min. Director: Edgar G. Ulmer; Writers: Aubry Wisberg, Jack Pollexfen; Cinematography: John L. Russell; Cast: Robert Clarke, Margaret Field, Raymond Bond, William Schallert, Roy Engel, Carles Davis.

THE MAN WHO FELL TO EARTH

In this 1976 film starring David Bowie, an alien arrives on earth from his drought-stricken planet and builds an industrial empire, with the idea of funding the construction of a spaceship to rescue his race and family. He falls victim to a woman, the government, which blinds, and a scientist who betray him so that he is unable to carry out his rescue plan. The basic situation seems to have been drawn from *The Man from Planet X,* the only other sci-fi film to be built around the theme of a space being who comes to earth in order to save his people, only to be rebuffed by terrestrials. In *The Man Who Fell to Earth,* however, the alien himself is partially to blame, participating in the "sins" of fallen humanity—a morality tale

about a fallen angel, in this case a fallen technological angel.

British Lion; 1976; 118 min. Director: Nicholas Roeg; Cast: David Bowie, Candy Clark, Rip Torn, Buck Henry, Bernie Casey.

MANDALA

A mandala, or mantra, is a visual diagram on which one focuses one's attention during meditation. The term is derived from *manas,* the Sanskrit word for "mind" or, more properly, for the "mind-stuff." Mandalas are common aids to meditation practice and are found in both Hinduism and Buddhism, particularly in the strands of these two traditions known as tantrism (Tantric Hinduism and Tantric Buddhism). Mandalas can contain elaborate pictures of the various worlds theorized by tantrism, or they can be rather stark geometric diagrams. The term "mantra" is derived from the same root word (*manas*) and refers to verbal formulas on which one focuses during meditation. Mandalas may usefully be thought of as visual mantras.

The psychologist Carl Jung adopted the term "mandala" to refer to one of the various categories of symbols—an archetypal dream image—that regularly appear in dreams. Jung postulated a drive toward self-realization and self-integration that he referred to as the "individuation process." The goal of this process was represented by the Self archetype, an archetype characterized by wholeness and completeness. One of the concrete manifestations of this archetype can be a circle, and it was various forms of the circle that Jung characterized as mandalas. According to Jung, mandala symbols emerge in dreams when the individual is seeking harmony and wholeness, which often occurs during periods of crisis and insecurity. Jung interpreted the phenomenon of flying saucers—which often appear in the form of circular disks—as mandala symbols, reflecting the human mind's desire for stability in a confused world.

See Also: Collective Unconscious; Jung, Carl
Further Reading:
Cavendish, Richard, ed. *Encyclopedia of the Unexplained: Magic, Occultism, and Parapsychology.* London: Arkana Penguin Books, 1989.

Jung, Carl Gustav. *Flying Saucers: A Modern Myth of Things Seen in the Sky.* Princeton: Princeton University Press, 1978.
———. *Memories, Dreams, Reflections.* New York: Vintage Books, 1965.
———. *Symbols of Transformation.* New York: Harper Torchbooks, 1956.

MANNA

Manna, the heavenly bread that feed the Hebrews during the Exodus, has been interpreted as being supplied by ufonauts. Manna is traditionally viewed as the food of angels. During the Exodus the Israelites feared that they had escaped Egypt

Manna from heaven, an incident described in Exodus that some have speculated was the result of a friendly action by extraterrestrials (American Religion Collection)

only to starve to death in the wilderness. God promised Moses that in the morning they would have bread in plenty:

"In the morning a fall of dew lay all around it. When the dew was gone, there in the wilderness, fine flakes appeared, fine as hoar-frost on the ground. When the Israelites saw it, they said to one another, 'What is that?,' because they did not know what it was. Moses said to them, 'That is the bread which the Lord has given you to eat'" (Exod. 16:13–15). "Manna" is Aramaic for "What is that?" A somewhat related story is the tale of Elijah's 40 days in the wilderness, during which he was nourished on food and water delivered to him by an angel—which, if we systematically follow out the ancient-astronaut line of interpretation of Exodus events, would be viewed as a ufonaut:

> He lay down under the bush and while he slept, an angel touched him and said, "Rise and eat." He looked, and there at his head was a cake baked on hot stones, and a pitcher of water. He ate and drank and lay down again. The angel of the Lord came again and touched him a second time, saying, "Rise and eat; the journey is too much for you." He rose and ate and drank and, sustained by this food, he went on for forty days and forty nights to Horeb, the mount of God. (1 Kings 19:5–8)

George Sassoon, an English linguist and electronics consultant, has suggested that manna, rather than being dropped from heaven by ancient flying saucers, was actually produced by a machine supplied by extraterrestrial visitors. Sassoon argues that a veiled description of this machine—referred to as the "Ancient of Days"—can be found in the *Zohar*, the foundation work of Kabbalistic mysticism.

See Also: Ancient Astronauts
Further Reading:
Downing, Barry H. *The Bible and Flying Saucers.* Philadelphia: J. B. Lippincott, 1968.
Goran, Morris. *The Modern Myth, Ancient Astronauts and UFOs.* South Brunswick, NJ: A. S. Barnes, 1978.

MARK-AGE

Charles Boyd Gentzel has channeled messages from the "Hierarchical Board" (the Ascended Masters), which governs the solar system, since the late 1950s. Together with Pauline Sharpe, a channel

Undated photograph of "Mark" (Mark-Age, Inc.)

also known as Nada-Yolanda, Gentzel organized a communication plan that spans through the last 40 years of the twentieth century. Such period is considered a transition phase from the Piscean to the Aquarian Age.

The Mark-Age Meta Center was established in Miami, Florida, in 1962, but subsequently changed its name to Mark-Age, Inc. It regards itself as a chosen point of contact with higher spiritual beings and is devoted to channeling and diffusing their messages through telepathy and automatic writing. Gloria Lee, who founded the Cosmon Research Foundation, the theosophical master El Morya, and John F. Kennedy all have provided messages to Mark-Age.

Communication with the Hierarchical Board also takes place through spaceships; Jesus is believed to have been orbiting in an ethereal earth orbit since 1885 and is expected to materialize after the cleansing of the planet. Messages channeled and the beliefs of the organization are published in several books, the fundamental source being *Mark-Age Period and Program.* In 1979 the organization settled in its new headquarters in Ft. Lauderdale, Florida.

See Also: Automatic Writing; Channeling; Contactees; The "I AM" Religious Activity; Religions, UFO.

Further Reading:

Lewis, James R. *The Encyclopedia of Cults, Sects, and New Religions.* Amherst, NY: Prometheus Books, 1998.

Melton, J. Gordon. *Encyclopedia of American Religions.* 5th ed. Detroit: Gale Research, 1996.

MARS

In 1877 Italian astronomer Giovanni Schiaparelli claimed to have found artificial structures on the surface of Mars. At that time, it was believed that the dark areas on Mars were bodies of water—oceans and seas. Schiaparelli saw what he thought were lines connecting the bodies of water, and he interpreted them to be waterways connecting the different seas and oceans. Although it was Schiaparelli who discovered the so-called canals, it was Percival Lowell in Arizona in 1894 who popularized the notion that the Martian canals were created artificially by intelligent beings.

On August 24, 1924, two American scientists ascended in a balloon high above Washington, D.C., and claimed to have made radio contact with Mars. They were David Todd, an astronomer at Amherst College, and C. Francis Jenkins, holder of more than 300 patents in radio and optics. Jenkins created a device—the "radio detective"—to listen for signals from Mars and record the signals optically. Todd and Jenkins chose August 24, 1924, for their ascent, because Mars was then at its closest point to earth. They flew up in the balloon with the radio detective. They had asked for complete radio silence from the armed services of the United States and received it. No transmissions were made from earth during the flight. They aimed their radio detective at Mars and recorded signals coming from that direction. A strange message coming from the direction of Mars was recorded on film. Todd and Jenkins brought the film back and began to analyze the markings on the film, which were very hard to decipher. There was something that looked like a face that was constantly repeated along one edge of the film. This so-called face-on-Mars code was the number-one topic of conversation in scientific circles in 1924. Dr. Todd submitted the film to William Friedman, the world's leading cryptologist. There is no evi-

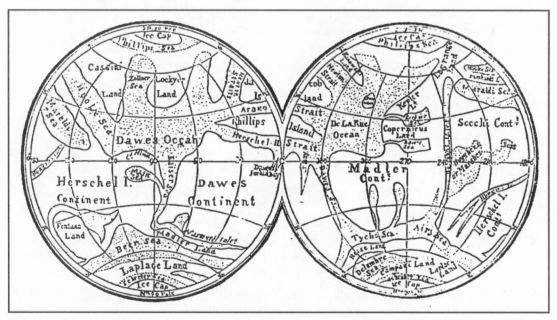

Richard Hoagland's speculations are part of a grand tradition that began with Percival Lowell's notion of canals in the Martian landscape. Pictured here is Richard A. Proctor's map of Mars, with landmarks named after astronomical explorers. (American Religion Collection)

dence in Friedman's file that he actually broke the code.

At a much later period, according to the controversial documents received by UFO researcher Jaime Shandera, the scientists who comprised Operation Majestic-12 suggested in 1947 that they were dealing with flying disks and extraterrestrial biological entities that might have originated on Mars. In 1947 there was a controversy surrounding the idea that the lines visible on Mars were a system of canals and oases. Some still maintained that because many of the straight lines ran for hundreds of thousands of miles, it was evidence that there was or had been intelligent life on Mars.

Between 1954 and 1956 earth and Mars were at their closest opposition in decades, and scientists thought they would have a good chance to study the red planet. The National Geographic Society and the Lowell Observatory cosponsored an international "Mars Patrol." Many Mars experts were hoping for photos to confirm that the mysterious lines on the surface of Mars were actually canals. However, no announcements from the international committee that observed Mars from 1954 to 1956 were ever made. The matter was quietly dropped without any explanation.

In November 1962 the Soviets launched a craft called Mars I and announced it would fly by Mars in June 1963. However, just 10 weeks before it was scheduled to arrive at its destination, the Soviets lost all contact. The United States launched Mariner 3 toward Mars in November 1964. Unfortunately, the craft's protective shroud wouldn't open; the craft was trapped inside and rendered useless. That same month, the Soviets launched a probe called Zond 2. Its purpose was to fly by Mars, but they lost contact with it in April 1965. As the failures mounted, U.S. space scientists began to joke nervously about the "Great Galactic Ghoul" lying in wait to gobble up anything on its way to Mars.

However, a turning point had been reached. Mariner 4 completed the first successful flyby of Mars in July 1965. It returned 22 images of Mars to earth. In 1969 Mariner 6 and 7 completed flybys, returning more than 200 photographs that detailed the planet's surface. It was finally proved that there were no canals on Mars. In 1971 NASA successfully placed Mariner 9 in orbit around Mars. It sent back some startling photographs of an area astronomers called Elysium, which clearly showed pyramid-like formations. Carl Sagan made much of this in his PBS series *Cosmos*. Sagan called for further unmanned exploration of Mars and the pyramids of Elysium.

Soviet scientists then announced that they were going to land on Mars. They launched Mars 2 and 3 in 1971; each craft carried rovers—small, remotely operated vehicles that could be sent across the planet's surface after touchdown. Two weeks after Mariner 9 went into orbit around Mars, the Soviet spacecraft arrived. Mars 2 flew into one of the great Mars duststorms and crashed. Mars 3, however, landed safely and deployed its rover. The Soviets were therefore the first to send pictures back to earth from the Martian surface. However, within two minutes of being deployed, the rover's transmitter went dead.

In 1975 NASA launched the Viking 1 and 2 probes. These craft sent back the most striking images ever seen of the surface of Mars. Huge volcanoes and canyons were identified. After studying the Viking images, several scientists announced that in all likelihood the surface of Mars was once covered with water. This led some scientists to suggest that Mars may have been habitable as little as 10,000 years ago.

Two of the photographs from the Viking probe raised a great deal of controversy. They showed a humanlike face on the surface of Mars. NASA discounted the photographs as mere tricks of light and shadow and did not study it. Vincent DiPietro, an electrical engineer with 20 years of experience in digital electronics and image processing, took the study of the images upon himself. DiPietro and Greg Molenaar, a Lockheed computer scientist, improved the image quality. The completed computer enhancement came to the attention of Richard Hoagland, a former NASA consultant. Hoagland believed that the mile-wide feature might have been formed by other than natural means. The more he investigated it, the more he became convinced that it could be an artifact from an ancient civilization.

DiPietro and Molenaar decided that what they needed were several more pictures of the face taken from different angles. Their search through the Viking library yielded another image taken 35 days later over the same area, identified by NASA as the Cydonia Plain, on the opposite side of the planet from the pyramids of Elysium. This photo was taken by the same satellite and the face appeared again, but with more detail than before. The images of the eyes showed pupils and the mouth area showed teeth. NASA insisted that the photograph showed naturally formed features of the Martian landscape.

Hoagland, fueled by this second image of the face, began a serious investigation of the phenomenon. He formed the Mars Mission with the aid of Erol Torun of the Defense Mapping Agency and Dr. Mark Carlotto of Analytical Sciences Corporation. In the early 1970s NASA prepared the Mars Observer, a new probe carrying a Mars Observer Camera (MOC), which had the capability of imaging objects as small as a coffee table from orbit with at least 50 times the resolution of the Viking probes. The purpose of Hoagland's Mars Mission was to make certain that the MOC would reimage the plains of Cydonia, the geographic area where the face was located. About 10 miles away from the face on the Cydonian Plain are pyramids of a very regular triangular shape. At each corner of each pyramid is a pyramid-shaped buttress. It would be incredible if these turned out to be natural formations.

Hoagland continued his study of the face and the pyramids on Mars and wrote a book about them: *The Monuments of Mars,* published in 1987. He found that the right side of the face, when mirror-imaged to form a complete face, bore a resemblance to the Sphinx at Giza. Upon further investigation, he found that recent archaeological and geological findings show that the Sphinx is at least 10,000 years old. This means that the Sphinx was created at a time when nobody on earth was supposedly able to accomplish anything of that magnitude. It also means that the Sphinx was created at a time when Mars was thought by some scientists to have been habitable. Hoagland began raising the question of whether the Sphinx on earth and the face on Mars had been made by the same race of beings.

Author and paranormal researcher David Percy believes that the Mars complex was deliberately designed and built by extraterrestrials. He has discovered a connection between the structures on Mars and other monuments on earth. In Avebury, in south-central England, there are 5,000-year-old stone structures of unknown origin. There are also enormous circular mounds, the purpose of which remains a mystery. This area has been the site of hundreds of UFO sightings dating back to the sixteenth century. It has the largest concentration of crop circles in the world. Percy took a survey map of the Avebury area and superimposed it over a NASA photograph of the Mars complex and found that it matched. The Mars crater on the east side of the complex is a match with the Avebury stone circle. They are the same size. Percy's theory is that the stone circle is a copy of the crater on Mars. The Mars spiral mound is a match for Silbury Hill. They are the same size. The spiral mound on Mars is the same relative distance to the crater that Silbury Hill is to the Avebury circle. In a document from the 1700s, Percy discovered that for a very long time Silbury Hill was called the Hill of Mars. Percy believes that Avebury is a model of Cydonia on earth.

Of course, many scientists reject the idea that any of the features on Mars were created by intelligent beings. Dr. Michael Malin of the University of Arizona, who was responsible for the imaging process on the Mars Observer, went on record with his opinion that there were no artificial structures on Mars. He went on to say that it was not the mission's objective to look for life there. Stanley McDaniel, professor emeritus at Sonoma State University in Arizona, investigated the entire controversy and concluded that NASA was mistaken in its rejection of the research of Hoagland, DiPietro, and Molenaar.

In October 1988 Phobos 1 and Phobos 2 were launched by a joint effort of the United States, the Soviet Union, and 13 European nations. Phobos 1 was lost, but Phobos 2 made it to Mars and seemed to be operating perfectly. It sent several images back to earth. On March 1, 1989, photographs were received at mission control that showed a strange gridwork of some sort on the surface of Mars. When the infrared images were overlaid on the optical photos and enlarged, the result looked very geometric and quite unnatural. On March 26 Phobos 2 sent back images taken just south of the Martian equator. They showed a long, elliptical, moving shadow through which other surface characteristics could be seen. These were the last images received from Phobos 2. The next day, something caused Phobos 2 to shut down. Three weeks later in a news conference, the head of the Soviet Space Agency made a comment that there was no flying saucer and that all that the scientists saw could be explained in natural, understandable and physical terms. In September 1989 British television did a special on the Phobos mission, reporting that the last images received from Phobos 2 showed an object coming toward the spacecraft that should not have been there.

Meanwhile, Richard Hoagland continued to press for a firm commitment on the part of NASA for the upcoming Mars Observer mission to reimage the entire Cydonia Plain and to look closer at the pyramids of Elysium. NASA did not commit themselves to this. They did, however, state that there would be a six-week delay in the public release of any photographs from the Mars Observer. This was an abrupt change in NASA policy, which had until that time simultaneously broadcast images it received.

Hurricane Andrew hit the coast of Florida just about the time the Mars Observer was being prepared for launch. After the storm, technicians checked the probe to make sure it had not been damaged by the storm. Despite the fact that the nitrogen system was equipped with special filters to prevent dust and debris from being taken into the system, bits of paper and dust and debris were found in the probe.

On September 25, 1992, the Mars Observer was launched into outer space. On August 21, 1993, at 6 P.M. Pacific Standard Time, the radio signals from the Mars Observer stopped. Not everyone believes the Mars Observer really died. Richard Hoagland hopes that a miraculous "recovery" will recur and that images will be received from the Mars Observer.

In 1996 NASA researchers announced that a chunk of Mars, which had fallen to earth in the form of a meteorite, contained carbonate globules—carbon-containing compounds and microscopic structures that looked like fossil bacteria.

Taken together, the compounds strongly suggested that life was once present on Mars. While people have long assumed that earth was the only planet in our solar system capable of sustaining life, scientists point out that microorganisms currently live in hot springs in Yellowstone and beneath the ice of Antarctica. Given the great adaptability of life on earth, it is certainly feasible that life exists on Mars.

See Also: War of the Worlds
Further Reading:
Craft, Michael. *Alien Impact.* New York: St. Martin's, 1996.
Hoagland, Richard. *Monuments of Mars: The City on the Edge of Forever.* Berkeley, CA: North Atlantic Books, 1987.
Randle, Kevin D. *The Randle Report: UFOs in the 1990s.* New York: M. Evans, 1997.

MARS ATTACKS!

In 1996 *Mars Attacks!* was released, somewhat later than the blockbuster *Independence Day.* This movie appears to be a spoof on the former. In actuality, *Mars Attacks!* was based on a series of 55 trading cards that vividly depicted earth being attacked by Martians. The cards also provided a horrifically detailed description of what these invaders did to folks. For five cents, your nickel got you five of these cards along with a stick of bubble gum. In 1962 these cards had been released in New England and Upstate New York. Although the sales were plentiful, outrage from parents caused them to be withdrawn from circulation after only six months. The movie, which features an all-star cast, is more a spoof of 1950s alien-invasion films originally entitled *Mars Attacks,* which plays on popular stereotypes about flying saucers and little green men from Mars.

Warner 1996; Director: Tim Burton; Writer: Jonathan Gems; Cinematography: Wynn Thomas; Cast: Jack Nicholson, Glenn Close, Michael J. Fox, Annette Bening, Martin Short, Danny De Vito, Rod Steiger, Paul Winfield, Tom Jones, Pam Grier, Natalie Portman, Pierce Brosnan, Lisa Marie, Lukas Haas, Sylvia Sydney, Joe Don Baker, O-lan Jones, Jack Black, Jim Brown, Janice Rivera.

MARS NEEDS WOMEN

In this 1966 low-budget film, a group of Martians comes to earth in search of women with

The alien "king" confronts the president of the United States (Jack Nicholson) in the 1996 film Mars Attacks! *(The Del Valle Archive)*

which to repopulate Mars. The military fights back with the result that the Martians finally escape without any women. From the standpoint of ufology, it is interesting how this film anticipates one of the themes of more recent UFO lore about alien abductions, namely, the notion that the DNA of extraterrestrials has somehow become exhausted and that the alien abductors renew themselves with human DNA. Perhaps this ufological notion had its origin in sci-fi films rather than vice versa.

Azalea 1966; 80 min. Director: Larry Buchanan; Writer: Larry Buchanan; Cinematography: Robert C. Jessup; Cast: Tommy Kirk, Yvonne Craig, Byron Lord, Roger Ready, Warren Hammack.

A MARTIAN IN PARIS

This is a 1961 French film (*Un Martien à Paris*) in which the Martians send one of their own to find out about the mysterious earth disease called "love" so that an antidote can be developed. Unfortunately, the Martian falls victim to the "disease" himself. From a ufological viewpoint, this is not a very sophisticated film. Nevertheless, it anticipates one of the themes of recent abduction literature, namely, that extraterrestrials are fascinated with human sexuality. Perhaps this notion had its origin in sci-fi films rather than vice versa.

Les Film Univers; France 1961; 87 min. Director: Jean-Daniel Daninos; Writers: Jean-Daniel Daninos, Jacques Vilfrid; Cinematography: Marcel Combes; Cast: Dary Cowl, Nicole Mirel, Henri Vilbert, Gisèle Segur, Michele Verez, Pierre Louis.

MEIER, EDUARD ALBERT "BILLY"

Eduard Albert Meier is the most prominent contemporary Adamski-style contactee. Born February 3, 1937, in Bulach, Switzerland, he acquired the nickname "Billy" as a result of his interest in classic American cowboy figures like Billy the Kid, Wild Bill Hickok, and Buffalo Bill. Meier had a troubled childhood, running away from home several times. As an adult he held several odd jobs, served briefly in the Foreign Legion, and did time for theft.

Meier claims to have been in contact with ufonauts since the age of five. The space people, who are human in appearance and who are from the Pleiades star system, eventually selected him as a "truth offerer." To prove their existence, they permitted Meier to take innumerable pictures of their "beamships." Though rejected by most ufologists, Meier acquired prominence as an occult celebrity by the mid-1970s due to coverage in European periodicals. In the late 1970s he entered into an agreement with a group of Americans who pro-

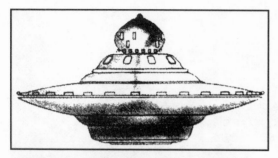

Drawing of the Pleiadean Beamship described by Billy Meier (American Religion Collection)

moted his books and other materials to the UFO–New Age community. Meier has also attracted several critics who accuse him and his associates of exploiting the credulous.

—*Jerome Clark*

See Also: Contactees; Hoaxes; New Age; Religions, UFO

MEN IN BLACK

Men dressed all in black seem to be a persistent element in folklore. Such figures appear, for example, in the data collected by Margaret Murray about the witch trials in Scotland and England. She interpreted them as being the cult's leader in disguise. More recent stories about men in black have come under study by professional folklorists.

Since 1953 there have been stories about men in black who appeared to ufologists and threatened them with dire consequences if they published what they knew. They typically wear all black and have unusual characteristics, such as bug-eyes, hairlessness, unblinking eyes, unmoving lips, and/or monotonous speech. They have been variously identified as agents of Satan, government agents, and aliens.

Men in black have been associated with the devil for several centuries. According to *A History of the Devil* by William Woods, "Sometimes the devil wears green or gray, but mostly he is dressed in black, and always in the fashion of the day."

In 1730 a Norwegian girl told witch hunters that she and her grandmother had flown on the back of a pig to attend a meeting with Satan. On the way they met three men dressed in black, whom the old woman called "grandfather's boys."

"Grandfather" was the term the woman used to refer to Satan.

The first report of men in black in a UFO context occurred in March 1905, when an exceptionally intelligent young rural woman was visited three nights in succession by a man dressed in black who delivered a message to the girl, which she was frightened to relate. This visitation occurred in the midst of a religious revival in Wales begun by Mary Jones, a 30-year-old farmer's wife who had recently converted to Christianity and become a preacher. Jones was accompanied on her travels through the Welsh countryside by mysterious lights.

The most famous men-in-black story was that told by Albert K. Bender, who in April 1952 formed the International Flying Saucer Bureau (IFSB), the most successful early UFO organization. It opened branches in other countries, published a magazine called *Space Review,* and had an active investigations unit. In late September 1953, after Bender had confided a UFO theory to an unnamed correspondent, three dark-suited men visited him. The men, whom Bender believed to be agents of the U.S. government, told Bender what the actual source of UFOs was and threatened him with imprisonment if he told anyone else. Bender was physically ill for three days after the men's visit. His ardent pursuit of information regarding UFOs ended with the visit of the men in black.

In 1956 Gray Barker, who had been chief investigator at IFSB, published *They Knew Too Much About Flying Saucers,* which launched the men-in-black legend in ufology. It tells of a sinister "Silence Group" that sent enforcers in dark suits to the residences of UFO researchers who got too close to the truth. He speculated that the silencers might be extraterrestrials.

South African contactee Ann Grevler in her book *Transvaal Episode* (1958) identified the "men in dark suits" who threaten those who know too much as evil space people seeking to thwart the efforts of benevolent extraterrestrials. That same year, George Hunt Williamson and John McCoy's book, *UFOs Confidential! The Meaning behind the Most Closely Guarded Secret of All Time,* was published. Williamson and McCoy maintained that the three men who contacted Albert Bender were the

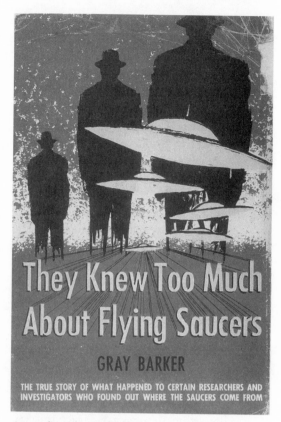

Cover of Gray Barker's 1956 novel, They Knew Too Much about Flying Saucers *(Mary Evans Picture Library)*

hired henchmen of the "international bankers" whose only duty was to suppress all men who would act as channels of truth. Williamson and McCoy maintained that "three men" have always been present during every great event of history.

Bender's own bizarre story came out in 1962 in his book, *Flying Saucers and the Three Men,* which Gray Barker published. He claimed that monstrous extraterrestrials had kidnapped him and flown him to the South Pole. Their mission on earth was to gather seawater and extract from it an element needed on their home planet in a distant solar system. They gave Bender a small disk with which they would monitor his activities until they were finished with their mission and on their way home. The three men in black were actually aliens in disguise. The aliens departed earth in 1960, freeing Bender to tell his story.

There were few who believed Bender's story as given in his book. Some believed that Bender's

original story as well as the book were fabrications. Those who knew Bender, however, recalled how frightened he had been in 1953; they believed that Bender's first story was true and that the book was a concoction to end pestering by UFO buffs or harassment by the government.

The possibility exists that Bender was actually visited by three men from the Central Intelligence Agency. In January 1953 the CIA had assembled a panel of five American scientists under the leadership of physicist H. P. Robertson. The scientists spent 12 hours reviewing data from the Air Force's Project Blue Book. The panel concluded that UFO reports represented a danger to national security and that civilian UFO groups should be watched because of their potentially great influence on public thinking. At the time of Bender's alleged visit by the three men in black, the Robertson panel's existence was classified as secret and unknown to anyone in the civilian UFO community. Moreover, IFSB was more than just a run-of-the-mill flying-saucer club. It was conducting scientific research on UFOs, including case studies, photo analyses, and metallurgy. It was plotting UFO flight paths in hopes of discovering their bases of origin. The hypothesis that Bender was visited by government agents will not be proven until someone finds the relevant documents in an official file.

In the mid-1960s occult journalist John A. Keel appeared on the UFO scene. To Keel, UFOs and their occupants represented a malevolent force that had been interfering in human affairs as long as *Homo sapiens* existed. He believed them to be paranormal entities associated with the UFO intelligences themselves. Keel chronicled the activities of individuals who usually wore dark suits and intimidated UFO witnesses. Some of them had dark complexions and Oriental features while others were pale and bug-eyed. Their behavior was frequently odd, as if they were operating in an alien environment. They often drove black Cadillacs or limousines. It was Keel who began referring to the men in black by the acronym "MIB."

Keel not only collected stories about men in black from witnesses; he had also encountered them personally. In the summer of 1967 he received a series of strange phone messages urging him to go by himself to an isolated location on

Long Island. There he found a black Cadillac occupied by two dark-skinned men in dark suits waiting for him. No contact with the men in black took place. Instead, the Cadillac drove off, followed by Keel. A cat-and-mouse game then took place in which the men in black and Keel pursued each other. Keel believes that the episode was staged by the men in black to convince him that they do exist.

In 1967 Colonel George P. Freeman, a Pentagon spokesman for Project Blue Book, reported that individuals had been posing as Air Force officers or government agents and threatening UFO witnesses, sometimes even confiscating photographs. Freeman said these men were committing a federal offense by posing as government agents and that he would like to catch them. However, he was unable to find out anything about them.

In January 1971 a Brazilian newspaper reported that UFOs had been repeatedly sighted in a rural location close to Brasilia. A local peasant was noted as saying that a man in black showed up regularly and looked for "little stones." The man arrived in a plane the peasant described as two dishes, one atop the other, which goes up in the air, changes color, and disappears.

In July 1971 a Spanish physician and his family were visiting friends near Caracas, Venezuela, when they saw two men wearing black step out of a new red Mustang. The men were wearing black berets and red ties with their black suits. The men stood there for about five minutes and then began to put on orange belts. A shining object suddenly appeared in the sky, descended rapidly, and stopped about two feet above the ground. It was about 90 feet in diameter and rapidly changed color from blue to orange to white. A staircase came down from underneath the UFO, and the two men used it to enter the saucer. The staircase was drawn up and the saucer flew away at incredible speed.

On May 3, 1975, a young man named Carlos de los Santos, who was flying a private plane near the Mexico City airport, experienced a near collision with three daylight disks. The incident attracted a lot of media attention. A week later, as de los Santos was driving down the freeway on the way to discuss the incident on a TV talk show, two large black limousines forced his vehicle to the side of the road. Four tall, pale men in dark suits emerged from the limousines and approached him as he sat in his car. They threatened his life and that of his family if he continued to speak of the sighting. De los Santos subsequently broke his appointment with the TV show. A month later, however, de los Santos was about to join visiting American astronomer-ufologist J. Allen Hynek for breakfast when one of the men in black appeared before him on the hotel steps. The man in black shoved de los Santos and told him that he had been monitoring his movements. De los Santos was intimidated into breaking his appointment with Hynek.

One night in September 1976, Dr. Herbert Hopkins of Orchard Beach, Maine, received a telephone call from someone who identified himself as the vice president of a New Jersey UFO organization. He wanted to discuss a UFO-abduction case that Hopkins had been probing using hypnosis of the abductee. Hopkins invited the man over. The man arrived immediately, without time for travel from wherever he had made his phone call. He was dressed in an impeccable black suit, was bald, and had no eyebrows or eyelashes. During their conversation, the man sat motionless and spoke flawless English in a monotone. After he had asked the doctor several questions, the man said that Dr. Hopkins had two coins in his pocket and asked him to remove one. Hopkins took out a penny and held it in the palm of his hand. Hopkins watched as the penny turned silver, then blue, became blurred, and faded from view. Hopkins admired the trick and asked the man if he could make the coin reappear. The man replied, "Neither you nor anyone else on this planet will ever see that coin again." The man in black then asked Dr. Hopkins if he knew why a certain patient had died. The doctor answered that it was the result of a long illness. The man in black, however, declared that this patient had died because he had no heart, just as Dr. Hopkins no longer had his penny. He then ordered Hopkins to destroy all tapes and other materials in his possession relating to the UFO-abduction case. Out of fear, Hopkins complied. The strange man announced that his energy was running low and that he had to leave. He walked out, down the steps, and around the corner of Dr. Hopkins's house. The man walked up the driveway, rather than down it toward the street, and disappeared.

Peter M. Rojcewicz was doing research for a Ph.D. thesis on the folklore of UFOs at the University of Pennsylvania library in November 1980 when a tall, thin, dark-complexioned man wearing a rumpled black suit approached him and sat down. The man asked what Rojcewicz was doing. Rojcewicz told him briefly and then attempted to return to his research. The man in black asked if Rojcewicz had ever seen a UFO. Rojcewicz replied that he was only interested in stories about UFOs, not in the question of whether UFOs existed. The man in black suddenly shouted, "Flying saucers are the most important fact of the century, and you're not interested?" Rojcewicz calmed the man down. Then the man stood up, placed his hand on Rojcewicz's shoulder, wished him well, and left. A few seconds later Rojcewicz was struck by the strangeness of the encounter and began to walk around through the library. He found no one there—no students, no librarians. Too prevent himself from panicking, he forced himself to go back to his desk. An hour later, when he left the library, librarians and patrons were there as usual.

In October 1981 in Victoria, British Columbia, a young man named Grant Breiland saw a UFO. Three days later he went to the business district to meet a friend. When the friend did not show up, Breiland called him from a pay phone at a popular department store. As he was about to leave the phone booth, he saw two men dressed in dark suits staring at him. They had tanned, expressionless faces and unblinking eyes. They began to ask him questions, and he noticed that their lips did not move as they spoke. They asked him his name, where he lived, and his "number." Breiland did not answer, and after a few seconds the two men left with a stiff, mechanical stride. Breiland followed them down the street until they entered a muddy vacant lot. As they crossed the lot, the men in black vanished. Breiland began to pursue them further until he noticed that they had left no footprints in the mud. He lost his nerve at that point and went home. During the entire time that he saw the men in black no other human beings were in view, even though this occurred during business hours in a normally busy area. There were cars parked on the street, but none driving on it. As soon as the men in black disappeared, the area was normally populated and traffic was normal.

—Jerome Clark

See Also: Bender, Albert K.; Conspiracy Theories; Mythology and Folklore; Satanism and UFOs
Further Reading:
Barker, Gray. MIB: The Secret Terror among Us. Clarksburg, WV: Saucerian Books, 1983.
———. They Knew Too Much about Flying Saucers. New York: University Books, 1956.
Barker, Gray, ed. Bender Mystery Confirmed. Clarksburg, WV: Saucerian Books, 1962.
Beckley, Timothy Green, ed. The UFO Silencers. New Brunswick, NJ: Inner Light Publications, 1990.
Evans, Hilary. Visions, Apparitions, Alien Visitors. Wellingborough, U.K.: Aquarian Press, 1984.
Glemser, Kurt. The Men in Black Report. Kitchener, Ontario, Canada: Galaxy Press, 1971.
Keel, John A. UFOs: Operation Trojan Horse. New York: G. P. Putnam's Sons, 1970.
Keith, Jim. Casebook on the Men in Black. Lilburn, GA: IllumiNet Press, 1997.

MEN IN BLACK

This 1997 film takes the name, but radically alters the meaning of, a popular figure in UFO lore. In "traditional" ufology dating back to the early 1950s, men in black suits showed up at the doors of ufologists and others, threatening them with dire consequences if they revealed what they knew about UFOs. It was suspected that these awkwardly behaving people were actually extraterrestrials.

The movie begins with the premise that the U.S. government has secretly entered into an agreement permitting a host of different beings from other worlds to live on the earth undercover—a bit like a cosmic witness-protection program. The men in black are the law-enforcement officials who watch over these alien "guests." The two intersecting plots of the film are the initiation of a new man in black by a seasoned veteran, and the recovery of an item stolen from one extraterrestrial by another (who also murders the first alien) before a spacecraft from the aggrieved star system destroys the earth.

1997; 98 min. Director: Barry Sonnenfeld; Writer: Ed Solomon; Cast: Will Smith, Tommy Lee Jones, Linda Fiorentino, Rip Torn.

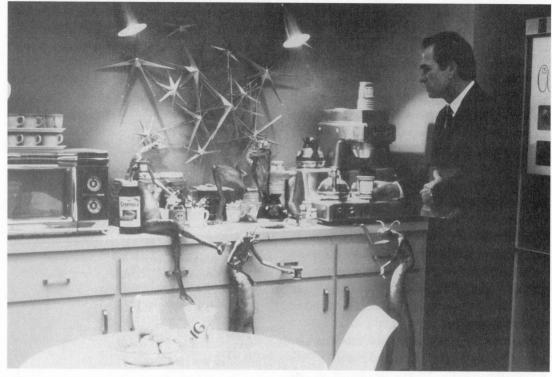

Tommy Lee Jones in a scene from the 1997 film Men in Black *(The Del Valle Archive)*

MENGER, HOWARD

Howard Menger was a world-famous contactee of the 1950s. Born in Brooklyn, New York, in 1922, Menger served in an armored division and later with U.S. Army intelligence in World War II. After he was discharged from the service in 1946, he formed a sign-painting company. He and his family lived on a farm near High Bridge, New Jersey.

In 1953 Howard Menger read *Flying Saucer's Have Landed* by George Adamski. On October 29, 1956, Menger appeared on the Long John Nebel radio show in the company of an already-well-known contactee, George Van Tassel. On the show, Menger stated that his contacts had started in childhood when he sighted flying disks and experienced flashbacks of life on another world. In 1932 he claimed to have met a beautiful blonde woman who read his mind and told him she and others were "contacting their own." He said that in 1946 he saw this woman step out of a flying saucer. The woman told Menger that she and other beings were coming to earth to help earthlings solve their problems. On August 4, 1956, he was invited

aboard one of the spaceships. He claimed to have taken photographs of some of the spaceships. Menger's appearance on the Nebel show led to more radio and TV appearances, including one on Steve Allen's popular show.

Those who examined Menger's photographs, including Civilian Saucer Intelligence of New York, found them to be obvious frauds. They were photographs of crude paintings. There were many unusual occurrences reported at the Menger property. One woman stated she saw three flying saucers, one of which landed. A man got out and talked to Howard Menger 20 feet from where the woman was standing. People were taken outside and shown spacemen in luminous ski pajamas in the apple orchard. Others saw disks lying on the ground amid the trees. Menger would not allow witnesses to shine flashlights on either the spacemen or the disks.

In late 1956 Connie Weber showed up at the Menger residence to attend a lecture by George Van Tassel. Soon Menger left his wife and married Weber, also known by her pen name, Marla Baxter.

When challenged by the National Investigations Committee on Aerial Phenomena to take a polygraph test, Howard Menger declined.

The year 1959 saw publication of Menger's *From Outer Space to You,* one of the most widely read contactee books of the time. Menger tried to market a four-foot radio-controlled saucer model in 1963. In 1966 Menger circulated a letter stating that years before he had sent UFO photographs to the Pentagon. A government agency had asked him to stage an elaborate UFO hoax in order to get an index of human reaction. In 1990 Howard and Connie Menger made an appearance at the national UFO Conference in Miami Beach, Florida, where they announced that they were writing a new book.

—*Jerome Clark*

See Also: Contactees; Hoaxes
Further Reading:
Keel, John A. *UFOs: Operation Trojan Horse.* New York: G. P. Putnam's Sons, 1970.
Menger, Howard. *From Outer Space to You.* Clarksburg, WV: Saucerian Books, 1959
Nebel, Long John. *The Way Out World.* Englewood Cliffs, NJ: Prentice-Hall, 1961.

A MESSAGE FROM MARS

A Message from Mars is a 1913 British film that was remade in the United States in 1921. The plot involves a Martian who sees the selfish actions of a particular earthling in a crystal ball and then comes to earth to reform the sinner. As a result of his efforts, the earthling is transformed into a generous, kind-hearted man. In this movie the alien is clearly a covert celestial being—a disguised "technological angel," to use Carl Jung's term.

Metro 1921; 69min. Director: Maxwell Karger; Writers: Arthur Zellner, Authur Maude; Cinematography: Arthur Martinelli; Cast: Bert Lytell, Raye Dean, Gordon Ash, Maude Milton, Alphonse Ethier, Leonard Mudie.

METAPHYSICAL

One strand of the contemporary interest in UFOs is associated with the occult-metaphysical subculture known as the New Age movement. Partly because of the vagueness of the term "New Age," and partly because the term has acquired negative connotations, members of this alternative spiritual subculture prefer to refer to themselves and their subculture by other names. One such euphemism is "metaphysical," although it has been applied so loosely that it has become as vague as the term it replaces.

The term "metaphysical" originates from the arrangement of Aristotle's works, in which Aristotle's speculations about the ultimate nature of reality were placed *after* (Greek: *meta*) his writings on physics—hence *metaphysics.* Throughout the history of Western philosophy, metaphysics has represented the aspect of a thinker's philosophical system that dealt with ultimate reality.

In contrast to reductionistic philosophers who declared that everything was material, as well as in contrast to dualistic philosophers who argued for the existence of mind and matter, several important thinkers—most notably Berkeley and Hegel—declared that the ultimate nature of reality was mind or spirit. The physical world appears real but, like the landscape of dreams, is actually a manifestation of our collective thoughts. This is the so-called idealist school of metaphysics.

One should also note that certain schools of South Asian philosophy, such as Advaita Vedanta, advocate a position that, while not the same as Western idealism, similarly denies the reality of the physical world as we experience it in our normal, everyday state of consciousness. Through the translation of Asian philosophical texts, these schools of thought were becoming known to the West and were sometimes referred to in discussions of philosophical idealism. South Asian thought systems also contributed the notion of karma to this admixture of ideas—a notion of cause and effect that could be interpreted to imply that the experiencer was ultimately responsible for everything that she or he experienced.

The basic thrust of these strands of philosophical theorizing was picked up by the popular nineteenth-century healing movement referred to as "mind cure." The mind-cure movement eventually generated several different denominational bodies, most notably Christian Science but also Unity, Science of Mind, and related New Thought churches. While few thinkers in the mind-cure movement delved into the intricacies of Western philosophy, they knew enough to be able to refer intelligently to philosophical idealism in their explanation of why the mind cure worked: If everything is simply thoughts in manifestation, then obviously illness is no more than a wrongheaded idea. Hence, replacing a sick idea with a healthy idea should effect a cure. It is this connection with philosophical idealism that led the various religious bodies arising out of the mind-cure movement to be referred to as "metaphysical" churches.

Members of these New Thought denominations often participate in the same general subculture as non–mind cure organizations, such as spiritualism and theosophy. The association of these diverse religious bodies with less formal expressions of the same kinds of spirituality constitutes what has been referred to as the "occult-metaphysical" subculture or tradition. It was this subculture that gave birth to the New Age movement. However, because of the negative connotations that have accrued both to New Ageism and occultism, "metaphysical" came to be adopted as a general term to refer to the entire subculture. Thus, for instance, bookstores that cater to members of this tradition of alternative spirituality are often called "metaphysical bookstores."

See Also: New Age; Occult
Further Reading:
Lewis, James R., and J. Gordon Melton, eds. *Perspectives on the New Age.* Albany: State University of New York Press, 1992.
Melton, J. Gordon, Jerome Clark, and Aidan Kelly. *New Age Encyclopedia.* Detroit: Gale Research, 1990.

MIDNIGHT MOVIE MASSACRE

At a drive-in movie in 1956, a Martian shows up in a flying saucer and wanders around gorily murdering patrons in this 1986 movie. A simple monster movie that substitutes an extraterrestrial for other kinds of monsters, this is an alien-as-technological-demon film.

Williams 1986; 86 min. Director: Mark Stock, Larry Jacobs; Writers: Roger Branit, John Chadwell, David Houston, Mark Stock; Cinematography: Ken Wheatly; Cast: Robert Clarke, Ann Robinson, David Staffer, Tom Hutsler, Margie Robbins, Brad Bittiker, Charity Case.

MILLENNIALISM

UFO religions are often millennialist in their orientation. Even much secular thinking about UFOs embodies quasi-religious themes, such as the notion that the world is on the verge of destruction and that ufonauts are somehow going to rescue humanity—either by forcibly preventing a nuclear Armageddon or by taking select members of the human race to another planet to preserve the species. The psychologist Carl Jung was referring to the latter portrayal of flying saucers when he called them "technological angels." The source of this religious mind-set lies in the Western religious tradition.

The terms "millenarianism" and "millennialism" are derived from Christian theology and refer to the paradisiacal 1,000-year period—the millennium—in which, according to the Book of Revelation, history and the world as we know it will terminate (sometimes conceived of as the reestablishment of the Garden of Eden). The ex-

Cover for issue 7 (1980) of UFO Review, *"Massive UFO Landings to Take Place: Will You Be Taken Onboard by the Aliens?" (Mary Evans Picture Library)*

pression "millenarian movement" is applied to groups of people who expect the imminent emergence of the millennium and whose religious life is saturated by this expectation. Although the term originated in the Christian tradition, by extension other, non-Christian religious movements that are characterized by such an expectation can be accurately referred to as either millenarian or millennialist movements (crisis cult and messianic movement are alternative names). Some researchers have argued that all religions with historically specifiable origins began as millenarian movements—movements that, after they became established, lost much or all of their millennial enthusiasm.

The New Age movement, although it often explicitly rejects Christianity, shares the millennialist emphasis of Christian thought. The New Age movement hopes and expects that the world of the dominant culture will be swept aside and replaced with a golden era. At an earlier stage of the movement the millennium was referred to as the Aquarian Age, which is an astrological notion that the planet is entering a new cosmic cycle in which "higher vibration" energies are being focused on the earth that will usher in a new era of peace and understanding.

One also finds a nonbiblical form of apocalypticism within the New Age movement, built around the theme of drastic upheavals in the earth that will supposedly occur around the year 2000. The most influential figure in this regard has been Edgar Cayce, a psychic who passed away in 1945 but whose readings were turned into a series of highly popular books by his son, Hugh Lynn Cayce. Cayce followers have even produced maps showing how the U.S. landscape will be changed, with much of what is now California becoming sea bottom. To this basic view, the popular writer Ruth Montgomery added the popular idea—supposedly revealed to her by her spirit guides—that these upheavals would occur because the North and South Poles of the earth would shift in 1999 (a date she since pushed back farther into the future). This apocalyptic scenario has become widely accepted within certain segments of the New Age community.

See Also: Apocalypse; Eschatology; New Age

Further Reading:
Cohn, Norman. *The Pursuit of the Millennium.* London: Oxford University Press, 1957.
Eliade, Mircea, ed. *Encyclopedia of Religion.* New York: Macmillan, 1987.
Lanternari, Vittorio. *The Religions of the Oppressed: A Study of Modern Messianic Cults.* New York: Mentor, 1956.

MINISTRY OF UNIVERSAL WISDOM

In January 1952 George W. Van Tassel began to receive messages from extraterrestrial entities. He had started having meditation sessions with his wife Doris three years earlier, during which he channeled messages. He channeled an entity named Ashtar, who was the commander of space station Schare. Ashtar and his companions were on a mission to save mankind from self-destruction. Van Tassel was instructed on how to build the Integratron, a structure where people could rejuvenate and experiments would take place to allow time travel and annul gravity. Giant Rock, California, where Van Tassel lived, became a meeting place for flying-saucer observers. An annual convention was held.

The messages he received embodied a theology according to which humankind was originally created on another planet; then the only-male Adamitic race came to inhabit the earth. Lord God, a figure that came after God, was himself from the Adamitic race and created Eve as a non–human being. The following mating between Eve and an Adamitic gave rise to the hybrid race humanity. Through the Ministry of Universal Wisdom, Van Tassel wanted to spread the message he had received from the space entities. He also established the College of Universal Wisdom, which managed the Integratron and its research activities. When he died at 60 in 1970, his wife managed the organization through the 1980s. It eventually ceased to exist, but other mediums now claim contact with Ashtar.

See Also: Ashtar Command; Channeling; Contactees; Giant Rock Spacecraft Convention; Hybrids, Alien-Human

Further Reading:
Melton, J. Gordon. *Encyclopedia of American Religions.* 5th ed. Detroit: Gale Research, 1996.

Van Tassel, George. *I Rode a Flying Saucer! The Mystery of the Flying Saucers Revealed.* Los Angeles: New Age Publishing, 1952.

MISSING TIME

The phrase "missing time" is used to describe testimony about one or more periods of time that cannot be recalled accurately by the narrator of a UFO encounter or an alien-abduction narrative (AAN). Although missing time is frequently treated as if it was a physical occurrence by some researchers, it is more accurate to call it a report of a failure of memory. In spite of this, it has come to represent one of the key elements of a typical AAN. Reports of periods of missing time are considered key evidence of alien intervention by several researchers. This has been criticized as spurious by others, who allege that gaps in one's memory of personal time are both normal and frequent. This is an area where an evident absence is not considered an absence of evidence but as near-proof.

Missing time is not a modern phenomenon. It also appears in legend and folklore in such disparate sources as the quest for the Holy Grail and the story of Rip Van Winkle, who falls asleep and upon waking discovers that many years have passed. In his book *Passport to Magonia,* researcher Jacques Vallee assembles many traditional folklore accounts that include missing time. Missing time can also indicate that a person has experienced a daydream, hypnotic trance (such as "highway hypnosis" while driving), fugue state, or epileptic seizure. For example, in petit mal ("mild") epilepsy—a fairly common illness of childhood—a person may experience up to 100 seizures a day, each approximately 10–60 seconds in duration. This experience of "turning off" many times a day can be socially disruptive and can lead to suspicious episodes of "missing time" even in the absence of seizures. In this regard, more research needs to be done on the childhood medical histories of alien-abduction narrators.

Time distortion is also a factor in the characterization of the UFO myth as millenarian. Such movements are concerned with the end of time both in history and social dynamics. Christianity made linear time important when measured as counting toward the Endtime. Before the Christian era, the source of transcendent meaning tended to be "outside" of time (or perhaps in "missing" time). Narrators now as then can see themselves as a new elect standing against the secular worldview. They may await "revealed" aliens to vindicate their experience of distorted time. While this may be interpreted by the larger society as irrational, such a dismissive interpretation is similar to the way that the educated Roman elites viewed the early Christians.

—*Scott R. Scribner*

See Also: Abductees; Alien-Abduction Narratives; Time Travel
Further Reading:
Fuller, John Grant. *Interrupted Journey: Two Lost Hours "Aboard a Flying Saucer."* New York: Dial Press, 1966.
Goodrich, N. L. *The Holy Grail.* New York: Harper-Collins, 1992.
Hopkins, Budd. *Missing Time: A Documented Study of UFO Abductions.* New York: Richard Marek, 1981.
Lewis, James R., ed. *The Gods Have Landed: New Religions From Other Worlds.* Albany: State University of New York Press, 1995.
Spanos, N., et al. "Close Encounters: An Examination of UFO Experiences." *Journal of Abnormal Psychology* 102 (1993): 624–632.
Vallee, Jacques. *Passport to Magonia: From Folklore to Flying Saucers.* Chicago: Contemporary Books, 1993.

THE MONITORS

The Monitors is a 1968 film about good-intentioned aliens that, in an unsuccessful attempt to foist love and peace upon humans, invade earth, only to fail. This is an alien-invasion film that inverts the moral character of the extraterrestrials. Although the theme of the film is distant from mainstream ufology, in some of the contactee literature one sometimes gets the sense that contactees look forward to the day when the saucers will land and establish peace on earth.

Bell and Howell 1968; 92 min. Director: Jack Shea; Writer: Myron J. Gold; Cinematography: William (Vilmos) Zsigmond; Cast: Guy Stockwell, Susan Oliver, Avery Screiber, Sherry Jackson, Shepperd Strudwick, Keenan Wynn.

MON-KA

In April 1956 Dick Miller, head of a contactee group called the Solar Cross Foundation, announced at the Giant Rock Spacecraft Convention that he possessed tape-recorded messages from a Martian. He claimed that the voice had appeared on the tapes even though they were inside sealed cans.

The message on the tape identified the speaker as Mon-Ka, head of the government on Mars. It said that on the evening of November 7, 1956, at 10:30 P.M. a Martian craft would be visible at 10,000 feet above Los Angeles. It requested that a radio station remove its carrier signal from the air for two minutes so the Martians could speak from their craft.

Despite the facts that Dick Miller was known to be a hoaxer and many conservative ufologists saw the tapes as manifestly bogus, interest in the tapes did not fade. In September a California contactee named Kenneth Kellar took the tapes with him to England and played them at a public meeting. The Associated Press picked up the story, which was run internationally.

A contingent of followers of Mon-Ka developed, and they held mass rallies in Los Angeles on October 13 and 27. As a publicity gimmick, two radio stations (one in San Luis Obispo and one in Los Angeles) went off the air at the predetermined time on November 7 at 10:30 P.M. A Los Angeles TV station sent a plane in the air to watch for the approaching spaceship. Contactee followers gathered on rooftops. Unsurprisingly, nothing happened.

See Also: Contactees; Giant Rock Spacecraft Convention; Hoaxes

Further Reading:

Beckley, Timothy Green. *Book of Space Contacts.* New York: Global Communications, 1981.

Tuella [pseudonym of Thelma B. Turrell], ed. *Ashtar: A Tribute.* 3rd ed. Salt Lake City: Guardian Action Publications, 1989.

MONOLITH MONSTERS

In this 1957 B-grade movie, a geologist discovers crystal fragments from a meteor shower that absorb silicon from anything, killing those who touch them and growing in the process. The huge crystals advance on a small town at the edge of the desert, causing it to be evacuated. The theme is somewhat a cross between *The Blob* and *The Andromeda Strain.*

1957; 76 min. Director: John Sherwood; Writers: Norman Jolley, Robert M. Fresco; Music: Joseph Gershenson; Cinematography: Ellis W. Carter; Cast: Grant Williams, Lola Albright, Les Tremayne, Trevor Bardette.

MONSTERS FROM THE UNKNOWN PLANET

In this 1975 Japanese film aliens that control monsters are served by an embittered scientist and his daughter. The aliens repaired the daughter after a fatal accident, and she now survives as a cyborg. The aliens launch their cyborg Godzilla and their Titanosaurus against earth. The two monsters are supervised and encouraged by the cyborg woman. The real Godzilla and a supersonic machine defeat the invasion.

Toho-Eizo, Jap. 1975; 83 min. Director: Inoshiro Honda; Writer: Yukiko Takayama; Cinematography: Motoyoshi Tomioka; Special Effects: Teruyoshi Nakano; Cast: Katsuhiko Uchida, Goro Mutsu, Kenji Sahara, Toru Kawane, Kazunari Mokri, Tatsumi Fuyamoto.

Poster for the 1957 film Monolith Monsters *(The Del Valle Archive)*

MOODY ABDUCTION

In 1975 Sergeant Charles L. Moody was abducted while watching for meteors in the New Mexico desert near Holloman Air Force Base. A metallic disk 50 feet by 20 feet fell out of the sky and moved toward Moody. Feeling uneasy, he got into his car, but the battery was dead. Through an oblong window on the disk's side, he saw shadowy movements of what appeared to be human forms. A numbness came over him, and before he knew it the disk was rising and taking off. When he again tried to start his car, it turned over almost immediately.

Arriving at his home, he was startled to note that it was much later than he had anticipated— approximately 90 minutes of "missing time." Unable to get the event out of his mind, he eventually wrote a magazine editor who put him in touch with the Aerial Phenomena Research Organization, directed by Jim and Coral Lorenzen. Moody also undertook some meditation, at the suggestion of a friend, in an effort to recall what happened during the missing 90 minutes.

The scenario Moody was able to recover was typical of many other reported alien-abduction experiences, except that Moody had fought with the humanoid extraterrestrials before they paralyzed him. After assuring him that they did not mean to hurt him, Moody's movement was restored, and he was given a tour of the ship. The alien leader talked down to Moody as "my child" or "my son" and noted that several different races were studying humankind. After being released, Moody never publicized his experience or sought to profit from it.

See Also: Abductees; Close Encounters; Time Travel
Further Reading:
Bullard, Thomas E. *UFO Abductions: The Measure of a Mystery, Volume 1: Comparative Study of Abduction Reports;* and *Volume 2: Catalogue of Cases.* Mount Rainier, MD: Fund for UFO Research, 1987.
Lorenzen, Coral, and Jim Lorenzen. *Abducted! Confrontations with Beings from Outer Space.* New York: Berkley Medallion, 1977.

MOON PILOT

This was a Disney film released in 1962. With three days to go before blasting off to the Moon, an astronaut is contacted by a female alien that warns him to beware of proton rays in space. A security agent is convinced that the alien is a spy. A film about the romance between an earthling and a "good" alien, *Moon Pilot* comes closest to ufology in the idea that extraterrestrials take inordinate interest in terrestrial space programs.

Walt Disney 1962; 98 min. Director: James Neilson; Writer: Maurice Tombragel; Cinematography: William E. Snyder; Cast: Tom Tryon, Brian Keith, Edmond O'Brien, Dany Saval, Tommy Kirk, Bob Sweeney, Kent Smith.

MORONS FROM OUTER SPACE

The premise of this 1985 film is that visitors from space, far from being geniuses by earth's standards, might well be morons. The film's inversion calls attention to the fact that our normal tendency is to project higher intelligence upon extraterrestrials.

Thorn EMI 1985; 97 min. Director: Mike Hodges; Writer: Griff Rhys Jones, Mel Smith; Cinematography: Phil Meheaux; Cast: Mel Smith, Griff Rhys Jones, Paul Bown, Joanne Pearce, Jimmy Nail, Dinsdale Landen, James B. Sikking.

MOTHMAN

There have been numerous sightings of strange, winged creatures, some of which have been linked with conventional UFOs. The so-called Mothman is the best known of these. Late on the evening of November 15, 1966, in Salem, West Virginia, contractor Newell Partridge was watching television when the screen went blank and it began making a loud, whining sound. Partridge's dog Bandit began to howl on the porch and kept howling even after Partridge turned the TV off. Partridge went outside and saw the dog facing toward the barn 150 yards away. He shined the light in that direction, and it picked up two red circles that looked like bicycle reflectors but much larger. The dog shot off toward the figure despite Partridge calling him to stop. Partridge went inside to get a gun but then decided not to go outside again.

Meanwhile, 90 miles away in Point Pleasant, West Virginia, two young married couples were driving near an abandoned dynamite plant when they spotted a large, humanlike figure with two eyes two inches in diameter and six inches apart. The figure had big wings folded against its back. As they saw the figure heading toward the plant door, they sped away in their car. Shortly thereafter they saw the same or a similar creature on a hillside near the road. This figure spread its wings, which looked like those of a bat, rose into the air, and followed their car. Although the car was now traveling at 100 miles per hour, the creature kept pace without even flapping its wings. At the Point Pleasant city limits they noticed the body of a large dog lying by the side of the road. Although the creature was apparently no longer pursuing them, they did not stop until they got to the Mason County Courthouse, where they told their story to a sheriff's deputy. The deputy accompanied the witnesses back to the plant, where they found nothing out of the ordinary.

The next morning, when Newell Partridge arose, Bandit was nowhere to be found. Partridge found the dog's tracks in the mud going in a circle as if he had been chasing his tail. The dog had still not shown up two days later when Partridge read a newspaper report of the sightings in Port Pleasant. The article mentioned the couples' sighting of the dog by the side of the road and said that when the deputy and witnesses went past that point on their way back to the dynamite plant a few minutes later, the dog was gone. Partridge's dog was never seen again.

Once the Port Pleasant–Salem story hit the press wires, a reporter immediately dubbed the creature "Mothman" after a villain on the *Batman* TV series. That was not the end of the Mothman sightings. Several more sightings were reported over the next year.

On November 16, 1966, three adults, one carrying a baby, were walking to their car after leaving a friend's house. Suddenly something rose up from the ground, startling one woman so badly that she dropped her baby. The witnesses described it as a big gray thing, larger than a man, with no discernible head, but with two large glowing red circles near the top and wings that unfolded from its back. The man grabbed the baby and rushed it and the two women inside the house they had just left. The witnesses could see the eyes of the creature peering in through the window. They called the police, but by the time they arrived the Mothman was gone.

In May 1967 a woman allegedly saw a flying creature with luminous red eyes approach a luminous object and vanish. In November of that year four hunters observed a giant gray manlike figure with red eyes gliding along the ground.

Although the 1966 sightings were the ones that gave Mothman his name, some reports of a similar creature predate this. A West Virginia woman said she had seen such a creature on a highway one evening in 1961. It stood in the middle of the road, its wings unfolded from its back to a width about equal to that of the road. Then it took off straight up and disappeared out of sight in seconds.

Mothman made only one appearance outside of Ohio and West Virginia. It occurred in England in November 1963, when four young people saw a golden, oval-shaped light floating a few feet above a field 80 yards from them. The UFO moved into a wooded area and out of view. Suddenly the witnesses saw a dark shape shambling toward them from across the field. It was black, human-sized, and headless, with wings that looked like those of a bat. The youths fled the scene.

The major chronicler of the Mothman stories was John A. Keel, a controversial writer on anomalous phenomena. He compiled a composite description of the Mothman from the accounts of at least 100 persons who saw the creature. It stood between five and seven feet tall and walked in a shuffling manner on humanlike legs. The eyes were set near the top of the shoulders. The wings were batlike but did not flap when the creature flew. Its color was described as brown or gray. It was said to emit a squeaky sound or a mechanical humming. It ascended straight up, like a helicopter.

Two possible mundane explanations have been put forth for the Mothman. One came from a West Virginia University biologist who suggested that witnesses had seen sandhill cranes. This was rejected by all of the witnesses. John Keel believes that a few of the witnesses mistook owls encountered briefly on dark country roads for the Mothman. Several other winged entities have been seen sighted, albeit none with the frequency of the Mothman sightings.

Several sightings of flying men occurred in 1948. In January of that year, a woman and some children allegedly saw what appeared to be a man with long silver wings fastened over his shoulder with a strap. He flew in an upright position, manipulating the wings with controls strapped to his chest. Using these controls he was able to hover and bank. In April in Longview, Washington, two people saw three flying men circling the city. They were dressed in khaki flying suits with helmets over their faces. In September near Grassy Butte, Oregon, two flying men were seen at dawn.

A U.S. Air Force private on guard duty at Camp Okubo, Japan, in 1952 heard flapping sounds and looked up to see what at first he thought was a bird. It got closer and hovered above him before starting to descend. The private could now see that it had the body of a man, over seven feet from head to feet; its wingspan was almost equal to its height. The private fired his rifle at it repeatedly. He thought he heard it hit the ground, but when he went to look for it, it wasn't there.

In 1956 a Falls City, Nebraska, man noticed something in the air about three blocks away while he was outside loading equipment into his pickup. He thought it was a loose kite, but as it came closer he realized that it was a large, winged human form. As it came even closer the witness could make out a frightening, demonic face. It had large, blue eyes and very wrinkled facial skin. The witness estimated its height at eight to nine feet. The wingspan was 15 feet. The wings looked like polished aluminum and were two feet wide close to the body and three feet wide at the outer edges. On the underside of the wings were blue, yellow, orange, and red lights. The wings were fastened on with a shoulder harness. A breastplate had dials on it that the flying man adjusted. A hissing sound accompanied the flying man.

In May 1968 in Galesburg, Illinois, a man and his wife saw three figures flying at a speed of about 30 miles per hour at a height of 500 feet. The figures appeared to have either feathers or scales with a metallic appearance. They had heads but no

necks and cone-shaped tails. Their wingspans were 15 to 20 feet. The couple saw two objects with pulsating red lights flying at about the same height as the "birds" and moving on a course to intercept them. Ten days later the same couple had a second sighting of one of the birdlike creatures.

In August 1969 a U.S. Marine private sitting in a bunker in South Vietnam saw what he at first thought was a huge bat. As it drew closer, he determined it to be a naked black woman with batlike wings. In Elma, New York, in October 1974 a witness allegedly saw an immense birdlike creature with a wingspan of nine or 10 feet, a humanlike body, and a grotesque head.

On the night of April 23, 1994, a man was driving in the foothills of Washington's Mt. Rainier when his engine abruptly died. Then a large object descended and landed with a thud in the road 30 feet ahead of his vehicle. It was nine feet tall with a humanlike torso covered with a bright, bluish fur. It had clawlike hands and feet like those of a bird. The face was like a wolf with yellowish eyes and a big mouth with white teeth. As the man watched, the beast's wings unfolded and began flapping. The creature rose and flew off toward the mountain. Shortly thereafter the man's truck started up by itself.

—*Jerome Clark*

See Also: Atmospheric Life-Forms; Bigfoot; Chupacabras
Further Reading:
Bord, Janet, and Colin Bord. *Alien Animals.* Harrisburg, PA: Stackpole Books, 1981.
Clark, Jerome. *Unexplained! 347 Strange Sightings, Incredible Occurrences, and Puzzling Physical Phenomena.* Detroit: Visible Ink Press, 1993.
Clark, Jerome, and Loren Coleman. *Creatures of the Outer Edge.* New York: Warner Books, 1978.
Keel, John A. *The Mothman Prophecies.* New York: E. P. Dutton, 1975.
———. *Strange Creatures from Time and Space.* Greenwich, CT: Fawcett Gold Medal, 1970.

MUNROE FALLS HIT-AND-RUN

In the wee hours of March 28, 1967, David Morris was on his way home in Munroe Falls, Ohio, from a graveyard shift at an electrical plant when his attention was distracted by a glowing, cone-like UFO in a wheatfield. Glancing back at the foggy highway, he discerned four or five glowing, unearthly "midgets" walking on the road, seemingly unaware of his car. Slamming on the brakes, Morris hit one of the short beings with his right-front bumper and saw a thumbless hand jut upward and then down. Coming to a stop some 10 feet beyond, he instinctively started to get out and try to help the victim when he realized what a strange situation he was in. Glancing backward as he sped away, he saw a group of the beings standing around as if they were standing around a body. The next morning, Morris found dents on the right-front side of his car.

See Also: Close Encounters
Further Reading:
Clark, Jerome. *The UFO Encyclopedia.* 2nd ed. Detroit: Omnigraphics, 1998.
Keyhoe, Donald E., and Gordon I. R. Lore Jr., eds. *Strange Effects from UFOs.* Washington, DC: National Investigations Committee on Aerial Phenomena, 1969.

MUSIC

Since the early years of the UFO age flying saucers—as befits their place in popular culture—have occasionally been the subject of songs.

In the early 1950s, for example, the Buchanan Brothers, a hillbilly gospel duo, averred in their song "When You See Those Flying Saucers" that UFOs were signs of Jesus's imminent Second Coming. Billy Lee Riley's 1957 hit "Flying Saucers Rock'n'Roll" was a rip-snorting rockabilly rave-up. The Byrds's mid-1960s "Mr. Spaceman" wed UFOs to psychedelic rock. A personal favorite is by an obscure singer-songwriter named Tom Pacheco, who on an RCA album, *The Outsider,* memorably performs his folk-rock composition "Judge Proctor's Windmill," a hilarious retelling of the famous (though, alas, untrue) story of the Martian airship that crashed in Aurora, Texas, in April 1897.

More recently, however, California folklorist Clark Branson has come upon the earliest known song about the sighting of a UFO. It appears in an 1867 work, *The Ballads and Songs of Derbyshire,* compiled by Llewellynn Jewitt. The book is a collection of old English broadside ballads, rhymes composed by songsmiths, sold by peddlers, and intended to be sung to familiar melodies. Many of these addressed topical matters, including politi-

cal events, murders, wars, and other subjects currently in the public eye. A few of these broadsides survived to enter (in altered form) oral tradition and become folk songs. But most were quickly forgotten, as was the case with one entitled "On the Strange and Wonderful Sight That Was Seen in the Air on the 6th of March 1716":

The sixth of March, kind neighbors this is true,
A wonder in the Sky came to my View;
I pray believe it, for I tell no Lye,
There's many more did see it as well as I.
I was on a Travel, and was very late,
To speak the truth just about Day-light's gate,
My Heart did tremble being all alone,
To see such wonders—the like was never known.
The first of all so dark it was to me,
That much ado my Way I had to see;
I turn'd me round to see some Lights appear,
And then I saw those Wonders in the air.
These Lights to me like great long spears did show,
Sharp at one end, kind neighbors this is true;
I was so troubled I could not count them o'er,
But I suppose there was above a score.
Then I saw like Blood it did appear,
And that was very throng among those spears;
I thought the Sky would have opened in my View,
I was so daunted I knew not what to do.
The next I saw two Clouds meet fierce together
As if they would have fought one another;
And Darkened all these Spears excepting one,
They gave a Clash and quickly they were gone.
The very last Day in the same month I am told
Many people did strange Sights behold;
At Hartington, the truth I will not spare,
That night they saw Great Wonders in the Air
This Hartington it is in Darbyshire,
And credible persons living there,
They have declared that Wonders they did view
The very last night in March it's certain true.
About Eleven a'Clock late in that Night,
A very dark Cloud which then; did them sore afright;
Great smoke there came, it was perfect to their view,
They cried out, O Lord, what must we do?
They saw Great Lights which did amaze them sore,
The like was never seen in any Age before,
They went into their Houses for to Pray,
We must Repent whilst it is call'd to Day.

Jewitt says that he found the ballad in a chapbook called "The Garland of Merriment," printed in

1716–1717. "The appearances were probably those of the Aurora Borealis," he suggests. If the urge to explain sounds familiar, note also the singer's need to attest to the reliability of the witnesses (not to mention his anticipation of the Buchanan Brothers's eschatological interpretation). Some things, it appears, never change.

The second oldest UFO song was inspired by some curious events in the mid–nineteenth century, when several Nebraska residents claimed to have seen a huge lighted serpent-shaped object flying or hovering overhead. The late Western historian Mari Sandoz, in her *Old Jules Country* (1965), quotes this fragment of an apparent folk ballad inspired by this early UFO flap:

> 'Twas on a dark night in Sixty-six
> When we was layin' steel.
> We seen a flyin' engine come
> Without no wing or wheel
> It came a-roarin' in the sky
> With lights along the side . . .
> And scales like a serpent's hide.

—Jerome Clark

See Also: Popular Culture
Further Reading:
Sandoz, Mari. *Old Jules Country.* New York: Hastings House, 1965 [repr. 1982 by the University of Nebraska Press].

MY STEPMOTHER IS AN ALIEN

Dan Aykroyd stars in this film as an astronomer intent on proving there is life on other planets. He sends a beam out to a faraway galaxy and gets a visit from an attractive woman in a flying saucer. Her mission is to seduce the astronomer and get the details of his experiments that could save her planet. The astronomer and the alien are married, but his daughter suspects something when she finds her stepmother eating batteries. An interesting, comic play on certain stereotyped images of extraterrestrials, the film has some excellent special-effects spaceships.

Columbia 1988; 108 min. Director: Richard Benjamin; Writers: Herschel Weingrod, Timothy Harris, Johnathan Reynolds; Music: Alan Silvestri; Cast: Dan Aykroyd, Kim Basinger, Jon Lovitz, Alyson Harrigan, Joseph Maher, Seth Green, Wesley Mann, Adrian Sparks, Juliette Lewis, Tanya Fenmore.

THE MYSTERIANS

In this 1957 Japanese film aliens come to earth in flying saucers and dispatch a robot bird that shoots death rays out of its eyes. The aliens are looking for women to breed with the aliens, whose planet was destroyed by a nuclear explosion. The theme of aliens needing human beings to reproduce their species, which is central to several different early sci-fi films, is eerily precognitive of an important theme of contemporary abduction literature.

Toho 1957; 85 min. Director: Inoshiro Honda; Music: Akira Ifukube; Cast: Kenji Sahara, Yumi Shirakawa, Takashi Shimura.

MYSTERIOUS SATELLITE

In this 1956 Japanese movie aliens looking like giant starfish with an eye in the middle of their body come to earth from a planet called Paira. Being friendly, they change into human shapes in order not to frighten people. Their leader admonishes the earthlings not to use nuclear weapons against each other but to join forces with Paira to destroy a fiery planet that is on a collision course with earth. Only after the approaching planet heats earth up disastrously, causing tidal waves, does a Japanese scientist develop a special bomb that is fired by the Pairans from their spacecraft, destroying the menacing planet. Also called *Warning from Space.*

A friendly-alien movie that contrasts sharply with the many hostile-alien movies produced by the Japanese, it demonstrates the point that it is not just Westerners who project images of both "good" and "bad" beings into the unknowns of outer space.

Daiei 1956; 87 min. Director: Koji Shima; Writer: Hideo Ogumi; Cinematography: Kimio Watanabe; Cast: Toyomi Karita, Keizo Kawasaki, Isao Yamagata, Shozo Nanbu, Buntaro Miake, Mieko Nagai, Kiyoko Hirai.

MYTHOLOGY AND FOLKLORE

UFOs—whatever they are—may or may not exist outside of the human imagination. It has proved impossible to verify the presence of the alleged phenomenon to everyone's satisfaction, and, simultaneously, it is impossible to prove that nothing is going on. From a philosophical point of view, UFOs are therefore an elusive subject that avoids, in a great many ways, rational interrogation. It is correct that UFO buffs and a series of UFO organizations over the years have claimed that the enigma of the "flying saucers," which was the original term used to designate unidentified flying objects in the late 1940s, has in fact been solved. Yet the proof provided to support such claims has always been meager, to say the least. Most apparently inexplicable UFO incidents, when investigated more closely, can be understood in mundane terms. Trained observers and analysts are able to explain most UFO witness accounts in terms of familiar things (aircrafts, stars, balloons, satellites, natural phenomena, misconceptions, hoaxes, psychological reactions, etc.). Focusing on the so-called high-strangeness observations, most of these cases are explained in similar ways. To put it bluntly: The proofs that are supposed to determine the existence of UFOs—let alone extraterrestrial visitation—would not stand up in court beyond a reasonable doubt.

This still does not prove that UFOs are merely figments of the imagination, but it provides circumstantial evidence to that effect. Furthermore, it places the modern notion of UFOs within the context of social-scientific research. Physics, astronomy, biology, and other disciplines in the hard sciences have not be able to solve the riddle of the UFO, but sociology, folklore, and the social-scientific study of religion have provided functional and well-argued explanations by changing the usual point of departure in the analysis of UFOs and UFO-related phenomena. Rather than looking for something "out there," the focus is human beings themselves and the processes taking place in human minds and society. In short, it seems that UFOs, apart from any other kind of identification that may become relevant, are a product of psychological and sociological processes.

Rather than remaining puzzled by the many weird tales of strange crafts hovering high above, human confrontations with benevolent beings from other worlds, horrifying abductions, and many other strange occurrences, historians and psychologists have tried to track down the origins of UFO-related tales and narratives. This kind of work has revealed that most UFO notions are antedated by similar ideas in traditional folklore and mythology and that nothing fundamentally new is being perceived. People have always claimed contact with superhuman or nonhuman entities, strange things have been reported floating in the air, and inexplicable events of all kinds are found in abundance in the recollections of earlier times. From this comparative perspective, it is worthwhile to approach the current interest in UFOs as a kind of myth adapted to conditions in contemporary society. Rather than looking into the sky for an explanation of this strange phenomenon, it should be identified in all arenas of modern culture—literature, film, cartoons, arts, fashion—but primarily in language and thus in the human imagination. The UFO myth is a collectively shared narrative with no formal authority to contain it and no priesthood to maintain it. It lives its own life, and anyone who so desires is able to share in ufological discourse.

This kind of noninstitutionalized, collectively shared occupation with things beyond human control is usually framed by the expressions "folk religion" or "folk mythology." Even if the belief in UFOs reveals important differences when compared with its counterparts of earlier times, it seems fair to designate it accordingly. The UFO is a core feature in contemporary Western society's popular culture and is thus folk religion or folk mythology. The sociological outcome of this shared belief sometimes leads to the emergence of special milieus or specific social organizations, but in most cases the elusive UFO has found its way into many peoples' everyday lives. Some 25 percent of adults in the United States believe in UFOs in one way or another, but the concept takes on real importance for a much smaller segment of the population. One therefore has to ask whether the balanced presence of the idea among the many is more significant than the intense awareness of the concept among the few. In fact, both perspectives are equally important; the actual UFO community—people who find UFOs and what goes along with them to be of utmost importance—draws on the peripheral interest among others, and vice versa. With no broad public awareness of the concept there would be no core group, and, with no subcommunity preoccupied with the subject, the average man or woman would rarely hear of the subject and therefore be less inclined to consider it at all.

The notion of UFOs has changed considerably since the concept of "flying saucers" was coined in American news media in the summer of 1947. It all began when people learned of a strange incident involving private pilot Kenneth Arnold, who died in 1984. After a flight over the Cascade Mountains in the state of Washington, on June 24, 1947, Arnold reported that he had encountered nine strange flying objects. Talking to a newspaper reporter about his experience, Arnold said that the objects were traveling at a tremendous speed and that they moved "like a saucer would if you skipped it across the water." Arnold was referring to the movements of the objects, but a headline editor interpreted it incorrectly, and the notion of "flying saucers" was subsequently presented to the public. Arnold's description of the objects, though, was in fact quite unlike saucers: He described them as "crescent-shaped." During the days following the incident, many newspapers carried the story, and a growing number of witnesses came forward with new reports: Apparently flying saucers had been spotted in many different places, and the image of the flying saucer had become a model of how subsequent sightings should be reported. The concept of flying saucers grew out of a highly fascinating tale brought to the public's attention through different media reports. In peoples' reading about the strange occurrences, flying saucers became social facts. In other words, we find a specific narrative at the outset of the modern flying-saucer myth—and nothing much but that.

But what kind of cultural and social circumstances caused the myth of the UFO to emerge? One possible answer is given in what we might term the "Cold War hypothesis." According to this line of interpretation, the image of the flying saucer arose as a response to the tensions between the United States and the Soviet Union in the wake of World War II. As the Cold War was heating up, people realized that their lives, and the very existence of humankind, was under permanent threat,

and the psychosocial climate became more and more difficult. In light of the unwillingness or inability of political authorities to curtail the proliferation of nuclear weapons, there arose a myth of extraterrestrials prepared to either prevent nuclear destruction or assist a surviving human remnant. The flying saucer, according to this theory, serves as a symbolic mediator between the two oppositional powers—but also as a mediator between the individual and the complex society of which he or she is a tiny part.

From this perspective, the flying saucer is a collective representation of widely shared concerns in popular culture. But other things also played an important role in the formation of the UFO myth: Most important were science fiction, new technologies, the emerging possibility of space travel, and sciences such as astronomy. The individual constituents of the UFO myth are typical to the age in which it originated and that still unfolds, but the Cold War is no longer the prime force behind it. In today's world the UFO narrative serves much more traditional, or "classical," purposes: Through the UFO motif the unknown, the superhuman, the divine, and the demonic acquire a face. Depending on how the concept is understood and interpreted, the UFO becomes a symbol of things otherwise addressed through religious myths, folklore, and tales of the twilight zone. In relating to things nonhuman or superhuman, people are able to talk of the world in ways that are otherwise impossible. Modern humanity has, for instance, abandoned previous generations' fears of creatures of the night, the strange beings of the woods, and the spirits of the dead, just to mention a few. The fear and wondering itself, however, are still there, but the unknown or strange creatures have changed their appearance. Today they come from deep space, from new kinds of realms beyond human reach. The structure is the same, but the specific narrative is designed for modern consumption. The situation is similar for positive aspects of the UFO myth: When benevolent space entities contact humans they act the parts previously played by angels, gods, guardian spirits, and the like. Mythological creatures of the past have been replaced by their modern equivalents. Consequently, it is ideas of "human versus nonhuman," "good

A parallel to extraterrestrial abduction: Travelers in the German countryside suddenly find they have become the playthings of a young giantess in this nineteenth-century engraving by J. B. Zwecker. (Mary Evans Picture Library)

versus evil," "meaning versus meaninglessness," and "understanding versus not understanding" that are at the epistemological heart of the UFO myth; spacecraft, aliens, and strange occurrences are the outward expressions of these issues. It is also quite apparent that the specifics of the myth are intimately related to concerns of people in the "real world." The abduction myth, for instance, mirrors problems with abortion, prenatal birth, medical technology, gene technology, repressed sexual desires, the dignity of the individual, mother-child relations, pain, and other ethical dilemmas and problems.

In the years following the first flying-saucer reports, there was no consensus regarding the nature of this phenomenon. People hypothesized that Soviet agents were infiltrating the United States by means of flying saucers; others believed secret government agencies were responsible or that surviving Nazi groups hiding under the ice cap of Antarctica were preparing an assault on the United States. Visitors from inside the earth was another theory, but most people simply did not know what to believe. The notion that flying saucers were vehicles carrying visiting aliens from other worlds was not present from the beginning. Indeed, the expressions "flying saucer," "flying disc," and "UFO"— which eventually came to mean "extraterrestrial spacecraft"—have changed in meaning over the years—a change paralleled by the creation and growth of a UFO community. The forming of the spaceship myth may thus be seen as a response to an otherwise intolerable situation where no explanation and no meaning regarding the nature of the alleged flying saucers could be found. By labeling the alleged objects "spaceships," they were transformed into less puzzling phenomena. They acquired a place in a meaningful taxonomy that made them psychologically manageable. The alleged flying saucers were captured in a secular myth with obvious parallels to religious systems of interpretation, and to many people this was all that was needed. The precise nature of the visiting aliens was still to be determined, but the phenomenon itself was accessible for discussion and judgment. A line of UFO organizations was established, books and journals were published, and the UFO community gradually took form.

Transcending the views of secular UFO proponents, George Adamski and his fellow contactees added spiritual and ethical dimensions to the whole thing and produced definite answers to many of the questions being posed. Secular UFO organizations were operating more or less within the theoretical and methodological boundaries of everyday logic and never seemed to get any closer to solving the enigma. Today the most effective argument presented by secular ufologists to prove that UFOs are real is the conspiracy myth. It is argued that government agencies withhold information and that U.S. leaders or secret agents have been in close contact with aliens. This explains why no real proof exists, and it gives people a reason for continuing to investigate UFO reports and other sorts of documentation. New elements are added to the ufological narrative all the time—most important, abduction tales turned traditional ufology upside-down during the 1990s—but the structure remains the same.

Religious ufology, however, has managed to take advantage of the myth in other ways. Religious discourse is special in the sense that no proof is needed. Religious authority is different from secular authority. Revelations, miracles, and the like are accepted as perfectly possible within most religious communities, and tales of human encounters with extraterrestrials in the shape of Cosmic Masters or highly developed souls are not provocative or problematic in and of themselves. Many UFO religions have come into being on that account, some traditional religions have to a certain degree been influenced by ufology, and much New Age spirituality is linked to a belief in human contact with entities from deep space. In effect, religious ufology rose out of a secular narrative as a more sonorous response to the questions being raised. Today ufology may be seen as either secular or religious, but it is important to note that the in-between position is just as likely. Many people will take secular as well as religious perspectives into account in addressing the issue. At any rate, it is important to remember that UFO buffs and deeply committed UFO devotees are very few compared with the numbers of people for whom UFOs play a lesser role. It is probably correct to say that the concept of the UFO, to most people, exists as a possibility, as a sociopsychological resource that may be triggered at times and—left alone—unnoticed at other times.

—*Mikael Rothstein*

See Also: Abductees; Adamski, George; Arnold, Kenneth; Contactees; New Age; Religions, UFO.

Further Reading:
Adamski, George, and Desmond Leslie. *Flying Saucers Have Landed.* New York: British Book Centre, 1953; London: Werner Laurie, 1953.
Bartholomew, Robert E. *Ufolore: A Social Psychological Study of a Modern Myth in the Making.* Stone Mountain, GA: Arcturus Book Service, 1989.
Bethurum, Truman. *Aboard a Flying Saucer.* Los Angeles: DeVorss, 1954.
Cohen, Daniel. *Myths of the Space Age.* New York: Dodd, Mead, 1977.
Curran, Douglas. *In Advance of the Landing: Folk Concepts of Outer Space.* New York: Abbeville Press, 1985.
Evans, Hilary. *Gods, Spirits, and Cosmic Guardians: A Comparative Study of the Encounter Experience.* Wellingborough, U.K.: Aquarian Press, 1987.
———. *Visions, Apparitions, Alien Visitors.* Wellingborough, UK: Aquarian Press, 1984.
Jung, Carl Gustav. *Flying Saucers: A Modern Myth of Things Seen in the Sky.* Princeton: Princeton University Press, 1978.

NAKED ALIENS

There are innumerable stories by contactees of meeting with unclad humanoid aliens. Except for the relatively small percentage of accounts that relate tales of explicit sexual encounters, in most of these cases the extraterrestrials—who seem to always have beautiful physical forms—accept their nakedness as naturally as earthlings accept the state of being clothed. The sense one gets from reading accounts of such contacts is that lack of clothes is symbolic of innocence and purity: The aliens live in an Eden-like state before the fall—in contrast to corrupt humanity.

See Also: Contactees; Sex; Thompson, Samuel Eaton
Further Reading:
Clark, Jerome. *The UFO Encyclopedia.* 2nd ed. Detroit: Omnigraphics, 1998.

NAZCA LINES

The Nazca people of Peru some 1,500–2,000 years ago developed an art form that created pictures by removing a layer of rock to reveal the light soil beneath it. Some of these pictures are immense and can be seen in their entirety only from the air. This fact has led some people to speculate that these pictures were intended to be seen by extraterrestrial visitors. Erich von Däniken proposed they were actually airfields where spacecraft landed and took off. The Nazca lines resemble figures created similarly in England about 3,000 years ago, which also could be seen only from the air. These artifacts could be the remains of a neolithic art form, the significance of which has been lost to time.

See Also: Ancient Astronauts; von Däniken, Erich
Further Reading:
Goran, Morris. *The Modern Myth, Ancient Astronauts and UFOs.* South Brunswick, NJ: A. S. Barnes, 1978.

von Däniken, Erich. *Chariots of the Gods? Unsolved Mysteries of the Past.* Trans. Michael Heron. New York: G. P. Putnam's Sons, 1970.

NEAR-DEATH EXPERIENCE

A near-death experience (NDE), sometimes also called the "pseudodeath" experience, refers to the seemingly supernatural experiences often undergone by individuals who have suffered apparent death and have been restored to life. Several recent observers have pointed out that there are structural and other parallels between NDEs and the alien-abduction experience.

The systematic scientific study of NDEs is recent, although accounts can be found in literature and historical documents dating back hundreds of years, such as those of ancient philosophers, like Plato, and of modern writers, like Melville and Tolstoy. A small number of cases was collected by in-

The tunnel reported in many near-death experiences resembles certain abduction experiences. (American Religion Collection)

terested investigators beginning in the late nineteenth century, especially by the pioneers of psychical research, such as Edmund Gurney, Sir William Barrett, and James H. Hyslop, who also studied the deathbed visions that constitute a common element of NDEs. However, it was only after the advent of medical techniques of resuscitation, like modern cardiopulmonary resuscitation measures, that NDEs became a widespread phenomenon.

The main impetus for modern studies on NDEs was the 1975 publication of the book *Life after Life,* by psychiatrist Raymond A. Moody, which followed earlier researches on this topic by other physicians such as Elisabeth Kubler-Ross and Russell Noyes. Also, NDEs had been discussed before as a subcategory of out-of-body experiences (OOBE, or OBE). The OOBE, in turn, became a topic of widespread discussion with Robert Crookall's work *Out of Body Experience* (1970), as well as Robert A. Monroe's popular work *Journeys out of the Body* (1972). At the time, "out-of-body experience" was the newly coined parapsychological expression for what an earlier generation of occultists had called "astral projection"—the practice of extracting one's consciousness from the physical body and traveling to a different location in a nonphysical body (an "astral" body that traveled in a different, nonphysical dimension).

Moody's work describes the results of more than 11 years of inquiry into NDEs and is based on a sample of about 150 cases, including persons who were resuscitated after having been thought or pronounced clinically dead by their doctors; persons who came very close to physical death in the course of accidents or severe injury or illness; and persons who, as they died, told their experiences to other people who were present.

Moody outlines nine elements that seem to occur generally but not universally in the NDE experiencers:

1. Hearing a buzzing or ringing noise while having a sense of being dead. At this initial stage of the NDE, the experiencers are confused and try, unsuccessfully, to communicate with other people at the scene of their death.

2. Peace and painlessness. While people are dying they may be in intense pain, but as soon as they leave the body the pain vanishes and they experience peace.

3. Out-of-body experience. NDEers often have the experience of rising up and floating above their own body surrounded by a medical team, and watching it down below, while feeling very detached and comfortable. They experience the feeling of being in a spiritual body that looks like a sort of living energy field.

4. The tunnel experience. The NDEers then experience being drawn into darkness through a tunnel, at an extremely high speed, or going up a stairway (or some other symbol of crossing a threshold) until they achieve a realm of radiant golden-white light.

5. Rising rapidly into the heavens. Instead of a tunnel, some NDEers report an experience of rising suddenly into the heavens and seeing the earth and the celestial sphere as if they were astronauts in space.

6. People of light. Once on the other side of the tunnel, or after they have risen into the heavens, NDEers meet people who glow with an inner light. Often they find that friends and relatives who have already died are there to greet them.

7. The Being of light. After connecting with these beings, NDEers meet a powerful, spiritual Being who some have referred to as an angel, God, or Jesus. Also, although NDEers sometimes report feeling scared, none feels that they either were on the way to hell or that they fell into it.

8. The life review. This higher Being presents NDEers with a panoramic review of everything they have done. In particular, they experience the effects of every act they have ever done to other people and come away feeling that love is the most important thing in life.

9. Reluctance to return. The higher Being sometimes says that the NDEer must return to life. In other experiences, the NDEer is given a choice of staying or returning. In

either case, NDEers experience a reluctance to return. The people who choose to return do so only because of loved ones they do not wish to leave behind.

Moody's work was anecdotal, and he was careful to point out that it should not be regarded as a scientific study, since the case histories presented were highly selective and the data were not subjected to any statistical analysis. The first book to report an investigation of NDEs from a scientific point of view was published in 1980 by psychologist Kenneth Ring. His *Life at Death* was based on the interviews with 102 near-death survivors. The statistical analysis of the data presented was supplemented by extensive qualitative materials in order to evaluate Moody's prior findings. Ring was concerned with comparing NDEs of illness victims, accident victims, and suicidals, and his book showed that NDEs were largely invariant over different conditions of near-death onset and that they had a high incidence of occurrence in all categories studied. In Ring's *The Omega Project,* he develops the parallels between NDErs and abductees.

See Also: Abductees; Astral Projection and UFOs; Jung, Carl Gustav

Further Reading:
Gallup, George. *Adventures in Immortality.* New York: MacGraw-Hill, 1982.
Greyson, Bruce, and Charles P. Flynn, eds. *The Near-Death Experience. Problems, Prospects, Perspectives.* Springfield, IL: Charles C. Thomas, 1984.
Moody, Raymond A. *Life after Life.* New York: Bantam, 1976.
———. *The Light Beyond.* New York: Bantam, 1989.
Ring, Kenneth. *The Omega Project: Near-Death Experiences, UFO Encounters, and Mind at Large.* New York: William Morrow, 1992.

NEPHILIM

The biblical term "Nephilim," which in Hebrew means the "fallen ones" or "those who fell," refers to the offspring of the "sons of God" (traditionally interpreted as being angels) and human females mentioned in Genesis 6:1–4. Many ufologists, whether or not members of the ancient-astronaut school, have speculated that these sons of Gods were ufonauts who carried out experimentation with human-alien hybridization to produce the

Nephilim. A fuller account of the generation of the Nephilim is preserved in the apocryphal Book of Enoch, which recounts how a group of angels desired mortal females, left heaven to mate with them, and taught humanity such heinous skills as the art of war. This particular story, which at one time was widely known, eventually disappeared from popular folklore because it clashed with what became the official church position, which was that angels were purely spiritual beings and thus could not engage in sexual intercourse.

The chief distinguishing characteristic of the Nephilim was their gigantic size. The descendants of these giants are mentioned several times in both the canonical and the noncanonical books. There is a particularly vivid image in the Book of Numbers, in which the wandering Israelites come upon a land occupied by the giants. The Hebrew scouts give the following report: "All the people that we saw in it are men of great stature. And there we saw the Nephilim (the sons of Anak, who come from the Nephilim); and we seemed to ourselves like grasshoppers, and so we seemed to them" (Num. 13:33). Other groups of exceptionally tall people who appear to have been descendants of the Nephilim, such as the Anakim and the Rephaim, are mentioned in the Book of Deuteronomy (2:11; 2:20; 3:11; 3:13) and the Book of Joshua (12:4; 13:12; 15:8; 17:15; 18:16). (The tallness of these peoples is clearer in the King James version of the Bible, which translates "Rephaim" as "giants.")

There were still descendants of the Nephilim around during King David's time. Four enormous members of the Philistine army are mentioned in 2 Samuel and in parallel verses in 1 Chronicles. The identification of these men as "descendants of the giants" clearly marks their ancestry as traceable to the Nephilim. These passages observe that at least one of these four men had six fingers on each hand and six toes on each foot—an interesting trait, considering that some images of ufonauts (e.g., in the alien autopsy film) portray them as having six digits.

The author of 2 Samuel also notes that "these four were descended from the giants in Gath" (21:22)—which was the homeland of Goliath, the most famous giant in the Bible—making Goliath a descendant of the Nephilim. Finally, there are other allusions to the descendants of the Nephilim in the apocryphal Book of Judith (16:6), the Book of Sirach (16:7), the Book of Baruch (3:26–28), and the Wisdom of Solomon (14:6).

See Also: Ancient Astronauts; Angels

Further Reading:

Davidson, Gustav. *A Dictionary of Angels: Including the Fallen Angels.* New York: Free Press, 1971.
Godwin, Malcolm. *Angels: An Endangered Species.* New York: Simon and Schuster, 1990.
Prophet, Elizabeth Clare. *Forbidden Mysteries of Enoch: Fallen Angels and the Origins of Evil.* Livingston, MT: Summit University Press, 1992.

NEVADA AERIAL RESEARCH GROUP

The Nevada Aerial Research Group is, according to leader "Val Valarian" (a/k/a John Grace), on a mission to "investigate negative factors in the social structure" and "all processes that impede evolution of the species." UFOs are part of that impeding process, which is in fact a worldwide conspiracy to enslave the human race. Aliens work with U.S. government drug traffickers to alter the human genetic system, making humans too docile and stupid to resist. The U.S. government is also involved in a "secret space program" that works with aliens and androids to secure control of civilizations beyond the earth.

According to the *Newsletter,* the group's publication, conspirators have infiltrated and now head UFO and contactee groups, occultism, major religions, peace groups, banks, Wall Street, TV, radio, *Playboy* and the *National Enquirer,* movies, police, the United Nations, the American Medical Association, Western politics, communism, aerospace corporations, universities, the Rotary Club, the Better Business Bureau, fraternities, European royal families, and economic organizations. This is, however, only a fragment of all parties involved. The group is located on the extreme right of the political spectrum.

The *Newsletter* also gives descriptions of the various extraterrestrial species, named grays, Draconians, Sirians, Essessani, and so on and informs us of what they are up to. For example, "The [grays] are an extremely old species . . . they are members of the 4th Invader force"; "the Draconi-

ans . . . use Pluto in our solar system for a way station and use bases on the Dark Side of the Moon for earth access"; "the Sirians are a negative force that use the Eye of Horus [eye in a triangle] as one of their symbols. The Sirians are humanoid." The relations between these groups is complex, and they are ultimately organized into the Federation, coming from all the various "densities." The earth is alleged to be the third density.

See Also: Conspiracy Theories; Contactees

Further Reading:

Lewis, James R. *The Encyclopedia of Cults, Sects, and New Religions.* Amherst, NY: Prometheus Books, 1998.
Melton, J. Gordon. *Encyclopedia of American Religions.* 5th ed. Detroit: Gale Research, 1996.

NEW AGE

The New Age movement is not an actual movement, and New Age ideology is not a single philosophy. Neither is New Ageism a specific religious system, although theosophy remains the strongest component. Thus the so-called New Age belief system is a syncretistic structure that encompasses many different elements into a coherent whole. To some people UFOs are a mandatory component in the eclectic fabric of New Age beliefs, but to others UFOs are of remote interest.

In sociological terms the New Age movement may be described as an informal, highly versatile network of people who share certain interests and beliefs. Sociologists of religion William Simms Bainbridge and Rodney Stark have labeled this kind of religiomythical network an "audience cult." Participants in such a network need not know one another, and they need not be in one another's presence. Common notions are absorbed through the same channels by all believers or contributors, namely, the popular media. Due to intensified communications in the modern world, people are able to share belief in the supernatural by means of common literary and visual media. In a world that is becoming more and more globalized—not least due to the fact that information is easily available and transmitted—such common beliefs are quickly diffused into many different societies. Thus, we may view the global community of believers in UFOs as one gi-

The New Age Movement has enthusiastically embraced the idea that benevolent "Star People" are overseeing the transformation of humanity. (UFO Magazine)

gantic "client cult." Indeed, the world has become "a single place." There are parallels to this development in earlier periods of history. It has, for instance, been suggested that the enthusiasm for UFOs today is in many ways similar to the so-called occult revival of the Renaissance, which can be understood as built upon the emergent phenomenon of the printing press. Similarly, it seems correct to say that the sociology of the gen-

eral UFO community is intimately linked with conditions in the modern, industrialized world, as is the concept of the UFO itself.

The image of the UFO has changed over the years. The spacecrafts allegedly seen and photographed by George Adamski were rather 1950ish in style. (The design of American cars of those days comes to mind.) Today, however, most UFO descriptions are more in tune with the technical designs of our age. This is wholly predictable, as all religious images are shaped according to the culture in which they belong. In the same way that the extraterrestrial visitors of the early contactees came from planets in our own solar system, extraterrestrials today tend to arrive from more distant—more exotic—worlds, perhaps stars thousands of light-years away or from our own future. Clearly, Mars is no longer attractive enough. It has been worn out by scientific progress.

In the New Age movement since the 1960s, the myth of the UFO has changed from a focus on hardware concerns (sightings, physical evidence, and the like) to an intense preoccupation with the so-called spiritual aspects. The teachings of the early contactees like George King point in that direction (although he met physically with the Masters, including Jesus, in spacecraft on several occasions), and the same emphasis is found in other contactee groups such as Mark-Age and Unarius Academy, but in the contemporary New Age movement it has become predominant. Today, for instance, very few people within the New Age movement claim to have been aboard spaceships, but it is quite normal that devout New Agers claim to have traveled to the stars by means of emotions, thoughts, or in their astral body. Emphasizing spiritual studies of UFOs, Swedish New Age writer Kristina Wennergren says: "It is hard to determine at what non-physical level you have these experiences. They are by no means less real because they are happening on a non-physical level through senses beyond the ordinary five senses. Actually it is likely that you glide between different levels and experience more than one. Perhaps we should not care too much about where we were in the nonphysical realm after we have had an experience of this kind."

In certain ways, such notions take religious ufology back to the times before UFO contactees emerged on the scene. In 1909, for instance, a book was published in Sweden entitled *On the Planet Mars 2000 Years Ago—The Solution to All Social Problems*. The publisher was Oscar Busch, but it presented itself as a study by one Engelbrekt Modin, who died in 1883. Busch had known Modin personally from his early years, and after Modin's death he would frequently visit Busch "in the spirit." One day Modin announced that he would go away for some time, and when he returned after more than 10 years, in 1908, he (i.e., the spirit of Modin) had a fantastic story to tell. Busch served as his "pen," and a book about his experiences was written. According to the deceased Modin, he traveled to Mars as an astral being to a point in time 2,000 years earlier, where he was shown every aspect of Martian culture and taught the ways of the Martians. Thus, his visit to another planet was not in his physical body, in contrast to Adamski and others. Modin's postdeath existence made it possible for him to transcend time and space and go to Mars 2,000 years earlier in his astral body, and Busch, by means of spiritual communication, served as his physical medium.

Kristina Wennergren adopts the basic structures of Modin's story (probably without knowing it), although the two belong to two very different times. The earlier narrative was conceived prior to any discussion of space travel as we know it, and visits to Mars had to be done by means of astral travel. This was in the happy days of spiritualism, a tradition stressing the importance of the nonphysical realm. Today, when space travel has become commonplace and the popular notion of UFOs as spacecraft is widely accepted, many New Agers have nevertheless embraced a cosmology similar to Busch's (i.e., Modin's). Reality is not perceived on a physical level. Rather, the physical world blocks the view of the "real" reality. It would be wrong to say that New Agers generally disregard the physical world, but the emphasis is laid on the nonphysical realm when the awaited spiritual transformation is discussed. It is not, however, the souls of the dead that are now the subject of attention, as it was in Modin's and Busch's time. Rather, it is extraterrestrial beings above the human level that approach us through different media.

One trend in religious ufology is the increasing importance of so-called channeling and other means of nonphysical communications. Of course, this in itself is not at all a newcomer to the history of religions. Since time immemorial people have claimed to communicate with gods or other divine beings by means of telepathy and similar phenomena. In this connection spiritualism, as we have seen, also needs to be considered as an important source of inspiration. Historian of religions Jennifer Porter has, for example, shown how the structure of traditional spiritualism has been transformed in a ufological context and that the channeling of extraterrestrial beings—which is very popular among many New Agers—may therefore be perceived as a prolongation of the otherwise worn-out interest for communication with the spirits of the dead.

In essence, the messages given by extraterrestrials to modern channelers are the same as those received by the more religiously inclined contactees of the 1950s encountering Martians or Venusians. Today, however, an important element has been added to the list: Ecological responsibility has become a most important topic. This, of course, is due to the fact that ecological problems are recognized today, whereas it was a rarely discussed issue in the early 1950s. According to modern New Agers, the Space Brothers are watching us carefully and adjusting their teachings accordingly. From the viewpoint of the historian of religion, this example indicates that religious notions are shaped and altered according to societal circumstances; thus, the Space Brothers are symbols of peoples' own consciousness and awareness regarding the problems of today's world.

The most obvious change from contactee lore to New Age mythology is the fact that the tangible flying saucer (i.e., a machine) has vanished; in its stead a much more spiritualized, and hence versatile, image of extraterrestrial beings has come to be emphasized. As we have seen, the vehicle of the visiting Masters from other planets may well be interpreted as a mediating link between what is human and what is above human. Contemporary channelers do not need this link—they are themselves the vehicle used by superhuman entities. By putting their bodies at the space being's disposal they automatically leave out the necessity for the Masters to land on Planet Earth in advanced machines. Deliberately or not, this idea of extraterrestrial communication avoids the delicate issue of proving one's claims. Adamski had to present photographs because he insisted that he had actually touched a flying saucer and talked person-to-per-son with its occupant. Modern channelers do not. Their challenge is of another nature: Like other religious preachers before them, they struggle to convince people that the *messages* they deliver are genuine.

In the early 1970s New Age author Brad Steiger launched a new perspective for religious ufology. In his book *Revelation: The Divine Fire,* he argues against technically interested ufologists and offers a clear-cut spiritualized understanding of extraterrestrial contact. The nuts-and-bolts UFO becomes of less importance while the channeled or telepathically transmitted messages from entities from other worlds come into focus. The extraterrestrials, Steiger claims, are helping people on earth accommodate to the new conditions in the Age of Aquarius. In subsequent books, Steiger explains that beings from other worlds are now accepting reincarnations on earth in order to live among humans in the shape of ordinary human beings. Such individuals are in fact the most active participants in New Age activities—they are the bringers of the New Age. They have extraordinary abilities, they are more sensitive, and they may feel alienated when confronted with the tedious or primitive ways of people on earth. However, such "Star People," as they are termed, have no clear memory of their origin. The psychological pressures would be much too difficult if they had a full awareness of their own history, it is claimed.

Steiger's ideas have been propagated in mass-market paperbacks, and it is quite normal to encounter people within the New Age milieu who have been profoundly inspired by him, although many people never realize that Steiger is their source of inspiration. It is easily to find persons in Europe or the United States who believe themselves to be from another world. This author has on record two examples of children who were brought up to believe that they have arrived from "the stars" to help people on earth. They were taught that they have a certain mission and that they are not like everyone else. Similarly, this author has met with individuals who believe they have come from distant worlds; they may have realized this during meditation, in hypnotic regression, or by a revelation of some kind. In every case, the social reaction is the same: They feel that they have a mission, they do not feel ordinary, and they have ways of dealing with various forms of alienation.

The same chords are struck by other New Age authors; for instance, Ruth Montgomery claims that earth has been incorporated into an intergalactic association, which means that quite a few Star People live among us. It has been so for a long time, and various religious notabilities such as Jesus and the Buddha were such guests. These myths of Star People are steadily developing into more and more complex systems. One of the more important recent innovations is the idea that beings from other worlds enter adult human beings and take over their bodies. This phenomenon, first developed by Montgomery in her book *Strangers among Us,* is referred to as "walk-ins" (a positive counterpart to the "body snatchers" of science fiction). Walk-ins, according to Montgomery, are "idealistic but not perfected souls, who, through spiritual growth in previous incarnations, have earned the right to take over unwanted bodies, if their overriding goal is to help mankind. The original occupants vacate the bodies because they can no longer maintain the physical spark of life or because they are so dispirited that they earnestly wish to leave." Moses, Lot, Joseph, Jesus, Muhammad, Christopher Columbus, Abraham Lincoln, Joseph Smith (the founder of Mormonism), and many more (including certain contemporary U.S. politicians) are considered to be or to have been such walk-ins.

On the basis of these notions, people at the core of the New Age milieu will frequently claim that they have in fact changed identity. The body and outer personality may be the same, but the soul that now inhabits the body is another. This author has experienced rather dramatic changes with a woman who insisted that she was an "Animah of another world." She felt compelled to help people on the threshold of the emerging Age of Aquarius, much like other walk-ins who may perceive themselves to be extraterrestrials in service to earth's awakening. In such cases, the UFO as an object is downplayed if it is present at all. Instead, traditional New Age concepts such as millennial visions, individual possibilities, spiritual evolution, reincarnation, karma, emphasis on the soul rather than body, and the like are framed by a ufologically inspired narrative focusing on extraterrestrial intelligences.

—*Mikael Rothstein*

See Also: Channeling; Extraterrestrial Walk-Ins; Star People
Further Reading:
Hanegraaff, Wouter. *New Age Religion and Western Culture: Esotericism in the Mirror of Secular Thought.* New York: E. J. Brill, 1996.
Heelas, Paul. *The New Age Movement.* Oxford, U.K.: Blackwell, 1996.
Melton, J. Gordon, et al. *New Age Almanac.* Detroit: Visible Ink, 1991.
Modin, Engelbrekt. *Paa Planeten Mars for 2000 Aar siden. Samfundsspørgsmaalenes Løsning.* Psykisk Forlag, København Oscar Bush, 1947 [orig. Swedish version publ. in 1909]
Montgomery, Ruth. *Strangers among Us: Enlightened Beings from a World to Come.* Pantheon, New York 1977.
O'Keefe, Daniel Lawrence. *Stolen Lightning: The Social Theory of Magic.* New York: Vintage Books, 1983.
Porter, Jennifer E. "Spiritualists, Aliens, and UFOs: Extraterrestrials as Spirit Guides." *Journal of Contemporary Religion* 12(3) (1996).
Stark, Rodney, and William Simms Bainbridge. *The Future of Religion: Secularisation, Revival, and Cult Formation.* Berkeley: University of California Press, 1985.
Steiger, Brad. *Revelation: The Divine Fire.* New York: Prentice-Hall, 1973.
———. *The Star People.* New York: Berkley Books, 1982.
Wennergren, Kristina. *UFO-Lexicon.* Göteborg, Sweden: no publisher, 1990.

NEW BEING PROJECT

Founded by New Age psychologist David Pursglove, the New Being Project seeks to establish groups of sensitive, creative individuals who are capable of "high quality communication with intelligences different from ourselves." Also known as "Other Consciousnesses" (OCs), these "intelligences" may be the key to a great evolutionary leap for the human race, according to Pursglove. Humans must exercise their paranormal abilities, and for this purpose Pursglove developed "calling circles," in which no more that eight members gather together to contact OCs through group telepathy, meditation, and other techniques. For the New Being Project, "E.T. . . . means *Evolutionary Transformation.*"

See Also: Humor and UFOs; New Age
Further Reading:
Pursglove, Paul David. *Zen in the Art of Close Encounters: Crazy Wisdom and UFOs.* Berkeley: New Being Project, 1995.

THE NIGHT CALLER

In this 1965 British film an alien is sent to earth to provide women for genetic experiments on his home planet. His modus operandi is to advertise for models and ship them back to his planet. Two scientists discover the alien's energy transmitter. One scientist is strangled by the alien when she discovers his whereabouts. The other scientist and a police inspector finally catch the alien. This film anticipates a major theme of later alien-abduction literature, namely, that extraterrestrials are involved in ongoing genetic and sexual experiments with human beings.

Armitage Films 1965; 84 min. Director: John Gilling; Writer: Jim O'Connolly; Cinematography: Stephen Dade; Cast: John Saxon, Maurice Denham, Patricia Haines, Alfred Burke, John Carson, Jack Watson.

NIGHT OF THE BIG HEAT

In this 1967 British film alien protoplasm takes over a British island and causes a winter heat wave so fierce that most of the island's inhabitants are burned to death. The survivors discover the energy-starved aliens, desperate for any heat source. The aliens finally are melted by a storm caused by the heat-saturated atmosphere.

Planet 1967; 97 min. Director: Terence Fisher; Writers: Ronald Liles, Pip Baker, Jane Baker; Cinematography: Reg Wyer; Cast: Christopher Lee, Peter Cushing, Patrick Allen, Sarah Lawson, Jane Merrow, William Lucas, Jack Bligh.

NIMROD

Nimrod was a hunter, the son of Cush, and the moving force behind the Tower of Babel. In the Book of Genesis, he is mentioned briefly in chapter 10: "Nimrod . . . was the first on earth to be a mighty man. He was a mighty hunter before the Lord; therefore it is said, 'Like Nimrod a mighty hunter before the Lord.' The beginning of his kingdom was Babel, Erech, and Accad" (Gen. 10:9–10).

According to Jewish legend, Nimrod was one of the Nephilim—the children of the angels who, as it says in Genesis verse 6:2, "saw that the daughters of men were fair and . . . took to wife such of them as they chose." If these "angels" were actually ufonauts, as the ancient-astronaut school of thought speculates, such a geneology would make Nimrod a descendant of aliens.

In addition to his celestial heritage, Nimrod is associated with ufological speculation through his connection with the Tower of Babel. According to biblical scholars, the Hebrews took a dim view of ziggurats—the pyramid-like temples of ancient Mesopotamia—and the story of Babel is said to embody their critique of such structures. Nimrod, in other words, was a builder of ziggurats. Where this ties into ancient-astronaut thinking is that certain authors, notably Zecharia Sitchin, view the original ziggurats as having been landing pads for alien spaceships. Thus, Nimrod, a descendant of the celestial "sons of God," would seem to have been involved in the construction of these landing pads.

See Also: Ancient Astronauts; Angels; Nephilim
Further Reading:
Ginzberg, Louis. *The Legends of the Jews.* Philadelphia: Jewish Publication Society of America, 1954.
Ronner, John. *Know Your Angels: The Angel Almanac with Biographies of 100 Prominent Angels in Legend and Folklore, and Much More.* Murfreesboro, TN: Mamre, 1993.
Sitchin, Zecharia. *The Twelfth Planet.* New York: Avon, 1976.

NINETEENTH-CENTURY AIRSHIP TALES

On January 12, 1836, in Cherbourg, France, a glowing, doughnut-shaped object two-thirds the size of the moon appeared to rotate on its axis as it flew by.

On July 13, 1860, citizens of Wilmington, Delaware, saw a 200-foot-long object at 100 feet altitude for about a minute. It moved in a straight line. In front of it was a black cloud and behind it at 100-foot intervals were three glowing red balls. The object gave off sparks in the manner of a rocket.

According to a Mr. Oleson of El Campo, Texas, in September 1862 the Danish brig *Christine* sank in the Indian Ocean, stranding five injured crew members, including Oleson, on a tiny, rocky island. High in the air the men saw what seemed to be an immense ship coming straight down toward them. It crashed against a cliff a few hundred yards away. They could see that the vehicle was propelled by four huge wings. The men found food in metal boxes, which saved them from starvation. They also found the bodies of more than a dozen men dressed in strange garments. The men were about 12 feet tall and they had long, silky hair and beards. Oleson took from one of the bodies a ring two and a quarter inches in diameter, which had been on the being's thumb. It was made of an alloy unknown to any jeweler who examined it and had two reddish stones that likewise could not be identified. The shipwrecked sailors built a raft of the wrecked spaceship and left the island. They were picked up within a few days by a Russian ship bound for Australia. The other men succumbed to their injuries before reaching port.

On March 22, 1870, in the Atlantic Ocean off the Coast of West Africa, the captain and crew of a ship saw a gray object shaped like a doughnut divided into four connected sections. There was a long hook trailing from its center. It was moving against the wind and was in view for 30 minutes.

In Marseilles, France, on August 1, 1871, an astronomer watched what he thought was a meteor at night for 18 minutes. It went rapidly eastward, suddenly slowed, and maintained the slower pace for the next seven minutes. Then it stopped, was motionless for a brief time, and headed to the north. Seven minutes later it stopped and headed east. It made one more short stop and then streaked toward the horizon and out of sight.

On January 22, 1878, an orange object was observed high in the morning sky near Denison, Texas. It approached, and when it was nearly overhead it appeared to be the size of a large saucer and at great height.

On June 6, 1884, cowboys rounding up cattle heard a whirring noise overhead and saw a blazing object plunging to earth. They rode over to where they could see the crashed vessel. There were fragments of machinery so hot as to make it impossible to approach it. The sand was fused over a 20-foot by 80-foot space and was still bubbling and hissing. One man's face was blistered and his hair

singed as a result of approaching too closely, and the cowboys left the scene to get medical help for him. On the morning of June 7 a party arrived on the scene to inspect the crash site. By this time the machinery had cooled enough to be approached but not handled. Several metal pieces were picked up using spades. Later the vehicle's remains were seen to vanish in a heavy rainstorm.

On August 31, 1895, in Oxford, England, renowned linguist and lexicographer James Augustus Henry Murray saw a brilliant luminous body emerge over the tops of some trees and move eastward across the sky. At first it looked like a brilliant meteor, larger than Venus, but then he thought it may be some artificial firework. It did not emit any spark or leave any trail. It became rapidly dimmer and disappeared behind a tree. Twenty-five minutes later two observers in London watched a star traverse a quarter of the sky.

On November 27, 1896, H. G. Shaw of Stockton, California, said he encountered three nude weightless aliens that tried without success to drag him into a nearby airship. In April 1897 there was a claim that a spaceship crashed in Aurora, Texas, and that its Martian occupant died.

On December 3, 1896, a dairy farmer in Stanford Heights, California, went out to investigate a loud noise and cries for help heard late in the evening. He found the wreckage of an airship and two injured occupants. One witness concluded the ship was a fake that had been dragged to the site as a hoax.

In Rhodes, Iowa, on April 9, 1897, a rapidly approaching bright light making mechanical noises plunged into a reservoir. The hissing could be heard for miles and the water became boiling hot.

At 4 A.M. on April 9, 1897, in Lanark, Illinois, a cigar-shaped airship plowed into the ground. Two of the occupants were killed outright. A third, dressed in robes, shouted hysterically and then lapsed into unconsciousness. He was taken into a nearby farmhouse, and the farmer started charging admission to see the crash remains. Soon the pilot regained consciousness, said he was from Mars, and went out to repair the ship. He flew away with the bodies of his companions.

In the early-morning hours of April 11, 1897, in Pavilion, Michigan, a fast-moving airship exploded overhead. Various pieces of machinery were found scattered throughout the town, with minute fragments reportedly penetrating roofing shingles.

In Decatur, Illinois, on April 14, 1897, a man saw a bright light moving in the sky as he was on his way to the barn to milk the cow. As he finished milking a loud crash was heard, and much of the roof was ripped off the barn. The frightened cow kicked the man in the head, rendering him unconscious. When he regained consciousness he told his wife he had glimpsed an airship crashing into the roof and sailing on.

In April 1897 in Humboldt, Tennessee, a man reported seeing an airship that had crashed in the woods, its occupant encased in ice.

On April 16, 1897, in Jefferson, Iowa, an airship fell to earth, leaving a large hole in the ground.

In Aurora, Texas, on the morning of April 17, 1897, residents saw an airship flying to the north over town before it collided with a windmill and exploded. Debris was scattered over several acres. A badly disfigured body was found in the wreckage, which a local signal service officer or blacksmith (reports vary) identified as a native of Mars. Subsequent investigations failed to turn up any evidence that the crash actually occurred.

—*Jerome Clark*

Further Reading:
Bullard, Thomas E., ed. *The Airship File: A Collection of Texts Concerning Phantom Airships and Other UFOs, Gathered from Newspapers and Periodicals Mostly During the Hundred Years Prior to Kenneth Arnold's Sighting.* Bloomington, IN: The Author, 1982.
———. *The Airship File, Supplement 2.* Bloomington, IN: The Author, 1990.
Chariton, Wallace O. *The Great Texas Airship Mystery.* Plano, TX: Wordware Publishing, 1991.
Cohen, Daniel. *The Great Airship Mystery: A UFO of the 1890s.* New York: Dodd, Mead, 1981.
Randle, Kevin D. *A History of UFO Crashes.* New York: Avon Books, 1995.

NO SURVIVORS PLEASE

This is a 1963 German film in which aliens take over the bodies of leading politicians and military men in order to create a war that will kill off all people on earth, clearing it for the inhabitants of another planet. The notion of aliens infiltrating important terrestrial positions as a prelude to invasion is widespread in the alien-invasion genre and echoes concerns expressed in a certain subgenre of UFO conspiracy literature.

Hans Alban Films 1963; 92 min. Director: Hans Albin, Peter Berneis; Cast: Maria Perschy, Uwe Friedrichsen, Robert Cunningham, Karen Blanguernon, Gustavo Rojo.

NORTH DAKOTA ALIEN SHOOTING INCIDENT

Four men were hunting in the Great Plains of North Dakota in 1961 when they had a bizarre experience with extraterrestrials. All men were professionals, "extremely reliable and responsible." Two of them noticed a descending glow, and, thinking it was an imminent plane crash, rushed to the scene. Arriving on the scene, they saw a "silo-appearing type craft" with four humanoid beings around it, about five feet tall and wearing white suits. They heard a loud explosion, and a being motioned them to stop.

The men left to get the police, who chased some glowing lights, found nothing, and left. The hunters, on their way back home, then saw the UFO a second time. One fired a rifle at an extraterrestrial and hit it in the shoulder. The being yelled, "Now what the hell did you do that for?" The hunter did not know why he had shot at an alien, and he could not remember what happened to the UFO or the extraterrestrials. He said, "All of us knew or had the feeling that something was missing there, and to this day we don't know what it was."

Later, strangers, who they took to be U.S. Air Force investigators because of their official demeanor, asked many questions—about what clothes the shooter had been wearing during the incident, whether he had gotten out of the car into the muddy field—asked to see his muddy boots, and told him not to say anything to anyone. These figures resemble the men in black of other UFO claims, who ask oddly detailed questions and seem to be Air Force officials.

See Also: Men in Black

Further Reading:
Hynek, J. Allen, and Jacques Vallee. *The Edge of Reality: A Progress Report on Unidentified Flying Objects.* Chicago: Henry Regnery, 1975.

Schwarz, Berthold E. *UFO-Dynamics: Psychiatric and Psychic Aspects of the UFO Syndrome.* 2 vols. Moore Haven, FL: Rainbow Books, 1983.

NOT OF THIS EARTH

The original film was released in 1956; a remake was released in 1988. An alien posing as a human being collects human blood for shipment back to his home planet—extraterrestrial vampires who need the blood to keep their dying race nourished. He dies because the high pitch of a motorbike siren causes him so much pain he crashes his car. The original film anticipates the idea that ufonauts need to draw sustenance from human genetic material extracted during the abduction of human beings.

Concorde 1988; 92 min. Director: Jim Wynorski; Writers: Jim Wynorski, R. J. Robertson; Cast: Traci Lords, Arthur Roberts, Lenny Juliano, Rebecca Perle, Ace Mask, Roger Lodge.

An alien agent played by Paul Birch is sent to Earth from the distant planet Davana to collect blood for his dying race in the 1956 film Not of This Earth. *(The Del Valle Archive)*

OCCULT

Most of the religious groups to arise around the fringes of the mainstream ufological community draw, to a greater or lesser extent, from much older strands of occult spirituality. The very term "occult" is, however, ambiguous.

In the same way in which the expression "New Age" came to have negative associations after the wave of media attention it received in the late 1980s, "occult" acquired negative connotations after a similar wave of media coverage in the 1970s. Also, because occultism encompasses a broad range of ideas and practices, it is difficult to adequately define or delimit the term. This is compounded by the negative connotations the term has acquired, both inside and outside of the metaphysical-occult subculture: "Occultism" calls to mind images of robed figures conducting arcane rituals for less-than-socially desired ends. As a consequence, very few participants in the metaphysical-occult subculture would identify themselves as occultists.

There have been innumerable attempts to define "occult," all of which are more or less inadequate. It derives from a root word meaning "hidden," and the original connotation of the word was that it referred to a body of esoteric beliefs and practices that in some sense were "hidden" from the average person in the street (e.g., practices and knowledge that remain inaccessible until after an initiation). An alternate meaning is that occult practices deal with energies that are normally imperceptible and thus hidden from the ordinary person (e.g., magical and astrological forces).

In the modern world, however, these meanings fail to encompass many occult phenomena. Thus occultism is a catch-all category for certain religious and psychic phenomena that fall outside the boundaries of mainstream society, science, and re-ligion. It includes religious bodies in the theosophical and spiritualist traditions, psi phenomena, and divinatory practices such as astrology. Metaphysical bodies in the nineteenth century "mind-cure" tradition (such as Religious Science and Unity) and certain Asian spiritual practices (such as yoga and meditation) are on the boundary and are also sometimes classified as being occult. UFO religions are a syncretistic, diverse lot that often draw on several of these traditions.

See Also: Metaphysical; New Age; Religions, UFO

Further Reading:

Bletzer, June G. *The Donning International Encyclopedic Psychic Dictionary.* Norfolk, VA: Donning, 1986.

Shepard, Leslie A., ed. *Encyclopedia of Occultism and Parapsychology.* Detroit: Gale Research, 1991.

OTHERWORLD

With the mysteries of the UFO phenomenon no closer to solution than during the first decades of the flying-saucer phenomenon, it is not surprising that several ufologists have abandoned the extraterrestrial hypothesis (ETH—the notion that UFOs are alien spaceships). In lieu of the ETH, some have gravitated to the idea that UFOs are spiritual or quasi-spiritual phenomena that flip into and out of our reality from another dimension. The basic idea of one or more spiritual otherworlds, or dimensions, existing alongside the world of our ordinary, everyday experience is taken for granted in almost every religious and cultural tradition. For many of these traditions, the spiritual realm is more important, and often more real, than the physical realm. Crossculturally and across many different historical periods, there is widespread agreement on certain important traits of this otherworld. One point of agreement is that living human beings—or their spiritual

An engraving of a spiritual pilgrim piercing the boundaries of this world and perceiving the spheres and secrets of the otherworld. (American Religion Collection)

essences—can journey to the otherworld. This is particularly true of the many cultures influenced by shamanism. So perhaps the Space Brothers are, at least figuratively, technological shamans.

See Also: Shamanism
Further Reading:
Eliade, Mircea, ed. *Encyclopedia of Religion.* New York: Macmillan, 1987.
Thompson, Keith. *Angels and Aliens: UFOs and the Mythic Imagination.* Reading, MA: Addison-Wesley, 1991.

OXFORD ABDUCTION

While David Stephens and Glen Gray were driving toward Lake Thompson, Maine, in October 1975, Stephens lost control of the car as it veered sharply in the direction of Oxford under the guidance of some outside force. Their ride was uncommonly smooth and quick, and they remember seeing cows shaking their heads back and forth. Moments later they saw a strange craft with blue, green, and yellow lights hovering above them, shining a blinding light on their car. They did not remember the next few minutes; they only felt their eyes burning painfully and noticed that each others' eyes had turned bright orange. They were also a mile farther down the road.

They thought the UFO had gone, but 45 minutes later they saw two lighted disks hovering over an island in a pond, which seemed to them like an ocean. In reality the pond is small and has no island. They felt they had been told something like, "We're not done with you yet." They drove frantically to Stephens's parents' house, where weird things continued to occur—an ashtray rose a foot in the air, a black cube hurdled across the room and disappeared into the wall, "golden wires" appeared over the TV screen, and they heard footsteps on the roof. The next morning, Stephens was visited by a stranger who said, "Better keep your mouth shut if you know what's good for you."

Gray and Stephens were hypnotized in an effort to recover their memories of the event. Gray became so upset that he refused to speak of it again and moved to Oklahoma. Stephens described a room with shiny gray walls, where he met a four-and-a-half-foot, mushroom-headed being, with large eyes, a nose, and no mouth, wearing a long black robe. He was led to an "operating room" where he had samples of blood, hair, and fingernails taken. He punched one of the aliens, but it didn't respond. The beings told him they had been watching him and would see him again, then returned him to the car.

Dr. Herbert Hopkins, who performed the hypnosis, received a strange, inhuman visitor later in the year—the face was "dead white," his head never moved, and he wore lipstick to create the illusion of lips. He told Hopkins that he was a UFO investigator, but the organization he named didn't exist. He ordered Hopkins to destroy the Stephens tapes and any written material, or he would be killed, just like Barney Hill (of the Hill abduction fame). After the being left Hopkins barely had the energy to walk, and he saw a strange, blue-white light at the end of his driveway and later found weird tread marks in his driveway. Hopkins destroyed the tapes as instructed. Investigators link this being with the so-called men in black.

See Also: Abductees; Close Encounters; Men in Black

Further Reading:
Beckley, Timothy Green. *Mystery of the Men in Black: The UFO Silencers.* New Brunswick, NJ: Inner Light Publications, 1990.
Bullard, Thomas E. *UFO Abductions: The Measure of a Mystery, Volume 1: Comparative Study of Abduction Reports;* and *Volume 2: Catalogue of Cases.* Mount Rainier, MD: Fund for UFO Research, 1987.
Lorenzen, Coral, and Jim Lorenzen. *Abducted! Confrontations with Beings from Outer Space.* New York: Berkley Medallion, 1977.

OZ FACTOR

The expression "Oz factor" refers to the sensation of being transported into another reality during a UFO sighting. Coined by author Jenny Randles in *UFO Reality* (1983), she describes the feeling as one of "being transported temporarily from our world into another, where reality is but slightly different." In a later book, *Sixth Sense* (1987), Randles hypothesizes that the Oz factor could be indicative of the observer's having entered an altered state of consciousness.

Further Reading:
Randles, Jenny. *Sixth Sense.* Topsfield, MA: Salem House Publishers, 1987.
———. *UFO Reality: A Critical Look at the Physical Evidence.* London: Robert Hale, 1983.

PADRICK, SID

Television repairman Sid Padrick was invited aboard a UFO while walking on Manresa Beach, California, in January 1965. When he first saw the UFO, he ran in terror, but a voice told him, "We are not hostile," and he decided to take a chance. He entered the craft and met a being who said, "You may call me Xeno," and told Padrick to ask any question he liked. There were nine beings on the ship, all in uniform, looking 20–25 years old, intelligent, and energetic. The only real difference from human features was their pointy chin and nose. They paid no attention to Padrick.

Xeno gave him a tour of the ship, which had two levels, an elevator, and 14 rooms. There were no corners, and light came through the walls. Xeno politely answered all of Padrick's questions and showed him a photograph of their city on a planet behind a planet visible from earth. There was no disease, crime, schools, or police on their home planet, and everyone was trained from childhood for one specific task. Xeno then brought him to the "consultation room," which resembled a chapel and said, "Would you like to pay your respects to the Supreme Deity?" When Padrick asked if this was the same as God, Xeno said, "There is only one." Padrick prayed and felt a holy presence for the first time in his life. He thought the beings might be on a spiritual mission.

U.S. Air Force investigators were certain that he was lying and abandoned the inquiry. Some ufologists pointed to a psychological explanation—a planet of his unconscious mind. As for Padrick, he continued to have contact with the aliens, gave some lectures, but mostly remained private and contented. "I have not had a day of sickness since then. I feel absolutely good every day," he said a few years after the incident.

See Also: Contactees; Healing

Further Reading:
Keel, John A. *UFOs: Operation Trojan Horse.* New York: G. P. Putnam's Sons, 1970.
Lorenzen, Coral, and Jim Lorenzen. *Encounters with UFO Occupants.* New York: Berkley Medallion, 1976.

PAJAMA PARTY

In this 1964 film a Martian pioneer arrives at a swimming-pool party and falls in love with Annette Funicello. One of the innumerable beach-party movies from the 1960s, it has no particular relationship with UFO thinking, though the all-too-human Martian could pass for the aliens that people much contactee literature.

AIP 1964; 85 min. Director: Don Weis; Writer: Louis M. Heyward; Cinematography: Floyd Crosby; Cast: Tommy Kirk, Annette Funicello, Elsa Lanchester, Buster Keaton, Harvey Lembeck, Jesse White, Dorothy Lamour, Frankie Avalon.

PALENQUE IMAGE

An ancient Mexican artifact—the lid of a sarcophagus found in a pre-Columbian temple in Palenque—has given rise to considerable speculation regarding the possibility of humanity's contact with ufonauts in the distant past. This coffin cover is decorated with an elaborate design that appears to show a person piloting some sort of mechanical craft, perhaps even a spacecraft. Erich von Däniken and many other writers in the ancient-astronaut school of thought have referred to it as one among many anomalies that resist explanation in terms of our current understanding of the human past.

See Also: Ancient Astronauts

Further Reading:
von Däniken, Erich. *Chariots of the Gods? Unsolved Mysteries of the Past.* Trans. Michael Heron. New York: G. P. Putnam's Sons, 1970.

The Palenque Image is an elaborate design on a coffin cover that appears to show a person piloting some sort of mechanical craft, perhaps even a spacecraft. (American Religion Collection)

PARANORMAL AND OCCULT THEORIES ABOUT UFOS

In 1758 Swedish scientist and mystic Emanuel Swedenburg published a book, *Earths in the Solar World,* on his observations of other planets and their occupants. He claimed to know this because he had traveled to these places in his astral body. Nineteenth-century occult teacher, writer, and medium Madame Helena Petrovna Blavatsky, founder of theosophy, theorized a complex cosmic spiritual order that engulfed such "Ascended Masters" as the Lords of the Flame from Venus. She claimed to have spoken with these godlike beings and taught their beliefs to earthfolk. Later Guy Ballard, who popularized theosophy for Americans, founded the I AM organization, perhaps the first religious group to make aliens the center of worship.

The UFO contactee subculture was rooted in Southern California. In 1945 Meade Layne of San Diego theorized that flying saucers were "etherships" piloted by "etherians." The etherians, Layne claimed, have the same physical features as we do, live on planets with stars and solar systems as we do, but are highly advanced. Some ufologists claimed that UFOs did not come from outer space but rather that they were visiting from a "fourth dimension." In 1948 the magazine *Fate* was founded by Curtis Fuller and Ray Palmer. *Fate* was dedicated to things such as UFOs, ghosts, and archaeological mysteries. Another saucer theorist was Thomas M. Comella, who believed that the reason flying saucers could not be accounted for by scientists is because they transcend our immediately perceptible world.

An English magazine, *Flying Saucer Review,* printed an article that pushed a demonological interpretation of the UFO phenomenon. Some claimed that Satan himself was behind UFOs. John Keel, a prominent writer for *Flying Saucer Review,* claimed that aliens were once gods and superkings of the earth. But when they mated with humans they lost their powers and have waged war on earth ever since. Some people believe that even hoaxers are not really making up their stories. They feel that hoaxers were set up by the aliens to make them look foolish so as to thwart humanity's knowledge of their existence. Even a confessed hoax is all part of the conspiracy. To many ufologists these claims were isolated voices, trying to explain one unexplainable phenomena with another.

In 1992 *The Omega Project* by Kenneth Ring was published. Ring believes that spacemen and monsters live in an "imaginal realm," a "third kingdom" between reality and fantasy, accessible through "certain altered states of consciousness." In extensive psychological testing of sample groups, Ring found that abductees and near-death experiencers are emotionally indistinguishable. Of all the occult theories, Ring's is the most compelling because he at least studied some real people instead of trying to just theoretically correlate near-death experiences and abductions.

—*Jerome Clark*

See Also: Near-Death Experience; Occult
Further Reading:
Ring, Kenneth. *The Omega Project: Near-Death Experiences, UFO Encounters, and Mind at Large.* New York: William Morrow, 1992.
Vallee, Jacques. *Dimensions.* Chicago: Contemporary Books, 1988.

PASCAGOULA ABDUCTION

After the Betty and Barney Hill case, the most famous alien abduction took place on the Pascagoula River in Mississippi on October 11, 1973. Although less dramatic than other abductions, this incident was made prominent by the large amount of publicity it received.

Sometime in the early evening Calvin Parker, 19, and Charles Hickson, 42, were fishing when they heard and then spotted a descending UFO about 30 feet across and 10 feet high. It landed in a clearing about 35 yards behind them. A door opened, and three eerie figures floated toward them. About five feet tall, the odd-appearing beings were gray-colored with wrinkled bodies and clawlike hands. Some observers later speculated that the beings were some kind of robot.

Parker fainted. Two of the entities grabbed Hickson by the arms, and the man felt himself becoming paralyzed. The third picked up Parker, and together the group moved back into the craft. Something like a giant "eye" the size of a football floated to within a half a foot of Hickson's face. He tried to cry out, "Please don't take me away!" but he was too paralyzed to talk. Then, almost as abruptly as it had begun, the kidnapping ended. The beings returned the two men to the dock. As they left, Hickson heard, "We are peaceful. We mean you no harm" inside of his head.

See Also: Abductees; Close Encounters
Further Reading:
Blum, Ralph, with Judy Blum. *Beyond Earth: Man's Contact with UFOs.* New York: Bantam Books, 1974.

Gansberg, Judith M., and Alan L. Gansberg. *Direct Encounters: The Personal Histories of UFO Abductees.* New York: Walker, 1980.
Hickson, Charles, and William Mendez. *UFO Contact at Pascagoula.* Tucson, AZ: Wendelle C. Stevens, 1983.
Hynek, J. Allen, and Jacques Vallee. *The Edge of Reality: A Progress Report on Unidentified Flying Objects.* Chicago: Henry Regnery, 1975.

PHANTOM EMPIRE

The original 1935 film serial by this name was influenced by hollow-earth theory. In it, bad guys want to force singing cowboy Gene Autry off his ranch so they can mine a secret radium deposit. Meanwhile, 25,000 feet underground, an advanced ancient civilization wants to avoid discovery and dispatches Thunder Riders to the surface to ward off nosy cowboys.

It was remade as a movie of the same name 53 years later. In this version, an expedition into Bronson Caverns to discover a lost city encounters a leather-suited alien queen accompanied by a robot, a group of ragged mutants, women in fur bikinis, and several dinosaurs.

Mascot 1935; 245 min. Director: B. Reeves Eason, Otto Brower; Cast: Gene Autry, Frankie Darro, Betsy King Ross, Smiley Burnette.

PHANTOM FROM SPACE

In this 1953 film an invisible alien crash-lands his flying saucer near a large U.S. observatory. He kills two men and some innocent picnickers. The police and scientists investigate the killings and find the alien's fatal flaw: In order to survive on earth he must wear a helmet containing air from his own world. The scientists lure the alien into their observatory and put him in an infrared light machine, which makes him visible. They then remove his helmet. A chase ensues, and the alien falls to his death from a ladder.

The theme of extraterrestrial invisibility, repeated in later films such as *Predator,* transforms hostile aliens into semispiritualized presences—an image of the alien Other in which extraterrestrials are characterized as "technological demons." One rarely finds invisibility attributed to ufonauts in UFO literature, although flying saucers often seem to fade into and out of existence, which is a trait suggestive of invisibility.

Planet Filmways 1953; 72 min. Director: W. Lee Wilder; Cast: Ted Cooper, Rudolph Anders, Noreen Nash, James Seay, Harry Landers.

THE PHILADELPHIA EXPERIMENT (PROJECT RAINBOW)

The story of the Philadelphia experiment originated in October 1955 with a series of letters mailed to Morris K. Jessup from a person who referred to himself either as Carlos Miguel Allende or Carl Allen. Written in multicolored ink and characterized by a peculiar style, the letters focused on levitation as a phenomenon that technology could control. Referring to Jessup's books and lectures on levitation and antigravity, Allende stated in further communications that experiments had been successfully conducted to achieve the invisibility of a destroyer: The ship had allegedly disappeared from its docking position to reappear in another harbor.

Allende claimed that a scientist, Franklin Reno, had accomplished this feat by connecting the twin forces of electromagnetism and gravity as a special application of Albert Einstein's unified field theory. Allende further claimed to have actually watched the destroyer, the USS *Eldridge,* disappear from Philadelphia harbor. The *Eldridge* supposedly reappeared in the Norfolk area. In a letter to Jessup dated January 13, 1965, Allende wrote:

> The result of the experiment was COMPLETE INVISIBILITY of a ship destroyer type, AND ALL its crew, while at sea [Oct. 1943]. The field was effective in an oblate spheroidal shape, extending 100 yards . . . OUT from each beam of the ship. Any person within that sphere became vague in form. . . . Somehow, also, the experimental ship disappeared from its Philadelphia dock and only a very few minutes later appeared at its other dock in the Norfolk, Newport News, Portsmouth area . . . the ship then AGAIN disappeared and went BACK to its Philadelphia dock.

Allende further noted that the experiment resulted in horrific side effects on the ship's crew. For example, according to Allende, some of these crewmen later disappeared into thin air during a fight at a bar.

A similar account of a disappeared ship was mailed as an annotated copy of Jessup's book *The Case for the UFO* to Admiral Furth of the Office of Naval Research. Although the admiral disregarded the annotations, some of his junior officers invited Jessup to examine the copy. Although three different persons—who identified themselves as A, B, and Jemi—had written the annotations, he immediately noticed a strong similarity between the letters he had received and the writing he was examining.

The annotated copy of *The Case for the UFO* and the letters were subsequently published by Varo Manufacturing Company, an electronics contractor for the U.S. Navy. The book—known as *The Varo Edition*—raised rumors of the navy being interested in the topic (though it was never more than the interest of some navy officers). A best-selling book about the Philadelphia experiment was published in 1979. More books were published and a movie was produced on the subject, and "The Experiment" became a permanent chapter of paranormal lore.

See Also: Antigravity; Hoaxes; Time Travel
Further Reading:

Jessup, M. K. *The Case for the UFO.* New York: Citadel Press, 1955.

Moore, William L., with Charles Berlitz. *The Philadelphia Experiment: Project Invisibility: An Account of a Search for a Secret Navy Wartime Project That May Have Succeeded Too Well.* New York: Grosset and Dunlap, 1979.

Story, Ronald D., ed. *The Encyclopedia of UFOs.* Garden City, NY: Doubleday, 1980.

Steiger, Brad, Sherry Steiger, and Alfred Bielek. *The Philadelphia Experiment and Other UFO Conspiracies.* New Brunswick, NJ: Inner Light Publications, 1990.

Steiger, Brad, and Joan Whritenour, eds. *The Allende Letters: A Challenging New Theory on the Origin of Flying Saucers.* New York: Universal, 1968.

Vallee, Jacques. *Revelations: Alien Contact and Human Deception.* New York: Ballantine Books, 1991.

PLAN 9 FROM OUTER SPACE

Aliens try to conquer earth by reviving the dead as zombies. This 1956 film—a cult classic—has been nominated as the worst film of all time. Cadillac hubcaps are used for flying saucers.

J. Edward Reynolds 1956; 78 min. Director: Edward D. Wood Jr.; Writer: Edward D. Wood Jr.; Cinematography:

Aliens plan to take over the Earth with an army of reanimated corpses in the 1956 film Plan 9 from Outer Space. *Vampira is pictured on a movie poster as one such zombie. (The Del Valle Archive)*

William C. Thompson; Cast: Bela Lugosi, Tor Johnson, Lyle Talbot, Vampira, Gregory Walcott, Duke Moore, Tom Keene.

POPDOWN

This is a film about two aliens sent to observe earth life that become fascinated with pop music in 1968 London. Not a remarkable film, but one that stimulates the thought: If UFOs really are extraterrestrial spacecraft, what is it about humanity and/or about our planets that so fascinates ufonauts?

Fremar Productions 1968; 98 min. Director/Writer: Fred Marshall; Cinematography: Oliver Wood; Cast: Diane Keen, Jane Bates, Zoot Money, Carol Rachell, Debbie Slater, Birl Aaron.

POPULAR CULTURE

Depending on how one delimits the UFO category, the impact of UFOs on popular culture has been either widespread or minimal. If one chooses to confine UFOs to the specific, contemporary phenomenon that began with Kenneth Arnold's sighting of flying disks on July 24, 1947, then UFOs have exercised comparatively little influence on the public imagination. There was, however, a much older interest in space travel and the possibilities of encounters with extraterrestrial beings that antedates the UFO modern craze by at least several centuries. This larger interest has had a much broader impact on our culture.

The theme of alien invasion, for example, which provides the basic plot for countless science-fiction novels and popular films, is at least as old as H. G. Wells's 1898 novel, *The War of the Worlds*. Thus, although the UFO phenomenon of the 1940s and 1950s may have stimulated writers to compose more alien-invasion stories, the basic plot of such tales has a much older origin. Even in the science-fiction literature of the last 50 years, one notes a

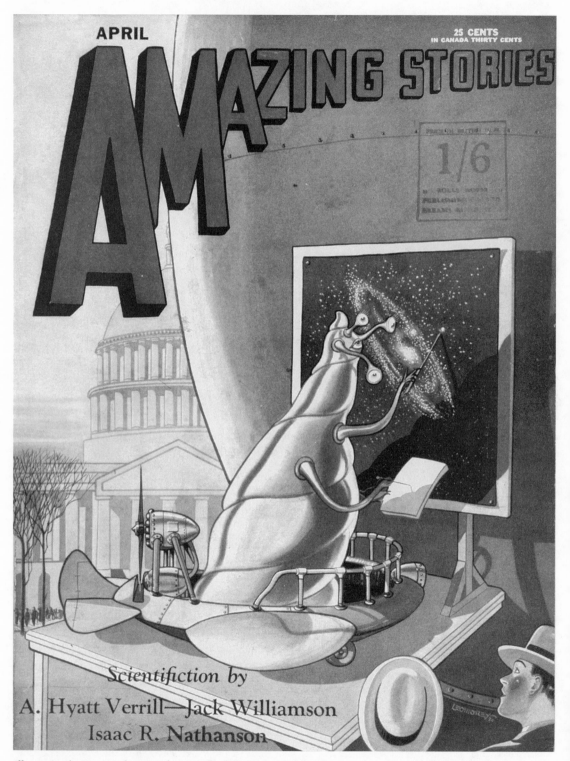

Illustration by Isaac Nathanson of an invader from Andromeda explaining where he comes from, from the cover of Amazing Stories *magazine, April 1930 (Mary Evans Picture Library)*

marked tendency to avoid bringing anything like contemporaneous UFOs into the narrative. This is because, as many observers have noted, the conscious goal of better sci-fi authors is to compose so-called plausible fictions—an aim that easily works at cross purposes with the flying-saucers-are-real! emphasis of most ufological literature.

The same observation holds true, though to a lesser extent, for films and TV narratives. More recent Hollywood productions, from movies like *Independence Day* to TV shows like *X-Files,* seem to reflect a trend toward a more conscious appropriation of UFO lore in imaginative productions. Comic books, in contrast—particularly those that feature superheroes who constantly need unusual enemies to battle—have been less reticent to regularly throw in stories that merged contemporaneous flying-saucer interest with the older *The War of the Worlds*–type alien invasion plot.

There has been even less impact in the sphere of popular music. The first UFO-inspired song to become a hit record was the rather inane "One-eyed, One-horned, Flying Purple People Eater" (which later inspired an even more innane movie by the same name). A more profound if overworked theme was articulated in Neil Young's song about flying saucers rescuing a select group of human beings ("Mother Nature's Silver Seed") from the destruction of the earth and flying them to a "new home in the sun." Striking a more humorous note was the Byrds's popular "Hey, Mr. Spaceman!" and, in a similar vein, the more recent "Rapture" by Blondie. The light-heartedness of the latter two songs reflects the popular perception of UFOs as topics of humor rather than subjects of fear and trepidation.

Like the phenomenon itself, interest in UFOs tends to come and go in waves. During previous waves, toy manufacturers produced innumerable flying-saucer toys. In Eric Nesheim and Leif Nesheim's tribute to popular interest in the UFO phenomenon, *Saucer Attack!,* the authors note that "swarms of tin wind-up and battery-operated flying saucers 'made in Japan' invaded the American toy market in the '50s and '60s." Several different manufacturers also turned out "saucer guns" and "ray guns" in an effort to cash in on the UFO craze of the 1950s. Other products regularly embodying

UFO and outer space–related themes were and are Halloween costumes and lunch pails.

One component of pop culture that has been deeply penetrated by the UFO imagination is conspiracy theories. Over the past several decades conspiracy-dominated ideology has broken out of the political fringe to become a significant force in American society. Since the late 1980s UFOs have become an increasingly important theme in popular conspiracy literature. Many such theories portray the government as having secretly entered into an agreement with aliens that have supposedly been given carte blanche to abduct citizens and mutilate cattle in exchange for providing the military with extraterrestrial technology. Most UFO conspiracy theories involve speculation about the Roswell incident, the Majestic–12 document, and Area 51. The popular TV show *X-Files* is probably the single most important factor contributing to the popularity of UFO-related conspiracy thinking.

The area of popular culture where UFOs have exercised the most influence, however, is in the arena of religion and folklore. From spiritual groups based around channeled messages from the Space Brothers to folklore about cattle mutilations and fairy-like abductions by extraterrestrial ufonauts, UFOs and their occupants play a prominent role in the religious imagination of contemporary society. In many ways, UFOs and aliens have become a integral theme within the occult/metaphysical/New Age subculture—as omnipresent as notions of karma and reincarnation. Many of the entries in this encyclopedia speak to this dimension of the UFO phenomenon.

Another indicator of popular culture: supermarket tabloids. Tabloid aliens, it turns out, are either unusually fascinating beings that are not particularly hostile, or beings that have come to earth to warn or to help humanity in some manner. As examples of the latter, one can simply list stories in which the headlines indicate "humanitarian" themes, such as "UFO ALIENS KIDNAPPED ME. . . . NOW I CAN HEAL WITH MIRACLE POWERS," "UFOS WARN OF ATOMIC DIASTER," and "UFO DROPS CHRISTMAS FOOD TO STARVING ETHIOPIANS."

Less frequently, one comes across negatively valenced narratives, such as "UFO VAMPIRES MAY

BE MURDERING FISHERMEN." However, even in tabloid stories that portray extraterrestrials as hostile, this character trait is always ameliorated in some way, either by their humanlike behavior or by the silliness of their actions. A useful example of this kind of amelioration can be found in Karl Bova's story that appeared in the *Weekly World News* of April 16, 1991, "A SPACE ALIEN RAPED MY ELECTRIC BROOM":

> Puerto Vallarta, Mexico—A Mexican gardener is living in fear because the space alien that beat him to a pulp and tried to mate with his weed eater returned to his house—and raped his electric broom! . . .
>
> "I thought I'd seen the last of him until [recently when] somebody ransacked my house while I was at work. . . . The next morning I heard gasping and grunting noises coming from my closet and when I opened the door I found the alien on top of my electric broom." He called the police, "but by the time they arrived the alien was gone and my electric broom was twisted like a corkscrew. I know it was the same space alien. You never forget a face like that."

Clearly it would be difficult for even the most serious readers of this story to feel threatened by such a ridiculous alien, no matter how hostile.

Some of these popular periodicals give clues regarding how to determine if one's acquaintances or neighbors are space aliens. An article published February 6, 1986, in the *National Examiner,* for example, provides a list of "telltale signs," such as:

> Work or sleep periods that are unusually long or short (because the length of a day on an extraterrestrial world is probably of a different duration than one of our days).
>
> Fear, a mood change, or some other reaction (e.g., a rash) when close to equipment emitting electromagnetic radiation.
>
> Constant gathering of information (as part of an alien's ongoing research into terrestrial life).
>
> Decorates or paints home in odd ways (because aliens are not familiar with human aesthetic criteria).

What should one do upon discovering that their next-door neighbor is an alien? The *National Examiner* recommends against raising a fuss. After all, tabloid aliens are rarely dangerous, as expressed in the concluding citation from Brad Steiger: "In my opinion, based on my research,

space aliens living here on Earth are on a goodwill mission that will usher in a Golden Age for humanity. So take no action, other than giving that alien support—through friendship, kindness, and neighborly goodwill." In a similar vein, the front-page story of *The Weekly World News* of June 7, 1994, reported "12 U.S. SENATORS ARE SPACE ALIENS!" In this special report by Nick Mann, one of the featured citations in a sidebar quotes Senator Phil Gramm as admitting, "It's all true. We are space aliens. I'm amazed that it's taken you so long to find out." Other extraterrestrials who have posed as U.S. congressmen are Christopher Dodd, Bennett Johnston, William S. Cohen, Dennis Deconcini, Orrin Hatch, Nancy Kassebaum, Alan Simpson, Howell Heflin, John D. Rockefeller IV, Sam Nunn, and John Glenn. This information was revealed to President Bill Clinton at a special meeting with an alien representative, and a prominent picture included with the story shows the president shaking hands with an (apparently unclothed) humanoid extraterrestrial.

However, rather than raise alarm at this partial takeover by otherworldly outsiders, the writer quotes a "UFO expert" as saying, "I'm not saying this is bad, because it might very well be good. . . . If nothing else, these space alien legislators can serve as our links to a world that is even more advanced than our own." Again, the basic tabloid assumption about extraterrestrials seems to be that space aliens are not really so bad and are probably here to help us anyway—so why get upset?

See Also: Advertising; Film and Television; Humor and UFOs; Literature and the Alien Image; Music

Further Reading:

Curran, Douglas. *In Advance of the Landing: Folk Concepts of Outer Space.* New York: Abbeville Press, 1985.

Guffey, George R. "Aliens in the Supermarket: Science Fiction and Fantasy for 'Inquiring Minds.'" In *Aliens: The Anthropology of Science Fiction.* Edited by George E. Slusser and Eric S. Rabkin. Carbondale: Southern Illinois University Press, 1987.

Jung, Carl Gustav. *Flying Saucers: A Modern Myth of Things Seen in the Sky.* Princeton: Princeton University Press, 1978.

PREDATOR

In this 1987 film a group of covert-action commandos in the Central American jungles are picked off one by one by an alien big-game hunter who tracks down human beings for sport. It comes down to Arnold Schwarzenegger versus the alien monster in the end. The movie projects a very human image—sportsman/big-game hunter—onto the alien being. This image is not found in UFO literature. However, like other Hollywood themes that anticipated later ufological themes, perhaps this idea will eventually make its way into the UFO community.

Fox 1987; 107 min. Director: John McTiernan; Writer: Jim Thomas, John Thomas; Music: Alan Silvestri; Cinematography: Donald McAlpine; Cast: Arnold Schwarzenegger, Jesse Ventura, Sonny Landham, Bill Duke, Elpidia Carrillo, Carl Weathers, R. G. Armstrong, Richard Chaves, Shane Black, Kevin Peter Hall.

PREDATOR II

This sequel is set in a 1997 Los Angeles ghetto overrun by warring drug cartels but maintains the premise of a big-game hunter from outer space going after a well-trained and armed team of he-men for sport.

Fox 1990; 105 min. Director: Stephen Hopkins; Writers: John Thomas, Jim Thomas; Cinematography: Peter Levy; Cast: Danny Glover, Gary Busy, Ruben Blades, Maria Conchita Alonso, Bill Paxton, Robert Davi, Adam Baldwin, Kent McCord, Morton Downey Jr., Calvin Lockhart, Teri Weigel, Kevin Peter Hall.

PSALMS, BOOK OF

Psalms 18:8–20 is a visionary description of the Lord riding a cherub down to rout the enemies of the writer and to rescue him. These verses have been interpreted as referring to UFOs or extraterrestrials. Psalms 29 describes a storm as if it were the activity of the Lord himself. Psalms 104:3 again uses the classical imagery of a god riding on clouds.

Further Reading:
Downing, Barry H. *The Bible and Flying Saucers.* Philadelphia: J. B. Lippincott, 1968.
Goran, Morris. *The Modern Myth, Ancient Astronauts and UFOs.* South Brunswick, NJ: A. S. Barnes, 1978.

PSYCHOSOCIAL HYPOTHESIS

Scientific explanations for UFO phenomena often focus on the physical evidence produced in de-fense of an account. From crop circles and burn marks to radar trackings and photos, it becomes simply a matter of accounting for the evidence as the product of a known terrestrial source. But what is the scientist to do about all the eyewitness accounts and stories of abduction that don't produce material evidence, thereby precluding any authoritative verification? How does one explain the almost continuous stream of UFO sightings in light of the overwhelming, if not complete, refutation of their material existence?

It is into this lacuna that psychosocial theorists have ventured. Attempting to explain UFO phenomena exhibiting no credible physical evidence, they have drawn upon a body of psychological and sociological literature to formulate a theory that focuses attention away from causal agents from outer space to the human psyche. To be sure, few of them have attributed these phenomena entirely to the human mind. Rather, the bulk of the theorists recognize the power of cultural contexts to trigger, shape, and define human perceptions. According to the theory, this cultural context in dialogue with individual emotional or psychological needs lays the foundation for the appearance of UFOs. For some theorists, they are the result of changes in consciousness. Others favor an emphasis on imagination. In any case, the opening of the sphere of explanation to workings of the human psyche has proved fruitful, at least in theory.

The earliest roots of this theory lie in Carl Jung's work. Jung, an eminent psychologist and philosopher from Switzerland, reflected late in his life on UFO-like images in dreams, paintings, and works of science fiction. In his *Flying Saucers: A Modern Myth of Things Seen in the Sky,* he discussed a "psychic change in the air," linking it to the uncertainties of the twentieth century and the concurrent tensions between the rational conscious and intuitive unconscious. Without completely ruling out the possibility of alien spacecraft having been with us on earth, he emphasized the evolution of human consciousness as a key factor in "seeing" them at this moment in history. He wrote that as a result of peoples' perception of an ever more threatened existence, they have unconsciously projected themselves on these heavenly phenomena, thereby giving them undue significance.

Jung's well-known notion of the archetype also comes into play, most clearly in his discussion of the circular shape of the projections. Jung believed people were drawing upon archetypal symbols that connote wholeness or completeness. In an unconscious effort to "compensate for the split-mindedness of our age," people focused on the simpleness and totality of the round form.

Jung's contribution, though substantial, still begs the question: What exactly are UFOs? An interesting, but less than definitive, solution can be found in the notion of "materialized psychisms." Jung appreciated the potential of these theoretical psychic phenomena with physical properties, but he ultimately ruled out the possibility of such mind-over-matter manifestations, citing a dearth of any evidence. It is interesting that in the years since Jung's death some evidence of just such phenomena (notably spoon-bending à la Uri Geller) has emerged. Nevertheless, psychistic explanation has generally remained marginal to the growing literature on psychosocial theories.

Soon after Jung's book several other scholars published works that departed from Jung's themes, but these reflected a similar disenchantment with extraterrestrial explanations for UFO phenomena. Among them was Jacques Vallee, an astrophysicist by training. Following two rather scientifically grounded volumes on UFOs in 1965 and 1966, Vallee wrote *Passport to Magonia,* a radical departure from scientism. In it, he spoke of the emotional needs and loneliness of humankind, from which the notion of Magonia—a place of gentle folks and magic—was generated. This human-centered notion of the fantastical became a fertile ground for further development of psychosocial theories.

Just six years later, in 1975, Clark and Loren Coleman published *The Unidentified,* explicitly rejecting the involvement of aliens in human UFO experiences. Drawing on their knowledge of UFO stories and Jungian analysis, they extolled the symbolic meanings in UFO claims and forwarded their hypothesis that UFO experiences were largely the product of unusual mental states, such as sleep deprivation or ecstasy. In Jung's tradition, they em-

phasized the human psyche's distress under the strict rationalism of the twentieth century and claimed that the collective unconscious, in seeking to right the imbalance, was bursting onto the scene.

This theme of altered states was echoed in French ufologist Michel Monnerie's work of the late 1970s. Monnerie was generally critical of witnesses and ufologists alike for propagating UFO stories. But instead of dismissing them as hoaxsters, he claimed that visions resulting from altered states of consciousness were the source. Another Frenchman, Bertrand Méheust, was a bit more sympathetic to witnesses but was similarly convinced that the inspiration for their accounts was this-worldly. In a work comparing old science-fiction stories with modern UFO accounts, Méheust asserted that science-fiction writers and UFO experiencers were drawing on a common pool of images in the human imagination. Certainly, we can see sparks of Jung's "collective unconscious" in this explanation.

Into the 1980s, variations on these three ideas—satisfaction of human needs, altered consciousness, and collective imagination or archetype—continued to surface, notably in the works of Peter Rogerson and Hilary Evans. Some theories were more credible than others. However, in 1989 an interesting counterargument to the psychosocial hypothesis emerged out of a large-scale comparative analysis of all know abduction narratives. Some of these narratives had been collected from standard sources, whereas others had been produced as part of an experiment involving the intentional inducement of experiences through hypnosis. In the comparative study, Thomas E. Bullard found significant distinctions between the former "real" stories and the latter "imaginary" cases. Contrary to previous interpretations of the hypnosis experiments' data, Bullard argued that the "consistency in context and narrowness of variation" of the real stories compared to the "much greater looseness and diversity of imaginary abductions" indicated a common source that theories based on cultural and personal factors could not account for.

Perhaps he would have agreed with a theory proposed in 1970 by John Keel, which posited that "ultraterrestrial" beings—incomprehensible intelligences from another reality—were the force behind UFO-encounter stories. Skirting the difficulties of both the extraterrestrial and psychosocial hypotheses, Keel had addressed the all-too-real experiences of UFO phenomena in a way that still pushes the frontier of the believable almost 30 years later. He claimed that ultraterrestrials, able to create and manipulate matter, had been behind stories of fairies and creatures in times past, and they were behind the visions of aliens today. In a display of astonishing audacity, and despite lack of concrete evidence to support his theory, he attacked UFO buffs for being so ignorant and frightened that they couldn't or wouldn't face the truth about ultraterrestrial intrusion on earth.

Keel would have been an interesting subject for a study carried out in 1988 that proposed to use the notion of "fantasy-prone personalities" in evaluating close-encounter claimants. Working from a hypothesis that all claimants of such encounters had this type of personality, they tested UFO participants and a control group of non-UFO witnesses. Surprisingly, they found no significant differences. Although far from dealing a fatal blow to psychosocial theories, the conclusion did serve to refocus explanations for UFO phenomena away from the human mind. Jerome Clark, author of *UFOs in the 1980s,* writes, "The problem with the psychosocial hypothesis is not that the quite real psychological and sociological aspects of the UFO problem are unworthy of attention; it is that the psychosocial hypothesis simply fails to deal plausibly with ufology's most interesting questions, the ones that brought it into being in the first place." He is referring to the physical evidence and independently witnessed events that continue to plague nay-sayers.

Whereas debunkers have brought valuable skepticism to dubious claims, and psychosocial theorists have provided interesting interpretations of culturally symbolic meanings in UFO stories, an explication encompassing the psychological and the material aspects integral to so many claims remains elusive.

—*Jerome Clark*

See Also: Abductees; Jung, Carl Gustav

Further Reading:
Clark, Jerome, and Loren Coleman. *The Unidentified: Notes Toward Solving the UFO Mystery.* New York: Warner Books, 1975.
Evans, Hilary. *Gods, Spirits, and Cosmic Guardians: A Comparative Study of the Encounter Experience.* Wellingborough, U.K.: Aquarian Press, 1987.
Hufford, David J. *The Terror That Comes in the Night: An Experience-Centered Study of Supernatural Assault Tradition.* Philadelphia: University of Pennsylvania Press, 1982.
Jung, Carl Gustav. *Flying Saucers: A Modern Myth of Things Seen in the Sky.* New York: Harcourt, Brace, 1959.

THE PURPLE MONSTER STRIKES

The Purple Monster Strikes was a 15-episode film serial from 1945. The title refers to a Martian in a purple, scaly suit that comes to earth to get plans for a reusable rocketship. (The Martians only have a one-way capsule.) As soon as the astronomer-inventor proudly turns his rocketship construction plans over to the supposedly friendly Martian, the purple monster kills him and takes over his body. He then continues construction of the craft with the help of earth criminals. If the Martian returns to his planet with the reusable craft technology, earth is surely doomed. A heroic lawyer attempts to foil the Martian plans through the remaining episodes. One of the interests of this film is how it anticipates later alien-invasion films years before the beginning of either the Cold War or the UFO era.

Republic 1945; 188 min. Director: Spencer Gordon Bennet; Cast: Dennis Moore, Linda Stirling, Roy Barcroft.

PURPLE PEOPLE EATER

Sheb Woolley's 1958 hit record inspired a movie by the same name 30 years later. A one-eyed, one-horned, flying purple people eater comes to earth to join a rock-and-roll band. The film features Sheb Woolley, Chubby Checker, and Little Richard.

Motion Picture Corporation of America 1988; 91 min. Director: Linda Shayne; Cast: Ned Beatty, Shelly Winters, Neil Patrick Harris, Kareem Abdul-Jabbar, Little Richard, Chubby Checker, Peggy Lipton.

PYRAMIDS

The mysterious monuments left by the ancient Egyptians have always intrigued people with an occult orientation. Pyramids, however, really came into their own in the metaphysical/New Age subculture in the wake of the publication of the book *Psychic Discoveries behind the Iron Curtain* in 1970. In this work, Sheila Ostrander and Lynn Schroeder reported the content of their meeting with Czech radio engineer Karel Drbal, who told them about a Frenchman named Bovis who claimed to have discovered, during a visit to the Great Pyramid in Egypt, bodies of animals that had strayed into the pyramid and gotten lost.

According to Bovis, there was something particular about these bodies, which were found in a garbage can in the pharaoh's chamber: The bodies of the animals were mummified in spite of the humidity of the site. He later decided to build a model of the pyramid and to conduct some experiments with organic material in order to determine if any mysterious power connected with pyramids interfered with normal processes of decay. When his model showed the same results, he concluded that a peculiar relation exists between the shape of the space inside the pyramid and the organic processes occurring inside that space, and he suggested that by using suitable shapes it should be possible to make processes occur faster or slower.

Another pyramid experiment was conducted in 1973 by Lyall Watson, who discovered that the speed of dehydration of organic materials is related to the substance involved as well as to the weather conditions. After observing that objects that had been put in the pyramid preserved better than objects in an ordinary box, Watson concluded that replicas of Cheops pyramids do have special properties. During the 1970s occult interest in pyramid energy became considerable. An example of this interest was represented by the advertisement for a pyramid product in *Fate* magazine, asserting that mystical powers were contained in the product, resulting in significant and rewarding benefits for its users.

This mysterious "pyramid power," whatever it is, represents a technical knowledge that contemporary science has not touched. For adherents to the ancient-astronaut view, it is clear that this lost knowledge of the Egyptians was but a fragment of the legacy bequeathed to humankind by ufonauts who visited the earth in the distant past. In the wake of the popularity of books like *Fingerprints of the Gods* and *The Orion Mystery,* interest in the ancient Egyptians has been kindled anew. Erich von Däniken, the premier author of books in the ancient-astronaut genre, recently wrote a book on the extraterrestrial-Egypt connection.

Contrary to popular belief, no mummy of any kind has ever been found in any Egyptian pyramid. This being the case, what was the purpose of these structures?

The Great Pyramid of Egypt (located in Khufu) is the largest construction on earth. It covers nearly 14 acres at its base and is nearly 500 feet high. It weighs some 700,000 tons. Because the Great Pyramid rests on a solid base of limestone underneath the sand, in 5,000 years it has settled less than one-half inch. It is composed of 2.3 million limestone blocks, each weighing from two and a half to 10 tons. The Great Pyramid contains enough stone to build 35 Empire State Buildings, with several tons left over. It was once covered with exterior casing stones that were highly polished and covered the entire structure with a smooth, gleaming surface. The stones were so closely fitted that a knife blade could not be inserted between them.

The Great Pyramid's alignment is just three minutes off of absolute true north. (The closest that modern science and construction methods have come to that kind of precision is in the Paris Observatory, which is off true north by six minutes.) The Great Pyramid is situated on the prime meridian of earth. Its east-west and north-south axes intersect the only lines of longitude and latitude in the world that equally divide the earth's land masses and oceans. The Egyptians—or whoever built this monument—could calculate the longitude and latitude of the earth many centuries before Europeans had discovered that the earth was in fact a sphere. The alignment of the three pyramids on the Giza Plateau duplicates the position of the stars in Orion's belt as they appeared in 10,500 B.C. The Pyramid Texts, ancient religious writings from the Fifth and Sixth Dynasties, contain continual references to Osiris. One passage states, "O Horus, these kings are Osiris, these pyramids are Osiris, these constructions of theirs are

Osiris." Osiris was the ancient Egyptian god of the underworld who possessed life-giving powers connected to the constellation Orion.

Inside the pyramid there are huge, 75-ton granite stones called "spirit stones." No one knows how these immense stones got in the pyramid or what their purpose is. A level passageway within the pyramid leads to an area called the Grand Gallery, 157 feet in length and 26 feet high. The walls are 62 inches wide at the bottom, gradually narrowing to 42 inches at the top. The Grand Gallery meets the specifications of a large observatory bisected by a meridian through the North Pole.

Despite the fact that the Egyptians were prolific record-keepers, they did not leave any hieroglyphs about the construction of the pyramids. The construction of the Great Pyramid is arguably the single greatest undertaking in the history of humankind, yet there is not one picture or drawing, not one artifact, to tell of its construction. The Egyptians left 3,000 years of written and pictorial history covering everything from birth to death, work to play. But there was nothing about the building of the pyramids. Is it possible that the Egyptians didn't build the pyramids? If they didn't build the Great Pyramid, then who did?

Many scientists agree that physically, mathematically, and scientifically the Great Pyramid could not have been built by human labor at all. Some argue that if the pyramid weren't already there, we would not have the scientific know-how and capability today to build it to such exacting and precise standards.

The Greek historian Herodotus made the first historical record of the pyramids in 425 B.C. He stated that the Great Pyramid of Khufu, also called Cheops, was built in 20 years by teams of 100,000 men working in three-month shifts. According to him, the pyramid was built at the direction of the Pharoah Cheops, his son Khafre, and his brother. This would place its construction at around 2500 B.C. Herodotus supposed that the huge stones were quarried from a gigantic limestone formation nearby. He suggested that some sort of huge leverage device was used to raise the stones to each succeeding level.

Two thousand years after Herodotus, Napoleon Bonaparte set an army of scholars, scientists, artists, and mathematicians to work upon the task of answering how and why the pyramids were built. By the time Napoleon saw them, much of the beautiful polished white limestone that covered the exterior of the pyramids had been removed to build the city of Cairo. That made it possible for the French scientists to measure and calculate the weight of individual stones used in the construction. Napoleon estimated that there were enough stones in the Great Pyramid to build a wall around France seven times.

Modern Egyptologists maintain that the quarried blocks were dragged or rolled over the sand on logs to the Giza Plateau. Many modern theorists believe the structure was raised by means of an earthen ramp that was constructed as the pyramid rose and was then dismantled from the top down, allowing workers to put the casing stones in place as the ramp receded.

John Anthony West has studied vertical erosion on the Sphinx and the Great Pyramid. He claims that vertical erosion can come only from continuous downpours of rain over long periods of time. No significant rainfall has occurred on the Giza Plateau, site of both the Sphinx and the Great Pyramid, since before 10,000 B.C. This leads West to believe that both structures were built more than 7,000 years prior to the age of the Egyptians.

It has long been the opinion of traditional Egyptologists that the building of the Great Pyramid was the culmination of hundreds of years of practice in the art of pyramid-building. In other words, the Egyptians first built the smaller pyramids, such as the "bent" pyramid (so called because of its irregular shape) and the step pyramids. In the process of building these pyramids, the Egyptians, according to this theory, solved the problems of pyramid construction using gradients, ending in triumph with the construction of the Great Pyramid of Khufu.

Dr. Herbert Haas, director of the Radiocarbon Laboratory at Southern Methodist University, has dedicated much time and effort to dating the construction of the pyramids and other ancient constructions. He announced based on established carbon-dating methods that the Great Pyramid of Khufu was at least 400 years older than Zoser's "bent" pyramid.

With the confirmation that the Great Pyramid is 400 years older than the other pyramids, it is possible to postulate that the Great Pyramid already existed when the Egyptians appeared on the scene. The other 80 pyramids scattered along the west bank of the Nile could simply have been failed attempts to copy the original.

Zechariah Sitchin, New York author of *The Earth Chronicles,* maintains that the Giza pyramids were built as beacons by extraterrestrials as part of a landing corridor ending at the space port in the Sinai Desert. As evidence, he cites Egyptian legends telling of an age when sky gods came down to earth, raised the land up from under mud and water, flew through the air in flying boats, and gave man laws and wisdom through a royal line of pharaohs. These ancient gods required food and clothing. Sitchin recounts how humanity's early history was shaped by visitors from a twelfth planet in our solar system. This planet is reportedly on a 30-degree inclined orbit to the parallax of our solar system, which takes it far into space, preventing viewing today. It comes close to earth every 3,600 years and is due back between the years 2060 and 2065. According to ancient Sumerian texts, a ruler from the twelfth planet was overthrown and fled to earth more than 400,000 years ago. The aliens mined gold and genetically manipulated early humans. About 10,000 years ago the aliens were either killed or left earth, leaving behind only ruins and legends.

Stories of 12 planets in our solar system are not as far-fetched as they at first seem. In 1981 astronomer Thomas Van Flandern reported to the American Astronomical Society that irregularities in the orbit of Pluto indicate that our solar system contained a tenth planet. In 1983 the Washington Post News Service reported, "A heavenly body possibly as large as Jupiter and possibly so close to the earth that it would be part of this solar system has been found in the direction of the constellation Orion by an orbiting telescope called the Infrared Astronomical Observatory."

The pyramids of Mexico and Central America are just as astonishing and just as mysterious as those in Egypt. South American legends tell of white, bearded beings that taught the indigenous natives the arts of civilization, producing intricate highways and other wonders. They lived among the native peoples for a time, eating, bathing, and behaving in a very human way.

Pyramids have been photographed on the surface of Mars by both the Mariner 9 probe and the more recent Viking probes. These pyramids have been found on opposite sides of Mars. (Cairo, the site of the two greatest pyramids, was originally named El-Kahira, from the Arabic El-Kahir, meaning "Mars.") They have a very regular triangular shape. At each corner of the pyramid there appears to be a buttress. The buttresses themselves are pyramid-shaped. The largest of the pyramids is five-sided and was named the D&M Pyramid after its discoverers, Vincent DiPietro and Greg Molenaar. Although NASA's official position is that all features photographed on the surface of Mars are natural, many others are convinced that the Martian pyramids were constructed by an intelligent life-form.

—*Kay Holzinger*

See Also: Ancient Astronauts; von Däniken, Erich
Further Reading:
Craft, Michael. *Alien Impact.* New York: St. Martin's, 1996.
Hoagland, Richard. *Monuments of Mars: The City on the Edge of Forever.* North Atlantic Books, 1987.
Sitchin, Zecharia. *Divine Encounters: A Guide to Visions, Angels, and Other Emissaries.* New York: Avon, 1995.
———. *The Twelfth Planet.* New York: Avon, 1976.
von Däniken, Erich. *Chariots of the Gods? Unsolved Mysteries of the Past.* Trans. Michael Heron. New York: G. P. Putnam's Sons, 1970.

QUATERMASS AND THE PIT

This is the third in the series of Quatermass films. While constructing a new subway, workers discover an ancient Martian spaceship with dead insectmen in the hull. Professor Bernard Quatermass investigates and discovers that the Martians landed at the dawn of earth's time in search of slaves and speeded up the process of evolution by advancing apes to men before dying out. The core theme comes directly from ancient-astronaut thinking as embodied in the work of Erich von Däniken.

Hammer 1967; 180 min. Director: Roy Ward Baker; Cast: Andre Morell, Cec Linder, James Donald, Barbara Shelley, Julian Glover.

QUATERMASS II

This 1957 film is a sequel to *The Quatermass Xperiment*. Alien invaders have all but taken over the British government and are on the verge of world conquest when Dr. Bernard Quatermass steps in. At the beginning of the film Dr. Quatermass is angry that funds for his moon-rocket project have been cut off. He is sent to a rural area to investigate some abnormalities. He finds soldiers and government officials in the area behaving like brainwashed zombies. There are many meteorites in the area, which erupt when approached. In the center of a cordoned area is a collection of pressure domes that look like the professor's own moon-base life-support system. It turns out that the meteorites contain tiny living organisms that have the ability to take over humans. The life-support system is being prepared for the waiting aliens by the zombies they have taken over in order to provide them with a habitable environment, the earth's atmosphere being unsuitable for them. Quatermass unravels the conspiracy, which reaches into the upper reaches of government and includes the commissioner of Scotland Yard. This *Invasion of the Body Snatchers*–type of film may reflect the fear of communist infiltration.

Hammer 1957; 84 min. Director: Val Guest; Writers: Val Guest, Nigel Kneale; Music: James Bernard; Cinematography: Gerald Gibbs; Cast: Brian Donlevy, John Longden, Sidney James, Bryan Forbes, William Franklyn, Vera Day, John Van Eyssen, Michael Ripper, Michael Balfour, Tom Chatto, Percy Herbert.

THE QUATERMASS XPERIMENT

In this 1955 British film the sole astronaut surviving a space mission returns to earth unknowingly carrying an alien infestation. He starts behaving strangely, and a fungus-like growth appears on his hand. The growth creeps all over his body until he is nothing but a living fungus. The organism spreads around London, killing everybody and growing larger by the hour until Dr. Bernard Quatermass corners it in Westminster Cathedral and electrocutes it. After the alien is killed, the film climaxes with a second rocket launch. This movie was released in the United States as *The Creeping Unknown* and may have been the direct inspiration for *The Blob*.

Hammer 1955; 78 min. Director: Val Guest; Writers: Richard Landau, Val Guest; Music: James Bernard; Cast: Brian Donlevy, Margia Dean, Jack Warner, Richard Wordsworth.

Richard Wordsworth plays an astronaut (Victor Carroon) who returns from space and begins a metamorphosis into an alien being bent on invasion in the 1955 film The Quatermass Xperiment, *released in the United States as* The Creeping Unknown. *(The Del Valle Archive)*

RADAR MEN FROM THE MOON

Radar Men from the Moon is a 12-episode serial released in 1952. In it, Captain Cody, Sky Marshal of the Universe, puts an end to the Moon monarch's plans of invading earth. Most of the action takes place on the Moon, where Captain Cody, in total disregard for scientific truth, needs no space suit and is unaffected by the reduced gravity.

The notion of extraterrestrials invading the earth, which became one of the most overused of Hollywood sci-fi plots, goes back at least as far as H. G. Wells's *The War of the Worlds* (1898), thus antedating the modern UFO era by half a century. This calls into question the oversimplified claim of many commentators that alien-invasion movies represent no more than Cold War fears of a communist invasion.

> Republic 1952; 12 Chapters. Director: Howard Hawks; Writers: Ben Hecht, Charles Lederer; I. A. L. Diamond; Cinematography: Milton Krasner; Cast: Cary Grant, Ginger Rogers, Charles Coburn, Marilyn Monroe, Hugh Marlowe, Henri Letondal, Larry Keating.

THE RAELIAN MOVEMENT

The Raelian Movement International (Raelian Religion in Canada), is the largest UFO "religion" in the world, currently numbering around 45,000 members with branches in 52 countries. It was founded by a Frenchman, Claude Vorilhon ("Rael") in 1976. Vorilhon (b. 1946) wrote in *Le livre qui dit la verité* (1974) about his encounter with an extraterrestrial during a walk in the volcanic Clermont-Ferrand mountain range. This "eloha" (from the planet of the Elohim) gave Vorilhon his name—Rael—and taught him the true meaning of the Bible. Humans were "implanted" on earth by a team of Elohim scientists that created us in laboratories from their own DNA mat-

ter. Rael was chosen as the messenger of the Elohim to warn humanity that, since the explosion at Hiroshima, we have entered the "Age of Apocalypse," in which we confront the choice of destroying ourselves through nuclear war, or learning to live in peace and tolerance and preparing to welcome our forefathers from space.

Originally, Rael founded MADECH (Mouvement pour Accueil des Createurs de l'Humanite) in 1974, which resembled a contactee circle. In 1976 there was a schism from whence the Raelian Movement, a full-fledged new religious movement, issued. In 1975 Rael wrote of his second encounter in *They Took Me to Their Planet* and described his journey to the nameless planet of the Elohim, where he was taught the sensual meditation technique and observed his own body being re-created from DNA in a vat. He also studied their system of government, the "geniocracy," or rule of the most intelligent, which were chosen for leadership on the basis of intelligence tests. Upon his return Rael instructed his followers in sensual meditation, a sensory-awareness exercise believed to enhance telepathy and harmony with the universe and to stimulate the growth of new brain cells. He also attempted to found a political party in France, La Geniocratie, but after weathering intense investigations and searches by the gendarme he abandoned the project. The symbol of the movement is the swastika inside the Star of David, worn by members on a medallion.

The Raelians do not believe in a god or an immortal soul; rather, they believe in an infinite progression of human scientists, who have achieved a relative immortality through cloning and travel throughout the universe creating life from DNA. Human beings who have made outstanding contributions to humanity (even non-Raelians) may be judged worthy to be re-created. Rael has proph-

Transmission of the cellular code, the Raelian Movement's "baptism" ceremony (Raelian Movement)

esied that the Elohim will return to earth sometime before the year 2035, if humanity fulfills the two goals of the movement: spreading the message, and building the embassy to welcome the 39 prophets and extraterrestrial scientists, who will then bequeath to their creations their wealth of scientific knowledge.

The Raelians participate in four annual festivals that commemorate Rael's various encounters and revelations. The initiation ritual, or baptism ceremony, is performed on these occasions as the "transmission of the cellular plan." Rael or one of his bishops will dip his hand in water and place it on the initiate's forehead in order to transmit their genetic code to the Elohim's machines, where it is stored for the future cloning process, if the aspirant is deemed worthy. The initiate must also make out a will designating the Raelian Movement as beneficiary and sign a contract with a local mortician so that their "third eye" (a chunk of frontal bone considered and essential ingredient for the re-creation process) can be cut out upon

their demise, packed in ice, and stored in a bank vault in Switzerland. Raelians are also advised to practice sensual meditation to a tape on a daily basis, and newcomers have the opportunity to try out the oxygenation and guided-relaxation stages of the meditation at the monthly meetings.

There are two levels of membership: the Raelians, who are loosely affiliated baptized members, representing many degrees of commitment and engagement; and the Structure leadership, who form a pyramid, descending from Rael who is the Guide of Guides, through the Bishop Guides, the Priest Guides, the Animators, the Assistant Animators, and the Probationers at the bottom. A Council of the Wise controls heresy and sanctions rule-breakers. All Raelians are expected to pay 10 percent of their income toward the construction of the embassy, but this rule is not enforced. In order to maintain a pure genetic code, Raelians are not permitted to drink alcohol or caffeine, smoke cigarettes, or use recreational drugs; they tend toward vegetarianism and health food. The pursuit of sexual pleasure with many partners of both sexes and all races is emphasized in the movement, and the marriage contract is rejected as oppressive. Birth control and precautions against sexually transmitted diseases are taught, and members of the Structure rarely breed.

Rael founded FIREPHIM (International Federation of Minority Religions and Philosophies), an organization dedicated to fighting "religious racism," and the Raelians regularly demonstrate against intolerance by participating in gay marches, by protesting racism and sexism, and by demonstrating outside anticult headquarters. In 1997 Rael (in the wake of the publicity surrounding the cloning of Dolly the sheep), set up Valiant Venture, a cloning company that for an investment of $250,000 and up promised to offer CLONAID as soon as that technology became available. The Raelians have constructed a museum of ufological lore in Valcourt, Quebec, for the purpose of fundraising for the eventual building of the Embassy; they have also founded a monastic order for women, Rael's Angels, in training to be the hostesses, companions, and lovers of the Elohim and Prophets and breeders of a new race of "giants of old."

Controversies surrounding the movement have focused on their freewheeling sexual mores, rejection of Charles Darwin's theory of evolution, the swastika symbol, and the utopian ideal of a geniocracy. However, because the Raelians do not live communally, are not sectarian, and have a history of defending their rights through lawsuits and public demonstrations, they have weathered media attacks and persecution in France (in the wake of the Solar Temple tragedy) with remarkable equanimity.

—*Susan J. Palmer*

See Also: Contactees; Cults, UFO; Hybrids, Alien-Human; Religions, UFO

Further Reading:
Palmer, Susan J. "The Raelians Are Coming: The Future of a UFO Religion." In *Religion in a Changing World.* Edited by Madeleine Cousineau. Westport CT: Praeger, 1998, pp. 139–146.
———. "Woman as Playmate in the Raelian Movement: Power and Pantagamy in a New Religion." *Syzygy: Journal of Alternative Religion and Culture* 1(3) (1992): 227–245.
———. "Women in the Raelian Movement: New Religious Experiments in Gender and Authority." In *The Gods Have Landed: New Religions From Other Worlds.* Edited by James Lewis. New York: State University of New York Press, 1995, pp. 105–136.
Vallee, Jacques. *Revelations: Alien Contact and Human Deception.* New York: Ballantine Books, 1991.
Vorilhon, Claude (Rael). *Let's Welcome Our Fathers from Space: They Created Humanity in Their Laboratories.* Tokyo: AOM Corporation, 1986.
———. *"Real" Space Aliens Took Me to their Planet.* Waduz, Lichtenstein: Face, 1975.

REINCARNATION

The term "reincarnation" refers to the rebirth of the soul after death into a new physical body, which can be human or animal as well as divine, angelic, demonic, vegetative, celestial, or, within certain UFO religions, extraterrestrial. Reincarnationists usually believe that the goal of reincarnation is to escape the cycle of rebirth and to go on to some other state of existence, although sometimes reincarnation is regarded as an unending process. In some traditions it is supposed to happen immediately after death, in others only after a certain period of time has passed, during which the soul dwells in some other plane of existence.

The notion of reincarnation is very ancient and is still widely prevalent in every part of the world, especially in parts of Asia and in the native societies of Africa and Australia. However, the most elaborate doctrines of rebirth and reincarnation belong to the ancient Greek and Indian traditions. In ancient Greece, where the idea of metempsychosis (reincarnation) was imported from the East, the concept of reincarnation is associated principally with the philosophies of Pythagoras, Empedocles, and Plato.

In India, belief in reincarnation is best known in connection with the teachings and practices of Hinduism and Buddhism, although all traditions native to the South Asian subcontinent accept reincarnation as one of their tenets. Hinduism regards present life as a preparation for life after death. According to the law of karma, the results of good and evil actions in previous existences determine the circumstances of any lifetime that are caused by the imperfections of the soul when it first comes into the world. A person can escape rebirth only by suppressing all desires except that for perfect unification with the universal self or with the divine.

In Western countries, belief in reincarnation vanished in the early Middle Ages, being incompatible with Christian orthodoxy, although it was periodically revived in such heretical movements as the Cathars and Albigenses, in groups such as the Knights Templars, Rosicrucians, and Freemasons, and among alchemists, Kabbalists, and others. Belief in reincarnation has returned to and grown in the modern West as a result of the impact of Eastern religions, which have become well known in the West as an unanticipated by-product of the European colonization of India and Buddhist countries. Reincarnation is a fundamental element of New Age and, more generally, of metaphysical philosophy, providing an alternative to traditional Christian belief in bodily resurrection and future existence in heaven.

As ideas about the inhabitants of UFOs and extraterrestrials were adopted by—and integrated into the ideology of—the West's metaphysical/New Age subculture, it was natural that speculation about possible incarnations on other planets would eventually be integrated into this subculture's general worldview. In more recent communications with the Other Side, New Age channels have even claimed to have received information from, among other sources, extraterrestrials. Thus, it is not uncommon to speak with members of this subculture who claim to have had lifetimes on other planets.

A more unusual notion is that two or more individuals who seem distinct because they occupy separate bodies have, in fact, but one soul among them. In more sophisticated formulations, this single group soul is conceived of as having several different aspects, or facets, each of which incarnates in a distinct series of embodiments. It is not unusual for some of these alternative embodiments to be on other planets. The purpose for such multiple embodiments is explained in different ways. If the purpose of a series of incarnations is to gain experiences that will help one to grow spiritually, then clearly the ability to enter simultaneously into several different embodiments allows one to speed up the process of spiritual growth.

See Also: Extraterrestrial Incarnations; Karma; New Age
Further Reading:
Banerjee, H. N., and W. C. Oursler. *Lives Unlimited: Reincarnation East and West.* New York: Doubleday, 1974.
Evans-Wentz, W. Y., ed. *The Tibetan Book of the Dead.* 3rd ed. London: Oxford University Press, 1960.
Hall, Manly Palmer. *Reincarnation: The Cycle of Necessity.* Los Angeles: Philosophical Research Society, 1956.
Head, Joseph, and S. L. Cranston, eds. *Reincarnation in World Thought.* New York: Crown Publishers and Julian Press, 1967.
Stevenson, Ian. *Twenty Cases Suggestive of Reincarnation.* 2nd ed. Charlottesville: University Press of Virginia, 1974.

RELIGIONS, UFO

A subculture now exists in every country, based on the idea that humanity has a higher destiny. You will find people . . . who have literally dropped out of city life . . . because they had received messages from space instructing them to do so. . . . Their lives have been changed by what they consider to be genuine extraterrestrial communication. . . . We are not here dealing with escapism—we are dealing with the next form of religion.

—*Jacques Vallee*

In H. G. Wells's story "Jimmy Goggles the God" a diver stomps onto the shore of a Pacific island in his diving suit (nicknamed "Jimmy Goggles"). The natives, seeing this unearthly being coming to them from the sea, unhesitatingly assume he is a god and proceed to worship him accordingly.

In our time, otherworldly beings are allegedly visiting our planet in considerable numbers. It tells us something about human nature that—almost from the first moment the flying saucers were reported—there were those who saw beyond the nuts and bolts of the surface phenomenon to its profounder and more spiritual dimensions. What seemed to most people simply a mirror of our own tentative ventures into space—manifestations of alien technology—carried for these others implications of a supernal reality.

Wells's natives lacked a frame of reference into which they could place the diver in his suit—so they placed him outside reference, they made him a god. In our time, science has failed to provide a

Unarian students listen to a reading of an inspired book beneath an image of Uriel overcoming Satan. (Michael Greeco)

satisfactory terrestrial explanation for the flying saucers and their occupants, so some of us have placed them outside science, in the realm of the divine. The flying saucers, these people suppose, must be piloted by gods, from which it is a simple step to worship, and the crystallization of the worshippers into UFO-related religious groups (URGs), more or less formal as the case may be.

Doubtless among Wells's islanders there were skeptics who questioned whether the diver was really a god. If so, Wells omits them from his fiction. Ours, however, is a skeptical culture, and only a tiny percentage of us is prepared to make the mental leap that translates the flying-saucer pilots into gods. But that tiny percentage adds up, in a head count, to a sizeable number. URGs proliferate, and they merit a chapter to themselves in sociological studies; TV documentaries love them.

It is often said that everyone needs religion. This can be widely interpreted, and proponents of a particular belief system are apt to exploit it as an argument for belief in general as the stepping-stone to belief in their particular religion. But of course the assertion, even if true, does not necessarily imply adherence to any belief system. The phrase could equally well—some would say better—be rephrased in some such formulation as "everyone needs some working hypothesis to account for his/her existence and place in the cosmos." Even if we grant—though it is by no means proven—that we all need such a working hypothesis as a basis for our lives, it does not follow that we all need to be a practicing member of an established religion. However, it appears that there is a sizeable proportion of humanity that does indeed feel such a need.

Some naturally will feel most comfortable as members of a majority religion, arguing, for instance, that so many billions of Christians can't be wrong, particularly with a 2,000-year tradition behind them. But the history of religious belief records many thousands of smaller, elitist groups that have come to think that to them and them alone has the truth been vouchsafed. The confidence of the Jews that they are the Chosen People is well known: But it is evident from a study of, say, the Doukhobors or the Skoptzy that these smaller religious groups see their limited numbers, far from being an indication that they are mistaken in their beliefs, as a validation of their privileged position.

There exists at least a minority of people for whom a working hypothesis is not sufficient yet feel the need for a more concrete belief shared with others. When Christians stand up in their churches, face the altar, and utter the creed aloud and collectively, they are making an affirmation of consensus belief that comforts and reassures them. And we can further recognize that it does not necessarily matter to the believer that his/her belief is shared only by a few.

So a URG, far from being a rare anomaly, can be seen as merely one of the innumerable esoteric cults that have arisen in human society as far back as history goes, some to flicker briefly and then fade away or be snuffed out, others who continued—and perhaps continue—to maintain a more or less precarious existence.

It can broadly be stated that until the seventeenth century most everyone shared the unquestioning view that religion is a basic fact of human existence and, indeed, is one that distinguishes man from the beasts. Doubters were few and usually short-lived; atheists were rarer still. Since the seventeenth century this assumption has been progressively questioned. Although until quite recent times it has been socially discreditable to proclaim disbelief—indeed, it still is in many communities—a few individuals have from time to time made a public stand, and today a substantial proportion affirms a total rejection of any orthodox belief. Moreover, of those who continue to label themselves Christians or whatever, it is clear that many are no more than nominal believers who for social or psychological rather than spiritual reasons are unwilling to make a final rejection. Of those who abandon traditional religions, some reject religion altogether, becoming agnostics or atheists. Others turn to alternative faiths.

Publicized cases occur of prominent converts from Protestant to Catholic Christianity, from Christianity to Judaism or Islam, and so forth, but it is their rarity that makes them notable.

An interesting development has been a swing to fundamentalist versions of traditional religions. In an extremist form of Tertullian's *credo quia impossibile,* many believers, notably in the Christian and Muslim religions, have adopted a position of total and unquestioning belief; for example, the Christian Bible is literally the word of God and its every word true—even its contradictions. In this context it is interesting to consider a remarkable statement by Douglas Curran, who spent several years traveling North America visiting URGs: "Every single flying-saucer group I encountered in my travels incorporated Jesus Christ into the hierarchy of its belief system." If URGs tend to incorporate Christian beliefs into their systems, the reluctance to shed them stems not from any fundamentalist conviction but from a perceived compatibility with the newer forms of spirituality—a compatibility that often involves distorting or cropping the Christian message to a degree that would make it unrecognizable to the orthodox.

In strong contrast to fundamentalism are the groups that could be described, generally, as "theosophist." From the nineteenth century onward, several parallel belief systems came into being, several of which still survive: Christian Science and the multitudinous varieties of theosophy proposed by such as Katherine Tingley, Manly P. Hall, Rudolph Steiner, Krishnamurti, and so on. The teachings of a charismatic figure such as Helena Blavatsky, whether one considers her a spiritual leader or a charlatan, were somewhat too esoteric to attract a wide public, but they can be seen as providing a philosophical framework for many of the URGs of the 1950s. As author Douglas Curran expresses it: "Adding flying saucers to the cosmic plan and expanding the Great White Brotherhood to include extraterrestrial masters known as the Space Brothers gave the traditional Theosophical beliefs a contemporary relevance."

When the flying saucers first appeared in our skies, many writers sought to link them with traditional religious beliefs. The reverend Barry Downing wrote: "UFOs are a modern form of religion, something quasi-scientific, which have taken the place of traditional ideas of angels and miracles." A good many writers, particularly those inclined to fundamentalist religious views, have argued that they might be the work of the devil; expecting the world to end, and Jesus to return, in the near future, these writers perceive the flying saucers as a last-ditch attempt by the forces of evil to sabotage the divine will. John Weldon and Zola Levitt subtitled their 1975 book *The Coming Invasion,* warning us that we should be making preparations to repel demonic aggression.

We might expect the candidate for godhead to possess and to display superhuman powers; to demonstrate superhuman knowledge and wisdom; and to be morally superior to us. The extraterrestrial aliens do, in large measure, fulfill these requirements. Simply by getting to earth from whencesoever they originate, they demonstrate a substantially advanced technology compared with ours. Indeed, the problems of travel beyond our immediate space environment are so formidable that some students of the subject consider them to be, in practice, insoluble. Exploration that has to be carried out over periods of light-years, so that results cannot be received by the generation that initiated the venture but only several generations later, is so inconceivable in practical terms, albeit feasible in scientific terms, that it savors more of science fiction than science. If these critics are right, then the achievements of the visiting extraterrestrials are, literally, superhuman.

Having got here, the extraterrestrials perform other feats, such as passing through walls, transporting human beings safely through the air, or controlling and directing humans at will. These and other such feats are as miraculous as any attributed to Buddha, Muhammad, and Jesus. When it comes to the healings that are widely regarded as evidence of divine intervention, the aliens seem to be equally efficacious as those just named, if no less arbitrary as to whom they choose to heal, and whom not.

The contactees—those who represent the first phase of contact between humankind and its otherworldly visitors—told stories that differed widely as to what the Space Brothers and Sisters looked like, what spaceships they flew in, and

where they came from. But all were in concordance on one thing: The beings they met are superior and benevolent—elders, masters of wisdom. They give their human contacts visions of other worlds that promise all kinds of goodies to be bestowed at such time as humanity shall show itself ready for them. Their knowledge and wisdom are displayed in two forms: either in direct communication, or through messages dictated, apparently, telepathically. Dutch businessman Stefan Denaerde, as a thank-you for assisting some aliens stranded beneath the Zuyder Zee, was taken aboard their spacecraft and instructed for hours on end: Yolanda-Nada is just one of many alien beings that have channeled voluminous texts to mankind. Even if, unlike George King, who in 1954 was told "you are to become the Voice of Interplanetary Parliament," a contactee was not allotted a specific role, the end result of these messages was to leave the individual convinced that she or he had a personal mission to alert the rest of us to the glorious future that can be ours if we behave ourselves. Contactee Gabriel Green, a candidate for the U.S. presidency in 1960, and president of the Amalgamated Flying Saucer Clubs of America, summarized the benefits promised by his otherworldly contacts:

> The scientific and technical knowledge to be gained from the Space People is a wealth of beneficial information, which could transform this world from its present chaotic state into a utopian-like society, far beyond today's most optimistic concepts. Some of the many amazing benefits of the knowledge already received from the Space People, or promised by them if we will welcome them in a friendly manner, are: elimination of disease, poverty, and smog; solving of the problem of automation and unemployment; a way to finance all public works projects and aid to other countries without taxation; an extended life span; a greater measure of personal freedom, economic security, and abundance; and for many living today, personal journeys to other planets beyond the stars.

Put like that, it seems as if the attitude of URGs toward aliens is on a not much higher level than those cargo cultists of the Pacific, whose perception of divinity was on a strictly materialist, what's-in-it-for-me level. But this would be unfair:

Although the material conditions of life on the visitors' planets are invariably painted in utopian colors, the moral and spiritual dimensions are always emphasized.

Among groups like Gabriel Green's—and such groups proliferated in the United States during the 1960s and 1970s—there is a widespread agreement that some kind of educational process is under way: that earth's population is being prepared for participation in cosmic affairs, instead of simply being concerned in our own relatively trivial concerns. It is comforting to be reassured by Jeanne Dixon, America's most respected prophet, that "the people in the UFOS" (who come from a planet beyond Jupiter) "are interested in us, but have avoided contacting us until now because we have not been mentally ready." Soon, soon, if we behave ourselves, if we learn to make love not war, if we renounce short-term materialism for long-term spirituality, we may earn the benevolence of the aliens; the cargo may be ours.

At the basis of every religion is a story, generally focused on a particular individual: Buddha, Confucius, Muhammad. The most elaborate and arguably the least implausible of these stories is that of Jesus, whose career while incarnate on earth involves wonders of all kinds—after an immaculate conception and virgin birth, the hero is visited by three kings bearing symbolic gifts, and he grows up to perform miracles and enunciate teachings, finally giving himself up voluntarily as a sacrifice to redeem humanity's sins, then ascending back to heaven.

The flying-saucer religions have nothing to offer to compare with this—but they do not set out to do that. If traditional texts that are the very basis of the world's leading religions are today widely relegated to the realm of folklore, it is understandable that many regard them as an inadequate foundation for the most important spiritual commitment of their lives. Still, the promoters of the established religions offer their potential customers a product so defective yet find so many takers, which tells us something about human nature; fewer and fewer are choosing to swallow the sales pitch, which tells us that a growing number of people are learning to back their own judgment rather than take on trust what they are instructed to believe.

The flying-saucer story, by contrast, is eminently suited to a space-age awareness. As we humans make our own first tentative ventures beyond the atmosphere of our planet, it is natural to imagine the reverse process—other inhabitants of the universe coming to visit us. Stories of otherworldly visitors have been told throughout history, but they have mostly come from heaven, hell, or other such fantasy places. What has enabled today's otherworldly visitors to get the edge over their predecessors is that they claim to come from worlds more or less like our own—not a pie-in-the-sky heaven, but a planet that would be acceptable to the most skeptical astronomer. That proposition that we should be visited by the inhabitants of such places is scientifically plausible, even to be expected.

What can be said, though, is why this type of religious belief attracts people today. Robert Ellwood has written: "The UFO experience has seemed for many fraught with spiritual or religious meaning. This is understandable, for the sense of wonder evoked by the thought of otherworldly visitants flows easily, for persons of a certain susceptibility, into those feelings of the presence of the numinous and the transcendent which characterizes religious experience." This has been adumbrated through this essay. To summarize, we can say that UFO sects offer a plausible story that conforms, superficially at least, with our knowledge of life in space. They do not require belief in traditional myths such as virgin birth or bread changing into flesh and wine into blood; their marvels are space-age marvels and not inconsistent with scientific possibility. At the same time, it must be said that even though the stories are scientifically credible there is as yet no evidence for them that could be considered scientifically valid. The new URGs require just as much a suspension of disbelief, just as venturesome an act of faith, as any of the old religions.

—*Hilary Evans*

See Also: Aetherius Society; Contactees; Cults, UFO; The Raelian Movement; Unarius

Further Reading:

Cohen, Daniel. *Myths of the Space Age.* New York: Dodd, Mead, 1977.

Curran, Douglas. *In Advance of the Landing: Folk Concepts of Outer Space.* New York: Abbeville Press, 1985.

Evans, Hilary. *Gods, Spirits, and Cosmic Guardians: A Comparative Study of the Encounter Experience.* Wellingborough, U.K.: Aquarian Press, 1987.

———. *Visions, Apparitions, Alien Visitors.* Wellingborough, U.K.: Aquarian Press, 1984.

Goran, Morris. *The Modern Myth, Ancient Astronauts and UFOs.* South Brunswick, NJ: A. S. Barnes, 1978.

Lewis, James R., ed. *The Gods Have Landed: New Religions From Other Worlds.* Albany: State University of New York Press, 1995.

Melton, J. Gordon. *The Encyclopedia of American Religions.* 3rd ed. Detroit: Gale Research, 1989.

Thompson, Keith. *Angels and Aliens: UFOs and the Mythic Imagination.* Reading, MA: Addison-Wesley, 1991.

Vallee, Jacques. *Messengers of Deception: UFO Contacts and Cults.* Berkeley: And/Or Press, 1979.

———. *Passport to Magonia: From Folklore to Flying Saucers.* Chicago: Henry Regnery, 1969.

ROACH ABDUCTION

In a lonely house outside Lehi, Utah, in 1973 Pat Roach and her seven children were visited by aliens and taken aboard their ship for experiments. Roach remembers waking at midnight with her five-year-old screaming that he'd seen a "skeleton." Her other children began to tell her strange things about what had just happened—events about which she remembered nothing. They said that space creatures had entered their home, taken them aboard, and warned them not to say anything. A year and a half later, Roach was hypnotized and began to vividly recall the story told by her children. The beings were in suits, had large eyes, slits for mouths, clawlike thumbs, and no noses. They mentally told her to undress. She remembered that they were cold and "businesslike," and she felt very hostile toward them, saying they treated her "like a guinea pig." She was given a gynecological exam, and a needle was put into her brain to read her thoughts. They were extremely curious about human emotions and seemed to have none themselves. They asked many questions, and Roach had the impression that they needed humans somehow. She was taken back to her living room and woke up, remembering nothing. Hypnotizing the children revealed the same story—being inside the craft, seeing their mother naked on an examining table, and receiving mental communications from the beings. Investigators found the family to be intelligent and honest and did not suspect a hoax. Later abduction cases have reported beings that were extremely interested in emotions and gynecology and performed physical examinations.

See Also: Abductees; Close Encounters

Further Reading:

Lorenzen, Coral, and Jim Lorenzen. *Abducted! Confrontations with Beings from Outer Space.* New York: Berkley Medallion, 1977.

Randle, Kevin D. *The October Scenario: UFO Abductions, Theories about Them, and a Prediction of When They Will Return.* Iowa City, IA: Middle Coast Publishing, 1988.

Turner, Karla. *Taken: Inside the Alien-Human Abduction Agenda.* Roland, AR: Kelt Works, 1994.

ROBOT MONSTER

Robot Monster is arguably the most famous bad movie of all time. Made in 1953, the film is set in the form of a dream of a ten-year-old boy. Seven people are the last survivors on earth after aliens have decimated the rest of the population with their rays. The reason the aliens invaded was that earth was on the threshold of space travel, and the aliens feared competition. The last seven humans are immune to the alien rays because one is a scientist who just invented total-immunization serum. Because of this, the alien has to track down the humans and physically kill them. At this point the boy wakes up and the dream is over. The alien in this picture is ridiculously outfitted in a gorilla suit and a deep-sea diver's helmet.

Although ufonauts may or may not fear human competition, it is arguable that they show a marked interest in terrestrial efforts at space travel because of the frequent reports of UFOs in the vicinity of rocket launches and other facilities associated with the space program.

1953; 62 min. Director: Phil Tucker; Writer: Wyott Ordung; Music: Elmer Bernstein; Cinematography: Jack Greenhaigh; Cast: George Nader, Claudia Barrett, Gregory Moffett, Selena Royle, George Barrows, John Mylong.

ROCKET MAN

In this 1954 film an orphan receives a ray gun from a spaceman (who wears Klaatu's suit from *The Day the Earth Stood Still*) that makes people tell the truth when it's fired. He uses the ray gun to prevent the villain from taking over the orphanage.

The notion that being compelled to tell the truth saves the day pushes this film in the direction of being a morality play. Like Klaatu, the alien in *Rocket Man* is a sort of "technological angel."

Panoramic Productions 1953; 79 min. Director: Oscar Rudolph; Writers: Lenny Bruce, Jack Henley; Cinematography: John Seitz; Cast: George Winslow, Spring Byington, Carles Coburn, Anne Francis, John Agar, Emory Parnell.

THE ROCKY HORROR PICTURE SHOW

When an engaged couple's car breaks down, they call for help at a nearby castle. It turns out that at this castle on this very night the annual convention of visitors from the planet Transsexual in the galaxy Transylvania is being held. The master of the castle, Dr. Frank-N-Furter, is completing an experiment in which he brings Rocky Horror, a handsome, muscular young man, to life. Dr. Everett Scott, who has a government contract to investigate UFOs, arrives at the castle. The cast dances for the conventioneers. The butler and maid, wearing space outfits, kill Frank with an antimatter laser blast. In the end, the castle takes off for space.

The widespread, cultlike popularity of this film indicates that its appeal is complex, in the sense that it cannot be reduced to only one type of explanation. One interpretive angle is that outer space and extraterrestrials can be a screen upon which we project the contents of our shadow selves. Here the spaceship, disguised as a castle, becomes an arena for the release of sexual and aggressive urges forbidden by conventional social mores.

Fox 1975; 105 min. Director: Jim Sharman; Writers: Jim Sharman, Richard O'Brien; Music: John Barry; Cast: Tim Curry, Susan Sarandon, Barry Bostwick, Meat Loaf, Little Nell, Richard O'Brien.

THE ROSWELL INCIDENT

In 1980 a book appeared alleging that an alien spacecraft had crashed in the vicinity of Roswell, New Mexico, in 1947 and that the U.S. government had kept the event hidden for more than three decades. During the next 20 years the so-called

Roswell incident became the subject of more than a dozen books, many articles in UFO journals and magazines, a TV docudrama, and a massive, 1,200-page government report.

The most substantive and detailed accounts of the Roswell incident are to be found in the books that appeared during this 20-year period, and although they all agree that something crashed in the New Mexico desert in 1947, they are sharply divided on the key issue of whether or not it was an alien spacecraft. In part this outcome appears attributable to the methodology employed by the authors to evaluate evidence. In books in which it is concluded that there was no crashed spacecraft, the authors base their reconstruction of the Roswell incident primarily on contemporary documents (i.e., those produced in the 1940s) and cite testimony obtained later (i.e., after 1977) from individuals involved in the 1947 incident only if it is consonant with information provided by the documents. In contrast, in those books that claim an alien spacecraft crashed, the authors rely chiefly on testimony obtained after 1977 and cite information in the 1940s documentation only when it is consonant with such testimony.

Books that purport to describe the Roswell incident can thus be categorized as either "documentary" or "testimonial," depending on the primary source of evidence cited to support the claims put forth. For purposes of exposition, below we offer generic accounts of the Roswell incident abstracted from books in both categories.

Documentary Reconstruction of the Incident

In 1946 only the United States had the atomic bomb, but officials suspected that the Soviet Union was developing one. So that U.S. officials could monitor the progress of the Soviets, research was initiated on instrumentation capable of detecting their first atomic-bomb test at great distances from the test site. Part of this top-secret research was a project code-named "Mogul" aimed at developing a balloon-borne sonic system that could listen to the high-altitude soundwaves produced by a Soviet test bomb. In support of the classified Project Mogul, the U.S. Army Air Force awarded New York University (NYU) an *unclassified* contract to develop the needed balloons—ostensibly for high-altitude research (university personnel received no information about Mogul).

In the spring of 1947 NYU technicians conducted preliminary trials at Alamogordo Army Air Field, New Mexico, where, over a period of a week, they launched several instrumented balloon trains. Each balloon train consisted of a linked cluster of two dozen conventional, five-foot-diameter, rubber "weather balloons." The balloon train launched on June 4 is relevant to this history because the payload included three radar reflectors that enabled ground radar to track the flight path during ascent and descent. Radar reflectors were kite-like constructions of paper and tinfoil supported on a frame of lightweight sticks. They were balloon-borne devices developed for the army's field artillery during World War II to measure the velocity of winds aloft via radar tracking—information essential for gunnery control—and they were unfamiliar to most Army Air Force personnel. They carried no identifying labels, since they were considered throwaway items, and were not readily identifiable as meteorological devices.

Charles B. Moore, one of the NYU technicians responsible for the launchings, later recalled that the June 4 balloon train drifted to the northwest on the usual summer winds and began to descend, a course that would place the impact point of the deflated and burst balloons and payload about 25 miles north-northwest of the town of Arabela. The land in this area was part of a ranch operated by William Brazel.

On June 14 Brazel was making his rounds of the ranch and, according to his account published a few weeks later in the local newspaper, about eight miles from his house he encountered "wreckage made up of rubber strips, tinfoil, a rather tough paper, and sticks." But because he was in a hurry to complete his rounds, he "did not pay much attention to it."

Ten days later and unknown to Brazel (who lived in isolation 70 miles from the nearest town and had no telephone), an event occurred that triggered what has been described as the modern era of flying-saucer sightings in the United States. On June 24 Kenneth Arnold, a private pilot flying from Chehalis to Yakima, Washington, reported seeing nine aerial objects traveling at unprece-

dentedly high speeds. This sighting received much publicity, and reporters coined the terms "flying saucer" and "flying disk" to refer to the objects. In the following weeks many similar sightings were reported around the country, and these also received media attention. Although a few newspapers mentioned the possibility of extraterrestrial visitors, a Gallup poll taken at the time indicates that virtually no one thought flying disks were from another planet. Instead, people attributed the reports to illusions, hoaxes, misinterpreted or unknown natural phenomena, or secret military aircraft. The last possibility excited Cold War fears that the disks might be of Soviet origin.

On July 5 Brazel visited the town of Corona, where he first heard about flying disks, and, according to his published account, he wondered if what he had found "might be the remnants of one of these." Two days later he visited the town of Roswell to sell some wool; while there he reported his discovery to the sheriff, who notified authorities at Roswell Army Air Field. Major Jesse Marcel, intelligence officer of the 509th Bomb Group, soon appeared accompanied by a counterintelligence officer, Captain Sheridan Cavitt, and they returned with Brazel to his ranch. These officers were unable to identify the wreckage, so they decided to collect it and take it back to the base. According to Brazel's account, when this material was gathered "the tinfoil, paper, tape, and sticks made a bundle about three feet long and 7 or 8 inches thick, while the rubber made a bundle 18 or 20 inches long and about 8 inches thick. . . . The entire lot would have weighed maybe five pounds."

This debris was taken to Roswell Army Air Field, and on the following day the base's public-relations office issued a press release indicating that a flying disk had been recovered and sent to higher headquarters. This press release was carried in leading newspapers, but at that time (according to polls) few people associated flying disks with extraterrestrial spacecraft. It thus appears that media interest was stimulated by the possibility that a terrestrial mystery was about to be solved.

When the debris arrived at the regional headquarters of General Roger Ramey, it was identified by Warrant Officer Irving Newton, the weather officer on duty at the time, as the remnants of balloon-borne radar reflectors. Newton was sure of his identification because he had used such devices during his wartime service overseas. That evening General Ramey announced on a newscast that the alleged wreckage of a flying disk was actually the remains of a radar reflector and fragments of the weather balloon that carried it aloft. The next day newspapers around the country carried headlines such as "FLYING DISK EXPLAINED."

So ends the documentary reconstruction of the Roswell incident. It faded quickly from public memory and entered the limbo of overpublicized nonevents, where it remained for the next 30 years. But during those 30 years the public perception of flying disks, or UFOs, as they came to be called, changed dramatically. Polls in the 1970s and 1980s reveal that a majority of U.S. adults had come to accept the notion that some UFOs were alien spacecraft. In this 1970s climate of public acceptance, former Major Jesse Marcel began to regale his friends with his tale of recovering the wreckage of something in 1947 that an official press release had described as a "flying disk," a term that in the 1970s had become a synonym for "alien spacecraft" in the minds of many. Through intermediaries, his story came to the attention of two writers who specialized in strange and unusual phenomena, Charles Berlitz and William Moore. In 1978 they interviewed Marcel, who told them that the wreckage he recovered had unusual properties (e.g., it could not be dented or burned) and that "it was nothing that came from earth." The writers uncovered other witnesses that confirmed and elaborated on Marcel's story. Most significant, the testimony of these individuals indicated that the debris found on Brazel's ranch was material torn from the hull of an alien spacecraft that subsequently crashed elsewhere. In 1980 these writers produced the first of the testimonial books on Roswell. In the years that followed, other investigators found new witnesses and produced more books in this category. In most respects, the accounts in these books are similar, and they all agree on extraterrestrial involvement, but they differ markedly on when and where the alien spacecraft crashed, what it looked like, and whether one or two crashed spacecraft were found. In the sum-

mary that follows, these differences are noted (Versions 1, 2, and 3, respectively).

Testimonial Reconstruction of the Incident
In the early summer of 1947 alien spacecraft, apparently intent on monitoring human scientific progress, were seen in the skies over the sites of atomic and rocket research near Alamogordo, New Mexico. Accounts of what happened next diverge at this point.

Version 1: On the evening of July 2, one of these spacecraft was struck by lightning over the town of Roswell, causing pieces of the hull to fall on a ranch operated by William Brazel. The stricken craft traveled more than 100 miles before crashing in a part of the desert called the Plains of San Agustin. The crash was observed on radar at the nearby White Sands Missile Range, and a search for the crash site was made on the following day. Before the troops arrived, however, the remains of a saucer-shaped craft and the small, humanoid bodies of its crew were found by some archaeologists who were working in the area. When the troops arrived they collected the bodies and wreckage, expunged all traces of the crash, and warned the archaeologists to remain silent about what they had seen. On July 3 Brazel found the wreckage that had been ripped from the spacecraft by the lightning strike, and the next day he went to Roswell, where he reported his discovery to the sheriff.

Version 2: On July 4 one of these spacecraft malfunctioned, causing it to touch down briefly on the ranch operated by William Brazel. Still malfunctioning after takeoff, the craft glanced the ground, leaving behind gouged earth and wreckage torn from the hull by the impact. The stricken craft rose in the air and managed to travel about 35 miles north of Roswell, where it crashed into the base of a cliff. Radar operators at White Sands monitored the crash, and a search was scheduled for the following day. But before the troops could arrive some archaeologists who were working in the area stumbled upon the crash site. The remains of the spacecraft indicated that it had a narrow hull with batlike wings. Amid the wreckage were the bodies of four small, humanoid aliens; one appeared to be still alive. One of the archaeologists phoned the sheriff at Roswell and reported the crash. Alerted by the sheriff, military personnel arrived and collected the bodies and wreckage, expunged all traces of the crash, and threatened the archaeologists with severe reprisals, including death threats, if they failed to remain silent about what they had seen. On July 5 Brazel found the debris resulting from the spacecraft's glancing contact with the ground near his ranch house. The next day he went to Roswell, where he reported his discovery to the sheriff.

Version 3: On the evening of July 2 one of these spacecraft malfunctioned, causing it to touch down briefly on a ranch operated by William Brazel. Still malfunctioning after takeoff, the craft exploded in the air, scattering wreckage on the ground below. At about the same time this event occurred, the remains of a *second* alien saucer-shaped spacecraft were found 150 miles away on the Plains of San Agustin by some archaeologists who were working in the area. Amid the wreckage were the bodies of four small, humanoid aliens; one appeared to be still alive. Alerted by radar, troops arrived and collected the bodies and wreckage, expunged all traces of the crash, and warned the archaeologists to remain silent about what they had seen. On July 5 Brazel found the debris scattered on his ranch by the spacecraft that had exploded, and on the following day he went to Roswell, where he reported his discovery to the sheriff.

Versions 1, 2, and 3 agree on what happened next.

The sheriff notified the authorities at Roswell Army Air Field of Brazel's discovery. Major Jesse Marcel, intelligence officer of the 509th Bomb Group, accompanied by another officer soon appeared. They returned with Brazel to his ranch and collected the wreckage, which included lightweight sheets of a metallic substance that was harder than any known terrestrial material; it could be neither dented nor burned. The wreckage was taken to Roswell Army Air Field and, on July 8 the base's public-relations office—as the result of error or an incredible lapse in security—issued a press release indicating that a flying disk had been recovered and sent to higher headquarters. Actually, the bodies and wreckage had been sent to several government laboratories for analysis. On that same day, military personnel carefully coached Brazel on a cover story to be given to reporters. Thus, his interview, which was published on the following day, was a tissue of lies. The official press release—mistakenly issued—was speedily repudiated by General Roger Ramey at his regional headquarters. The wreckage he displayed to reporters was indeed that of a crashed radar reflector and weather balloon that had been substituted for the wreckage of the alien spacecraft. Ramey was thus able to state in an evening newscast that the alleged flying disk was merely the remnants of a downed weather balloon. This cover story points to a calculated government policy to deny the existence of alien visitations. This policy was dictated partly by the fear that widespread panic would follow in the wake of any disclosure of the truth, partly by the military's desire to keep secret the advanced technology gleaned from the wrecked alien spacecraft. This policy, however well-meaning at the time, has continued to the present day, and it now constitutes an unconscionable abuse of the security system that denies us proof at last that we are not alone in the universe.

Commentary

Books on the Roswell incident can be generally characterized as documentary or testimonial, but there is at least one that does not fall in either category. Rather, the author attempts to reconcile the information in 1940s documentation with testimony obtained after 1977 by pointing to the likelihood that an alien spacecraft collided with a Mogul balloon in the sky over the Brazel ranch. In this reconstruction of the incident, the debris found by Brazel was a mixture of wreckage from the crashed balloon and pieces torn from the hull of the damaged spacecraft, which later crashed in another location. The authors of documentary and testimonial books, however, make no such attempt to reconcile conflicting data and instead offer various reasons for accepting some sources of information and rejecting others.

As can be seen, documentary and testimonial books represent drastically different perspectives on the Roswell incident. Moreover, within the category of testimonial books there are significant differences in the reconstructions of the incident, largely because their authors have made different assessments of the credibility of certain witnesses.

Books in both categories have their partisans. Proponents of the documentary reconstruction of the incident reject testimonial books by claiming that some of the testimony on which they are based is unreliable for a variety of reasons (e.g., faulty memory, misinterpretation of valid memories, deliberate lying, etc.); and by pointing out that some of the individuals who handled the debris found by Brazel (notably Sheridan Cavitt, the officer who went with Jesse Marcel to the Brazel ranch) testified later (i.e., after 1977) that the debris did not exhibit any of the unusual properties attributed to it by Marcel.

For their part, proponents of the testimonial reconstruction reject the documentary books by claiming that such books merely promulgate the government's false cover story; and by pointing to the cumulative significance of the thousands of unexplained UFO sightings by credible witnesses that have been reported over the years since 1947.

In sum, the Roswell incident remains highly controversial. Those who wish to form an opinion on this topic are thus well advised to read both documentary and testimonial books.

—*Charles A. Ziegler and Benson Saler*

See Also: Alien Autopsy Film; Area 51; Conspiracy Theories; Hangar 18; Majestic 12

Further Reading:

Berlitz, C., and W. L. Moore, *The Roswell Incident.* New York: Grosset and Dunlap, 1980.

Friedman, S. T., and D. Berliner. *Crash at Corona.* New York: Paragon House, 1992.

Korff, K. K. *The Roswell UFO Crash.* New York: Random House, 2000.

Randle, K. D., and D. R. Schmitt. *The Truth about the UFO Crash at Roswell.* New York: Avon Books, 1994.

Saler, B., C. A. Ziegler, and C. B. Moore. *UFO Crash at Roswell.* Washington, DC: Smithsonian Institution Press, 1997.

United States Air Force. *The Roswell Report.* Washington, DC: U.S. Government Printing Office, 1995.

SAMPLE-TAKING INCIDENT

In 1975 numerous UFO sightings in or near North Hudson Park (near the border of New York and New Jersey) were reported, but the closest encounter was that of George O'Barski, 72. He was driving through the park when he saw an object that looked like a "great big pancake that had puffed up." It was brightly lit and 30 feet long, hovering 10 feet above the ground. A door opened, and small beings in suits came down a ladder and began filling bags with soil, totally ignoring O'Barski. After a few moments they scurried into the UFO and took off.

Doormen at the Stonehenge Apartments across the street also saw, on varied occasions, strange lights and round, humming objects in the park area. One doorman, a few months after the first sighting, saw a small figure in a suit carrying a bag and bending over. An entire family also witnessed a UFO with square windows and a dome just north of the park.

Further Reading:

Clark, Jerome. *The UFO Encyclopedia.* 2nd ed. Detroit: Omnigraphics, 1998.

Hopkins, Budd. *Missing Time: A Documented Study of UFO Abductions.* New York: Richard Marek, 1981.

SANTO VERSUS THE MARTIAN INVASION

In this 1966 Mexican film Martians land in Mexico because it is such a peaceful country and demand an end to nuclear testing and space shots. Their intentions appear to be less than peaceful, however, when they threaten to and in fact do disintegrate people with rays and kidnap several earthlings to study their physiological construction. Santo rescues the kidnapped earthlings and blows up the spaceship, killing all the aliens. *Santo versus the Martian Invasion* reflects several themes found in UFO literature, from aliens' interest in terrestrial nuclear testing to the kidnapping and physical examination of human beings.

Producciones Cinematograficas 1966; 85 min. Director: Alfredo B. Crevenna; Writer: Rafael Garcia Traversi; Cinematography: Jorge Stahl Jr.; Cast: Maura Monti, Eve Norvind, Wolf Ruvinskis, Belinda Corell, Gilda Miros, Benny Galan, Natanael Leon Frankenstin.

SATANISM AND UFOS

Satanism, the worship of the Christian devil, has traditionally been associated with several practices that parody Roman Catholic Christianity. Among its rituals is the black mass, which usually includes the profaning of the central acts of worship, the repeating of the Lord's Prayer backward, the use of a host that has been dyed black, the slaughter of an animal, which is usually a cat or a dog, in order to parody the crucifixion, or the rape of a woman upon the altar. The worship usually culminates with the invocation of Satan for the working of malevolent magic.

The satanic tradition was created and sustained by generation after generation of antisatanic writers—above all, conservative Christians, who authored several books about satanism, describing its practices in great detail, although none had ever seen a satanic ritual or met a real satanist. The satanism portrayed in the Christian literature has been reproduced by groups and individuals over the last two centuries. Christian authors, convinced that diabolical plots underlie anything perceived as occult, have also not been reluctant to portray the UFO phenomenon as a demonological manifestation.

An increase in the number of ritual remains found in graveyards, church break-ins and vandalism, and mutilated bodies of animals has been reported since the early 1970s. The focus on the remains of mutilated animal bodies attracted the attention of law-enforcement officials who, in late 1973, were investigating deaths of cattle in Kansas and Minnesota under apparently mysterious circumstances. There seemed to be no visible cause of death; soft body parts had been removed with surgical precision; the blood had been drained; and there were no footprints near the carcasses. In December a group of sheriffs met and decided, from essentially no evidence, that the deaths were probably the work of so-called cultists. Other law-enforcement officials were more skeptical, and the Kansas State University Veterinary Hospital proved that the animals had died of blackleg, a bacterial disease. Nevertheless, many rural people had come to believe that satanists had sacrificed the cattle, and this rumor persisted.

By the late 1970s these rumors had spread to other states and into Canada. Newspapers were claiming thousands of deaths. The four major schools of thought on the causes of the deaths blamed them on cultists, secret government experiments, UFOs, and hysteria. Circumstantial evidence began to turn up that seemed to link cultists with these supposed deaths. In 1975 Donald Flickinger, an agent for the U.S. Bureau of Alcohol, Tobacco, and Firearms, was assigned to investigate reports of a nationwide satanic network engaged in animal and human sacrifice. He could find no supporting evidence. Investigations of speculations about government experiments led to a similar dead end.

In 1980 a documentary entitled "Strange Harvest" by Linda Moulton Howe, a Denver filmmaker, gave new impetus to the UFO theory. Theories about extraterrestrials that mutilated cattle merged with abduction beliefs. By the early 1990s there had arisen a subculture believing firmly in a complex mythology that asserted evil aliens were in cahoots with the U.S. government and were being permitted to abduct cattle and humans in exchange for advanced technological information. This school of thought eventually won out over the satanic-ritual theory.

See Also: Cattle Mutilations; Demonological Explanations of UFOs

Further Reading:
Clark, Jerome. The UFO Encyclopedia. 2nd ed. Detroit: Omnigraphics, 1998.
Richardson, James T., Joel Best, and David G. Bromley, eds. The Satanism Scare. New York: Aldine de Gruyter, 1991.

SAUCERS

Saucers was a digest-sized quarterly magazine published from June 1953 through Winter 1960. Edited by Max B. Miller, it covered the widest range of viewpoints of any UFO periodical. Included in its pages were scientific analyses of UFO evidence and contactee reports. Saucers published the first account of Truman Bethurum, who claimed contact with aliens in the Nevada desert. Saucers's parent company was Flying Saucers International, which sponsored the first Giant Rock Spacecraft Convention in August 1953.

See Also: Bethurum, Truman; Giant Rock Spacecraft Convention

SCHIRMER ABDUCTION

In Ashland, Nebraska, on December 3, 1967, at 2:30 A.M. police Sergeant Herbert Schirmer noticed red lights on the highway. When he went to investigate he saw a metallic disk hovering six to eight feet above the road. With a high-pitched whine and blue flame coming from underneath, the UFO rose and zoomed off, leaving an open-mouthed Schirmer to stand and stare. He was surprised to find that a half hour had elapsed—it seemed like only 10 minutes. He began to feel sick and noticed a red welt under his ear.

Three years later a psychologist hypnotized him, and he remembered that aliens had emerged from the craft. They were about five feet tall, had long, thin heads, slitlike eyes that never blinked, flat noses, and no lips. They were seeking power from a nearby power plant. Schirmer was given a tour of the ship and was told that the beings were from a nearby galaxy and had bases on Venus as well as on earth, off the coasts of Florida and Argentina. The beings were friendly and wanted to help humans, they said, but were waiting until earthlings were more accustomed to the idea of extraterrestrials before they came out in the open.

Driving near Geneseo, Illinois, Rex Ball sees a strange object in a field. He falls asleep but is vaguely aware of small, hairy, Japaneselike aliens who abduct him. (Mary Evans Picture Library)

Schirmer was told by the leader to say nothing about what he had seen and that he would be contacted again twice. When they left, Schirmer remembered nothing.

An interesting detail in this case is Schirmer's report of winged serpents depicted on the space suits. At least three other close encounters describe the same or similar emblem. It is especially strange because a winged serpent is a familiar image in earthly mythology.

See Also: Abductees; Close Encounters
Further Reading:

Blum, Ralph, with Judy Blum. *Beyond Earth: Man's Contact with UFOs.* New York: Bantam Books, 1974.

Bryan, C. D. B. *Close Encounters of the Fourth Kind: Alien Abduction, UFOs, and the Conference at M.I.T.* New York: Alfred A. Knopf, 1995.

SCHMIDT, REINHOLD

On November 5, 1957, 60-year-old grain buyer Reinhold Schmidt was driving along the Platte River near Kearney, Nebraska, when he saw a flash of light in the sky. Looking closer, he observed a blimp-shaped object resting on the ground. It was 100 feet long, 30 feet wide, and 14 feet high. When he got close to it his car engine died. He got out of the car and started walking toward the object, but he was hit by a beam of light, which briefly paralyzed him. Two men came out of the craft and ushered him inside.

In the craft he met the crew of four men and two women, all conventionally dressed. They spoke German to each other and German-accented English to Schmidt. There was brief conversation about the U.S. space satellite. Then Schmidt was asked to leave, and the craft departed. Afterward, Schmidt went to the sheriff's office. A sheriff and policeman accompanied Schmidt to the site and found three sets of footprints and a greenish, greasy substance on the ground.

A background check on Schmidt revealed that he had served time for embezzlement in a Nebraska penitentiary in 1938 and 1939. They found an empty can of green motor oil in Schmidt's trunk. Schmidt refused to take a polygraph test. The day after the contact, two psychiatrists examined Schmidt and decided that he was mentally ill because he believed what he was saying. He was placed in a state mental hospital and released a few days later.

Schmidt was soon on the contactee circuit, lecturing with Wayne S. Aho. He began claiming additional contacts by the same crew he had met previously, who turned out to be from Saturn. In May 1961 a film dramatization of the Schmidt story called *Edge of Tomorrow* was released.

In October 1961 Schmidt went on trial in Oakland, California, for grand theft in having bilked a widow out of $5,000. The money was to go into a mining venture, as Schmidt claimed to have viewed quartz crystals from a spaceship. Schmidt acknowledged having collected more than $25,000 from elderly women. Notable at this trial was young astronomer Carl Sagan, who testified that Saturn could not possibly harbor human life as Schmidt had claimed. The jury convicted Schmidt, and he was imprisoned; thus ended his four years on the UFO circuit.

See Also: Contactees; Hoaxes

Further Reading:

Bryan, C. D. B. *Close Encounters of the Fourth Kind: Alien Abduction, UFOs, and the Conference at M.I.T.* New York: Alfred A. Knopf, 1995.

Schmidt, Reinhold O. *Edge of Tomorrow: A True Account of Experiences with Visitors from Another Planet.* Hollywood, CA: The Author, 1963.

SCIENTOLOGY

It has been disputed whether or not Scientology is a religion in the standard sense, despite the many claims to this effect by founder L. Ron Hubbard (1911–1986) and most members and institutional organs of Scientology. Although the starting point of this organization and its idea of salvation is basically a therapeutic concept and practice (cf. *Dianetics* and the promised state "clear"; from 1950 onward), it nevertheless has to be placed within the growing ufological stream of the late 1940s and early 1950s. In light of several purported UFO sightings and supposed contacts of that time (cf. so-called close encounters of the fourth kind), esoteric-theosophical concepts of reincarnation, the striving for psychological and spiritual liberation, and the fascination with paranormal faculties became fused with ideas of ancient astronauts, sunken continents, science-fiction motifs, Christian millenarism, and the like and soon advanced to the stage of a popular fad. This was true not only for individual writers and prophets of a dawning millennium but also in terms of socially organized UFO groups. Scientology can even be viewed as a group representation of certain ufological motifs. It is no mere coincidence that one of the first public presentations of Hubbard's *Dianetics* was published in Joseph Campbell's famous sci-fi magazine *Astounding Science Fiction,* in which a few of his early sci-fi writings had already appeared between 1938 and 1950. Some contactees and esoteric ufologists of the formative period after World War II had also been in touch with Scientology for some time—as in the case of Mrs. Keech (a pseudonym for Dorothy Martin, also known as Sister Thedra of the Association of Sananda and Sanat Kumara), who was the subject of the classic sociopsychological study *When Prophecy Fails* (1955).

Scientology's ufological strands can be illustrated by the following observations, which relate to (1) the group's basic anthropological framework, (2) a specific science-fiction mythology as founding myth, (3) the alleged recollection of "memories of the future" along the disclosure of "Whole Track" memories, (4) the amalgamation of spiritual progress and scientific-technological perfection, and (5) the important role of Hubbard's sci-fi novels for Scientologists.

Scientology's Concept of the Person (Anthropology)

In a typical representation of UFO faith motifs, Scientology shares the widespread ufological assumption that human souls are originally spiritual "implants" from other galactic realms. In direct analogy to the extraterrestrial "walk-ins" or so-called "star seeds" of esoteric ufology, which are supposed to mature spiritually in the earthly garden (e.g., the Ashtar Command: "You are not human beings, having a spiritual experience, but you are a spiritual beings, having a human experience"), Scientology speaks of a "Thetan" as the true spiritual core of the person: This Thetan is currently "wearing" a human body and a mind. According to Hubbard's writings and lectures, the person's Thetan has a (normally unconscious or hidden) "track" of memories stretching back into primordial interstellar times. The Thetans once became trapped into the physical universe, which is represented by matter, energy, space, and time (MEST), and they forgot to make use of their original superhuman freedom and strength. Surpassing the original scope of mere dianetics, it is the basic intention of Scientology to awaken the Thetans from their sleeplike state and to free them from their captivity in the material, three-dimensional world. In realization of this program, the Thetan is to be transformed into a so-called Operating Thetan (OT): a spiritual being who—in the course of several stages (OT I, OT II, and so on)—will resume the "state of full cause" over MEST. As in other representations of ufology (cf. the esoteric concept of ascension), a great range of paranormal faculties will then be at his/her hands. Similar to the prologue of the Star Wars movies, the history of Thetans stretches back to a once-upon time in a remote galaxy, and Hubbard's estimations indeed go far beyond the scope of modern scientific astrophysical assumptions.

The Founding Myth

The founding myth of Scientology's anthropological framework is part of the organization's secret doctrines (such arcane teachings are common to many secret societies, mystery religions, and lodges). However, much of the material has already become known to the wider public through the disclosures of former members, several court trials, and critical publications in print as well as on the Internet. The basic story, which has a special place within secret OT III teachings, can be summarized in brief: About 75 million years ago a fierce intergalactic ruler named Xenu seized billions of Thetans and brought them unto earth (Teegeeack in those times), where he arrested them. From those times onward, after a severe struggle and hypnotically implanted false memories, today's earthly Thetans began to dwell in this region of the universe, and they started to inhabit human bodies in innumerable circles of reincarnations ("past lives" in Scientology terminology). Although the details of this account are supposed to remain secret, many other aspects of the typical incidents around this "space opera" (Hubbard's own term) were already described publicly by Hubbard in his works on the cosmic history, or "track" of theta-memories.

Space-Opera Memories of the Whole Track

Hubbard's most "mythological" public writings, Scientology—A History of Man (1952) and Have You Lived before This Life? (1960), as well as his lecture series Time Track of Theta and Whole Track (available as audiocassettes), portray portions of a very extensive ufological scenario. Hubbard takes it for granted that earthly Thetans have large memories from past lives during terrestrial times and from extraterrestrial regions of the universe. With the "religious technology" of Auditing, Hubbard claims to have gained access to these locked memories and to have proved their truth scientifically. He even felt that he was able to sketch the basic "incidents" of the time-track that are most common to all earthly Thetans' memory banks. Such incidents incorporate memories "before earth," "between-lives areas" on other planets, the experience of magic forces and electric tortures, and many more. Apart from these apparently collective memories there is an abundance of individual memories dealing with past lives in interstellar regions (cf. esp. Have You Lived Before This Life?). To the outside observer, however, such alleged recollections seem to have more affinity to the phenomena of guided fantasies than real memories. Nevertheless, it is the basic conviction of Scientology therapy, or "processing," that the individual can (and should) be freed from all traumatic "engrams" (a class of traumatic memories), "forgetter implants," and the like on the track in order to resume the state of a free Operating Thetan.

Amalgamation of Spiritual Progress and Scientific-Technological Perfection

The amalgamation of spiritual progress and scientific-technological perfection is a result of this outlook. Similar to several other esoteric ufological teachings, Hubbard's Scientology claims to complete all religion and much of science by offering a truly integral approach to life for all humanity. Scientology is indeed presented as *the* integral science of humankind—incorporating science, philosophy, religion, and technology simultaneously. Hubbard's spiritual technology is said to fulfill the teachings of Buddha (cf. esp. Hubbard's *Hymn of Asia,* 1965); ancient extraterrestrial memory implants explain the existence of other religious beliefs. The whole notion and atmosphere of cool technology dominant in Scientology publications and products is mixed with the promise of ultimate spiritual perfection and freedom. The OTs are supposed to be increasingly capable (again) of various (dormant) paranormal faculties—like teleportation, telepathy, time travel, bilocation, astral projection, and so on. Many Scientology brochures and commercial advertisements for specific courses and religious techniques allude to these alleged and apparently attractive faculties. In auditing procedures, candidates are supposed to learn the employment of certain faculties like "exteriorization" and astral projection.

Hubbard's Science Fiction

Hubbard's science fiction is another component of the ufological undercurrent in Scientology. Although the sci-fi novels are of a different genre than the other technological disclosures of Hubbard, they are highly appreciated by participants, and the organization is very keen to promote Hubbard's literary output in this realm. Therefore, one could at least speculate about the influence of these literary sci-fi topics on the stimulation of an extraterrestrial imagery during auditing sessions. For example, a shy and fragile woman might reconstruct memories of being a former space commander of the toughest sort, as Hubbard points out in one of his lectures (*Whole Track*). Because of

connections between some motifs in Hubbard's sci-fi novels and specific Scientology teachings, one might perceive Scientology even as one of the rare instances where science fiction (or fantasy literature generally) is related to the successful formation of a new spiritual movement.

—Andreas Gruenschloss

See Also: Contactees; Cults; UFO; Religions, UFO

Further Reading:

A Series of Lectures on the Whole Track. Los Angeles: L. Ron Hubbard/Church of Scientology, 1984–1985 (six lectures from the years 1959–1963; six audio-cassettes).

Atack, Jon. *A Piece of Blue Sky: Scientology, Dianetics, and L. Ron Hubbard Exposed.* Secaucus, NJ, and New York: Lyle Stuart, 1990.

Frenschkowski, M. "L. Ron Hubbard and Scientology: An Annotated Bibliographical Survey of Primary and Selected Secondary Literature." *Marburg Journal of Religion* 4(1) (July 1999).

Hubbard, L. Ron. *Have You Lived Before This Life?* Los Angeles: Bridge Publications, and Copenhagen: New Era Publications, 1989.

———. *Scientology—A History of Man.* Los Angeles: Bridge Publications, and Copenhagen: New Era Publications, 1988.

———. *The Time Track of Theta—More on the History of Man: A Series of Lectures by L. Ron Hubbard.* Los Angeles: Scientology/Golden Era Productions, 1978 and 1988 (lectures given in 1952; four audio-cassettes).

What Is Scientology? Based on the Works of L. Ron Hubbard. Los Angeles: Church of Scientology, and Copenhagen: New Era Publications, 1998.

SEX

Since UFO witnesses and researchers are human, and humans are sexual creatures, it comes as no shock that sex plays a role in the UFO mystery. More and more abduction cases are being reported each year, including more reports claiming intimacies between abductees and abductors. In 1837 and 1838 in London and its general vicinity, several women complained that a strange and powerful man attacked them and ripped off part or all of their clothing. They described the man as a tall, thin, caped figure with pointed ears. His eyes were like "red balls of fire." He wore tight-fitting oilskin attire and a metal helmet. They also claimed that he vomited blue and white flames from the mouth, which either stunned the women

Cover for issue 8 of UFO Review *(1980), "True Sensual Encounters with Aliens" (Mary Evans Picture Library)*

or made them unconscious. He also had the ability to leap great distances and to scale walls and roads with ease. This ability earned him the title "Springheel Jack" and kept him from being caught by the authorities. Jack's attacks continued into 1838, then resumed in 1843. In 1845 he killed a prostitute in front of many witnesses. Sightings were also recorded in 1877 and 1904 in England, then in 1953, 1964, and 1975 in the United States. Although Jack was never accused of any violation other than ripping off clothes, he was the first known otherworldly being interested in the sexuality of the human race.

At 1 A.M. on October 16, 1957, a young Brazilian man, Antonio Villas-Boas, who lived in Minas Gerais, claimed to be dragged from his tractor into a UFO by humanoid aliens. They removed his clothes and sponged his skin with a thick, odorless liquid. After they took a blood sample, a naked woman who was human in appearance, except for long, slanted eyes and pointed chin, walked in and had intercourse with Villas-Boas twice. Before

leaving she pointed to her belly and then to the sky indicating that their baby would be born on another world.

During the evening of May 2, 1968, a teenage girl, Shane Kurz, saw a cigar-shaped object. Half an hour later she fell into a deep sleep. A couple of days later she noticed two reddish, ring-shaped marks on either side of her lower abdomen and a line running from her navel down. She had other symptoms, such as burning eyes and disruption of her menstrual cycle, which led her to seek medical attention. In 1974 Shane wrote to Hans Holzer, a popular writer on psychic phenomena. Holzer placed her under hypnosis and told her to go back to the night in 1968. Shane recalled being transported into an oval-shaped UFO by a warm light. Inside what looked like a hospital room, she encountered a small humanoid being. He told her that she was special and ordered her to lie on a table and to take off her blouse. She was led into another room, where they stuck a needle into her navel. She was told that she will have a humanoid baby. Then a different being walked in and rubbed a warm, jellylike substance on her chest that he claimed would stimulate her. The being, whose body and sex organ was humanlike, entered her. Afterward she hit him and accused him of rape. She was then released.

In *Secret Life* (1992) David M. Jacobs introduced a new twist to the alien sexual phenomenon: alien-directed human-to-human sexual intercourse. Jacobs found that aliens have considerable interest in human sexuality. Sometimes they will appear in a couple's bedroom and watch them make love, or one member of the couple will be under some type of hypnotic state controlled by the aliens. In one of Jacobs's cases, the victim recalled that as a 15-year-old girl she was forced into having sex with a middle-aged man who was "absolutely out of it. . . . His eyes were glazed over, cloudy, unfocused."

—*Jerome Clark*

See Also: Abductees; Hybrids, Alien-Human; Springheel Jack; Villas-Boas Encounter

Further Reading:

Bryan, C. D. B. *Close Encounters of the Fourth Kind: Alien Abduction, UFOs, and the Conference at M.I.T.* New York: Alfred A. Knopf, 1995.

Jacobs, David M. *Secret Life: Firsthand Accounts of UFO Abductions.* New York: Simon and Schuster, 1992.

Mack, John E. *Abduction: Human Encounters with Aliens.*
New York: Charles Scribner's Sons, 1994.
Randles, Jenny. *Abduction: Over 200 Documented UFO
Kidnappings Investigated.* London: Robert Hale, 1988.

SHAMANISM

Shamans are the religious specialists of hunter-gatherer cultures. They are particularly associated with the aboriginal peoples of Central Asia and the Americas and are perhaps most familiar as the medicine men of traditional Native American cultures. As several observers have pointed out, UFO contactees reflect certain shamanic traits.

Although the terms "shaman" and "shamanism" have come to be used quite loosely, in the disciplines of anthropology and comparative religion shamanism encompasses a fairly specific set of ideas and practices that can be found in many, but not all, world cultures. The word "shaman" comes from *saman,* the Tungusic term for this religious specialist. The term was originally coined by an earlier generation of scholars who were studying societies in Siberia and Central Asia; it was later extended to similar religious complexes found elsewhere in the world. Depending on how one interprets the archaeological evidence, shamanism is many thousands of years old.

Characteristically, the shaman is a healer, a psychopomp (someone who guides the souls of the dead to their home in the afterlife), and more generally a mediator between her or his community and the world of spirits. As a system, shamanism frequently emphasizes contact and communication with spirits in the other world. It is in this latter role that contactees parallel shamans, in that contactees frequently deliver messages from the Space Brothers, who are conceptualized as quasi-spiritual beings.

There are several different traditional ways in which one becomes a shaman. Often it is simply inherited. At other times, the person to become a shaman is chosen by spiritual forces and compelled against her or his will to become a shaman. This supernatural election frequently involves a serious illness in which the chosen person comes close to death, making this part of the process a kind of initiatory death in which the old person

"dies" to her or his former self. The death theme is emphasized in certain traditions in which the chosen individual has a vision of himself as being slain, dismembered, reconstructed, and revived. In other traditions, the initiate is swallowed alive and regurgitated (e.g., the biblical story of Jonah has shamanic overtones). The parallel between shamanic election and the contactee who is abducted against her or his will and put through a kind of initiatory "torture" before assuming a role as a mouthpiece for ufonauts is fairly obvious.

People, when playing their role as shamans, enter an altered state of consciousness in order to contact nonordinary reality. This altered state can be brought on by diverse techniques, from drumming and chanting to fasting and sweat baths. When available, shamans sometimes make use of mind-altering drugs. Once in their altered frame of mind, shamans can see or sense normally invisible realms and are also able to serve as mediums. In this nonordinary state, they can travel to the realm of the gods—usually conceived of as in the heavens—and serve as intermediary between their community and divine beings. Once again, the connection between shamanic trances and the contemporary channeling phenomenon by UFO contactees is transparent.

See Also: Contactees; Initiation
Further Reading:
Eliade, Mircea. *Shamanism: Archaic Techniques of Ecstasy.*
Princeton: Princeton University Press, 1964.
Grim, John A. *The Shaman: Patterns of Siberian and
Ojibway Healing.* Norman: University of Oklahoma
Press, 1983.
Harner, Michael. *The Way of the Shaman.* New York:
Bantam, 1986.
Hultkrantz, Ake. "A Definition of Shamanism." *Temenos* 9
(1973): 25–37.

SHAVER MYSTERY

In 1943 Richard S. Shaver of Barto, Pennsylvania, wrote a letter to *Amazing Stories,* a pulp science-fiction magazine. Editor Howard Browne read the letter, which purported to reproduce an ancient alphabet from the lost civilization of Lemuria, a hypothetical continent thought by some to have existed long ago in the Indian Ocean. Browne considered the letter to be from a crackpot and threw it in the trash. Thus, what came to be known as the Shaver mystery might never have come to light had editor Ray Palmer not retrieved the letter from the wastebasket and published the alphabet in the January 1944 issue of *Amazing Stories.*

Upon seeing the alphabet in print, Shaver sent a long manuscript entitled "A Warning to Future Man" to Ray Palmer. Palmer worked the manuscript into a science-fiction novella called *I Remember Lemuria!* This introduction to the Shaver mystery was published under Shaver's byline in the March 1945 issue of *Amazing Stories.* The story began in the 1930s, when Richard Shaver began hearing mental voices that he learned came from "deros," depraved creatures that delighted in torturing people. Unable to turn off the voices in his head, Shaver quit his job as a welder and spent time in mental hospitals and prisons.

From the dero voices Shaver learned that both human beings and deros were descended from a race of giants known as the Titans, who lived on earth in the distant past. Then some 12,000 years ago the sun began emanating deadly radiation, and the Titans had to withdraw into vast subterranean caverns. The most favored members of the Titans boarded spaceships and moved to distant planets. Those who remained behind either adapted to the sun's rays and returned to the surface (the present human race) or continued to live in the caverns (the deros). The cavern-dwellers became sadistic cannibals.

Unlike many other unexplained phenomena, the so-called Shaver mystery really has no physical evidence it can point to for support. The closest thing to supporting evidence came from Ray Palmer, who went to Pennsylvania to meet Richard and Dorothy Shaver. Palmer claims that during the night he was at the Shaver house he heard five voices discussing tearing a woman apart in a nearby cave. Palmer said it was impossible for those voices to have come from Richard Shaver's lips.

Over the next three years *Amazing Stories* devoted a significant portion of the magazine's content to the Shaver mystery. Ray Palmer credited the Shaver mystery for increasing the magazine's circulation from 135,000 to 185,000 over that period. Another editor, however, claims that an audit indicated that there was no change in circulation during that time.

The Shaver mystery was controversial due in part to its sadomasochistic content. People either loved it or hated it. Chester S. Geier, a regular contributor to *Amazing Stories,* directed the Shaver Mystery Club, which was joined by some *Amazing* readers. Some readers claimed that they had been in the caves where the hideous creatures lived. Fred Crisman, who in 1947 was involved in the Maury Island hoax, even wrote that he had fought his way out of such a cave with a submachine gun.

While some readers became hooked on Shaver mystery stories, others were outraged by them, believing that they appealed only to the lunatic fringe of science fiction and fantasy enthusiasts. Most found Shaver's stories bizarre and unpleasant. Those who knew Shaver were convinced of his sincerity, even if they didn't believe his stories.

In 1948 Ziff-Davis, publisher of *Amazing Stories,* ordered the Shaver series to be dropped, apparently in response to complaints from readers. By then Ray Palmer had started publishing another magazine called *Fate,* which featured "true mysteries." *Fate* ran one article on the Shaver mystery, but Palmer's partner in *Fate,* Curtis Fuller, was not fond of the subject, and no further articles appeared in that publication.

In 1949 Ray Palmer moved to Wisconsin, where Shaver now lived, and started a rival magazine to *Fate,* called *Mystic,* in which pieces by Shaver continued to appear into the 1950s. It was in *Mystic* that Shaver shared his theory of flying saucers. He said there were three kinds of saucers. Some were projectiles from machines operated by the deros in their caverns. Others came from space to see the sights or loot the caverns in which the deros live. A third kind have lived on earth in hiding for centuries.

In 1961 Ray Palmer released the first issue of *The Hidden World,* a quarterly magazine entirely devoted to the Shaver mystery. It was published until 1964. Richard Shaver died in 1975, and Palmer died in 1977. With their passing, the Shaver mystery has for the most part died out. A newsletter called *Shavertron* is issued by Richard Toronto from time to time, and references to it can occasionally be found when the hollow-earth theory is discussed.

—*Jerome Clark*

See Also: Inner Earth
Further Reading:
Crabb, Riley. *The Reality of the Underground.* Vista, CA: Borderland Sciences Research Associates, 1960.
Gardner, Martin. *The New Age: Notes of a Fringe Watcher.* Buffalo, NY: Prometheus Press, 1988.
Kafton-Minkel, Walter. *Subterranean Worlds: 100,000 Years of Dragons, Dwarfs, the Dead, Lost Races, and UFOs from Inside the Earth.* Port Townsend, WA: Loompanics Unlimited, 1989.
Norman, Eric [pseudonym of Eugene Olson, a.k.a. Brad Steiger]. *The Under-People.* New York: Award Books, 1969.
Walton, Bruce A. *A Guide to the Inner Earth.* Jane Lew, WV: New Age Books, 1983.

THE SILENCE OF DR. EVANS

In this 1973 Russian film three aliens from a peaceful planet come to earth and find nothing but violence, injustice, and grief. The female alien is killed, causing the others to realize that their visit was premature—earth is still far too primitive a civilization—and they leave.

The Silence of Dr. Evans embodies a theme found in several sci-fi films, which is that extraterrestrials are morally superior to earthlings. The savagery of humanity is one of the reasons sometimes given for why the Space Brothers have not yet announced themselves and established formal relations with our planet.

Mosfilm 1973; 90 min. Director/Writer: Budimir Matalnikov; Cinematography: Yuri Sokol, Vladimir Bondarev; Cast: Sergey Bondarchuck, Zhanna Bolotova, I. Kuznetsov, Leonid Obolenski, Irina Skobtseva.

SIRIUS MYSTERY

In the late 1940s four priests of the Dogon, a people in Mali, supposedly of Egyptian descent, told two French anthropologists the following facts about the star Sirius: that it has a companion star (Sirius B) that is invisible to the human eye; that Sirius B orbits around Sirius A every 50 years; that it is small and incredibly heavy; and that it rotates on its axis. All these statements are true, but they had only been recently discovered by Western as-tronomers. How did the Dogon know of them only a few years later?

The Dogon also had detailed information about the planets in our solar system. They state that they got this information from the Nommos, reptile-like beings that arrived in fiery ships from a planet that revolves around another star (Sirius C) that also revolves about Sirius A. The Nommos lived mostly in the sea, were somewhat fishlike, and were the sources for Mediterranean depictions of gods resembling merfolk.

Skeptical Westerners claimed that the Dogon must have gotten this information from Western astronomers. The French anthropologists are sure this is not true; they have artifacts, centuries old, that depict the Sirius configuration. The skeptics ignore such arguments, as usual. The Sirius mystery remains unsolved.

See Also: Ancient Astronauts
Further Reading:
Clark, Jerome. *The UFO Encyclopedia.* 2nd ed. Detroit: Omnigraphics, 1998.
Temple, Robert K. G. *The Sirius Mystery.* Rochester, VT: Destiny, 1976.

THE SOCIOLOGY OF UFOLOGY

Is it possible to study science and parascience (commonly disparaged as pseudoscience), black holes and flying saucers, the theories of a scientist, and the beliefs of a saucerian (ufologist) with the same sociological tools? Is it possible to explain them with the very same kind of explanations?

Not so very long ago, subjects like sorcery were relegated to the ranks of studies of human ignorance. It took all of the energy of researchers like Jeanne Favret-Saada to show how biased this approach was and how it reflected researchers' prejudices. The anthropology of flying saucers is in the same state as the analysis of peasant witchcraft before Favret-Saada. Most scientists shelve the phenomenon away as irrational and/or pathological. This makes the subject a sociological "untouchable." Is it possible to do a sociology of flying saucers without reducing them to a sociopsychological phenomenon? Though all too rare, a few attempts have nevertheless been made by sociologists, historians, and folklorists. They have made some progress. Let us review briefly these efforts.

The majority of sociological studies of UFOs has focused on UFO cults, UFO contactees, and their followers. These studies take a radically different approach from the reductionist and psychiatrically oriented approach of the 1960s. Such psychiatrically oriented diagnoses as H. Taylor Buckner's—who claimed that UFO enthusiasts he observed are either "young schizophrenics or aged with advanced senility. I have never seen a male saucerian who could make a successful presentation of normalcy"—have been severely criticized by sociologists like John Lofland, who studied the same groups without noticing the people Buckner claimed he saw. Roy Wallis in his study of the Aetherius Society, and R. W. Balch and D. Taylor in their ethnography of Bo and Peep's followers (Heaven's Gate), showed that such people are not abnormal. David Stupple and William McNeece remark that "this pathological model of cult membership is both gratuitous and inaccurate." The many different reasons that might bring someone to join a cult show that "it is faulty to assume that cult members are alike in psychological or sociological characteristics." In the wake of these studies, academic treatments of contactees took a nonpsychiatric turn.

The sociology of the parasciences has also made significant progress. This was made possible because of the emergence of science studies in the 1970s and 1980s. The history and sociology of science advanced the analysis of controversies on scientific anomalies by moving the analysis from epistemology to sociology, from the content to the context, from the facts to the people who study them, from scientific *thinking* to scientific *practice*. This was done not in order to replace classical epistemology with a more fashionable sociology but to demonstrate how social factors are more important than alleged epistemological factors in the acceptance or rejection of facts, how content cannot be separated from context, and how observers construct the facts (not simply "discover" them) thanks to their practice of science and not thanks to some improbable rules of scientific thinking.

Some historians and sociologists of science also focused on controversies over scientific anomalies and on disciplines like parapsychology

and ufology. In the wake of social studies of science that explain the way error and truth are constructed in science, these studies of parasciences created the conditions for a balanced, symmetrical analysis of science and parascience, moving from the idea of pathological science to the idea that in parascience, "nothing unscientific is happening," as Harry Collins and Trevor Pinch remarked in regard to parapsychology. Ron Westrum showed that we could study controversies on scientific anomalies without making a priori assumptions about the difference between UFO facts and scientific facts. They showed that there is no great divide, no sharp distinction, between pseudoscientific and scientific minds. By moving from psychological arguments about pseudoscience to the description of the material conditions in which their work is produced, they have demonstrated the role of social factors in the acceptance or rejection of anomalies and that the same factors are necessary in the determination of scientific facts. By taking into consideration context, cultural setting, and social factors, they have shown that the latter play a role in the emergence of truth, of reality, and of new phenomena.

A third group of UFO spokespersons has been much less studied: the skeptics. Although their importance in maintaining the controversy is particularly important, they have been the focus of relatively few studies. Paul McCarthy was the first to take into consideration the work of Thomas Kuhn to study the career of University of Arizona professor James McDonald and, with the same tools in the same dissertation, to study the work of skeptical astrophysicist Donald Menzel and skeptical journalist Philip Klass.

In the 1970s UFO groups generated a new category of UFO investigators: the new ufologists, who tended to consider UFOs as a purely sociopsychological phenomenon. On the one hand studies of UFO cults have made progress by abandoning psychiatrically oriented explanations; on the other studies of ufology have made progress by abandoning the asymmetry between science and parascience (or between skeptics and advocates of the reality of UFOs). Instead, the line has moved to an asymmetry between ufology and UFO contactees. Sociologists who study contactees tend not to study ufology, and sociologists who study ufology either do not study contactees or debunk them. The two domains remain, for the most part, ignorant of each other. There is no debate on the feasibility or the necessity of a symmetrical study of both domains. The problem has never been raised or discussed. It is as if there were no problem, or as if the solution is clearly that there is some sort of a great divide—a fundamental difference between *minds*—between ufology and UFO cults.

A sociologist who moves from a description of ufology to a denunciation of UFO contactees is like a scientist who uses Newton's and Laplace's laws when he studies the physics of planetary orbits and then makes moral judgments when he speaks about "threatening" asteroids that may strike the earth. He *describes* the motion of the planets but *accuses* the asteroids of being dangerous. The latter is not an explanation. A physical description of meteorites gains nothing by a consideration of their dangerosity. What is added to a sociological explanation of UFO contactees when we pronounce the judgment that contactees are hoaxers or pathological liars? A sociologist of contactees should ask how the notion of fraud is constructed and not simply assume it as a self-evident characteristic. What is most obvious for members of the tribe should be the more strange for the analyst. But strangely enough, no sociologist has ever tried to analyze the social construction of hoaxing.

There is a final distinction made between UFO witnesses and UFO investigators (whether skeptics or believers). We have seen how much time and effort it took to suspend psychological explanations for ufologists and cultists and to treat them with the same sociological tools we use to study skeptics and scientists. But questions raised by UFO witnesses tend to be relegated to the domain of psychologists. The great divide we have been chasing manifests again. When someone asks "Why do people see UFOs?" social scientists and science spokespersons usually consider that the answer lies in the psychology of perception. But we do not use psychology to explain why scientists see scientific facts. Why not place the perceptions of a UFO witness and the perceptions of a

scientist on par with one another? The classic reply is that scientists see the world the way it is, without interpreting it, without being under the influence of their belief systems (except, of course, when they make mistakes), whereas the UFO witness makes the mistake of misperceiving natural or artificial phenomena due to the influence of her or his familiarity with science fiction. On one side is a neutral scientist; on the other, a UFO witness. The problem with this explanation of UFO sightings is that it simply assumes that UFOs do not exist and that if there is a such wide gap as the one between reality and fantasy we must use incommensurably different explanations for these two sets of facts—explanations that turn out to be overly complicated and impossible to falsify. The asymmetry of these explanations is their most important weakness. Is it possible to describe the perception of a scientist (astronomers are often mentioned when UFOs are discussed) and the perception of a UFO witness without using radically different kinds of explanation? Is it possible to use the same explanation for both categories of witness?

The problem is to contribute to a sociology of UFOs without reducing any aspect of it to a sociopsychological phenomenon. The trap to avoid is an obvious one: that of leaving the sociology to one side and concentrating only on the ufology, and the opposite trap of abandoning ufology by smothering it with a sociological explanation. But the most obvious traps are often the most deadly. Above all, one must use the accounts of the witnesses to furnish their own explanations. One should not presuppose any one actor is a priori more significant, or more truthful, than any other. On the contrary, one should attempt (within the limits of the available sources) to show how the actors themselves reach their conclusions and by what mechanisms they define who is right and who is wrong, who is off base and who is credible. Instead of imposing these differences or simply telling a story, the analyst should attempt to construct his or her account so that the actors themselves create the differences. In other words, the different protagonists should do the sociology, rather than the sociologist.

We need to study the circulation of the saucer story. The reality or falsity of UFOs is not a prize awarded by the external observer at the end of the process; it is the very thing at stake for all the protagonists while they dispute. It is this dispute itself that will gradually construct and deconstruct the phenomena. At one moment the narrative may collapse under the weight of certain actors; at another it may regain its reality. It is not for the analyst to decide in advance whether the saucers are real or not. As a sociologist, one must follow the tribulations of ufologists, skeptics, and contactees.

—*Pierre Lagrange*

Further Reading:
Balch, R. W., and D. Taylor. "Seekers and Saucers: The Role of the Cultic Milieu in Joining a UFO Cult." *American Behavioral Scientist* 20(6) (July-August 1966): 839–860.
Bartholomew, Robert. "The Romantic versus Enlightenment Debate within the Social Sciences." Ph.D. Thesis, Flinders University of South Australia, 1989.
Bloor, D. *Knowledge and Social Imagery.* London: Routledge and Kegan Paul, 1976.
Boureau, A. "L'église médiévale comme preuve animée de la croyance chrétienne." *Terrain* 14 (March 1990): 113–118.
Buckner, H. Taylor. "The Flying Saucerians: An Open Door Cult." In *Sociology and Everyday Life.* Edited by Marcello Truzzi. Englewood Cliffs, NJ: Prentice Hall, 1968.
———. "Flying Saucers Are for People." *Trans-Action* 3(4) (May-June 1966): 10–13.
Chevalier, G. "Parasciences et procédés de légitimation." *Revue française de Sociologie* 27 (1986): 205–219.
Collins, H. M., and T. J. Pinch. "The Construction of the Paranormal: Nothing Unscientific Is Happening." In *On the Margins of Science: The Social Construction of Rejected Knowledge.* Edited by R. Wallis. Keele: University of Keele, 1979.
Evans-Pritchard, E. E. *Witchcraft, Oracles, and Magic among the Azande.* London: Oxford University Press, 1951.
Favret-Saada, J. *Deadly Words: Witchcraft in the Bocage.* Paris: Maison des Sciences de l'Homme, 1980.
Festinger, L., H. W. Riecken, and S. Schachter. *When Prophecy Fails.* Minneapolis: University of Minnesota Press, 1956.
Lagrange, P., ed. "Science-parascience: preuves et épreuves." *Ethnologie française* 23(3) (1993).
Latour, B. "Comment redistribuer le Grand Partage ?" *Revue de Synthèse* 104 (April-June 1983): 203–236.
———. *Science in Action.* Cambridge: Harvard University Press, 1987.
Lewis, James R., ed. *The Gods Have Landed: New Religions from Other Worlds.* Albany: State University of New York Press, 1995.
Lofland, J. "Normal Flying Saucerians?" *Trans-Action* 3(5) (July-August 1966): 54–55.
McCarthy, P. "Politicking and Paradigm Shifting: James E. McDonald and the UFO Case Study." Ph.D. diss., University of Hawaii, December 1975.
Schmitt, J. C. *Les Revenants. Les vivants et les morts dans la société médiévale.* Paris: Gallimard, 1994.
Schnabel, Jim. "Puck in the Laboratory: The Construction and Deconstruction of Hoaxlike Deception in Science." *Science, Technology, and Human Values* 19(4) (1994): 459–492.
Shapin, S. "History of Science and Its Sociological Reconstruction." *History of Science* 20 (1982): 157–211.
Stoczkowski, W. *Des Hommes, des dieux et des extraterrestres: Ethnologie d'une croyance moderne.* Paris, Flammarion, 1999.
Stupple, D. "The Man Who Talked to Venusians." In *Proceedings of the First International UFO Congress.* Edited by C. Fuller. New York: Warner Books, 1980.
Stupple, D., and W. McNeece. "Contactees, Cult, and Culture." *MUFON Symposium Proceedings,* Seguin, TX, 1979.
Wallis, Roy. "The Aetherius Society: A Case Study in the Formation of a Mystagogic Congregation." *Sociological Review* 22(1) (1974): 27–44.
———. "Science and Pseudo-science." *Social Science Information* 24(3) (September 1985): 585–601.
Westrum, R. "Social Intelligence about Anomalies: The Case of UFOs." *Social Studies of Science* 7(3) (1977): 271–302.

SOLAR LIGHT RETREAT

The Solar Light Retreat began as the Santa Barbara Space Craft Research Society. When the founders moved to southern Oregon in 1965, the Solar Light Center (later changed to Solar Light Retreat) was incorporated as a vehicle for the director's (Aleuti Francesca, originally Marianne Francis) activities as a channel for ufonauts. Francesca's principal contact is with the Saturn Council. Like many other UFO-channeling groups, the Solar Light Retreat teaches standard occult doctrines such as reincarnation and the reality of a spiritual hierarchy of beings.

See Also: Channeling; New Age; Occult; Religions, UFO

Further Reading:

Lewis, James R. *The Encyclopedia of Cults, Sects, and New Religions.* Amherst, NY: Prometheus Books, 1998.

Melton, J. Gordon. *Encyclopedia of American Religion.* 5th ed. Detroit: Gale Research, 1996.

SOLEM, PAUL

In 1948 Paul Solem made his first telepathic contact with UFOs while three hovered over his ranch in Idaho. Four years later he met Paul 2, a Venusian, who, standing next to his spacecraft, gave Solem the mission of preaching the coming Day of Purification to the Indians of North and South America. For over 20 years Solem spoke with the tribes of the western United States, gaining small groups of followers, especially among the Hopi, whose religion prophesies the Day of Purification. On this day, the faithful will be saved from the earth's destruction by "ships without wings." Chief Dan of the Hopi Sun tribe and other traditionalist Hopis believed Solem completely, but the younger members only laughed, and the clan split.

In 1970 a wave of UFO sightings occurred in Prescott, Arizona, where Solem was staying while he communicated with Paul 2 and other beings. A reporter who saw the UFO wrote that Solem repeated words regarding Hopi prophesy that he received telepathically from UFO beings. Many witnesses reported seeing a strange, brilliant light darting around in the sky on numerous occasions. When UFO sightings ceased, however, Solem lost popularity and was scolded by the Venusians for not spreading the message quickly enough.

Solem soon arranged for a close encounter with the media to show the world he was telling the truth, but the Venusians never showed up, and Solem later disappeared from public view. Chief Dan was removed as leader of the Sun Clan by the Hopi Tribal Council for making them look foolish.

See Also: Apocalypse; Contactees; Hoaxes

Further Reading:

Clark, Jerome. *The UFO Encyclopedia.* 2nd ed. Detroit: Omnigraphics, 1998.

Katchongva, Chief Dan. *Hopi Prophecy.* Hotevilla, AZ: Hopi Independent Nation, 1970.

Waters, Frank. *Book of the Hopi.* New York: Viking Press, 1963.

SPACE BROTHERS

In 1952, George Adamski claimed, he met a Venusian in Southern California. This set off a wave of claims to have been contacted by beings from outer space, who were usually here representing the Galactic Federation and worrying about how primitive humans still were. These Space Brothers intend, the contactees believe and preach, to educate humans to prepare them for admission to the Galactic Federation and/or preserve some of them from an imminent catastrophe that will befall the earth. The contactees have a complex theology, largely adapted from theosophy. By the 1960s claims of physical contact began to be replaced by claims of psychic contact, and the phenomenon of channeling the Space Brothers' wisdom began to occur. The contactee movement thus overlaps the New Age movement.

See Also: Adamski, George; Ascended Masters; Channeling; Contactees; New Age; Religions, UFO; Theosophy

Further Reading:

Lewis, James R., ed. *The Gods Have Landed: New Religions From Other Worlds.* Albany: State University of New York Press, 1995.

Vallee, Jacques. *Messengers of Deception: UFO Contacts and Cults.* Berkeley: And/Or Press, 1979.

THE SPACE CHILDREN

In this 1958 movie a peace-seeking space brain controls the children of technicians and space scientists on a U.S. base and compels them to sabotage the launch of a rocket that will place a hydrogen bomb in outer space. The notion that ufonauts are concerned about our nuclear capabilities is a theme often found in UFO literature.

William Alland Productions 1958; 69 min. Director: Jack Arnold; Writer: Bernard C. Shoenfeld; Cinematography: Ernst Laszlo; Special Effects: John P. Fulton; Cast: Adam Williams, Peggy Weber, Michael Ray, Jackie Coogan, John Crawford.

SPACE MASTER X-7

This is a 1958 film told in semidocumentary style. Two security agents are sent to investigate a space probe that returns to earth covered in fungus. When mixed with blood, the fungus grows to enormous proportions and consumes everything in its path, killing the scientist in charge and tak-

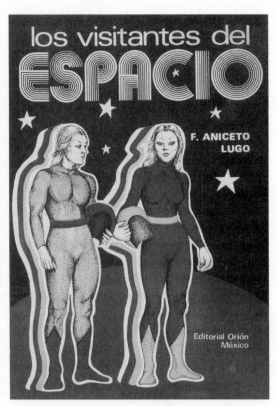

Cover of F. Aniceto Lugo's Los Visitantes del Espacio *(1978), a popular Mexican survey of the UFO phenomenon proposing that visitors from space are responsible for numerous sightings (Mary Evans Picture Library)*

ing over the body of his fiancée, who becomes antisocial. Finally, one of the security guards finds a decontamination antidote that destroys the fungus and restores the woman to her former state. The idea that aliens can take over human beings and control them is an old notion that one finds in such contemporary dramas as the TV series *Dark Skies.* This film takes its influence from *The Quatermass Xperiment* (1955).

Regal 1958; 71 min. Director: Edward Bernds; Writers: George Worthington Yates, Daniel Mainwaring; Cinematography: Brydon Baker; Cast: Bill Williams, Lyn Thomas, Robert Ellis, Paul Frees, Joan Barry, Thomas B. Henry.

SPACE TECHNOLOGY AND RESEARCH FOUNDATION

The Space Technology and Research Foundation (STAR) was set up to spread the message of the Ogatta group—aliens that psychically communicate with Greta Smolowe, who cofounded STAR with her husband, Dick Smolowe. The Ogattans anticipate apocalyptic earth changes in the not-too-distant future that will kill off the majority of the population but that will also prepare the world for the New Age. Smolowe has authored two books under the name Greta Woodrew, *On the Side of Light* (1981) and *Memories of Tomorrow* (1988), that report her experiences and express the message of the Ogattans. STAR also publishes a bimonthly newsletter, the *Woodrew Update.*

See Also: Apocalypse; Channeling; Contactees
Further Reading:
Clark, Jerome. *The UFO Encyclopedia.* 2nd ed. Detroit: Omnigraphics, 1998.
Melton, J. Gordon. *Encyclopedia of American Religion.* 5th ed. Detroit: Gale Research, 1996.

SPACED INVADERS

On the fiftieth anniversary of Orson Welles's radio broadcast of *The War of the Worlds,* an Illinois radio station airs it again in this 1990 film. The signal happens to be picked up by a passing Martian spaceship. The alien crew, thinking their comrades are mounting a mass invasion of earth, come down to Illinois to join in the fun. Since it is Halloween, everyone assumes that the aliens are just trick-or-treaters. This is an interesting take on an event that many have looked to as a paradigm for what might happen if the UFOs ever really did land on the White House lawn.

1990; 102 min. Director: Patrick Read Johnson; Writer: Scott Lawrence Alexander; Cast: Douglas Barr, Royal Dano, Ariana Richards, Kevin Thompson, Jimmy Briscoe, Tony Cox, Debbie Lee Carrington, Tommy Madden.

SPECIES

In this 1995 film human scientists create a human-alien hybrid, which turns out to be one-half blonde bombshell and one-half crazed killer. The movie's premise is particularly interesting, as it reflects an important theme of contemporary UFO lore: human-extraterrestrial hybridization.

MGM 1995; 108 min. Director: Roger Donaldson; Writer: Dennis Feldman; Music: Christopher Young; Cinematography: Andrzej Bartowiak; Cast: Ben Kingsley,

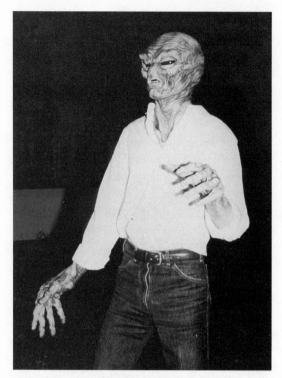

One of several aliens from the 1990 film Spaced Invaders *who land on Earth thinking an invasion is taking place after picking up a radio station broadcasting Orson Welles's* War of the Worlds. *(The Del Valle Archive)*

Michael Madsen, Alfred Molina, Forest Whitaker, Marg Helgenberger, Natasha Henstridge.

SPERMULA

This 1976 French sex film features a race of virgin vampire women from a distant planet that lives on sperm rather than blood. When they arrive on earth, they set about making slaves of mankind until one of them falls in love with an earthling. This film is representative of the tendency to project our subconscious fears and desires onto the great unknown of space.

> Film An Co./Paralafrance, Fr. 1976; 105 min. Director: Charles Matton; Writer: Charles Matton; Cinematography: Jean-Jacques Flori; Cast: Dayle Haddon, Udo Kier, Georges Geret, Ginnette Lecler, Joycelyne Boisseau, Francois Dunoyer, Isabelle Mercanton.

SPRINGHEEL JACK

In September 1837 outside London four separate but similar assaults on women occurred. The as-sailant in each case was a figure cloaked in darkness. The next month a young woman saw a huge, cloaked figure standing on a hill. The figure suddenly bounded toward her, taking enormous leaps. When he came near, she saw a man with glowing eyes who spat blue flames into her face. He ripped the top of her dress off and left scratches on her belly with ironlike fingers. The figure then laughed loudly and leaped away.

This figure became known as Springheel Jack. His victims described him as tall and thin with a prominent nose, pointed ears, and fiery eyes. He had enormous strength and the ability to leap enormous distances. He wore a black, flowing cloak and a metal helmet. Although he attacked women, frequently ripping off their clothes, he never raped them. Often he merely frightened his victim before walking away.

The most publicized attack occurred in 1838, when a young woman answered a ringing at the gate in front of her house. A man who said he was a policeman asked for a light because he had caught Springheel Jack in the lane. When she gave the man the candle he held it up to himself and spat blue and white flames from his mouth. His eyes resembled red balls of fire. He wore a large helmet and tight-fitting, white, oilskin garments under his cloak. The man grabbed the young woman by her dress, but her sister ran out to help her, pulling her indoors. The assailant fled across a field.

Springheel Jack's attacks occurred from 1837 to 1839. There were no further attacks until 1843. In 1845 the first murder was blamed on Springheel Jack. A 13-year-old London prostitute was thrown off a bridge and into an open sewer, where she drowned. There were no further attacks by Springheel Jack or someone like him until 1877 in Caistor, Norfolk. He was seen bounding through town or on rooftops. This time he was wearing what looked like a sheepskin. That same year he was seen by guards at an army base in Hampshire wearing a tight oilskin suit and helmet. He jumped right over the guards' heads and spat flames. The guards fired on him with no effect.

Several sightings of Springheel Jack or a similar person were made in Everton, England, in September 1904. Several people saw a man dressed in a flowing cloak and black boots pass down the street in a series of high leaps. Later the man frightened several girls, springing in front of them, laughing and bounding away. Once he leaped 25 feet to the roof of a building and then jumped from rooftop to rooftop in front of many witnesses. After that no trace of him was found.

A connection between Springheel Jack and UFOs occurred in 1953 in Houston, Texas. At 2:30 A.M. three people saw a man about six and a half feet tall, dressed in gray or black tight-fitting clothes, a black cape, and boots who leaped up into a pecan tree. One witness claimed that he had large wings folded at his shoulders. Fifteen minutes later the figure seemed to melt away. Then they heard a swoosh and saw a rocket-shaped object shoot upward while trailing white smoke.

—Jerome Clark

See Also: Mythology and Folklore; Sex
Further Reading:
Ashton, John. *Gossip in the First Decade of Queen Victoria's Reign.* London: Hurst and Blackett, 1903.
Haining, Peter. *The Legend and Bizarre Crimes of Spring Heeled Jack.* London: Frederick Muller, 1977.
O'Donnell, Elliott. *Ghosts of London.* New York: E. P. Dutton, 1933.

SPRINKLE, RONALD LEO

Ronald L. Sprinkle was born August 31, 1930. He earned his B.A. in 1952 and his M.A. in 1953 from the University of Colorado, then in 1961 received his Ph.D. from the University of Missouri. After teaching at the University of North Dakota for three years, he joined the faculty of the University of Wyoming and later became director of counseling and testing there. He left the university in 1989 to enter private practice as a psychologist.

Sprinkle had sighted a UFO in the daytime in 1951 and another one five years later with his wife. In 1962 he became a consultant to the Aerial Phenomena Research Organization and, a few years later, to the Condon Committee, the University of Colorado UFO project sponsored by the U.S. Air Force. He began investigating attitudes of people interested in UFOs; by using hypnosis he uncovered one of the first known cases of an abduction experience. After further investigations of such experiences, and of those of contactees in general, he

hosted the first Rocky Mountain Conference on UFO Investigation at the University of Wyoming in Laramie in 1980. This brought contactees together to discuss their beliefs and experiences, and it was an annual event until recently. He identifies himself as a contactee and has encouraged his professional colleagues to study contactee psychology.

—Jerome Clark

See Also: Contactees
Further Reading:
Clark, Jerome. *The UFO Encyclopedia.* 2nd ed. Detroit: Omnigraphics, 1998.
Sprinkle, R. Leo, ed. *Proceedings of the Rocky Mountain Conference on UFO Investigation.* Laramie: School of Extended Studies, University of Wyoming, 1980.

STAR BEACON

Star Beacon, edited by Ann Ulrich, is a New Age–oriented UFO newsletter that is published once a month. In addition to UFOs, the newsletter also reports on other New Age topics, from crystals to channeling. Ulrich is the author of *Intimate Abduction* (1988), a romance novel about alien abduction.

See Also: Channeling; New Age

STAR LIGHT FELLOWSHIP

Star Light Fellowship is an organization in the general "I AM" lineage that is centered in New York City. The leaders channel a variety of Master Teachers and Ascended Masters, including certain Space Brothers. Like many other UFO-channeling groups, the Star Light Fellowship teaches standard occult doctrines such as reincarnation and the reality of a spiritual hierarchy of beings.

See Also: Ascended Masters; Channeling; The "I AM" Religious Activity; New Age; Occult; Reincarnation; Religions, UFO
Further Reading:
Lewis, James R. *The Encyclopedia of Cults, Sects, and New Religions.* Amherst, NY: Prometheus Books, 1998.
Melton, J. Gordon. *Encyclopedia of American Religion.* 5th ed. Detroit: Gale Research, 1996.

STAR PEOPLE

The "Star People"—a notion popularized by Brad Steiger—can refer either to individuals who believe that they are descendants of human-alien breeding experiments, or to people who believe that they are extraterrestrial souls reincarnated in human bodies. Many thousands of contemporary terrestrials attribute their feeling that they do not belong on this planet to the fact that they have an extraterrestrial lineage.

Steiger claims that Star People are distinguished by unusually acute senses, above-average intelligence, and experience with supernatural phenomena. They need much less sleep than others, are uncomfortable in crowds, and are overly sensitive to loud sounds. Physically they tend to have heavy-lidded eyes, RH-negative blood type, lower-than-normal body temperatures, spinal problems, and, sometimes, even a extra vertebrae.

Many Star People gravitate to channeling groups or start one themselves. The majority are women, who believe that they are here to "improve the stock" and to uplift the human race with their greater spiritual awareness. The marked predominance of women later led Steiger to coin the expression "Star Maidens."

See Also: Extraterrestrial Incarnations; Hybrids, Alien-Human; New Age
Further Reading:
Steiger, Brad. *Starborn.* New York: Berkley Books, 1992.
———. *The Star People.* New York: Berkley Books, 1982.

STAR TREK

Although the highly successful *Star Trek* series and its various spin-offs are not about aliens invading earth or flying-saucer sightings, it has, like *Buck Rogers,* heavily influenced our image of space travel and of extraterrestrials. It should also be mentioned that at least two episodes have incorporated contemporary ufological concerns. There is, for example, a *Next Generation* episode in which aliens from another dimension are abducting crew members and performing experiments on them—an episode clearly inspired by the abduction phenomenon. Also, in a *Deep Space Nine* episode, Quark inadvertently goes back in time while traveling to earth and makes a forced landing near Roswell, New Mexico, in 1947; he thereby becomes the Roswell incident. *Star Trek* movies began coming out in 1979. The first involves a

quasi-religious encounter with a blended terrestrial-extraterrestrial starship.

Paramount 1979; 143 min. Director: Robert Wise; Music: Jerry Goldsmith; Cast: William Shatner, Leonard Nimoy, DeForest Kelly, James Doohan, Stephen Collins, Perses Khambatta, Nichelle Nichols, Walter Koenig, George Takei.

STARMAN

In the 1984 film *Starman* an alien takes the form of a recently deceased earthman while attempting to get to his rendezvous point. Love develops between the alien and the widow of the man whose form he has taken while the authorities are attempting to track the former down. The good alien is helped by good earthlings and hunted by bad earthlings until he returns to space at a site in the desert where a meteor crashed millennia before. This film later became the basis for a TV series.

Col/Delphi Productions II 1984; 115 min. Director: John Carpenter; Writers: Bruce Evans, Raynold Gideon; Special Effects: Industrial Light and Magic, Rick Baker; Cast: Jeff Bridges, Karen Allen, Charles Martin Smith, Richard Jaeckel, Robert Phalen, Tony Edwards.

STEIGER, BRAD

Brad Steiger, born Eugene Olson in 1936, is a prolific author of books on UFOs, anomalies, occult phenomena, New Age practices, and the like. He is also a very popular lecturer on the New Age circuit. A college teacher in the 1960s, he moved within a few years into full-time writing and is probably the best-known author in America on these subjects. He is currently living in Phoenix, Arizona, with his wife.

See Also: New Age; Star People
Further Reading:
Steiger, Brad. *Starborn.* New York: Berkley Books, 1992.
———. *The Star People.* New York: Berkley Books, 1982.

STRANGE INVADERS

This is a 1983 film in which aliens, during their initial exploration of earth in 1958, assume the bodies of Midwestern farmers and return in that form 25 years later in New York on a search for a couple of their number that stayed behind. The theme of aliens blending in with humanity reflects a similar theme found in UFO literature.

Orion/EMI 1983; 94 min. Director: Michael Laughlin; Writers: Michael Laughlin, William Condon; Cinematography: Lois Horvath; Special Effects: John Muto, Robert Skotak; Cast: Paul Le Mat, Nancy Allen, Diana Scarwid, Michael Lerner, Louise Fletcher, Wallace Shawn, Fjiona Lewis.

THE STRANGER FROM VENUS

This is a 1954 British film in which a woman crashes her car and is approached by a stranger who tells her he is from Venus. The Venusian tells the woman that he has been sent to earth because the Venusians are concerned about our misuse of atomic power. The woman's fiancé sets up an electronic trap for the alien spaceship, but the Venusian threatens retribution from the mothership. The fiancé gives up, and the Venusian sends his backup fleet away despite the fact that the earth's atmosphere is killing him. He disappears in a melodramatic death scene.

The mid-1950s saw the height of the Cold War scare about nuclear self-destruction. Like *The Day the Earth Stood Still* and several films of this era, *The Stranger from Venus* embodies both our fears (of atomic warfare) and hopes (of rescue from beyond). It is as if we wanted God to intervene to save us from ourselves. Viewing aliens in this way gives them a quasi-religious status as "technological angels" (to use Jung's term)—superior beings for an age that has difficulty grasping the reality of God.

Rich and Rich Productions/Princess Productions 1954; 78 min. Cast: Patricia Neal, Helmut Dandtine, Derek Bond.

STRIEBER, WHITLEY

Whitley Strieber (b. 1945) was a well-known writer of Gothic and futuristic fiction when, in 1985, he had an abduction experience. Working with neighbor Budd Hopkins under hypnosis, he was able to recall more of the events. He turned them into a book, *Communion,* which hit and stayed on the best-seller lists. Strieber insists the book was factual; skeptics claim it is a novel. In two succeeding books Strieber argued for his belief that the aliens that abduct humans are benevo-

Whitley Strieber talks about his book Communion *during a conference.* (UFO Magazine)

lent; other abductees do not believe this, and skeptics do not believe the aliens are anything. Strieber briefly ran the Communion Foundation, then shut it down, denounced ufologists as being mean-spirited, and went back to writing horror novels. More recently, he has been busy as a featured lecturer on the UFO circuit.

See Also: Abductees; Close Encounters; Hopkins, Budd
Further Reading:
Strieber, Whitley. *Communion: A True Story.* New York: Morrow/Beech Tree Books, 1987.
———. *Transformation: The Breakthrough.* New York: Morrow/Beech Tree Books, 1988.

SUPERMAN: THE MOVIE

This legend from the comic strips and comic books debuted in a TV series in the 1950s and came alive in the movie *Superman* in 1978. The story is about a being who came to earth from the doomed planet Krypton. He masquerades as an ordinary man and behaves like a nerd to avoid revealing his special powers of steel. Our government and local authorities are continually indebted to Superman, who always miraculously flies down from the sky to save our communities and citizens from evil—criminals, cataclysmic threats, and bad aliens. This movie was followed by three sequels. The plots always revolve around attempts to destroy Superman, who never gets to settle down with the girl yet always emerges the victor and keeps the secret of his identity from everyone but the audience. There are two themes in the Superman stories that resonate with the ideas found in the UFO community: Aliens are superior beings here on earth to help and save us; and aliens are walking around among us disguised as human beings.

> Warner Bros. 1978; 144 min. Director: Richard Donner; Writers: Leslie Newman, Mario Puzo, Robert Benton, David Newman; Music: John Williams; Cinematography: Geoffrey Unsworth; Cast: Christopher Reeve, Margot Kidder, Marlon Brando, Gene Hackman, Glen Ford, Susannah York, Ned Beatty, Valerie Perrine, Jackie Copper, Marc McClure, Trevor Hoard, Sarah Douglas, Terence Stamp, Jack O'Halloran, Phyllis Thaxter.

SWAN, FRANCES

On October 31, 1953, Frances Swan of Eliot, Maine, was standing on a ladder hanging decorations in the Grange Hall. When a distinguished looking stranger walked in, Swan engaged him in polite conversation. For no apparent reason, the man impressed Swan, and she remembered him vividly.

About six months later Swan began hearing a whistling sound in her left ear. She felt herself compelled to write, "We come will help keep peace on earth do not be frightened." Three days later she received another message by automatic writing. The communicator identified himself as Affa from Uranus and said he was the stranger she had met at the Grange Hall on Halloween. Swan continued to get messages from Affa as well as other beings that belonged to the Universal Association of Planets.

On May 18, 1954, Affa asked Swan to write a letter to the U.S. Navy, which would be able to receive his radio communications. Swan's next-door neighbor was Admiral (ret.) Herbert B. Knowles,

and she related the story to him. Admiral Knowles heard her out. He had trouble believing the reality of her contacts, despite Swan's obvious sincerity. Swan told him that Affa had promised a personal appearance at Swan's home at a specific time on May 26, and he agreed to be there. The time of the scheduled appearance came and went without event. Thirteen minutes after the scheduled time, Swan received a message via automatic writing apologizing for his inability to appear. Knowles had prepared a list of questions for Affa. He asked these of Swan, and the answers were written down by her swiftly and smoothly with no hesitation.

On May 19 Admiral Knowles wrote to Rear Admiral C. F. Espe, head of the Office of Naval Intelligence, enclosing some of the messages written by Swan. Knowles passed on Affa's request that the navy try to communicate with Affa on a particular band with a particular message. Espe did not respond, and Knowles wrote to him again on June 6. On June 8, 1954, two officers from the Office of Naval Intelligence called on Swan and, through her, interviewed Affa. Affa declined to appear personally but stated he would communicate via radio at 2 P.M. on June 10. No such transmission came through, and Rear Admiral Espe wrote Knowles that the navy would pursue the matter no further.

Knowles's letters regarding Swan were turned over to the navy's Bureau of Aeronautics, where they were read by a security officer, John Hutson. Hutson developed a personal interest in the case and contacted Knowles, who invited him to visit. Hutson stayed at the Knowles residence on July 24 and 25. When he returned to Washington, Hutson reported to the FBI on his visit. Hutson was interviewed by an agent of the FBI, which took no further action in the matter. Five years later navy Commander Julius Larsen came across the material in a file and decided to follow up on it. On July 5, 1959, he called on Admiral Knowles and spent the evening interviewing Swan. Larsen had a keen interest in spiritualism and tried his hand at automatic writing, with some success.

Larsen returned to Washington the next day and headed for the office of Arthur Lundahl, the director of the CIA's Photographic Intelligence Center. Lundahl and his assistant, Robert

Neasham, listened carefully to Larsen and urged him to try to contact the extraterrestrials then and there. Larsen entered a mild trance state and asked questions aloud. When he heard the answers inside his head he wrote them down. Neasham challenged Affa to appear before them or let them see his spacecraft. Larsen said, "Go to the window." Lundahl saw nothing out of the ordinary, but Neasham claimed a spaceship was hiding behind some clouds. Neasham also claimed that there was evidence that something had blocked out radar reception in the quadrant where the UFO had appeared. Neasham contacted Major Robert Friend, the acting director of Project Blue Book and urged him to come to Washington immediately for a briefing. Friend arrived on July 9 and heard Neasham's version of the incident and saw Larsen talking to the space people. Friend prepared a report on the subject and sent it to his superiors, who took no further action on it.

See Also: Automatic Writing; Contactees
Further Reading:
Emenegger, Robert. *UFOs Past, Present, and Future.* New York: Ballantine Books, 1974.
Jacobs, David M. *The UFO Controversy in America.* Bloomington: Indiana University Press, 1975.
Williamson, George H., and Alfred C. Bailey. *The Saucers Speak! A Documentary Report of Interstellar Communication by Radiotelegraphy.* Los Angeles: New Age Publishing, 1954.

SWEDISH CONTACTEE HOAX

Hans Gustafsson, 25, and Stig Rydberg, 30, claimed that while driving home to Helsingborg, Sweden, at 2:55 A.M. on December 20, 1958, they saw a strange light in a glade on their right. They left their car, walked toward it, and discovered that it was a disk 16 feet in diameter resting on three legs.

Rydberg said they were then attacked by four gray, jellylike creatures, about four feet high and 14 inches wide, having no extremities. The creatures, despite lacking extremities, allegedly grabbed the two men and attempted to drag them to the saucer. Rydberg and Gustafsson fought off the aliens, Gustafsson grabbing onto a pole and Rydberg running to his car and blowing the horn. The aliens then boarded their craft, which flew off with a high-pitched sound.

The men's account was published on December 31 in the *Helsingborgs Dagblad;* that same day Rydberg and Gustafsson were interviewed on a Swedish national radio news program. On January 8, 1959, the two men were examined by a doctor, who certified that they were sane. The following day military and police investigators interviewed Rydberg and Gustafsson for 12 hours, noting contradictions in their stories. Investigators also examined the scene of the alleged incident. Their official report, which was published on January 16, found neither man a credible witness.

Yet Sweden's most prominent ufologist, K. Gosta Rehn, and Coral Lorenzen of the Aerial Phenomena Research Organization were convinced of the authenticity of the story. Rydberg and Gustafsson began making lecture tours and public appearances. They also read at least three contactee books by George Adamski and Daniel Fry. After this they told an audience in Denmark that recently they had seen a flying saucer land. They boarded the vehicle, flew into space, and conversed with friendly space people, who were suspiciously similar to those described in Adamski's books.

In June 1959 Rydberg attempted to sell K. Gosta Rehn a set of UFO photos. Within months of the December contact, Rydberg and Gustafsson had a falling-out and were no longer on speaking terms. On November 12, 1960, Gustafsson fell off a boat while drunk and drowned. He was 27; Rydberg was found dead in his apartment on March 4, 1984, at the age of 56. The cause of his death was pneumonia, which he had contracted after being beaten unconscious and left for dead on a cold street. In the late 1980s Hans Gustafsson's brother, Artur, had been told in confidence by Hans that the story was a hoax. Artur said that Hans had been planning to confess to the hoax publicly but had died before he summoned the courage to do so.

See Also: Contactees; Hoaxes
Further Reading:
Lorenzen, Coral E. *Flying Saucers: The Startling Evidence of Invasion From Outer Space.* New York: New American Library, 1966 [expanded version of *The Great Flying Saucer Hoax,* 1962].
———. *The Great Flying Saucer Hoax: The UFO Facts and Their Interpretation.* New York: William-Frederick Press, 1962.

SYLPHS

Sylphs are winged fairies associated with the element of air. They are said to be light, airy, almost transparent beings that reside in the atmosphere. They are responsible for all movements of air, from the slightest breeze to the mightiest hurricane. In the occult tradition, air is traditionally associated with the mental body, and air elementals (i.e., sylphs) are said to work with human beings to inspire creativity, high thoughts, and intuition. In ceremonial magic, the sylphs are the air elementals of the east who are called upon to witness rituals.

There is also a tradition of sylphs traveling in aerial vehicles rather than propelling themselves through the atmosphere via the power of their own wings. Such beings were said to sometimes abduct human beings and give them a tour of the world of the sylphs, eventually returning them to earth. There is a clear parallel between these activities and the reported behavior of ufonauts, supporting the contention that modern UFO lore is little more than traditional folklore in contemporary garb.

See Also: Elementals; Fairies

Further Reading:

Andrews, Ted. *Enchantment of the Faerie Realm: Communicate with Nature Spirits and Elementals.* St. Paul: Llewellyn, 1993.

McCoy, Edwin. *A Witch's guide to Faery Folk.* St. Paul: Llewellyn, 1994.

TEENAGERS FROM OUTER SPACE

In this 1959 film teenage aliens invade earth in their flying saucers to graze and breed their lobster-like space cattle. The leader of the teenage pilots makes the fatal mistake of falling in love with an earthling; despondent, he guides his companions' saucers into a mountainside, killing himself and all of them— an invasion film in the tradition of good earthlings and good aliens versus bad aliens.

Topar Corp. 1959; 86 min. Director: Tom Graeff; Writer: Tom Graeff; Cinematography: Tom Graeff; Cast: Dave Love, Tom Graeff, Dawn Anderson, Harvey B. Dunn, Bryant Grant, Tom Lockyear.

TELEPATHY

Telepathy is a paranormal form of communication (a form of extrasensory perception) in which one person's mind communicates directly with another person's mind, independently of language or any other obvious medium of exchange. Telepathic communications are often reported in close-encounter and abduction experiences. In almost all instances, it is the alien being who initiates the exchange. One striking case of a communication with ufonauts initiated by human beings was an image of three circles connected in a triangular pattern by three lines that a group of crop-circle investigators "mentally sent" to the beings believed responsible for the crop-circle phenomenon. Their experiment was judged a success when a pattern matching the one they were visualizing appeared in a nearby field. It is phenomena such as this that make one wonder whether UFOs are nuts-and-bolts machines piloted by flesh-and-blood beings, or whether UFOs are actually paranormal phenomena masquerading in physical form.

See Also: Occult; Paranormal and Occult Theories about UFOs

Further Reading:
Good, Timothy. *Alien Update.* New York: Avon, 1993.
Ritchie, David. *UFO: The Definitive Guide to Unidentified Flying Objects and Related Phenomena.* New York: Facts on File, 1994.

THE TERRORNAUTS

This is a 1967 juvenile film from Great Britain. An alien spaceship takes five earthlings to a strange fortress constructed as a warning to future generations by man's alien forebears, just before they were defeated by their old alien enemies. The fortress warns that the ancient enemy forces will resume hostilities as soon as man leaves his planet and starts exploring the solar system. The theme of humanity's alien ancestors appears to be taken more or less directly from ancient-astronaut speculations.

Amicus 1967; 77 min. Director: Montgomery Tully; Cast: Simon Oates, Zena Marshall, Charles Hawtrey, Stanley Meadows.

TERRORVISION

TerrorVision is a 1986 movie in which a mutant monster from outer space is beamed to earth and emerges from the many TV sets in the house of a satellite-obsessed family. It spoofs some standard devices found in sci-fi movies. Although the monster is from outer space, this film is more about consumerism than alien encounters.

Empire/Altar 1986; 83 min. Director: Ted Nicolaou; Writer: Ted Nicolaou; Cinematography: Romano Albani; Special Effects: John Buechler; Cast: Mary Woronov, Gerrit Graham, Diane Franklin, Chad Allen, Johnathan Gries, Jennifer Richards, Alejandro Rey, Bert Remsen, Randi Brooks.

THEOSOPHY

The metaphysical/New Age subculture—the principal carrier of UFO interest—grew out of several

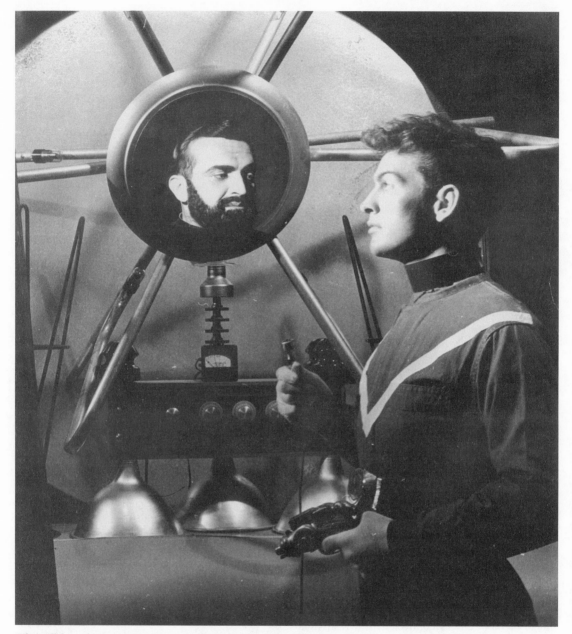

Film still from the 1959 movie Teenagers from Outer Space, *also released under the titles* The Gargon Terror *and* Invasion of the Gargon *(The Del Valle Archive)*

different nineteenth-century movements, including theosophy. Although the term "theosophy" has more than one meaning, in contemporary usage it refers to the particular synthesis of ideas from the philosophical systems of China and India with the works of Gnostics, Neoplatonists, and Kabbalists, manifested in the Theosophical Society, which was founded in New York in 1875 by Madame Helena Blavatsky.

Theosophy postulates a complex view of the universe within which humanity's origins, evolution, and ultimate destiny are delineated in some detail. The visible world arises from the ultimate, immutable Source—an immaterial reality of which, as in Hindu philosophy, the universe is the manifestation and from which it guided. The process of cosmic manifestation is characterized by two phases, the first being involution, during which a multitude of spiritual units emerge from the Source and, after becoming more and more involved in matter, finally achieve self-consciousness in the physical world. During the second phase—evolution—the human monads (souls) develop their inner potentials, free themselves from matter, and return to the Source with an increased consciousness. In many New Age scenarios, the Space Brothers are here to help speed up humanity's spiritual evolution.

The eternal human spirit attains mastery through cycles of reincarnation in accordance with karma, the moral law of cause and effect. In each incarnation new experiences are attained, leading to the development of the soul to a degree that is proportionate to the use made of each experience. According to theosophy, a long series of reincarnations is required for the soul to achieve its supreme aim.

Like the ancient Gnostics, who are viewed as predecessors, theosophists populate the cosmos with innumerable spiritual entities. At the head of this diverse assortment are the Ascended Masters—highly evolved beings who oversee the spiritual unfoldment of ordinary humanity.

It is commonly acknowledged that UFO contactees owe much to theosophy. The Space Brothers of contactee narratives, for instance, have the same features as the Ascended Masters, or Mahatmas, of theosophical lore—not only in behavior and intent but also in the way they are physically depicted. Contrary to the traditional Mahatmas, the Space Brothers need physical machines for transportation, which makes them somewhat less mysterious, but the fact that mediumistic or telepathic communication also occurs in contactee narratives shows that the classical Mahatmas and the Space Brothers are part of the same continuum. The metaphysical Mahatmas were to a certain degree secularized as the contactees translated them into physical beings with physical needs, but both groups are often located to Venus. The cosmology taught by the contactees also resembles that of theosophy. The gospel of spiritual evolution, "cosmic brotherhood," and peace that is

so typical of the contactees' message is also standard fare in theosophy, where it was originally conceived.

The role of the contactee also resembles the role of theosophical leaders; in traditional theosophy only a chosen few would receive messages from the Adepts, and it would be the obligation of these individuals to pass on to others what they had learned. Further, theosophical leaders would serve as preachers themselves and guard the Mahatmas' message on a daily basis, just as the contactees would undertake the responsibility for spreading the Space Brothers' message. Concepts such as cosmic wisdom, typical of theosophy, are therefore also very common in contactee literature. Thus, through ufology, traditional theosophy has been modernized.

—Mikael Rothstein

See Also: Ascended Masters; Evolution of the Soul; The "I AM" Religious Activity; New Age; Reincarnation
Further Reading:
Lewis, James R., ed. *The Gods Have Landed: New Religions From Other Worlds.* Albany: State University of New York Press, 1995.
Melton, J. Gordon, Jerome Clark, and Aidan Kelly. *New Age Encyclopedia.* Detroit: Gale Research, 1990.
Shepard, Leslie A., ed. *Encyclopedia of Occultism and Parapsychology.* Detroit: Gale Research, 1991.

THEY CAME FROM BEYOND SPACE

In this 1967 British film alien invaders arrive on earth with a meteorite shower and start sending humans to the Moon, where they are put to work repairing their crippled spaceships. A scientist rescues his girlfriend from them and finally establishes friendship with the aliens. This represents another example of alien abduction being established in the human imagination years before such abductions became the central focus of the UFO phenomenon.

Amicus 1967; 86 min. Director: Freddie Francis; Cast: Robert Hutton, Michael Gough.

THEY LIVE

In this 1988 film a drifter accidentally discovers an alien conspiracy to take over the country under the guise of Reaganism, capitalism, and yup-

John Nada (Roddy Piper) makes a stand against the invading aliens who have disguised themselves as human beings in the 1988 film They Live. *(The Del Valle Archive)*

piedom. This is a humorous takeoff on the time-worn alien-invasion-by-infiltration theme, which small segments of the UFO community still take seriously.

Alive 1988; 88 min. Director: John Carpenter; Writer: John Carpenter; Music: John Carpenter, Alan Howarth; Cinematography: Gary B. Kibbe; Cast: Roddy Piper, Keith David, Meg Foster, George Flower, Peter Jason, Raymond St. Jacques, John Lawrence, Sy Richardson, Jason Robards III, Larry Franco.

THE THING

The first movie called *The Thing* was made in 1951. A science-fiction classic, it begins with an alien spacecraft embedded in the Arctic ice. A research team discovers the ship and the creature within it. When the creature accidentally thaws, it begins to suck life from everything around. A good movie to illustrate the idea of outer space as a canvas upon which we project our fears, it is based on the short story "Who Goes There?" by John W. Campbell, editor of *Astounding Science Fiction*.

The 1982 film of the same name is more faithful to Campbell's short story. The scene has been shifted to the Antarctic, where a team of scientists discover a buried spaceship and an alien, which, it turns out, is able to take over humans at will.

Wincester Pictures 1951; 87 min. Directors: Christian Nyby, Howard Hawks; Writer: Charles Lederer; Music: Dimitri Tiomkin; Cast: James Arness, Kenneth Tobey, Margaret Sheridan, Dewey Martin.

THOMPSON, SAMUEL EATON

On March 28, 1950, Samuel Eaton Thompson, a poorly educated retired railroad worker in his seventies, was walking along an old logging trail near Mineral, Washington, when he claims he saw a large, saucer-shaped craft hovering just above a clearing. It was about 80 feet in diameter and 32 feet in height and it glowed.

Thompson said there were steps leading from an open door on the side of the craft; well-tanned naked children with long, blond hair played on these steps. When he got within 50 feet of the ship he could feel heat emanating from it. Adults (also nude and well-tanned with long blond hair) came to the door of the spaceship and saw him. Although apparently frightened at first, they invited him into the ship after being reassured by Thompson. The spaceship had only one door but had several rooms.

Thompson found out that the inhabitants of the spaceship were from Venus. There were 10 men, 10 women, and 25 children. The Venusians revealed to Thompson that the reason for the earth's problems is that earthlings are all born under different astrological signs. On other planets, all the people are of the same astrological sign—that of the planet. It seemed that all earthlings had lived lives on other planets before being exiled to the earth. Thompson learned that all people who fulfill their mission in life return to the planet of their sign when they die.

The Venusians told Thompson that they live long, disease-free lives because of their raw vegetarian diet. The Venusian spaceship served as their dwelling place even when they were at home on Venus. The controls of the ship were very simple and consisted of just a few levers to make it ascend, descend, accelerate, and decelerate. The Venusians' purpose in coming to earth was to contact earth people one at a time in order to eventually establish peace.

Thompson claims to have slept overnight in the spaceship. The next morning he went home and returned with a camera. None of his photographs came out, however, due to the bright light emanating from the spaceship. Two days after he had first seen the ship in the clearing, Thompson and the Venusians parted company.

The next day a brief account of the alleged contact appeared in a small local paper, the *Centralia Daily Chronicle*. A few days later Kenneth Arnold interviewed Thompson. Arnold was convinced of Thompson's sincerity but had difficulty believing in the literal occurrence of the events Thompson described. No further story on Thompson's contact was published until 30 years later, when Kenneth Arnold made available to *Fate* magazine the tape of his interview with Thompson. *Fate* characterized Thompson's encounter as a visionary experience.

There are some interesting similarities between Thompson's Venusians and the aliens encountered by other contactees. The most famous contactee of all, George Adamski, had apparently never heard of Thompson (at least he never made any reference to Thompson in his voluminous writings). Although Adamski's first contacts occurred two and a half years after Thompson's, there is little likelihood that Adamski ever happened upon the only published account of Thompson's contact (the *Centralia Daily Chronicle* article). Even in the unlikely event that Adamski did read that article, it consisted of only 11 paragraphs and did not include many of the details that were reported much later in *Fate*. Perhaps it is pure coincidence that Adamski's contacts were also with peace-loving, blond, long-haired Venusians who ate natural foods and did not get sick.

A similar contact that preceded Thompson's occurred on April 16, 1897. As reported in the *St. Louis Post-Dispatch* on April 19, 1897, a St. Louis man named W. H. Hopkins had encountered two beautiful nude Martians in Springfield, Missouri. The man and woman both had long hair. Although the temperature was cool, the Martians, who did not speak English, were fanning themselves as if overheated. Whatever the explanation for Samuel Thompson's claim of contact with extraterrestrial beings, he did not make the claim for personal fame or financial gain. His was one of the most obscure stories in UFO history.

See Also: Adamski, George; Astrology; Contactees; Naked Aliens

Further Reading:

Adamski, George. *Inside the Space Ships.* New York: Abelard-Schuman, 1955.

Clark, Jerome. *The UFO Encyclopedia.* 2nd ed. Detroit: Omnigraphics, 1998.

THE THREE STOOGES IN ORBIT

This is a typical Three Stooges film in which they defeat the plans of Martians to steal secret plans for a multipurpose vehicle. The basic plot of good earthlings defeating bad aliens supplies the setting for an unexceptional Stooges movie.

Normandy Productions 1962; 87 min. Director: Edward Bernds; Writer: Elwood Ullman; Cinematography: William F. Whitley; Cast: The Three Stooges (Moe

290

The Three Stooges befriend aliens Ogg and Zogg when they accidentally launch a spaceship in the 1962 film The Three Stooges in Orbit. *(The Del Valle Archive)*

Howard, Larry Fine, Joe DeRita), Carol Christensen, Edson Stoll, Emil Sitka.

THREE TORNADOES

This Italian film was released in 1992. When his best friend disappears in a cloud of light, a NATO flyer becomes obsessed with UFOs and initiates further close encounters, finally climbing a European mountain for an alien epiphany.

Clemi Cinematografica; It. 96 min. 1992; Director: Tony B. Dobb (Antonio Bido); Writer: Gino Capone; Cinematography: Maurizio Dell'Orco; Cast: Dirk Benedict, Patsy Kensit, Ted McGinley, David Warner.

TIME TRAVEL

Time and time travel are relevant to the UFO phenomenon in several ways. In close encounters with ufonauts, for example, individuals report that events experienced as taking place in a short period of time actually take much longer, or vice versa. Most familiar is the so-called missing time, in which abductees report the experience of finding that several hours have transpired without conscious recall of the events that transpired during that period. This particular trait is also a traditional attribute of fairy abductions.

UFOs have also been imaginatively linked to time travel. Writers have, for example, often hypothesized that UFOs are actually temporal visitors from the distant future. Others have gone so far as to speculate that perhaps UFOs represent visitors from the legendary civilizations of the past, such as Atlantis, which, in some writers' accounts, are technologically more advanced than the present.

See Also: Abductees; Atlantis; Missing Time
Further Reading:
Hopkins, Budd. Missing Time: A Documented Study of UFO Abductions. New York: Richard Marek, 1981.
Ritchie, David. UFO: The Definitive Guide to Unidentified Flying Objects and Related Phenomena. New York: Facts on File, 1994.

TOMEY ABDUCTION

Under hypnosis Debbie Tomey (who, under the pseudonym Kathie Davis, was the subject of Budd

Hopkin's book Intruders) related that on June 30, 1983, she saw lights searching the yard of her house. After going to investigate, she claimed to have been hit by a blast of radiation and abducted aboard the UFO. A probe was inserted into her abdomen and an object was implanted into her nose. She claimed to have been abducted again on October 3, 1983. The aliens showed her a child that they told her was a result of her impregnation by the aliens. Another abduction was claimed three years later in which Tomey maintained that the aliens told her they had impregnated her nine times. Tomey had a history of physical ailments, and it is likely that either she imagined the event or that the aliens implanted the memories rather than the fetuses.

See Also: Abductees; Close Encounters; Hopkins, Budd.
Further Reading:
Hopkins, Budd. Intruders: The Incredible Visitations at Copley Woods. New York: Random House, 1987.

THE TRICKSTER

Anyone who examines UFO reports for any length of time can understand the feeling of some researchers who have been led to entertain the thought that ufonauts have a keen sense of humor and enjoy making humanity the fall guy for their tricks. It would not, in fact, be going too far to view the UFO phenomenon in terms of that familiar figure found throughout world mythology—the trickster. Tricksters are powerful spirits or divinities who, as the name implies, delight in all sorts of pranks and jokes. Although not actually an evil spirit, the impact of the trickster's activity is often unpleasant. Because tricksters are shape-shifters, they are also symbols of transformation. This particular characteristic is also relevant, as the UFO phenomenon seems to always be altering form, particularly in those moments when we seem to have it pinned down.

See Also: Humor and UFOs; Mythology and Folklore
Further Reading:
Leach, Maria. Standard Dictionary of Folklore, Mythology, and Legend. San Francisco: HarperSan Francisco, 1984 [orig. publ. 1949].
Pursglove, Paul David. Zen in the Art of Close Encounters: Crazy Wisdom and UFOs. Berkeley: New Being Project, 1995.

TUNGUSKA EVENT

In 1908 a meteor entered earth's atmosphere and became so overheated from friction that it exploded in the air above Siberia. Forests were blown down for miles, the destruction extending some 375 miles outward. A pillar of fire rose into the air, and heat waves ignited fires in towns and forests. When Soviet scientists finally came to look at the site in 1921, they found there was no impact crater and concluded that the meteor or comet had exploded in midair. In 1946 a Russian science-fiction writer published a story about a Martian spaceship exploding over Tunguska. This set in motion a line of investigation and speculation that led many people to believe that this is what happened. Many have thought it must have been an atomic explosion, but there is no increase of radioactivity in the area.

See Also: Ancient Astronauts

Further Reading:

Goran, Morris. The Modern Myth, Ancient Astronauts and UFOs. South Brunswick, NJ: A. S. Barnes, 1978.

Ritchie, David. UFO: The Definitive Guide to Unidentified Flying Objects and Related Phenomena. New York: Facts on File, 1994.

TURNER ABDUCTION

Trucker Harry Joe Turner claimed he was taken on a trip through space by a UFO in 1979. He was traveling with a load of mustard and ketchup headed for a warehouse 80 miles away when he heard a terrible screeching noise and was grabbed by an alien while doing 70. He shot the alien with a pistol, but nothing happened. Suddenly Turner found himself at the warehouse—his watch read 11:17 A.M. but the warehouse clock read 3 P.M. A filmy substance covered his truck. He began to remember what happened: His truck was beamed into a UFO, where he saw humanlike figures with numbers on their faces. A being named Alpha La Zoo Loo told him they were going to visit a planet light-years away. He didn't remember the trip back. After the alleged incident, Turner began to suffer from hysteria, thinking aliens were chasing him or physically attacking him. He took heavy doses of tranquilizers and smoked constantly. Results from tests on his truck revealed human, not alien, tampering.

See Also: Abductees; Close Encounters

Further Reading:

Bullard, Thomas E. UFO Abductions: The Measure of a Mystery, Volume 1: Comparative Study of Abduction Reports; and Volume 2: Catalogue of Cases. Mount Rainier, MD: Fund for UFO Research, 1987.

Clark, Jerome. The UFO Encyclopedia. 2nd ed. Detroit: Omnigraphics, 1998.

THE TWELVE HANDED MEN OF MARS

The Twelve Handed Men of Mars is an Italian comedy about four Martians who come to earth in human form to prepare for an eventual invasion only to find earth more congenial than Mars. One becomes a real-estate developer, one a politician, one falls in love, and the other becomes a science-fiction writer—an unconventional take on the alien-invasion theme.

Produzione D. S./Epoca Films 1964; 95 min. Directors/Writers: Franco Castellano, G. Pipola; Cinematography: Alfio Contini; Cast: Paolo Panelli, Carlo Croccola, Enzo Garinei, Alfredo Landa, Magali Noel, Cristini Gajonia.

20 MILLION MILES TO EARTH

In this 1957 film a mission returning from Venus crashes into the sea off the coast of Italy, leaving one survivor, who is desperately concerned that the canister containing a specimen of Venusian life has been lost. Eventually a child discovers the canister and removes the jellylike substance, which hatches into a tailed creature. A local zoologist puts the creature in a cage. Twenty-four hours later the creature is already four feet tall. It escapes and kills a dog and a farmer but is recaptured and taken to a laboratory, where it keeps growing. It escapes a second time, batters an elephant to death, and climbs to the top of the Colosseum, where the military kills it with mortar and bazooka fire. The creature is portrayed as an innocent victim of circumstance rather than an evil monster—a marked departure from comparable films.

Morningside Productions 1957; 84 min. Director: Nathan Juran; Writers: Bob Williams, Christopher Knopf; Cinematography: Irving Lippman, Carlos Ventigmillia; Cast: William Hopper, Joan Taylor, Frank Puglia, John Zaremba, Thomas Browne Henry, Titu Vuolo.

The first spaceship to visit Venus crash lands in the sea, freeing a native Venusian creature called the Ymir, seen here threatening the city of Rome in 20 Million Miles to Earth, *1957. (The Del Valle Archive)*

THE 27TH DAY

In this 1957 film an alien gives five different people in five different countries a box of capsules capable of destroying human life because his own planet is dying and his people want to make earth their home. He explains that it is against his race's ethics to destroy intelligent life, but as humankind seems intent on destroying itself, he will assist them. Only the mind of each person can open his or her capsule. Once open, however, anyone can order the three concentrated radiation pellets anywhere on earth to instantly vaporize all humans within a 1,500-mile radius. Anything not human will be totally unharmed. The death of the holder renders the capsule harmless, and the capsules will automatically become harmless after 27 days. One woman throws her capsule into the sea. The other woman commits suicide and her capsule turns to dust. One of the men is shot and his capsule turns to dust. When nuclear war is declared, the remaining capsules are released to destroy the Soviets. The survivors invite the aliens to earth to found a new society based on peace and love.

This movie, shaped by the black-and-white thinking of the Cold War, lacks any sense that the mass destruction of whole peoples is a bad or even a morally ambiguous action. The notion that extraterrestrials might step in to save the planet and destroy evil reflects a simplistic idea of what the "god" of America should have done in the 1950s to set things right, meaning that the aliens in this movie play the role of quasi-divine beings.

Ronson Productions 1957; 75 min. Director: William Asher; Writer: John Mantley; Cinematography: Henry Freulich; Cast: Gene Barry, Valerie French, George Voskovec, Arnold Moss, Stefan Schnabel, Ralph Clanton, Friedrich Ledebur, Mari Tsien, Azenath Jani.

2 + 5

This is a 1966 Italian film in which a group of humans is kidnapped by aliens in a spaceship. The two races learn to coexist as they battle an array of space monsters. In this film, as in other films, it is interesting to see how often the theme of alien abduction crops up in the products of the human imagination before that theme becomes significant in the UFO mainstream.

> Golden Motion Pictures 1966; 95 min. Director: Pietro Francisci; Writers: Pietro Francisci, Aldo Calamara, Ermano Curti; Cinematography: Silvano Ippoliti; Cast: Leaonara Ruffo, Anthony Freeman, Kirk Morris, Roland Lesaffre, Leontine Snell, Gordon Mitchel.

2001: A SPACE ODYSSEY

2001 was a 1968 film based on Arthur C. Clarke's novella *The Sentinel*. Additionally, it was said that director Stanley Kubrick referred to the structure outlined in Joseph Campbell's *The Hero with a Thousand Faces* when he was putting together the movie, making the story more like an archetypal myth than a simple work of fiction. It was the first film to feature a vast space station and the everyday aspects of space travel, such as the space toilet, which succeeded in making space travel seem believable. In the film, never-seen aliens that are clearly humanity's superiors continually help the race along.

In the opening scenes an ape—presumably our distant forebear—glances back and forth between an obelisk (which we somehow know was placed there by an alien intelligence) and a long bone in his hand. In a flash, the ape suddenly understands that the bone can be used as a weapon and/or as a hammer-like tool, thus stepping over the threshold between dumb animal and intelligent toolmaker. Like the friendly extraterrestrials imagined by members of the New Age movement (as well as by certain segments of the ancient-astronaut school), the unseen aliens of *2001* are clearly involved in stimulating the evolution of the human race.

The basic theme of *2001*—namely, alien involvement in prompting the development of humanity—is also the organizing theme of Arthur C. Clarke's most celebrated novel, *Childhood's End*. The quasi-religious overtones of *2001* are more explicit in *Childhood's End*, particularly when the evolving human race merges into the "cosmic source" at the end of the latter work. When these two narratives are juxtaposed, it is easy to see that extraterrestrials have come to play the role of divine beings, intervening in history as a way of guiding humanity.

The film *2001* appeared the same year as the first German edition of Erich von Däniken's classic *Chariots of the Gods?* (the most influential book on the ancient-astronaut hypothesis)

In the year 2001, the SS Discovery *and its crew and onboard computer, HAL-9000, are sent on a mission to find a possible alien force in* 2001: A Space Odyssey, *based on an Arthur C. Clarke story. (The Del Valle Archive)*

and two years before the publication of the English translation. Given the widespread dissemination of Clarke's ideas and of similar notions put forward by other science-fiction writers, it is easy to see why *Chariots of the Gods?* should had been so favorably received by von Däniken's readership—namely, that the basic thesis had already been popularized by works of fiction like *2001*.

MGM 1968; 139 min. Director: Stanley Kubrick; Writers: Stanley Kubrick, Arthur C. Clarke; Cinematography: Geoffrey Unsworth; Visual Effects: Douglas Rain; Cast: Keir Dullea, Gary Lockwood, William Sylvester, Dan Richter, Leonard Rossiter.

U.F.O.

This film is about a man who is abducted into a flying saucer and convicted of crimes against womankind by feminist aliens. He is sentenced to live through multiple pregnancies. As in the films of previous eras, extraterrestrial aliens are used as characters in a morality play.

Polygram/George Foster 1993; 79 min. Director: Tony Dow; Writer: Richard Hall, Simon Wright, Roy "Chubby" Brown; Cinematography: Paul Wheeler; Cast: Roy "Chubby" Brown, Sara Stockbridge, Amanda Symons, Shirley Anne Field, Elizabeth Hickling, Roger Lloyd Pack, Sue Lloyd.

UFO CONTACT CENTER INTERNATIONAL

The UFO Contact Center International (UFOCCI) was begun in 1978 by Aileen Bringle (née Edwards) in Washington State as a meeting place and therapy center for abductees. In 1989 there were 36 centers across the United States and Canada, with the headquarters located in Arizona. Every month abductees gather to discuss their experiences, and many are hypnotized by Bringle. On Labor Day, UFOCCI holds its annual Jorpah, which, according to Dr. Greta Woodrew's book, *On a Slide of Light,* means "universal gathering" or "cosmic gathering." The group publishes a monthly newsletter, *The Missing Link,* which reprints articles on UFOs and New Age topics from various sources, with a prominent readers' letters section.

UFOCCI is willing to accept even the most outrageous UFO tales and encourages wide-ranging speculation. "Along with human extraterrestrials," they write, "we have discovered 'animal-beings,' 'insect-beings,' and other forms of life which we alternately find interesting or repulsive. All of these are currently visiting, staying, have been here, and/or coming periodically. They have interests in earth people, the planet, or need our resources."

Pleiadians have bases on earth, in mountainous regions, and live for 900 years. Grays are concerned with "interstellar research and life analysis. . . . They . . . abduct, at will, many humans for genetic purposes."

See Also: Abductees; New Age
Further Reading:
Clark, Jerome. *The UFO Encyclopedia.* 2nd ed. Detroit: Omnigraphics, 1998.

ULTRATERRESTRIALS

Defined as supernatural beings from a higher dimension of existence by occult-minded ufologist John Keel, ultraterrestrials are able to control matter, human life, and history. They come from intelligent energy fields, called the "superspectrum," and appear to humans as gods, angels, poltergeists, demons, monsters, aliens, and the like. They have only contempt for humanity and wish to enslave the human race or use us as pawns against warring ultraterrestrial groups. They are completely negative; Keel associates them with devils and demons. These "imposters," according to Keel, are behind all UFO phenomena, as well as all religions on earth.

See Also: Demonological Explanations of UFOs; Fairies
Further Reading:
Keel, John A. *UFOs: Operation Trojan Horse.* New York: G. P. Putnam's Sons, 1970.
———. *Our Haunted Planet.* Greenwich, CT: Fawcett Publications, 1971.

UMMO

Ummo is considered to be a major hoax by serious ufologists. It has probably been perpetrated by Fernando Sesma, a contactee who directed the Society of Space Visitors. He claims to have received documents written by residents of Ummo, a planet revolving around the star Iumma, which is 14.6 light-years from us.

Photographs of Ummo vehicles were demonstrated to have been faked. Ufologists have received more than 600 pages of letters and Ummo science and society, mailed from countries around the world. All were in Spanish (or French written by a Spanish-speaking person). Jacques Vallee has said that none of this material reveals any knowledge beyond that current on earth. Ummo has what amounts to a cult following around the world. Followers believe that the Ummites are sequestered in the French Alps, observing the human race, though for what reason is not agreed upon by all members of this movement.

—*Jerome Clark*

See Also: Contactees; Hoaxes
Further Reading:
Vallee, Jacques. *Revelations: Alien Contact and Human Deception.* New York: Ballantine Books, 1991.
Vallee, Jacques, with Martine Castello. *UFO Chronicles of the Soviet Union: A Cosmic Samizdat.* New York: Ballantine Books, 1992.

UNARIUS

The Unarius Academy of Science, located in El Cajon, California, uses channeling techniques to contact beings in outer space. These beings, collectively referred to as the Space Brothers, guide Unarius members in their cosmic "fourth-dimensional science." Unarius also boasts a prophecy of the landing of 33 starships, or flying saucers, in the year 2001. Although "communicating" with extraterrestrials remains an important practice, Unarius also focuses on healing and spirituality. Unarius considers its science a corrective therapy that can help anyone. As a benefit of the science, followers believe they can heal themselves of all physical as well as spiritual maladies. Historically, Unarius had three major leaders: Ernest L. Norman (1904–1971), Ruth Norman (1900–1993), and Charles Speigel (1921–1999). Members call themselves "students"; the core members call themselves the "nucleus." Since all the major leaders have passed away, their center is now being managed by the remaining students in a the form of a board of directors.

Unarius began in 1954 when Ernest Norman (the Moderator) met Ruth Norman (also known as Uriel) at a psychic convention. Ernest, who had worked with spiritualist churches, did a psychic reading for Ruth. In Unarian lore, the initial earthly meeting of these two ascended beings inaugurated the Unarian Mission. The mission is to bring peace and love to earth through the teaching of the celestial science of logic and reason. This science was brought to earth by the channeling efforts of Ernest Norman. His large treatises, *The Cosmic Continuum* (1956) and *The Infinite Concept of Cosmic Creation* (1960), are used as the basis for course curricula.

Originally titled the Unarius Science of Life, the group went through several major transitions. Throughout the 1950s Ernest Norman channeled various books; the most widely read is *The Voice of Venus* (1954), about a clairvoyant tour of Venus. Ruth typed manuscripts while Ernest occupied the limelight. She "transmitted," or channeled, her first book, *Bridge to Heaven,* in 1969. Until Ernest's death, they held classes and gave psychic readings through the mail. During this time they discovered their many past lives, including one "cycle" when Ernest lived as Jesus of Nazareth and Ruth was Mary of Bethany (Mary Magdeline). When Ernest passed away, Ruth took over the organization.

With the help of two of her students, Cosmon (Thomas Miller) and Antares (other names include Louis Spiegel, Charles or Vaughan Spaegel, Charles von Spraegel, and Sir Charles), Ruth channeled many more messages from the Space Brothers. Ruth's status rose to that of Cosmic Visionary. Cosmon occupied a leadership role for a few years but was evidently expelled from the organization, as was his successor, Arieson (Stephan Yanconski). In 1973 Ruth had a revelation that Antares had been Satan in his past life. Antares became Ruth's most devoted student, and he remained her close assistant while also directing the center until his own demise. His past life as Satan won him great affection from Uriel, because he had supposedly come to her to be healed and transformed by her powers.

Ruth opened the Unarius Center in 1972. Originally, she called it the Academy of Parapsychology, Healing, and Psychic Science. By 1975 Unarius incorporated as an educational foundation, and the organization bought the building that houses it

Cofounders of the Unarian Society Ruth and Ernest Norman (Unarius Academy of Science)

today. The center includes offices, classrooms, a library, a print shop, and a video studio. The most adept students learned to channel "higher intelligence" and transmit messages from the Space Brothers. The transcripts of these channelings, as well as testimonials about past lives, supply the content of Unarian books that are printed on the premises. During 1973 Unarians held a gala celebration at an upscale San Diego hotel to re-create one of Uriel's visions. Uriel and Antares reenacted the celestial marriage of Ioshanna (one of Ruth Norman's personas) and Michiel (a member of their spiritual hierarchy). This vision where "two God forces unite" is transcribed in the book *Conclave of Light Beings* (1973). At this point, she announced that she progressed in her evolution enough to be crowned Healing Archangel on the inner dimensions, or Queen Uriel.

In 1973–1974 the channeling of messages from outer space began to rapidly increase. Ruth received messages from dead scientists from other dimensions in the universe, specifically the planet Eros. She established the contact with beings on 32

previously unknown planets, and she also spoke to the crews of flying saucers through her channeling mediumship. Ruth proclaimed that an interplanetary confederation had been formed. Unarians believed that the 32 planets in this confederation were now readying themselves to send their starships to earth. Around this time, Ruth purchased 67 acres of land in the mountains near the center in order to establish a landing strip for flying saucers. The prophecy of the spacefleet landing went through several revisions. The first date in 1975 was hastily disconfirmed. A new date was set in March 1976. Ruth and some of her students wagered $4,000 with Ladbrokes, a British bookmaker, that the spaceships would land on earth within a year. The prophecy became a regular news item for the tabloid press. Ruth eventually lost that bet, but the organization endured to set a new date—Ruth's 101st birthday (i.e., 2001; Ruth was expected to live long enough to greet the Space Brothers when they touched down).

Ruth's contact with the Space Brothers was only part of her legacy. Ruth's higher self was consid-

Uriel (Ruth Norman) and her space Cadillac at the UFO landing site. Unarius purchased 67 acres to serve as a landing place for the Space Brothers, who will purportedly initiate a golden age in 2001. (Michael Grecco)

ered to be a supernatural being by her followers. In all respects, her charismatic authority was absolute in the organization. Throughout the years, her past lives revealed themselves; only a few are cited here. According to Unarius, she had been the inspiration for the Mona Lisa. In ancient Egypt as the goddess Isis, she brought the fourth-dimensional science to her followers. Long ago, she reigned as Ioshanna, the Peacock Princess of Atlantis. Some 800,000 years ago she came as Dalos to the planet Orion. In 1975 she received knowledge from the inner worlds that she lived in the spiritual dimensions as the Spirit of Beauty, Goddess of Love. In this form she held aloft the Sword of Truth while projecting healing rays from her eyes. In 1979 Ruth Norman received a mental transmission that she, as Uriel, was crowned Prince of the Realm, a higher rank than her previous title of archangel. As such, she would rule as one of the Lords of the Universe on the planet Aries.

Much of Unarian cosmology and lore revolves around the past lives of Uriel. While she was alive she was treated with the greatest of deference by her pupils. As Uriel, Ruth Norman appeared costumed in long capes with high collars. Wielding a royal scepter, she also acted out her charismatic persona, crowned in a tiara of glittering stars. Her students immortalized her in paintings that adorn the Unarius Academy. Now that she has passed away, it was expected that she would return with the spaceships in 2001. Uriel is believed to be closer than ever, because she is now free from the bonds of earthly energy.

Currently, Unarius is passing through a transitional period. Uriel was supposed to greet the Space Brothers at the beginning of the new millennium. Until 1991, members believed that she would live to be well over 100 years old. However, in that year she suffered so many health problems that she longed for release from her physical body. The first transitional problems were solved by

Ruth Norman herself. About two years before she died, she began to prepare her students for her passing with dissertations from a Space Brother named Alta. Antares channeled the messages from Interplanetary Ambassador, Alta of the Planet Vixall that gave her permission to die. Her mission, according to Alta, was accomplished: She was free to leave her body. In the interim, students rededicated themselves to the Unarius Mission. They adjusted to the fact that Antares would be left in charge. Ruth Norman died quietly in her sleep on August 12, 1993. Before making it to the millennium, Antares passed away on December 22, 1999.

Most Unarian beliefs and practices come from an oral tradition that has been improvised over the years. The practice of channeling mediumship endures as the accepted pathway to higher knowledge. Channeling or "inspiration" is considered the best way to bring forth "infinite intelligence." The emphasis on flying saucers obscures the spiritualist roots of the group that are evident in the belief system. Unarians have also borrowed from such diverse ideologies as scientism, Theosophy, the cultic milieu, and Swedenborg. Unarians give credence to: reincarnation, karma, progressive evolution, lost continents, The White Brotherhood, messages from ascended masters, and scientific rationalism, among a host of other beliefs. Their philosophy has been elaborated upon and altered over the years so as to synthesize these older notions with the emergent revelations of Ruth and Ernest Norman.

At the Academy, Unarian science and its branches, the "psychology of consciousness" and past-life therapy, remain the courses of study. The Academy is open to anyone. Art therapy classes are also held regularly. The most adept pupils learn to channel higher intelligence and transmit messages from the Space Brothers. Few actually acquire this ability. Students attend classes at the center about three nights a week. At home they study their science through books, audio-tapes, and videos. Those who live too far away engage in home study and correspond with the group. Students receive guidance by reading the texts of channeled messages and by obtaining psychic readings from leaders. In October the students annually celebrate the formation of the Interplanetary Confederation. Members accept that they have always been students of Uriel on other planets or in different civilizations throughout time and space. Outwardly, the group pursues an ordinary lifestyle with a few exceptions. These exceptions include dressing in costumes for celebratory events, such as Interplanetary Confederation Day, or for the making of films. Celebrations and films memorialize the core beliefs of their worldview.

While waiting for starships to arrive in 2001, Unarius serves the expressed function of spiritual growth and healing. Most dedicated students "get healings" and adopt lifestyle changes, such as giving up drugs, alcohol, and cigarettes. Most students share apartments and homes with each other out of economic necessity and for social support. In addition, some members regularly go on radio and television talk shows to let the world know of their teachings. In several cities in Southern California, the local public access channels carry weekly showings of Unarian films. Unarians distinguish themselves from similar groups by their profuse cultural productions in the area of book publishing, art, and film-making. They have produced over a 150 books that explain their teachings. Unarius does a brisk mail-order business in books, tapes, and pins. Many books are handsomely illustrated by student artwork. Murals and paintings decorate the inside and outside of the center. Jewelry, in the form of handmade flying saucer pins, are produced by volunteers and sold through the center. All Unarian films use students as actors. Some films, such as *The Arrival*, can compete with any "B" movie, although others are blurry and amateurish. Producing books, art, and films are at the heart of Unarian projects.

Unarian films are essentially psychodramas wherein students act out their past lives. The plots of the films sometimes utilize student testimonials of healings. Often the films celebrate stories about the "accomplishments" of Uriel, while other videos herald the prophesied landing or depict legends of colonization from outer space. One of the most easily understood films is called *The Arrival*. In this film, a student acts out his past life as Zan, a primitive man of Lemuria. He is visited by the Space Brothers in their dazzling spaceship. The Brothers enlighten him by giving him the memory of his previous life on the planet Orion when he had commanded a battle cruiser that destroyed other civilizations. Zan receives a healing by Uriel, who comes to him out of a vortex of stars.

Paintings and videos about flying saucers and outer space often interest outsiders, but understanding the complicated nature of Unarian thought can prove more difficult. Unarians interpret events on the basis of their specific presuppositions about reality. Sociologically speaking, their science involves an elaborate interpretive framework that gives rise to a continuous narrative. Their science uses electronic metaphors for social and spiritual interaction. Their storytelling runs the gamut from the sublime to the ridiculous. During meetings or in everyday conversation one can hear how earthlings battled Mars millions of years ago, how messages have been transmitted from scientists in outer space, how the Space Brothers are polarizing earth, how Uriel oscillates energies to other planets, or how osteoporosis is caused by space travel during a past lifetime. Though seemingly random, the Unarian accounts revolve around established tenets and stories and ways of explaining experience. Unarius is basically an oral tradition improvised over the years and transcribed into books and films. This oral tradition contains a strong mythological component, some of which is borrowed from world history, television, movies, and the tabloid press. The remainder relies upon direct revelation from channeling mediumship.

Through independent invention, Unarians have constructed origin myths that group members formally act out and recount to others. In these stories, Uriel and the flying saucers are the foremost symbols. The myths account for a member's role in other universes and civilizations throughout time, but most of all they place members in mythic history in relation to their leader, Uriel. Dozens of stories involve colonization from outer space. The tales differ from ordinary fantasies in as much as they function as the collective biographies of Unarian members who are believed to have followed their interplanetary leader, Uriel, throughout time. From their point of view, Unarians practice a objective, rational science that brings them face to face with their past lives and gives them the tools for "progressive evolution."

According to research by sociologists R. George Kirkpatrick and Diana Tumminia, some demographic information exists about Unarians. Findings from a survey and subsequent field research show that the core group has never numbered more than 65 people. Although Unarius has reportedly gained thousands of members around the world, their "nucleus" has averaged around 45 to 50 people per year until recently when it began to decline. Two small satellite centers exist, one in North Carolina and one in Nigeria. Those who live too far away from El Cajon engage in home study and correspond with the group. Almost every student is white. Women slightly outnumber men. Most Unarians are unmarried; those who choose to marry do so within the group. The majority of students hold working-class jobs or incomes. In the years subsequent to Uriel's death, dedicated membership in the group has waned. A significant portion of long-time, dedicated students have defected from the core group. With the death of Antares in 1999, their future seems uncertain.

—*Diana Tumminia*

See Also: Atlantis; Channeling; Contactees; Cults, UFO; Reincarnation; Religions, UFO; Space Brothers

Further Reading:

Norman, Ernest L. *The Voice of Venus.* Los Angeles: New Age Publishing, 1956.

Kirkpatrick, R. George, and Diana Tumminia. "California Space Goddess: The Mystagogue in a Flying Saucer Cult," In *Twentieth Century World Religious Movements in Neo-Weberian Perspective.* Edited by William H. Swatos. Lewiston, NY: Edwin Mellen Press, 1992, pp. 299–311.

———. "Space Magic, Techno-Animism, and the Cult of the Goddess in a Southern Californian UFO Contactee Group: A Case Study in Millenarianism." *Syzygy: Journal of Alternative Religion and Culture* 1(2) (1992): 159–172.

Tumminia, Diana, and R. George Kirkpatrick. "Unarius: Emergent Aspects of an American Flying Saucer Group." In *The Gods Have Landed: New Religions from Other Worlds.* Edited by James R. Lewis. Albany: State University of New York Press, 1995.

UNEARTHLY STRANGER

In this 1963 film a scientist working on a secret space project discovers his wife is an alien, partly because she sleeps with her eyes open. After several space scientists are murdered, his wife confesses to him that she's spearheading an alien invasion and that he should die next, but she finds she can't kill him because she's fallen in love with him. The idea that alien infiltrators come to like earthly life is a regular theme in alien-invasion films.

Independent Artists/A. Julian Wintel-Leslie Parkyn Production 1963; 74 min. Director: John Krish; Writer: Rex Carlton; Cinematography: Reg Wyer; Cast: John Neville, Gabriella Licudi, Phillip Stone, Patrick Newell, Jean Marsh, Warren Mitchell.

UNIDENTIFIED FLYING OBJECTS

Modern sightings of unidentified flying objects (UFOs) began in 1947, when pilot Kenneth Arnold reported seeing nine disk-shaped objects flying over Mt. Rainier, Washington. A reporter labeled them "flying saucers," and modern English acquired a new phrase. The more neutral expression "unidentified flying objects" was later coined by someone in the U.S. Air Force. These phenomena were not actually new, as newspaper accounts of airships from the 1890s shows, and similar reports go back to about 1800, when the concept of artificial flying devices entered the public consciousness.

The most popular theory about UFOs is that they are the spacecraft of extraterrestrial visitors. Mainstream scientists consider this concept to be, although not impossible, so exceedingly unlikely as to deserve no investigation. They point out that there is simply no definite evidence of the existence of such visitors. As a result, projects ostensibly intended to be objective investigations of these phenomena, such as those by the Air Force, instead played down and explained away public rumors and fears about UFOs. Devout skeptics maintain a campaign of ridiculing and preventing attempts to investigate such phenomena scientifically. After every attempt to explain reports in ordinary terms, there remains an inexplicable residue, evidence that something extraordinary does occasionally happen.

Contactee groups have arisen since 1947, centered around claims, memories, or perhaps experiences of having been kidnapped and manipulated

Cover of J. Arturo Abril's Contactos y Mensajes Extraterrestres en Guatemala, *1989 (Mary Evans Picture Library)*

by aliens; some of these have been sincere, others simple cons or hoaxes. Another variety of this movement focuses on the channeling of messages from extraterrestrials by clairvoyants. Some members of these movements subscribe to conspiracy theories that the U.S. government is in cahoots with aliens in order to obtain otherworldly technology. This type of activity has helped give rise to the paraphysical theory about UFOs: that the phenomena are "real," at least psychologically, but not extraterrestrial. Instead, they arise from the archetypal level of the mind and share continuity with other kinds of legends of strange beings and things that fly.

Recently, investigation of data supposedly retrieved under hypnosis has led to the concept of false-memory syndrome, investigation of which overlaps with claims of ritual abuse by satanic cults, memories of past lives, and various psychic abilities. The next step in dealing with the UFO phenomenon may be to study it as a type of religious movement, since it has many of the characteristics of a religion as defined by sociologists.

See Also: Archetype; Arnold, Kenneth; Contactees; Extraterrestrial Hypothesis
Further Reading:
Clark, Jerome. *The UFO Encyclopedia.* 2nd ed. Detroit: Omnigraphics, 1998.
Ritchie, David. *UFO: The Definitive Guide to Unidentified Flying Objects and Related Phenomena.* New York: Facts on File, 1994.

UNIDENTIFIED FLYING OBJECTS

Unidentified Flying Objects was one of the most factual popular films on UFOs. Its producer, Clarence Greene, did a great deal of research on the subject after seeing a UFO himself over Los Angeles in 1952. Greene interviewed former Pentagon press officer for UFO-related inquiries Albert M. Chop and former Project Blue Book director Edward J. Ruppelt. He contacted Nicholas Mariana and Delbert C. Newhouse, obtained copies of the UFO films they had taken, and had them analyzed.

Greene-Rouse Productions began work in May 1954 on this docudrama, with Winston Jones directing. The main character was Albert Chop, played by *Los Angeles Examiner* reporter and aviation journalist Tom Towers. The movie traced Chop's career from skeptical public information officer serving at Wright-Patterson's Air Materiel Command desk in 1950 to Pentagon UFO press spokesman who comes to understand the seriousness of the UFO phenomenon.

The film was made for less than $200,000 and used no professional actors, although it did feature the voice of actor Harry Morgan as a pilot communicating with radar operators as he attempted to intercept UFOs over Washington. UFO witnesses Delbert Newhouse, Nicholas Mariana, and Willis Sperry played themselves; Los Angeles policemen stood in for Air Force officers.

The movie included the first public showings of the recently declassified Montana and Utah films (of alleged UFO flights). It received many favorable reviews but lost money, possibly because it was not sensational enough to attract a large audience.

UNIVERSARIUM FOUNDATION

The Universarium Foundation was established in Portland, Oregon, in 1958 by Zelrun and Daisy Karlsleigh. They organized meetings during which they received telepathic messages; such ability was developed as well by other members of the group. Sri Souda, Lord Michael, and Koot Hoomi have been the most frequent communicators.

The foundation has established a sanctuary in Tucson, Arizona, and publishes a monthly magazine; its main goal is the illumination and improvement of mankind, obtainable through emancipation from confusion and fear. A board of seven directors oversees the activities of the organization, which includes the sale of metaphysical books.

See Also: Ascended Masters; Channeling; New Age
Further Reading:
Melton, J. Gordon. *Encyclopedia of American Religions.* 5th ed. Detroit: Gale Research, 1996.
Prins, Ethera. *Miracle of Love and Life.* Portland, OR: Universarium Foundation, 1974.

UNIVERSE SOCIETY CHURCH

Before acquiring its present name the Universe Society Church (UNISOC) was founded as the Institute of Parapsychology in 1958 (later, it became the Universe Society). Its founder is Hal Wilcox, a medium who was ordained spiritualist minister. In the 1950s, together with other mediums, he began channeling Master Fahsz and other masters from the Ancient Brotherhood of Fahsz (TABOF). The masters introduced the group of mediums to understanding the role of mankind within the universe and taught them particular techniques that put them in contact with INO and other space entities.

According to TABOF teachings, the universe, created by God, is made up of seven sectors, each containing seven galaxies. UFOs are spaceships traveling among galaxies and establishing links among the various inhabited planets.

UNISOC began a seven-step project that has led to the discovery of past covenants, the most important of which is the unveiling of a Japanese religion of the nineteenth century, called Tenrikyo. The first project began in the 1950s and was completed in 1963 with the ordination of Wilcox as a Tenrikyo minister. Six projects had been completed as of 1987; the last one regards America and is currently in progress.

UNISOC has developed a computer interface that in 1978 has allowed the printout of an extraterrestrial communication. Sessions are held weekly in the Hollywood, California, center, and instructional material is published by Galaxy Press along with some 60 books written by Wilcox.

See Also: Ascended Masters; Channeling; New Age
Further Reading:
Melton, J. Gordon. *Encyclopedia of American Religions.* 5th ed. Detroit: Gale Research, 1996.
Wilcox, Hal. *Contact with the Master.* Hollywood, CA: Galaxy Press, 1984.

"V"

"*V*" (for "Visitors") was a TV series (NBC, 1984–1985) about lizardlike aliens that ostensibly came to earth as friends but covertly planned to dominate humanity. The aliens are particularly nasty-looking creatures that eat human beings, but some of them defect to help humankind. On the other side of the coin, some human beings become alien allies. Instead of the usual good humans versus bad aliens, in "*V*" we have the unusual spectacle of good humans and good aliens versus bad humans and bad aliens.

NBC 1983; 120 min. Director: Kenneth Johnson; Writer: Kenneth Johnson; Cast: Marc Singer, Jane Badler, Faye Grant, Robert Englund, Michael Durrell, Peter Nelson, Neva Paterson, Andrew Prine, Richard Herd, Rafael Campos.

VAN TASSEL, GEORGE W.

George Van Tassel was a contactee and promoter of other contactees. Born on March 12, 1910, in Jefferson, Ohio, he moved to California in 1930. He worked for Douglas Aircraft until 1941, when he became the personal flight inspector of experimental aircraft for Howard Hughes. In 1943 Van Tassel went to work for Lockheed as a flight inspector on Constellation aircraft.

In 1947 Van Tassel and his wife and three daughters left Los Angeles and moved to the Mojave Desert. There, in the early 1930s, Van Tassel's friend Frank Critzer had blasted out living quarters in a seven-story boulder known as Giant Rock. Critzer had lived in Giant Rock until 1942 when he committed suicide by blowing himself up with dynamite. Van Tassel installed electricity and made other improvements to his family's new home. In due course, he opened a restaurant, an airport, and a dude ranch.

Beginning in January 1952 Van Tassel claimed that he received psychic messages from extraterrestrial starship commanders. That year he published the book *I Rode a Flying Saucer!* The title was misleading because at that time Van Tassel was only a psychic contactee. It wasn't until August 24, 1953, that he claimed to have set foot on a flying saucer, and that was a tour of the craft rather than a flight.

Early in 1953 Van Tassel began holding weekly Friday-night channeling sessions at Giant Rock, and that spring he hosted the first of many annual Giant Rock Spacecraft Conventions. Some of these conventions attracted up to 10,000 attendees. Through these conventions and his appearances on radio and television, Van Tassel became the major promoter of other contactees.

The space people gave Van Tassel the plans for an electrical rejuvenation machine, and he began raising funds for its construction. The machine, which would be called the Integratron, would not outwardly return a person's body to youth but would recharge its cells. By 1959 the Integratron, a four-story domed structure, was in place. It was 55 feet in diameter and was built mostly of wood and without nails, screws, iron, or steel. The Integratron functioned also as a time machine, receiving strange images and TV signals from other times. However, the Integratron was still incomplete when George Van Tassel died suddenly of a heart attack in 1978.

In 1979 Van Tassel's widow, unable to pay the taxes, sold the property to a San Diego real-estate developer, who announced that he would turn the Integratron into a disco. Van Tassel's outraged followers raised the money to buy the land back in 1981.

—Jerome Clark

See Also: Contactees; Giant Rock Spacecraft Convention; Religions, UFO

Further Reading:

Curran, Douglas. In Advance of the Landing: Folk Concepts of Outer Space. New York: Abbeville Press, 1985.

Flammonde, Paris. The Age of Flying Saucers: Notes on a Projected History of Unidentified Flying Objects. New York: Hawthorn Books, 1971.

Reeve, Bryant, and Helen Reeve. Flying Saucer Pilgrimage. Amherst, WI: Amherst Press, 1957.

Van Tassel, George W. I Rode a Flying Saucer! The Mystery of the Flying Saucers Revealed. Los Angeles: New Age Publishing, 1952.

VENUSIAN CHURCH

This religious group dates back to 1975, when it was founded by Seattle businessman Ron Peterson. Formerly a member of the Seventh-Day Adventist Church, Peterson followed a personal development that led him to realize the importance and the divinity of sexuality. His experience brought him to begin a career as a pornographer and to share with others the need to explore the potential of sexuality and human creativity; in this research he was joined by therapists and counselors.

Members of the church met first in the Temple of Venus in Seattle; later on they established a center, Camp Armac, in which seminars, social events, and religious services were held. During such meetings sexual experiments were conducted, pornographic films were shown, and the church's attitude toward sexual matters was communicated to the general public. In 1981 an old warehouse near Redmond, Washington, was purchased and converted into a church, named the Longhouse.

The church's activities and its opinions on sex prompted several attacks from legal authorities, who have repeatedly arrested members of the church, as well as from the Internal Revenue Service; the latter has denied the church its tax-exempt status, thus causing financial difficulties that have limited the progress of the church. In line with the fundamental neopagan creed, the Venusian Church sets as its goal the reestablishment of the links with the natural archetypes, lost through the development of civilization.

See Also: Archetype

Further Reading:

Lewis, James R. The Encyclopedia of Cults, Sects, and New Religions. Amherst, NY: Prometheus Books, 1998.

Melton, J. Gordon. Encyclopedia of American Religions. 5th ed. Detroit: Gale Research, 1996.

VILLAS-BOAS ENCOUNTER

On October 5, 1957, in Brazil, young farmer Antonio Villas-Boas rose from bed at 11 P.M. to open a window. Outside he saw a bright silvery fluorescent reflection. After a short period of time, the light started moving toward the window. Villas-Boas slammed the shutters shut. The light appeared through the crevices of the shutters, lighting up the darkness of the room. Then the light disappeared. On October 14 Villas-Boas was plowing when he saw a blindingly bright object hovering 300 feet above the end of the field. When he tried to approach it, it evaded him and then disappeared.

The next night, at 1 A.M., he saw a big, red, egg-shaped object that accelerated toward him until it was 160 feet above his head, shining as bright as daylight. Villas-Boas watched the object land. He described it as an elongated egg with three metal bars sticking out of it. Above the egg, something rotated rapidly. As the object descended, three legs extended from its underside to support it on the ground. Villas-Boas started to flee but felt someone grab his arm. He turned around to see a small figure, which he shoved to the ground. Three others grabbed him, lifted him off the ground, and carried him to the machine. There was a door in the object that opened from top to bottom, forming an entry ramp with a ladder on the end. Despite his struggles, Villas-Boas found himself inside a room with metal walls.

The figures communicated with each other via growling sounds. They were covered from head to toe with clothing. Even their eyes were partially obscured with glasses. The helmets they wore gave the appearance that their heads were twice the size of human heads. Three tubes ran between their helmets and their suits, which were made of a striped gray material. The figures grabbed Villas-Boas and undressed him without hurting him or tearing his clothes. They spread a thick odorless liquid all over his body and then took a blood sample from under his chin.

The figures then left him alone for awhile. A gray smoke emanating from metal tubes in the ceiling made Villas-Boas violently ill, and he vomited. Then a nude woman entered the room. She and Villas-Boas had intercourse twice. She had whitish-blonde hair, a wide face, pointed chin, and big blue eyes. The woman left the room, a man returned with Villas-Boas's clothes, and he was given a tour of the ship. He was then ushered out of the ship and watched as it flew off at 5:30 A.M. Over the next month Villas-Boas suffered from unusual sleepiness and bouts of nausea.

In November 1957 Villas-Boas wrote Brazilian journalist Joao Martins, who had written articles on UFOs in a popular magazine. Martins arranged for Villas-Boas to come to Rio de Janeiro, where Martins and ufologist Olavo T. Fontes interviewed Villas-Boas and his sworn statement was taken. Fontes and Martins were impressed with Villas-Boas's intelligence, straightforward manner, and sincerity, but they still found his story difficult to believe.

Fontes, who was also professor of surgery at the National School of Medicine of Brazil, examined Villas-Boas thoroughly and found two small spots on each side of the chin consistent with having had a blood sample drawn about a month earlier. This turned out to be the only physical evidence of the encounter. After his meeting with Fontes and Martins, Villas-Boas did not attempt to attract publicity and returned to his home. A short article on the case appeared in the bulletin of a Brazilian UFO group in 1962. The story first appeared in English in *Flying Saucer Review* in 1965. In 1978, 20 years after the incident, Villas-Boas made his first public appearance on a Brazilian TV show.

See Also: Abductees; Close Encounters; Sex
Further Reading:
Bowen, Charles, ed. *The Humanoids: A Survey of Worldwide Reports of Landings of Unconventional Aerial Objects and Their Alleged Occupants*. London: Futura Publications, 1974.
Jacobs, David M. *Secret Life: Firsthand Accounts of UFO Abductions*. New York: Simon and Schuster, 1992.
John E. *Abduction: Human Encounters with Aliens*. New York: Charles Scribner's Sons, 1994.

VIMANAS

Vimanas are the flying machines described in ancient Hindu religious literature. They have often been referred to as indicating the possibility of contacted with ufonauts in humanity's distant past. *Alien Identities,* a relatively recent book by a member of the Hare Krishna movement, systematically presents the evidence for such a view.

When Bhaktivedanta Swami Prabhupada (1896–1977), the founder of the Hare Krishna movement, brought Gaudiya-Vaisnavism to the West in 1965, he was presumably unaware of the ongoing UFO debate. His biographer does not mention anything that could indicate any awareness of the concept of UFOs, and nothing is to be found in his writings, although he occasionally discusses issues of "spiritual migration" to other realms or planets within classical philosophy. However, one of his disciples, Sadapuda Dasa, has with great enthusiasm and very skillfully related ufology to Bhaktivedanta's teachings. Under his civil name, Richard L. Thompson, he wrote *Alien Identities* based on the theory that UFOs, and whatever goes along, are wholly explicable in terms of Vaisnava theology. According to Thompson, strange flying crafts are minutely described in ancient Hindu texts such as the Puranas; UFOs are, in fact, the vehicles of the gods—their Vimanas. He refers to a large number of religious texts in support of his thesis and suggests why they are being seen, what they are doing, and so on.

This, of course, does not make ufology an International Society for Krishna Consciousness (ISKCON) discipline. However, as Sadapuda Dasa is a well-known devotee in ISKCON and one of the

Model of a Vimana (Ancient Astronaut Society)

more visible intellectuals (he is a trained scientist) in the movement, many people listen to him. Interestingly enough, the focus is not on what people may see in the skies. On the contrary, devotees argue that if things are described in the sacred texts, then they are real. Therefore, UFOs should be real. In this way, the interest in UFOs supports the traditional idea of the sacred texts and adds to ISKCON's theology. Usually it is the other way around when people try to prove the existence of UFOs with references to ancient scripture.

At the same time, Sadapuda Dasa has reached a new audience not familiar with ISKCON's position, namely the larger UFO audience who—according to reviews—accepted his book with enthusiasm.

—*Mikael Rothstein*

See Also: Ancient Astronauts
Further Reading:
Thompson, Richard L. *Alien Identities.* Alachua, FL: Govardhan Hill Publishing, 1995.

VISIT TO A SMALL PLANET

This 1960 film stars Jerry Lewis as a rational visitor from outer space who has confrontations with emotional humans. The longer he stays on earth, the more human he becomes. Some variation on the basic notion of extraterrestrials mixing with humanity in human form and becoming human as a result is one of Hollywood's staple plots. It might be noted that the idea that ufonauts are nonemotional beings interested in human emotions is a standard theme found in alien-abduction literature.

Paramount/Wallis-Hazen Production 1960; 85 min.
Director: Norman Taurog: Writers: Edmund Beloin, Henry Garson; Cinematography: Loyal Griggs; Cast: Jerry Lewis, Joan Blackman, Earl Holliman, Fred Clark, Lee Patrick, Gale Gordon.

VON DÄNIKEN, ERICH ANTON

Erich von Däniken (b. 1935), the most prominent advocate of the ancient-astronaut hypothesis, underwent a mystical experience at age 19 that left him convinced the earth had been visited by extraterrestrials. His obsession with this idea led him into debt, and in 1968 the Swiss police arrested him for fraud. He was convicted of it in 1970, but by this time his enormously popular book *Chariots of the Gods?* had appeared, so that he was able to pay his debts and be released early. Many sequels followed.

Von Däniken's books argue that the gods of existing religions were actually visitors from outer space that—either by interbreeding or direct genetic manipulation—created *Homo sapiens* from our unintelligent progenitors. They were also responsible for all the archaeological and architectural wonders of the ancient world. Critics have pointed out that his ideas are not very original; they can be found in at least a dozen books by previous authors, especially in the theosophical writings of H. P. Blavatsky and those of 1950s contactees. However, von Däniken is the one who pulled them all together into a fairly coherent philosophy.

See Also: Ancient Astronauts; Gods and UFOs; Theosophy
Further Reading:
Goran, Morris. *The Modern Myth, Ancient Astronauts and UFOs.* South Brunswick, NJ: A. S. Barnes, 1978.
von Däniken, Erich. *Chariots of the Gods? Unsolved Mysteries of the Past.* Trans. Michael Heron. New York: G. P. Putnam's Sons, 1970.

WALTON ABDUCTION

One of the most controversial abduction cases of all time took place in a remote mountainous region of east-central Arizona in 1975. Travis Walton was working late on a forestry project with six other crew members. As they were driving home, they saw a strange light through the trees, which turned out to be a disk-shaped craft hovering about 20 feet above the ground. Walton jumped out of the truck and walked toward it until it began making strange sounds and wobbled violently. As he turned to leave, a laserlike beam struck him, raised him into the air, and tossed him to the ground. The crew sped away in terror, and when they returned Walton was nowhere to be found.

They went straight to the police, who at first suspected murder. Later, authorities decided it was hoax, even though according to lie-detector tests all the witnesses were found to be telling the truth about seeing a UFO. A full-scale manhunt came up with nothing. Five days later Walton's brother-in-law received a phone call from Walton, who said he was hurt and needed to be picked up immediately. He was shaking, 10 pounds thinner, and spoke of beings with terrifying eyes. He thought he had been gone for only a few hours.

Walton took many lie-detector tests and passed all except one, which was used against him by his most aggressive accuser, Philip Klass (an archskeptic of UFOs). Most authorities did not believe his story and attributed the experience to an LSD trip or a hoax. To this day, the controversy has not subsided. Amid all the media fanfare and accusations, what Walton said he experienced aboard the craft was all but ignored.

After being taken up into the craft, he awoke inside the craft and saw three figures in orange suits who had huge, bald heads, huge eyes, and looked like "fetuses." Walton struck one being, and they left. He saw a humanlike being through the door and obeyed its motion to come nearer. Walton was led in silence to a room with other human-looking creatures that smiled at him and led him to a table. They put a mask over his face; he lost consciousness and woke up on the side of the road 20 miles from the abduction site.

—Jerome Clark

See Also: Abductees; Close Encounters; *Fire in the Sky*
Further Reading:
Gansberg, Judith M., and Alan L. Gansberg. *Direct Encounters: The Personal Histories of UFO Abductees.* New York: Walker, 1980.
Klass, Philip J. *UFO Abductions: A Dangerous Game.* Updated ed. Buffalo, NY: Prometheus Books, 1989.
Lorenzen, Coral, and Jim Lorenzen. *Abducted! Confrontations with Beings from Outer Space.* New York: Berkley, 1977.
Stein, Gordon. *Encyclopedia of Hoaxes.* Detroit: Gale Research, 1993.
Walton, Travis. *Fire in the Sky: The Walton Experience.* New York: Marlowe, 1996.

WAND

In some close-encounter cases, ufonauts reportedly paralyze contactees with a wandlike device. The wand image is interesting because of its parallels to traditional folklore. A wand is one of the basic working tools of magicians and witches. It is used, among other purposes, for invoking spirits. The wand is a pointer, a director of magical energy, and a magical rod of power. The wand is also a tool of transformation. It invokes the power of the spirit who transforms everything in the universe into something else.

See Also: Contactees; Occult
Further Reading:
Clark, Jerome. *The UFO Encyclopedia.* 2nd ed. Detroit: Omnigraphics, 1998.

Lewis, James R. *Witchcraft Today: An Encyclopedia of Wiccan and Neopagan Traditions.* Santa Barbara, CA: ABC-CLIO, 1999.

WAR OF THE PLANETS

In this 1965 Italian film incorporeal beings from Mars attack earth and its ring of defensive satellites by taking over humans. The notion of disembodied entities capable of possessing human beings is, of course, a standard item of traditional religious lore. As psychologist Carl Jung pointed out, however, modern people seem incapable of seriously entertaining such notions, so we substitute extraterrestrials for spiritual beings. Here, the Martians are clearly a kind of "technological demon."

Mercury Film International/Southern Cross Productions 1965; 99 min. Director: Antonio Margheriti; Writers: Ivan Reiner, Renato Moretti; Cinematography: Riccardo Pallottini; Cast: Tony Russell, Lisa Gastoni, Carlo Giustini, Massimo Serato, Michel Lemoine, Franco Nero.

WAR OF THE SATELLITES

In this 1958 film the United Nations tries to send a manned rocket into orbit. Aliens, however, set up an impassible space barrier and warn the nations of our planet that if they go forward with the project earth will be obliterated. The scientist in charge of the expedition dies in an automobile accident, but the extraterrestrials bring him back to life to help stop the project. The rocket launch occurs nevertheless, and when the resurrected scientist attempts to crash it into the barrier, he is prevented from doing so by the crew. The idea that human beings are barbarians not fit to be accepted as equals among the nations of the galaxy is one of the explanations for why the Space Brothers have not established formal relations with earth.

Roger Corman Productions 1958; 66 min. Director: Roger Corman; Writer: Lawrence Louis Goldman; Cinematography: Floyd Crosby; Cast: Susan Cabot, Dick Miller, Richard Devon, Robert Shayne, Jerry Barclay, Eric Sinclair, Jay Sayer.

WAR OF THE WORLDS (FILM)

This was a 1953 film adaptation of H. G. Wells's classic novel, but it was based more on Orson Welles's

Illustration of the alien invasion portrayed in H. G. Wells's story War of the Worlds *(American Religion Collection)*

radio broadcast than on the book. The setting was changed from the English countryside in the 1890s to Southern California in the 1950s. H. G. Wells's Martian war machines, in the shape of walking tripods, were replaced by flying saucer–like craft. The plot begins with meteors landing all over the earth. Flying machines with death rays arise from the meteors and begin destroying everything in sight. They appear to be invincible, but when complete destruction looms the Martian machines collapse, their pilots having succumbed to bacteria to which they have no immunity. *War of the Worlds* was later made into a TV series.

George Pal Productions/Paramount 1953; 85 min. Director: Byron Haskin; Cast: Gene Barry, Ann Robinson, Les Tremayne, Lewis Martin, Robert Cornthwaite, Sandro Giglio.

"WAR OF THE WORLDS" (RADIO BROADCAST)

On the night before Halloween in 1938, a radio announcer in New York broadcast the startling news

A Martian from director Byron Haskins's landmark adaptation of the H. G. Wells classic novel War of the Worlds, *about the invasion of the earth by aliens, 1953 (The Del Valle Archive)*

that Martians had invaded the United States. Thousands of innocent people had already been slain by ray guns and by clouds of noxious gas released by the aliens. From their landing area in New Jersey—the announcer asserted—the Martians were rapidly advancing in all directions, setting the countryside on fire, and quickly overpowering any opposition to their onslaught. The broadcast set off a wave of hysteria across the Eastern Seaboard.

The announcer was Orson Welles, a brilliant actor who was reading an adapted-for-radio version of H. G. Wells's 1898 novel, *The War of the Worlds*. Because a popular entertainer on a competing radio program had been replaced for the evening with a relatively unknown singer, many of the listeners who changed channels and tuned into Welles's broadcast missed the introduction in which the fictional nature of the play had been explained. The program was also carried out in an alarmist style— "We interrupt this program . . ."—which, in combination with the broadcaster's considerable talent, cloaked the drama with a marked atmosphere of realism. An embarrassed Welles, fearful that his career had been ruined, quickly offered a contrite public apology for the broadcast.

Many analysts later concluded that the panic set off by the broadcast could be explained in terms of America's prewar jitters: The nation was on the edge of its seat as a result of events in Europe that were leading to world war. The fictional Martian invasion seemed to embody widespread but vague anxieties about a possible assault by the fascist powers. These ambiguous fears were thus tapped and brought to the fore of the nation's consciousness by Welles's groundbreaking broadcast.

See Also: Mars
Further Reading:
Clark, Jerome. *The UFO Encyclopedia.* 2nd ed. Detroit: Omnigraphics, 1998.
Thompson, Keith. *Angels and Aliens: UFOs and the Mythic Imagination.* Reading, MA: Addison-Wesley, 1991.

WARLORDS OF ATLANTIS

In this 1978 film two Victorian antiquarians descend to the lost civilization of Atlantis, do battle with an octopus and a bizarre mutant dinosaur, and foil a villain's plans to conquer the upper world. They also learn that the Atlanteans came from Mars. The connection between ancient mythological civilizations like Atlantis and extraterrestrials reflects a theme found in ancient-astronaut literature.

EMI/John Dark–Kevin Connor Productions 1978; 96 min. Director: Kevin Connor; Writer: Brian Hayles; Cinematography: Alan Hume; Cast: Doug McClure, Peter Gilmore, Shane Rimmer, Lea Brodie, Daniel Massey, Cyd Charisse.

THE WATCHER IN THE WOODS

In this 1980 Disney movie a benign alien reunites an old woman with her daughter, who has been missing for 30 years while trapped in another dimension. This is another example of an extraterrestrial playing a quasi-spiritual role, not unlike a fairy godmother who intervenes in human affairs to set things aright.

Disney 1980; 83 min. Director: John Hough; Writer: Brien Clemens, Harry Spalding, Rosemary Anne Sisson; Cinematography: Alan Hume; Cast: Bette Davis, David McCallum, Carol Baker, Lynn-Holly Johnson, Kyle Richards, Ian Bannen, Frances Cuka.

WHEELS OF LIGHT

Some observations of aerial phenomena have reported structures like huge wheels of light. There have been at least 100 such reports since the mid–nineteenth century. These would appear to be merely a particular variety of UFO sighting. They are reported as complete circles or arcs of circles, sometimes with a hub, spokes, and rim structure, all giving off almost blinding light. They are sometimes accompanied by parallel bands of light as well. Among UFO observations, they are among the more inexplicable.

See Also: Nineteenth-Century Airship Tales; Unidentified Flying Objects
Further Reading:
Clark, Jerome. *The UFO Encyclopedia.* 2nd ed. Detroit: Omnigraphics, 1998.
Ritchie, David. *UFO: The Definitive Guide to Unidentified Flying Objects and Related Phenomena.* New York: Facts on File, 1994.

WHEN PROPHECY FAILS

Earthlings will awaken to . . . the lake seething and the great destruction of tall buildings. . . . The scenes of that day will be as mad . . . the event will begin at dawn and end swiftly as a passing cloud. . . . When the resurrected have been resurrected or taken up . . . it will be as a great burst of light. . . . In the midst of this it is to be recorded that a great wave rushes into the mountains. . . . The slopes of the side to the east will be the beginning of a new civilization upon which will be the new order, in light.

In this prophecy one finds many familiar apocalyptic elements, from the theme of universal de-

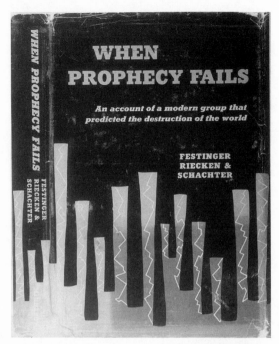

Cover of Festinger, Riecken, and Schachter's book When Prophecy Fails, *published in 1956 by the University of Minnesota Press (Mary Evans Picture Library)*

struction to the postapocalypse vision of a dawning new order. One can well imagine that these words spilled unbidden from the trembling lips of an ecstatic, Middle Eastern prophet. Alternately, perhaps they were uttered by a fiery preacher in harsh, dramatic tones from the pulpit of some backwoods church.

Instead, however, this prediction was one of the central transmissions of Space Brother Sananda (a.k.a. Jesus) to Marian Keech, a middle-aged, middle-class suburbanite who transcribed them via the medium of automatic writing in the comfort of her own living room. In other messages, Sananda assured Keech that Keech and a select group of followers would be taken up by a flying saucer in a kind of technological rapture before the destruction commenced on December 21, 1954. Needless to say, neither the rapture nor the predicted apocalypse occurred—a dramatic nonevent, the significance of which was captured in the title of the first and only study of the group, *When Prophecy Fails,* by sociologists Leon Festinger, Henry W. Reicken, and Stanley Schachter.

According to the authors, the study was conducted in order to test one of the implications of the theory of cognitive dissonance. This implication was that—in the face of a failed religious prophecy—one tactic the core community around the prophet might take to reduce the dissonance induced by the prophetic failure would be to increase their proselytizing activities. In other words, confronted with evidence that calls into question the validity of their belief system, the community's ability to convert new believers provides counterevidence that its system of belief is in fact correct after all.

Following up on a short newspaper article that provided basic information on the Keech group, members of the research team subsequently infiltrated the group by posing as believers. The bulk of *When Prophecy Fails* is a detailed description of events leading up to the failed prophecy. When the predicted date came and went, Marian Keech channeled an explanation from the Space Brothers to the effect that God had called the cataclysm off as a direct result of the little group's intense faith. In other words, Keech and her followers had saved the world.

Although the message was gratifying, the group was left with the difficult task of explaining the noncataclysm to the news media. Congruent with the sociologists' research hypothesis, the group closest to Keech accepted the modified revelation and immediately became engaged in intense (though ineffective) proselytizing activities. Believers who were not among the core group tended to become disenchanted and dropped out of the circle of people surrounding the prophetess. Marian Keech (whose real name is Dorothy Martin) went on to found a formal religious group.

See Also: Apocalypse; Automatic Writing; Channeling; Contactees

Further Reading:

Festinger, Leon, Henry W. Riechen, and Stanley Schachter. *When Prophecy Fails.* Minneapolis: University of Minnesota Press, 1956.

Lewis, James R., ed. *The Gods Have Landed: New Religions From Other Worlds.* Albany: State University of New York Press, 1995.

Melton, J. Gordon. *Encyclopedia of American Religion.* 5th ed. Detroit: Gale Research, 1996.

Vallee, Jacques. *Messengers of Deception: UFO Contacts and Cults.* Berkeley: And/Or Press, 1979.

WHITE STAR

In 1954 Doris C. LeVesque read a book on flying saucers and shortly after began to channel entities, among which was the Ashtar Command, also channeled by George Van Tassel of the Ministry of Universal Wisdom. She founded White Star and in 1957 began publishing the *White Star Illuminator.* In her teachings, LeVesque stresses the value of love as a means to avoid the destruction of nature. She also focuses on the achievement of higher spiritual levels that are characterized by the presence of more light; meditation sessions are meant to visualize light.

See Also: Ashtar Command; Channeling; Contactees; Van Tassel, George W.

Further Reading:

Lewis, James R. *The Encyclopedia of Cults, Sects, and New Religions.* Amherst, NY: Prometheus Books, 1998.

Melton, J. Gordon. *Encyclopedia of American Religion.* 5th ed. Detroit: Gale Research, 1996.

WHITMAN, STUART

Stuart Whitman claimed that he was contacted by aliens during a blackout in New York City and much of the Northeast in 1965. He said he was standing by the window of his Manhattan hotel room at dawn when he heard a whistling and saw two UFOs—one orange, one blue. The beings spoke to him, saying that "earthlings were messing around with unknown quantities and might disrupt the balance of the universe." They told him the blackout was a demonstration of their power, a warning to earth. They chose Whitman because he had no hate and told him to fight prejudice and injustice.

See Also: Contactees

Further Reading:

Keel, John A. *UFOs: Operation Trojan Horse.* New York: G. P. Putnam's Sons, 1970.

WILLIAMSON, GEORGE HUNT

George Hunt Williamson was born in Chicago on December 9, 1926. He had psychic experiences in his teenage years and a spontaneous out-of-body experience as a college student. In 1951 Williamson became interested in UFOs after reading Donald Keyhoe's *The Flying Saucers Are Real.* He subsequently immersed himself in saucer literature.

In 1952, when he and wife Betty were living in Prescott, Arizona, they were visited by fellow occult enthusiasts Alfred and Betty Bailey of Winslow, Arizona. The four conducted an automatic-writing experiment and received a message from an extraterrestrial aboard a spaceship. This being and other space people communicated to them over the next days and weeks by automatic writing and through a Ouija board. Bailey was instructed by the contactors to ask the help of ham-radio operator Lyman Streeter in picking up a space signal that they would broadcast on August 22. On that date, Streeter saw unusual lights over Winslow and heard strange signals on the frequency he had been instructed to monitor. Messages regarding imminent landings and apocalyptic warnings continued to be received by the Streeters, Williamsons, and Baileys via radio and mental telepathy.

George Adamski's name came to Williamson's attention when he read *The Coming of the Saucers* by Kenneth Arnold and Ray Palmer. Williamson got Adamski's address from Palmer and began corresponding with him. Adamski invited Williamson to visit him at Palomar Gardens in Southern California. During the fall of 1952 the Williamsons and the Baileys regularly traveled between Arizona and California. Adamski began channeling space messages in the presence of the Williamsons and the Baileys.

On November 18, 1952, Adamski called Williamson and said the space people had told him there would be a physical meeting in two days. On the morning of November 20, Adamski and two associates set out from Palomar Gardens. They met the Williamsons and the Baileys at Blythe, California, on the Arizona border. They drove off together deep into the desert. Allegedly, as his six companions watched from a distance, Adamski met a Venusian named Orthon who arrived in a flying disk.

The first account of Adamski's encounter with the Venusian was published in the *Phoenix*

Gazette on November 24, 1952. It made Adamski instantly famous. The faithful began making pilgrimages to Palomar Gardens. The Williamsons moved there to be close to Adamski, who seemed to have changed, becoming secretive and remote. When Adamski discouraged Williamson from channeling extraterrestrial communications, saying that he could handle all the channeling that needed to be done, Williamson left Adamski and linked up with other psychic contactees.

The year 1954 saw the publication of Williamson and Bailey's book, *The Saucers Speak!,* which related their radio and telepathic communications with extraterrestrials in Arizona in 1952. In 1955 Williamson and fellow psychic contactee Dick Miller started the Telonic Research Center to reestablish radio and light contact with extraterrestrials. The two men quarreled and parted that same year. In 1956 Williamson got involved with the Brotherhood of the Seven Rays, a metaphysical colony in Peru whose members included several other channelers.

Williamson's *Other Tongues—Other Flesh* was published in 1957. It was one of the first ancient-astronaut books. It was followed by two similar books, *Secret Places of the Lion* (1958) and *Road in the Sky* (1959). In these three books Williamson presented his UFO-age revisionist history of the human race. He contended that space people had interacted with humans throughout history and that some people—for example, the Hopi—had their origins on another planet. In *Road in the Sky* he was among the first to suggest that Peru's Nazca lines were markers to guide something arriving from outer space.

The February 1959 issue of *Saucer News* exposed the fact that Williamson's educational claims in *Who's Who in America* and *American Men of Science* were fictitious. Williamson's assertions about undergraduate and doctoral degrees proved false. Later that year, Williamson legally changed his name to Michel d'Obrenovic, which he claimed was his family's original name. Thereafter, he disappeared from the contactee circuit but occasionally delivered restrained lectures on ancient-astronaut themes under his new name.

In 1961 Williamson's book *Secret of the Andes* was published under the pseudonym Brother Philip. George Hunt Williamson's death in Long Beach, California, in January 1986 came as a surprise to most UFO enthusiasts who had lost track of him after he changed his name.

—*Jerome Clark*

See Also: Adamski, George; Contactees; Occult
Further Reading:
Brother Philip [pseudonym of George Hunt Williamson]. *Secret of the Andes.* Clarksburg, WV: Saucerian Books, 1961.
Leslie, Desmond, and George Adamski. *Flying Saucers Have Landed.* New York: British Book Centre, 1953.
Norkin, Israel. *Saucer Diary.* New York: Pageant Press, 1957.
Williamson, George Hunt. *Other Tongues—Other Flesh.* Amherst, WI: Amherst Press, 1953.
———. *Road in the Sky.* London: Neville Spearman, 1959.

WITHOUT WARNING

In this 1981 terror movie an aggressive alien flings bloodsucking organisms at its victims. A pure horror flick that substitutes a demonic extraterrestrial for more ordinary monsters, it has little connection to UFO lore.

Filmways 1980; 89 min. Director: Greydon Clark; Writers: Lyn Freeman, Daniel Grodnik, Ben Nett, Steve Mathis; Cinematography: Dean Cundy; Cast: Jack Palance, Martin Landau, Tarah Nutter, Christopher S. Nelson, Cameron Mitchell, Neville Brand.

WORLD UNDERSTANDING

Daniel Fry founded this group in 1955, five years after his meeting with an extraterrestrial being named A-Lan, who took him on a flight aboard a flying saucer from New Mexico to New York. A-Lan, who was on an exploratory mission to earth, became the source of inspiration for several books that Fry authored. The organization studies in particular those assumptions and human behaviors that are common to all cultures and races around the world, its goal being the individuation of a guide for the behavior of mankind. In the 1970s World Understanding moved its headquarters to Tonopah, Arizona, and there absorbed the Universal Faith and Wisdom Association; recently the organization moved to New Mexico.

See Also: Contactees; Fry, Daniel

Further Reading:
Fry, Daniel W. *Alan's Message: To Men of Earth.* Los Angeles: New Age Publishing, 1954.
Melton, J. Gordon. *Encyclopedia of American Religion.* 5th ed. Detroit: Gale Research, 1996.

X-FILES

The immensely popular TV series *X-Files* began airing in 1993. As of this writing, it appears to be going strong. The first *X-Files* movie, *Dark Horizons,* came out in 1998; the second, *Invasion,* was released in 2000. The title of the series refers to a designation—attributed to the days of J. Edgar Hoover—of FBI cases that seemed to have a paranormal component.

Roughly one in three episodes is about aliens and UFOs. The opening graphics begin with shots of a shadowy UFO crossing the sky. Fox Mulder, one of the two chief protagonists, is an FBI agent whose interest in the paranormal was initiated by the abduction of his sister at a young age. And the story that forms the background narrative for the entire series, as well as for the *X-Files* movies, revolves around a vast government-alien conspiracy. No other paranormal phenomenon is as significant in the *X-Files* as UFOs.

The ufology of *X-Files* is distinctly the so-called new ufology. Whereas traditional ufology encompasses reports of sightings (the "hardware" orientation) and contactees who claim to relate messages from concerned extraterrestrials ("soft" ufology), new ufology focuses on the abduction phenomenon and paranoid conspiracy theories about government collusion with hostile aliens. The writers and producers of *X-Files* have picked up on the latter themes and helped to popularize them.

The broad cultural awareness of abduction by extraterrestrials and UFO-related conspiracy theories is primarily, though not entirely, the result of the entertainment media. Without shows like *X-Files,* items of data reflecting new ufology might have remained confined to the UFO subculture. There is thus more discussion about UFOs today than during any previous era.

X-Files works by not providing a definitive answer to many of the phenomena investigated by Mulder and his partner, Dana Scully, thereby allowing viewers to revel in the mystery. Shows like *Dark Skies*—transparent *X-Files* wannabes—were flops precisely because they failed to perceive the importance of ambiguity and mystery. *X-Files* was also successful because of the creative tension between Mulder—the feminine male whose attitude is captured in the caption of his "I want to believe" poster—and Scully—the masculine female who gives expression to the skeptical, scientific voice. The inclusion of this latter point of view in the narrative—a perspective that is invariably undermined by the *X-File* storyline—paradoxically serves to silence the skeptical voice in the mind of the viewer, enhancing the suspension of disbelief that is essential to the success of good fiction.

Another key to the success of *X-Files* is found in its creative blend of genres—mystery, cop show, sci-fi, horror—to deal with themes out of folklore, both traditional (e.g., vampires and satanists) and contemporary (e.g., the Bermuda Triangle and UFOs). The juxtaposition of traditional and contemporary folklore in different *X-Files* episodes creates what Leslie Jones has referred to as "narrative osmosis," in which "the characteristics of one category seep into another and all narrative traits become interchangeable": "Science begins to seem much less objective when its products bear such strong resemblance to the monsters of myth and nightmare. Likewise, the juxtaposition of ancient legend and modern UFO belief reinforces and emphasizes the mythological axis of the alien stories." *X-Files,* in other words, contributes to what we might call the "mythologization" of conspiracy theories, UFOs, and other paranormal phenomena, contributing to a process that psychologist

Carl Jung, folklorists, and other observers noted as early as the 1950s.

See Also: Film and Television; Popular Culture

Further Reading:

Badly, Linda. "The Rebirth of the Clinic: The Body as Alien in the *X-Files.*" In *"Deny All Knowledge": Reading the X Files.* Edited by David Lavery, Angela Hague, and Maria Cartwright. Syracuse: Syracuse University Press, 1996.

Jones, Leslie. "'Last Week We Had an Omen': The Mythological *X-Files.*" In *"Deny All Knowledge": Reading the X Files.* Edited by David Lavery, Angela Hague, and Maria Cartwright. Syracuse: Syracuse University Press, 1996.

XTRO

In this 1982 film a man returns home after he has been abducted by a UFO. He infects his son with alien spores and leaves his wife with a brood of look-alike offspring. Eventually the man transforms into an alien shape. The central themes of this film flow directly out of UFO abduction literature.

Ashley Productions 1983; 80 min. Director: Harry Bromley Davenport; Writers: Lain Cassle, Robert Smith; Cinematography: John Metcalfe; Cast: Bernice Stegers, Philip Sayer, Danny Brainin, Simon Nash.

YOG—MONSTER FROM SPACE

In this 1970 Japanese film a group of visitors to a Pacific island are attacked by a giant squid, a giant crab, and a giant turtle. The animating force behind all these creatures is an alien life-form brought back to earth by a unmanned spaceship that passed through a mysterious blue mist. The monsters are all eventually destroyed by a volcano. The notion of a disembodied alien intelligence that takes over human beings or other terrestrial creatures is a standard theme of sci-fi movies. The movie's notion of disembodied entities capable of possessing living beings is a standard item of traditional religious lore, making the possessing alien a kind of "technological demon."

Toho 1970; 81 min. Director: Inoshiro Honda; Cinematography: Taiichi Kankura; Cast: Yoichi Manoda, Akira Kubo, Atsuko Takahashi, Toshio Tsuchiya, Kenji Sahara, Noritake Saito, Yukihiko Kobayashi, Satoshi Nakamura, Yuko Sugjihara.

Z

ZECHARIAH, BOOK OF

Verse 5:2 describes a "flying scroll" that is 20 cubits long and 10 cubits wide, that is, roughly 30 feet by 15 feet. It is described by the angel who is speaking to the narrator as a curse that will consume all the thieves and perjurers of the world. Its description roughly matches the reports of cigar-shaped craft.

Verses 6:1–6 describe "four chariots coming out from between two mountains of bronze." They were drawn by horses—red, black, white, and spotted. An angel tells the narrator these are the four winds of heaven, coming forth and being reviewed by the Lord of all the earth. Three fly away to the north, the one with the spotted horses to the south. It would be easy to interpret this as a UFO report.

See Also: Ancient Astronauts
Further Reading:
Downing, Barry H. *The Bible and Flying Saucers.*
    Philadelphia: J. B. Lippincott, 1968.
Goran, Morris. *The Modern Myth, Ancient Astronauts and*
    UFOs. South Brunswick, NJ: A. S. Barnes, 1978.

ZONE TROOPERS

In this 1986 film five American GIs in World War II–ravaged Europe stumble upon a wrecked alien spacecraft. The alien pilot is dead, but the copilot manages to get away. Soon the soldiers find themselves confronted by an alien rescue party—the Zone Troopers—that has come to save their injured comrade. The aliens join with the Americans to defeat attacking Nazis.

The role of flying saucers as weapons seems to have an obvious perspective to take on UFOs. In the early days of the UFO phenomenon, both the Soviets and the United States feared that the unidentified flying objects were a secret weapon of the other side. Among people who buy into notions of U.S. government–alien conspiracies— the idea that the U.S. government has entered into a secret, cooperative arrangement with extraterrestrials to obtain their technology—is quite common.

Empire Altar 1986; 86 min. Director: Danny Bilson; Visual
    Effects: John Carl Buechler; Cinematography: Mac
    Ahlberg; Cast: Danny Bilson, Paul DeMeo, Tim
    Thomerson, Timothy Van Patten, Art La Fleur, Biff
    Manard, William Paulson.

ZONTAR, THE THING FROM VENUS

In this 1966 film a scientist is contacted by a Venusian intelligence and, convinced that its intentions are benevolent, begins doing its bidding. When the alien arrives, however, it turns out to be a large, batlike monster—Zontar—that hides in a cave and takes over peoples' wills with small replicas of itself, which plant control devices in their victims' necks. This is another *Invasion of the Body Snatchers*–type of film that commentators have related to fears of communist infiltration.

Azalea 1966; 80 min. Director/Writer: Larry Buchanan;
    Cinematography: Robert B. Alcott; Cast: Larry Buchanan,
    H. Taylor, John Agar, Susan Bjorman, Anthony Houston,
    Patricia DeLaney, Warren Hammack.

BIBLIOGRAPHY

Adamski, George. *Cosmic Philosophy*. Freeman, SD: Pine Hill Press, 1972.

———. *Flying Saucers Farewell*. New York: Abelard-Schuman, 1961.

———. *Inside the Space Ships*. New York: Abelard-Schuman, 1955.

———. *Pioneers of Space: A Trip to the Moon, Mars, and Venus*. Los Angeles: Leonard-Freefield, 1949.

Adamski, George, and Desmond Leslie. *Flying Saucers Have Landed*. New York: British Book Centre, 1953; London: Werner Laurie, 1953.

Aetherius Society. *Temple Degree Study Courses*. Hollywood, CA: Aetherius Society, 1982.

———. *The Aetherius Society Newsletter*, 1992–1999.

———. *Cosmic Voice*, 1956–1999.Aho, Wayne S. *Mojave Desert Experience*. Eatonville, WA: New Age Foundation, 1972.

Aldrich, Jan L. *Project 1947: A Preliminary Report on the 1947 UFO Sighting Wave*. Chicago and Mt. Rainier, WA: Seguin and UFO Research Coalition, 1997.

Allingham, Cedric [pseudonym of Patrick Moore]. *Flying Saucer from Mars*. London: Frederick Muller, 1954.

Alper, Frank. *Exploring Atlantis*. Farmingdale, NY: Coleman Publishing, 1982.

Andersson, Pia. "'Fringe Archaeology': Contextual Truths about Our Prehistoric Past—A Closer Study of Pseudoscientific Archaeology." Seminar paper in Archaeology, Institution of Archaeology, Stockholm University, Stockholm, 2000 [English transl. by Olof Ribb].

Andrews, Ted. *Enchantment of the Faerie Realm: Communicate with Nature Spirits and Elementals*. St. Paul: Llewellyn, 1993.

Angelucci, Orfeo. *The Secret of the Saucers*. Amherst, WI: Amherst Press, 1955.

———. *Son of the Sun*. Los Angeles: DeVorss, 1959.

Anka, Darryl. *Bashar: Blue Print for Change—A Message from Our Future*. Simi Valley, CA: New Solutions Publishing, 1990.

Arguelles, Jose. *The Transformative Vision*. New York: Muse Publications, 1992 [orig. ed. 1975].

Arnold, Kenneth, and Ray Palmer. *The Coming of the Saucers: A Documentary Report on Sky Objects That Have Mystified the World*. Boise, ID, and Amherst, WI: The Authors, 1952.

Ashton, John. *Gossip in the First Decade of Queen Victoria's Reign*. London: Hurst and Blackett, 1903.

Atack, Jon. *A Piece of Blue Sky: Scientology, Dianetics, and L. Ron Hubbard Exposed*. Secaucus, NJ, and New York: Lyle Stuart, 1990.

Avery, Michael. *UFOs: Opposing Viewpoints*. San Diego: Greenhaven Press, 1989.

Axtell, James. *The European and the Indian: Essays in the Ethnohistory of Colonial North America*. Oxford: Oxford University Press, 1981.

Badly, Linda. "The Rebirth of the Clinic: The Body as Alien in the *X-Files*." In *"Deny All Knowledge": Reading the X Files*. Edited by David Lavery, Angela Hague, and Maria Cartwright. Syracuse: Syracuse University Press, 1996.

Baker, Robert A., and Joe Nickell. *Missing Pieces: How to Investigate Ghosts, UFOs, Psychics, and Other Mysteries*. Buffalo, NY: Prometheus Books, 1992.

Balch, R. W., and D. Taylor. "Seekers and Saucers: The Role of the Cultic Milieu in Joining a UFO Cult." *American Behavioral Scientist* 20(6) (July-August 1966): 839–860.

Banerjee, H. N., and W. C. Oursler. *Lives Unlimited: Reincarnation East and West*. New York: Doubleday, 1974.

Barker, Gray. *Gray Barker at Giant Rock*. Clarksburg, WV: Saucerian Publications, 1976.

———. *MIB: The Secret Terror among Us*. Clarksburg, WV: Saucerian Books, 1983.

———. *The Silver Bridge*. Clarksburg, WV: Saucerian Books, 1970.

———. *They Knew Too Much about Flying Saucers*. New York: University Books, 1956.

Barker, Gray, ed. *Bender Mystery Confirmed*. Clarksburg, WV: Saucerian Books, 1962.

————. *The Strange Case of Dr. M. K. Jessup.* Clarksburg, WV: Saucerian Books, 1963.

Barrow, J., and Tipler, F. *The Anthropic Cosmological Principle.* New York: Oxford University Press, 1986.

Bartholomew, Robert. "The Romantic versus Enlightenment Debate within the Social Sciences." Ph.D. Thesis, Flinders University of South Australia, 1989.

————. *Ufolore: A Social Psychological Study of a Modern Myth in the Making.* Stone Mountain, GA: Arcturus Book Service, 1989.

Baugher, J. *On Civilized Stars: The Search for Intelligent Life in Outer Space.* Englewood Cliffs, NJ: Prentice-Hall, 1985.

Beckley, Timothy Green. *Book of Space Contacts.* New York: Global Communications, 1981.

Beckley, Timothy Green, ed. *The Smoky God and Other Inner Earth Mysteries.* New Brunswick, NJ: Global Communications, 1993.

————. *The UFO Silencers.* New Brunswick, NJ: Inner Light Publications, 1990.

Bender, Albert K. *Flying Saucers and the Three Men.* Clarksburg, WV: Saucerian Books, 1962.

Bequette, Bill. "Boise Flyer Maintains He Saw 'Em." *East Oregonian,* June 26, 1947, p. 1.

————. "Experts Reach Deep into Bag to Explain 'Flying Discs.'" *East Oregonian,* June 28, 1947, p. 1.

————. "He'll Get Proof Next Time, Flyer Declares." *East Oregonian,* June 27, 1947, p. 1.

Berlitz, Charles. *The Bermuda Triangle.* Garden City, NY: Doubleday, 1974.

Berlitz, C., and W. L. Moore, *The Roswell Incident.* New York: Grosset and Dunlap, 1980.

Bernard, Raymond [pseudonym of Walter Siegmeister]. *The Hollow Earth: The Greatest Geographical Discovery in History.* New York: Fieldcrest Publishing, 1964.

Besant, Annie, and Leadbeater, C. W. *Man—Whence, How, and Whither: A Record of Clairvoyant Investigations.* Madras: Theosophical Publishing House, 1913.

Bethurum, Truman. *Aboard a Flying Saucer.* Los Angeles: DeVorss, 1954.

Billig, Otto. *Flying Saucers—Magic in the Sky: A Psychohistory.* Cambridge: Schenkman, 1982.

Biographical Sketch of Gabriel Green. Northridge, CA: Amalgamated Flying Saucer Clubs of America, 1974.

Birdsall, Mark Ian. *A Research Paper Pertaining to the Phenomenon Known as Ghost Rocket and Foo Fighter.* Leeds, U.K.: Quest Publications, 1988.

Bletzer, June G. *The Donning International Encyclopedic Psychic Dictionary.* Norfolk, VA: Donning, 1986.

Bloecher, Ted. *Report on the UFO Wave of 1947.* Washington, DC: The Author, 1967.

Bloor, D. *Knowledge and Social Imagery.* London: Routledge and Kegan Paul, 1976.

Blum, Ralph, with Judy Blum. *Beyond Earth: Man's Contact with UFOs.* New York: Bantam Books, 1974.

Bord, Janet, and Colin Bord. *Alien Animals.* Harrisburg, PA: Stackpole Books, 1981.

————. *Life Beyond Earth? Man's Contacts with Space People.* London: GraftonBooks, 1991.

Boureau, A. "L'église médiévale comme preuve animée de la croyance chrétienne." *Terrain* 14 (March 1990): 113–118.

Bowen, Charles, ed. *The Humanoids: A Survey of Worldwide Reports of Landings of Unconventional Aerial Objects and Their Alleged Occupants.* London: Futura Publications, 1974.

Boylan, Richard. *Close Extraterrestrial Encounters: Positive Experiences with Mysterious Visitors.* Tigard, OR: Wild Flower Press, 1994.

Briggs, Katharine. *An Encyclopedia of Fairies.* New York: Pantheon, 1976.

Brittin, Wesley E., Edward U. Condon, and Thurston E. Manning. *A Proposal to Air Force Office of Scientific Research for Support of Scientific Study of Unidentified Flying Objects.* Boulder: The Authors, November 1, 1966.

Brother Philip [pseudonym of George Hunt Williamson]. *Secret of the Andes.* Clarksburg, WV: Saucerian Books, 1961.

Brugger, Karl. *The Chronicle of Akakor.* New York: Delacorte Press, 1977.

Bryan, C. D. B. *Close Encounters of the Fourth Kind: Alien Abduction, UFOs, and the Conference at M.I.T.* New York: Alfred A. Knopf, 1995.

Buckle, Eileen. *The Scoriton Mystery.* London: Neville Spearman, 1967.

Buckner, H. Taylor. "Flying Saucers Are for People." *Trans-Action* 3(4) (May-June 1966): 10–13.

————. "The Flying Saucerians: An Open Door Cult." In *Sociology and Everyday Life.* Edited by Marcello Truzzi. Englewood Cliffs, NJ: Prentice Hall, 1968.

————. *Electric UFOs.* London: Blandford, 1998.

Budden, Albert. *UFOs: Psychic Close Encounters.* London: Blandford, 1995.

Bullard, Thomas E. *The Sympathetic Ear: Investigators as Variables in UFO Abduction Reports.* Mount Rainier, MD: Fund for UFO Research, 1995.

————. *UFO Abductions: The Measure of a Mystery, Volume 1: Comparative Study of Abduction Reports;*

and *Volume 2: Catalogue of Cases.* Mount Rainier, MD: Fund for UFO Research, 1987.

Bullard, Thomas E., ed. *The Airship File: A Collection of Texts Concerning Phantom Airships and Other UFOs, Gathered from Newspapers and Periodicals Mostly During the Hundred Years Prior to Kenneth Arnold's Sighting.* Bloomington, IN: The Author, 1982.

———. *The Airship File, Supplement 2.* Bloomington, IN: The Author, 1990.

Cavendish, Richard, ed. *Encyclopedia of the Unexplained: Magic, Occultism, and Parapsychology.* London: Arkana Penguin Books, 1989.

Cayce, Edgar. *Edgar Cayce on Atlantis.* New York: Paperback Library, 1968.

Chariton, Wallace O. *The Great Texas Airship Mystery.* Plano, TX: Wordware Publishing, 1991.

Chen, Hon-ming. *Practical Evidence and Study of the World of God and Buddha.* Privately published, 1996.

Chevalier, G. "Parasciences et procédés de légitimation." *Revue française de Sociologie* 27 (1986): 205–219.

Chevalier, Jean, and Alain Gheerbrant. *The Penguin Dictionary of Symbols.* London: Penguin, 1996.

Cirlot, J. E. *A Dictionary of Symbols.* New York: Dorset Press, 1991.

Clark, Jerome. *The UFO Encyclopedia.* 3 vols. Detroit: Omnigraphics, 1990, 1992, 1996.

———. *The UFO Encyclopedia: The Phenomenon from the Beginning.* 2nd ed. Detroit: Omnigraphics, 1998.

———. *Unexplained! 347 Strange Sightings, Incredible Occurrences, and Puzzling Physical Phenomena.* Detroit: Visible Ink Press, 1993.

Clark, Jerome, and Loren Coleman. *Creatures of the Outer Edge.* New York: Warner Books, 1978.

———. *The Unidentified: Notes Toward Solving the UFO Mystery.* New York: Warner Books, 1975.

Clayton, William. "It Looked Like a Football Field!" In *Flying Saucers.* Edited by David C. Whitney. New York: Cowles Communications, 1967, pp. 18–19.

Cohen, Daniel. *The Great Airship Mystery: A UFO of the 1890s.* New York: Dodd, Mead, 1981.

———. *Myths of the Space Age.* New York: Dodd, Mead, 1977.

Cohn, Norman. *Cosmos, Chaos, and the World to Come: The Ancient Roots of Apocalyptic Faith.* New Haven: Yale University Press, 1993.

———. *The Pursuit of the Millennium.* London: Oxford University Press, 1957.

Collins, H. M., and T. J. Pinch. "The Construction of the Paranormal: Nothing Unscientific Is Happening." In *On the Margins of Science: The Social Construction of Rejected Knowledge.* Edited by R. Wallis. Keele: University of Keele, 1979.

The Comforter Speaks. Potomac, MD: Cosmic Study Center, 1977.

Commander X. *Underground Alien Bases.* New Brunswick, NJ: Abelard Productions, 1990.

Cook, Ryan J. "Reporters in Godland, TX: The Role of the Mass Media in a New Religious Movement's Adaptation to Suburban America." Paper presented at Center for Studies on New Religions annual conference, Bryn Athyn College of the New Church, Bryn Athyn, PA, 1999.

Corrales, Scott. *Chupacabras and Other Mysteries.* Murfreesboro, TN: Greenleaf Publications, 1997.

———. *The Chupacabras Diaries: An Unofficial Chronicle of Puerto Rico's Paranormal Predator.* Derrick City, PA: Samizdat Press, 1996.

Crabb, Riley. *The Reality of the Underground.* Vista, CA: Borderland Sciences Research Associates, 1960.

Craft, Michael. *Alien Impact.* New York: St. Martin's, 1996.

Craig, Roy. *UFOs: An Insider's View of the Official Quest for Evidence.* Denton: University of North Texas Press, 1995.

Cremo, Michael A., and Richard L. Thompson. *Forbidden Archeology.* Los Angeles: Bhaktivedanta Book Publishing 1996 [orig. pub. 1993; condensed and reissued as *The Hidden History of the Human Race*].

Curran, Douglas. *In Advance of the Landing: Folk Concepts of Outer Space.* New York: Abbeville Press, 1985.

Daniels, Ted. *A Doomsday Reader: Prophets, Predictors, and Hucksters of Salvation.* New York: New York University Press, 1999, chap. 12.

Davidson, Gustav. *A Dictionary of Angels: Including the Fallen Angels.* New York: Free Press, 1971.

Davies, P. *The Accidental Universe.* Cambridge: Cambridge University Press, 1982.

Davis, Isabel, and Ted Bloecher. *Close Encounter at Kelly and Others of 1955.* Evanston: Center for UFO Studies, 1978.

Davis, Natalie Zemon. *Les Cultures du peuple. Rituels, savoirs er résistances au 16e siècle.* Paris: Aubier, Collection Historique, 1979.

Dean, Jodi. *Aliens in America: Conspiracy Culture from Outerspace to Cyberspace.* Ithaca and London: Cornell University Press, 1998.

Delaney, John J., ed. *A Woman Clothed with the Sun: Eight Great Appearances of Our Lady in Modern Times.* Garden City, NY: Hanover House, 1960.

Delgado, Pat, and Colin Andrews. *Circular Evidence.* London: Bloomsbury, 1989.

Derenberger, Woodrow W., and Harold W. Hubbard. *Visitors from Lanulos.* New York: Vantage Press, 1971.

Devereux P., A. Roberts, and D. Clarke. *Earth Lights Revelation.* London: Blandford, 1989.

DeVore, Nicholas. *Encyclopedia of Astrology.* New York: Philosophical Library 1949.

Dickinson, Terence. *Zeta Reticuli Update.* Fredericton, New Brunswick, Canada: UFO Research Institute, 1980.

Donnelly, Ignatius. *Atlantis: The Antediluvian World.* New York: Harper and Brothers, 1882.

Donner, Valerie. URL: http://www.thegroundcrew.com.

Dove, Lonzo. *The "Straith" State Department Fraud.* Broadway, VA: The Author, 1959.

Downing, Barry H. *The Bible and Flying Saucers.* Philadelphia: J. B. Lippincott, 1968.

Eberhart, Georges M. *UFOs and the Extraterrestrial Contact Movement: A Bibliography—Unidentified Flying Objects.* Metuchen, NJ, and London: Scarecrow Press, 1986.

Eliade, Mircea. *Shamanism: Archaic Techniques of Ecstasy.* Princeton: Princeton University Press, 1964.

Eliade, Mircea, ed. *Encyclopedia of Religion.* New York: Macmillan, 1987.

Ellwood, Robert. *Islands of the Dawn: The Story of Alternative Spirituality in New Zealand.* Honolulu: University of Hawaii Press, 1993, pp. 92–94.

Emenegger, Robert. *UFOs Past, Present, and Future.* New York: Ballantine Books, 1974.

Evans, Christopher. *Cults of Unreason.* New York: Farrar, Straus, and Giroux, 1974.

Evans, Hilary. *Gods, Spirits, and Cosmic Guardians: A Comparative Study of the Encounter Experience.* Wellingborough, U.K.: Aquarian, 1987.

———. *Visions, Apparitions, Alien Visitors.* Wellingborough, U.K.: Aquarian Press, 1984.

Evans, Hilary, and John Spencer, eds. *UFOs, 1947–1987: The 40-Year Search for an Explanation.* London: Fortean Times, 1987.

Evans-Pritchard, E. E. *Witchcraft, Oracles, and Magic among the Azande.* London: Oxford University Press, 1951.

Evans-Wentz, W. Y., ed. *The Tibetan Book of the Dead.* 3rd ed. London: Oxford University Press, 1960.

Favret-Saada, J. *Deadly Words: Witchcraft in the Bocage.* Paris: Maison des Sciences de l'Homme, 1980.

Ferguson, William. *A Message From Outer Space.* Oak Park, IL: Golden Age Press, 1955.

Festinger, Leon, Henry W. Riechen, and Stanley Schachter. *When Prophecy Fails.* Minneapolis: University of Minnesota Press, 1956.

Feuerstein, Georg. *Encyclopedic Dictionary of Yoga.* New York: Paragon House, 1990.

Fiore, Edith. *Encounters: A Psychologist Reveals Case Studies of Abductions by Extraterrestrials.* New York: Doubleday, 1989.

Flammonde, Paris. *The Age of Flying Saucers: Notes on a Projected History of Unidentified Flying Objects.* New York: Hawthorn Books, 1971.

A Flight to the Land Beyond the North Pole: The Missing Diary of Admiral Richard E. Byrd. New Brunswick, NJ: Inner Light Publications, n.d.

Foght, Paul. "Inside the Flying Saucers . . . Pancakes." *Fate* 14(8) (August 1961): 32–36.

Fort, Charles. *The Book of the Damned.* Revised by Mr. X. London: John Brown Publishing, 1995.

———. *The Books of Charles Fort.* New York: Henry Holt, 1941.

Frenschkowski, M. "L. Ron Hubbard and Scientology: An Annotated Bibliographical Survey of Primary and Selected Secondary Literature." *Marburg Journal of Religion* 4(1) (July 1999).

Friedman, S. T., and D. Berliner. *Crash at Corona.* New York: Paragon House, 1992.

Friedrich, Christof [pseudonym of Ernst Zundel]. *Secret Nazi Polar Expeditions.* Toronto, Ontario, Canada: Samisdat, 1978.

Fry, Daniel W. *Alan's Message: To Men of Earth.* Los Angeles: New Age Publishing, 1954a.

———. *The White Sands Incident.* Los Angeles: New Age Publishing, 1954b.

Fuller, Curtis G., et al., eds. *Proceedings of the First International UFO Congress.* New York: Warner Books, 1980.

Fuller, John Grant. *Interrupted Journey: Two Lost Hours "Aboard a Flying Saucer."* New York: Dial Press, 1966.

Gallup, George. *Adventures in Immortality.* New York: MacGraw-Hill, 1982.

Gansberg, Judith M., and Alan L. Gansberg. *Direct Encounters: The Personal Histories of UFO Abductees.* New York: Walker, 1980.

Gardner, Martin. *Fads and Fallacies in the Name of Science.* New York: Dover Publications, 1957.

———. *The New Age: Notes of a Fringe Watcher.* Buffalo, NY: Prometheus Press, 1988.

Gauch-Keller, W., and Th. Gauch-Keller. *Aufruf an die Erdbewohner* [Appeal to Earth Dwellers]. *Erklärungen zur Umwandlung des Planeten Erde und Seiner Menschheit in der Endzeit.* Ostermundingen/CH, 1992.

Genzlinger, Anna Lykins. *The Jessup Dimension.* Clarksburg, WV: Saucerian Press, 1981.

Gibbons, Gavin. *They Rode in Space Ships.* London: Neville Spearman, 1957.

Gilbert, Violet. *My Trip to Venus.* Grants Pass, OR: Cosmic Star Temple, 1968.

Gillmor, Daniel S., ed. *Scientific Study of Unidentified Flying Objects.* New York: Bantam Books, 1969.

Ginzberg, Louis. *The Legends of the Jews.* Philadelphia: Jewish Publication Society of America, 1954.

Ginzburg, Carlo. *The Cheese and the Worm (Le Fromage et les vers, l'univers d'un meunier du XVIth siècle).* Paris, Flammarion, 1980.

Girvan, Waveney. *Flying Saucers and Common Sense.* New York: Citadel Press, 1956.

Glemser, Kurt. *The Men in Black Report.* Kitchener, Ontario, Canada: Galaxy Press, 1971.

Godwin, Malcolm. *Angels: An Endangered Species.* New York: Simon and Schuster, 1990.

Good, Timothy. *Above Top Secret: The Worldwide UFO Cover-up.* New York: William Morrow, 1988.

———. *Alien Update.* New York: Avon, 1993.

Goodrich, N. L. *The Holy Grail.* New York: Harper-Collins, 1992.

Goran, Morris. *The Modern Myth, Ancient Astronauts and UFOs.* South Brunswick, NJ: A. S. Barnes, 1978.Gordon, Stuart. *The Encyclopedia of Myths and legends.* London: Headlione, 1993.

Grattan-Guinness, Ivor. *Psychical Research: A Guide to Its History, Principles, and Practices.* Wellingborough, U.K.: Aquarian Press, 1982.

Green, Celia, and Charles McCreery. *Apparitions.* London: Hamish Hamilton, 1975.

Green, Gabriel, and Warren Smith. *Let's Face the Facts about Flying Saucers.* New York: Popular Library, 1967.

Greyson, Bruce, and Charles P. Flynn, eds. *The Near-Death Experience. Problems, Prospects, Perspectives.* Springfield, IL: Charles C. Thomas, 1984.

Grim, John A. *The Shaman: Patterns of Siberian and Ojibway Healing.* Norman: University of Oklahoma Press, 1983.

Gross, Loren E. *Charles Fort, the Fortean Society, and Unidentified Flying* Objects: Fremont, CA: The Author, 1976.

———. *UFOs: A History—1946: The Ghost Rockets.* 3rd ed. Fremont, CA: The Author, 1988.

Gruenschloss, Andreas. "'When We Enter into My Father's Spacecraft'—Cargoistic Hopes and Millenarian Cosmologies in New Religious UFO Movements." *Marburg Journal of Religion* 3(2) (1998); URL: www.uni-marburg.de/fb03/religionswissenschaft/journal/mjr/ufogruen.html

Guffey, George R. "Aliens in the Supermarket: Science Fiction and Fantasy for 'Inquiring Minds.'" In *Aliens: The Anthropology of Science Fiction.* Edited by George E. Slusser and Eric S. Rabkin. Carbondale: Southern Illinois University Press, 1987.

Guiley, Rosemary Ellen. *The Encyclopedia of Ghosts and Spirits.* New York: Facts on File, 1992.

Gurney, Edmund, F. W. H. Myers, and Frank Podmore. *Phantasms of the Living.* London: Kegan Paul, Trench, Trubner, 1918.

Haining, Peter. *The Legend and Bizarre Crimes of Spring Heeled Jack.* London: Frederick Muller, 1977.

Hall, Calvin S., and Vernon A. Nordby. *A Primer on Jungian Psychology.* New York: New American Library, 1973.

Hall, Manly Palmer. *Reincarnation: The Cycle of Necessity.* Los Angeles: Philosophical Research Society, 1956.

Hall, Micheal D., and Wendy A. Connors. *Alfred Loedding and the Great Flying Saucer Wave of 1947.* Albuquerque, NM: Rose Press, 1998.

Hall, Richard. *Uninvited Guests.* Santa Fe, NM: Aurora Press, 1988.

Hall, Richard H., ed. *The UFO Evidence.* Washington, DC: National Investigations Committee on Aerial Phenomena, 1964.

Hamilton, William. *Cosmic Top Secret.* New Brunswick: Inner Light Publications, 1991.

Hancock, Graham. *Fingerprints of the Gods.* New York: Crown, 1995.

Hanegraaff, Wouter. *New Age Religion and Western Culture: Esotericism in the Mirror of Secular Thought.* New York: E. J. Brill, 1996.

Harner, Michael. *The Way of the Shaman.* New York: Bantam, 1986.

Hawking, S. *A Brief History of Time: From the Big Bang to Black Holes.* New York: Bantam, 1988.

Head, Joseph, and S. L. Cranston, eds. *Reincarnation in World Thought.* New York: Crown Publishers and Julian Press, 1967.

Heard, Gerald. *The Riddle of the Flying Saucers: Is Another World Watching?* London: Carroll and Nicholson, 1950.

Heelas, Paul. *The New Age Movement.* Oxford, U.K.: Blackwell, 1996.

Hesemann, Micheal. *The Cosmic Connection: Worldwide Crop Formations and ET Contacts.* London: Gateway Books, 1996.

Hickson, Charles, and William Mendez. *UFO Contact at Pascagoula.* Tucson, AZ: Wendelle C. Stevens, 1983.

Hoagland, Richard. *Monuments of Mars: The City on the Edge of Forever.* Berkeley, CA: North Atlantic Books, 1987.

Hopkins, Budd. *Intruders: The Incredible Visitations at Copley Woods.* New York: Random House, 1987.

———. *Missing Time: A Documented Study of UFO Abductions.* New York: Richard Marek, 1981.

Howe, Linda Moulton. *An Alien Harvest: Further Evidence Linking Animal Mutilations and Human Abductions to Alien Life Forms.* Littleton, CO: Linda Moulton Howe Productions, 1989.

Hubbard, L. Ron. *Have You Lived Before This Life?* Los Angeles: Bridge Publications, and Copenhagen: New Era Publications, 1989.

———. *Scientology—A History of Man.* Los Angeles: Bridge Publications, and Copenhagen: New Era Publications, 1988.

———. *A Series of Lectures on the Whole Track.* Los Angeles: L. Ron Hubbard/Church of Scientology, 1984–1985 (six lectures from the years 1959–1963; six audio-cassettes).

———. *The Time Track of Theta—More on the History of Man: A Series of Lectures by L. Ron Hubbard.* Los Angeles: Scientology/Golden Era Productions, 1978 and 1988 (lectures given in 1952; four audio-cassettes).

Hufford, David J. *The Terror That Comes in the Night: An Experience-Centered Study of Supernatural Assault Tradition.* Philadelphia: University of Pennsylvania Press, 1982.

Hultkrantz, Ake. "A Definition of Shamanism." *Temenos* 9 (1973): 25–37.

Hunter, Don, with René Dahinden. *Sasquatch.* Toronto, Ontario, Canada: McClelland and Stewart, 1973.

Hynek, J. Allen. *The UFO Experience: A Scientific Inquiry.* Chicago: Henry Regnery, 1972.

Hynek, J. Allen, and Jacques Vallee. *The Edge of Reality: A Progress Report on Unidentified Flying Objects.* Chicago: Henry Regnery, 1975.

Introvigne, Massimo. *Heaven's Gate: Il paradiso non può attendere.* Turin, Italy: Editrice Elle Di Ci, 1997.

Jacobs, David M. *Secret Life: Firsthand Accounts of UFO Abductions.* New York: Simon and Schuster, 1992.

———. *The UFO Controversy in America.* Bloomington: Indiana University Press, 1975.

James, William. "Notes on Automatic Writing." In *The Works of William James: Essays in Psychical Research.* Edited by Frederick Burkhardt (gen. ed.) and Fredson Bowers (text ed.). Cambridge: Harvard University Press, 1986 [orig. publ. 1889].

Jessup, M. K. *The Case for the UFO.* New York: Citadel Press, 1955.

Jones, Leslie. "'Last Week We Had an Omen': The Mythological *X-Files.*" In *"Deny All Knowledge": Reading the* X Files. Edited by David Lavery, Angela Hague, and Maria Cartwright. Syracuse: Syracuse University Press, 1996.

Jung, Carl Gustav. *Flying Saucers: A Modern Myth of Things Seen in the Sky.* Princeton: Princeton University Press, 1978.

———. *Memories, Dreams, Reflections.* New York: Vintage Books, 1965.

———. *Psychological Types.* London: Routledge, 1933.

———. *Symbols of Transformation.* New York: Harper Torchbooks, 1956.

Kafton-Minkel, Walter. *Subterranean Worlds: 100,000 Years of Dragons, Dwarfs, the Dead, Lost Races, and UFOs from Inside the Earth.* Port Townsend, WA: Loompanics Unlimited, 1989.

Kagan, Daniel, and Ian Summers. *Mute Evidence.* New York: Bantam Books, 1984.

Kaku, M. "A Theory Of Everything?" In *Mysteries of Life and the Universe.* Edited by W. Shore. New York: Harcourt Brace Jovanovich, 1994.

Katchongva, Chief Dan. *Hopi Prophecy.* Hotevilla, AZ: Hopi Independent Nation, 1970.

Keel, John A. *Disneyland of the Gods.* New York: Amok Press, 1988.

———. *The Mothman Prophecies.* New York: E. P. Dutton, 1975.

———. *Our Haunted Planet.* Greenwich, CT: Fawcett Publications, 1971.

———. *Strange Creatures from Time and Space.* Greenwich, CT: Fawcett Gold Medal, 1970.

———. *UFOs: Operation Trojan Horse.* New York: G. P. Putnam's Sons, 1970.

Keith, Jim. *Casebook on the Men in Black.* Lilburn, GA: IllumiNet Press, 1997.

Keyhoe, Donald E. *Flying Saucers from Outer Space.* New York: Henry Holt, 1953.

Keyhoe, Donald E., and Gordon I. R. Lore Jr., eds. *Strange Effects from UFOs.* Washington, DC: National Investigations Committee on Aerial Phenomena, 1969.

King, George. *Life on the Planets.* Hollywood, CA: Aetherius Society, 1958.

———. *The Nine Freedoms.* Hollywood, CA: Aetherius Society, 1963.

———. *The Twelve Blessings.* Hollywood, CA: Aetherius Society, 1962.

———. *You Are Responsible!* Hollywood, CA: Aetherius Society, 1961.

King, George, with Richard Lawrence. *Contacts with the Gods from Space: Pathway to the New Millennium.* Hollywood, CA: Aetherius Society, 1996.

King, Godfre Ray [Guy W. Ballard]. *Unveiled Mysteries.* Chicago: Saint Germain Press, 1934.

Kirkpatrick, R. George, and Diana Tumminia. "California Space Goddess: The Mystagogue in a Flying Saucer Cult," In *Twentieth Century World Religious Movements in Neo-Weberian Perspective.* Edited by William H. Swatos. Lewiston, NY: Edwin Mellen Press, 1992, pp. 299–311.

———. "Space Magic, Techno-Animism, and the Cult of the Goddess in a Southern Californian UFO Contactee Group: A Case Study in Millenarianism." *Syzygy: Journal of Alternative Religion and Culture* 1(2) (1992): 159–172.

Klarer, Elizabeth. *Beyond the Light Barrier.* Cape Town, South Africa: Howard Timmins, 1980.

Klass, Philip J. *UFO Abductions: A Dangerous Game.* Buffalo, NY: Prometheus Books, 1988 [updated ed. 1989].

Klimo, Jon. *Channeling.* Los Angeles: Jeremy P. Tarcher, 1987.

Knight, Damon. *Charles Fort: Prophet of the Unexplained.* Garden City, NY: Doubleday, 1970.

Korff, K. K. *The Roswell UFO Crash.* New York: Random House, 2000.

———. *Spaceships of the Pleiades: The Billy Meier Story.* Amherst, NY: Prometheus Books, 1995.

Kusche, Lawrence David. *The Bermuda Triangle Mystery—Solved.* New York: Harper and Row, 1975.

Lagrange, Pierre. "Enquêtes sur les soucoupes volantes. La construction d'un fait aux Etats-Unis (1947) et en France (1951–1954)." *Terrain, Carnets du Patrimoine Ethnologique* 14 (March 1990): 92–112.

———. "A Forgotten Sociologist Named Kenneth Arnold." *Fortean Studies* 7 (2000).

———. "It Seems Impossible, but There It Is." In *Phenomenon: From Flying Saucers to UFOs—Forty Years of Facts and Research.* Edited by John Spencer and Hilary Evans. London: Futura Publications, 1988, pp. 26–45.

———. "L'affaire Kenneth Arnold. Note sur l'art de construire et de déconstruire quelques soucoupes volantes." *Communications* 52 (November 1990): 283–309.

Lagrange, P., ed. "Science-parascience: preuves et épreuves." *Ethnologie française* 23(3) (1993).

Lanternari, Vittorio. *The Religions of the Oppressed: A Study of Modern Messianic Cults.* New York: Mentor, 1956.

Lara Palmeros, Rafael A. "Chupacabras: Puerto Rico's Paranormal Predator." *INFO Journal* 76 (Autumn 1996): 12–16, 18.

Latour, B. "Comment redistribuer le Grand Partage ?" *Revue de Synthèse* 104 (April-June 1983): 203–236.

———. *Science in Action.* Cambridge: Harvard University Press, 1987.

Leach, Maria. *Standard Dictionary of Folklore, Mythology, and Legend.* San Francisco: HarperSan Francisco, 1984 [orig. publ. 1949].

Lee, Gloria. *The Changing Conditions of Your World, by J. W. of Jupiter, Instrumented by Gloria Lee.* Los Angeles: DeVorss, 1962.

———. *Why We Are Here: By J. W., a Being from Jupiter through the Instrumentation of Gloria Lee.* Los Angeles: DeVorss, 1959.

Leslie, Desmond, and George Adamski. *Flying Saucers Have Landed.* New York: British Book Centre, 1953.

Lewis, J., ed. *The Gods Have Landed: New Religions from Other Worlds.* Albany: State University of New York Press, 1995.

Lewis, James R. *Astrology Encyclopedia.* Detroit: Gale Research, 1994.

———. *Cults in America.* Santa Barbara, CA: ABC-CLIO, 1998.

———. *Doomsday Prophecies.* Amherst, NY: Prometheus Books, 1999.

———. *The Encyclopedia of Afterlife Beliefs and Phenomena.* Detroit: Gale Research, 1994.

———. *The Encyclopedia of Cults, Sects, and New Religions.* Amherst, NY: Prometheus Books, 1998.

———, ed. *The Gods Have Landed: New Religions From Other Worlds.* Albany: State University of New York Press, 1995.

———. *Witchcraft Today: An Encyclopedia of Wiccan and Neopagan Traditions.* Santa Barbara, CA: ABC-CLIO, 1999.

Lewis, James R., and Evelyn Dorothy Oliver. *Angels A to Z.* Detroit: Gale Research, 1995.

Lewis, James R., and J. Gordon Melton, eds. *Perspectives on the New Age.* Albany: State University of New York Press, 1992.

Lofland, J. "Normal Flying Saucerians?" *Trans-Action* 3(5) (July-August 1966): 54–55.

Lore, Gordon I. R. Jr., and Harold H. Deneault Jr. *Mysteries of the Skies: UFOs in Perspective.* Englewood Cliffs, NJ: Prentice-Hall, 1968.

Lorenzen, Coral E. *Flying Saucers: The Startling Evidence of Invasion From Outer Space.* New York: New American Library, 1966 [expanded version of *The Great Flying Saucer Hoax,* 1962].

———. *The Great Flying Saucer Hoax: The UFO Facts and Their Interpretation.* New York: William-Frederick Press, 1962.

Lorenzen, Coral, and Jim Lorenzen. *Abducted! Confrontations with Beings from Outer Space.* New York: Berkley Medallion, 1977.

———. *Encounters with UFO Occupants.* New York: Berkley Medallion, 1976.

Maccabee, Bruce, and Edward Walters. *UFOs Are Real . . . Here's the Proof.* New York: Avon Books, 1997.

Mack, John E. *Abduction: Human Encounters with Aliens.* New York: Charles Scribner's Sons, 1994.

Mackal, Roy P. *Searching for Hidden Animals.* Garden City, NY: Doubleday, 1980.

Mapes, D. O. *Prince Neosom, Planet: Tyton* [sic]. Buffalo, NY: The Author, January 22, 1959.

Mark-Age MetaCenter. *Cosmic Lessons: Gloria Lee Channels for Mark-Age.* Miami, FL: Mark-Age MetaCenter [1969–1972].

———. *Gloria Lee Lives! My Experiences Since Leaving Earth.* Miami, FL: Mark-Age MetaCenter, 1963.

Matyi, J. Robert. *My God, They're Real!* Port Washington, NY: Ashley, 1979.

McCarthy, P. "Politicking and Paradigm Shifting: James E. McDonald and the UFO Case Study." Ph.D. diss., University of Hawaii, December 1975.

McClure, Kevin. *The Evidence for Visions of the Virgin Mary.* Wellingborough, U.K.: Aquarian Press, 1983.

McCoy, Edwin. *A Witch's guide to Faery Folk.* St. Paul: Llewellyn, 1994.

McDannell, Colleen, and Bernhard Lang. *Heaven: A History.* 1988; New York: Vintage, 1990.–

Meaden, George Terence. *The Circles Effect and Its Mysteries.* Bradford-on-Avon, U.K.: Artetech, 1989.

Melton, J. Gordon. *Encyclopedia of American Religions.* 5th ed. Detroit: Gale Research, 1996.

———. *The Encyclopedia of American Religions.* 3rd ed. Detroit: Gale Research, 1989.

———. *An Encyclopedic Handbook of Cults in America.* New York: Garland, 1992.

Melton, J. Gordon, et al. *New Age Almanac.* Detroit: Visible Ink, 1991.

Melton, J. Gordon, Jerome Clark, and Aidan Kelly. *New Age Encyclopedia.* Detroit: Gale Research, 1990.

Melton, J. Gordon, and George M. Eberhart, eds. *The Flying Saucer Contactee Movement, 1950–1990.* Santa Barbara, CA: Santa Barbara Centre for Humanistic Studies, 1990.

Menger, Howard. *From Outer Space to You.* Clarksburg, WV: Saucerian Books, 1959.

Michel, Aimé. "The Strange Case of Dr. 'X'." In *UFO Percipients: Flying Saucer Review Special Issue No. 3* (September 1969): 3–16.

———. "The Strange Case of Dr. 'X'—Part 2." *Flying Saucer Review* 17(6) (November-December 1971): 3–9.

Michell, John. *Eccentric Lives and Peculiar Notions.* San Diego: Harcourt Brace Jovanovich, 1984.

Modin, Engelbrekt. *Paa Planeten Mars for 2000 Aar siden. Samfundsspørgsmaalenes Løsning.* Psykisk Forlag, København Oscar Bush, 1947 [orig. Swedish version publ. in 1909]

Montgomery, Ruth. *Aliens among Us.* New York: Putnam's, 1985.

———. *Strangers among Us: Enlightened Beings from a World to Come.* New York: Coward, McCann, and Geoghegan, 1979.

———. *Threshold to Tomorrow.* New York: G. P. Putnam's Sons, 1983.

Moody, Raymond A. *Life After Life.* New York: Bantam, 1976.

———. *The Light Beyond.* New York: Bantam, 1989.

Moore, William L., with Charles Berlitz. *The Philadelphia Experiment: Project Invisibility: An Account of a Search for a Secret Navy Wartime Project That May Have Succeeded Too Well.* New York: Grosset and Dunlap, 1979.

Moseley, James W. "UFOs Out West." In *UFOs, 1947–1997: From Arnold to the Abductees: Fifty Years of Flying Saucers.* Edited by Hilary Evans and Dennis. London: John Brown Publishing, 1997, pp. 53–59.

Muhl, Anita. *Automatic Writing.* New York: Helix Press, 1963.

Muldoon, Sylvan J., and Hereward Carrington. *The Phenomena of Astral Projection.* London: Rider and Company, 1969.

———. *The Projection of the Astral Body.* New York: Samuel Weiser, 1970.

Myers, Frederic W. H. *Human Personality and Its Survival of Bodily Death.* Vols. 1 and 2. New ed. New York: Longmans, Green, 1954 [orig. publ. 1903].

Nebel, Long John. *The Way Out World.* Englewood Cliffs, NJ: Prentice-Hall, 1961.

Nelson, Buck. *My Trip to Mars, the Moon, and Venus.* Mountain View, AR: The Author, 1956.

Nesheim, Eric, and Leif Nesheim. *Saucer Attack! Pop Culture in the Golden Age of Flying Saucers.* Los Angeles: Kitchen Sink Press, 1997.

Neugebauer, O. *Astronomy and History: Selected Essays.* New York: Springer-Verlag, 1983.

Newman, L., and Baumeister, R. "Toward an Explanation of the UFO Abduction Phenomenon: Hypnotic Elaboration, Extraterrestrial Sadomasochism, and Spurious Memories." *Psychological Inquiry* 7 (1996): 99–126.

Nickell, Joe, with John F. Fischer. *Secrets of the Supernatural: Investigating the World's Occult Mysteries.* Buffalo, NY: Prometheus Books, 1988.

The Night Sky: The Science and Anthropology of the Stars and Planets. San Francisco: Sierra Club Books, 1981.

Norkin, Israel. *Saucer Diary.* New York: Pageant Press, 1957.

Norman, Eric [pseudonym of Eugene Olson, a.k.a. Brad Steiger]. *The Under-People.* New York: Award Books, 1969.

Norman, Ernest L. *The Voice of Venus.* Los Angeles: New Age Publishing, 1956.

Noyes, Ralph, ed. *The Crop Circle Enigma.* Bath, U.K.: Gateway Books, 1990.

O'Donnell, Elliott. *Ghosts of London.* New York: E. P. Dutton, 1933.

O'Keefe, Daniel Lawrence. *Stolen Lightning: The Social Theory of Magic.* New York: Vintage Books, 1983.

Owen, Nancy H. *Preliminary Analysis of the Impact of Livestock Mutilations on Rural Arkansas Communities.* Fayetteville: University of Arkansas Department of Anthropology, January 1980.

Palmer, Susan J. "The Raelians Are Coming: The Future of a UFO Religion." In *Religion in a Changing World.* Edited by Madeleine Cousineau. Westport CT: Praeger, 1998, pp. 139–146.

———. "Woman as Playmate in the Raelian Movement: Power and Pantagamy in a New Religion." *Syzygy: Journal of Alternative Religion and Culture* 1(3) (1992): 227–245.

———. "Women in the Raelian Movement: New Religious Experiments in Gender and Authority." In *The Gods Have Landed.* Edited by James Lewis. New York: State University of New York Press, 1995, pp. 105–136.

"Panorama: Major Wayne S. Aho." *Flying Saucer Review* 4(3) (May/June 1958): 30.

Persinger, M. A., and G. F. Lafreneire. *Space Time Transients and Unusual Events.* Chicago: Nelson Hall, 1977.

Peters, Ted. "Exo-theology: Speculations on Extraterrestrial Life." In *The Gods Have Landed: New Religions from Other Worlds.* Edited by James R. Lewis. Albany: State University of New York Press, 1995.

Planetary Activation Organization, URL: http://www.paoweb.com.

Plank, Robert. *The Emotional Significance of Imaginary Beings: A Study of the Interaction Between Psychopathology, Literature, and Reality in the Modern World.* Springfield, IL: Charles C. Thomas, 1968.

Porter, Jennifer E. "Spiritualists, Aliens, and UFOs: Extraterrestrials as Spirit Guides." *Journal of Contemporary Religion* 12(3) (1996).

Prins, Ethera. *Miracle of Love and Life.* Portland, OR: Universarium Foundation, 1974.

Prophet, Elizabeth Clare. *Forbidden Mysteries of Enoch: Fallen Angels and the Origins of Evil.* Livingston, MT: Summit University Press, 1992.

Pursglove, Paul David. *Zen in the Art of Close Encounters: Crazy Wisdom and UFOs.* Berkeley: New Being Project, 1995.

"Rael." *Space Aliens Took Me to their Planet.* Waduz, Lichtenstein: Face, 1975.

Randle, Kevin D. *A History of UFO Crashes.* New York: Avon Books, 1995.

———. *The October Scenario: UFO Abductions, Theories about Them, and a Prediction of When They Will Return.* Iowa City, IA: Middle Coast Publishing, 1988.

———. *The Randle Report: UFOs in the 1990s.* New York: M. Evans, 1997.

Randle, K. D., and D. R. Schmitt. *The Truth about the UFO Crash at Roswell.* New York: Avon Books, 1994.

Randles, Jenny. *Abduction: Over 200 Documented UFO Kidnappings Investigated.* London: Robert Hale, 1988.

———. *Sixth Sense.* Topsfield, MA: Salem House Publishers, 1987.

———. *UFO Reality: A Critical Look at the Physical Evidence.* London: Robert Hale, 1983.

Randles, Jenny, and Paul Fuller. *Crop Circles: A Mystery Solved.* London: Robert Hale, 1990.

Randles, Jenny, and Peter Hough. *The Complete Book of UFOs: An Investigation into Alien Contacts and Encounters.* New York: Sterling, 1996.

Ransom, Josephine. *A Short History of the Theosophical Society.* Adyar: Theosophical Publishing House, 1938.

Reeve, Bryant, and Helen Reeve. *Flying Saucer Pilgrimage.* Amherst, WI: Amherst Press, 1957.

Richardson, James T., Joel Best, and David G. Bromley, eds. *The Satanism Scare.* New York: Aldine de Gruyter, 1991.

Ring, Kenneth. *The Omega Project: Near-Death Experiences, UFO Encounters, and Mind at Large.* New York: William Morrow, 1992.

Ritchie, David. *UFO: The Definitive Guide to Unidentified Flying Objects and Related Phenomena.* New York: Facts on File, 1994.

Roberts, Jane. *The Seth Material.* Englewood Cliffs, NJ: Prentice Hall, 1970.

Rodeghier, Mark, Jeff Goodpaster, and Sandra Blatterbauer. "Psychosocial Characteristics of Abductees: Results from the CUFOS Abduction Project." *Journal of UFO Studies* 3 (new series, 1991).

Rogo, D. Scott. *The Haunted Universe: A Psychic Look at Miracles, UFOs, and Mysteries of Nature.* New York: Signet, 1977.

Rogo, D. Scott, ed. *UFO Abductions: True Cases of Alien Kidnappings.* New York: Signet, 1980.

Rojcewicz, Peter M. "The 'Men in Black' Experience and Tradition: Analogues with the Traditional Devil Hypothesis." *Journal of American Folklore* 100 (April-June 1987): 148–160.

Rommel, Kenneth M. *Operation Animal Mutilation.* Report of the District Attorney, First Judicial District, State of New Mexico. Santa Fe: District Attorney, June 1980.

Ronner, John. *Know Your Angels: The Angel Almanac with Biographies of 100 Prominent Angels in Legend and Folklore, and Much More.* Murfreesboro, TN: Mamre, 1993.

Rovin, Jeff. *Classic Science Fiction Films.* New York: Citadel Press, 1993.

Ryerson, Kevin, and Stephanie Harolde. *Spirit Communication: The Soul's Path.* New York: Bantam Books, 1989.

Sachs, Margaret. *The UFO Encyclopedia.* New York: G. P. Putnam's Sons, 1980.

Saler, B., C. A. Ziegler, and C. B. Moore. *UFO Crash at Roswell.* Washington, DC: Smithsonian Institution Press, 1997.

Saliba, John A. "The Earth Is a Dangerous Place—The World View of the Aetherius Society." *Marburg Journal of Religion* 4(2) (December 1999): 1–20.

———. "Religious Dimensions of the UFO Phenomenon." In *The Gods Have Landed: New Religions From Other Worlds.* Edited by James R. Lewis. Albany: State University of New York Press, 1995.

Samuels, Andrew, Bani Shorter, and Fred Plaut. *A Critical Dictionary of Jungian Analysis.* London: Routledge and Kegan Paul, 1986.

Sanderson, Ivan T. *Abominable Snowmen: Legend Come to Life.* Philadelphia: Chilton Books, 1961.

Sandoz, Mari. *Old Jules Country.* New York: Hastings House, 1965 [repr. 1982 by the University of Nebraska Press].

Saunders, David R., and R. Roger Harkins. *UFOs? Yes! Where the Condon Committee Went Wrong.* New York: World Publishing, 1968.

Schmidt, Reinhold O. *Edge of Tomorrow: A True Account of Experiences with Visitors from Another Planet.* Hollywood, CA: The Author, 1963.

Schmitt, J. C. *Les Revenants. Les vivants et les morts dans la société médiévale.* Paris: Gallimard, 1994.

Schnabel, Jim. *Dark White: Aliens, Abductions, and the UFO Obsession.* London: Hamish Hamilton, 1994.

———. "Puck in the Laboratory: The Construction and Deconstruction of Hoaxlike Deception in Science." *Science, Technology, and Human Values* 19(4) (1994): 459–492.

Schwarz, Berthold Eric. "The Man-in-Black Syndrome." *Flying Saucer Review* 23(4) (1977): 9–15 (pt. 1); 23(5) (1978): 22–25 (pt. 2).

———. *UFO-Dynamics: Psychiatric and Psychic Dimensions of the UFO Syndrome.* 2 vols. Moore Haven, FL: Rainbow Books, 1983.

Scully, Frank. *Behind the Flying Saucers.* New York: Henry Holt, 1950.

Shapin, S. "History of Science and Its Sociological Reconstruction." *History of Science* 20 (1982): 157–211.

Shepard, Leslie A., ed. *Encyclopedia of Occultism and Parapsychology.* Detroit: Gale Research, 1991.

Sitchin, Zecharia. *Divine Encounters: A Guide to Visions, Angels, and Other Emissaries.* New York: Avon, 1995.

———. *The Twelfth Planet.* New York: Avon, 1976.

Slate, B. Ann, and Alan Berry. *Bigfoot.* New York: Bantam Books, 1976.

Slotkin, Richard. *Regeneration through Violence: The Mythology of the American Frontier, 1600–1860.* Middletown, CT: Wesleyan University Press, 1973.

Slusser, George E., and Eric S. Rabkin, eds. *Aliens: The Anthropology of Science Fiction.* Carbondale: Southern Illinois University Press, 1987.

Spanos, N., et al. "Close Encounters: An Examination of UFO Experiences." *Journal of Abnormal Psychology* 102 (1993): 624–632.

Sprinkle, R. Leo, ed. *Proceedings of the Rocky Mountain Conference on UFO Investigation.* Laramie: School of Extended Studies, University of Wyoming, 1980.

Stark, Rodney, and William Simms Bainbridge. *The Future of Religion: Secularisation, Revival, and Cult Formation.* Berkeley: University of California Press, 1985.

Steiger, Brad. *Revelation: The Divine Fire.* New York: Prentice-Hall, 1973.

———. *Starborn.* New York: Berkley Books, 1992.

———. *The Star People*. New York: Berkley Books, 1982.

Steiger, Brad, Sherry Steiger, and Alfred Bielek. *The Philadelphia Experiment and Other UFO Conspiracies*. New Brunswick, NJ: Inner Light Publications, 1990.

Steiger, Brad, and Joan Whritenour, eds. *The Allende Letters: A Challenging New Theory on the Origin of Flying Saucers*. New York: Universal, 1968.

Stein, Gordon. *Encyclopedia of Hoaxes*. Detroit: Gale Research, 1993.

Steiner, Rudolph. Lecture No. 14, Dornach, May 13, 1921. In *Materialism and the Task of Anthroposophy*. Hudson, NY: Anthroposophic Press.

Steinman, William S., and Wendelle C. Stevens. *UFO Crash at Aztec: A Well Kept Secret*. Tucson, AZ: UFO Photo Archives, 1986.

Stevens, Wendelle C., and William James Hermann. *UFO . . . Contact from Reticulum: A Report of the Investigation*. Tucson, AZ: Wendelle C. Stevens, 1981.

Stevenson, Ian. "Some Comments on Automatic Writing." *Journal of the American Society for Psychical Research* 72(4) (October 1978): 315–332.

———. *Twenty Cases Suggestive of Reincarnation*. 2nd ed. Charlottesville: University Press of Virginia, 1974.

Stillings, Dennis, ed. *Cyberbiological Studies of the Imaginal Component in the UFO Contact Experience*. St. Paul: Archaeus Project, 1989.

Stoczkowski, W. *Des Hommes, des dieux et des extraterrestres. Ethnologie d'une croyance moderne*. Paris, Flammarion, 1999.

The Story of the Aetherius Society. Hollywood, CA: Aetherius Society, n.d.

Story, Ronald D., ed. *The Encyclopedia of UFOs*. Garden City, NY: Doubleday, 1980.

Strieber, Whitley. *Communion: A True Story*. New York: William Morrow, 1987.

———. *Transformation: The Breakthrough*. New York: William Morrow, 1988.

Stringfield, Leonard H. *Situation Red, the UFO Siege!* Garden City, NY: Doubleday, 1977a.

Stupple, David. "Mahatmas and Space Brothers: The Ideologies of Alleged Contact with Mahatmas and Space Brothers." *Journal of American Culture* 7 (1984): 131–139.

———. "The Man Who Talked to Venusians." In *Proceedings of the First International UFO Congress*. Edited by C. Fuller. New York, Warner Books, 1980.

———. "The Man Who Talked with Venusians." *Fate* 32(1) (January 1979): 30–39.

Stupple, D., and W. McNeece. "Contactees, Cult, and Culture." *MUFON Symposium Proceedings*, Seguin, TX, 1979.

Teets, Bob. *West Virginia UFOs: Close Encounters in the Mountain State*. Terra Alta, WV: Headline Books, 1995.

Temple, Robert K. G. *The Sirius Mystery*. Rochester, VT: Destiny, 1976.

Thompson, Keith. *Angels and Aliens: UFOs and the Mythic Imagination*. Reading, MA: Addison-Wesley, 1991.

Thompson, Richard L. *Alien Identities: Ancient Insights into Modern UFO Phenomena*. Alachua, FL: Govardian Hill Publishing, 1993.

Tromf, Garry, ed. *Cargo Cults and Millenarian Movements*. Berlin and New York: Mouton de Gruyter, 1990 (esp. "Introduction" and the essay "The Cargo and the Millennium on Both Sides of the Pacific").

Tuella [pseudonym of Thelma B. Turrell], ed. *Ashtar: A Tribute*. 3rd ed. Salt Lake City: Guardian Action Publications, 1989.

Tulien, Thomas, ed. *The Sign Proceedings of Historical Group UFO History Workshop*. Scotland, CT: Sign Historical Group, 1999.

Tumminia, Diana, and R. George Kirkpatrick. "Unarius: Emergent Aspects of an American Flying Saucer Group." *In The Gods Have Landed: New Religions from Other Worlds*. Edited by James R. Lewis. Albany: State University of New York Press, 1995.

Turner, Alice K. *The History of Hell*. New York: Harcourt Brace, 1993.

Turner, Karla. *Taken: Inside the Alien-Human Abduction Agenda*. Roland, AR: Kelt Works, 1994.

United States Air Force. *The Roswell Report*. Washington, DC: U.S. Government Printing Office, 1995.

Vallee, Jacques. *Confrontations: A Scientist's Search for Alien Contact*. New York: Ballantine Books, 1990.

———. *Dimensions*. Chicago: Contemporary Books, 1988.

———. Vallée, Jacques. *Dimensions*. New York: Ballantine, 1989.

———. *Messengers of Deception: UFO Contacts and Cults*. Berkeley: And/Or Press, 1979.

———. *Passport to Magonia: From Folklore to Flying Saucers*. Chicago: Contemporary Books, 1993.

———. *Revelations: Alien Contact and Human Deception*. New York: Ballantine Books, 1991.

Vallee, Jacques, with Martine Castello. *UFO Chronicles of the Soviet Union: A Cosmic Samizdat*. New York: Ballantine Books, 1992.

Van Der Leeuw, G. *Religion in Essence and Manifestation, Volume 1*. Gloucester, MA: Peter Smith, 1967 [transl. of first German ed., 1933].

Van Tassel, George W. *I Rode a Flying Saucer! The Mystery of the Flying Saucers Revealed*. Los Angeles: New Age Publishing, 1952.

VanDerBeets, Richard. *The Indian Captivity Narrative*. Lanham, MD: University Press of America, 1984.

Volpe, Anthony, and Lynn Volpe. *Principles and Purposes of Delval UFO, Inc*. Ivyland, PA: The Authors, n.d.

von Däniken, Erich. *Chariots of the Gods? Unsolved Mysteries of the Past*. Trans. Michael Heron. New York: G. P. Putnam's Sons, 1970.

Vorilhon, Claude (Rael). *Let's Welcome Our Fathers from Space: They Created Humanity in Their Laboratories*. Tokyo: AOM Corporation, 1986.

Wallis, Roy, "The Aetherius Society: A Case Study in the Formation of a Mystagogic Congregation." *Sociological Review* 22 (1974): 27–44.

———. "Science and Pseudo-science." *Social Science Information* 24(3) (September 1985): 585–601.

Walters, Ed, and Frances Walters. *The Gulf Breeze Sightings: The Most Astounding Multiple Sightings of UFOs in U.S. History*. New York: William Morrow, 1990.

Walton, Bruce A. *A Guide to the Inner Earth*. Jane Lew, WV: New Age Books, 1983.

Walton, Travis. *Fire in the Sky: The Walton Experience*. New York: Marlowe, 1996.

Waters, Frank. *Book of the Hopi*. New York: Viking Press, 1963.

Weldon, John, and Zola Lewitt, *UFOs: What on Earth Is Happening?* Irvine, California: Harvest House, 1974.

Wennergren, Kristina. *UFO-Lexicon*. Göteborg, Sweden: no publisher, 1990.

Westrum, R. "Social Intelligence about Anomalies: The Case of UFOs." *Social Studies of Science* 7(3) (1977): 271–302

———. "UFO Reporting Dynamics." In *UFO Phenomena and the Behavioral Scientist*. Edited by Richard F. Haines. Metuchen, NJ, and London: Scarecrow Press, 1979, pp. 147–163.

———. "Witnesses of UFOs and Other Anomalies." In *UFO Phenomena and the Behavioral Scientist*. Edited by Richard F. Haines. Metuchen, NJ, and London: Scarecrow Press, 1979, pp. 89–112.

What Is Scientology? Based on the Works of L. Ron Hubbard. Los Angeles: Church of Scientology, and Copenhagen: New Era Publications, 1998.

Wheeler, G., and S. Scribner. "Take Me or Leave Me Alone: Frames, Filters, and Paradigms for the Age of First Contact." *Continuum* 4(1) (1996): 10–14.

———. "Remembering Shadows in Plato's Cave." *Continuum* 5(2) (1997): 8.

Wicker, Christine. "Leader Tells Listeners That They Are God." *Dallas Morning News*, April 1, 1998.

Wilcox, Hal. *Contact with the Master*. Hollywood, CA: Galaxy Press, 1984.

Wilkins, Harold T. *Flying Saucers on the Attack*. New York: Citadel Press, 1954.

Williamson, George Hunt. *The Brotherhood of the Seven Rays*. Clarksburg, WV: Saucerian Books, 1961.

———. *Other Tongues—Other Flesh*. Amherst, WI: Amherst Press, 1953.

———. *Road in the Sky*. London: Neville Spearman, 1959.

Williamson, George H., and Alfred C. Bailey. *The Saucers Speak! A Documentary Report of Interstellar Communication by Radiotelegraphy*. Los Angeles: New Age Publishing, 1954.

Wilson, Sheryl C., and T. X. Barber. "The Fantasy-Prone Personality: Implications for Understanding Imagery, Hypnosis and Parapsychological Phenomena." In *Imagery: Current Theory, Research, and Application*. Edited by Anees A. Sheikh. New York: John Wiley, 1983, pp. 340–387.

Zangger, Eberhard. *The Flood from Heaven*. New York: William Morrow, 1992.

Zimmer, Heinrich. *Philosophies of India*. New York: Bollingen, 1951.

A note on sightings: Although the modern UFO era formally began in 1947 with Kenneth Arnold's sighting of nine objects in the sky near Mt. Rainier, Washington, prior to that there were innumerable sightings and encounter reports that have been retrospectively viewed as UFO events. Recorded accounts reaching back into the mid–nineteenth century have been included in this chronology; pre-nineteenth-century reports of aerial phenomena have not.

1837   Springheel Jack legend begins when four separate but similar assaults on women occurred. Some later claim that Jack was an alien.

1860   Citizens of Wilmington, Delaware, see a 200-foot-long object at 100 feet altitude for about a minute. The object gives off sparks in the manner of a rocket.

1870   In the Atlantic Ocean off the coast of West Africa, the captain and crew of a ship see in the sky a gray object shaped like a doughnut divided into four connected sections with a long hook trailing from its center.

1871   In Marseilles, France, an astronomer watches what he thinks is a meteor at night for 18 minutes until it begins slowing, stopping, and changing direction.

1878   An orange object is observed high in the morning sky near Denison, Texas. It approaches, and when it is nearly overhead it appears to be the size of a large saucer and at great height.

1882   Publication of Ignatius Donnelly's *Atlantis: The Antediluvian World*. Although the notion of Atlantis goes at least as far back as Plato, contemporary interest in the Atlantis legend begins with Donnelly. It will not be until the latter half of the twentieth century that Atlantis comes to be viewed as a possible point of origin for UFOs.

1884   Cowboys rounding up cattle in Nebraska hear a whirring noise overhead and see a blazing object plunging to earth that turns out to be a crashed aerial vessel.

1892   Recovery of the *Mary Celeste* off the coast of Portugal with no crew members. The mystery of the crew's disappearance was retroactively incorporated into the Bermuda Triangle legend.

1895   At Oxford, England, renowned linguist and lexicographer James Augustus Henry Murray sees a brilliant, luminous body emerge over the tops of some trees and move eastward across the sky.

1896   Two men are confronted by seven-foot-tall naked beings that try to carry them into a nearby airship. The attempt reportedly fails because the aliens were weightless and therefore unable to carry the men.

An airship crashes into a windmill, killing its Martian pilot, which is reportedly buried in the local cemetery.

1896   In Rhodes, Iowa, a rapidly approaching bright light making mechanical noises plunges into a reservoir. The hissing could be heard for miles and the water became boiling hot.

In Lanark, Illinois, a cigar-shaped airship plows into the ground. Two of the occupants are killed outright. A third, dressed in robes, shouts hysterically, lapses into unconsciousness, and eventually flies back to Mars with the bodies of his companions.

In the early-morning hours in Pavilion, Michigan, a fast-moving airship explodes overhead. Various pieces of machinery are found scattered throughout the town, with minute fragments reportedly penetrating roofing shingles.

In Decatur, Illinois, an airship crashes into the roof of a barn and then sails on.

In Humboldt, Tennessee, a man reports seeing an airship crash in the woods.

In Jefferson, Iowa, an airship falls to earth, leaving a large hole in the ground.

In Aurora, Texas, residents see an airship flying to the north over town before it collides with a windmill and explodes. A badly disfigured body is found in the wreckage; a local signal service officer identifies it as a native of Mars.

Three men report seeing the occupants of an airship rustle a calf, the remains of which are found the next day in a neighbor's pasture.

A newspaper in British Columbia carries a story about the sighting of a "monkey man" by a Vancouver Island lumberman, perhaps the first modern Bigfoot tale. Only later will Bigfoot become associated with flying saucers.

1898   Publication of H. G. Wells's novel *War of the Worlds;* its basic alien-invasion plot will be repeated in numerous subsequent novels and films.

1900   Near Reedsburg, Wisconsin, a 14-year-old sees the outline of a large, dark, dirigible-shaped object. It passes at a low altitude over some poplar trees. As it does so, the trunks of the trees bend dramatically, and the object makes a loud swishing sound.

1903   In Helmer, Indiana, a farmer and his 12-year-old daughter see a huge, glowing, cigar-shaped object. It has eight windows in the side and light inside illuminating the ship.

In Stratford, Indiana, residents see a cigar-shaped object high in the late-afternoon sky. It circles the town and then flies east. Someone

using binoculars sees a canopy at the top-center, with two figures moving backward and forward underneath it.

1904   In Dixboro, Michigan, two men spot a large object moving to the west at a low altitude in the sky. The shape of the object reminded one man of the Confederate gunboat *Merrimack.*

1905   In Silsbee, California, a man driving some pigs to market sees a bright light flash from a huge airship 70 feet long. It has a brilliant searchlight and huge wings that move up and down.

1906   On Maui, Hawaii, a green object appears from behind the Wailuku Mountains. It is visible for five or six seconds before disappearing behind Mount Haleakala.

In Hallock, Minnesota, an airship alternately hovers and moves as it flies overhead, finally vanishing into the darkness.

Hundreds of Indianapolis residents see a cigar-shaped object over the city.

In Oklahoma, five cotton-pickers spot a fiery object shaped like a stovepipe about 10 inches in diameter and 16 feet long. A series of objects passes within 16 feet of the men at eye level.

1907   In Burlington, Vermont, witnesses hear an explosion and look up to see a torpedo-shaped object suspended in the air about 50 feet above the tops of the buildings. It is about six feet long and eight inches in diameter, with tongues of fire issuing from spots on the surface in various places.

1908   A meteor enters the atmosphere of the earth and becomes so heated from atmospheric friction that it explodes in the air over Siberia. There are many speculations that this was actually an alien spacecraft.

Over Long Island, a series of lights like a string of beads is seen in the late-evening sky.

Repeated sightings of unidentified airships over Denmark. They are sometimes seen flying against the wind. Some have wings and searchlights. Other reports are of odd-shaped clouds from which bright lights sweep the ground.

The skipper of a small boat 35 miles off the coast of England notices a large star that appears to be approaching. The crew can see the outline of a sausage-shaped airship.

1909 A constable in Peterborough, England, hears what he takes to be a motorcar. Then he looks up and sees a light at an altitude of about 1,200 feet and makes out the outline of an oblong and narrow object traveling rapidly.

In Essex, England, a man sees a large dark object cross the sky and remain stationary in front of his window. He sees the outline of a torpedo-shaped airship a quarter of a mile above the houses and trees.

In Northamptonshire, England, three men traveling in a car hear a motor. Looking up they spot an oblong airship 100 feet long flying about 500 feet above them.

In Suffolk, a woman hears a motorcar in the middle of the night and looks out her window. She sees a long, dark, bottle-shaped object pass by at a low altitude.

In Norfolk a man bicycling home around midnight sees the trees and hedges near him light up briefly in a bright-blue light. Then he looks up to see a long, cigar-shaped object 300–400 feet overhead.

A New Zealand farmhand is feeding horses when a loud whirring sound from an airship frightens the animals. The object is 150 feet long and moving fast.

Four men at the Fisher's Island lifesaving station off the New England coast sight an airship 60 feet long and 20 feet wide. It moved rapidly against the wind.

In Indiana, a huge object shaped like one bowl inverted on top of the other, with a row of lights across the center, shines a blinding light on some people in a horse-drawn wagon. The horses rear up in terror.

Residents of Worcester, Massachusetts, see a light emanating from an object 1,000 feet in the sky.

A man in Revere, Massachusetts, sees an airship at an altitude of 400 feet. He hears engines and sees searchlights at either end.

1910 In Utah, a man riding a horse sees a row of lights a few feet above the ground. The lights are attached to a huge, hovering disk.

In East Providence, Rhode Island, two objects that look like luminous pumpkins perform aerial loops, circling and diving while traveling in a generally southeasterly direction.

1912 In Alameda, California, a 15-year-old and two friends see three round objects traveling parallel to the horizon. They are in vertical formation, one above the other, and pale green.

1913 A fast-moving airship sails over a Lansing, Michigan, racetrack while a race is in progress.

1914 In Manchester, England, a man observes a black, spindle-shaped object crossing the sun.

1916 The series of Marian apparitions referred to as the Fatima apparition begins in Fatima, Portugal. About half a century later the apparitions are reinterpreted to be UFO phenomena.

1918 In Waco, Texas, soldiers see a cigar-shaped object 100–150 feet long coming toward them. It flies directly overhead at an altitude of 500 feet.

1920 In Iowa, a fisherman spots a soundless blue disk-shaped object about two feet in diameter that flies across the pond and lands 15 feet away from him.

Two hundred persons in Kansas and Missouri see a cylindrical object flying at an altitude of 75 feet. They see it make a sharp right turn before disappearing into a cloud.

1924 Two people in Oklahoma see a beam of light shining on the snow. The source of the light is a large oval object with lights on the side and a blue flame at the stern.

1925   Near Chicago, a 300-foot-long, cigar-shaped object flies toward the city. It is multicolored, and red sparks are flying away from its nose.

1926   In Mongolia, a mountain climber sees a huge oval moving through the sky at great speed from north to south. It has a shiny surface that reflects the light of the sun.

1927   A child in Illinois sees a bright, flashing disk approaching silently. It stops and hovers over a house across the street, about 100 feet away.

1928   In North Dakota, a metallic object like a soup bowl turned upside down flies by about 15 to 20 feet above the ground. It has four or five lights that illuminate the ground below it.

1930   Guy Ballard, founder of the "I AM" Activity, meets St. Germain while he was working near Mt. Shasta and later attends a meeting featuring spiritual masters from Venus. These events from the early 1930s are reported in Ballard's *Unveiled Mysteries.*

1931   In Sardinia, two young men see an object the size and shape of a soccer ball pass in front of them. It enters a thick growth of trees, which part as the object approaches and close together afterward.

Over the Tasman Sea, Sir Francis Chichester looks out the cockpit of his Gypsy Moth aircraft and sees a series of flashes. Then he sees the dull, gray shape of an airship. It vanishes.

The Fortean Society, dedicated to the examination of so-called Fortean phenomena—strange animals, archaeological mysteries, UFOs—is established on January 26 in New York City by Tiffany Thayer, a close friend of anomalist Charles Hoy Fort.

1932   Charles Fort dies.

In Pennsylvania, a farmer sees a bright speck of light about 400 yards away. It moves toward him until it is within four feet of him at eye level. It is a brilliant, blue-silver ball 14 inches in diameter.

1933   In Pennsylvania, a man repairing a flat tire notices a faint violet glow in a field to his right.

He walks toward it and sees a ball-shaped craft 10 feet in diameter and six feet high.

1934   A French tourist in England sees the ground around him become illuminated. The light comes from a white disk, too bright to be looked at directly. The light turns blue, white, yellow, orange, and red before the object takes off rapidly and disappears.

1935   In Virginia, a woman sees flashes of light in the southwestern sky. She watches and determines that they are emanating from a brightly glowing ball that is moving along the horizon.

1936   George Adamski founds the Royal Order of Tibet, the model for the teachings he later claims to receive from the Space Brothers.

1937   The Fortean Society begins publication of *The Fortean Society Magazine,* which changes its name to *Doubt* in 1944.

1938   "War of the Worlds" radio broadcast sets off a wave of hysteria across the Eastern Seaboard.

1940   In Illinois, five disks are seen traveling together at 100–200 miles per hour before they disappear into a cloud.

1942   First sightings of unidentified flying objects by military personnel that come to be referred to as "foo fighters."

In New Jersey, three adults see a cigar-shaped object hovering over them. It has two rows of windows through which colored lights shine.

In Mississippi, an army radio operator spots a tiny red dot high in the sky, descending rapidly. Soon the object is very large and hovers over trees.

1943   In Santa Barbara, California, a woman notices a huge dark object approaching soundlessly in the sky. From the front of the object a beam shoots down to the ground. The beam appears to swing from side to side as if scanning the ground.

Richard S. Shaver relates through *Amazing Stories* magazine his interactions with a race of giants that lives in a vast series of underground caverns. According to Shaver, this race had superior science and technology and possessed spaceships that were sometimes seen in our atmosphere.

1944   In New York, a cigar-shaped object, longer and slimmer than a blimp, is spotted. It appears to be made of smooth metal and has no windows, openings, or gondola on its underside.

In Minnesota, two women see a shiny-brown, bullet-shaped object 20 feet above their heads. The object makes a crackling noise, turns right, and ascends rapidly.

1945   Disappearance without a trace of Flight 19, consisting of five U.S. Navy Avenger bombers. An official report on the incident notes that the Avengers had disappeared "as if they had flown to Mars." This becomes the seminal event for the Bermuda Triangle legend.

N. Meade Layne founds the Borderland Sciences Research Foundation.

A pilot about to land in Texas sees a 30-foot-long gray object 500 feet above the ground. The hull is featureless, with no wings, windows, or tail.

1946   In Ontario, a family ice-fishing watches 12–14 small disks descend at a 45-degree angle 75 feet from them. They come spinning down on the ice, rise two feet into the air, and come down again.

In New York, two men see a metallic, cigar-shaped object with sharply pointed ends. It is 300–400 feet long and at 5,000–10,000 feet in altitude. It is smooth with no protrusions.

1946   In Florida, a man sees a dark, football-shaped object, 15–20 feet in diameter flying at 125 miles per hour at an altitude of 1,500 feet. It makes a whistling sound and has no appendages (wings, propellers, tail, etc.) and no trail of smoke.

Nearly 1,000 sightings of cigar-shaped "ghost rockets" are reported in Northern Europe.

1947   Kenneth Arnold's sighting of nine objects in the sky near Mt. Rainier, Washington, launches the modern UFO craze. The expression "flying saucers" is first used by headline writers for this story.

A flying saucer crashes near Roswell, New Mexico. Remains from the crash, including bodies of dead ufonauts, are allegedly picked up by the military. This event, which the Army Air Force asserts is nothing more than the crash of a weather balloon, will become the starting point of one of the most famous UFO legends of all time.

Admiral Richard E. Byrd flies over the North Pole. Hollow-earth enthusiasts believe that he flew into an opening at the top of the world that led into a world in the interior of our planet that is the home base for UFOs.

Fred L. Crisman contacts science-fiction editor Ray Palmer, claiming that he and Harold Dahl had seen doughnut-shaped UFOs disgorge metallic materials.

The Air Force orders Project Sign to be set up under the Air Materiel Command at what is now Wright-Patterson Air Force Base in Dayton, Ohio. Its purpose is a detailed study of flying disks (UFOs).

At Muroc Air Base (now Edwards Air Force Base) in Southern California, there are four different UFO sightings by four different, independent military witnesses.

1948   According to a story that appeared in *Weekly Variety* under Frank Scully's byline in 1949, a flying saucer crashed on a rocky plateau east of Aztec, New Mexico, on March 28, 1948. The story of the Aztec crash will rival Roswell in notoriety.

Aerial phenomena described as "green fireballs" are sighted in the southwestern United States, just as the UFO craze is beginning to grow.

Captain Thomas F. Mantell Jr. dies when his F-51 crashes southeast of Franklin, Kentucky, while pursuing a UFO.

The U.S. Air Force's first UFO project, Project Sign, drafts an intelligence report—an "estimate of the situation." The report reviews reports from scientists, pilots, and other credible observers and concludes that UFOs have an extraterrestrial origin. The Air Force later denies the existence of this document.

1949 Dr. Clyde W. Tombaugh, his wife, and his wife's mother are stargazing in the backyard of the Tombaugh home in Las Cruces, New Mexico, when they see a geometrical group of faint blue-green rectangles of light moving in a southeasterly direction until they fade from view. Dr. Tombaugh was the astronomer who discovered the planet Pluto in 1930.

Project Sign, the Air Force's UFO investigation wing, is taken over by personnel who are convinced that all UFO reports can be accounted for in conventional terms. The Project is renamed Grudge.

1950 Samuel Eaton Thompson is walking along an old logging trail near Mineral, Washington, when he sees a large, saucer-shaped craft hovering just above a clearing. Later he meets naked, well-tanned, humanoid aliens that advocate astrology and a vegetarian diet.

Near McMinnville, Oregon, Mr. and Mrs. Paul Trent see a slow-moving metallic disk. Mr. Trent has the presence of mind to grab a camera and is able to take two photographs before the object disappears.

1951 Release of *The Day the Earth Stood Still,* an influential sci-fi film in the "technological angel" tradition of friendly aliens warning earthlings to stop atom-bomb testing.

Three Texas Technical College professors in a Lubbock backyard see a fast-moving semicircular formation of 20–30 blue-green lights that traverse the sky and disappear in seconds. Five other individuals, two of them college professors, report similar sightings.

In New Jersey, an unidentified flying object is tracked by radar at Fort Monmouth. Around the same time in the same area, a round, flat, silver object the size of a fighter plane is sighted by an Air Force lieutenant and a major flying in a T-33 jet trainer. The object is flying at an altitude of

5,000–8,000 feet at a speed of about 900 miles per hour. Both men watch as the UFO banks and flies out of sight over the ocean.

1952 The encounter that gives rise to the Flatwoods Monster, one of the most famous alien encounters of all time, takes place near Flatwoods, West Virginia.

Among the most famous of the channeled Space Brothers, Ashtar begins transmitting to George Van Tassel, perhaps the most influential flying-saucer contactee.

Albert K. Bender forms the International Flying Saucer Bureau (IFSB) to gather information about flying saucers and publishes the first issue of *Space Review,* the IFSB magazine.

Project A is formed in July 1952 by the administration and faculty of Ohio Northern University to solve the UFO mystery by examining the available evidence.

Project Blue Book, the Air Force's Aerial Phenomena Group, is born.

Captain William B. Nash and copilot William H. Fortenberry are flying a Pan-American airliner above Chesapeake Bay when they see six red disks 100 feet in diameter and 15 feet thick in an echelon formation.

Aerial Phenomena Research Organization (APRO), an independent organization for investigating UFO reports that for many years would publish the popular *APRO Bulletin,* is founded by Leslie James and Coral Lorentzen in Sturgeon Bay, Wisconsin.

1953 Publication of George Adamski and Leslie Desmond's *Flying Saucers Have Landed,* one of the most popular flying-saucer books ever written. This book claims to report Adamski's telepathic contacts with a humanoid Venusian.

The annual Giant Rock Spacecraft Convention first held at Giant Rock in the desert of Southern California. Hosted by George Van Tassel, it quickly becomes the most important contactee gathering on the circuit.

The first stories appear about men in black who appear to ufologists and threaten them with dire consequences if they publish what they know.

A barber in Atlanta, Georgia, buys a monkey, kills it, shaves it, cuts off its tail, and claims that it is the occupant of a flying saucer he had run over.

An air-traffic controller at Washington, D.C.'s National Airport spots seven blips clustered together in a corner of his radarscope. He quickly alerts the senior air-traffic controller for the Civil Aeronautics Administration, joking about the objects being flying saucers. A rash of sightings follows. Interceptor jets find nothing.

Saucers, a digest-sized quarterly magazine, begins publication. Edited by Max B. Miller, it covers the widest range of viewpoints of any UFO periodical.

The CIA assembles a panel of scientists headed up by physicist H. P. Robertson to deal with the problem of UFOs. The panel comes to the conclusion that further investigation would be a waste of time and that the air force should embark on a debunking campaign. The conclusions and recommendations of the panel set government policy on UFOs for years to come.

An Air Defense Command radar at Kinross Air Force Base in Michigan detects a UFO. An F-89 interceptor jet is dispatched. At 8,000 feet over Lake Superior, the blip of the F-89 and that of the UFO merge, then fade from the screen. Nothing more is heard of the interceptor and no trace of it is ever found, despite an extensive search. The radar officer who witnesses the event is later quoted as saying, "It seems incredible, but the blip apparently just swallowed our F-89."

1954 James W. Moseley starts the monthly magazine *Nexus.*

George King founds the Aetherius Society, which, until the Heaven's Gate suicides, is the most well-known and well-organized flying-saucer religion.

Flying Saucer from Mars by Cedric Allingham is published and attracts much attention. In this book, Allingham claims that he had seen a spaceship land in Scotland in February 1954 and had talked to a humanoid Martian from the spaceship.

Publication of Truman Bethurum's *Aboard a Flying Saucer,* recounting his encounters with ufonauts from the planet Clarion.

The Cosmic Circle of Fellowship is formed in Chicago by William A. Ferguson.

Publication of Daniel Fry's *White Sands Incident,* an account of Fry's ride on a flying saucer.

Ernest L. Norman meets his future wife, Ruth, at a psychic convention. In Unarian lore, this earthly meeting of the two ascended beings inaugurated the Unarius Society.

Ted Bloecher, Isabel Davis, and others found Civilian Saucer Intelligence in New York.

Passengers and crew aboard a British Overseas Airways plane flying from New York to London observe a large cigar-shaped object and six smaller black ovals moving at about 230 knots on a course parallel to that of the airplane. The sighting attracts wide publicity.

1955 Orfeo Angelucci, an enthusiastic amateur scientist, publishes his book *The Secret of the Saucers.*

The Kelly-Hopkinsville incident takes place during which strange creatures from a flying saucer besiege a farmhouse and are repeatedly repelled with gunfire.

The legend of the Philadelphia experiment originates in October 1955 with a series of letters mailed to Morris K. Jessup from a person referring to himself as either Carl Allen or Carlos Miguel Allende.

Daniel Fry founds the group World Understanding five years after his meeting with an extraterrestrial being named A-Lan who took him on a flight aboard a flying saucer.

U.S. Senator Richard Russell of Georgia (head of the Senate Armed Services Committee) and Lieutenant Colonel E. U. Hathaway sight a UFO while on a Soviet train passing through the Transcaucasus region.

1956 South African Elizabeth Klarer takes off with a man whose name is Akon from the planet Meton in the Alpha Centauri system. She lives on Meton for four months, gives birth to her and Akon's son, but cannot bring him back to earth.

The Brotherhood of the Seven Rays is established by George Hunt Willamson. Williamson and some associates travel to Peru to establish the Abbey of the Seven Rays.

Publication of Gray Barker's *They Knew Too Much About Flying Saucers,* one of the principal sources for modern men-in-black folklore.

Release of *Earth Versus the Flying Saucers,* one of the first popular films to use the expression "flying saucers" and one of the first films to recast the classic *War of the Worlds* alien-invasion theme in terms of the emergent flying-saucer phenomenon, transforming ufonauts from beings of ambiguous intent into hostile enemies.

Invasion of the Body Snatchers, a film about an invasion of parasitic aliens that replace humans with soulless counterfeits, is released. Although not the first film to feature people being taken over by alien invaders, it is the most influential, and the notion subsequently becomes a staple theme in the UFO subculture.

Howard Menger, who would become a world-famous contactee, gets his start when he appears on the Long John Nebel radio show in the company of well-known contactee George Van Tassel.

Donald E. Keyhoe and Physicist T. Townsend Brown incorporate the National Investigations Committee on Aerial Phenomena (NICAP). Before disbanding in 1980, it would serve as a conservative forum for UFO reporting, inquiry, investigation, and speculation.

1957 Antonio Villas-Boas, a Brazilian farmer, claims to be abducted and forced to have sex with an alien. This is one of the very first UFO abduction accounts to receive widespread attention.

Wayne Aho sights a UFO and receives a "cosmic initiation" in the desert of Southern California.

Reinhold O. Schmidt claims to meet ufonauts along the Platte River near Kearney, Nebraska. This meeting is later dismissed as a hoax.

Silvery UFOs appear to monitor atmospheric tests being conducted by the Brazilian navy on the unoccupied island of Trindade, 600 miles off the coast of Bahia, Brazil, in the middle of the South Atlantic. A photographer is able to snap three shots.

An Air Force RB-47 flying over the Gulf Coast near Gulfport, Mississippi, has a series of dramatic visual and radar sightings of a UFO.

An airplane pilot flying over Brazil sees an unusual red light. The pilot goes to investigate when some of the plane's equipment abruptly stops functioning and the UFO disappears. Less than an hour later at the Brazilian army's Itaipu Fortress, two soldiers see a brilliant orange light and are hit by a wave of heat. Their screams rouse other soldiers as the electrical system at the fort goes out. Some observers see the UFO streak away.

Conference on the last weekend in June for UFO contactees.

Pedro Saucedo and Joe Salaz are driving along Route 116 four miles west of Levelland, Texas, when they spot a flash of light that rises from a field and accelerates toward them. Their truck's lights and engine die. Similar close encounters with electrical disturbances take place in a series of similar incidents throughout West Texas.

Olden Moore is driving in northeastern Ohio when he sees a lighted object. The object splits in two, with one part settling to the ground in a nearby field, making a whirring sound. Moore watches the object for 15 minutes, but when he returns after going to get his wife the object is gone.

1958   At Loch Raven, Maryland, Alvin Cohen and Phillip Small are driving near Loch Raven Dam when they see a large, flat, egg-shaped object hovering above the lake. Their car dies and its electrical system goes out. The two men watch the object as it flashes a brilliant white light and makes a sound like a thunderclap. The men feel heat on their faces as the object rises and disappears.

Bigfoot appears in conjunction with a sighting (widely considered a hoax) of giant tracks in northern California. Speculation links this creature with UFOs as being possibly an extraterrestrial creature.

A popular TV show, *The Armstrong Circle Theater,* broadcasts a program called "UFO: The Donald E. Keyhoe Enigma of the Skies" in which the broadcast of the keynote speaker, Donald Keyhoe, is cut short, sparking a controversy about government secrecy and censorship.

The Universarium Foundation is established by Zelrun and Daisy Karlsleigh in Portland, Oregon.

Universe Society Church founded under the original name Institute of Parapsychology.

1959   English publication of Carl Jung's *Flying Saucers: A Modern Myth of Things Seen in the Skies,* one of the most influential psychological treatments of UFOs.

Gloria Lee, a contactee for J. W., a resident of Jupiter, establishes the Cosmon Research Foundation to publish and distribute J. W.'s teachings, including Lee's first book, *Why We Are Here!,* which was widely read in contactee circles.

In Papua, New Guinea, Anglican missionary Father William Booth Gill and 38 people watch as a large, four-legged, disk-shaped object hovers overhead. On top of the disk, four humanlike figures, their bodies surrounded by illumination, are busy performing some task. Two months later the UFO returns. This time a group of a dozen people watches and waves at the ufonauts; the ufonauts wave back before taking off and leaving the area.

1960   The Cosmic Star Temple is founded in Santa Barbara, California, by Violet Gilbert. It later relocates to Grants Pass, Oregon.

Two California Highway Patrol officers attempt to follow a UFO in their patrol car after spotting a metallic, football-shaped object over 100 feet long with red and white lights darting around in the sky. Many other witnesses verify the officers' perceptions.

1961   Joe Simonton, a 54-year-old plumber from Eagle River, Wisconsin, receives pancakes from crew members of a UFO temporarily parked in his driveway.

On a cloudless afternoon by witness accounts, a disk-shaped object approximately 50 feet in diameter and roughly 10 feet thick appears in the sky over Salt Lake City. From the air, pilot Waldo J. Harris observes it alternately hovering and rapidly moving up and away from him. About a dozen witnesses on the ground give similar descriptions.

1962   The Mark-Age Meta Center (subsequently Mark-Age, Inc.) is established in Miami, Florida. Communication with the Hierarchical Board takes place through spaceships.

The family of Rivalino Mafra da Solva awakes to floating, nonhuman entities half the height of a human being in their home. The next morning Rivalino sees two balls in the sky that merge, begin discharging yellow smoke, and engulf Rivalino. He is never seen again.

In Great Britain it is discovered that the Ministry of Defense, the principal investigative unit of UFOs for the British government, destroys its UFO files every five years. The houses of Parliament order that this practice cease, and that the ministry makes the files public after 30 years.

1963   The Betty and Barney Hill abduction occurs, one of the earliest instances of abduction claims later "recovered" by hypnosis.

1964   A photograph taken of a little girl in a marsh near Carlisle, England, reveals a strange, otherworldly image when it is developed. The photographer, the girl's father, says no one was near the field at the time of the photo, but the photo shows a large figure in a white spacesuit and a helmet standing behind the little girl. Soon afterward, the father has a men-in-black encounter.

Driving near the Georgia–South Carolina border, Beauford E. Parham sees a UFO that looks like a giant top that emits a hissing sound. The saucer flies back and forth in front of Parham's headlights. When the object flies off for the final time it leaves an odor like embalming fluid and a gaseous vapor that is deposited as an oily substance on his car. He also feels his arms beginning to burn, seeming to be the result of some sort of radiation.

Horace Burns sees a UFO that looks like a bubble or beehive 80–90 feet high; it consists of six concentric circular levels of metallic material with bluish-white lights at its base. It lands near Route 250. Later, Burns and two engineers measure levels upwards of 17–18 milliroentgens in the area.

1965   George Adamski, the first contactee of modern times, dies.

Two deputy sheriffs outside Damon, Texas, see a triangle-shaped UFO 150 feet away and 100 feet high. The next day one of the deputies is approached by two menacing strangers who tell him not to repeat the story.

Television repairman Sid Padrick was invited aboard a UFO while walking on Manresa Beach in California.

Stuart Whitman claims he is contacted by aliens during a blackout in New York City. They tell him the blackout was a demonstration of their power—a warning to earth.

Near the town of Valensole, France, farmer Maurice Masse has a close encounter with beings that paralyze him and pick lavender in his garden.

The UFO Bureau, a nonprofit research organization with the goal of informing the public about such things as UFOs, Bigfoot, extraterrestrials, psychic phenomena, animal mutilations, and other strange phenomena, is founded.

A New Mexico police officer follows a light to a ravine, where he sees a white craft and two small figures inspecting it. The craft later ascends, causing a loud roar and emitting blue flame. There are four impressions in the earth and small footprints. There is a strange, crescent-shaped symbol in the footprints.

John F. Reeves reports an encounter with a UFO and its occupant near Brooksville, Florida, and claims to have papers with alien writing on them. His report, though later dismissed as a hoax, receives much attention at the time.

While hunting in the Everglades, James Flynn spots a glowing, inverted cone–shaped hovering object about 25 feet high and 50 feet in diameter. He approaches the ship and is knocked out by a wind and an intense beam of light. He returns to the site several weeks later to find a burned circle 72 feet in diameter and scorched cypress all around.

Norman Muscarello sights five powerful flashing red lights in a circular formation floating up and down over a field. After catching a ride to the Exeter, New Hampshire, police station, he is joined by Officer Eugen Bertrand, who reports a similar experience. Both return to the site and see the lights once again floating back and forth over a nearby barn.

William Blackburn arrives at an archery club near his home in Virginia. Outside the club he sees two flying saucers land and three humanoid beings emerge from one of the ships. They speak unintelligibly and return to their craft.

1966   UFO Research, an Australian UFO organization, begins publication of *UFO Encounter*, a bimonthly journal that is edited by Martin Gotschall.

Woodrow W. Derenberger, a salesman living in Parkersburg, West Virginia, begins having a series of encounters with beings from the planet Lanulos. He is briefly in the national news as the latest contactee and then fades back into obscurity.

Two Ohio sheriff's deputies engage a UFO in a high-speed chase across two counties and the state line.

William Laxon is driving to work when he notices a bright light off to the side of the road eight miles south of Temple, Oklahoma. Coming closer, he sees a large, fish-shaped structure in the middle of the road. A door is open and a ladder leads up to an occupant, which looks like a human being bent down on one knee underneath it. Other witnesses see the same vehicle within a two-mile radius of Laxon's sighting.

1967 UFOCAT is created by psychologist David Saunders in 1967 as a comprehensive database for the classification of UFO phenomena and reports.

The first animal mutilation to be linked to UFOs is reported on September 9 in the San Luis Valley in Colorado when rancher Harry King finds his sister's horse decapitated near his home.

Death of William Ferguson, founder of the Cosmic Circle of Fellowship.

Fourteen-year-old Ronnie Hill of North Carolina sends a color photograph of a spacesuit-clad, large-headed little man holding an unknown device and standing in front of a spherical UFO to John Keel, a writer on UFOs. Although the photo passes examinations by experts, it is a hoax.

In Ashland, Nebraska, police Sergeant Herbert Schirmer is abducted from his police car. Schirmer is given a tour of the ship and told that the beings are from a nearby galaxy and have bases on Venus as well as on earth.

Stefan Michalak is prospecting near Falcon Lake, Manitoba, when he sees two red, cigar-

shaped objects in the sky, one of which lands near. The UFO appears to be hot stainless steel, whirring, hissing, and emitting purplish light from horizontal slits. Michalak accidentally touches the walls, causing the UFO to take off, blasting Michalak with hot gas that burns his shirt, undershirt, and chest.

A rash of sightings takes place in Great Britain. During one incident, police officers chase a cross-shaped light buzzing through the sky in Devon and Cornwall, which is later interpreted as the planet Venus.

1968 The Condon Committee, under the direction of University of Colorado physicist Edward U. Condon, issues a report of a study of the UFO phenomenon that began in 1966. The report, which announces that all UFOs can be explained by ordinary means, is widely assailed by critics.

On Lake Champlain in Vermont, a 16-year-old boy and a 19-year-old woman experience a typical abduction and "medical examination" by beings they identify as aliens.

A physician in southern France, Dr. X (so called because of his wish to remain anonymous), begins having a series of strange experiences linked to UFOs.

Release of the highly successful film 2001—A Space Odyssey. The unseen aliens of 2001 are clearly involved in stimulating the evolution of the human race, a widespread theme in the UFO subculture.

1969 Walter H. Andrus Jr., a regional officer of the Aerial Phenomenon Research Organization, starts a rival group, the Midwest (later the Mutual) UFO Network, which rapidly becomes an important UFO group on the international scene.

A 24-year-old Brazilian soldier named Jose Antonio da Silva claims to be paralyzed and abducted by beings who, in sharp contrast to most such accounts, were very hairy and had long, pointed noses.

The UFO Newsclipping Service is established by Rod Dyke and Lucius Farish.

Truman Bethurum dies on May 21 in Landers, California.

1971 Ernest L. Norman, cofounder of the Unarius Society, dies.

In the small town of Delphos, Kansas, 16-year-old Ronald Johnson is tending sheep when he sees a multicolored domed object in the sky giving off a loud, whining, mechanical noise. When he later brings his parents to where the UFO had appeared, they find a circle of glowing trees and warm soil. The parents touch the soil, and their hands temporarily go numb.

1972 Astronomer and ufologist J. Allen Hynek proposes a three-tiered classification system for UFO sightings, which subsequently becomes standard nomenclature—close encounters of the first, second, and third kinds.

Delval UFO, Inc., a New Age contactee group, is founded by Anthony and Lynn Volpe.

1973 "In Search of Ancient Astronauts," a TV special based on Erich von Däniken's *Chariots of the Gods?*, airs in January.

The Ancient Astronaut Society, an organization that actively promotes the concept of ancient astronauts as inspired by Erich von Däniken, is founded by Gene M. Phillips in Chicago.

Rael (Claude Vorihon), said to be the offspring of a human mother and an alien being, founds the Raelian Movement as a result of an encounter with space aliens.

The so-called Pascagoula abduction, one of the most famous of alien abductions, takes place on the Pascagoula River in Mississippi.

The Roach abduction takes place outside Lehi, Utah, when Pat Roach and her seven children are visited by aliens and taken aboard their ship for experiments.

The Center for UFO Studies is founded by astronomer J. Allen Hynek and Sherman Larsen as a forum for scientists and other professionals to deal with UFO research in a responsible manner. It is still one of the largest UFO groups in the United States.

In the midst of a major wave of UFO sightings, Falkville, Alabama, police chief Jeffrey Greenhaw responds to a report. Once there, he takes several photographs and speaks with a silver-suited figure in his headlights, who soon afterward flees the site on foot. Refusing to admit that he is hoaxing his story, he is eventually forced to resign, has his house burned down, and leaves town.

1974 E. Carl Higdon Jr. travels with "men" who take him to their home planet following an encounter during a hunting outing.

Edwin Fuhr of Langenburg, Saskatchewan, Canada, is harvesting his crop when he sees five UFOs hovering over some grass. He walks to within 15 feet and notices that the objects are spinning. Afterward he notices the grass they were spinning over is compacted in a clockwise fashion. The grass is twisted as if something had been probing around in it.

1975 Human Individual Metamorphosis—later known as Heaven's Gate—makes its first headlines following a public lecture in Waldport, Oregon, when more than 30 people recruited by Marshall Applewhite and Bonnie Lu Nettles vanish overnight.

On August 12 Sergeant Charles Moody, an airman at Holloman Air Force Base in New Mexico, experiences a sighting that later, through hypnosis, he reconstructs as an abduction experience.

Jackie Larson, Terry O'Leary, and Sandy Larson experience what they later believe was an alien abduction during a trip from Fargo to Bismarck, North Dakota.

Travis Walton is abducted while other members of his logging crew watch. Five days later Walton calls his brother-in-law from a phone booth in nearby Heber, Arizona, and asks to be picked up. The story of this incident becomes the basis for the popular film *Fire in the Sky*.

Eduard Albert "Billy" Meier claims contact with ufonauts from the Pleiades star system that select him as their "truth offerer." Featuring innumerable pictures of their "beamships," Meier becomes the most successful Adamski-style contactee.

George O'Barski is driving through North Hudson Park, New York, when he sees a brightly lit object about 30 feet long from which small beings in suits came come down a ladder, fill bags with soil, scurry back into the UFO, and take off.

The Venusian Church is founded by Seattle businessman Ron Peterson.

1976   The so-called Kentucky abduction takes place in which three friends driving home are abducted, arrive with no memories of the abduction, and experience a significant interval of "missing time." Later, under hypnosis, they recall being examined by aliens, with a scalding liquid being poured over them.

Residents around the Mehrabad airport in Iran see a multicolored aircraft hovering at 6,000 feet and phone the air-traffic controller. A flight of F-4 planes is then dispatched to rendezvous with the object. Each plane experiences electrical failure in the vicinity of the UFO.

Many Moroccans reported seeing luminous disks and tube-like UFOs. The same flying objects had apparently flown over Iran several hours earlier.

1977   The film *Close Encounters of the Third Kind* makes astronomer J. Allen Hynek's expression a household word. The commercial and critical success of this movie makes interest in UFOs less marginal and puts writer-director Steven Spielberg on the way to becoming the most popular film director in recent history.

1978   The UFO Contact Center International is begun by Aileen Bringle (then Edwards) in Washington State as a meeting place and therapy center for abductees.

While flying his single-engine Cessna from Victoria, Australia, to King's Island, Frederick Valentich reports that he is having engine trouble and that a strange metallic craft with

green lights is hovering above him. Controllers hear a loud scraping sound before the transmission cuts off. Valentich and his plane are never seen again.

UFOlogy Research of Manitoba begins publication of *Swamp Gas Journal.*

The Pinecastle Electronic Warfare Range Tracking Station, a U.S. Navy facility in Florida, tracks a UFO on its radar screens at the same time civilians call, reporting strange phenomena, flare-like lights, and flying saucers.

Several different pilots radio Wellington Air Traffic Control in New Zealand to report strange white lights in the sky. A Melbourne reporter, with a camera crew, hires a plane and films the lights. The film is later the focus of intense controversy.

Sergeant Jeffrey Morse sights a short, slender, gray-brown being in the training area of Fort Dix Army Camp in New Jersey. Morse and a state patrol officer, who is pursuing a low-flying oval object that is a glowing blue-green, find the corpse of the being, dead of gunshot wounds, in the woods. The corpse is quickly removed by a team from Wright-Patterson Air Force Base in an atmosphere of secrecy, and Morse is sworn to secrecy.

1979   The Fund for UFO Research, a nonprofit tax-exempt research foundation chaired by physicist and longtime ufologist Bruce S. Maccabee, is founded to provide grants for scientific and educational projects dealing with UFOs and related topics.

A UFO seen by seven witnesses, including one American, appears over the pumping equipment of the Kuwaiti Oil Company. The equipment, geared to shut down during dangerous malfunctions and not restart except manually, shuts down when the craft appears; it restarts on its own when the saucer leaves.

Deputy Val Johnson's police car is hit by a UFO. Later, he doesn't remember anything. Investigators notice that his car's clock and his wristwatch are both running 14 minutes late.

Trucker Harry Joe Turner claims to be taken on a trip through space by a UFO.

England's House of Lords debates various theories on the existence of UFOs, the possibility of races outside our universe, and their religious implications. The discussion is inconclusive.

1980   The first article on crop circles appears, describing flattened circles found in a field of oats in Wiltshire, England.

In England, Lieutenant Colonel Charles Halt, a U.S. Air Force deputy base commander at RAF/USAF Woodbridge near Ipswich, Suffolk, issues a report of a UFO sighting by some of his patrolmen. Media interest peaks in 1983 after Halt's memorandum is released and an article appears in *News of the World,* although the major British papers debunk the story.

Publication of *World Messages from the Coming Decade* by Tuella (Thelma B. Terrell), who claims to channel the Ashtar Command. In it, Tuella describes the contacts she had with this group of space entities, which lives in spaceships hovering around the earth.

Myra Hansen, along with her six-year-old son, report seeing a cow mutilation and then being abducted, examined, and taken to an underground base filled with vats full of floating human body parts.

A debate between leading UFO proponents and debunkers, long demanded by the debunking camp, is staged at the Smithsonian Institute in Washington, D.C.

Institute for UFO Contactee Studies is founded.

George Blackwell, caretaker of White Acres farm in Victoria, Australia, sees a domed object, 15 feet high and 25 feet long with a white top and blue and orange lights, hovering over a concrete water tank. The next morning he discovers that the water tank has been emptied of 10,000 gallons of water.

U.S. Air Force officers at RAF bases in Great Britain encounter UFOs and find physical trace evidence.

1981   In the village of Trans-en-Provence, France, Renato Nicolai witnesses an airship landing while he is working in his garden. Although the encounter is brief and otherwise uneventful, this becomes an important incident because of the thoroughness of the subsequent investigation and testing of the soil and vegetation where the UFO set down.

First reports of the Hessdalen lights, in the Hessdalen Valley in central Norway, reach ufologists. Strange lights hover over the region for up to an hour at a time, then disappear at incredible speeds. The lights are variously described as being cigar- or bullet-shaped, spherical, and cone-shaped, white or yellowish-white, sometimes with a smaller red light leading the others.

1982   *E.T. The Extra-Terrestrial,* one of the most successful movies of all time, is released, breaking the mold for alien-contact films.

Publication of Brad Steiger's *Star People,* popularizing the notion that there are individuals who are descendants of human-alien breeding experiments.

Beginning of a four-year period of UFO sightings collectively known as the Westchester sightings. Though centered in Westchester County, New York, these sightings are spread across seven densely populated counties in New York and Connecticut. The Westchester UFO is shaped like a giant V, or a boomerang, with lights along its periphery. Thousands of people witness the UFO, which often moves slowly at low altitudes with little or no accompanying sound.

In Kazakhstan, two UFOs hover over the Baikonur Cosmodrome spaceflight center, site of the first Soviet space-shuttle mission. One of the UFOs comes down toward one of the launch pads while the other stays near the housing complex. The gantries at the launch pads have rivets sucked out of them as well as welded joints, and thousands of windows are shattered at the housing complex.

1983   Linda Moulton Howe, Denver-based producer of the documentary "Strange Harvest" and the most prominent person investigating the UFO angle on cattle mutilations, becomes the target of an elaborate intelligence campaign designed to discredit her and to spread disinformation to the larger UFO community.

Englishman Alfred Burtoo, 78, is taken aboard a UFO in Aldershot, Hampshire, by two short creatures wearing pale-green overalls and green helmets with black visors. The aliens, however, ultimately decide not to abduct him because, he is told, he is "too old and infirm" for their purpose.

1984   Jaime Shandera, a member of a research team looking into the reality of flying saucers, receives a package containing undeveloped photographs of documents purporting to be briefing papers on the subject of Operation Majestic 12 that become keystones in subsequent conspiracy theories involving what the government supposedly knows about UFOs.

1985   Publication of *Aliens among Us,* in which Ruth Montgomery develops her notion of extraterrestrial walk-ins—the idea that souls from other planets have come to earth to take over the bodies of human beings. This idea, building on her earlier writings about walk-ins, becomes widely accepted in New Age circles.

Residents of six towns near Bulawayo, Zimbabwe, see a UFO. Bulawayo airport personnel follow the UFO on radar while observers on the ground are able to see it with the naked eye. Military aircraft chase it until the object shoots away at high speed.

1986   Japan Airlines Flight 1628 is en route from Iceland to Anchorage, Alaska, when pilot Kenju Terauchi sights moving lights that appear to be following his plane. One of the two large crafts appears to be the size of two aircraft carriers. Both the airliner's radar and ground radar pick up unidentified objects. Terauchi later describes one of the UFOs as shaped like a walnut and about twice the size of an aircraft carrier.

UFO Magazine (originally *California UFO*), the first commercially produced, newsstand-quality magazine in the United States to factually address the UFO subject, is founded by Southern California journalists Vicki Cooper Ecker and Sherie Stark.

The Extraterrestrial Earth Mission begins when the extraterrestrial spirit, Avinash, walks into the body of John, a channel and metaphysical teacher in Seattle.

Military and civil radars show numerous UFOs in the vicinity of São Paolo and Rio de Janeiro, Brazil. Pilots report sightings and radar detection.

1987   Publication of Whitley Strieber's *Communion.* Interest in abductions and abductees explodes. Strieber's account, written with skill by an accomplished author, presented the bizarre details of UFO abduction in an accessible way, spurring the book to the top of the *New York Times* best-seller list.

Budd Hopkins's book *Intruders* lands on the best-seller list, causing interest in abductions to dominate the field of ufology.

The harmonic convergence takes place, a period of a few days during which many New Agers believed that a strong cosmic force would climax, leading to a collective shift in human mental orientation. During the convergence, many participants, including Jose Arguelles, the person who laid the theoretical foundation for the gathering, saw UFOs—implying that the Space Brothers were somehow aware of and participating in the event.

Publication of the first edition of Richard Hoagland's influential *The Monuments of Mars,* which focuses on a Martian surface formation on the Cydonian Plain that appears to be a human face.

Edward Walters, a well-to-do businessman in the construction industry in the small city of Gulf Breeze, Florida, has a series of UFO encounters spread out over several months. These include seeing and photographing UFOs on about 17 occasions, seeing aliens a few feet away, being immobilized by blue beams from a UFO, hearing alien voices in his head, and being abducted.

1988   In Tetbury, Gloucestershire, England, a man goes out of his house to investigate a light he sees across a field. Suddenly he is surrounded by a glow and finds himself in a conversation with an unknown entity that warns him that if humankind does not clean up its act that the aliens will have to take measures against it, such as introducing a bacterial disease.

On the Nullarbor Plain in western Australia a UFO lands on the roof of a traveling car. The car starts to rise off the ground. The UFO then lets go of the car, which crashes to the ground and bursts a tire.

Two articles by Keith Basterfield and Robert Bartholomew are published in *International UFO Reporter,* offering an original and controversial hypothesis for abduction phenomena—the fantasy-prone personality hypothesis.

Two military jets are reported to disappear near a large, yellow UFO that had appeared over the community of San Germán, Puerto Rico. Subsequently, two smaller UFOs emerge from the first and speed away. A similar incident takes place at Cabo Rojo.

1989   Whitley Strieber, author of *Communion: A True Story* and *Transformation: The Breakthrough,* founds the Communion Foundation.

The Soviet news agency Tass reports five to seven UFO encounters in different parts of the Russian city of Voronezh, an industrial city 300 miles southeast of Moscow. The incident attracts international attention. Western observers conclude that the new freedoms set in motion by glasnost are being put to trivial ends, such as allowing the Soviet media to print *National Enquirer* kinds of stories.

British UFO enthusiast Henry Azadehdel leaks a top-secret document allegedly prepared by the South African Air Force claiming that two South African fighter planes pursued a UFO and shot it down over the Kalahari Desert on the Botswana border. It is later dismissed as a hoax.

1990   Budd Hopkins, author of *Missing Time: A Documented Study of UFO Abductions* and

Intruders: The Incredible Visitations at Copley Woods, founds the Intruders Foundation in New York City.

Many sightings are reported around Laguna Caragena near Boquerón, Puerto Rico. This rash of sightings gives rise to speculation that an underground UFO base is located nearby.

1991   Douglas Bower and David Chorley hoax a crop circle in England. They are subsequently able to trick a prominent crop-circle expert into declaring their artificially constructed wheat circle genuine. The hoax makes international headlines, and skeptical debunkers have a field day.

Space Shuttle *Discovery* is flying mission No. STS-48 while its cable channel, called NASA Select, is transmitting a live broadcast. Recorded by Donald Ratch of Dundalk, Maryland, he later notices anomalous objects moving in the background.

1992   The International UFO Museum and Research Center in Roswell, New Mexico, opens, reflecting the increasing interest in the Roswell incident.

1993   Publication of Michael A. Cremo and Richard L. Thompson's *Forbidden Archeology,* a popular work on the origins of the human race and material culture that calls certain views of establishment science into question. The ancient-astronaut school is quick to embrace the book as tending to support the hypothesis of early contact between humanity and extraterrestrials.

Release of *Fire in the Sky,* a box-office film based on the Walton abduction in 1975. *Fire in the Sky* is probably more responsible for making the public aware of the alien-abduction phenomenon—particularly as a negative, frightening experience—than any other single mainstream production before the *X-Files* TV series.

Ruth Norman, cofounder of the Unarius Society, dies quietly in her sleep.

1994   At Arial School in Ruwa, Zimbabwe, 12 miles outside the capital city of Harare, 62 school children see a brilliant UFO and claim to have made contact with the alien beings that emerged from the craft.

1995   First public showings of the "Alien Autopsy Film," a film purporting to show an autopsy being performed on the body of an alien that was recovered from the flying-saucer crash at Roswell, New Mexico, in 1947.

The first of a series of mysterious animal deaths reported in Puerto Rico becomes the basis for folklore about the Chupacabras ("Goat Sucker"), a creature that some writers later claim is an extraterrestrial animal purposefully or accidentally released on our world by aliens.

1996   Release of *Independence Day,* an alien-invasion film in the grand tradition that broke previous box-office records. For the UFO buff, one of the interesting aspects of the film is that it draws in everything from the Roswell incident to Area 51,

reflecting the growing public awareness of and interest in UFO-related conspiracy theories.

1997   On March 26 the bodies of 39 men and women are found inside a posh mansion outside San Diego, the result of a mass suicide. Messages left by this group, Heaven's Gate, indicate they believed they were stepping out of their physical "containers" in order to ascend to a UFO that was arriving in the wake of comet Hale-Bopp.

George King, founder and leader of the Aetherius Society, dies.

1998   Hon-ming Chen, the leader of the Taiwanese UFO religion Chen Tao, announces that God will appear on television on March 25 and then in person on March 31 in Garland, Texas. The media whips up public fear of another Heaven's Gate tragedy, and the group briefly makes world headlines.

Although the particular synthesis preached by Marshall Herff Applewhite and Bonnie Lu Nettles cannot be described as typical, most of the themes in the Heaven's Gate ideology are also found in the teachings of other UFO religions. Thus, without intending to imply that other UFO groups are thereby candidates for mass suicide, we are justified in examining the teachings of "the Two" (as they sometimes called themselves) as representative of UFO spirituality.

Although the basic doctrines of Heaven's Gate seem to have remained constant, the details of the ideology were flexible enough to undergo modification over time. For example, in the early days Applewhite and Nettles taught their followers that they were extraterrestrial beings. However, after the notion of walk-ins became popular within the New Age subculture, the Two changed their tune and began describing themselves as extraterrestrial walk-ins.

The walk-in idea—a notion implying a radical disjunction between soul and body—would have provided Applewhite with an essential ideological component in his rethinking of the ascension scenario. In other words, after the death of Nettles, Applewhite had to come to grips with the fact that his spiritual partner—under the physical-ascension scenario that had been a cornerstone of their teachings for almost two decades—would miss the chance to escape the planet with the rest of the group. This option was, however, unimaginable to Applewhite. Hence, by the time of the mass suicide, Applewhite had reconceptualized the ascension as an event in which Heaven's Gate members let go of their physical containers and ascended *spiritually* to the waiting saucers. Once aboard, they would consciously "walk into" a new physical body and join the crew of the Next Level spacecraft. This scenario is related in one of the group's Internet statements: Their final separation is the willful separation from their human body, when they have changed enough to identify as the spirit-mind-soul—ready to put on a biological body belonging to the Kingdom of Heaven. (This entering into their "glorified," or heavenly, body takes place aboard a Next Level spacecraft, above the earth's surface.)

Presumably, these new physical bodies would be supplied to Heaven's Gate members out of some sort of "cloning bank" kept aboard the spaceships.

Another notion the Two picked up from the metaphysical subculture of their day was the ancient-astronaut hypothesis, though Applewhite and Nettles taught a slightly modified version: Aliens planted the seeds of current humanity millions of years ago and have come to reap the harvest of their work in the form of spiritually evolved individuals who will join the ranks of flying-saucer crews. Only a select few members of humanity will be chosen to advance to this transhuman state. The rest will be left to wallow in the spiritually poisoned atmosphere of a corrupt world.

Applewhite would later teach that after the elect had been picked up by the space brothers the planet would be engulfed in cataclysmic destruction. Although Applewhite's apocalyptic teachings might at first appear to be derived entirely from his biblical background, his decidedly this-worldly vision of our planet's end suggests that his ideology was influenced by the New Age subculture and by the discussions, found in contemporary popular culture, of colliding asteroids.

Yet another theme Applewhite and Nettles absorbed from the metaphysical subculture was the view that the spiritual life is a series of learning experiences culminating—in the case of Heaven's Gate—in a "graduation" to the next evolutionary kingdom. Members of the group thought of themselves as students, their fellows as classmates, and Applewhite as their tutor. These educational metaphors would have been particularly comfortable and natural for a man who had been a popular university teacher during the first part of his adult life.

Like other religious and cultural systems, the worldview of the contemporary New Age movement is held together by a shared set of symbols and metaphors—shared images of life reflected in the discourse of participants as a set of commonly used terms. For example, due partly to a vision of metaphysical unity inherited from theosophy and from Asian religious philosophy—but also due to this subculture's reaction against the perceived fragmentation and alienation of mainstream society—the New Age movement emphasizes the values of unity and relatedness. These values find expression in such common terms as "holistic," "oneness," "wholeness," and "community." This spiritual subculture also values growth and dynamism—an evaluation expressed in discourse about evolution, transformation, process, and so forth.

The image of education is related to the growth metaphor (e.g., one of our linguistic conventions is that education allows a person to grow). If we examine the metaphysical subculture through the lens of the education theme, we discover that the dominant New Age "ceremonies," in contrast to so many other religious movements, are actually workshops, lectures, and classes rather than traditional worship ceremonies. Even large New Age gatherings such as the While Life Expo resemble academic conferences more than camp meetings.

It is also interesting to note the extent to which educational metaphors inform New Age thought. In terms of the way the Western metaphysical tradition has interpreted the ongoing process of reincarnation, spiritual growth and even life itself are learning experiences. To cite some of examples of this, Katar, a New Age medium, channels such messages as, "Here on Earth, you *are* your teacher, your books, your lessons, and the classroom as well as the student." This message is amplified by J. L. Simmons, a sociologist who in *The Emerging New Age* describes life on the physical plane as the "Earth School" and asserts that "we are here to learn . . . and will continue to return until we 'do the course' and 'graduate.'" It would not be going too far to assert that in the New Age vision of things the image of the whole of human life—particularly when that life is directed toward spiritual goals—can be summed up as a learning experience:

Each of us has an Inner Teacher, a part of ourselves which knows exactly what we need to learn, and constantly creates the opportunity for us to learn just that. We have the choice either to cooperate with this part of ourselves or to ignore it. If we decide to cooperate, we can see lessons constantly in front of us; every challenge is a chance to grow and develop. If, on the other hand, we try to ignore this Inner Teacher, we can find ourselves hitting the same problem again and again, because we are not perceiving and responding to the lesson we have created for ourselves. [It] is, however, the daily awareness of and cooperation with spirit [that] pulls humanity upwards on the evolutionary spiral, and the constant invocation and evocation of spirit

enables a rapid unfolding of human potential. When the Inner Teacher and the evolutionary force of the Universe are able to work together with our full cooperation, wonders unfold. [From a flyer put out by the Findhorn Foundation in 1986]

In these passages we see not only the decisive role of the educational metaphor but also how this metaphor has itself been reshaped by the spiritual subculture's emphasis on holism and growth. In other words, the kind of education this subculture values is the "education of the whole person," sometimes termed "holistic education," and this form of education is an expression of the "evolutionary force of the Universe" (a parallel, in more traditional language, might be called the "redemptive activity of the Holy Spirit"). Thus, despite the marked tendency to deploy images drawn from the sphere of formal education—a tendency that has created a realm of discourse saturated with metaphors of classrooms, graduations, and the like—the metaphysical subculture's sense of the educational process has tended to be more informal (more or less equivalent to learning in the most general sense), as well as more continuous—a process from which there may be periodic graduations but never a final graduation after which the learning process ceases. Even for Heaven's Gate members, graduation from the earth plane represented entering a new sphere of never-ending personal evolution—the Evolutionary Kingdom Level above Human.

As is evident from even the most casual perusal of the group's writings, Heaven's Gate was dominated by the educational imagery found in the contemporaneous New Age subculture. As has already been noted, Applewhite viewed himself as a teacher: His followers were students, their spiritual process was likened to an educational process (in their "metamorphic classroom"), and their goal was frequently referred to as a "graduation." The group's writings, published on the Internet, discuss how their "Teachers" on the Next Level had an "extremely detailed lesson plan" designed for their personal growth. Then, toward the end, they received signals that their "classroom time" was over and that they were ready to graduate to the Next Level.

Thus, with the exceptions of (1) suicide being the means by which the transition to the next evolutionary sphere is to take place, and (2) the next sphere being a literal, physical realm (a spacecraft), the basic concepts informing the Heaven's Gate thought world would be recognizable to any serious metaphysical seeker. However, even the notion of a physical spaceship being a quasi-heavenly realm is already implicit in the marked tendency of the New Age movement to portray ufonauts as spiritual beings. Furthermore, the widely accepted walk-in notion provides a readily understandable mechanism by which such a transition could be accomplished.

This leaves only suicide as the one anomalous component of Applewhite's synthesis. We should note, however, that there are many phases of the New Age movement that portray death—if not suicide—in a positive light. For example, the basic metaphysical/New Age afterlife notion is reincarnation, although this process is regarded somewhat differently by the New Age than by the Asian religions from which the notion is derived. Whereas in a tradition like Buddhism reincarnation is viewed negatively—as a process that brings one back into the world to suffer—in the metaphysical subculture reincarnation is viewed as part of an extended education program stretched across many lifetimes and is thus part of a positive process. In the same vein, the interest that many participants in occult-metaphysical spirituality express in learning about their past lifetimes—in the hope of discovering that they were some famous or otherwise exalted personality—would be anathema to a traditional Buddhist.

The New Age movement is also home to advocates of conscious dying. This expression refers to an approach to dying in which death is regarded as a means of liberation of one's own consciousness—as a means of achieving enlightenment. This approach, ultimately inspired by Tibetan Buddhism, was popularized in the New Age subculture through the work of Baba Ram Das and Stephen Levine. In line with the New Age emphasis on spiritual-unfoldment-as-education, dying thus acquires a positive valence as part of the larger learning process.

Finally, it is within the metaphysical subculture that one finds the most interest in the near-death experience (NDE). That expression, sometimes called the "pseudo-death experience," refers to the seemingly supernatural experiences often undergone by individuals who have suffered apparent death and been restored to life. The main impetus for modern studies on NDEs was the publication in 1975 of the book *Life after Life* by psychiatrist Raymond A. Moody, which followed earlier researches on this topic by other physicians such as Elizabeth Kubler-Ross and Russell Noyes.

Moody's work describes the results of more than 11 years of inquiry into NDEs and is based on a sample of about 150 cases. He outlines nine elements that seem to occur generally (but not universally) in NDE experiencers. The near-death experience has attracted extensive public interest because of its seeming support for the notion of life after death. The overall picture of the dying process to emerge from NDE studies is quite positive, even attractive. Furthermore, it should also be noted that Moody's fifth trait sounds like it could have been (though I actually doubt that it was) the immediate source of Applewhite's idea that his group could die and ascend to a waiting spacecraft. Instead of a tunnel, some NDEers report rising suddenly into the heavens and seeing the earth and the celestial sphere as if they were astronauts in space.

In this regard, in another one of his books, Moody mentions an ecstatic vision Carl Jung experienced during an apparent NDE. Following a heart attack, Jung found himself 1,000 miles above the surface of the earth, on the threshold of entering a floating temple in which he would finally discover the answers to all of his questions. In this vision Jung vividly describes the terrestrial globe, his sense of letting go of everything associated with earthly life, and his sense of anticipation of the glories awaiting him upon his entrance into the temple. Finally, Jung notes his profound disappointment when his doctor brings him back to his body before he has a chance to cross the threshold.

Again, with only a little interpretation (e.g., temple equals spacecraft), the whole experience could be taken as almost a blueprint for what Heaven's Gate members believed would happened after their deaths. This is not, of course, to assert that either NDE research or the writings of Carl Jung encourage people to take their own lives. It is, however, clear that reports of NDEs, if taken seriously, paint a positive enough portrait of dying to take the sting out of death. Thus, far from being crazy or irrational, even the final dramatic exit of Heaven's Gate becomes understandable in terms of the thought world of the metaphysical subculture from which Applewhite drew his theological synthesis.

This appendix reproduces three different kinds of Heaven's Gate documents, each reflecting different aspects of the group's ideology. The first is a recruiting poster announcing a public talk. The second comes from the Heaven's Gate website. The third is a transcript of one of the group's final videotapes.

Meeting Poster

UFOs, Space Aliens, and Their
Final Flight for Earth's Spoils
All reproducing space aliens—including
mammalian—use Earth's humans simply for their
own interests (and have been for thousands of years).

- They intentionally keep humans falsely
  "programmed"—"in the dark"—primarily

through corrupt religious concepts, and secondarily, through reproductive and "humanitarian" concerns.

- They support these preoccupations by transmitting images and thoughts into Earth's atmosphere
- These "Luciferians" abduct humans for genetic experimentation, "rob" healthy human specimens for their own next "suit of clothes," and induct humans into their service.

In spite of these facts, there is a true Kingdom of "God"—a truly Evolutionary Kingdom Level Above Human, above all mammalian or any other reproductive species. It is a many-membered Kingdom that exists in the literal Heavens, with its own unique biological "containers" or bodies, and modes of travel—spacecrafts of "UFOs." It is, in fact, more physically real than the world of the space aliens or humans. This Kingdom Level created the physical world, as we know it, as a "holographic classroom," and the human-mammalian kingdom as a stepping stone. That hologram is about to be "rebooted"—canceled and restarted—for its usefulness and serviceability as a classroom has come to an end.

- All religions were designed as "prep" for this day, but the "adversary forces" have corrupted them.
- Two thousand years ago, an Older Member in the real "Kingdom of Heaven," left behind His Next Level (non-mammalian) Body and incarnated into a "picked" and "prepped" human body at approx. its 29th year. He brought with Him the souls that His Father's Kingdom had nurtured in the past, in order that He might help them incarnate and change over their bodies. That formula for being born into the Evolutionary Level Above Human requires the shedding of all human-mammalian behavior, such as all forms of sexuality; ties to family, human relationships, and possessions; addictions of all types; habits; and self-concerns.
- That formula was brought again in 1975/76 by two Older Members from that same Kingdom (who incarnated when the bodies, that were "picked" and "prepped" for them, were in their early [forties]). They took the names "Bo and Peep" and later, "Te and Do." They put out a "call" for the crew—the souls who came with them—and helped them incarnate (take over their bodies), while in isolation (separated from the world) for approx. 18 years.
- The "Older Member" of the two (Te) left His human female body in 1985, returned to the physical

Kingdom of "God" to re-enter His body in that next Evolutionary Level (from whence He still serves this project). This finds them once again, in the same relationship with the crew—and each other—that they were in 2—years ago (the "Father," His Son Jesus, and their disciples).

- That "birthing" or incarnating procedure requires "midwifing"—personal tutoring—by an Older Member from that Kingdom who is incarnate in the human kingdom. When a soul—one brought here by the Next Level—incarnates, it must take control of a body (one that was "prepped" for it) to the degree that it ceases to perform as a human, sufficiently to establish and sustain a well-founded loyalty to the Next Level through that Older Member. It is that loyalty and personal relationship with that Older Member that motivates those behavioral changes and makes that "newborn" viable.
- A very accelerated "classroom" (for incarnating), is now being offered for the third and last time in this civilization, by those representatives from the 1975/76 "yield" to the remainder of the souls that have been saved from a previous time by the Next Level. In other words, the first crew is gathering the remainder of their crew—holding meetings as of January '94—before exiting.
- If this "strikes a chord" in you, you have received a "chip" (of recognition) from the Next Level— though the hard work of "changeover" can only be done by your unending effort under the supervision of the reps here now.
- The two representatives who came in the early 1970's, and their crew (student reps), all came and will leave in spacecrafts or "clouds of light"—the same way the representatives left 2,000 years ago.

Representatives from that "Next Level" will speak at:

7 pm, Tuesday, July 26
Univ. of Illinois @ Chicago-East Campus
Behavioral Sciences Bldg, Room 140
1007 W. Harrison, Chicago

7 pm, Tuesday, July 28
Holiday Inn
1250 Roosevelt (at Finley)
Glen Ellyn, IL

Reading material will be available. Come EARLY if you want to know more about us.

FREE ADMISSION
YOUR ASSISTANCE IS WELCOME

Website Posting

What Our Purpose Is—The Simple "Bottom Line"
Two thousand years ago, a crew of members of the Kingdom of Heaven who are responsible for nurturing "gardens," determined that a percentage of the human "plants" of the present civilization of this Garden (Earth) had developed enough that some of those bodies might be ready to be used as "containers" for soul deposits. Upon instruction, a member of the Kingdom of Heaven then left behind His body in that Next Level (similar to putting it in a closet, like a suit of clothes that doesn't need to be worn for awhile), came to Earth, and moved into (or incarnated into), an adult human body (or "vehicle") that had been "prepped" for this particular task. The body that was chosen was called Jesus. The member of the Kingdom of Heaven who was instructed to incarnate into that body did so at His "Father's" (or Older Member's) instruction. He "moved into" (or took over) that body when it was 29 or 30 years old, at the time referred to as its baptism by John the Baptist (the incarnating event was depicted as " . . . the Holy Spirit descended upon Him in bodily form like a dove"—Luke 3:22). [That body (named Jesus) was tagged in its formative period to be the receptacle of a Next Level Representative, and even just that "tagging" gave that "vehicle" some unique awareness of its coming purpose.]

The sole task that was given to this member from the Kingdom of Heaven was to offer the way leading to membership into the Kingdom of Heaven to those who recognized Him for who He was and chose to follow Him. "The Kingdom of Heaven is at hand" meant "since I am here, and I am from that Kingdom, if you leave everything of this world and follow me, I can take you into my Father's Kingdom." Only those individuals who had received a "deposit" containing a soul's beginning had the capacity to believe or recognize the Kingdom of Heaven's Representative. They could get to His Father only through total reliance upon Him. He later sent His students out with the "Good news of the Kingdom of Heaven is at hand," and His followers could then help gather the "flock" so that the "Shepherd" might teach others what was required of them to enter His Father's House—His Father's Kingdom—the Kingdom of Heaven—in the literal and physical Heavens—certainly not among humans on Earth. Leaving behind this world included: family, sensuality, selfish desires, your human mind, and even your human body if it be required of you—all mammalian ways, thinking, and behavior. Since He had been through this metamorphic transition Himself from human to Level Above Human—under the guidance of His Father—He was qualified to take others through that same discipline and transition. Remember, the One who incarnated in Jesus was sent for one purpose only, to say, "If you want to go to Heaven, I can take you through that gate—it requires everything of you."

Our mission is exactly the same. I am in the same position to today's society as was the One that was in Jesus then. My being here now is actually a continuation of that last task as was promised, to those who were students 2,000 years ago. They are here again, continuing in their own overcoming, while offering the same transition to others. Our only purpose is to offer the discipline and "grafting" required of this transition into membership in My Father's House. My Father, my Older Member, came with me this time for the first half of this task to assist in the task because of its present difficulty.

Looking to us, and desiring to be a part of my Father's Kingdom, can offer to those with deposits that chance to connect with the Level Above Human, and begin that transition. Your separation from the world and reliance upon the Kingdom of Heaven through its Representatives can open to you the opportunity to become a new creature, one of the Next Evolutionary Level, rightfully belonging to the Kingdom of Heaven.

Why It Is Difficult to Believe or Accept Us

We don't know if you believe in the real existence of negative or "lower" forces. If you do, then you may be able to understand or relate to some of what we are about to say. It seems that how your "programming" permits you to see or identify those forces, determines the limit of your acceptance or understanding. Many believe that there are "evil" acts or even "evil" individuals, but would draw the line before they would believe in evil spirits, evil discarnates, negative influences, malevolent space aliens, "Luciferians," or Satan and his fallen angels.

The generally accepted "norms" of today's societies—world over—are designed, established, and maintained by the individuals who were at one time "students" of the Kingdom of Heaven—"angels" in the making—who "flunked out" of the classroom. Legends and scriptures refer to them as fallen angels. The current civilization's records use the name Satan or Lucifer to describe a single fallen angel and also to "nickname" any "evil presence." If you have experienced some of what our "classroom" requires of us, you would know that these "presences" are real and that the Kingdom of God even permits them to "attack" us in order for us to learn their tricks and how to stay above them or conquer them. The space aliens, or Luciferians, use the discarnate spirits (the minds that are disembodied at the death of a body) as their primary servants—against potential members of the Kingdom of God. These "influences," or discarnates, are constantly "programming" every human "plant" (vehicle or body), to accept a set of beliefs and norms for behavior during a lifetime. From our point of view, this "programming" finds that body, and the vast majority of all human bodies, barely usable by students of the Kingdom of Heaven.

As the above example can serve to testify, the "lower forces" would—through their "norm" concept—what is "socially acceptable," what is politically correct— have you not believe in spirits, spirit possession, negative space aliens, Satan, etc. They would have you believe that to even dabble in these ideas is of the "occult," satanic, or at the least, giving credence to "fringe" topics. That's where they would also categorize any mental search of Eastern religions, astrology, metaphysics, paranormal, UFOs, etc., etc. In other words, they (these space aliens) don't want themselves "found out," so they condemn any exploration. They want you to be a perfect servant to society (THEIR society—of THEIR world)—to the "acceptable establishment," to humanity, and to false religious concepts. Part of that "stay blinded" formula goes like this: "Above all, be married, a good parent, a reasonable churchgoer, buy a house, pay your mortgage, pay your insurance, have a good line of credit, be socially committed, and graciously accept death with the hope that 'through His shed blood,' or some other equally worthless religious precept, you will go to Heaven after your death."

Many segments of society, especially segments of the religious, think that they are not "of the world," but rather that their "conversion" experience finds them "outside of worldliness." The next statement that we will make will be the "Big Tester," the one that the "lower forces" would use to clearly have you discredit or disregard us. That statement is: Unless you are currently an active student or are attempting to become a student of the present Representative from the Kingdom of Heaven—you ARE STILL "of the world," having done no significant separation from worldliness, and you are still serving the opposition to the Kingdom of Heaven. This statement sounds—to humans who have been so carefully programmed by the "lower forces"—arrogant, pompous, or egotistical at the least—as if by taking this stand we had something to gain—as if we were seeking recognition as "Deity" or as self-appointed prophets.

That Luciferian programming has truly been effective, for we don't even want to voice to you the statement in question. However, believe it or not, it is only for your sake—the sake of prospective recipients of the Kingdom of Heaven—that we must "tell the truth," openly identify to you as Representatives of the Kingdom of Heaven, well aware of the "fallout" of that position.

The hard facts or bold statements in a nutshell, that are so difficult to accept or "digest"—come down to: If you want or ever expect to go to Heaven—here is your window. That window opportunity requires: 1) an incarnate (as human) Representative of the Kingdom of Heaven; 2) that all who hope to enter Heaven become active students of that Representative while the Representative is present; 3) those who endure the "transition classroom" until it ends (adequately bonding or "grafting" to that Representative) will go with that Representative—literally LEAVE the human kingdom and Earth as He is about to do. Staying behind, for any significant period, could jeopardize that "graft." That window to Heaven will not open again until another civilization is planted and has reached sufficient maturity (according to the judgment of the Next Level).

We can't blame you for "buying into" the "Luciferian" program. What else has been available during those periods when no Representative was present? Almost nothing—save some warnings in the Scriptures, i.e., Luke 20:34–36, Luke 21:23, Mark 12:25, and Mark 13:17–19. Check these out.

Another fact is that what someone is into during the time a Representative is not present really doesn't matter that much, except that they are found unprepared when One comes—the only time when the Kingdom of Heaven can be offered to you.

The dilemma is we are here and most humans are thoroughly "hooked" to humanity. However, the same "grace" that was available at the end of the Representative's mission 2,000 years ago is available now with our presence. If you quickly choose to take these steps toward separating from the world, and look to us for help, you will see our Father's Kingdom.

It is clear to all of us, that to the Anti-Christ—those propagators of sustained faithfulness to mammalian humanism—we are, and will be seen as, their Anti-Christ. This is certainly to be expected, and it will not delay our return to our Father's Kingdom. It might even accelerate that return.

We will, between now and our departure, do everything we can for those who want to go with us.

But we cannot allow them to interfere with or delay our return to Him.

The Present Representative
Do

Videotape Transcript, October 5, 1996

Planet about to Be Recycled—Your Only Chance to Survive—Leave with Us

This is a very exciting time for us. Who is us? I'm "Do" [pronounced "Doe"] for starters, and I have in front of me a number of students, or my classroom, or in old language of a couple of thousand years ago, my disciples—those who are trying to prepare themselves for entry into the Evolutionary Level Above Human, synonymous with the Kingdom of God, the Kingdom of Heaven. We're going to talk to you about the most urgent thing that is on our mind, and what we suspect is the most urgent thing on the minds of those who will connect with us.

We'll title this tape, "Planet Earth about to be Recycled—Your Only Chance to Evacuate Is to Leave with Us." Planet Earth about to be recycled—Your only chance to survive or evacuate is to leave with us. Now, that's a pretty drastic statement—pretty bold—in terms of religion, in terms of anybody's intelligent thinking. To most people who would consider themselves intelligent beings, they'd say, "Well, that's absurd. What's all this doomsday stuff? What's all this prophetic, apocalyptic talk?" You know, intelligent human beings should realize that all things have their own cycle. They have their season. They have their beginning, they have their end. We're not saying that planet Earth is coming to an end. We're saying that planet Earth is about to be refurbished, spaded under, and have another chance to serve as a garden for a future human civilization.

Now, the reason this is such an interesting time is not only because we're on the threshold of the end of this civilization (because it's about to be recycled), but because of where that finds us, and where that finds you—where that finds those who would judge us— how we would speak of them, and how they would speak of us. Now, you might say, "You keep saying 'us'? Who do you think you are?" Well, I, in all honesty, to address that must first acknowledge who my Father is. My Father is not a human father. My Father is a member of the Evolutionary Level Above Human—the Kingdom of God—the Kingdom of Heaven. My Father—long before this civilization began—gave me birth into that Kingdom Level Above Human, that Kingdom of Heaven, that Kingdom of God.

Now, you can say, "I can't believe that!" Well, it's up to you whether you believe that or not. That's not important to me, even though I wish that you could believe it for your sake. For those who do believe it stand a possibility of having a future beyond this recycling time. Now, you say, "According to religious literature, I thought there was someone else who was going to come and be our "Savior" here at these last days—that that was going to be Christ's return?" Well, the name "Christ" or the name "Jesus" might be a little confusing. Because the name "Jesus," of course, was merely the name given to the body that that mind (that was indeed from the Kingdom of Heaven) incarnated into. That mind was here 2,000 years ago, and that mind came for the express purpose of teaching humans how they could be "saved"- how they would not be plowed under at the End of the Age. Well, we're now at the End of the Age. So that mind that was in Jesus—What? That mind, that spirit, that soul is me, and in this body called "Do" that you're looking at? You'll have to decide that for yourself. I must admit that I am here again. That I'm here saying exactly the same thing that I said then, trying to say it in today's language, trying to hope that, for your sakes, you can see what we have to offer you. For the Next Level, through my Father and through me, is offering you LIFE for the first time—and we're not talking about human life.

Now, the planet is about to be recycled, and we say we see the planet as a steppingstone—planet Earth as a steppingstone. Just as with a civilization, that civilization can evolve upwards—each segment within that civilization has the option to become more civilized, less barbaric. It would be better for them if they took more civilized options. Not that they necessarily do. Sometimes they seem to appear to be more civilized when, in fact, they have become more barbaric, more quick to condemn the rest of the world, more quick to kill the rest of the world that does not think as they think.

Well, I know what I said a few moments ago. I said that I am the return of the Son of my Father. I'll tell you something that's even more remarkable: my Father came with me this time. He came in the early '70's, took on a human form—an adult female human form. He helped me "get into" an adult human form, in the early '70's. And we together helped those who came with us (our students, who were also here 2,000 years ago as disciples) get in the bodies that they are presently wearing—so that they could rid themselves of human behavior, human activity, human thinking—so that they could be ready at this time to move into the

Kingdom of Heaven or the Evolutionary Level Above Human.

These that are sitting before me have been students of Ti and Do—Ti, my Father—and they are still students of Ti and Do, even though Ti returned to the Heavens in 1985. Ti is my Heavenly Father and is the One who gave me birth into that Kingdom before this civilization began. Now, I'm not here to sell you on that, or who I am or who these are. I'm here to offer you, as these are, an opportunity to know the Truth, so that if you can connect with it, at any level, then you might survive the re-spading or the recycling that is about to occur.

We made a tape just shortly ago, and in that tape we said that there are three types of individuals who will survive the recycling. One type is those individuals who have overcome their humanness enough that when the End of this Age is complete, when the war is over (the spading complete, there is nothing left here except for recycling), when the end of that occurs, that first type will have reached a condition of having overcome human behavior, human thinking, human desires—desiring only to be in the Kingdom of Heaven, in the Evolutionary Level Above Human, being of service in that Kingdom. When they have done that overcoming to that degree, at that point they are a match for a physical body belonging to that Kingdom.

Humans think that this is a flesh body world, and it is. But, more importantly, it is a human flesh body world. The Kingdom of God, the Kingdom of Heaven, the Evolutionary Level Above Human also has bodies. I wouldn't say flesh bodies because they have different characteristics. But it is a physical body, a biological body, and in a sense, it is equivalent to a human body for that next Evolutionary Level. It doesn't need the kind of fuel that humans need, for it's not a mammalian body. It doesn't reproduce. It's not male nor female. It probably would look like what you might consider a very attractive "extraterrestrial." Most of the illustrations of extraterrestrials these days have been grotesque—looked like giant insects, or slimy reptilians, or have eyes so big that you could fall into them. An extraterrestrial that we would consider a genuine extraterrestrial is not a "fallen angel," is not a "space alien."

We see fallen angels and space aliens as synonymous—fallen angels and space aliens are synonymous. And the Next Level—the only real extraterrestrials—have a body similar to the human body. The human body was made from the same basic design, the same general form, except the human body is more animal than that Next Level form. The human body has hair, needs teeth, has physical characteristics that are appropriate to this environment. When you go into an environment that does not require eating things that you have to pull off the bone, or crack the shells off the nut, then certainly teeth are not needed. A Next Level body in a non-earthly environment also needs no hair. That Next Level body is a creature that looks very attractive, has two eyes, some remnant of a nose, some remnant of ears—what you would call remnants—even though they function very well as nose, as ears. They have a voice box, but don't really need to use it, for they can communicate by thought—communicate with their minds. And that's an extraterrestrial—that is the "body" belonging to a member of the Evolutionary Level Above Human, the Kingdom of Heaven, the Kingdom of God. It's true, they could seem unattractive to you if you're really "into" human flesh bodies and see them as beautiful.

You know, there are sayings that there is seed of flesh, or there are things that are born of flesh, and there are things that are born of spirit. Also, born of water is synonymous with being born of flesh. If people really understood the more accurate of the religious literature, and could read it as it was intended to be read, they would know it clarifies that seed of flesh (human) was and is, literally, seed of the negative, the opposition, the space aliens, the fallen angels. Therefore, to the Next Level, human flesh has become a product of the lower forces, and is of the kingdom level beneath the Kingdom of God—that kingdom level that rightfully should be only a steppingstone leading to the Kingdom of Heaven.

Now, this understanding isn't meant to put you down or to say that an individual is necessarily "evil" just because they're wearing a human vehicle. I'm wearing a human vehicle, because I have to wear one for this task. I don't like it. It doesn't match me. And those who sit in front of me don't like their human vehicles that they have to wear for this task. But they have to wear them, because the task of overcoming the human kingdom requires that they overcome human flesh—the genetic vibrations, the lust of the flesh, the desire to reproduce, the desire to cling to offspring, or spouse, or parents, or house, or money, or fame, or job, or, or—that could go on and on—overcoming the human flesh and its desires—even its religious desires. There is not a religion on the face of the globe that is of God, as it is today. All of those ideologies that are called religions use corrupted records and corrupted interpretations of man's relationship with someone from the Kingdom of God, the Evolutionary Level Above Human.

In other words, it's like the religious literature (the Bible, the Torah, the Koran, etc.) are written as time manuals. So that ancient religious literature, with its laws and rules, was appropriate to the time that it was written in and to that phase of civilization. Less ancient literature, with its laws, was appropriate to its own particular age. What did the "Lord" God—the one who was here long before the Messiah came—say to His people? Through His prophets, He said, "I will send a Savior, a Messiah to help you get out of the human kingdom," knowing that some humans should certainly reach a condition where they would be ready to move up into His Kingdom by that period in time when His Representative—the Messiah—would be sent. When the One He sent came as the "Messiah," truly some in the civilization at that time were prepared for the information—the steps, the requirements—that that Messiah had to offer to those who would seek His Father's Kingdom.

Well, that Savior came, that Messiah came. And after a brief teaching period with those He picked—those who were His disciples/students—He said, "I will come again." And His Father sent Him again. And for me to say that I was and am He, is to most, utter blasphemy. In other words, what I say to you now is a direct, present, current transmission—information from the Kingdom Level of My Father, the Level Above Human, the Kingdom of God, the Kingdom of Heaven.

Today's Christians say they are Christians and think they are Christians. And yet they seldom quote the most important things that Jesus said. Jesus said, "If you want to know My Father, if you want to move into My Father's Kingdom, then shed everything of this world—leave everything behind—and come and follow Me. And unless you hate everything of this world, your sister, your mother, your brother—everything of this world—you will not know the Kingdom of Heaven. You have to graft to Me, you have to cling to Me, if I am to literally take you into My Father's house." Most Christians, world over, mostly frequently quote Paul—who never sat with that Representative (Jesus), nor was Paul ever a student of that Representative. Christians say, "Oh, I love Jesus. He's in my heart. I'm filled with Jesus. Jesus wants me to live an abundant human life. He wants me to have riches. He wants me to have more children so that I can bring them up with Christian family values." I don't remember Jesus ever saying that, "What I want you to do is to go get married, have families, have children, and together bring all of them and I will take them into the Kingdom of Heaven." He only spoke to individuals—and said, "The only way out of here is for you to know that as an individual this human world is not for you—that tie that binds you to the human kingdom is not for you. If you know it is not for you, then come to Me—and My Father will feed Me information that can nourish you—and help you overcome this world—and we'll leave this world, and we'll go to My Father's Kingdom."

Remember, we're not talking about a spiritual kingdom—no clouds, no harps—even though we are talking about in the heavens. But the Heavens are no more spiritual than when you go out at night and look at the Heavenly bodies and see them. They are literally there. They are physical. My Father's Kingdom also moves or travels in spacecrafts (some of which are even organic). You could say, "Oh, my goodness, that's outrageous." Well, you don't like the illustrations of chariots of fire or wheel within a wheel? You don't like the illustrations that are in your religious literature that tell of spacecrafts of my Father's Kingdom? "Clouds of light"—at that time they didn't know what else to call them. Even when they saw angels that they said had wings—how else could they have described that they fly? That didn't necessarily mean they had feathers on their backs (though that possibility exists as well). Certainly some of these illustrations mean that they came to Earth in a flying object and they left aboard that flying object. And when they saw Jesus ascend, they said, "He went up into that cloud of light."

Now, I'm not trying to make a big deal over the means of transportation issue. For a spacecraft—belonging to the Level Above Human—is much more than a piece of transportation. It is a very valuable work station. It is commonly a place of service to the Level Above Human. These students that are leaving this kingdom level to go with me to my Father's Kingdom, to my Father's house, these will not go into houses on some planet like Earth, and reproduce, and have families and sit and watch television and make scrambled eggs. They're going to be genderless individuals, in service—full time—for whatever need the Level Above Human, the Kingdom of Heaven has for them. And the tools they use, the workstations that they use are spacecrafts—all sizes. Spacecrafts that are so small that a very small crew could fit into them because that small spacecraft is best suited for that given task. Spacecrafts that are so large you can't even see the outer extremities of them. They could look like something larger than a planet to the observers, because that size craft is best suited for whatever laboratory work or experimentation is going on. All sizes are used for a variety of purposes.

How can these students be effective servants in that Kingdom if they're worried about their children, or their dogs, or their horses, or their cats, or how much time they have to put in at the Rotary, or such things as that. As individuals they serve one or two individuals—older Representatives of that Next Kingdom—who are their instructors for their assigned tasks. Just as in the task that we're in now with this classroom—these look to me as their Older Member, their instructor, for everything. I look to my Older Member for everything—to fill me in on what these students' needs are and how I might be used to instruct them. I'm not just talking about their physical needs, but their mental/spirit/soul needs—how they can most effectively make their change from human into the Kingdom Level Above Human.

Now, this is not to say that we know that there is a guarantee that we will all go on board a craft together, in order to leave before this spading under occurs. We will definitely go on board a craft to leave before the "spading under" occurs. You could say, "Well, what's the difference?" Well, the difference is that we don't yet know if we are going to take these flesh bodies on board that craft or if we will leave these flesh bodies behind before we board. We don't believe that Our Father's Kingdom has much need for these flesh bodies. But, it's possible that a spacecraft will come down, and we'll walk on board that craft, and they'll take these bodies from us, and issue us the ones that belong to that Level so that we might begin our service. It is also possible that part of our test of faith is our hating this world, even our flesh body, to the extent to be willing to leave it without any proof of the Next Level's existence, other than what we have come to know: that we have nothing to fear; that we are in Good keeping; that we can leave the body that we're in and Be that soul, that identity, which totally survives that separation—whether it is by martyrdom, because someone went crazy over our "righteous blasphemy," or whatever event that might separate us from that human body that we are wearing. Our faith is primarily based upon our trust in our Older Members. We do know one thing—we don't care to cling to the life of this body until it naturally "gives up." We don't care to be aborted by the body that we're wearing. We care more to abort it in proof to our Heavenly Father that we trust Him and are ready to leave this place. We're ready to go into His Kingdom. And they, these students, have to say to my Father, "We trust your Son. We trust the One You sent for our sakes. Even so much that we have no hesitation to leave this place—to leave the body that we are wearing. We know that whatever happens to us

after we leave this body is a step forward from what we were, and that we don't care to be here any longer."

Earlier in this tape I spoke to you of three types of individuals who can be salvaged from this re-spading. One type that I mentioned was those who have overcome enough that they will get an issue of a physical body belonging to the Next Level, and go into service, as a crew member, working for the Next Level. A second type of individual that can be salvaged from this planet at this time are those who don't quite reach that point of overcoming by the time it is time to leave. But they are still faithful to the best of their ability in their effort of breaking away, leaving their humanity, and looking to us—looking to me, looking to my Father, looking to the Next Level—to give them the strength and the understanding of how they can break away more quickly. So wherever they are, to the best of their capability, at the time of our exit, even if they are not ready for issue of a Next Level body—they may have to experience a time in a civilization that is yet to come and do more overcoming of the human kingdom. But they will be in the keeping of the Kingdom Level Above Human, just as these have been in the keeping of the Kingdom Level Above Human—not just here at this time, in this generation, with me and with Ti.

"Ti" isn't Ti's name, by the way. "Do" isn't Do's name. I'm not even given to tell you what my name or Ti's name is. The Next Level wouldn't have humans know what our real names are. I had to put that in for the record, so that you would understand.

Back to the previous subject, the second type of individual who can go into the Kingdom of Heaven is one who, at the time we leave, has not completed their human overcoming to the satisfaction of the Next Level, and therefore the Next Level will bring them back when a civilization is at its development point to be a "match"—at the point where those individuals might pick up where they left off. Then they will reach "issue time" for a Next Level body by or before the end of the next civilization.

The third type of soul or individual who can go to the Kingdom of Heaven now, with us, and be in the keeping of that Kingdom, are those who either hear our voice right at the end of our task, or have received this information and don't know where it's coming from. In other words, some might hear our voice and might know where it is coming from, might know that I exist in physical form here, about to leave. Others might not make contact, but something tells them, "I've got to break away, I can't stand to stay here. I've got to put my life on the line for the Kingdom of Heaven."

The lower forces' whole effort is to have potential members of the Next Level not succeed in remaining faithful to the end so that they might prevent them from coming into the keeping of the Kingdom of God, the Kingdom of Heaven.

So, here we are. We're going public with this information once again, right before we leave. This is like putting ourselves right out on the chopping block where the lower forces will have a chance to try to demean us, have the world turn against us, and try to do us in. It will challenge all those who are religious minded to look at us and say, "Hmmm, how could that possibly be the Truth, is this not the Anti-Christ or the spurious Messiah?" "Spurious Messiah" is the term that some prominent television/satellite ministries use in describing the Anti-Christ, who, they say, is to arrive on the scene before Christ returns. So, in their eyes, since the Anti-Christ has not yet arrived, then Christ's return must be at a later time. Well, I hate to tell you, but the Anti-Christ—the spurious Messiah—has been on the scene ever since my Father and I left 2,000 years ago. And he and his helpers have worked as hard as they could through religions, through governments, through "acceptable" morality, through "responsibility as a human," to brainwash humans to expect "Heaven on Earth." Those lower forces have "programmed" humans, especially Christians, to see our arrival "on the scene" as the Anti-Christ. Those fallen angels—those humanoid space aliens—would have humans not look to or expect to go to a Kingdom of Heaven, but to look for a Heaven on Earth—where they might reign as your Christ—to work toward the future—to be preoccupied with replicating or reproducing children—and laying aside enough money to take care of those children so that they will have a future, and they will have a future, and they will have a future. A future in what?—the human kingdom? What an abomination! To the Next Level the human kingdom is, at its best, nothing more than a potential steppingstone. It's clear that anyone who wants to stay in the human kingdom—and make it some sort of divinity—is looking to some "spurious Messiah," an anti-Christ indeed.

Now, I know that those who are expecting the arrival of the "spurious Messiah"—"the anti-Christ"—if they become aware of this tape and of Do sitting here saying what I'm saying now, they'll say, "That's the one. Because I warned you that the spurious Messiah would say, 'I'll take you out of here. I'll rapture you into my Father's Kingdom.'" And that's what I'm saying. I'm saying that, "If you can believe my Father's information, if you can believe the Truth that we share

with you, and if you believe it enough that you can put your trust in me—and that could be a "big dose" for some—you will soon find yourself in the safekeeping of the Kingdom of Heaven." These students in front of me know me well. If you have some of my Father's mind in you, you can have recognition as well, even with only this brief viewing, though I'll remind you that the lower forces will do everything they can to have you lose or doubt that recognition.

We have a website now, you know, it's the popular thing—everybody has to have a website. Our website on the Internet is called Heaven's Gate. Heaven's Gate—oh, of course, .com. Everything is .com. We're not .org, we're .com. So if you want to, you can learn more about who we are, what we have to say, what I have to say, what my Older Members can share with you through what we have said, and know of our history. We have nothing to hide. Even though to some, we might be a dangerous cult. We understand that. Why dangerous? Because we threaten the family, we threaten the established norm of family values. If you knew Jesus 2,000 years ago, you would know that exactly the same thing occurred. And that the reason for getting rid of Him was because if people really began to follow Him to any significant degree, it would threaten the political, and certainly the religious norm. His teachings were clearly against what the mainstream was teaching, what the norm was in the governments or the family, and certainly against the religion of that time.

Religion today is an interesting thing. Remember how we said a moment ago that the religious literature like the Bible, the Koran, the Torah, are time manuals. In the time that something was written, as the Lord or as God related to man, it was appropriate for them at that time. And yet we have the bulk (if not the vast majority) of humans on the planet today who are very religious living exactly as they were trying to live some 5,000 years ago, or some 4,000 years ago. They never made it to 2,000 years ago. But 2,000 years ago, a chance to get out of here, was available to those who listened to what the Next Level's Representative had to say. A chance to get out of here—out of the human kingdom—whenever it is offered, requires everything of you—that you, as an individual, go join some cult—that you leave everything behind—that you ignore the members of your family—that you ignore the responsibility to your community—that you ignore your career—and that hearts will be broken.

I don't mean to make light of that, "that hearts will be broken." I know that hearts are broken. I also know that anyone who leaves to go to my Father's Kingdom, that any heart that is broken in the process of that transition, can easily be more than healed, if that heart looks to my Father for healing, and looks to my Father for understanding. That soul does not need to see this as a terrible experience. Many times, the worst things in the human kingdom that can happen to us, end up being the best things that could happen to us. Because we learn "in depth" lessons as a result of those difficult times. Every life that was touched by these who are sitting in front of me—every life that was hurt or experienced pain by their leaving and becoming students of mine and of my Father's—was hurt, severely hurt. Some of them still hurt. They could actually say, "Thank you, God, for the lesson that is mine to learn in this experience. And as far as that individual that I used to call my son or daughter, or my husband or wife, I put them in Your trust. I cannot tell them what they must do with their life. That is their decision."

We cannot judge each other. I cannot judge you. I don't care to judge you. You will judge yourselves by how you respond to what we have to say, by what you can accept and what you can't. In some cases, it's almost better that you never see me, or hear what we say, for that will put you to the test of whether or not you will condemn me, whether or not you will judge me. You cannot hurt me. You cannot hurt these. We can only be hurt if we displease our Heavenly Father.

It's funny that the world—the mainstream human world—is so quick to condemn and judge (those who are not like them) as if they were God Almighty. They would also judge those who would follow us, determining the worthlessness of any that would join some cult, assuming that that is the worst thing that anyone could possibly do, for they are being brainwashed and led down the wrong track into some occult camp, and they're going to the devil. What is the devil like? Know your literature. What do the fallen angels like? They like the pleasures of the human flesh—the aspirations of this world.

What is told to you in all religious literature—that you will find if you ever reach the Kingdom of Heaven? There, there will be no males, no females, no children, no families other than your relationship with God—your Lord. Your Lord is whichever Member of His Kingdom He has given to you, assigned to you as your Helper, your Instructor, your Teacher. This is so simple that it sounds unreal—unspiritual. This information would be easier to accept if it were more spiritual, if it were more complicated, if it had more ritual with it, or more trappings of religion. In my Father's house, no incense is required, no flowing robes, no tinkling bells,

no genuflecting, no sitting in the lotus position, no things of "spirituality," even though our Father's Kingdom requires cleansing of the spirit/the mind. It requires ridding ourselves of the mind of the human kingdom—ridding ourselves of the lusts of the human world, and of the binds to the human level.

"Being filled with spirit" is an interesting thing for you to think about. What happened when the illustration was made that Jesus was with John the Baptist, and was being baptized, and a dove descended and He was "filled with the Holy Spirit"? "Filled with the Holy Spirit" meant that the major portion of Jesus' mind, His Next Level identity, was entering the body that He was wearing to the degree that the vehicle's human mind was no longer affecting Him—He had aborted that mind of the human kingdom. He was "filled" with the mind of His Father. The mind of His Father is "Holy Spirit." Any mind of the Level Above Human is pure Spirit—is Holy Spirit. To think of "being filled with the Holy Spirit" as something that comes-and-knocks-you-down-and-makes-you-fall-on-the-floor-because-somebody-is-trying-to-heal-your-broken-knee, is an abomination. It is anything but the "Holy Spirit" that you're being "filled with." Likewise, to "babble" in some indiscernible "mumbo-jumbo" and call it "speaking in tongues" or "being filled with the Holy Spirit" is also an outrage. It might be an experience of being "filled with the spirit," but it certainly is not the Holy Spirit.

You know, a soul is another very interesting thing, because my Father's Kingdom plants souls. And souls become the great separator as they are planted. My Father's Kingdom plants souls in many humans each time a Representative of the Kingdom Level Above Human is to be incarnate on planet Earth—plants many souls in many human plants. Now, even though they're planted in the flesh, because the flesh is what has to be overcome, they are really planted in the spirit of that flesh. The spirit being the mind or the intelligence of that flesh. And you can say, "Well, does that mean that everybody doesn't have a soul?" Yes, that's exactly what it means. But it also means that anybody can have a soul that can believe in my Father—the reality of my Father, the reality of His Son, and the reality of His Kingdom.

In other words, those who are given the responsibility and the task of planting those souls, plant them in all of the human plants who have a potential of making that step—using that steppingstone—and getting out of the human kingdom and into that Next Kingdom Level. That soul, as the separator, helps the individual, in their mind (in their spirit), abort human thinking, human evaluation, human behavior, and replace it with the mind that they get from the Representatives—the mind of the Next Level—fill it up, fill it up, fill it up. When it is so filled and enough aborting of human mind has occurred—then that individual has come into viability—has come into bloom enough that that individual is ready to go to "quartermaster" when they leave this planet, and be issued a body, of service, belonging to the Kingdom of my Father.

Now, let me say this: all human plants—even in their genetic structure—have a little bit of Heavenly mind, or mind of the Kingdom of God, mind of the Evolutionary Level Above Human (I have to say all of those each time I say it, just to remind you I'm talking about the same thing). Each human plant has a little bit of that Next Level mind in it. So theoretically, and this is true, that if there is a human listening to me who, in fact, may not at this moment have a soul, but that plant listens to me, and says, "Could it be true, what Do is saying? It sounds crazy, but I wonder if that's true?" Even that degree of curiosity would attract the attention of the Next Level crew which is assigned to planting souls. That crew will be sure that a separator (a soul) is immediately made available to that individual. So that deposit of a soul could happen very, very quickly. They're not going to let it happen, that any potential recipients of their Kingdom not have the needed receptacle of Next Level spirit coming into full blossom as pure spirit, pure mind, of the Kingdom of Heaven.

Now, let's go back to the topic of urgency. I don't know if you are aware that a great deal of literature used by many scholars today, says that the calendar that humans use is off by 4 years. And that Jesus was born in 4 B.C. Now, if Jesus was born in 4 B.C., and this is [1996] A.D., could this be the year 2000—the millennium, the beginning of the end? That's why we're talking. For us to surface with who we are and the information that we are surfacing with, we know, could challenge you to want to squelch us. It's interesting that we see the world—we see the world—as the anti-Truth, the anti-Christ, the spurious Messiah. The world—those who want to stay in the world—will see us as anti-Truth, anti-Christ, spurious Messiah. We're prepared for that. We know that that is inevitable at this time. That was inevitable 2,000 years ago—that is what found Jesus sentenced to die on a cross.

Remember, we said that the third type of person who can actually be salvaged at the end, can be taken into the keeping of the Next Level, simply because they believe in what we say. That simple belief is what

occurred in the mind of the thief who was on the cross next to Jesus. When Jesus recognized his belief, He told him that, "this day he would, upon their departure, be with Him in paradise." He knew that he seriously believed. And He knew that is all that it took—is for him to believe who He was. Even believing Him in a condition when He was being killed as a heretic—against the Church, against the system. The Church today certainly will see us as against the Church. The Church of today is not of God. Though once the true followers—the Church—were of God. The only true Church of today are those who are connected with the present existence of the Next Level, the Kingdom of God, the Kingdom of Heaven—and the Representative from that Kingdom.

This time is so exciting to us, even though we know that it is close to our end, and that is why it is exciting to us. We don't expect to or want to build a Church on this planet. We don't want any gothic Cathedral. We don't want any membership roll. We don't want to help you reproduce so that we have more children to put on the Sunday school roll in our Church. We are a group of believers in the Kingdom Level Above Human, who want to leave and enter that Kingdom, and become of significant service to that Kingdom.

This does not mean that when in the human kingdom, that a strong humanitarian drive is not a healthy thing. Because really a strong humanitarian drive is motivated to improve. But if you could only see that a human condition is a temporary condition, a steppingstone, an opportunity to get out of this kingdom, then you could accept this Truth. This is as scientific—this is as true as true could be—but you have to know me, you have to trust me, you have to believe me. Some can know me now. Some can even know me for the first time when they see this tape and say, "I don't know what there is, but there's something in my head that makes me know that fellow, and makes me know that what he's saying is true. And I may be wrong, but I'm going to try to find more out and see if that's what I need to be a part of. Because I know that this Earth has become something that is not where I belong."

It's funny—not funny—it's really sad that a segment of my Father's Kingdom, in particular my personal Heavenly Father, related to a community that is today considered the early Jewish community, and worked with them preparing them for my presence here 2,000 years ago and now. And yet, the Jewish community of then and now, would certainly see me as anything but a Representative of God. The Muslims, who are considered by some to be the enemy of the Judeo-Christians, many of them have sustained a more real connection with God—with some higher standards of behavior, and with more restraint. You know, one of my students reminded me just today that they came in contact with a Muslim who said, "Look, you know you people of the West have a wrong idea of what we are. We don't praise Mohammed. We don't worship Mohammed. We consider Mohammed a prophet of many prophets. Many of the books of our literature are about Jesus. And I say, 'Great is God' more than 50 times a day, because God means so much to me." God means so much to many of them that they are more modest in the clothing that they wear. Many are more on guard against sensuality and "worldly" things. God means so much to many of them that they are willing to die for God and justify that frame of mind more quickly than they would a willingness to die for nation, or die for world. I'm not saying that Muslims are the ones who are going to inherit God's Kingdom any more than anyone else. In the eyes of the Kingdom of Heaven, there's no such thing as race or color or religious background. It doesn't matter—none of it matters. If the extent of your religious background was Star Trek—that in itself could be the best background you could have, if you could accept this as Truth, if you could accept this as reality.

This is a test time. You could easily say, "Here's a little bitty classroom, with some old fellow with a prune face sitting here, calling himself Do, saying, 'I'm a Representative of the Kingdom of God.' How can I believe that?" If you have some of my Father's mind in you, you will have some recognition of us and this information. Even though once you recognize me, the forces of this world will dive in with all their might to have you lose that recognition, to have you not trust me, to have you come to your senses, and come back into the service of this world.

I hope this tape session with you will be the beginning of our relationship. If this tape session is used to validate your seeing us as anti-God, the Anti-Christ, so be it. That's part of what we expect. That's part of the necessity of what comes at this time. It's the common thing for us to see each other as opposites of what we believe we are.

I'm so happy, because my time is short here. If you come with us, your time here can be shortened. When Jesus left 2,000 years ago—or the one who was in Jesus, or when I left 2,000 years ago—only a very short time after that, Truth was significantly corrupted. So that no matter who tried to use the name of "Jesus," or of "Christ," or His information—seeing it as true, seeing it as real, referring to what had been said of what it takes to come into my Kingdom—that fell apart, that deteriorated, that became unimportant. It's a miracle that His Teachings can still be found in the gospels—they're still there—you'd be amazed, you should read them again. Likewise this time, after I'm gone, when we leave, when we enter into my Father's spacecraft in order to go into service in His Kingdom, the Truth will deteriorate as fast as we depart. It will leave this atmosphere within a very short time.

I hope for your sake that you will, at least, ponder this—don't ask your neighbors, your friends, what they think of this. Instead, go into the privacy of your "closet" and see if you can connect with the purest, highest source that you might consider "God," and ask: "What about this? Is this information for real? Is this for me? If it is, then please give me the strength I need to pursue it." As soon as you tell anyone else, they will likely be used by the lower forces as their instruments to have you not believe, to have you stay in this world and wait for the "Heaven on Earth."

We hope to be of some service to you in this short time before our departure. We believe it to be a very short time. So our thoughts will be of you. We hope that your thoughts will be of our Father's Kingdom.

APPENDIX C: UFO-RELATED
ORGANIZATIONS AND PERIODICALS

Aerial Anomalies International
Robert D. Boyd, director
Box 66404
Mobile, AL 36606

Alien Spacecraft and Planetary Data
John R. Frick, director
Box 0705
Melbourne, FL 32902

Ancient Astronaut Society
Gene M. Phillips, director
1921 St. Johns Avenue
Highland Park, IL 60035
Publishes *Ancient Skies*

The Anomalist
Patrick Huyghe and Dennis Stacy, editors
Box 577
Jefferson Valley, NY 10535

Anomaly Research Centre
Mark Moravec, director
104 Howitt Street
Ballarat, Victoria 3350, Australia
Publishes *UFO Report Survey* and *Project OVNI Update*

Arcturus Book Service
Box 831383
Stone Mountain, GA 30083

Athene Newsletter
Endymion Beer, editor
Tawside, 30 Part Avenue
Barnstaple, Devonshire EX31 2ES, UK

Australian International UFO Flying Saucer Research,
    Inc.
Colin Norris, director
Unit 3/114 Cross Road
Highgate, South Australia 5063, Australia
Publishes *National International*

Borderland Sciences Research Foundation
Riley Hansard Crabb, director
Box 429
Garberville, CA 95440
Publishes *Journal of Borderland Research*

Center for Scientific Anomalies Research
Marcello Tuzzi, director
Department of Sociology/Eastern Michigan University
Ypsilanti, MI 48197
Publishes *Zetetic Scholor*

Center for the Study of Extraterrestrial Intelligence
Steven Greer, director
Box 15401
Ashville, NC 28813
Publishes *CSETI Newsletter*

Citizens Against UFO Secrecy
Barry Greenwood, editor
Box 176
Stoneham, MA 02180
Publishes *Just Cause*

Committee for the Scientific Investigation of Claims of
    the Paranormal
Paul Kurtz, chairman
Box 703
Buffalo, NY 14226
Publishes *Skeptical Inquirer*
Kendrick Frazier, editor

Communion Foundation
Whitley Strieber, director
Box 1975
Boulder, CO 80306

Contact International
J.Bernard Delair, president
Box 23
Wheatley, Oxfordshire OX311FL, UK
Publishes *Awareness*

Geoffrey Ambler, editor
Also publishes *UFO Register*
Francis Copeland, editor

Earth Star Publications
Ann Ulrich, editor
Box 117
Paonia, CO 81428
Publishes *The Star Beacon*

The Eclectic Viewpoint
Cheyenne Turner, editor
Box 802735
Dallas, TX 75380

Fate
Terry O'Neil, editor
Box 63483
St.Paul, MN 55164

FSR Publications, Ltd.
Gordon Creighton, editor
Box 162 High Wycombe
Buckinghamshire HP13 5DZ, UK
Publishes *Flying Saucer Review*

Fortean Times
Bob Rickard and Paul Sieveking, editors
Box 2409
London NW5 4NP, UK
Publishes *Fortean Studies*
Steve Moore, editor

Fund for UFO Research, Inc.
Richard Hall, director
Box 277
Mount Rainier, MD 20712

The Gate
Beth Robbins, editor
Box 43516
Cleveland, OH 44143

Global Communications
Timothy Green Beckley, editor
Box 1994
New York, NY 10001
Publishes *UFO Universe* and *Unsolved UFO Sightings*

The Hollow Earth Insider
Dennis G. Crenshaw, editor

Box 918
Yulee, FL 32041

Intergalactic Spacecraft-UFO-Intercontinental
    Research and Analytic Network
Colman S. Von Keviczky, director
35-40 75th Sreet, Suite G
Jackson Heights, NY 11372

International Fortean Organization
Phillis Benjamin, president
Box 367
Arlington, VA 22210
Publishes *Info Journal*
Michael T. Shoemacker, editor

International UFO Museum and Research Center
Walter G. Haut, president
400–402 North Main
P.O. Box 2221
Roswell, NM 88202

Intruders Foundation
Bud Hopkins, director
Box 30233
New York, NY 10011
Publishes *Bulletin of the Intruders Foundation*

Irish UFO and Paranormal Research Association
Patrick J. Delaney, director
Box 3070
Whitehall, Dublin 9, Ireland
Publishes *IUFOPRA Journal*

J.Allen Hynek Center for UFO Studies
Mark Rodeghier, scientific director
2457 West Peterson Avenue
Chicago, IL 60659
Publishes *International UFO Reporter*
Jerome Clark, editor

Journal of UFO Studies
Stuart Appelle, editor
Magonia
John Rimmer, editor
John Dee Cottage, 5 James Terrace
Mortlake Churchyard, London SW14 8HB, UK

Midohio Research Associates, Inc.
William E. Jones, director
Box 162
5837 Karnic Square Drive

Dublin, OH 43016
Publishes *Ohio UFO Notebook*

Mutual UFO Network, Inc.
Walter H. Andurs Jr., international director
103 Oldtowne Road
Seguin, TX 78155
Publishes *Mufon UFO Journal*
Dennis Stacey, editor

National Investigations Committee on UFOs
Frank E, Stranges, director
14617 Victory Boulevard, Suite 4
Van Nuys, CA 91411
Publishes *UFO Journal*

New Being Project
David Pursglove, director
Box 11542
Berkeley, CA 97401

Northern Anomalies Research Organization
Andrew P. Blunn, secretary
41 Somerset Road
Droylsden, Manchester M43 7PX, UK
Publishes *NARO Minded*

Northern UFO News
Jenny Randles, editor
1 Hallsteads Close, Dove Holes, Buxton, Derbyshire
    SK17 8BS, UK

Northern UFO Research and Investigation
Dave Newton, director
2A East Cheap
Heaton, Newcastle Upon Tyne NE6 5UA, UK
Publishes *Strange Daze*

Omega Communications
John White, director
Box 2051
Cheshire, CT 06410

Orbiter
Jim Melesciuc, editor
43 Harrison Street
Reading, MA 01867

Organization for Paranormal Understanding and
    Support
Eugene Lipson, director
Box 273273

Concord, CA 94527
Publishes *OPUS Newsletter*

Kathi Hennesey, editor
Outter Hear Productions
Mark Lee Center, director
39834 Wheatly Drive
Murrieta, CA 92563

OVNI-Presence
L'Association d'Etude sur les Soucoupes Volantes
B.P. 324
F-13611 Aix-en-Provence
Cedex 1, France

Paranet
Michael Corbin, director
Box 928
Wheat Ridge, CO 80034

Phenomenon Research Association
Omar Fowler, director
94 The Circle
Sinfin, Derbyshire DE24 9HR, UK
Publishes *OVNI*

Pricer UFO Library
Don Pricer, curator
2260 East Florance Avenue
Deland, FL 32724
Publishes *The Blue Book of UFO Publications*

Project Awareness
Buddy Crubley, Patty Crubley, and Vickie Lyons,
    directors
Box 730
Gulf Breeze, FL 32562

Project 1947
Jan Aldrich, director
Box 319
Canterbury, CT 06311

Promises and Disappointments
Kevin McClure, editor
23 Strawberrydale Avenue
Harrogate, North Yorkshire HG1 5EA, UK

Research Institute on Anomalous Phenomena
Vladimir V. Rubtsov, director
P.O. Box 4684
310022 Kharkov-22, Ukraine

Samizdat
Scott Corrales, editor
Box 228
Derrick City, PA 16727

Saucer Smear
James W. Moseley, editor
Box 1709
Key West, FL 33401

Skeptics Society
Michael Shermer, director
2761 North Marengo Avenue
Altadena, CA 91001
Publishes *The Skeptic*

Skeptics UFO Newsletter
Phillip J. Klass, editor
404 N Street SW
Washington, D.C. 20024

Society for Scientific Exploration
Peter A. Sturrock, president
Box 5848
Stanford, CA 94309
Publishes *Journal for Scientific Exploration*
Bernhard Haisch, editor

Strange Magazine
Mark Chorvinsky, editor
Box 2246
Rockville, MD 20847

Surrey Investigation Group on Arial Phenomena
Gordon Millington, director
126 Grange Road
Guildford, Surrey GU2 6QP, UK
Publishes *Pegasus*

Treatment and Research on Experienced Anomalous
    Trauma
Rima E. Laibow
13 Summit Terrace
Dobbs Ferry, NY 10522

Tristate Advocates for Scientific Knowledge
Terry Endes, director
239 East State Road
Cleves, OH 45002
Publishes *Task Researcher*

UFO Bureau
Billy J. Rachels, director

516 Colton Avenue
Thomsville, GA 31792

UFO Enigma Museum
6108 South Main
Roswell, NM 88202

UFO Information Network
Box 5012
Rome, OH 44085
Publishes *UFO Ohio Newsletter*
Dennis Pilchis, editor

UFO Investigation Centre
Bill Chalker, director
Box W42
West Pennant Hills, New South Wales 2125,
    Australia

U.F.O.
Vicki Cooper Ecker, editor
P.O. Box 1053
Sunland, CA 91041

UFO Magazine
Graham W. Birdall, editor
1st Floor, 66 Boroughgate
Otley near Leeds LS21 1AE, UK

UFO Museum and Research Center
Deon Crosby, director
114 North Main
Roswell, NM 88201
Publishes *IUFOMRC Monthly Newsletter*

UFO Newsclipping Service
Lucius Farish, editor
2 Caney Valley Drive
Plumerville, AK 72127

UFO Research Queensland, Inc.
Tino Pezzimenti, chairperson
Box 222, 50 Albert Street
Brisbane, Queensland 4002, Australia
Publishes *UFO Encounter*
Martin Gotschall, editor

UFOlogy Research of Manitoba
Box 1918 GPO
Winnipeg MB R3C 3R2, Canada
Publishes *Swamp Gas Journal*
Chris Rutkowski, editor

UFOs Tonite! (radio show)
Don Ecker, host
P.O. Box 1053
Sunland, CA 91041

United Aerial Phenomena Agency
Alan J. Manak, director
Box 347032
Cleveland, OH 44134-7032
Publishes *Flying Saucer Digest*
Robert Easley, editor

Victorian UFO Research Society
Judith Magee, director
Box 43
Moorabbin, Victoria 3189, Australia
Publishes *Australian UFO Bulletin*

X: The Unknown
Patrick O'Donell, editor
Box 14
Matawan, NJ 07747

Films

There are abundant popular, documentary-style videos on UFOs but no academic treatments of which I am aware. Most of these present the evidence for the real existence of UFOs and, almost invariably, make the assumption that they are extraterrestrial spacecraft. The same genre encompasses videos on government UFO conspiracies and alien abductions. Most are higher-quality productions than one might anticipate. One can almost always find at least some of these at video stores.

A company with a large collection of UFO and alternative videos is Underground Video: Box 527, Beverly Hills, CA 90213; Phone: 800-769-7077.

Some websites through which UFO videos can be ordered are:

Lightworks, www.ufos.com
Lone Zone, www.lonezone.com
Genesis III, www.genesis-3.com

Almost all of the larger UFO religions offer numerous videos and other material on their particular group. (See relevant website addresses below.)

Websites

It has been said that there are more websites dealing with UFOs than almost any other subject. This may or may not be the case, but there is a decided abundance of such sites. I have included a selection of website addresses, with the caveat that this medium is constantly changing. Old sites go out of existence and new sites come into being on a daily basis. Thus, many of the following websites may have disappeared or relocated by the time the reader opens these pages. However, any good search engine will turn up hundreds of relevant websites.

General
International Society for UFO Research
www.isur.com

The ISUR is an old-style UFO organization. It has a particularly useful link page.

Road Kill Cafe, UFO Links
www.calweb.com/~roadkill/ufo.html

The Road Kill Cafe is a link site covering more than just UFOs.

UFO Folklore
www.gtm.net/~geibdan/framemst.html

As this book goes to press, there are no websites of which I am aware that approach UFOs and aliens academically in terms of folklore and popular-culture studies. The UFO Folklore website comes the closest.

MUFON
www.rutgers.edu/~mcgrew/MUFON/

MUFON is perhaps the largest UFO membership organization.

UFO Magazine
www.ufomag.com

UFO Magazine is a high-quality magazine available at newsstands.

Flying Saucer Review
www.fsreview.net

Flying Saucer Review is an online magazine.

Art Bell Website
www.artbell.com

Popular radio-show host Art Bell maintains a large website containing much UFO-related information.

Jeff Rense Website
www.sightings.com/www.rense.com

Jeff Rense hosts a popular radio program comparable to the Art Bell show, which also contains abundant UFO material.

Citizens Against UFO Secrecy
www.caus.org

Citizens Against UFO Secrecy is, as the name suggests, an organization that believes the government is hiding what it knows about UFOs and aliens.

Committee for the Scientific Investigation of Claims of the Paranormal
www.csicop.org

If you want a dose of skepticism about all this, go to the CSICOP website.

UFO Religions
Jeffery Hadden New Religion Page
cti.itc.virginia.edu/~jkh8x/soc257/home.html

Jeff Hadden, who teaches sociology at the University of Virginia, maintains the most ambitious site on new religious movements—a category that encompasses UFO groups—on the web.

UFO Mind
www.AliensOnEarth.com (formerly www.ufomind.com)

Whereas most general websites deal only with sightings, conspiracy theories, abductions, and the like, Aliens On Earth (formerly UFO Mind) contains useful data and links on contactees and UFO religions. This is easily the best website for researching the latter topics on the web.

Heaven's Gate
www.webcoast.com/heavensgate.com
www.zdnet.com/yil/higher/heavensgate/index.html

Immediately following the "exit" of Heaven's Gate members in 1997, innumerable mirror sites sprung up that replicated the group's website information. These are gradually disappearing as interest in Heaven's Gate wanes, but more than a few contained this information as of this writing.

Following are the official websites for the organizations indicated:

Billy Meier group
www.figu.ch (Switzerland)/www.billymeier.com (USA)

Mark-Age
www.islandnet.com/~arton/markage.html

Adamski Foundation
www.gafintl-adamski.com

Aetherius Society
www.aetherius.org

Unarius Academy
www.unarius.org

Raelian Movement
www.rael.fr/www.rael.org

Ashtar Command
www.ashtar.org

Ground Crew
www.thegroundcrew.com

Chen Tao
trueway-chentao.homepage.com

INDEX